Studies and documents on cultural policies

For a complete list of titles see page 90

Cultural policy
in Bulgaria

Kostadine Popov

The Unesco Press

Published in 1981 by the United Nations Educational,
Scientific and Cultural Organization,
7 place de Fontenoy, 75700 Paris
Printed by Imprimerie des Presses Universitaires
de France, Vendôme

ISBN 92-3-101939-2
French edition: 92-3-201939-6

Preface

The purpose of this series is to show how cultural policies are planned and implemented in various Member States.

As cultures differ, so does the approach to them; it is for each Member State to determine its cultural policy and methods according to its own conception of culture, its socio-economic system, political ideology and technical development. However, the methods of cultural policy (like those of general development policy) have certain common problems; these are largely institutional, administrative and financial in nature, and the need has increasingly been stressed for exchanging experiences and information about them. This series, each issue of which follows as far as possible a similar pattern so as to make comparison easier, is mainly concerned with these technical aspects of cultural policy.

In general, the studies deal with the principles and methods of cultural policy, the evaluation of cultural needs, administrative structures and management, planning and financing, the organization of resources, legislation, budgeting, public and private institutions, cultural content in education, cultural autonomy and decentralization, the training of personnel, institutional infrastructures for meeting specific cultural needs, the safeguarding of the cultural heritage, institutions for the dissemination of the arts, international cultural co-operation and other related subjects.

The studies, which cover countries belonging to differing social and economic systems, geographical areas and levels of development, present therefore a wide variety of approaches and methods in cultural policy. Taken as a whole, they can provide guidelines to countries which have yet to establish cultural policies, while all countries, especially those seeking new formulations of such policies, can profit by the experience already gained.

This study was prepared for Unesco by Kostadine Popov, of the Committee for Culture.

Contents

Introduction

Bulgaria, which today covers 111,000 square kilometres and has 8,850,000 inhabitants, has existed as a state since 681, when this, the first Slav state, came into existence in an area where various tribes and cultures intermingled. This is in fact a region where ancient and modern history join hands, and the original Bulgarian culture, though it first emerged in those far-off times thirteen centuries ago, itself sent down roots into the culture of those peoples who had previously inhabited the land.

This area had formerly been occupied by the Thracians, a vigorous and energetic people, who created an art imbued with realism and freshness. According to Homer, the Thracian chief Rheusos went to the aid of Troy 'bearing arms worthy of the gods themselves'. The style of Thracian art can be seen in low-relief stone carvings, in gold objects, in the architecture of the tomb discovered near Mezek, in the frescoes of the famous domed tomb of Kazanlak—in short, in all the monuments of the period that have resisted the ravages of time. How many Thracian gladiators there once were is unknown, but history has immortalized the memory of one of their number, Spartacus, who was the leader of the greatest of the slave revolts against the Roman legions.

Later on, the country came within the orbit of Rome. By the middle of the first century of our era the whole of the Balkan peninsula was under Roman rule and Roman architecture has left a deep impression in Bulgaria itself: the ancient town of Abritus near Razgrad, Nicopolis ad Istrum near the village of Nikyip, Marcianopolis, Augusta Trajana, Philippopolis, the Roman villa of Armira, and so on.

A Slavo-Bulgar settlement was subsequently established on the ruins of Abritus after the arrival of the Slavs, who brought with them their own art forms that drove Byzantine cultural influences out of this area. Later the Slavs were joined by the Bulgars of Khan Asparukh. The fusion of these two ethnic groups, the Slavs and the Proto-Bulgars, gave birth to a new community, which was to become known over the centuries as the

Bulgarian people. The assertion of their identity brought into being a new culture that was one of the most original in southern Europe during the Middle Ages.

The Proto-Bulgars brought with them their art and their own conception of beauty. Referring to the battle of Anhialo, the Byzantine chroniclers could not pass over in silence the fact that 'the Bulgars [were] richer than the Thracians'.

In 681, the Byzantine Empire gave official recognition to the Bulgarian state. Hardly was Khan Asparukh, the first Bulgarian sovereign-ruler, installed on the throne than he began the construction of his capital, Pliska, which was surrounded with battlements of massive stone blocks and had a palace decorated with marble columns, mosaics and friezes.

His successors built an even more imposing city as their capital, Preslav, whose architecture was outstanding for its beauty and imagination. Not only were the Bulgars traditionally great builders, but they also attained a very high standard in the decorative arts, as can be seen from the treasure comprising twenty-three magnificent gold objects, discovered at Nagy-Szent-Miklos in Hungary, which gives eloquent proof of the genius of Bulgarian artists.

This is the period from which date the oldest Bulgarian written records: columns covered with inscriptions, of which so far sixty examples are known. The inscription of Tchatalare is carved on a column 6 metres high. It mentions the sculptured figures and the copper lions that decorated the khan's palace. The language is rich and full of imagery, and these stones, as if they were brought to life by the thinking and poetic vision of our forefathers, stand forth as original literary works. On one column dating from the time of Khan Omurtag (816–31) can be read the words: 'A man, even when he has lived well, dies and another is born. Let him who is alive today look on this inscription and remember its author. . . .'

Also dating from this same period is a monument that is the only one of its kind in Europe: the *Madara Horseman*. This enormous low-relief sculpture carved in the rock on the face of an immensely high cliff represents a horseman followed by a dog, and a lion pierced by a spear. It is surrounded by inscriptions glorifying the state and its culture.

In the ninth century, the first Bulgarian apostles, Cyril and Methodius, invented a new Slav script (the Cyrillic alphabet). Until then, in accordance with the dogma of the three sacred languages, the people had to write in Latin, Greek or Hebrew—languages they hardly understood at all—and thus any new ideas likely to contribute to their culture were condemned from the start. Once this dogma had been rejected, the new Slav script spread rapidly in Bulgaria, encouraged by the existence of a strong state, with a firmly established centralized government, in which the Slavs and the Proto-Bulgars formed an almost homogenous community, which the Pope himself referred to as 'a people' (the reply of Pope Nicolas to questions from the Bulgarians in 866). From this time onwards Old Bulgarian (Old

Church Slavonic) became the fourth written language of the country. Cyril and Methodius invented the new alphabet because they were convinced of the importance of culture in the life of a nation and, in so doing, they also showed an awareness of the ideas which were later to come to fruition in the Renaissance. Bulgaria, as the birthplace of the new script, was to become the centre of medieval Slav literature and, in fact, writers of talent, including Bishop Constantine, Chernorizetz Krabar and John the Exarch, lived and worked in the royal palace.

More than two thousand manuscripts have come down to us, revealing the thoughts and feelings that moved the writers of that period. In seven years Clement, a disciple of Cyril and Methodius, taught 3,500 people to read and write. This was the golden age of Old Bulgarian literature and culture. The writers used the popular, living language, whose rich and expressive vocabulary enabled them to convey abstract ideas and to describe different states of mind. In addition to religious works there were also works of a secular nature. It was at this period that Bulgarians first became acquainted with Homer's poetry through translations of the chronicles of Troy. John the Exarch translated fragments of Aristotle's works and Constantine of Preslav more than once quotes Plato. Aesop's fables were also translated. Bulgarian literature had its own particular themes and spirit and sought to reflect the nation's social and historical destiny. From the very beginning it attempted to serve the people and showed an interest in contemporary problems. The classic works of Old Bulgarian literature—the *Zograph Gospel*, the *Marinska Gospel*, the *Assemane Gospel*, the Sinai *Psalter*, etc.—date from the tenth and eleventh centuries. Whenever the Bulgarian's creative mind felt hemmed in by the set forms of religious literature, he threw off their bonds and broke through into the field of the apocryphal writings, which gave free rein to the imagination, to the lyrical impulse and to pathos. One of the masterpieces of this type of writing is the *Secret Book* of the Bogomils, which was translated into Latin.

Bogomilism, which was essentially a social and philosophical doctrine, originated in Bulgaria and later spread through neighbouring countries as far as Italy and France. In 1111, or 489 years before Giordano Bruno and 304 before Jan Hus, the Bogomil preacher Vassil Vrach, a defender of freedom of speech and freedom of conscience, was found guilty of heresy and burnt at the stake in Constantinople. But Bogomilism was also an attempt to defend those forms of art and literature that were closest to the people and to their dreams and aspirations.

A flowering of the plastic arts went hand in hand with a flowering in literature. From the tenth century we have the ceramic image of Theodore Stratilatus, an outstanding masterpiece of the old Bulgarian School, unique in the art of the whole world.

The finest examples of ancient Bulgarian art are to be seen in Turnovo. This magnificent city was not only the capital of the kingdom but also a centre of culture. The famous school of artists of Turnovo broke out of the straitjacket of orthodox forms, took upon itself greater freedom in creation, and was characterized by the vitality, elegance and richness of its decoration. Among the works of art of this school is one of the oldest mural calendars in the world, *The Forty Martyrs*, painted in one of the churches of Turnovo. Very typical products of the art of Turnovo are the frescoes in the old churches in the town, which abound in free, vigorous figures, richly coloured and lovingly portrayed. The search for realism in portraiture continued and is particularly evident in the frescoes of the church at Boyana (1259), one of the most remarkable monuments of this school. The painter of these frescoes, the Master of Boyana, anticipates the Renaissance in Western Europe by several centuries, painting not only saints, but also lay figures, such as the sebastocrat Kaloyan and his wife Desislava, King Constantine Asen and Queen Irena. The scene of the 'rescue of the fishermen in danger', in which the painting of their bodies, their gestures and the expressions on their faces suggests the drama of the fishermen's situation, is particularly remarkable. The figures in the fresco showing Christ in the midst of the doctors in the temple convey an amazing impression of gentleness and spiritual nobility.

The Master of Boyana has also left a particularly interesting 'Last Supper'. So as to stress the close links between the men of his time and those partaking of the Last Supper, he has shown the table spread with vegetables which formed part of everyday Bulgarian food.

At a time when stereotypes were prevalent in art, the frescoes in the church at Boyana, showing figures which are full of life and of marked individuality, glorify mankind. There were other painters too who dealt with interesting subjects. Particular mention should be made of the artist of genius who painted the beautiful frescoes in the rock church in the village of Ivanovo, which display a really astonishing interest in the classical world and the nude.

Magnificent examples of thirteenth- and fourteenth-century Bulgarian miniature art have been preserved, including the mid-fourteenth-century *Chronicle of Manasses* (Vatican Museum) and the *King Ivan Alexander Gospel* of 1356 (British Museum). The illustrations in the *Chronicle of Manasses* show a highly developed sense of colour. This work contains nineteen appendices representing episodes from Bulgarian history and includes the most ancient view of Turnovo in existence. The *King Ivan Alexander Gospel* has 366 miniatures, all of remarkable elegance. Some of them are of great historical interest as they include portraits of the king and of his family and because they provide information about the way of life and the architecture of the period.

From the same period date the churches of Trapezitsa (the boyars' quarter of Turnovo), the well-preserved Bachkovo ossuary, near the monastery of the same name (eleventh century), the Church of St John the Evangelist in the monastery of Zemen (eleventh and twelfth centuries), the churches of the Holy Virgin (fourteenth century), of the Forty Martyrs

12

(thirteenth century) and of SS. Peter and Paul (fourteenth century), in Turnovo, etc.

The architecture at Turnovo, the churches at Nesebūr, Asen Castle, the Hrelu Tower at the Rila Monastery, the *Chronicle of Manasses*, the literary works of Theodosius of Turnovo, of the Patriarch Ephtimi, of Constantine of Costenetz and of Grigori Tsamblak, the musical production of the composer and cantor Ivan Kukuzel—all these are evidence of the flowering and range of Bulgarian culture, over which the shadow of Ottoman domination was soon to fall.

The invasion of the Ottoman Turks broke like a devastating storm over the whole country, which was put to fire and the sword. The great library at Turnovo, to which the conquerors set fire, burnt for a whole month. A large number of old books, golden seals and manuscripts were destroyed in the flames. Castles, palaces and churches were razed to the ground. Works of all kinds, created by inspired minds and skilful hands, disappeared for ever. Very little trace of Bulgarian culture was left after the conquerors finished their work of destruction: their fanaticism wreaked terrible havoc.

Thus subject to Ottoman domination, the Bulgarian people suffered serious losses and the material products of their culture were pillaged. Throughout this terrible ordeal, however, they preserved their dignity as a nation and their faith in life, though quite clearly the opportunities for the spread of cultural enlightenment, for the construction of architectural monuments and for artistic expression of any kind were extremely limited.

The invaders mercilessly oppressed the people in the desire to deprive them of their identity. Having observed that the Bulgarians were better and more richly attired than they were themselves, the occupying forces even forbade the local inhabitants to wear luxurious and brightly coloured clothes and tall hats.

Despite the enslavement of the country, Bulgarian culture was not completely annihilated. Monasteries, remote from the great highways, tucked away in the mountains, attracted men of letters, painters and sculptors. Many works of art were created in such places during those hard years of enslavement. At Rila Monastery, for example, a master sculptor, using only a needle, took ten years to carve a magnificent cross out of a piece of wood. On it were represented many different scenes and a multitude of minute human figures with individual expressions, the whole embellished with rich and refined decoration.

The creative strength of the people found expression in various ways. Simple things of everyday life were transformed into works of art. Wood-carvings, wrought ironwork, pottery and stone sculptures exhibit admirable combinations of shape and colour. And what is there to say of the cloths and embroideries! To sum up, Bulgarian artists managed to introduce original conceptions into many different fields of the applied arts.

The sufferings the people underwent sharpened their memories and stimulated their imagination. Folklore was passed on from generation to

13

generation and the most beautiful folk-songs took shape at this period. Though the conquerors might carry off girls, women and children and massacre the finest of the young men, the Bulgarians could still give vent to their heaviness of heart in singing. Thus songs were born in which the deepest wisdom of the people fused with their strongest feelings and was then reproduced in an inimitable poetic form.

In modern times, over a hundred and fifty thousand folk-songs have been collected and recorded. Together with the surviving folk-tales they constitute a rare treasure of folklore. Thus in one of the ballads recalling the memory of the legendary hero Krali-Marko, it is said that he wished to pit his strength against God's by raising the earth in his hand. So great was his audacity that the evening star took fright, and hid behind a cloud. This theme goes back a long way in Bulgarian folklore and expresses man's aspiration for freedom and his belief in his own strength. The injustice of their historical fate and their centuries-long suffering drove the people to feats of audacious courage, to measuring themselves against God and breaking all written and unwritten rules. Their fighting spirit upheld their faith, gave them strength and guided them in all their cultural activities and creative work.

In different places the inhabitants erected small religious buildings at their own expense—the invaders only allowed the construction of buildings of very limited size—with walls decorated with frescoes of great artistic merit. Such buildings were the monasteries of Dragalevtsi (1476), Kremikovtsi (1483), Poganovo (1476), etc. They contain interesting portraits, enhanced with details from everyday life. One noticeable feature of the artists of this time is the tendency to go their own way and reject classical solutions and designs. The same tendency is also evident in literature.

Under Ottoman domination literature developed more slowly, but more than ever it became stamped with a democratic spirit. Vladislav the Grammarian (fifteenth century), Pop Pejo and Mathei the Grammarian (sixteenth century) exalted the moral stamina of the Bulgarian people and their spirit of freedom and independence.

In 1762 the monk Paissi finished his *History of the Bulgarian Slavs*, which was destined to be the first secular work to become widely known. Proud of being Bulgarian and a son of the people, Paissi wrote his book for the people. It is a masterly work, totally free of any trace of vanity on the part of the author, though its composition required not only talent and learning, but also extraordinary daring; and it is imbued with a keen awareness of the importance of the ordinary people.

This was the beginning of the Bulgarian national revival. New and much larger churches and monasteries were built, as were more spacious new houses, with ceilings decorated with suns and garlands of flowers, the work of fine wood sculptors. In 1865, after having a number of churches and public buildings built to his own plans, the father of the new Bulgarian architecture, Kolio Ficheto, personally supervised the construction over the River Yantra, near the town of Byala, of the most noteworthy nineteenth-century bridge in the entire Balkan peninsula. With its fourteen arches and its piers decorated with stone-carvings, this bridge is a structure of exceptional beauty.

The increasing demand for artistic works caused several schools of art to be opened—at Tryavna, Samokov and Boyana—whose alumni not only travelled all over Bulgaria itself but also throughout the Balkan peninsula. The wood carvings on church altars represent branches in blossom, bunches of grapes and birds singing. Each bears the mark of an individual talent. The admirable portraits that we owe to the painters Stanislav Dospevski, Zacharias Zographe, Nicolai Pavlovich and others celebrate the triumph of the free man, his dignity, moral strength and nobility.

The development of literature at the time of the Bulgarian national revival is closely linked with the awakening of national consciousness in the people, which it both influences and reflects at the same time. The literature of this period, which is represented by such writers as Neophyte Bozveli, Petar Beron, Nayden Guerov and Ivan Bogorov, acted as a spiritual force in the struggle for national liberation.

The old Balkan Mountains, in which more than one generation of rebels had taken refuge during the time of foreign domination, jealously preserved the memory of the patriotic ballads of the poet Dobri Chintulov. Against the panorama of the struggle for national liberation stand out the great figures of revolutionaries, poets and writers: Georg Rakovski, Vasil Levski, Lyuben Karavelov and Christo Botev, an impetuous spirit, outstanding poetic genius and great patriot, who died fighting the Turks. This union of poetry with the national struggle, this love for one's country coupled with a readiness to die for it, were to be exemplified anew later on in the life and work of poets such as Gueo Milov, Christo Yasenov and Nikola Vaptsarov.

The Bulgarian people, although they had lost their state and been deprived of political power and of freedom, still had in their midst poets, writers, painters and scholars. Despite the barbaric conditions in which they lived, they found ways of acquiring education. Obstinately and steathily they kept alight the flames of learning in the schools, whose number had risen to 1500 by the eve of the Russo-Turkish War of Liberation of 1877–1878. With the same perseverance they set up reading centres, conscious of their importance for the liberation movement, wrote into their calendar a festival for the celebration of education and culture (a festival unique in the world) and established a theatre, not to provide entertainment for a privileged few, but to awaken national consciousness. Perhaps because of their country's historical destiny, Bulgarian artists and intellectuals have always stood alongside the people in the constant quest for social and cultural advance. Intellectual snobbery and the desire to create for an élite have always been foreign to them. This was as true of the icon painters and men of letters of the Middle Ages as of the artists of the

Bulgarian national revival. These men of marked individuality whose hearts were open to truth and justice saw no conflict between their own fate and the destiny of the people; the aristocratic concept of the independence of art from life and social conflicts had no hold over them.

Once the country had been freed from Ottoman domination, Bulgarian culture and art remained attached to realistic folk traditions. The Bulgarian state did its best to overcome the backwardness that resulted from the long foreign domination: it put in hand a number of large-scale projects and founded new cultural institutions.

However, instead of the 'pure and holy republic' that the men of the Bulgarian national revival had dreamed of, a monarchy was instituted, which, three times in the space of seventy years, involved the country in devastating wars. However, by dint of unremitting effort, those responsible for promoting education and culture worked to set the country back on its feet and to bring it prosperity. They managed for the most part to control the passing passions and the effects of petit-bourgeois attitudes, and many of them succeeded in overcoming artistic subjectivism thanks to the positive influence of the working class and of the Communist Party. Hatred of hypocrisy and conservatism in thought and practice brought artists and men of culture together even when they belonged to different ideological groups. Poets and writers, artists and actors all protested with one voice against Fascism. The burning aspirations of popular struggle found expression in their works, its intensity being matched by their love of mankind. Most Bulgarian creative artists remained faithful to the basic traditions of Bulgarian culture, which had always been close to the spirit of the people. This bond with the people, which was given a new meaning with the growth of the working class, favoured rapid artistic development along the path of socialist realism and the appearance of revolutionary proletarian art, in the very midst of the struggle for a just world where people could live happily and in peace.

A real turning-point in the country's history was reached on 9 September 1944, the date on which the People's Republic of Bulgaria was proclaimed.

Aims and principles
of cultural policy

The overthrow of Fascism and the victory of the Socialist Revolution on 9 September 1944 were of great importance for the socio-historical evolution of the Bulgarian people, and in particular for the development of their culture. The main lines of the cultural programme of the People's Republic of Bulgaria were laid down in the Declaration of the First Government of the Patriotic Front. It provided for revolutionary reforms in all aspects of cultural life and the development of a democratic popular culture, accessible to the working masses.

This wide-ranging programme of reform helped to establish a social climate conducive to respecting, maintaining and enriching democratic cultural traditions, satisfying the cultural interests and needs of the people, promoting artistic creation and activity and fostering the work of cultural institutions. The driving force behind this programme of cultural development was the profound conviction that the strength of a country resides in the culture of its citizens, their creativity and their capacity and desire to work towards the achievement of common aims, for the masses possess enormous creative resources to which free rein must be given. To achieve this, two series of measures had to be taken: in the first place, the material foundations and the conditions necessary for general cultural development had to be established, which meant creating a huge network of cultural and educational institutions, giving members of the intelligentsia material security and improving the living conditions of the workers; in addition, cultural activity as a whole had to be democratized, a more lively interest in culture awakened and developed in all social strata and steps taken to strengthen the workers' participation in social activities and creative work. A consistent and well-organized programme of action was necessary to bring about radical changes in the intellectual life of society. In fact, these changes were natural and inevitable, for what was required was not solely to raise educational standards and produce a quantitative increase on the plane of cultural values, but to transform fundamentally the character of

17

culture and its function and mission in society. Such reforms were an integral part of the revolutionary socio-economic changes brought about by the country's commitment to the path of socialist development, and they were conditioned by the fact that the Bulgarian Communist Party had become the guiding socio-political force in the country and that its policies reflected the aspirations and interests of the masses.

The changes that occurred in the field of culture were the result of concrete socio-economic forces and were but one component of the universal changes that took place. For cultural development, by the very nature of culture itself, is closely linked with many other aspects of the life of society. It is determined by a number of economic and political factors, by national traditions and the national character, the ethical code, law, the nature of inter-personal relationships, the educational system, social mobility, etc.

Thanks to these revolutionary changes, the right to work, to education, to social security, to free development and human cultural rights—in the widest sense of the term—were actually put into practice.

This cultural leap forward was favoured by a whole series of circumstances. In fact, primary education had for a long time been compulsory in the country and there was a large, ready-made network of reading-rooms and public libraries. The Bulgarian people had a rich cultural heritage. Nevertheless, the cultural inequalities between the various social groups, which were due to basic differences in their economic and social situations, had to be overcome. To this end, the government set about the task of democratizing the educational system, establishing different kinds of educational institutions offering a wide range of specialized training and increasing the number of cultural institutions.

Particular importance attaches to the fact that in the course of the struggle against Fascism the monarcho-Fascist ideology had been discredited. Moreover, many of the intelligentsia had taken part in the struggle against Fascism alongside the people; in fact those who were of a progressive, democratic turn of mind had never cut themselves off from the masses, but on the contrary had felt it their duty to promote cultural progress among the people. While the new state had none the less to take appropriate steps to build up the numbers of the intelligentsia, these factors, pertaining to the historical development of the nation and the national character, had a favourable influence on the transformation of the cultural life of the country.

During the first few years after the victory of the Socialist Revolution in Bulgaria, the educational system, the libraries, publishing, the press, radio, museums and the applied arts were reorganized according to new, democratic and progressive principles. At the same time, efforts were made to bring about a rapid development of the network of cultural institutions. For example, the state sought to encourage creative activities and intellectual work by bringing cultural education and the treasures of the cultural

18

heritage within the reach of all sections of society. Artistic creativity in all its forms was supported and encouraged.

Towards the end of 1947 industrial firms and the banks were nationalized. Shortly afterwards, similar measures were taken in the field of culture. All theatres and cinemas, the publishing houses and other means of spreading culture came under the control of the state. This act, which had important social consequences, was in accordance with the interests of the majority of the population, since all sections of society aspired to wider and freer access to culture and education. The promotion of culture and the democratization of the means of spreading culture satisfied this aspiration. The state took over the running of all schools. Education became free in all educational institutions from primary schools to the universities. Henceforth all citizens had an equal opportunity to acquire education.

The progressive reorganization of the publishing houses, the theatre, the cinema and all other cultural institutions was carried out in a comparatively short period. New cinemas and theatres were opened and the number of publishing houses increased. This was accompanied by changes in the principles underlying their activities, fundamental changes in their repertories and output and the appearance of new tendencies in their development. A new way was found to solve the problems of the libraries and museums: a unified system of museums was established and the state took over responsibility for the collections in the reading-rooms and in the archaeological societies.

The transformation of the existing museums into active educational, cultural and scientific institutions took place at the same time as new institutions of this kind were being established. Thus during the period from 1944 to 1948 fundamental democratic changes took place in the cultural field. New laws were passed so as to encourage the masses to take advantage of the cultural facilities available.

The concentration of the material infrastructure of culture in the hands of the state, of society, brought numerous advantages. It made it possible to plan the provision of cultural amenities, to examine the problems to do with culture as a whole and to deal with them in accordance with general needs and concrete economic and political imperatives. Favourable conditions already existed for the co-ordination of cultural activities, for experimentation and the introduction of new forms, for the efficient organization of the various cultural departments and services, and for the establishment of rational, fruitful relationships between them.

To the same ends the state assumed responsibility for the legal protection of artistic creation, set up a system of social assistance for creative artists and enacted several laws placing the different branches of culture under its protection. All the laws relating to cultural development were introduced by the government and passed by the supreme legislative bodies. Thus, concern for the protection of the cultural heritage was given legal backing by the law on the protection of cultural monuments, arts and crafts and popular folk arts were encouraged by the law on the development of arts and crafts, and creativity was likewise encouraged by the law on copyright.

In this way the basic principles of the new cultural policy of the socialist state were put into force. Though inseparable from society's socio-economic progress and the general trends of its development, cultural policy is also indissolubly linked with science. It is based on sociological research and forecasts, planning and scientific analysis of the present situation and of future prospects. In spite of these constant improvements and additions at each stage of development, it still conforms to objective tendencies and obeys the principle of continuity. If certain nuances are evident in cultural policy, they are due to the choice of forms and the methods used to make culture more widely available, but these in turn are always related to national and social needs. Because it rests on scientific foundations, such a cultural policy is likely to produce positive results and enjoy the support of both the intelligentsia and the masses.

Cultural policy takes as its main starting-point the idea that the masses play a decisive role in cultural development. But, at the same time, culture has a corresponding effect on society: it contributes to the individual's personal development and increases his opportunities for participation in the economic and social life of the country. Although it is determined by certain economic factors, it also inevitably expresses man's attitudes towards the ideas inherited from the past as well as those existing in the present. The objective determination of events is not isolated from subjective factors. There are two processes at work here, an interaction which favours the quantitative increase in artistic expression and the rise in the level of education, as well as the transformation of the individual's mentality and his relations with others.

The implementation of the state's cultural policy is based on the assumption that an adequate infrastructure has already been created. This includes the building and financing of schools, theatres and other cultural institutions; the forecasting of their development; the training of personnel; the moral and material encouragement of creativity in the arts; and the creation of conditions favouring the activities of cultural and educational organizations and of artists' and writers' associations.

At any given time culture is influenced by the problems, events and social tendencies of the period, which passes on to it some of its own characteristic features. At the same time, culture is a continuous process whereby man deepens his knowledge of the world and then uses this knowledge so as to transform reality. Each period critically examines its cultural inheritance handed down from the past and then makes its own contribution to it. This is the basis of the historical continuity of cultural development. During the process of building socialism in Bulgaria the importance of the cultural heritage was fully appreciated. This is why socialist culture has not deviated from the national cultural traditions and from the evolution of world culture. In keeping with the laws of continuity, modern

Bulgarian culture has borrowed from the past everything that was most valuable and progressive. Benefiting from historical experience, it has preserved for future generations all the genuine spiritual values built up during the nation's past. Thus, many cultural and artistic achievements that had long remained forgotten were brought to light and their humanistic importance was fully revealed.

This progressive and democratic culture is one of the factors that have gone to mould society and left their mark on the individual's mind and consciousness and his relationship with the community as a whole. Humanism is the distinctive feature of modern Bulgarian culture. It is of a realistic, practical bent, summed up in the expression: 'To do everything for the good of mankind!' By helping to make society more cohesive, to alter the nature of work and to develop man's full potentialities on the scientific, technical, psychological and moral planes, culture speeds up the progress of mankind. It pursues a noble end—the achievement of man's harmonious development.

The state is steadily adding to the material infrastructure in order to ensure the development and cultural progress of society. The forms and methods employed to spread culture and the arts are being constantly extended and diversified. In this way many problems in regard to satisfying the cultural needs of all workers and ensuing their free access to the treasures of the human spirit have been happily solved. However, these cultural needs should not be regarded as adding up to a given level of demand, fixed once and for all. Cultural needs grow and change at different rates. New interests appear as man evolves and as the material possibilities of a richer, more varied life increase. The solution of some problems has been followed by the appearance of other, even more complex problems arising from the first. What has henceforth to be done is to convert the consumers of the fruits of artistic activity into producers of such fruits, to develop the artistic creativity of the people and ensure the full flowering of their creative talents.

In this context it should not be forgotten that a man's cultural relations with other people are based on predetermined social positions, embracing his convictions, his needs and his ideals, and that in all he does he reveals his own personal attitude towards culture.

Raising the educational and cultural level of the workers entails a change in their role and their place not only in the field of material production but also with regard to cultural matters and creativity. The individual's views of the world and of the meaning of life are changed, and his notions of happiness take on new colours. He escapes from the strait-jacket of his professional interests and widens the horizons of his creative activities. Thus the process whereby man is transformed is an integral and essential part of cultural progress. This process has many different sides and includes knowledge and know-how, capabilities and interests, needs and ideals, consciousness, the will and feelings, the net result being to

21

contribute to modifying the entire thrust of the individual's personality.

The period in which we live is characterized by the speed of scientific and technical progress. Discoveries made by the human spirit introduce new intellectual and aesthetic dimensions into life. The individual's intellectual opportunities are constantly increasing thanks to the flow of information he receives. Science, the arts and politics become an integral part of his life, as he gradually draws closer to the intellectual interests of all mankind. Nowadays, time imposes an unheard-of speed in his development and the material possibilities for such development are constantly increasing. Whether these possibilities are to be realized depends on the proper implementation of the cultural policy of the state and, at the same time, on the subjective factor—on the will and energy of the individual. For man is not a passive object of culture; he must act himself if he is to make any cultural progress.

Gaining access to culture is a continuing process that goes beyond the mere assimilation of knowledge and skills, beyond the development of physical and intellectual capabilities, and becomes instead a lifelong process for the full development, education and training of the individual.

The cultural activity that takes place in Bulgaria is intended to make people aware of their own spiritual and intellectual value; it is directed against passivity and inertia and aims to make people creative.

The harmonious development of man's faculties and abilities is no longer a dream or a distant ideal, but an immediate individual and social objective. It is, however, clearly a long-term process that requires certain objective pre-conditions and much individual effort. Its possibilities of fulfilment rest on the social environment that conditions the development of the individual and on the educational opportunities and the means of satisfying cultural needs that are available.

Every year thousands of workers are brought into the educational system through evening classes and correspondence courses, while at the same time continuing in their regular employment. In this way they improve their general knowledge and further their training. Once their studies are finished, they are given a new job in keeping with the training they have received, with the result that their place in industrial production and in society changes. Even if they continue in their old jobs, they are given different work of a higher intellectual level. Social mobility facilitates the movement of workers from one category to another. The steady increase in the number of people with specialized secondary or higher education has changed public attitudes towards culture.

Creative activity is steadily increasing in all areas of life. The number of inventors and innovators is becoming larger and larger. Currently, thousands of innovations and 'rationalizations' (schemes to apply more rational working methods) are being introduced each year and this increases the productive capacity of industry.

The fact that a worker exercises a trade does not prevent him from participating in the creation of spiritual values. The introduction of workers to intellectual activities, which is one of the determining factors of progress, greatly strengthens this participation.

At the present time, 2 million people have received secondary education and more than 350,000, higher education.

The democratization of culture involves the liberation of man's personality and this implies the development of all his individual talents and of all his creative potential. Obviously, the aim is not to level out individual abilities (that would be both impossible and useless), but to encourage man's creativity and give free rein to his need to fulfil himself throughout his life. Creativity represents for him a fundamental way of broadening his horizens. The richer and more varied a man's interior life is, the more this is reflected in all his activities. In fact, his aspiration towards creative work of social importance and towards the social assertion of his personality is strengthened. At the same time, each person's creative talents find a better outlet. All this results from the fact that not only do people receive an aesthetic education that enables them to understand works of art, but they seek to live in harmony with the great moral principles reflected in such works, and to create in accordance with the laws of beauty. It is particularly important to transform the ideas expressed through art and culture into personal convictions and to inculcate such elevated thoughts and feelings as will have a positive effect on behaviour.

Culture and art are now within reach of a huge public. Workers, in their daily life, move among cultural events and works of art, and become in the full sense heirs to mankind's spiritual patrimony.

The new attitude of the workers towards culture and the vigour of their cultural interests make themselves apparent in many different ways, though they cannot be examined independently of the important changes that have occurred in the composition of Bulgarian society. The working class has grown in size and 83.5 per cent of all workers now work in the field of material production. The internal structure of the working class has also changed as a result of the increase in the number of people working in industry, building, transport and communications, and of the rise in their level of education and in their occupational qualifications. The number of members of the intelligentsia who are playing an increasingly important role in social life, and in particular of those working in the fields of technical and scientific progress, has grown considerably. The proportion of experts who have received secondary and higher education is steadily rising. This phenomenon is accompanied by the gradual elimination of the differences between social groups as they come together in a spirit of social equality, as well as by an increase in the intellectual content of manual work and the strengthening of the links between science and production, in line with the continually increasing participation of the workers in cultural life. However, this phenomenon should not only be seen in quantitative terms; it also has a qualitative side, connoting an enormous moral advance. The ordinary man's attitude towards cultural progress is founded on civic consciousness, evinced in his active participation in cultural life, in the formation and development of the new culture, in the increase in the number of people taking part in artistic creation, in the many amateur artistic activities and in the life of cultural organizations. No longer is it a question of mere passive access to culture; the present trend, which is growing steadily stronger, is for the masses to be encouraged to participate actively in creative work of social relevance.

This movement whereby the people and art have come closer together has been characteristic of life in Bulgaria during the last few decades.

On the one hand, the people's level of education and general culture is steadily rising, their aesthetic education is broadening and art penetrates more and more deeply into their daily lives, while on the other hand, art itself comes closer to the people on account of the problems with which it deals, the new images it creates and the ideas, conceptions and aspirations it embodies.

The part that writers and artists play in national life is apparent in their artistic evocation of patriotism, heroism and idealism in action. As well as laying increased demands on personal artistic skills, this new national role gives rise to new forms of communication through the intermediary of culture.

The general socio-historical character of manual and intellectual work and the workers' participation in the socialist transformation of life strengthen the spiritual bonds already existing between them and contribute to the unity of the community. The activity of creative artists forms an integral part of the work of the people as a whole and creates new bonds between them and the workers. These relationships between writers and artists and the general public have undergone considerable changes, resulting naturally in a continually rising quality in regard to all types of cultural activity, in respect of both the works of art themselves and the standard of execution. This phenomenon, which necessitates appropriate community action and friendly co-operation between the different sectors of society for the sake of the overriding common objectives, is the result of the rise in cultural standards and the higher level attained by socialist man in general and, more particularly, the mature judgement the workers can now bring to bear on aesthetic values, their vision of culture and art having been transformed as a result of the evolution of their intellectual capabilities.

The stimulation
of cultural activity

Practical activity in the field of culture is conducted on the basis of planning, the general principles of which are applied by cultural institutions. Cultural development is also planned according to the state's cultural policy, but there is no administrative interference in the work of artists and other members of the intelligentsia. The five-year national economic development plans regulate and co-ordinate the development of culture at the national level. They lay down the broad lines of cultural expenditure, provide for new institutions and new buildings to be opened and new equipment to be supplied, determine the number of books to be published and of films to be made, etc.

The country's economic expansion and the rapid increase in the national income make it possible to devote considerable—and annually increasing—resources to cultural purposes.

The relationship existing between the economy and culture, between economic progress and cultural development, is attested by the steady rise in capital expenditure for education, culture and the arts, as well as in the budgetary appropriations and special funds specifically earmarked for culture. Economic management and the assistance given by the state to cultural activities make it possible to use the economic resources available in the most efficient way so as to create the optimum conditions for cultural development.

The economic relationships in the cultural field are identical to those existing in other areas of the national economy, since they all rest on the same social base. They contribute to efficient utilization of all human, material and financial resources with a view to encouraging the fullest possible cultural activity.

Many of the activities concerned with artistic creation and interpretation also have a productive and economic side. The two sides are closely connected, though priority is given to the requirements in regard to the aesthetic and ideological aspects of artistic creation. The value of any cultural activity is measured primarily by its aesthetic impact, and this determines the way in which cultural institutions are organized and managed. Naturally, the co-ordination of creative activities with the economy as a whole is carried out within a specific framework delimited by the level of revenue from cultural activities and the financial assistance the state is in a position to extend to cultural institutions.

From the point of view of funding, Bulgarian cultural institutions are divided into the following types: (a) those run entirely at the expense of the state and the local authorities; (b) those subsidized by the state and the local authorities; (c) institutions which operate on a self-supporting basis.

With regard to state aid for cultural development, various forms of material and psychological incentive play an important part. These incentives bear witness to the profoundly human attitude shown towards particularly talented people, as well as to the interest and public recognition they receive; their purpose is to encourage writers and artists and cultural institutions to realize their creative potential to the full. In addition to the award of prizes and honorary titles, material incentives are given in the form of contracts granting financial assistance for the creation of literary, musical and artistic works. The highest material reward, and also the highest honorary title, which is given for the most distinguished achievements in the field of literature and the arts or in artistic interpretation, is the Dimitrov Prize. In addition, the trade unions, the artists' and writers' associations and some departmental and municipal councils award prizes once a year. Thus, the Sofia City Council awards annual prizes to the authors of literary and artistic works, to performers and theatrical producers.

Another type of reward for artistic creation is the award of honorary titles: Emeritus Promoter of Culture, Emeritus Artist, People's Artist, Emeritus Painter, People's Painter, etc.

Alongside these material incentives there are also various forms of moral encouragement, such as formal eulogies, decorations, medals, certificates, etc. They give public recognition to those taking an active part in cultural life and to creative achievements in the arts.

The authorities are constantly seeking new ways of encouraging cultural activity. Thus, special funds have been set up, such as the Aid to Creativity Fund (under the auspices of the Committee for Culture), which is designed to encourage writers, painters, scientific research-workers, etc. and to support creative activities through the organization of artistic and literary events, festivals, competitions, exhibitions, research programmes, etc. and by giving loans for specialized training courses, scholarships, prizes and so on. Similar funds have also been set up by the various artists' and writers' associations. Prizes for artistic creation are also awarded by other social institutions such as the trade unions, the town councils, the Youth Association, etc.

One facet of the administrative measures taken by the state to encourage creative work and to ensure that creative artists enjoy the material conditions allowing them to give full rein to their talents is the policy applied in the matter of fees. This is based on the constitutional principle whereby all work must be paid for. It is this principle which underlies the legislation governing the use made of literary, scientific and artistic works in Bulgaria.

Fees to be paid to authors and performers have been set out in a schedule approved by the Council of Ministers of the People's Republic of Bulgaria and this schedule must be applied by all public bodies, organizations and institutions which make use of works or organize public events with the aid of performers. The schedule fixes the amount of the fee according to the character and type of the work or performance in question, the use made of it and the social aim envisaged.

The schedule sets out the royalties paid to literary authors and authors of scientific works or books about art in relation to a range setting minimum and maximum amounts per printed page of 2,000 signs. In the case of some (e.g. literary) works, it also lays down different royalty rates depending on the number of copies printed. Translators' fees are fixed in the same way; under the copyright law, translators are regarded as the authors of their translations and possess all the rights laid down by the law.

The schedule also lays down the fees for authors of dramatic, operatic, musical or other works intended for public performance. These fees are payable independently of the box-office takings from public performance of the works in question.

Bulgarian legislation does not provide for any complete and final abrogation of copyright, by virtue of which publishing houses, institutes and other bodies become joint owners of the copyright and divide the royalties with the author. Copyright law in Bulgaria strictly observes the socialist principle whereby the author is the sole owner of copyright. Even to the extent that copyright can be ceded, cession is limited by the law to a maximum of five years. Thus the author has an absolute right to receive the whole of the profits that ensue from the use made of his work.

On the same principle, government bodies, organizations and institutions for which an author has created works in the performance of his normal duties or on the basis of a commission cannot acquire the copyright. Here too, the author remains the owner of the copyright and receives the royalties due for the use made of his work in accordance with the conditions laid down by law and in the schedule, even where it is being used by the institution, government body or organization in question.

In addition, the rate of taxation on authors' and performers' fees is much lower than on other income.

The protection of creative artists' copyright and legitimate interests is the responsibility of a special body, the Directorate for the Protection of Copyright, whose main tasks are *inter alia* to facilitate the judicious application of the regulations laying down standard scales for authors' fees, issue directives with regard to their application and work out new draft regulations.

The People's Republic of Bulgaria is a member of the International Union for the Protection of Literary and Artistic Works (the Berne Union), and thus ensures the protection of the copyright of foreign authors whose works are made use of by Bulgarian publishers, theatres and other organizations and institutions, in accordance with the provisions of the Berne Convention for the Protection of Literary and Artistic Works.

The publication and use of works by foreign authors in Bulgaria form the subject of contracts made with the authors or their representatives, whereby the fees and royalties the authors will receive for the use of their works are fixed. The amounts to be paid to foreign authors are fixed by agreement, on the basis of international practice and reciprocity. In principle, such payments are made in the currency of the country to which the authors in question belong or in which they live.

The People's Republic of Bulgaria is taking all necessary steps to ensure that creative artists enjoy their legitimate rights, in accordance with the obligations incumbent on it under Article 27, paragraph 2, of the Universal Declaration of Human Rights.

The administration
of cultural activities by the state
and semi-public bodies

Since the administration of cultural activities is related to numerous aspects of everyday life, it cannot remain static but must be continually adapted and improved in such a way as to achieve a dynamic balance with the general system of social administration, and keep in time with the changes in the development of society and economic and social conditions. It must also necessarily reflect the existing cultural level of society and the extent to which social and cultural needs are being satisfied.

Not only is the state responsible for promoting general cultural development and artistic creation; it is also part of its task to take the necessary steps enabling the organization and administration of cultural activities to be improved.

Of all the manifold ways in which people can develop their creative potential, not the least is by participating in the management of public affairs. Because the state is organized and operates in a democratic fashion, it is possible for the masses to be encouraged to play a full and regular part in administration, such as they are now capable of playing thanks to the continuous rise in their intellectual and cultural level and the broadening of their social interests. Socialism in Bulgaria has developed not only in terms of political organization, but also in terms of the economic and cultural organization of society. As socialism is built, the conditions and forms of participation by the people in all spheres of public life, including the running of society, are being continually changed and improved.

During the last decade, certain functions previously carried out by state bodies have been transferred to semi-public bodies such as trade unions, youth associations, etc. The democratization of the management of the national economy and of all aspects of social life has also shown itself in the cultural field. It was natural to seek the most effective structure for all the different cultural organizations and try to find more suitable and more flexible working methods, the more so since their social role was

29

becoming much more important at this stage of social development. These changes were in harmony with the basic evolution of the socialist system and the gradual elimination of the differences between physical and intellectual work and between the countryside and the town. In order to achieve this harmony, the administration of culture and the arts had to be brought into line with the laws governing social development and the role of the state and other social agents in bringing about the progress of society.

In 1967, in order to achieve the best possible balance between cultural affairs and the administration of society as a whole, a general reorganization was carried out of all the administrative bodies in the field of culture and far-reaching changes were made in both their structure and their character. As a result of a study on the new situation and the new tendencies in the socio-economic and political life of the country, certain conclusions of a scientific nature were reached. At the same time an analysis was made of the state of national culture and of current needs, taking into account the historical, social and moral changes which had taken place in Bulgarian society, the prospects for cultural development and the complexity and growth potential of society in the modern world. The reorganization carried out in the cultural field was designed to serve the vital interests of society, the spiritual development of the people and the aspirations of creative artists, for the very best system of social organization was necessary if the talents of creative artists were to flower and if their work was to make an impact on society and fulfil a real social function. The aim of this reorganization of the administration of cultural affairs was not merely to make improvements in an imperfect system, but to replace it with an entirely new administrative system. National characteristics, which have never been underestimated, determined the particular nature of the system chosen and the intrinsic contribution that popular progressive traditions had to make to it.

This reorganization of the administrative bodies in the cultural field is in keeping with historical development and represents an original solution to the problems of social and cultural development. A basic aim of the new system is that it should have close ties with popular traditions, with contemporary social developments and with the changes affecting the individual on the moral and cultural planes. At the same time, this reorganization forms part and parcel of the evolution of the socialist state and thus represents one of the possible ways of improving the social structure and its administrative machinery.

The distinctive feature of the present system for administering cultural affairs is that it combines social (semi-public) and state elements, and is eminently democratic, since it is based on an elective principle. It is the start of a new stage in the socialist cultural development of the country, characterized by democratization of the organization of cultural activities at all levels, and by the active participation of creative artists and the promoters of culture in the administration of cultural and national affairs.

30

The new system takes account of the special characteristics of culture and of the process of artistic creativity. It is relatively independent, though as an integral part of the social system it is naturally subject to the general principles operating within this system. The principles governing the structure and the operation of the system for administering cultural affairs are identical with the general principles for the scientific management of socialist society, in particular the elective principle and the principle of democratic centralism, which combines centralized administration with a considerable degree of freedom for local bodies.

Representatives from the arts have the right to elect the members of all the local and higher administrative bodies in the cultural sphere, including the Chairman of the Committee for Culture, who has ministerial rank. Thus, at the First Congress of Bulgarian Culture, held in 1967, and at the Second Congress in 1972, a completely new model for the administration of culture by state and semi-public bodies was drawn up and put into practice.

The Third Congress of Culture, held in May 1977, was attended by 1,810 delegates representing the arts from all over the country. The congress, by secret ballot, elected the Committee for Culture as a joint state and semi-public body with responsibility for studying the problems of culture and directing policy in this field. The committee's statutes were also adopted at this congress. Set up in accordance with the principle of democratic centralism, the Committee for Culture has top-level responsibility for administering cultural affairs. It reports on its work to the Congress of Culture (the supreme body responsible for the administration of culture in the People's Republic of Bulgaria) and to the Council of Ministers. It is responsible for directing, co-ordinating and supervising the conduct of cultural activities decided upon by the congress.

The committee encourages the search for and the introduction of new methods of directing cultural activity. It also promotes experimentation on the basis of rigorous scientific analysis of the natural laws of cultural development. Its main functions include:

Directing and guiding cultural policy and cultural development, as well as cultural relations with foreign countries.

Examining and trying to solve the problems that arise in the fields of culture and communications.

Laying down guidelines for the development of socialist art and aesthetic education.

Supervising and directing the work of creating, preserving and disseminating works of art and artistic values in the following fields: (a) publishing and the sale and distribution of books, multi-media materials, photography, the production of records and audio-visual material, the making, conservation and distribution of films; (b) television, radio broadcasting, the press and other mass media; (c) music, the theatre, the circus and amateur artistic activities; (d) research and conservation

31

work on cultural monuments; (e) the activities of libraries, artistic and
cultural institutions, reading-rooms, museums and amateur groups.

Approving the programme and the repertoire of cultural institutions and
helping to co-ordinate the various national plans for culture and the
arts.

Organizing co-operation and cultural exchanges with foreign countries.

Ensuring, in accordance with the laws and international conventions in
force, the protection of copyright in the fields of literature, the arts
and science.

Ensuring, jointly with the trade unions, that the officials working for the
Committee for Culture are paid regularly and have job-security;

Helping to draw up legislation in the realm of arts and culture (all regulations affecting the interests of individual artists and writers and
cultural associations and organizations are first discussed with the
associations and organizations concerned).

The members of the Committee for Culture are elected every five years by
the Congress of Culture. In 1977, 217 writers, painters, musicians, journalists, artists, architects, scientific experts and officials were elected. The
Executive Board, which consists of a chairman, a number of vice-chairmen
(having the rank of deputy ministers), a secretary-general with the rank
of vice-chairman and several ordinary members, is elected from among the
members of the committee. The Chairman of the Committee is a member
of the government. The Executive Board reports to the committee on all
the organizational, ideological and cultural activities of the committee's
sections and organs, and also on the action taken in pursuance of the
decisions of the Congress of Culture. The Congress of Culture assembles
every five years. Its date of convocation and its agenda are announced
three months in advance. On the initiative of the Committee for Culture,
or at the request of a minimum of one-third of its members, extraordinary
congresses may also be called. The congress is empowered to approve the
activities of the Committee for Culture, alter its statutes, dissolve its
elected bodies and elect new ones, and also lay down the main guidelines
for its future work. Between meetings of the congress, the committee may
hold national conferences to consider important questions relating to arts
and culture. It holds at least two plenary sessions each year. During such
sessions decisions are taken on matters of fundamental importance concerning the allocation of budgetary resources, long-term plans are adopted
and so on.

As is clearly apparent, the Committee for Culture is a complex social
entity and this affects the ways and means by which it performs its functions. Of particular importance for the administration of cultural activities
are the councils that have been set up under the aegis of the general
directorates of the Committee. The members of these councils are chosen
from among creative artists and the most highly qualified specialists in the
various branches of the arts. The relationships that exist between the coun-

cils and the directorates are not administrative but functional; their aim is
to co-ordinate and systematize the activities planned so as to find the best
way of dealing with any problems that might arise. The councils are highly
competent bodies with great prestige. Their composition is a guarantee of
the soundness of their ideological and aesthetic views. For example, the
Music Council consists of twenty composers, conductors, choral directors,
musicologists and specialists in the teaching of music. Since such figures
are aware of the major theoretical problems and the specific needs of
musical institutions, they are able to make valid assessments with a view
to laying down rational policies in the musical field.

The Musical Council supervises the repertoire of the opera houses, the
light-opera theatres and the state symphony orchestras. It also supervises
the development of musical ensembles, studies the problems relating to
symphonic music and to the foundation of musical institutions, etc.

The Fine Arts Council consists of twenty of the most famous painters
and art theorists. It studies the basic problems affecting the arts in the
country and is responsible for the planning of national exhibitions of
graphic or applied arts and of exhibitions of Bulgarian painters abroad,
for pre- and in-service training, for the state of art galleries, for periodical
publications on problems in art and so forth.

All these councils are distinguished by their spirit of initiative, their
energy and their awareness of their responsibilities. They report on their
activities to the Committee for Culture and to the corresponding artists'
associations.

The provincial, communal and municipal councils of culture correspond
to the administrative subdivision of the country. They are elected in secret
ballot by provincial or communal conferences for a period of two and a half
years—that is, half the interval between two meetings of the Congresses of
Culture. Their members can be relieved of their responsibilities before the
expiration of their term of office if they fail to carry out their tasks, or
prove unworthy of the trust bestowed upon them. Their dismissal may be
decided on at a plenary session of the provincial council concerned, by a
simple majority on a show of hands. Members representing the sections of
the artists' associations or the socio-political organizations can be relieved
of their mandate on the proposal of the association or organization
concerned.

The councils of culture are special joint state and semi-public bodies,
constituted on an elective basis, which come under the Committee for
Culture and the corresponding People's Councils. They are responsible for
directing all cultural and artistic activity within the province, commune or
municipality concerned.

The composition of the councils is extremely important. In principle it
must rest on agreement between the administrative authorities and those
they administer, without which any effective activity would be impossible.
In fact, analysis of the number of their members, their level of education

and their qualifications proves that such agreement does exist. The present composition of these local councils is, therefore, such as to encourage a scientific approach to cultural problems and ensure productive results.

The number of members of the councils of culture varies according to the size of the area for which they are responsible. The communal councils number between nine and twenty-one members, the municipal councils between nine and thirty-one, and the provincial councils between forty-one and eighty-one.

Every provincial council of culture has an operational arm, the executive bureau, drawn from members of the council. The bureau consists of a president, a vice-president, a secretary and several ordinary members.

Sections similar to those established in the writers' and artists' associations and in the directorates of the Committee for Culture also exist in the local bodies responsible for cultural affairs. The members of these sections are representatives of local cultural circles. Their structure and numerical composition vary, as does the distribution of responsibilities within each council, according to the economic and geographical characteristics of the provinces or towns. The existence of these sections enables many problems to be solved, not through administrative channels, but directly, with regard for local conditions and needs. Their decisions are taken on the basis of collective experience and understanding.

The provincial councils of culture hold from two to four plenary sessions each year, which bring together a large number of writers, artists and so on. These sessions are devoted to the consideration of important problems relating to cultural development and of current issues, such as cultural activity in the countryside, art education, the conservation of cultural monuments and property, libraries, amateur artistic activities, etc.

At the plenary sessions the members of the councils consider the work done in the various sectors, take appropriate measures for the implementation of the projects proposed, exchange opinions and views and lay down guidelines for future activities. For creative artists from the individual provinces thus to take an active part in the consideration of so many questions affecting cultural life is an entirely new phenomenon.

In order to carry out their task, these joint state and semi-public bodies enjoy conditions that give them freedom of initiative and increasing independence. Their work is of an innovative nature and much energy, imagination and sense of responsibility are required to carry it out. The councils of culture provide a rational framework linking the various levels of cultural activity. Their structure, functions and powers are so conceived as to reconcile the principle of planning with the intellectual worker's spirit of initiative. Those elected to the councils carry out their duties without remuneration and are fully conscious of their moral responsibility and of the need to minister honestly to the interests of society.

At the present time, the councils of culture number 18,000 members—writers, painters, artists, journalists, composers, musicians, architects, librarians, teachers and officials. This vanguard working on behalf of culture participates directly and fully in the government of the country. The councils of culture impart a new quality to the social structure. By their very nature and their duties they are part of the state apparatus, yet at the same time, because they are elected, they are democratic bodies representing the organized opinion of the working masses. Consequently, they serve as a link between the state and the writers' and artists' associations, to strengthen the bonds between intellectual and other workers and also to promote creative activity.

With the setting up of these joint state and semi-public bodies to direct cultural activities, the position and the role of the artists' and writers' associations in the process of cultural development have altered. Their rights, and equally the say they have in the solution of cultural problems, have taken on a new dimension and their role in the country's social life has considerably increased. The associations in question are the following: the Bulgarian Writers' Association, the Bulgarian Painters' Association, the Bulgarian Journalists' Association, the Bulgarian Artists' Association, the Bulgarian Composers' Association, the Bulgarian Musicians' Association, the Bulgarian Cinema Artists' Association, the Bulgarian Translators' Association and the Bulgarian Architects' Association. They are independent, democratic organizations with their own statutes and rules and bring together on a non-remunerated basis artists and writers, etc. from the various branches of culture. They organize and promote the creative activities of their members, help with their professional training and further training and strive to improve their living and working conditions. The associations have at their disposal funds which enable them to give material aid to their members, encourage young talent, organize competitions, award prizes, etc. Much of their work is devoted to discussing the problems of artistic creation, considering literary and scientific works and so on.

The associations, which now have more than 20,000 members, are powerful bodies within society. Their responsibilities are wide-ranging. They have considerable financial resources at their disposal and possess their own newspapers or journals. The Bulgarian Writers' Association and the Bulgarian Painters' association even have their own publishing houses. The associations have been in existence for many years and enjoy great prestige. As they now play an integral part in the administration of cultural affairs, their responsibilities and sphere of action have been considerably extended. By successfully discharging their own particular functions, they help the state in the fields of culture and education and also play a concrete part in the administration of cultural affairs. The Bulgarian Writers' Association participates in preparing thematic plans for the publication of Bulgarian literary works, while the other associations also have a share in the planning of publications coming within their respective provinces. In addition, the associations are responsible for promoting the activities of amateur artists.

The Committee for Culture, in collaboration with the artists' and writers' associations, draws up all the documents affecting these associations. Co-operation between the joint state and semi-public bodies and the associations is particularly important in connection with the periodic reviews of ongoing activities in the field of drama, opera and ballet, or on the occasion of national singing and music competitions, international festivals and competitions and so on.

Since the Committee for Culture became a joint body, relations have become even closer between it and such semi-public bodies as the professional associations, the Youth Association, etc. One of the chief benefits of this collaboration is that it involves the young in cultural activities, and at the same time enables them to become aware of their cultural heritage and of contemporary artistic values.

In order to achieve closer co-operation between the Committee for Culture, the writers' and artists' associations and other semi-public bodies, co-ordinating committees have been set up under the aegis of the Committee for Culture, bringing together the presidents of the artists' and writers' associations, the representatives of the semi-public bodies, the representatives of government departments, etc.

The work of these co-ordinating committees covers the main areas of cultural affairs—creative work in the arts and the preservation and dissemination of cultural values. As permanent bodies under the auspices of the Committee for Culture they help to improve the administration of the arts and encourage continuity of action in this field.

Cultural development makes it necessary to study the changes taking place within society and also to deal with many problems of a scientific and technical character. The specialized scientific institutes accordingly have their place in the administration of cultural activities. Among the bodies operating under the auspices of the Committee for Culture are the Institute of Scientific Research on the Arts, the National Centre for Scientific Information on Cultural Matters, the Centre for Research on the Material and Technical Foundations of Culture and the Scientific Institute for the Protection of Cultural Monuments. There are also research units concerned with different art forms or cultural activities, and these too come under the appropriate sections of the committee.

Ever since it was set up, the Committee for Culture has sought to establish better relations between the state, the artists' and writers' associations and individual creative artists. As its activities have developed, it has sought new ways to raise the standard of cultural life. Thus, in 1974 the national structure 'artistic creativity, cultural activities and the mass media' was set up and the Committee for Culture instead of being a mere administrative organ became a joint state and semi-public body responsible for dealing with general problems in the arts.

Administration of cultural activities
by the state and semi-public bodies

In its organization, its machinery and its principles of action this national structure embodies the idea of the unified organization and administration of artistic and cultural activities. It includes various state, scientific, economic, social, artistic and other semi-public bodies that operate at various levels and are united in their aim to encourage the flowering of Bulgarian culture, to satisfy the cultural needs of the people and to maximize the development of the individual and of his creative capabilities, through the spread of artistic values, introduction to the different forms of cultural activity and the use of the media.

Thus the structure includes government departments, artists' and writers' associations, scientific institutions and other semi-public bodies. By bringing together all these varied bodies on a functional basis, it is possible to harmonize overall cultural policy with the administration of activities in particularly important and relatively specific fields. Without intervening directly in the affairs of the state organs, the artists' and writers' associations and other semi-public bodies which make up this structure, the Committee for Culture, by virtue of its super-sectoral character, co-ordinates activities in all the different cultural sectors, and organizes and directs the material and creative resources available so as to overcome the basic problems concerning the cultural development of the country and of the people.

As a joint state and semi-public body, the Committee for Culture is responsible for providing methodological guidance and supervision in regard to the cultural activities of the ministries, government departments and the artists' and writers' associations and other semi-public bodies, the public authorities and the specialized administrative bodies concerned with artistic creativity, cultural activities and the media.

With the progressive improvement in the administration of cultural affairs and the organization of the national structure, solutions are being found to the major problems confronting the local councils of culture. Measures have been taken with a view to strengthening the role of the provincial and communal councils of culture, making them solely responsible for the co-ordination, direction and supervision of all cultural affairs in their respective areas. Since 1977 local structures have been established in the country in order to bring all cultural activity within a unitary system providing for joint administration by state and semi-public bodies. Each provincial council of culture has control over the structure in its territory and is responsible for all activities connected with artistic creativity, cultural affairs and the mass media within the province.

This new system of administration seeks to make rational use of the experience acquired and, with due regard to the new objectives, to promote ways and means likely to maximize the development of culture and the arts.

The experience acquired during the last few years in setting up and developing the new joint system of administration (by state and semi-public bodies) has confirmed its viability, warranting the extension of this system to the administration and development of national education. The first congress of National Education, held in May 1980, elected a Higher Council of Education. This is again a joint state and semi-public body, responsible for studying the main problems in the educational field and, if it considers necessary, submitting them to the Council of State and the Council of Ministers. In collaboration with the Higher Council of Education, the Ministry of National Education, the Councils for General and Vocational Education and their special directorates and sections are responsible for implementing the state's educational policy. At the same time, local (provincial and communal) bodies have been set up in the field of national education, again on a joint state/semi-public basis, to direct and supervise all the organizational, pedagogical and methodological activities of educational institutions, and also to draw up and implement educational programmes. Such measures have strengthened the efforts already being made with a view to overcoming the problems in regard to national education and its democratization.

The National Programme
for Popular Aesthetic Education

Aesthetic education has existed in one form or another throughout history. Nowadays, however, it has become a vital necessity, and because of the improved material conditions and the constructive spirit prevailing in society it has become easier to provide it. In fact, only a society where all production of material goods and spiritual values is centred on man is likely to pursue such an aim and be able at the same time to create the conditions necessary to achieve it. Thus, in the National Programme for Popular Aesthetic Education, which has been drawn up in Bulgaria, aesthetic education is seen as forming a whole, comprising not only work, social life and the arts, but also the traditional and modern means of spreading information and culture, together with the activities of the appropriate organizations in this field. For it is essential to promote awareness of the wealth of ideological, aesthetic and moral conceptions which art transmits, in order that these may be evinced in the individual's work, in his behaviour and in his relationships with other members of society. Naturally, aesthetic education of this kind is inconceivable unless people are informed in such a way as to enable them to assimilate such ideas.

The idea of drawing up a national unified programme of aesthetic education stems from this conception and is a reflection of the increased opportunities of both a material and a spiritual nature in Bulgarian society. Thus, we are witnessing the emergence of a new tendency which is growing stronger and stronger: the closer material consumption approaches traditional, scientifically based norms, the more man's spiritual concerns increase and the more necessary it becomes to satisfy his growing cultural and aesthetic needs. This is an objective process to which the lofty humanitarian objectives of an advanced socialist society properly correspond, namely to bring out and develop all the individual's creative faculties, to awaken the artist—the connoisseur and creator of beautiful things—which exists in every man, and to encourage his aspirations to transform reality in accordance with the laws of beauty.

The National Programme for Popular Aesthetic Education is directed towards the whole population and tries to take into account their different cultural levels, personal tastes and aesthetic needs.

The distinctive feature of this programme is that aesthetic education is regarded not only as a means whereby the individual may broaden his general culture and acquire artistic awareness, but also as one of the essential factors in the flowering of his creative capabilities and in the development of his personality. At the same time, aesthetic education is seen as reflecting the aesthetic level achieved in the production of spiritual values, with the result that the processes of education and artistic creation are fused together in a single whole.

The aim is not to produce a passive consumer attitude towards aesthetic values, nor to encourage mere knowledge of the arts, but to stimulate people to take action in the field of culture and the arts.

Consequently, everything is based on the natural linkage that exists between the aesthetic and educational functions of material and spiritual production, of work and of the environment. Aesthetic education is related to the efforts being made to improve the aesthetic level of the means of production, work processes and the articles produced. This is even more important in view of the situation created as a result of the scientific and technological revolution, as there is a danger that the individual's intellect will be developed at the expense of his feelings. Clearly, modern man must possess scientific knowledge, but this must be leavened by artistic insight.

It is extremely important that aesthetic education should stimulate artistic creativity. It is in this context that the programme is likely to influence cultural development, bearing in mind the place and the role of each art form and of artistic creativity within the process of aesthetic education, for the increasing interaction between the various forms of artistic activity provides numerous opportunities for the improvement of aesthetic education.

The programme of aesthetic education encourages the development of the personality and the awakening of the creative talents. Its specific aim is to ensure the development of the individual's tastes and aesthetic needs and thereby raise the level of consciousness and of artistic activity of the whole community.

By virtue of its essence, and its principal aim, aesthetic education nowadays is thus bound up with creation of all the conditions necessary for the harmonious development of the individual, the increasing satisfaction of his material and spiritual needs, training in artistic sensitivity and the awakening and stimulation of the basic feelings for art which exist in all human beings. It is necessary to develop within each individual a yearning for beauty in his work, in his way of life and in his relationships with other people and thus induce him to broaden his spiritual horizons.

It is for this reason that the programme is based on a few essential principles. It is primarily a general programme, aimed at all sections of society, all generations and all the institutions concerned. The programme is of a universal nature both with regard to the content of aesthetic education and also with regard to the forms that impart a particular character to it, within the framework of society as a whole. Other principles underlying the programme are continuity, sequentiality, permanency and co-ordination. There should be continuity in the methods and means which are employed and also in regard to the activities directed to different age-groups. Continuity in aesthetic education involves the use of traditional forms of expression and of permanent values, while at the same time making use of the new ideas which have come to the fore in the arts. Continuity in the impact of aesthetic education presupposes the concerted action of all those responsible for cultural activities at all levels and in all fields, as well as harmonization of the planned objectives with the methods and means adopted to attain them.

The national programme does not regard the individual merely as an object of aesthetic education and experience, but seeks instead his active participation in the very process of aesthetic education, which must therefore include the principle of self-improvement. In other words, the individual is also regarded as an active agent in the process of aesthetic education.

However, before becoming an agent of aesthetic education and beginning to educate himself, the individual has already been influenced by the environment, traditions and public opinion. His tastes and his aesthetic needs, so formed, may be satisfied by what society provides and by his own interior impulses. This determines the extent to which he assimilates aesthetic values, the range of his aesthetic responses and the depth of his critical judgements.

Nowadays, the cultural and educational differences between the different sections of society are being progressively eliminated. Sociological studies and statistics show that these differences are due to cultural inequalities inherited from the past and that there are older people whose educational level is still not very high. There are also differences in the amount of interest taken in the arts and these in turn give rise to differences in people's receptivity to culture.

The implementation of the programme of aesthetic education is a long-term process which is continually being refined and improved in response to the dynamics of life and the needs of social development. It is for this reason that it includes a large number of subprogrammes. All the provinces have introduced their own programmes of aesthetic education in accordance with their own particular circumstances. There are also programmes at the communal and municipal levels and special programmes for the various trades and professions. These are carried out with the aid of various government departments and institutions, including the Ministry of National Education, the Council of State for Scientific and Technical Progress, the Bulgarian Academy of Sciences, the artists' and writers' associations, the Youth Association, etc. The task of co-ordinating all the projects organized as part of these programmes is the responsibility of the Committee for Culture, which also deals with the problems of publicity and methodology and carries out scientific research in this field.

The projects planned as part of the provincial programmes are extremely wide-ranging and include:

The role of art in the aesthetic education of different age-groups and segments of the population.

Aesthetic education in everyday life and in interpersonal relationships.

Aesthetic education for workers (during and after working hours).

Aesthetic education and man's everyday, natural environment.

The structural and material prerequisites for the implementation of the programme.

The programme of aesthetic education is accompanied by wide-ranging scientific and methodological research work, which seeks to build on the experience acquired, evaluate the results obtained and draw conclusions which will benefit future projects. A number of conferences and symposia on the theoretical and practical aspects of this subject have been organized in the various provinces and also at the national and the international level. Special mention should be made of the Bulgarian-Soviet symposium on 'Aesthetic Education for the Young', the international symposium on 'Culture and the Harmonious Development of the Individual in the Modern World' (1978), the symposium on 'The Child, Creativity and Evolution', held on the occasion of the 'Banner of Peace' International Assembly of Children (1979), etc.

The programme also draws on the riches of worldwide culture and the major attainments of the human spirit. Guided by the idea that culture is an open system that can borrow its models from anywhere and can assimilate and adapt what it takes so as to raise the level of national achievement, the authors of this programme consider culture and the arts to be among the most important factors in bringing about mutual understanding and harmony between people in the name of peace, friendship and co-operation.

It is with this end in view that a long-term programme has been devised and is now being put into practice which assigns to culture and the arts an even larger role in the harmonious development of the individual. It includes a number of projects intended to show the life and work of some great creative figures. These projects encourage people's aspiration towards harmonious development and try to help them to give better expression to their creative powers in the various areas of social life. The first project of this kind sought to introduce the Bulgarian people to the work of Nikolai Rörich, the great Russian painter and writer. A retrospective exhibition of his paintings was organized and translations of his works were published. In addition, over a period of several months attempts were made through the mass media to bring his literary and artistic works to the attention of the public. The artists' and writers' associations studied his creative work and attempted to make it known to their members, while, for their part, scientific circles organized an international symposium highlighting the relevant factors conducive to development of an all-round personality.

Numerous projects were also organized in order to publicize the life and work of Leonardo da Vinci. They revealed the universal nature of his work and his importance as an innovator. Among the events organized in this connection mention should be made of an exhibition of original paintings by Leonardo da Vinci and painters of his school, an exhibition on *The Scientific and Technical Heritage of Leonardo da Vinci*, an exhibition of pictures by Bulgarian painters on the subject *Leonardo da Vinci and Us*, etc. A series of lectures was organized with the participation of Bulgarian and foreign art historians and another series of lectures on science and technology. As part of this same programme, a debate on 'Science, Technology, the Arts and the Harmonious Development of the Personality' was held with the participation of the artists' and writers' associations, the media and the Bulgarian Scientific and Technical Association. An international conference was held to discuss 'The Historical Destiny of Humanism in Eastern Christian Culture During the Renaissance in Western Europe', which was illustrated in an original fashion by an exhibition bearing the same name.

Television, radio and the press gave wide coverage to these events, as well as dealing themselves with all aspects of the work of this genius of the Renaissance. The Ivan Vazov National Classical Theatre put on a Bulgarian play about Leonardo da Vinci. Material from his literary and philosophical works, reproductions of his paintings and many general and specialist works on Leonardo da Vinci and Italian Renaissance art were published.

All these projects provided a wealth of material affording the Bulgarian people closer acquaintance with this remarkable all-round creative genius, and the eternal artistic values represented by his work.

The Vladimir Ilyich Lenin Programme was also organized as part of the long-term programme of aesthetic education, for this intellectual giant, ardent revolutionary and popular leader is one of the most famous figures of our time and is, of course, especially well known in Bulgaria. It is for this reason that the aim of the programme was not so much to make known his life and work, but rather to make people more aware of the qualities which made Lenin the greatest figure of his time, and of his contribution to world culture. Lenin played an outstanding role in the creation of the communist ideal, namely the harmonious development of the personality. The implementation of his ideas established the social foundations necessary for the attainment of this ideal at the present stage in the construction of an advanced socialist society, in which, in keeping with Lenin's teachings, increasing emphasis is laid on the creative potential of the new system and its genuine humanistic content.

Starting with the commemoration of the 110th anniversary of Lenin's birth, the V. I. Lenin Programme extended over several months and included numerous national events, a succession of special features in the

media, performances of plays about Lenin, film shows, a visit to the
V. I. Lenin Museum in Moscow, the organization by the national museums
of an exhibition entitled *Lenin and Bulgaria*, etc. Other events that were
also organized at the same time included an international assembly of
representatives of the arts, science and culture on 'Lenin and Artistic
Creativity', an international symposium on 'Leninism, a Symbol of the
Socialist and Spiritual Renewal of the World', and an interdisciplinary
seminar on 'Lenin and the Harmonious Development of the Modern
World'. The competition 'Lenin's Century is my Century' sought to
encourage writers and artists to make use of Lenin's ideas in their works.

The main events included in this programme took place in Sofia and in
other towns throughout the country. Arts festivals were also organized in
numerous other places in order to pay homage to Lenin. All the artists'
and writers' associations and other semi-public bodies and many government departments took part in this programme, which thus involved the
participation of all cultural circles, as well as being aimed at all segments of
the population and stimulating creativity, especially among the young.
In all, it gave the Bulgarian people the opportunity to see the whole range
of Lenin's personality and assess his importance as a synthesis of universal
cultural values in addition to being the prime initiator of the contemporary
historical process.

Plans are now being made to organize other cultural events devoted
to Constantine Cyrillus the Philosopher, Lomonosov, Einstein, Peter
Beron, etc. The aim is to show how the creative potentialities of these
historical figures developed in a harmonious way, and their relevance to our
present day when socialist society is giving increasingly full scope for all-
round development of the personality. On the same subject, mention should
be made of the National Centre for Culture and the Arts, which is now
being set up. Its task will be to define the special role, the importance and
the place of culture and the arts in the evolution of world civilization and
also the contribution of the Bulgarian people to world culture.

As part of the events planned to mark the International Year of the
Child, in 1979, the People's Republic of Bulgaria organized and was host to
the 'Banner of Peace' International Assembly of Children, whose aim was
to bring together children from all over the world in the name of peace,
creativity and beauty.

The very nature and the specific objectives of this event meant that it
was closely connected with the national programme of aesthetic education,
as well as forming an integral part of the ongoing activities whose purpose
is to detect, guide and stimulate children's creative talents and develop
them to the full.

Bulgarian children were able to give full rein to their musical, artistic
and literary talents on the occasion of the assembly. Some 300,000 children
took part in the events organized at the communal or municipal level,
more than 50,000 in the provincial events and 5,000 in the national events;

of these, 1,000 went on to the assembly, which was also attended by 1,321 children from seventy-six foreign countries. For this occasion, more than 13,000 children from eighty-four countries sent to Bulgaria 17,000 works of art, which were of considerable value. Among the events organized were an international exhibition of children's drawings, a review of children's writings, an international festival of musical composition and performance and an exhibition of photographs taken by children. The children were able to attend concerts, an international children's carnival and a special final concert. During the assembly an international symposium on 'The Child, Creativity and Evolution' was attended by seventy-six scholars from twenty-four countries, who assembled in order to study the different ways in which society can encourage talented youngsters.

All in all, the assembly served as eloquent proof of Bulgaria's interest in the development of children's creative talents, and the events held under its auspices left both the young participants and the adults with fond memories, for they brought the joy of making contact with art in its purest and most sincere form, in a search to penetrate the mysteries of the unknown.

The expansion
of cultural activities

Culture by its very nature encompasses contemporary ideas, problems and aspirations, the distinctive features of the national character and the force and the individuality of the creative spirit. At the same time it affords evidence, in the richness and variety of its manifestations, as to the social climate prevailing at the time of its genesis and development.

If we examine the path of socialist development followed by Bulgarian culture, it is clear that this has been as it were rekindled by the open-hearted spirit of our times. This open-hearted spirit is evinced in several ways—in the liberty given to creative artists, in the concern and interest shown in encouraging individual talent, in the responsibility assumed for the future direction of culture no less than in the warm reception given to new achievements in the arts.

Without society's concern in raising the cultural level, and without the socialist environment, the Bulgarian people would never have been able to show so fully its love of learning and would not have been able to attain the high level of education it enjoys today.

Education

The Bulgarians' love for learning and culture dates from the earliest times. As early as the ninth century, once Bulgarian was adopted as the official written language, there were two great schools of literature—at Preslav and Okhrida—which were responsible for educating the first Bulgarian scholars. Later, at the time of the Bulgarian national revival, with the establishment of new secular schools a vast popular movement grew up in favour of education. On the eve of the liberation from Turkish domination, in 1878, there were more than 1,500 schools paid for by the population itself, and more than 450 textbooks had been published for use in the schools. In 1869 a number of Bulgarian intellectuals founded, in the

Romanian town of Braila, a Bulgarian literary society which, after the liberation, moved to Sofia and became the Bulgarian Academy of Sciences.

Education in Bulgaria has always drawn its strength from democratic traditions which, despite frequent attempts, have never been entirely destroyed. Even when Fascism held sway in the country, the people maintained an interest in spiritual values and a thirst for knowledge.

After the victory of the Socialist Revolution on 9 September 1944, the structure of the educational system, and especially the educational syllabus, underwent radical changes. In 1948 the National Assembly enacted a law on public education, which laid down the principles of the new socialist system of education.

The principles are set out in the Constitution of the People's Republic of Bulgaria. Since 1922 school attendance had been compulsory up to the age of 14 (seventh grade). Since 1966 it has been compulsory up to the age of 15 (eighth grade). Conservative ideas are entirely foreign to education in Bulgaria. It develops in accordance with the needs of the times, taking into account the requirements of the rising generations whom it seeks to prepare for life. Changes with this end in view were introduced by the law of 1959 on 'the strengthening of links between education and life'. Under this law, it is the duty of education to train the young in the performance of activities that benefit the community and contribute to personal development.

In 1969 General Regulations for the Reform of the Educational System were issued. The aim of this reform was the progressive introduction of universal secondary education. In this way education has been more closely linked with social development and the construction of a socialist society. This reorganization has made it possible to apply improved methods in educating individuals for the social and occupational duties which await them.

In the course of these changes, which took place as part of the dynamic social development of the country, considerable experience was acquired and many of the guiding principles in education were redefined. In 1978 new reforms were planned and in May 1979 draft regulations were studied and subsequently adopted by the Central Committee of the Bulgarian Communist Party meeting in plenary session.

The prime objective of our educational system is to educate people so that they are able to fulfil themselves in life thanks to having a good general education, well-developed creative capabilities, sound political and ideological views and appropriate occupational training qualifying them to participate in work for the benefit of the community. The young should start their working lives with their personalities fully developed and enriched by the spiritual values acquired, have a wide range of interests and the wish to improve themselves at all times. It is for this reason that the education they receive must fit them to play a useful role in society.

Thus, the free and spontaneous actions of the individual are shown to be related to social needs and forces.

The regulations accord a special role to the new secondary schools of general and technical education, where education is provided at three different levels. At the first level (from the first to the tenth grade) the pupils acquire the basic knowledge and the general culture which form the foundations of any specialized training. At the second level they receive general work-training and acquire a wide range of technical knowledge. At the third level they are trained for a particular occupation. Thus, it is the role of general secondary education to ensure every individual's access to knowledge and to the occupation of his choice.

Higher education has also undergone reforms and, as a result of the new objectives which have been laid down, changes have been introduced in the administration of education. The whole educational system has been reorganized according to the principle of joint control by the state and semi-public bodies. How the new regulations are to be put into practice was discussed by the first National Educational Congress, held in 1980.

Education is completely free in all educational establishments. The school system includes establishments of pre-school education, secondary schools of general education, polytechnics (some of which specialize in teaching languages and the natural sciences), vocational and technical secondary schools, art schools and institutions of post-secondary and higher education. This variety enables young people to choose their course in accordance with their own interests and personal tastes. Special schools are provided for physically or mentally handicapped children, who also receive compulsory basic education and vocational training. For children who are predisposed towards certain illnesses or have suffered from serious infectious diseases, so-called climatic schools have been opened in certain areas. For children of pre-school age, throughout the country there are crèches and nursery schools, where children can be sent by the day or by the week; there are also a substantial number of seasonal nursery schools open during the summer. Over 336,000 children of pre-school age attend 6,406 establishments designed in accordance with the requirements of modern theories on child-care.

Boarding schools, homes for children and adolescents, semi-boarding schools and study facilities also form part of the educational system. Study facilities are available to pupils after their classes, for them to do their preparation, read, play, etc., under the supervision of a teacher. At semi-boarding schools the children stay on for several hours after classes have finished.

Out-of-school activities are very varied. For the most part they take place in 'pioneer' halls, which are cultural centres in which the pupils are introduced to art. They have rooms for film-shows and concerts, play rooms and workshops in which young people make model planes or ships, take an interest in radio technology and so forth. Children may also take dancing, music or drawing lessons, join handicraft classes in which they do modelling, embroidery, poker-work, wood carving, etc., or else take part in drama groups, puppet performances, children's choirs or orchestras, etc.

The members of the Radio Sofia Children's Choir, the Pionneria (young pioneers) Symphony Orchestra and the Bodra Smiana (younger generation) Children's Choir have given concerts in several foreign countries. In addition to the pioneer halls, there are special interest centres for those interested in technical subjects, the natural environment and tourism.

All the schools throughout the country have playgrounds and sports grounds. More than 600,000 pupils, distributed among 8,900 physical culture groups, take an active part in sport. Each year the schools form mathematics, physics, chemistry, biology, radio and other groups. There are a large number of choirs and orchestras, theatre groups and dance troupes, which give young people the chance to develop and display their talents.

At Sofia there is a Centre for Literature and Art, the main purpose of which is to study the literary and artistic works intended for young people and to develop methods of putting these works to optimum use as part of the aesthetic education of the younger generation and of contributing to the flowering of children's artistic talents. This centre includes sections for children's literature, artistic sections, a section responsible for providing guidelines for children's libraries, and a publishing section that brings out a bulletin (*Children, Art, Books*) and also collections, directories and year-books, such as *Problems in Literature for Children* and *Problems of Aesthetic Education*. The Centre for Literature and Art arranges poetry recitals, story-telling evenings and meetings between young readers and poets, writers and painters. Its library contains a wide range of interesting books for children. With the help of educational experts, writers, art theorists, creative artists and leading figures in the promotion of the arts, the Centre for Literature and Art organizes discussions on works of art intended for children, guides the children's reading and so on.

During the academic year 1979/80, primary and secondary schools and institutions of higher education were attended by 1,453,995 students. Unesco statistics show that Bulgaria is among the leading countries in the world in terms of the number of children enrolled in school as a proportion of the total population. To convey the rate at which higher education is expanding one need only quote the fact that during the academic year 1979/80, the number of students rose to 87,494 in the institutions of higher education and to 19,225 in those of post-secondary education, as against 10,169 in 1939/40. Before the Second World War there were five institutions of higher education in the country. Today there are twenty-eight institutions of higher education and thirty-four of post-secondary education. There are nine times as many specialized technical courses as there were in 1944/45. This rise has been brought about by the need for highly qualified personnel in the main branches of material production:

energy, metallurgy, engineering and chemistry. In Bulgaria today there are 2 million people who have completed their secondary education and more than 350,000 have received higher education.

Education in the arts is provided by the following institutions:

Institutions of higher education: the Bulgarian State Conservatory in Sofia, the Higher Institute for the Plastic Arts, Sofia, the Higher Institute for the Dramatic Arts, Sofia, and the Higher Institute for Educational Methods, Plovdiv.

Institutions of post-secondary education: three post-secondary teacher-training institutes, in Varna, Blagoevgrad and Kardjali; one post-secondary institute in Sofia for training musicians and choreographers; one post-secondary institute in Sofia for training bibliographers.

Secondary schools of music: seven secondary schools of classical music, in Sofia, Plovdiv, Varna, Pleven, Ruse, Stara Zagora and Burgas, and two secondary schools of folk music, in Kotel and Shiroka Lake.

Secondary schools of art: two schools of the plastic arts, in Sofia and Plovdiv, and seven schools of the applied arts, in Sofia, Plovdiv, Smolian, Kotel, Triavna, Kazanlak and Troyan.

A secondary school for teaching the languages and culture of the ancient world, in Sofia.

A national experimental school for art education, also in Sofia.

From 1949 onwards, correspondence courses were introduced in the institutions of higher education, at first in some specialized subjects only, then in a wider range of subjects. This gives many workers the chance to be trained in new skills. They are granted paid leave for the period they need to spend at university in order to work for and sit the examinations.

Before the Socialist Revolution the total number of professors, lecturers and assistants teaching in the universities was 453, whereas by 1979 it had risen to 12,505. In all institutions of higher education, the rectors, the deans and their deputies are elected.

Nowadays, students work in enviable material conditions. As early as 1948, a law was passed on student social security. The funds that the state allocates to higher education increase each year; they are used for building purposes, for the provision of laboratories, experimental installations and libraries, for the award of scholarships, for the establishment of student residences, etc. More than 45 per cent of the students hold scholarships. The institutions of higher education also have funds available to reward students who have done outstandingly well in their studies. About half the students take their meals in the canteens, which are paid for by the state; in addition, many students live in halls of residence on the university campus, where they have excellent working conditions and can take advantage of sports facilities, etc.

Children of married students can be left in crèches free of charge on weekdays; if only one of the parents is a student there is a very small charge. Medical treatment is free to the whole population. In the halls of residence there are student health centres. During their holidays students can stay at special rest-homes in mountain or bathing resorts or other holiday centres.

The development of scientific and technical institutions is related to the rise in the general level of education, to the greater intellectual demands of work and to the modernization of plant. There now exist in Bulgaria 494 organizations and bodies carrying out scientific research, including 168 research institutes, 32 institutions for research, planning and construction, 19 research groups, 115 technical development units, 31 experimental centres, etc. More than 70,000 people are employed in the scientific field and there are 126,000 teachers.

Publishing

In 1855, when the country was still under Ottoman rule, a Bulgarian, Christo G. Danov, showed great initiative by founding, in Plovdiv, the first Bulgarian publishing house. Until that date, all Bulgarian books had been published abroad. (The first book to be published in modern Bulgarian was printed in Rome in 1651.) This event marked a turning-point in the country's cultural history, as henceforth the Bulgarian people were able to take advantage of one of the most remarkable achievements in the history of world civilization—the invention of printing. In spite of the unfavourable circumstances, 111 books written in Bulgarian were published in 1869 alone. After the liberation (1878), by which time 1,800 titles had been published abroad, publishing expanded rapidly, although there were ups and downs.

Nowadays, books are the inseparable companions of Bulgarian men and women and play an essential role in their daily lives. Publishing has continued to show a rapid development and it is interesting to draw some comparisons with the past: in 1939, i.e. the last pre-war year, 2,169 titles were published, with a total print-run of 6,488,000, whereas today there are twenty-four publishing houses in Bulgaria, publishing eight times as many books as in 1938. Many of the books published are specialist works: literary works, translations, books for children and young people, books on art, science, music and medicine, technical literature, works on farming techniques, etc. The publishing houses belong to the state or to various scientific institutions and semi-public bodies such as the trade unions, the Bulgarian Academy of Sciences, the Bulgarian Writers' Association, the Bulgarian Painters' Association, the Youth Association, etc.

Nowadays, more than six books per inhabitant are published each year in Bulgaria and the number of titles is constantly increasing: in 1960, 3,369 titles were published, representing a print-run of 30.2 million copies; the corresponding figures for 1972 were 3,978 titles and 42 million copies and for 1979 4,337 and 51 million.

A rapid glance through a list of the books published shows a considerable increase in the number of books dealing with the social sciences, philosophy, history and economics. Scientific works and popular science books have also shown an increase. A balance has been struck between the publication of Bulgarian and foreign classics and of contemporary works. Literary works occupy a considerable place among the books published for adults and also for children and adolescents.

The classics of world literature are widely available. The publishers catalogues always contain the names of the greatest writers, poets and playwrights of all times, though Bulgarian readers can also obtain the works of contemporary authors from all over the world. Each year, works belonging to more than thirty-five different national literatures are translated into Bulgarian and published. Between 1944 and 1976, Bulgarian publishing houses published 694 works by French authors, 488 works by American authors, 477 works by British authors, 192 works by Italian authors, etc. During 1976 alone, 651 works by foreign authors, representing a total print-run of 12.5 million copies, were published. Overall, more than 10,000 works by Soviet authors and authors from other socialist countries, representing a total print-run of over 100 million copies, have been translated since the Socialist Revolution.

Publishers have also had successes in the field of book illustration and design. In May each year there is a book and book-art exhibition, which has become traditional, and in the autumn Sofia holds an international book fair, which helps to strengthen the ties between Bulgarian publishing houses and those of near-by and far-off countries. For their part, Bulgarian publishers take part in international book exhibitions and fairs in Moscow, Leipzig, Warsaw, Belgrade, Frankfurt am Main, Bologna, Cairo, etc. and have already won several prizes at such events.

Progress in publishing is matched by similar progress in the Bulgarian press. Here again, comparisons with the past are relevant. In 1939 there were 513 newspapers in Bulgaria with an annual total of 130,097,000 copies, whereas in 1972, there were already 681, printing a total of 900,363,000 copies, and in 1975, 498 printing a total of 843,603,000 copies. In 1979 the annual total was 870 million copies. In 1939, 393 periodicals were being published, with an annual total of 11,208,000 copies; in 1972, there were 909, with a total of 50 million copies; in 1973, 826 with a total of 51.2 million copies, and in 1979, 957 with a total of 57,741,000 copies. In addition to these periodicals there are specialist journals published by the Committee for Culture, the artists' and writers' associations, the reading-centres and so on.

Literature

Bulgarian literature, which possesses an extremely long tradition, experienced a glorious period in the ninth century, which has been called 'the golden age of ancient Bulgarian literature'. In addition Bulgaria possesses a wonderful treasury of folklore.

The best of the works written after the liberation from Ottoman domination remained attached to realism and to popular traditions. Literature then took a great new leap forward; different literary forms were introduced, and new literary trends appeared. The writers evoked episodes of the people's struggle for national liberation and glorified the battles and the legendary heros. Ivan Vazov's novel *Under the Yoke*, the memoirs of Zacchary Stoyanov, *Notes on the Bulgarian Insurrections*, *In Prison* by Constantin Velichkov and Pencho Slaviekov's poem, *Song of Blood*, all date from this period. Some writers, such as Ivan Vazov, Aleko Konstantinov, Stoyan Mikhailovski, Georgy Stamatov, Mikhalki Georgiev and Anton Strachimirov, severely criticized certain types of behaviour that resulted from the social development of the country. Other writers, such as Peyo Yavorov, Tsanko Tserkovski and Eline Peline, took a particular interest in the social problems of the period and the life of the peasants.

At the end of the last century the worker made his first appearance in social literature as the young hero and the bringer of new values, and writers were inspired by a new form of revolutionary romanticism. Among such writers mention should be made of the outstanding contributions of Dimitri Blagoev, the founder of the Marxist theory of literature, Dimitri Polyanov, the father of proletarian and revolutionary poetry, and Georg Kirkov, who was a great prose writer in the new progressive vein. They were followed by a company of talented authors, such as Christo Yasenov.

Between the end of the First World War and the end of the Second World War there were a large number of progressive writers in Bulgaria who produced works bearing a democratic stamp. They include Yordan Yovkov, Ludmil Stoyanov, Stoyan Zagorchinov, Georgy Raichev, Konstantin Petkanov, K. Konstantinov, Emmanuil Popdimitrov and so on. With great courage they criticized capitalist society and raised their voices against Fascist ideology.

However, it was proletarian literature that most strongly attacked Fascism through such authors as Christo Radevski, Nikola Chrelkov, Mladen Isaev, Georgy Karaslavov and Orlin Vassilev. This type of literature, which reflected the revolutionary struggles of the people, developed particularly during the 1930s.

The work of Nikola Vaptsarov is an outstanding example of the Bulgarian national spirit and of revolutionary, proletarian poetry. Vaptsarov and a group of talented young poets, such as At. Mantchev, V. Vodenitcharski, Tzvetan Spassov and Ivan Nivyanin, combined their poetry with lives of action and laid down their lives for the sake of freedom.

Bulgarian literature has always sought to show the extraordinary destiny of the Bulgarian people and has associated itself with national struggles, joys and hopes. It remains closely attached to the efforts made by the people to achieve ever more perfect forms of social life, as well as reflecting contemporary events and the changes that have occurred in the destiny of mankind. Bulgarian writers are fully aware of their social responsibilities and, though addressing themselves to the founders of a new world, their works deal not only with the great social transformations which have occurred but also with the lives and everyday problems of ordinary people. While the outstanding events of the nation's history and of the contemporary situation provide the subject-matter for very many literary works, contemporary writers have accordingly sought to show the life of the people and to reveal the mind of modern man. They are particularly aware of moral and ethical problems and of the development of the spiritual side of man. They make judgements and look for the meaning behind people's actions, their behaviour and their relationships with one another.

Great novels such as *Ordinary People* by Georgy Karaslavov, *Tobacco* and *Damned Souls* by Dimitri Dimov, *The Iron Candlestick*, *The Bells of Prespa*, *Ilinden* and *I Hear Your Voices* by Dimitri Talev, *For Life and Death* by Dimitri Angelov, *Ivan Kondarev* by Emilian Stanev and many other such works, which deal with important events and have people with progressive ideas as their heroes, are now part of the Bulgarian literary heritage. These remarkable works are imbued with humanism and faith in mankind.

Bulgarian writers take a great interest in the history of the people, and this has inspired works like *The Time of Separation* by Anton Donchev, *For Liberty* and *The Road to Sofia* by Stefan Dichev, *Last Day* and *Boyana Fair* by Stoyan Zagorchinov, *Antichrist* and *The Legend of Sibin* by Emilian Stanev, *Annals of Troubled Times* and *The Djem Affair* by Vera Mutafchieva, *The Golden Age* by Andrei Guliashki, etc. The attraction of real-life subjects has also brought about an increase in the writing of memoirs—particularly during the last ten years—which are characterized by the wealth of background material and by the immediacy with which events are described. During the last thirty years, profound social changes and important demographic movements have taken place in Bulgaria. The reorganization of the economy on socialist foundations, emigration from the countryside to the towns and the rise of the working class have been accompanied by the formation of a new morality and a new spirit.

More and more, literature has come to represent the problems of modern man and has dealt with the different aspects of these problems in numerous works of all kinds. The new hero—the builder of socialism, the man with broad spiritual horizons, conscious of his responsibilities towards the community as a whole—has at last come into his own in literature. The problems of contemporary life are dealt with in the works of

Kamen Kalchev, Bogomil Rainov, Stoyan Daskalov, Pavel Vejinov, Diko Fuchedjiev, Ghencho Stoev, Athanas Nakovski, Kosta Strandjev, etc.

In addition to the novel, mention should be made of the success achieved by other literary genres, the novella and the short story, which contain many new and varied elements. These genres have been extremely successful in the hands of such talented writers as Nikola Haitov, Yordan Radichkov and Ivailo Petrov.

All this literary activity has become even more important because it has served as the foundation for the development of other arts. Thus poetry has encouraged the development of song-writing, film scripts that of the cinema, and plays have had the same effect on the theatre. The Bulgarian theatre has made great progress through the work of such playwrights as Orlin Vasilev, Kamen Zidarov, Lozan Strelkov and Todor Ghenov. Representatives of the following generation, Georgy Djagarov, Emil Manov, Dragomir Asenov, Rangel Ighnatov, Ivan Radoev, Kolyo Georgiev and Georgy Svejine, together with some young writers such as Nedialko Yordanov, Nicolai Parushev, Milko Milkov, Doncho Tsonchev, Stanislav Stratiev and Georgy Danailov, have also produced dramatic works of great value.

This new period of creativity in Bulgarian literature is also due to poets such as Christo Radevski, Dimitri Metodiev, Mladen Isaev, Georgy Djagarov, Damar, Elisaveta Bagriana, Venko Markovski, Dora Gabe, Veselin Hanchev, Lubomir Levchev, Pavel Matev, Botidar Boyilov, Blaga Dimitrova, Stanka Pencheva, Vladimir Golev, Evtim Evtimov, Slav Chr. Karaslavov and Orlin Orlinov. The face which Bulgarian literature now presents to the world has thus been formed by writers of several different generations, each with an artistic style of his own and showing marked individuality.

Bulgarian writers have thousands of readers and admirers abroad, as is shown by an analysis of the foreign editions of Bulgarian books. The immortal novel by Ivan Vazov, *Under the Yoke*, is still the most translated Bulgarian book abroad. The main languages into which Bulgarian literary works are translated are Russian, German, Italian and French.

Between 1944 and 1956, 658 Bulgarian books were translated into foreign languages. Between 1956 and 1968 the figure was 1,452. In 1979, 250 translations of Bulgarian books appeared. The works of authors belonging to several different generations have been translated into sixty-five foreign languages. The classic author of Bulgarian literature, Ivan Vazov, has been translated into forty-four languages, Eline Peline into thirty languages, Yordan Yovkov into twenty languages, and Nikola Vaptsarov, who was posthumously awarded the prize of honour by the World Peace Council, has been translated into forty-three languages. Contemporary Bulgarian writers such as Georgy Karaslavov, Ludmil Stoyanov, Dimitri Dimov, Stoyan Daskalov, Andrei Guklyashki, Veselin Hanchev and Emilian Stanev, have been translated into about forty foreign languages, while other authors whose works have been translated widely abroad include Dimitri Talev, Bogomil Rainov, Georgy Djagarov, Lubomir Levchev, Dimitri Metodiev, Elisaveta Bagriana and Blaga Dimitrova. Such recognition is indeed evidence of the extremely high quality of Bulgarian literature.

In addition, a large number of Bulgarian books have been translated into foreign languages and published in Bulgaria. The press, cinema and photographic agency, Sofia Press, which was set up by the Bulgarian writers', journalists', painters' and composers' associations, published a very large number of literary, scientific, socio-political and other works and arranges for them to be distributed in many foreign countries.

Theatre

The traditions of Bulgarian dramatic art are continously being nourished by new creative efforts. It is well known that the Slavs of ancient times were already familiar with dramatic spectacles and the literature of the tenth century shows that ideas of the 'theatre' and the 'actor' were not unknown at the time.

The Bulgarian national theatre was born at the time of the Bulgarian national revival. During the first few decades of the nineteenth century, school feast days often included performances of original or translated plays.

In 1856 the first theatrical performances given by amateur groups took place in the towns of Shumen and Lom and the number of such performances quickly increased. The repertoire of these groups was chosen from among the works of Dobri Voinikov, Vasil Drumew, Ilia Blaskov and Luben Karavelov.

After the country was freed from Ottoman rule, many professional companies with much more varied repertories came into being. The works of Shakespeare, Ibsen, N. Ostrovski, Tolstoi and Chekhov were already being performed and Bulgarian plays also occupied an important place thanks to the works of Ivan Vazov, Peyo Yavorov, Racho Stoyanov, St. L. Kostov and Yordan Yovkov.

The beginning of this century saw the appearance of such gifted playwrights as Vasil Kirkov, Adriana Budevska, Krestu Sarafov, Sava Oghnianov, Zlatina Nedeva, A. Kirchev, Vera Ighnatieva, E. Snejina, etc.

The 1930s were marked by the appearance of several great actors, such as Vladimir Trandafilov, Konstantin Kisimov, Ivan Dimov, Georgy Stamatov, Zorka Yordanova and Petia Gerganova, who contributed to the growth of critical realism in theatrical art. Since its very beginning, the Bulgarian theatre has shown strong democratic tendencies and has closely reflected the hopes and aspirations of the times. Thus, it rapidly became the vehicle for the progressive and humanist ideas that were to become so powerful during the years of socialist development.

56

Rhyton from the gold treasure of Panaguirshte.

A view of the Rila Monastery.

The Ivan Vazov National Classical Theatre, Sofia.

The Cyril and Methodius National Library at Sofia.

Nikolai Ghiaurov, a People's Artist, in the title role
of Mussorgsky's opera *Boris Godunov*.

A Peasant Girl: a painting by Vladimir Dimitrov the Master,
a People's Artist.

A Thracian dance performed by an amateur group.

The Banner of Peace Monument, near Sofia.

Nowadays the Bulgarian people are enthusiastic theatre-goers. That is due to a large extent to the development of a national drama. During the last few decades, playwrights have dealt with a large number of important subjects and problems of vital interest in their plays, thereby helping to extend the dramatic repertoire. An important place is occupied by those plays devoted to the people's struggle against Fascism; these include *The Struggle Continues* and *The First Blow* by Krum Kyuliavkov, *Alert* and *Happiness* by Orlin Vasilev, *Recognition* and *Unforgettable Days* by Lozan Strelkov, *Blockade* by Kamen Zidarov, *Each Autumn Evening* by Ivan Peichev, *Conscience* by Emil Manov, etc. During the last few years there have been staged many plays devoted to the Bulgarian people's heroic past, such as *Ivan Shishman, Kaloyan* and *Cain the Magician* by Kamen Zidarov, *Samuil* by Magda Petkanova, *The Monk and his Sons* by Milko Milkov, *The Legend of Gotse* by Venko Markovski, etc.

Contemporary problems have been tackled in such plays as *Love* and *The Shining Dawn* by Orlin Vasilev, *Women with a Past* by Dimitri Dimov, *Journey towards Truth* by Lozan Strelkov, *This Small Earth* by Georgy Djagarov, *Everybody's Mother* by Georgy Karaslavov, *The Red and the Brown* by Ivan Radoev, *Thirst* by Velicho Neshkov, *Our own Judges* and *Journey towards the Future* by Kolyo Georgiev, *The Court of Honour* by Rangel Ighnatov, *An Inexplicable Love* by Nedialko Yordanov, *The Supply of Gold* and *The End of the Day* by Dragomir Asenov, *Romantics* and *Radiation* by Georgy Svejin, *January* and *Trial Take-off* by Yordan Radichkov, *The End Remains for You* by Georgy Danailov and *Music of Shatrovets* by C. Iliev.

Alongside classic and modern Bulgarian works, plays by foreign authors occupy a prominent place in the repertoire. Shakespeare, Lope de Vega, Carlo Goldoni, Tirso de Molina, Molière, Schiller, Gogol, Ostrovski, Chekhov, Gorki, Shaw and Ibsen are regularly performed. Bulgarian theatre-goers also know the works of Bertolt Brecht, Arthur Miller, Sean O'Casey, Eugene O'Neill, Friedrich Dürrenmatt, etc.

Bulgaria is the homeland of fine actors, such as Ruya Delcheva, Stephen Getsov, Georgy Kaloyanchev, Lubomir Kabakchiev, Asen Milanov, Margarita Duparinova, Tania Mesalitinova, Georgy Georgiev-Gets, Slavka Slavova, Stoicho Mazgalov, Georgy Radanov, Georgy Partsalev, Elena Stefanova and many others. Many of them have been awarded the title of People's Artist or Emeritus Artist. The new generation of actors, producers and theatre theoreticians is trained in the Krestiu Sarafov Higher Institute of Dramatic Art, which has a theatre where students can act in front of an audience. Every year, the best of the Institute's diploma-winners bring a breath of fresh air into the theatrical companies which they join.

Before the Second World War there were thirteen theatres in Bulgaria, only four of which were subsidized by the state. In 1956, there were already forty-five, and at the present time the number is fifty-eight, including the Young Theatre-Goers' Theatre, the Satirical Theatre, etc. The Ivan Vazov

National Classical Theatre plays a leading role in this field. Some theatres have both a small and a large auditorium. The theatres in the various provinces regularly do tours round their province, so that there is almost no town or village that is not visited by a theatrical company at one time or another.

A major role in raising professional standards in the theatre is played by such special events as the special festivals (for example, the periodical festivals of children's theatre, the national festival of plays for young people, the historical drama festival) and the Drumev drama festivals held regularly at Shumen. National festivals devoted to contemporary Bulgarian drama, in which all the theatres in the country take part, were started a few years ago. This competition takes place in two stages: regional festivals are held in a number of cities, after which a final festival is held in the capital, in which the best companies take part. A jury, representing a wide range of people from the theatrical world, awards prizes for playwriting, producing, stage design and acting (male and female roles). The six national festivals held in 1952, 1959, 1964, 1969, 1974 and 1979 have made an especially valuable contribution to the development of dramatic art. At the fifth festival 120 plays by Bulgarian writers were performed. All this shows that the public's interest in the theatre has been steadily rising. In 1979 alone, 6.5 million people went to the theatre, and it is clear that the ties between the theatre and its audiences are becoming closer and closer.

Music

Music occupies a particularly interesting place in Bulgarian history. In the Middle Ages, music had already started to flourish. At Veliko-Turnovo there was a national school of liturgical chant, which had a strong influence on the music of other countries. It was there that, in the fourteenth century, the singer, composer and theoretician Ivan Kukuzel lived and worked. He made an important contribution to the development of religious singing in the Eastern Church.

Popular Bulgarian music is original, melodic and possesses a remarkable variety of rhythms, with typically Bulgarian tempi, such as 5/8, 7/8, 11/8, etc.

There is also a rich stock of traditional folklore, and many popular songs deal with the struggles of the Bulgarians against Ottoman domination. Since the Liberation, popular works have remained the basis of professional music and have never lost their attraction.

Musical composition and performance developed in Bulgaria from 1890 onwards. Opera appeared a little later and it was in 1900 that Emanuil Manolov composed the first Bulgarian opera. A little later, Georgy Atanasov-Maestro composed six major operas in the space of a few years. At that time, Bulgarian composers wrote, above all, choral and solo works. That was the case of Emanuil Manolov, A. Bukureshtliev, P. Pipkov and A. Morfova. At

58

this point mention should also be made of the considerable contribution of Dobritar Christov at the beginning of the twentieth century.

The third decade of this century was marked by the appearance of symphonic and operatic works, choral songs and other musical works of merit, written by composers such as Petko Stainov, Pancho Vladigerov, Lubomir Pipkov, V. Stoyanov and Marin Goleminov, but it was after the victory of the Socialist Revolution in Bulgaria that music really began to flourish.

Modern Bulgarian composers like to work on a broad canvas and their works are of very high quality. A number of them have enjoyed well-deserved success on Bulgarian and foreign stages: the opera *Ivailo* and the ballet *Kaloyan's Daughter* by Marin Goleminov, *Albena, July Night, The Gay Blade* and *Summer 893* by Parashkev Hadjiev, *Momchil* and *Antigone 43* by Lubomir Pipkov, *Hitar Petar* (Peter the Sly) and the ballet *Pope Joan* by Veselin Stoyanov, *The Master of Boyana* by Konstantin Iliev, and the ballets *The Song of the Haiduks* by Alexander Raichev, *The Legend of the Lake* by Pancho Vladigerov, *Orpheus and Rhodope* by Tsvetan Tsvetanov, etc. Choral songs and other genres, such as the cantata and the oratorio, have drawn upon contemporary events for their subjects. Among such works, the cantatas *September the Ninth* by Philip Kutev, *He Dieth Not* and *Friendship* by Alexander Raichev, *Let the Day Be* by V. Stoyanov, *Sing, Land of my Birth* and *The Struggle for Peace* by S. Obretenov and *Oratorio for Our Time* by Lubomir Pipkov are particularly famous. Highly gifted composers, such as Asen Karastoyanov, Dimitri Petkov, Georgy Zlatev-Cherkin, Todor Popov and Georgy Dimitrov, have written various kinds of symphonic works, such as symphonies, overtures, symphonic poems, etc.

A large number of symphonies have been composed and performed during the last two decades. This intense activity in the field of composition has been matched by the increasing skills of performers and the growth in the number of professional musical institutions. Mention should also be made of the particular impulse provided by the twelve state symphony orchestras, several major ensembles and a number of choirs (such as the Svetoslav Obretenov choir), the Sofia Popular Song and Dance ensemble, directed by People's Artist Philip Kutev, the Pirin Ensemble, the Thracian Ensemble in Plovdiv, etc.

In Bulgaria there are seven opera houses and two operetta theatres, which give performances of all the best classic works. The National Opera and Ballet Theatre in Sofia is the country's foremost opera house. It was there that such new Bulgarian operas as *Momchil, Hitar Petar, Ivailo* and *The Gay Blade* were first performed. Legend has it that the Thracian singer Orpheus, who could enchant men and also tame wild animals, lived in Bulgarian territory. Perhaps for this reason, Bulgaria has become famous for the wonderful voices of its singers. Here it is sufficient to quote the names of Boris Christoff, Nikolai Ghiaurov, Christo Brambarov, Mikhail Popov,

Raina Kabaivanska, Gena Dimitrova, Julia Viner, Nikolai Nikolov, Nikolai Ghuselev, Dimitri Petkov, Anna Tomova-Sintova, etc.

Many Bulgarian instrumentalists have also won various international prizes, for example, Emil Kamilarov, Boyan Lechev, Luba Encheva, Petr Christoskov, Dina Schneiderman, Stoika Milanova, Dora Milanova and Milena Mollova.

In 1979, seventy-nine Bulgarian instrumentalists and singers took part in thirty-five international competitions and won thirty-eight prizes.

The most famous opera houses in the world frequently welcome Bulgarian singers such as Nikolai Ghiaurov, Nikolai Nikolov, Nikolai Guselev and Raina Kabaivanska, who are very highly esteemed by audiences in Europe and the United States. During the last few years, the Sofia National Opera has given performances in the USSR, Romania, Hungary, France, Spain, Switzerland, the Federal Republic of Germany, Lebanon, Italy, Belgium, Greece and so on. The *corps de ballet* has made visits to Italy, India and France. Groups of Bulgarian singers have given performances in Belgium, Austria, the Netherlands, Denmark, etc. The Sofia State Philharmonic Orchestra, the Bulgarian Radio and Television Symphony Orchestra, the Sofia Chamber Music Orchestra, the Bulgarian Radio Chamber Music Choir and the Svetoslav Obretenov Choir have made numerous tours abroad. The Pioneer's Symphony Orchestra, the Bulgarian Radio Children's Choir, the Popular Song and Dance Ensemble, the Bodra Smiana Pioneer's Choir, the Varna Opera and the Ruse Philharmonic Orchestra have already gained an international reputation. Space does not allow us to list here all the foreign tours made by Bulgarian singers, conductors, instrumentalists and producers, who have gained the public's esteem.

Similarly, famous singers, soloists and conductors from various countries give performances in Bulgaria, concerts being arranged in various Bulgarian towns, for a wide range of opera singers, choirs, orchestras, singers and different types of ensembles.

Bulgaria organizes and plays host to a number of important cultural events: the Varna International Ballet Competition, the Sofia International Contest for Young Opera Singers, the Varna Summer International Music Festival, the International Music Festival held in conjunction with the 'Sunshine Coast Holiday Weeks', the Golden Orpheus International Singing Contest, the Plovdiv International Chamber Music Festival and the Alen Mak International Festival of Political Song in Blagoevgrad. These new events are eloquent proof of the intense activity of national cultural life.

Contemporary Bulgarian culture is marked not only by the numerous successes it has achieved, but also by the fact that the whole population takes part in cultural activities, even in the most remote regions of the country. It has already become a tradition in Bulgaria to organize special events to celebrate the anniversaries of famous composers and musicians.

There are many annual festivals of an original character that testify to the intensity of Bulgaria's musical life: those most worthy of mention are the March Music Festival in Ruse, the Lilac Music Festival at Lovech, the Black Sea Summer, the ten-yearly Symphony Festival at Burgas, the Katia Popova Prize-Winning Musicians' Festival at Pleven, the Golden Diana Festival of Chamber Music Choirs at Yambol, the Gabrovo Chamber Music Festival, the Sofia Music Festival, the Nedialka Simonova Music Festival and many others. The music to be performed is chosen so as to make the Bulgarian people familiar with the great musical classics of the world, the works of contemporary composers and, in particular, the works of Bulgarian composers, which benefit from being performed by the best orchestras and soloists. It is becoming more and more common to put on series of concerts of educational interest, and lectures on music and opera. They help to develop the public's taste, to introduce them to the history of music and to different musical forms and to familiarize them with the work of individual composers and the styles of different musical traditions. This is the intention behind the work of the Young Music Lovers' Association, which has expanded considerably in recent years. The many musical events that take place throughout the country—operas, concerts and festivals—and the number of people who attend them bear witness to the Bulgarian people's great interest in music. For example in 1979 the professional orchestras and ensembles in the country gave more than 15,000 concerts, which were attended by 6.4 million people.

The development of musical activity has been encouraged by the periodic holding of large-scale competitions and national festivals. The Festival of the State Symphony Orchestras, the Bulgarian Opera, Operetta and Ballet Festival and the national competitions for singers and instrumentalists reflect the expansion of musical activity and encourage young talents.

Cinema

The Bulgarian cinema is relatively young. Before the Socialist Revolution, several hundred short-length films and fifty full-length feature films had been produced. It was, however, only after 1944 that the cinema really began to develop, having chosen to take the path of socialist realism. The Bulgarian cinema is deeply imbued with the spirit of humanity; it is concerned with the contemporary situation and with everything new in life.

Conditions are now wholly conducive to the development of the cinema. Modern equipment is available at the Sofia Film Centre, which comes under the Bulgarska Kinematografia, a large organization for the production and distribution of feature films, popular science films, animated cartoons and newsreels. The Bulgarska Kinematografia is also responsible for the distribution of films abroad. There is a Special Institute for Film Archives and a Film Library.

Over the last two decades, the production of feature films and of medium- and short-length films has considerably increased. Each year the Kinematografia produces more than sixty full-length feature films and about 450 short-length films for the cinema and for television.

Bulgarian films deal with a wide range of topics: historical and revolutionary subjects are tackled at the same time as the psychological and moral problems of modern man. Thanks to the cinema, many literary classics and modern works have acquired a new popularity. It would be difficult to list all the films that have marked the development of the Bulgarian cinema, but the following in particular are worth mentioning: *Young Though we Were, The Peach Thief, The King and the General, The Inspector and the Night, Sun and Shadow, The Longest Night, Tango, The Eighth, The White Room, The Black Angels, Mr. Nobody, There's Nothing Finer than Bad Weather, The Goat's Horn, The Best Man I Know, Love, The Last Word, Between the Devil and the Deep Blue Sea, Ivan Kondarev, A Difficult Love, Examinations at the Ungodly Hour, The Soldier of the Troop Train, Julia Vrevska, Surgeons, The Fence,* etc.

Particular mention must be made of Bulgarian animated cartoons, which have emerged as an original genre with a wealth of different subjects and possessing a universal character. *Jealousy, The Apple, Marguerite, Perpetuum Mobile, The Large Box, De facto, The Three Fools, The Musical Tree, Commission, The Star, Aquarium, Horoscope* and *Opera for a Hazelnut* have all won major international prizes.

Popular science films also bear witness to their makers' wish to deal with some of the problems that arise in our society and in modern science. Particularly worthy of mention are *Extraordinary Physics, One Hundred Years of Immortality, Peasants, Life in the Saltworks,* etc.

Nowadays, the cinema is continuing to make progress as an art-form thanks to such directors as Zacchary Jandov, Todor Dinov, Valo Radev, Christo Christov, Borislav Charaliev, Christo Piskov, Rangel Valvalchanov, Lubomir Sharlandyiev, Nikola Korabov, Ludmil Kirkov, Ivanka Grabcheva, Binka Jeliazkova, Metodi Andonov, Christo Kovachev, Iuli Stoyanov, Doniu Donev, etc.

The Bulgarian cinema has strengthened its ties with other national cinemas by buying films, organizing festivals and film weeks and participating in co-productions. It has become traditional to hold Bulgarian film festivals in the USSR and in other socialist countries. Bulgarian film weeks are held in Algeria, Denmark, Finland, France, the Federal Republic of Germany, India, Iraq, Japan, Pakistan, Peru, Sweden, Switzerland and the United Kingdom. Bulgarian film festivals take place in Paris, London, New York, Calcutta, Lausanne, Stockholm, etc. Festivals of documentaries and popular science films and also a national film festival take place each year in Bulgaria and film weeks are held so as to show the most outstanding foreign works. Bulgarian feature films and documentaries are shown in eighty countries. Every year, the Bulgarian cinema takes part in some thirty international film festivals for feature films and shorts. A large number of Bulgarian films have won international awards. During the last five years they have carried off 179 international prizes. *The Last Summer* achieved great success at the San Remo Festival in Italy and at the Karlovy Vary Festival. The film *Examinations at an Ungodly Hour* won four prizes at the Gijón Festival in Spain and *The Counting of the Hares* obtained a prize at the Lucerne Festival in Switzerland. At the end of the International Festival for Politically Committed Films, held at Avelino in Italy, the first prize was awarded to the film *Between the Devil and the Deep Blue Sea*. In short, many international prizes have been awarded to Bulgarian directors, cameramen and actors for their virtuosity and for the humanitarian ideas expressed in their films.

The development of the art of the film in Bulgaria is not unconnected with the expansion of the network of cinemas throughout the country. In 1939 there were 213 cinemas, situated mainly in the towns. By 1960, their number had risen to 1,515, by 1972 to 3,337, and by 1979 it had reached 3,600. In addition, there are touring cinemas, which allow films to reach the most remote villages. Despite the rapid spread of television, film attendances have remained high. Whereas in 1939 the attendance figure was 13 million, by 1979 it had risen to 110 million. Bulgarian audiences show as great an interest in foreign films as they do in Bulgarian films.

Radio and television

Radio and television play an important part in cultural development and these modern means of spreading culture and information occupy an ever more important place in the daily life of our society. This is due, on the one hand, to the rise in the standard of living and, on the other hand, to the growth in cultural needs and the increasing interest in culture. The development of radio and television is shown by the increase in the number of programmes and by the higher technical quality of the broadcasts.

As national cultural institutions, radio and television have a part to play in raising cultural standards, for they contribute to the spread of cultural values and also encourage cultural activity.

Today, Bulgarian Radio broadcasts more than 114 hours a day on ten channels and also sends out foreign broadcasts in twelve languages. It has fifty-two transmitters. The number of receiving sets is over two million. As for television, there are twenty-four transmitters. The number of television sets, which stood at 1.7 million in 1979, is constantly increasing. Bulgarian Radio and Television maintain permanent contacts with thirty-eight countries in accordance with agreements and treaties for co-operation and also co-operate with fifty-two radio and television broadcasting organizations all over the world.

Plastic arts

At all times, the plastic arts in Bulgaria have transmitted aesthetic and moral ideas of unquestionable value. Though both the artist who created the extraordinary ceramic icon of Saint Theodore, dating from the tenth century, and the painter, a precursor of the Renaissance, whose remarkable frescoes in the church of Boyana (1259) show such a realistic approach to religious subjects, are remote from us in time, contemporary artists possess the same exceptional sense of colour, together with expressive vigour and a love of mankind. The artistic tradition which imbues the ancient icons, frescoes and miniatures is equally evident in the works created during the time of the people's revolutionary struggles. The national movement (the Bulgarian national revival) favoured the birth of a national art and thus it was that various national schools, such as those of Triavno, Samakov, Bansko and Debar, came into being. The icon-painters and wood-sculptors who had been taught in these schools worked all over the country. They gave expression to new artistic ideas and tendencies, ignored the rules and displayed ever increasing individuality in their works. Art gradually managed to free itself from the straitjacket of religious mysticism so as to win acceptance in people's homes. This is particularly true of wood-carving.

Zachary Zographe, an illustrious representative of the artists of the Bulgarian national revival, introduced, with unprecedented boldness, elements from everyday life into his religious frescoes. He was imitated by a whole group of painters—Nikola Pavlovich, Stanislav Dospevski, Christo Tzokev, D. Dobrovich—who produced many portraits, pictures and lithographs on historical subjects, in order to stir up the people's patriotic fervour. Revolutionary graphic art experienced a particularly brilliant period during the 1860s.

After Bulgaria's liberation from Ottoman domination, artistic activity increased. The painters Ivan Angelov and Anton Mitov acquired great renown towards the end of the nineteenth century, as too did Ivan Mrkvitchk and Yaroslav Vechin.

At the beginning of the twentieth century, the range of subjects and styles was extended even further in the words of A. Nikolov, T. Todorov and A. Bojinov.

The various tendencies that have emerged in Bulgarian painting have each in their way influenced the different forms of expression. The representatives of these tendencies—Vladimir Dimitrov the Master, Ivan Milev, Sirak-Skitnik, Tzanko Lavrenov—had different styles, but their works reflected the same humanitarian and democratic spirit. The progressive tendencies in art even survived during the period of Fascist dictatorship.

Nowadays, Bulgarian painting can express itself in a great variety of ways. Today's painters create works of talent in all genres—from still life and landscapes to large historical compositions, from caricatures to essays in graphic art, from small ornamental panels to large-scale painting.

Alongside the salons which are traditionally held each year, various exhibitions have recently been organized to commemorate certain important historical anniversaries and events. Nor should the periodic exhibitions of painting, graphic art, caricatures and posters be forgotten. They make it possible to observe the continuing development of the visual arts in Bulgaria, the range of subjects tackled and the skills of many original artists of all ages. Finally, in addition to the exhibitions devoted to the recent works of individual artists, retrospective exhibitions trace the way they have developed from their beginnings.

The number of exhibitions and of visitors to them increases yearly. In 1965, 174 art exhibitions were held; in 1966 there were 344, and in 1979 353, viewed by 3,070,000 visitors.

The best works by Bulgarian painters and sculptors are on display in the National Fine-Arts Gallery in Sofia.

Bulgarian painting and sculpture are at present experiencing a period of remarkable development, thanks to such outstanding artists as Ilya Petrov, Tzanko Lavrenov, Zlatyu Boyadjiev, Dechko Uzunov, Stoyan Venev, Naiden Petkov, Alexander Poplivov, Svetlin Rusev, Mara Georgieva, Christo Neikov, Sekul Krumov, Todor Panayotov, Velichko Minekov, Dora Boneva and many others. Some of them have been awarded the title of People's Painter or Emeritus Painter.

Several artists of the younger generation, members of the numerous branches of the Bulgarian Painters' Association, have brought themselves to the attention of art-lovers on account of their enthusiastic work and their contribution to art.

Mention should be made of the creative vitality of those specializing in the applied arts, whose works are periodically exhibited.

The opening of more than thirty-five galleries over the last two decades shows the increasing interest taken by the public in the plastic arts. Several provincial towns—Plovdiv, Burgas, Varna, Vidin, Sliven, Stara Zagora and Kustendil—possess rich galleries. The number of villages with their own art collections is constantly increasing, the idea of organizing exhibitions in the villages having met with a favourable response from the public.

Among the great international exhibitions of recent years, it is worth singling out two: *Treasures of the Bulgarian Museums* and 2,500 *Years of Art on Bulgarian Territory*; both were put on show in Austria, Belgium, France, the Federal Republic of Germany, Japan, Poland, the USSR, etc. In Paris, the exhibition *2,500 Years of Art on Bulgarian Territory* was the subject of numerous articles in the French press, and André Malraux said of it, 'The history of art must be revised, the Bulgarians have their *Mona Lisa*'. The exhibition *Thracian Art on Bulgarian Territory* was shown in Paris, Moscow, Leningrad, Vienna, London, Mexico, Berlin, Prague, the United States of America, the Federal Republic of Germany, etc.

Every year, Bulgarian painters hold private exhibitions abroad or take part in international exhibitions (Paris, Venice, Brno, Cracow, Stettin, Stuttgart). Some of them have taken part in the Biennial Exhibition of Graphic Arts in Brazil. Several individual and joint exhibitions of Bulgarian works have been held in Czechoslovakia, Greece, Romania, Turkey, the USSR, etc. The works of Bulgarian artists have been shown in Canada, Colombia, Japan, Luxembourg, Peru and elsewhere. Works by Zlatyu Boyadjiev and Vladimir Dimitrov the Master have been shown in Paris; by Dechko Uzunov in Bucharest and Paris; by Ilya Petrov, Lubomir Dalchev, Svetlin Rusev, Zlatka Dabova and Georgy Baev in London; by Naiden Petkov, Boris Angelushev, Stoyan Venev and Ilya Petrov in Berlin; by Jova Raevska, Evgeni Burgaev, Petar Urumov, Mana Parpulove, Vladimir Goev and Boris Tzenov in Hungary and Czechoslovakia. On the occasion of the exhibition devoted to Vladimir Dimitrov the Master in Paris, the visitors' book included such comments as 'What expressiveness there is in the purity of the lines!', 'It's an enormous pleasure to see these paintings'!, 'How beautiful Bulgarian women are!'. In the newspaper *L'Humanité*, Lucien Cursy wrote, 'The sixty canvases by Vladimir Dimitrov, called the Master, the most representative of the Bulgarian painters of the first half of the century, show us an accomplished art, born in a climate of pastoral lyricism'.

During the last three years, Bulgarian painters have taken part in over eighty international artistic events; they have put on more than a hundred private exhibitions abroad and won sixty international prizes. In 1979 alone, forty exhibitions by Bulgarian artists were held abroad.

Architecture

Bulgarian architecture was born in the seventh century, when the Bulgarian state was founded, and it derives from the merging of the Proto-Bulgar and Slav traditions with those of the peoples who had previously lived on the same soil. The establishment of a centralized state encouraged the appearance of monumental architecture, as shown by the remains of the two ancient Bulgarian capitals, Pliska (ninth century) and Preslav (ninth/tenth centuries). One of the main features of architecture between the eleventh and the fourteenth centuries was the widespread use of decorative forms: frescoes and multicoloured ornamentation in stone, brick and glazed ceramic-work.

During the period of Ottoman domination, many monuments were destroyed and the architectural traditions fell into disuse. It was only at the time of the Bulgarian national revival in the eighteenth century that architecture was able to rise again, thanks to the improvement in the economic circumstances of a part of the population. The isolation in which Bulgarian architects had found themselves as a result of the country's

66

subjugation was offset by the development of an individual national style, which was characterized by its variety of forms, in the construction both of public buildings and also of private houses.

After the Liberation, the traditions peculiar to the Bulgarian national revival gradually gave way before the growing tendency to borrow from Western sources and, in fact, during the period between 1910 and 1918 many of the public buildings constructed in Bulgaria were the work of foreign architects.

The young architects who had studied abroad gave Bulgarian architecture a new look after the First World War. A certain amount of eclecticism still existed, at least as far as public buildings were concerned, but a tendency to recreate the styles of the past was already beginning to appear and became particularly strong during the 1930s.

After the Second World War, the socialist development of the country conferred a modern appearance on Bulgarian architecture. Bulgarian painters and architects combined their efforts to embellish towns and villages. Architecture and decorative mural painting already have helped to alter the face of the towns in keeping with the needs of the environment.

As a result of the fundamental changes that have occurred in the social and economic life of the country, Bulgarian architecture is constantly developing and extending its range, while its styles reflect a deep concern for human beings. Intensive programmes for the construction of housing and public buildings have offered Bulgarian architects great opportunities to express themselves. New residential areas and cultural centres have sprung up all over the country. Along the Black Sea coast beautiful new complexes have arisen, such as those of Drujba (Friendship), Zlatni Piassatsi (Golden Sands), Slanchev Brjag (Sunshine Coast) and Albena.

Under socialism the state has taken a special interest in architectural embellishment of urban areas. The construction of buildings to act as cultural centres and museums has given architects the opportunity to develop a more fluid and light-hearted style, to use some elements of the national architectural heritage and to seek formulas that are in harmony with the building materials used and with the natural environment. This has helped to improve the overall appearance of Bulgarian villages in particular and of socialist architecture in general.

Bulgarian architecture enjoys exceptional prestige abroad. At various international competitions, the boldness and innovative spirit of Bulgarian architects have been apparent. Many of them work on large buildings projects in Asia, Africa and the United States. In their research, as in their actual projects, they concentrate on achieving a graceful and harmonious style, meeting the artistic needs of society.

Museums

Mankind's cultural development has naturally given rise to the need to establish special institutions responsible for conserving the treasures of the past, for the peoples of the world do not exist only in the present. More than a century ago, in 1856, the first museum collection in Bulgaria was inaugurated in the reading centre of a small town situated on the banks of the Danube called Svishtov. After the end of Ottoman domination, several new museums were set up, usually owing to the efforts of enlightened patriots. Alongside the state museums, museum collections were assembled in reading centres, schools and archaeological societies.

The Bulgarians of today see themselves as the heirs of the cultural monuments created over the centuries by both known and anonymous masters. In their eyes, therefore, everything bearing on the people's past is precious, and great efforts are made to seek out and conserve the cultural treasures of the past.

Within the vast network of Bulgarian cultural and educational institutions, the museums have a central role to play. Several of them possess unique products of the national genius. Their exhibitions illustrate the heroic and legendary deeds of the sons of the Bulgarian people, and reflect their long struggle for liberty and national independence. Today, there are 207 state museums and art galleries, among which we may single out the national archaeological and ethnographical museums, the Central Army Museum, the Museum of the Bulgarian Revolutionary Movement, the Georgy Dimitrov National Museum, the National Museum of the Rila Monastery, the Shipka-Buzdludja National Park and Museum, the Etara Park and Ethnographical Museum, the historical museums set up in the chief towns of the provinces, a large number of houses designated as national monuments in Sofia and elsewhere, the museums of Madan and Dimitrovgrad on the building of socialism, the Natural History Museums of Sofia, Plovdiv and Kotel, the National History Museum, the National Polytechnical Museum in Sofia, etc.

In addition, there are more than 400 museum collections in reading centres, schools, firms, churches and monasteries, etc. Private citizens also own collections of paintings, coins or old books. The museum collections are being continually enriched, thanks to the unceasing archaeological excavations and research work. Today the museums have more than three million items of great historical, artistic and cultural value.

The state gives considerable material assistance to the museums, increasing each year the appropriations for research and restoration work, and for new buildings.

The protection of antique remains, together with historical and architectural monuments, is the responsibility of the state, and whole localities like Jeravna, Koprivshtitsa, Melnik, Bojenci, etc. are classified as historical sites. The same is true of the old quarters of Plovdiv, Nesebar, Lovech, etc.

In 1979, museum admissions totalled 15.5 million. The ties between museums and visitors are constantly growing stronger. The interest shown in exhibitions is a further mark of the nation's vigorous cultural life, backed by extensive information; moreover, it is developing with the aid of the cinema, radio, television, the press, books and photographs.

The museums often play host to scientific meetings and conferences and organize exhibitions, discussion evenings and meetings with scholars, writers, art theoreticians and painters. They also bring out publications, produce documentary films, and seek to develop new methods not only the better to conserve their treasures but also to bring them to the knowledge of an increasingly wide public.

Libraries

The rise in the level of education and the people's love of culture have also led to the expansion of the library services. In addition to the increase in the number of libraries and the building-up of their collections, a series of new measures has brought about an improvement in the methods used for distributing literary and scientific works. The work of the libraries is established on scientific foundations. Apart from the state libraries, the largest of which is the Cyril and Methodius National Library in Sofia, there are libraries in the reading centres, schools, industrial enterprises and other institutions. The National Library's collection is particularly large and interesting, comprising as it does 1.2 million books and periodicals, a rich collection of old Bulgarian books, historical documents on the Bulgarian national revival, an impressive collection of maps, portraits and photographs, scores and records. The library has an excellent information service where information on all world literature is available. In addition, the library acts as a central clearing-house with regard to other Bulgarian libraries.

The Bulgarian Academy of Sciences has a collection of more than 950,000 volumes and the libraries of the institutions of higher education contain more than 1.5 million books. There are 10,305 public libraries, with collections totalling 70 million volumes, which annually issue 51 million books to their readers. In addition, there are 5,621 public libraries in the villages. Bulgaria occupies one of the leading positions in the world in the provision of library services in rural areas. Many qualified librarians work in the rural areas and there is one librarian per 3,000 people. There has also been a considerable increase in the size of the collections held by scientific and technical libraries.

The rapid expansion of library services, the foundation of new types of establishment, the increase in total holdings and the home-lending service combine to make the libraries an important component of cultural activity in Bulgaria.

Amateur artistic activities

Over the centuries the Bulgarian people have managed to preserve a vast treasury of folk-songs and dances, the fruit of genuine feeling and a profound sense of beauty. During the last few years, as a result of changing attitudes and modes of thought, increasing importance has come to be attached to whatever contributes to the expression of the individual's personality, his opinions, interests and personal aspirations. This is particularly true of amateur artistic activities, which play an important part in Bulgarian cultural life. Their development stems as much from popular traditions as from the progress of the human spirit. Hundreds of thousands of workers, from every walk of life, devote themselves to artistic activities during their leisure hours. In this way they can experience new pleasures and give fuller expression to their personalities.

Amateur activities are practised by people of all ages. The standard achieved compares favourably with that reached by professionals, as it has to do if it is to measure up to what people now expect. These activities encourage creativity, enrich the intellectual life of the workers, contribute to their aesthetic education and help new talents to emerge. They represent a mass movement in favour of culture which introduces a new element into the cultural life of the country. More than 500,000 people, united by their interest in and their common love for art, together make up 17,800 artistic groups (choirs, ballet companies, orchestras, drama groups, light music ensembles, folk-singing and folk-dancing groups, etc.). In Bulgaria there are 4,477 choirs, 2,167 singing groups, 2,581 orchestras, 508 drama groups, 148 puppet-theatre groups, 2,469 dance troupes, 184 music groups, etc.

The different forms of artistic expression to which amateurs devote themselves in the fields of music, dance and drama, as well as the works created by amateur artists in the fields of the plastic and applied arts, are too numerous to be mentioned fully here. Collective and individual exhibitions of works by amateur artists are held each year. Large-scale participation by the workers in such activities has a favourable influence on their individual development and on the part they play in social life generally. Thus it is that the state takes every opportunity to encourage amateur activities.

The general organization of these activities is undertaken by the National Centre for Amateur Artistic Activities in Sofia and by the appropriate bodies in the provinces. Each year the National Centre publishes six collections of divers repertoires, so as to help amateur groups in their choice of what they wish to perform. These groups put on more than 100,000 shows and concerts a year, with an audience of over 30 million people.

Periodically, amateurs have the opportunity, at national festivals, to show off their talents and compare their achievements. These festivals take place in several stages in villages throughout the country. A jury judges the best performances in the final, and prizes are awarded. The national festivals of 1948, 1965, 1974 and 1979 have shown that the standard of amateur artistic activities has been steadily rising.

Some groups of amateur artists have been invited to tour abroad. Whether in Belgium, Cyprus, France, Iraq, Ireland, Italy, Japan, the United Kingdom or the USSR, they have everywhere received a warm welcome from the public and the critics alike. They have also taken part in international folk-arts competitions. For some years now, Bulgarian folk-art groups have consistently carried off the major prizes at the Llangollen International Eisteddfod in Wales (United Kingdom). Others have been leading prize-winners at the Middlesborough International Competition (United Kingdom), the Dijon International Folk-Arts Competition (France) and the Debrecen International Competition for Choral Singing (Hungary). In 1977, amateur groups won twenty-seven prizes at thirty-three international festivals; in 1979, thirty-two groups won twenty-six prizes at thirty-six international competitions. Bulgarian amateur artists have won prizes at Agrigento and Gorizia (Italy), Neerpelt (Belgium), Cork (Ireland), Charleroi (Belgium), Zakopane (Poland), Bonn (Federal Republic of Germany), Carthage (Tunisia), etc.

Amateur artistic activities help to awaken the workers' talents and their needs for artistic expression. Moreover, they encourage the entry of young talent into establishments providing education in the arts and into professional cultural and artistic institutions, thereby contributing to the formation and education of new generations of professional artists.

Reading centres

In their struggle for national independence, the Bulgarian people aspired as much to education and culture as to freedom. It was this urge which was at the root of the idea to set up reading centres, whose establishment and subsequent growth are closely bound up with the cultural history of Bulgaria. Founded 125 years ago on the initiative of scholarly patriots, they have long experience behind them and are deeply rooted in everyday life. The first secular libraries were set up in these reading centres, which also saw the birth of drama groups, amateur musicians' groups and archaeological collections and played a major role in the popularization of scientific knowledge. At the time of the Bulgarian national revival the reading centres were true centres of education and culture, and their importance has in no way diminished since then. The names of some of the greatest sons of the people—writers, politicians and promoters of culture—are linked with the history of these reading centres.

The reading centres are cultural and educational organizations to which all workers, without distinction of nationality, religion or sex, have access. Each centre has independent legal status and may own real estate, library collections, museum items, etc. The centres are administered by a governing body elected at the annual general meeting; its term of office covers the period between two successive general meetings. Today, as in the past, reading centres make an important contribution to the spread of art and culture. They are subsidized by the state and the provincial authorities.

By 1939, there were 2,610 reading centres in the country. Today they total 4,272. The increase has been particularly marked in the villages, where there were 3,830 centres in 1977, as against 2,334 in 1944. Museum collections, picture galleries and radio and television clubs have been set up in these centres and amateur film-making and photography courses, language courses, music and ballet classes for children and meetings of literary and artistic circles are also held there. The study of local history and the investigation and recording of legends, ancient customs and folk-songs are all extremely popular with the public. The reading centres also act as centres of amateur artistic activities. In 1979, more than 120,000 amateur artists took part in 28,000 shows before a total audience of 8 million people.

Bulgarian workers have at their disposal 265 Houses of Culture and more than 1,800 cultural clubs, equipped with cinemas, concert-halls and reading-rooms and affording scope for pursuing a variety of hobbies, such as amateur film-making, photography, etc.

Several new forms of cultural activity have recently been introduced: popular universities, popular public lectures, discussion meetings, folk-singing competitions, etc. The Houses of Culture and cultural clubs, like the parks for rest and culture, are increasingly proving their worth as places for education and culture, where workers can spend their leisure hours in a pleasant and profitable way.

The popular universities and public lectures give everyone the opportunity to gain a wide range of knowledge on literature, art and the technical and social sciences, attend film-shows, join in discussions on problems in culture and the arts or literary works, etc.

Today, there are 2,140 popular universities operating under the auspices of the reading centres; they have 961,364 members, for whom 15,850 courses were arranged in 1979.

Local cultural festivals

Cultural development favours the appearance of new forms of expression, which serve to improve the quality of life in many different localities. They include cultural festivals linked to the history of the localities or to the lives of writers and important figures who lived there. The Ruse Music Festival, the Lilac Music Festival at Lovech, the summer festivals of

72

Varna and Burgas, the Drama Festival at Vidin, where historical plays are performed in the natural setting of the ancient citadel—these are only a few of the many events which testify to the richness of cultural life, stirring up interest among the people at large and encouraging the workers to take an active part in the promotion of cultural progress. Some commemorate anniversaries, centenaries or particular episodes in the heroic history of the Bulgarian people.

These festivals help to forge closer links between cultural life in the towns and in the villages. They help to give the people some knowledge of great works of art and to develop and strengthen progressive folk traditions, comprising as they do dramatic performances, concerts, art exhibitions, competitions, carnivals and all kinds of entertainment. This great variety at the same time satisfies and stimulates the cultural interests of the working masses. In the field of music or the theatre, there are no longer what used to be called 'the provinces', because the state is constantly seeking to create conditions which will ensure vigorous cultural life throughout the country. Organizing cultural festivals is inseparable from the development of art and amateur activities. Sometimes, in the programmes of such festivals, new musical works are played for the first time, or the première of a dramatic work is performed. In many cases, these festivals combine the most easily accessible art-forms with other art-forms that require wider knowledge and a higher level of culture. The opening and closing ceremonies are organized with good taste and a lot of imagination, so as to leave lasting impressions in the minds of the public.

It is quite obvious that local cultural festivals help to improve the artistic standards of those who take part in them. The competitions that are organized as part of such festivals, to reward the best work, the best performance or recital, etc., often have the effect of transforming ordinary men and women into creative artists spreading cultural values.

The Spring Cultural Festivals at Kustendil include a wide range of cultural events. For ten days, on the town's main square, the festival continues at full swing. Amateur artists give poetry readings and musical recitals and there are several exhibitions, a carnival and literary evenings. Meetings are organized which enable the local inhabitants to exchange ideas with local writers and artists, etc.

The poetry festival at Sliven, the so-called 'Slivenski ogniové' (Fires of Sliven), also takes place during the spring. A large number of poets and writers visit the towns and villages of the province, giving poetry readings and holding meetings with the public.

It is in the springtime, too, that the Yambol Golden Diana Festival of Chamber Music Choirs is held. This brings together the best chamber music choirs from all over the country.

Other notable local cultural festivals include the Vasil Drumev Drama Festival at Shumen, the Humour and Satire Festival at Gabrovo, the Yavorov Festival, dedicated to the poet Peyo Yavorov, at Pomorie. In the

Dobrudja Folk-Arts Festival, many concerts are given in the towns and villages of the area. Also worthy of mention are the Rose Festival at Stara Zagora and Plovdiv, the cultural festivals at Smolian, the art festivals in May at Razgrad, 'Thrace Sings and Dances' at Haskovo, 'Lights over Rhodope' at Kardjali, the gathering of choirs from towns along the Danube at Silistra, the male-voice choir festival at Gabrovo, 'The Thracian Lyre' and the light music festival at Stara Zagora, the pioneers' choir festivals at Shumen, etc. In addition to all this, there is the 'Sea and Man' poetry contest held at Nesebur, a town on the Black Sea coast which is famous for its remains of classical art and architecture. At Kuzanluk, a month-long painting festival includes, in addition to exhibitions, lectures on painting problems, meetings between young artists and the masters of modern Bulgarian painting, and other cultural events.

The provincial authorities often organize cultural festivals in the villages during the winter months, by calling on artistic groups, theatre companies, writers, etc. They seek in this way to introduce more variety into the cultural life of the towns and villages.

All these types of activity form a link between the people and art, and at the same time help to raise the citizens' standards of artistic culture.

The humanism
of Bulgarian culture

As old as the human race itself, culture has always served the needs of social life. It has always been, and still remains, a driving force which guides and transforms everyday practice and seeks to satisfy the needs and the deep-seated urges for development of both society and the individual. In the complex process of contemporary political development, culture plays an active role, contributes to our understanding of events and thus provides man with new information, which helps him to acquire an overall vision of the world.

In order to realize its essentially humanist vocation, which stems also from the fact that it satisfies man's need to communicate, culture requires social conditions that allow it to express itself in various ways and to exercise an influence on the development of the individual human being.

In Bulgaria, the basic conditions necessary to ensure the development and full realization of the individual have been created. Humanism and the love of peace inspire the whole social and cultural policy of the country, as well as imbuing the way in which the activities of the cultural institutions and cultural development itself are organized, spontaneity being harnessed in the interests of a rising tide of consciously planned cultural action involving the participation of the public as a whole.

The democratization of culture has a profoundly humanistic meaning: it is not solely a question of making culture accessible to the masses, but also of awakening in them a lasting interest in cultural values and giving free rein to their creativity. Thus, by encouraging the manifold expansion of the individual's relationships with the surrounding world, culture affirms a truly humanistic ideal, that of transforming interpersonal relationships on the basis of noble and exalted principles.

The humanism of contemporary Bulgarian culture is also shown by the fact that in line with its fixed resolve to contribute to the maintenance of peace, it deals openly with the most complex of life's philosophical problems and solves them in a bold and original manner.

In a socialist society under construction, freely creative work directed towards noble social objectives is the main factor in man's development. Cultural policy is governed by the principle that creativity is inherent and available to all men, whatever their age or occupation. Participation in cultural activities develops and increases their opportunities for creative expression. This presupposes an appreciation of the individual's worth and of what he can contribute. Based on these principles, creativity involves increasingly varied forms of activity until he has received a real opportunity to employ and display his talents, in different areas of life, in the solution of social problems. The task of bringing culture to the public at large is a continuous, never-ending process; it goes beyond the mere assimilation of knowledge and skills, beyond attainment of a certain level of development of physical and intellectual capabilities, to become a process for the lifelong education and self-education of the individual. The blossoming of individual talents and the increase in personal individuality take place concurrently with a deepening of communal relationships, of the relationships between the individual and society and between the individual and the whole of mankind. What characterizes Bulgarian society today is that, with the increase in social activities, the workers are displaying social sentiments, such as a sense of community, a spirit of mutual assistance, humanism, patriotism and internationalism.

The expression of the individual's talents, knowledge and experience serves humanity's most exalted and noble principles as well as the ideals of peace, understanding and peaceful co-operation between nations.

Contemporary Bulgarian culture exercises an increasingly unifying influence on society, on account of the role it plays in certain extremely important social processes, such as the gradual elimination of the differences between physical and intellectual work and between the town and the country. This unifying influence extends beyond national frontiers, since it includes the overriding principle of the affirmation of life itself. In addition to its specifically national characteristics, the basic content of culture and the ideas behind it are universal and respond to the aspirations of millions throughout the world.

Bulgarian culture is a humanistic culture. It combines the perpetuation of the democratic and progressive traditions of the people with a critical evaluation of its cultural heritage. It has a keen awareness of history and takes a profound interest in the life of the people. It is this which determines its attitude towards socialist reality and the innovative spirit in which it defines and seeks to solve the problems raised by the construction of socialism and contemporary human life. On the basis of concrete historical analyses of the processes of development, culture and the arts point to certain general conclusions and show the contribution made to these processes by different social groups.

Contemporary Bulgarian culture and art, because of their constructive attitude to the situation actually obtaining in Bulgaria and throughout the world, contribute to the solution of various historical, social, cultural and artistic problems of our times. Their universality stems from their peace-loving spirit, from their sympathy towards all those fighting for their freedom and social rights, and from their respect for the beauty and nobility of the human personality. They are imbued with a sense of his-torical optimism and with an interest in the cultures of all peoples of the world, large or small, and in the cultural treasures of the whole of mankind. Their attitude to these universal cultural treasures shows that they have inherited the progressive traditions of the past. Since it appeared in the second half of the ninth century, Bulgarian literature has included many translations of religious, secular and scientific works. As a result, the Bulgarian people have been able to acquire a knowledge of the works of the ancient philosophers and gain access to the culture of classical Greece. This perhaps explains the constant interest taken by the Bulgarian people in the works of art created by the genius of peoples both near and far. However, the Bulgarian, in looking upon such works, has always been guided by his love for mankind and for artists who sincerely search for truth in the world and who believe in man and in his creative powers. He has always sought to understand the spiritual values existing at different periods, possessing an astonishing sense of their real worth and a discriminating eye for what is transitory and what is destined to endure. He has always appreciated human genius, whether it appeared in the remote or recent past, in a distant or nearby country.

Optimism is one of the essential features of art. It derives from the artists' philosophical viewpoint, their conception of the world, their tem-perament and their organic ties with the life of the people.

Culture, which is a many-sided phenomenon, helps to satisfy man's need to communicate and to form relationships with his fellow men. Com-munication is, above all, a social phenomenon, in which culture plays the role of an objective regulator. On the one hand, culture transmits, dissemi-nates and brings within the individual's reach a constant flow of infor-mation; on the other, it lays down forms and principles of communication that help to control and harmonize the various activities carried out in different human communities. Thanks to the function culture performs in communication, time, space and national and linguistic barriers are overcome.

Within the complex system of social relationships, the communicative role of culture helps to harmonize men's individual aspirations with the interests and objectives of society and also to regulate the motives behind his behaviour. Culture does not therefore serve merely to enhance com-munication between people by contributing to the exchanges of ideas and spiritual values and, consequently, to the general development of the individual, but it also plays a decisive role in social integration, since it conditions the appearance of common factors influencing man's behaviour, consciousness and mental life in general. Culture fulfils this function on an international scale within a given aesthetic framework which reflects society's cultural ideals and its artistic experience, though it also includes some subjective elements. In this way, it contributes to the socialization of the individual, by making him aware of the socio-historical realities of the times and the constraints that stem from them.

In the light of these considerations there is no denying the exceptional importance of the provisions of the Final Act of the Helsinki Conference concerning the part culture plays in communication at the international level and in relation to the fundamental problems of the contemporary situation.

Cultural relations have always given a strong impetus to the development of national cultures. In addition, the great cultural movements have always been international in their scope—in this connection mention need only be made of the Renaissance, the Enlightenment, etc. The progressive tendency to combine the efforts now being made on behalf of peace with cultural communication is extremely promising. Of course, cultural exchanges are not a new phenomenon. In spite of national, linguistic, psychological and other differences, cultural exchanges have always existed, on account of the general laws of social development and the community of material and spiritual interests, notwithstanding social and other differences, deriving from the fact that all men have the same material and spiritual needs. Without these common factors in human existence and development, which survive despite the most striking social differences, it would not be possible to talk of universal culture, which is the result of interaction and cultural co-operation, whether spontaneous or organized.

The contemporary situation provides new opportunities for co-operation in areas concerned with spiritual growth and the development of the human personality. Solution of the problems relating to contacts between people and to information, culture and education creates favourable conditions for the establishment of a climate of trust and security, of better intellectual communication between peoples and of deeper mutual knowledge and respect. On the one hand, international détente contributes towards the improvement and strengthening of international relations in culture and the arts, while, on the other hand, cultural relations bring about positive changes in international affairs and contribute towards détente.

At this time of peaceful co-existence between states with different social systems, culture and the arts are playing an increasingly important role in the quest for peace and international understanding.

The People's Republic of Bulgaria has always been of the opinion that cultural relations should be founded upon reciprocity, mutual esteem, trust and respect for national traditions. It is on the basis of these principles, and with an awareness of the part played by cultural co-operation in achieving a better understanding of mankind and other countries, that Bulgaria displays its own cultural possessions and traditions and gives a welcome to the cultural treasures of other countries.

International scientific and cultural co-operation is growing: there are joint scientific research projects at the international level, the exchange of ideas is increasing and countries are combining their efforts in such fields as the natural sciences, medicine, environmental protection, etc.

The last few years have been marked by a considerable increase in the various forms of scientific, ideological and intellectual co-operation between the countries of the socialist world, whose cultures reap mutual benefit from discussion, symposia, meetings and festivals of friendship, as well as from the organization of exhibitions, national culture months, etc.

The cultures of these countries help to bring peoples closer together, since the ideas they transmit respond to the vital needs of mankind and of human progress. They resemble each other in their common historical objectives, their ideological positions and their vision of the world and of mankind.

The development of socialist culture is conditioned by the fact that the countries concerned have increasingly similar problems to solve and that there are common traits marking their evolution. At the same time, it is necessary to stress the importance of the identical attitudes taken by the socialist countries towards major contemporary problems, and also the importance of their feelings of solidarity and of the assistance which they give one another in order to build a new society. The last few decades have been marked by the appearance of an increasing number of new factors in the political, economic and social life of the socialist countries and by the harmonization of their levels of development. This conformity finds expression in the extension and strengthening of their economic, scientific, technical, socio-political and cultural co-operation. The strengthening of the ties between the socialist countries is to be seen in all areas of intellectual life.

Similar phenomena, processes and tendencies are noticeable in all socialist cultures, though in their actual expression they maintain their national identity and originality.

The systematic, conscious realization of all potentialities for cultural development, in their interlocking national and international aspects, confers a special character on socialist culture. The national cultures of the socialist countries have elements in common, which are not to be found in the cultures of other social systems. At the same time, each socialist culture has its own specific features. The link between the national and international aspects shows the importance of both the specific and the common features of socialist culture and contributes to the strengthening of cultural exchanges, which are undertaken on the basis of the increasingly close relations between the socialist countries. Such exchanges are of a new type and new quality.

The development of the national cultures of the countries following the path of socialism is indissolubly linked to the general intellectual creativity of the entire socialist community. Where an advanced socialist society is being constructed, cultural development exhibits an increasingly striking similarity, consisting in the dialectical unity of what is particular and specifically national and what exists in common. The cultures of socialist nations assimilate and build on what is democratic in the cultures of all nations, in addition to the best national traditions, drawing strength from their experience. This fusion of national and universal elements gives rise to the appearance of new cultural phenomena and progressive, popular traditions, each nation seeking to raise its cultural level by drawing upon its own traditions and renewing them in such a way as to assimilate the experience and accumulated wisdom of other nations. In this way the distinctive national elements are brought into harmony with the international elements and enriched as a result.

Contemporary Bulgarian culture encourages this linking of the national and the international aspects, bearing in mind that the creative process contains both a personal element and a common element: the individual viewpoint and the aesthetic vision of the age. There exists a dynamic process for the strengthening of cultural co-operation between the socialist countries, in accordance with their national and international interests; the signing of bilateral agreements for exchanges and cultural co-operation leads to closer cultural relations between them, to the mutual enrichment of their respective cultures and consequently to the strengthening of their common features.

Today, the People's Republic of Bulgaria maintains cultural relations with forty-nine countries, on the basis of intergovernmental agreements and cultural exchange programmes. It also maintains contacts and organizes cultural exchanges with associations and famous writers, artists and musicians in various countries with which it has not yet signed agreements. In total, Bulgaria has cultural exchanges with more than a hundred countries. In this field it has never raised barriers of a political nature. The Bulgarian people respect the national identity of every other culture. Thus, Bulgaria has cultural exchanges, on the basis of equal rights and mutual benefits, with many non-socialist countries, including Belgium, France, the Federal Republic of Germany, Japan, the Netherlands, Norway, Portugal, Spain, Sweden, the United Kingdom, the United States of America and many others.

Socialist culture is an open form of culture. That is why it seeks to become acquainted with all genuine artistic values in the world and all the different forms of artistic expression of other nations. Bulgarian workers are better informed about cultural development and the latest artistic trends in Western countries than the peoples of these countries are about Bulgarian culture.

The cultural activities organized by Bulgaria both inside and outside Europe are particularly important. Bulgarian cultural events abroad, which often turn into festivals of Bulgarian socialist art, as well as the organization within Bulgaria of many events devoted to the cultures of other countries, encourage the growth of mutual trust and strengthen the desire for peaceful coexistence and co-operation.

All the different forms and specific instances of international cultural co-operation help towards the creation of a climate of public opinion hostile to those dangerous forces that have an interest in trying to maintain an atmosphere of animosity between states and of tension in international relations.

Heir to an ancient culture and possessing a strong social conscience, the Bulgarian people are well aware of contemporary international problems and are convinced that if international détente is to be strengthened, then the forces of peace and progress must endeavour to undertake common action in the field of culture as well.

Conclusion

The present flowering of culture and the arts in Bulgaria will ensure still greater success in the years ahead. Cultural development will henceforth keep pace with Bulgaria's social and economic progress. It will be marked by a tendency towards the steady democratization of culture and towards an increase in the number and variety of the forms and means employed to spread culture among the people.

At the same time, efforts will be made to encourage forms of artistic action linked to productive work and to improve the environment, while close attention will also be paid to the need to bring greater beauty into normal work, to increase the intellectual content of work, to make daily life more attractive and to ennoble man. The fact that this tendency is evinced in human behaviour bears out the idea that emancipated work is indissolubly linked to beauty and the quest for perfection. The linking of work with beauty—an association which is forcing itself more and more strongly on public consciousness—displays both ethical and aesthetic aspects. At the same time, efforts are being directed towards the creation of better conditions for introducing workers to the arts and enabling them to play an active part in cultural development.

Artistic activity will continue to reflect the demands and the tendencies of historical evolution, give expression to the workers' interests and call the masses to action, while at the same time reflecting the extraordinary diversity of contemporary life and the aspirations and ideals of modern man. The general guidelines laid down by the Eleventh Congress of the Bulgarian Communist Party and by the Third Congress of Bulgarian Culture have opened up new horizons for the expansion of the arts in Bulgarian society and for the spiritual development of the individual.

As part of the task of building an advanced socialist society, cultural development is directed towards improving the minds and the creativity of the workers. It would hardly be possible to overestimate the importance of the fact that the development of the socialist economy, the increase in the benefits conferred by society and the steady rise in the standard of living and in real and nominal incomes bring about profound changes of both a qualitative and a quantitative nature in cultural life and in the patterns of the individual's cultural needs and interests. This generates a favourable climate for the establishment of even firmer and more harmonious relations between cultural development and the sum total of social processes. And when we talk of the cultural objectives and type of culture proper to an advanced socialist country, we should not restrict ourselves to a rigidly determined field, as within such a society culture can and must play a part in all fields of life. Thus, it embraces the exceptional wealth of material goods and spiritual values, ideas and knowledge through his assimilation of which man is able to develop his creative talents.

The social impact of cultural activities has always been very important, but now they have a new and even larger role to play, as the general development of socialist society provides people with exceptional opportunities for their real emancipation and harmonious development. The enrichment of cultural life and the qualitative changes which are at present taking place within it are likely to make it even more intense and varied in the future.

Appendix

Statistics

	School years			
	1960/61	1970/71	1975/76	1979/80
Total number of pupils	1 416 882	1 554 306	1 530 654	1 453 995
Schools of general and technical education				
Schools	5 877	4 197	3 747	3 611
Pupils	1 212 383	1 154 630	1 098 889	1 075 960
School for physically and mentally handicapped children				
Schools	66	116	125	139
Pupils	7 080	16 870	18 139	17 595
Vocational and technical schools				
Schools	236	132	8	5
Pupils	42 123	47 253	9 708	1 854
Vocational and technical secondary schools				
Schools	236	196	307	299
Pupils	42 123	83 038	136 566	153 105
Polytechnics and art schools				
Schools	231	246	246	221
Pupils	93 944	152 919	141 518	98 762
Post-secondary institutes				
Institutes	18	20	28	34
Students	6 187	10 265	19 779	19 225
Institutions of higher education				
Institutions	20	26	24	28
Students	54 965	89 331	106 055	87 494

Source: Statistical Yearbook of the People's Republic of Bulgaria, Sofia, 1980.

Appendix

TABLE 2.   Nursery schools and the number of children attending: development between 1970 and 1979

	1970	1975	1977	1978	1979
Nursery schools					
Total	8 037	7 550	6 807	6 602	6 406
Permanent	4 508	5 562	5 590	5 587	5 563
of which, on a daily basis	1 757	2 938	3 142	3 239	3 387
Seasonal	3 529	1 988	1 217	1 015	743
Children (in thousands)					
Total	332	393	397	404	419
Permanent	216	327	358	373	395
of which, on a daily basis	105	209	253	274	294
Seasonal	116	66	39	31	24

TABLE 3.   Books published: development between 1939 and 1979

	1939	1948	1956	1966	1975	1979
Number of titles	2 169	2 322	2 900	3 500	3 669	4 337
Number of copies printed annually (in thousands)	6 484	19 893	21 141	39 000	49 100	51 080

TABLE 4.   Periodicals published

	1939	1948	1956	1966	1975	1979
Number of titles (including bulletins)	393	246	105	640	830	957
Number of copies printed annually (in thousands)	11 208	10 421	9 443	27 000	49 961	57 741

TABLE 5.   Newspapers published

	1939	1948	1956	1966	1975	1979
Number of titles (including house journals)	513	92	80	600	498	454
Number of copies printed annually (in thousands)	130 297	345 905	498 782	680 000	843 603	870 000

TABLE 6.   Theatre: development between 1939 and 1979

	1939	1948	1956	1966	1975	1979
Total number	13	21	45	38	55	58
Attendances (in thousands)	1 521	1 651	4 662	4 780	6 000	6 500

Appendix

TABLE 7. Cinema: development between 1939 and 1979

	1939	1948	1956	1966	1975	1979
Total	155	448	1 076	2 712	3 689	3 517
Attendances (in thousands)	13 103	32 047	69 374	124 326	114 225	110 275

TABLE 8. Exhibitions: development between 1963 and 1979

	1963	1970	1974	1979
Total	190	260	315	353
Attendances	729 000	1 048 000	2 015 000	3 070 000

TABLE 9. Amateur artistic activities: development between 1958 and 1979

	1958	1966	1975	1979
Groups	12 303	14 229	11 774	17 800
Performers	370 506	451 311	362 902	436 158
Performances	63 535	72 022	69 642	115 200
Attendances (in thousands)		19 333	21 380	33 100

TABLE 10. Libraries: development between 1952 and 1979

	1952	1956	1965	1975	1979
Libraries holding more than 500 volumes	4 434	5 759	10 813	10 500	10 305
Book collections (volumes in thousands)	8 138	38 443	36 034	59 462	70 000

TABLE 11. Reading centres: development between 1952 and 1979

	1952	1956	1965	1975	1979
Reading centres	4 168	4 502	4 513	4 268	4 254
Members (in thousands)	575	779	958	1 051	1 101

TABLE 12. Museums: development between 1939 and 1979

	1939	1956	1966	1975	1979
Total	13	96	144	181	209
Attendances	—	—	7 419 760	12 897 000	15 744 854

89

Titles in this series:

The serial numbering of titles in this series, the presentation of which has been modified, was discontinued with the volume *Cultural policy in Italy*

Human Rights in International Relations

This fourth edition of David P. Forsythe's successful textbook provides an authoritative and timely analysis of the place of human rights in an age of upheaval in international politics. Human rights standards are examined at the global, regional, and national levels, with separate chapters on transnational corporations and advocacy groups. Completely updated and revised, the fourth edition takes account of new sources and recent scholarship, as well as recent events, such as the Syrian war, the rise of ISIS, refugee flows, South Sudan crises, and the resurgence of nationalism. A new chapter has been added on the media and human rights, covering both traditional and social media. Examining attempts to protect human rights by various actors, such as the United Nations, the European Union, transnational corporations, and the media, the book stresses that the open-ended fate of universal human rights depends on human agency in context. Containing further reading suggestions and discussion questions, this textbook is a vital resource for courses on human rights in an international context.

DAVID P. FORSYTHE is University Professor Emeritus and Charles J. Mach Distinguished Professor of Political Science at University of Nebraska-Lincoln. He has been a visiting professor at universities in Geneva and Utrecht and in 2008 he held the Fulbright Distinguished Research Chair of Human Rights and International Studies at the Danish Institute of International Studies, Copenhagen. He has also been on staff for the United Nations University in Tokyo and has been a consultant to both the UN Office of the High Commissioner of Refugees and the International Red Cross and Red Crescent Movement. In 2012, he was given the career achievement award by the Academic Senate of the University of Nebraska-Lincoln, and the Phi Beta Kappa national office in Washington, DC selected him as a national Visiting Scholar for 2013–2014.

Themes in International Relations

This new series of textbooks aims to provide students with authoritative surveys of central topics in the study of International Relations. Intended for upper level undergraduates and graduates, the books will be concise, accessible and comprehensive. Each volume will examine the main theoretical and empirical aspects of the subject concerned, and its relation to wider debates in International Relations, and will also include chapter-by-chapter guides to further reading and discussion questions.

Human Rights in
International Relations

Fourth Edition

David P. Forsythe

CAMBRIDGE
UNIVERSITY PRESS

CAMBRIDGE
UNIVERSITY PRESS

University Printing House, Cambridge CB2 8BS, United Kingdom

One Liberty Plaza, 20th Floor, New York, NY 10006, USA

477 Williamstown Road, Port Melbourne, VIC 3207, Australia

4843/24, 2nd Floor, Ansari Road, Daryaganj, Delhi – 110002, India

79 Anson Road, #06-04/06, Singapore 079906

Cambridge University Press is part of the University of Cambridge.

It furthers the University's mission by disseminating knowledge in the pursuit of education, learning, and research at the highest international levels of excellence.

www.cambridge.org
Information on this title: www.cambridge.org/9781107183919
DOI: 10.1017/9781316874929

First published 2000
Second edition 2006
Third edition 2012
Fourth edition 2018

Printed in the United Kingdom by Clays, St Ives plc

A catalogue record for this publication is available from the British Library.

Library of Congress Cataloging-in-Publication Data
Names: Forsythe, David P., 1941– author.
Title: Human rights in international relations / David P. Forsythe.
Description: Fourth edition. | Cambridge, United Kingdom : Cambridge University Press, 2017. | Includes bibliographical references and index.
Identifiers: LCCN 2017014550 | ISBN 9781107183919 (Hardback : alk. paper) | ISBN 9781316635186 (pbk. : alk. paper)
Subjects: LCSH: Human rights–Political aspects. | International law and human rights. | International relations.
Classification: LCC K3240 .F67 2017 | DDC 341.4/8–dc23 LC record available at https://lccn.loc.gov/2017014550

ISBN 978-1-107-18391-9 Hardback
ISBN 978-1-316-63518-6 Paperback

Contents

Preface to the fourth edition

My preface to the third edition was written at the time of the Arab Spring, with its popular demand for more democracy and human rights, but before its widespread failure. One can note the reinstitution of military rule in Egypt, humanitarian disaster in Syria, and chaos in Libya. Five years after 2011, there are ample reasons to be cautious if not pessimistic about the future of human rights. This is not only because of developments in the Arab-Islamic world, but also because of clear repressive trends in important states like China and Russia. Even in the West, almost every democratic government was under pressure from nativist and xenophobic forces hostile to – or at the least indifferent to – the notion of universal human rights. Many persons felt threatened by international forces, often described as socio-economic globalization. In addition, the prevalence of terrorism in much of Asia, Africa, and the Middle East, and its occasional occurrence in the West, created a political climate conducive to violation of many human rights in the name of national security. Counter-terrorism policies led at times to enforced disappearances, torture, administrative detention, and trial in military commissions offering "rough justice."

Broad feelings of alienation and insecurity are not conducive to protection of human rights. Yet defense of the individual, his integrity and her dignity, is most needed precisely in those times of stress. It is easy to be in favor of human rights in times of peace and prosperity. The challenge is to respect the fundamental dignity and autonomy of persons in times of violence and economic distress. This means finding some workable and relatively humane blend of national security, economic prosperity, sustainable development, *and* human rights. This is what international law requires and this is what many governments profess to endorse. But making the law on the books into the law in reality is no easy path – especially given the insecurities and competitions inherent in the nation-state system of world affairs.

The objective of the fourth edition is finding the right synthesis between positive and negative developments in the quest for a more rights-protective world. All governments go through the motions of paying lip service to this goal. All states have accepted the 1949 Geneva Conventions designed mainly to protect human dignity in war. At the United Nations, the acceptance rate of most human rights treaties is about 70 percent. States want to be associated with the idea of human rights. Even China and Russia go through the motions of holding (controlled) elections. Yet numerous rights violations are evident.

In part because the commercial media emphasizes the negatives ("if it bleeds, it leads"), we tend to overlook areas of progress on rights – e.g., more international trials for atrocities, more abstract agreement on limiting state sovereignty in the name of rights, more tolerance for gay rights at least in Europe and the Americas.

The fourth edition seeks to establish the right balance between optimism and pessimism on internationally recognized human rights, arguing throughout that the future of rights depends on human agency in changing contexts. Nothing is guaranteed.

I would like to update the list of those who gave me helpful comments on various draft chapters for this fourth edition, with many thanks to: Charlyne Berens, Roger Clark, Barb Flanagan, John Gruhl, Courtney Hillebrecht, Ari Kohen, Patrice McMahon, Kurt Mills, Mahmood Monshipouri, and Jay Ovsiovitch.

Preface to the third edition

My preface to the first edition explains the objectives of this book, and they have not changed. My preface to the second edition explains the considerations that guide revisions, and they have not changed either. As before, revisions seek both to clarify the presentation and to incorporate recent developments. In particular I have now added some brief case studies to provide more specificity to certain rights in political context. My overall approach, hence the structure of the book, remains unchanged.

From the origins of this work as a gleam in the author's eye, the tension between personal rights and the workings of the state system of world affairs has been highlighted. If anything, the new edition emphasizes this tension even more. It is now even clearer that when states perceive a serious threat to their interests, above all their physical security, it becomes more difficult to get serious attention to human rights, especially the rights of those perceived as enemies. Moreover, when ruling elites elevate perceived challenges to the level of existential threats, sometimes to the nation but often just to the nature of their rule, serious attention to human rights suffers. Complicating analysis is the fact that some non-state actors see the existing situation as so objectionable that unrestricted violence is justified. This then feeds into a downward spiral of animosity and violence that tends to push human rights to the margins of public policy. Pursuit of victory in total war is not a mindset conducive to human rights.

Still, such is the power of the idea of human rights, defined to include humanitarian law, that states continue to profess their commitment to at least some of those standards, even as their record of compliance is often far short of what it should be. And armed non-state actors who attack civilians and kill prisoners face an uphill journey as they try to explain why they should be considered the new legitimate elite with the right to rule. The Arab Spring of 2011, with its demand for more democracy and other human rights, was a rejection of the militancy of Al Qaeda and other Islamist violent actors. Al Qaeda and its allies were not completely spent forces, but they were mostly irrelevant to major developments in Tunisia, Egypt, and many other places.

After the demise of European communism some thought the world had entered a golden age of human rights. Forces such as militant Islam and the globalized but impersonal for-profit corporation, however, showed that the promised land remained distant. But the story is yet to be concluded, and the competing tensions are yet to be fully resolved. This third edition is an attempt to indicate the contemporary synthesis between clashing trends over human rights.

As the cliché has it, one thing is perfectly clear. Not only in the West but around the world the teaching of human rights in schools and universities has increased. There are now more scholarly journals focused on human rights, and more articles are being published on human rights in disciplines such as political science. Even in places such as China and Iran, human rights is now a subject of lively and officially sanctioned discussion. This gives some reason for long-term optimism. In the meantime, I sadly note the passing of some of those educators who led the way in this domain, such as Louis Henkin and Richard P. Claude in the United States, Kevin Boyle in the United Kingdom, and Peter R. Baehr in the Netherlands. Three of the four were affected by their family origins whether in Belarus, Northern Ireland, or Nazified Berlin. The lives of each of these three demonstrated that repression can produce human rights progress over time through personal commitment. Surely it is now evident that it is precisely human wrongs that lead to the demand for more practice of human rights, and that this dynamic has yet to run its course. (This is a good spot to refer the reader to Richard Pierre Claude, "Right to Education and Human Rights Education," in David P. Forsythe, ed., *Encyclopedia of Human Rights* [New York: Oxford University Press, 2009], vol. II, 97–107.)

As with earlier editions I had the help of many persons who called material to my attention or who were kind enough to read passages for accuracy and clarity: Danny Braaten, Jack Donnelly, Kathleen Fallon, Barb Flanagan, John Gruhl, Jorge Heine, Courtney Hillebrecht, Rhoda Howard-Hassmann, Mark Janis, Alice Kang, Bert Lockwood, Peter Malcontent, Jay Ovsiovitch, Scott Pegg, David Rapkin, David Richards, Bill Schabas, Fusun Turkmen, Andy Wedeman, David Weissbrodt, and Jake Wobig.

As before, the production team at Cambridge University Press was efficient and helpful, especially my editor John Haslam.

Part I

The foundations

Part 1

The Foundations

1 Introduction: human rights in international relations

Human rights are widely considered to be those fundamental moral rights of the person that are necessary for a life with human dignity. Human rights are thus means to a greater social end, and it is the legal system that tells us at any given point in time which rights are considered most fundamental in society. Even if human rights are thought to be inalienable, a moral attribute of persons that public authorities should not contravene, rights still have to be identified – that is, constructed – by human beings and codified in the legal system.[1] While human rights have a long history in theory and even in spasmodic practice, it was the American and French revolutions of the eighteenth century that sought to create national polities based on broadly shared human rights. Despite the rhetoric of universality, however, human rights remained essentially a national matter, to be accepted or not, until 1945 when they were recognized in global international law.

This book is about the evolution and status of human rights in international relations at the start of the twenty-first century. Thus this extended essay is about the effort to liberalize international relations – to make international relations conform to the liberal prescription for the good society. In the classical liberal view, the good society is based on respect for the equality and autonomy of individuals, which is assured through the recognition and application of the fundamental legal rights of the person. In this book liberalism is a synonym for attention to personal rights. But in international relations it has been widely believed that the state, not the individual, is the basic unit. And the core principle has been said to be state sovereignty and non-interference in the domestic affairs of states. In this book realism is a synonym for attention to state interests – foremost among which is security – and state power. The subject of international human rights thus projects liberalism into a

[1] Jack Donnelly, "The Social Construction of International Human Rights," in Tim Dunne and Nicholas J. Wheeler, eds., *Human Rights in Global Politics* (Cambridge: Cambridge University Press, 1999), 71–102.

3

realist world – a world dominated for several centuries by states and their collective interests.[2]

To paraphrase Charles Dickens, human rights in modern international relations represents both the best of times and the worst of times.[3] During the half-century after World War II, truly revolutionary developments occurred in the legal theory and diplomatic practice of internationally recognized human rights. Human rights language was written into the United Nations Charter, which was not the case with the Covenant of the League of Nations. Member states of the United Nations negotiated an international bill of rights, which was then supplemented by other treaties and declarations codifying that human beings had certain fundamental legal rights that were to be respected. By the first decade of the twenty-first century more than 160 states (United Nations membership was 193 in 2016) had formally adhered to the International Covenant on Civil and Political Rights and the companion International Covenant on Economic, Social, and Cultural Rights. Some regional developments were even more impressive. The Council of Europe (made up of forty-seven states in 2016) manifested not only a regional convention on civil and political rights, widely accepted in that region, but also an international court to adjudicate disputes arising under that treaty. The Western Hemisphere was also characterized by a regional treaty on human rights and a supranational court to give binding judgments. The 1949 Geneva Conventions were formally accepted by all states; they enshrined the view that certain personal protections were to be respected even by parties engaged in armed conflict. In the fall of 1993 the UN General Assembly approved the creation of a High Commissioner for Human Rights. In the mid-1990s the UN Security Council created international criminal courts to try individuals for violations of the laws of war, genocide, and crimes against humanity in the former Yugoslavia and Rwanda, thus rejuvenating international criminal responsibility after the Nuremberg and Tokyo trials of the 1940s. In the summer of 1998 a diplomatic conference in Rome approved the statute for a standing international criminal court with jurisdiction similar to the two *ad hoc* courts. In 2005 a United Nations summit meeting affirmed the principle of the responsibility to protect (R2P). Henceforth, while sovereign states had the primary responsibility for protecting human rights in their jurisdictions,

---

[2] For an excellent discussion of varieties of liberalism and realism, see Michael W. Doyle, *Ways of War and Peace* (New York: Norton, 1997), especially 41–48 and 205–213.

[3] Lynn Miller, *World Order: Power and Values in International Politics*, 3rd edn. (Boulder: Westview, 1994), ch. 1.

if states proved unwilling or unable to prevent gross violations, outside parties had the responsibility to become involved.

Other developments also indicated the central point that human rights was no longer a matter necessarily or always within state domestic jurisdiction. In principle, states were to answer to the international community for their treatment of individuals. International relations regularly entailed not only subjects like war and trade, but also human rights. Human rights had been internationalized, and at least some attention to internationally recognized rights had become routinized. International relations involved aspects of governance in the sense of public management of policy questions.[4] Attention to human rights was part of this international governance. Concerns about the equal value, freedom, and welfare of individuals had long affected many national constitutions and much domestic public policy. From 1945 those same concerns about individual autonomy and respect and welfare also began to affect international relations in important ways – regardless of whether the distribution of power was bipolar, multipolar, or unipolar.[5]

The other side of the coin, however, merits summary attention as well. Perhaps no other situation captures so well the inhumanity that occurs in the world as the famine in China between 1958 and 1962, induced by Mao's regime, that claimed approximately 30 million lives.[6] Not only did the international community not respond, but also many outsiders even denied that a catastrophe of major proportion was occurring or had occurred. If one judges events by number of human lives lost, Mao's famine made him a greater mass murderer than either Hitler or Stalin. The twentieth century, with its record of mass murder and mass misery, was plainly not a good era for the practice of liberal values in many ways. It has been estimated that some 35 million persons were killed in armed conflict during the twentieth century; but perhaps 150–170 million persons were killed by their own governments through political murder or mass misery that could have been ameliorated.[7] The journalist David Rieff was quite perceptive when he wrote that

---

[4] James N. Rosenau and Ernst-Otto Czempiel, eds., *Governance Without Government: Order and Change in World Politics* (Cambridge: Cambridge University Press, 1992).

[5] Lea Brilmayer, *American Hegemony: Political Morality in a One-Superpower World* (New Haven: Yale University Press, 1994).

[6] For an introduction, see Andrew Wedeman, "China: The Famine of the 1960s," in David P. Forsythe, ed., *Encyclopedia of Human Rights* (New York: Oxford University Press, 2009), vol. I, 321–328. See further Jasper Becker, *Hungry Ghosts: China's Secret Famine* (London: J. Murray, 1996).

[7] R. J. Rummel, *Death by Government* (Somerset, NJ: Transaction Publishers, 1996).

the twentieth century, by comparison to those that came before, had the best norms and the worst realities.[8]

Even after the collapse of European communism and the demise of communist economics in other places like China and Vietnam, a number of persons embraced the traditional view that international relations remained a dangerous game, and that those who wanted decisive international action for human rights were naively optimistic.[9] The historian Samuel Moyn considered the push for international human rights one more utopian project akin to the panaceas of communism and national liberation from colonialism.[10] In the post-Cold War world, the rise of Islamic jihadists – or militant Islamists if one prefers – seemed to confirm this dark view of the perpetual human condition. Thus the end of the Cold War did not mean the demise of "realists" who argued that pursuit of human rights in international relations had to take a back seat to the self-interested pursuits of the territorial state. It was ironic but nevertheless true that democratic realists like Henry Kissinger, however much they might be philosophical liberals at home in their support for democracy and human rights, were prepared to sacrifice foreign rights and foreign democracy to advance the interests of their state. Democratic societies surely had a collective right to defend themselves. The rub came in whether a democratic society should sacrifice the human rights of others to advance its own security and prosperity. Even commentators sympathetic to universal human rights agreed that anarchical international relations, without central government, meant that it was not easy to interject human rights considerations into the small policy space left over from intense national competition.[11]

This book, focusing on human rights in international relations since World War II, will present an analysis of competing liberal and realist perspectives. It will also chart the enormous gap between legal theory and political behavior, as public authorities both endorsed human rights standards and systematically violated – or failed to correct violations of – the newly emergent norms. The following pages will explain why legal and diplomatic progress transpired, analyzing both moral and expediential influences. It will also outline major sources of

---

[8]   *A Bed for the Night: Humanitarianism in Crisis* (New York: Simon & Schuster, 2002), 70.

[9]   E.g., John Mearsheimer, "Disorder Restored," in Graham Allison and Gregory Treverton, eds., *Rethinking America's Security: Beyond Cold War to New World Order* (New York: Norton, 1992), 213–237.

[10]   Samuel Moyn, *The Last Utopia: Human Rights in History* (Cambridge, MA: Belknap for Harvard University Press, 2010).

[11]   Stanley Hoffmann, *Duties Beyond Borders: On the Limits and Possibilities of Ethical International Politics* (Syracuse: Syracuse University Press, 1981).

opposition to the consolidation of the legal-diplomatic revolution. The analysis will hence trace the successes and failures of international action for human rights, with the latter being frequently more visible than the former. Along the way we will pay attention to critiques of liberalism other than realism, such as some versions of feminism and Marxism.

The long-term vision that emerges from the pages that follow is open-ended. The future of human rights depends on agency in context: nothing is set in stone. We should keep in mind that contemporary international relations is characterized by much turbulence, with ample evidence of contradictory findings and trends.[12] Nevertheless, for pragmatic liberals such as the author who regard international human rights as good and proper, but whose application must be matched to contextual realities thus leading to difficult policy choices, the twenty-first century holds both dangers to, and promise for, human rights. I am guarded about a liberal world order in the long term.[13] I believe that the future of human rights in international relations is not predetermined by structural (meaning fundamental or systemic) factors but depends on choice by humans. In the light of what social scientists call the agent–structure problematique, I believe that agents have some freedom of choice even while structures cannot be discounted. Racism remains strong, but Nelson Mandela showed that individuals could make progress toward a multi-racial and rights-protective polity.

In addressing this subject, one has to admit that the topic of human rights in international relations is too big and complex for one macro-thesis – aside from the general argument that human action for or against human rights will determine. Four smaller themes, however, permeate the pages that follow. The first is that some international concern with human rights is here to stay. The second is that one should appreciate human rights as important and pervasive soft law, not just the occasional hard law of court pronouncements. The third is that private parties merit extensive attention, not just public authorities. The fourth is that the notion of state sovereignty is undergoing fundamental change, the "final" form of which is difficult to discern. But, as never before, to be "sovereign" entails the duty to protect human rights. At least this is the endorsed principle.

---

[12] James N. Rosenau, *Turbulence in World Politics: A Theory of Change and Continuity* (Princeton: Princeton University Press, 1990).

[13] Max Singer and Aaron Wildavsky, *The Real World Order: Zones of Peace, Zones of Turmoil*, 2nd edn. (Chatham, NJ: Chatham House Publishers, 1996).

Human rights as end of history?

There is no reasonable prospect of a return to the international relations of, say, the early nineteenth century. As mentioned above, and as will be shown in some detail in Chapters 2 and 3, human rights standards and basic diplomatic practices have been institutionalized in international relations.[14] The first and most simple explanation for this is that there are now so many treaties, declarations, and agencies dealing with internationally recognized human rights that especially the last fifty years of international interactions cannot be undone. But there are deeper and more interesting explanations, some accepted, some debated.

Second and relatedly, western power has made a difference. Liberal democracies still constitute the most important coalition in international relations. The affluent liberal democracies which comprise the core of the Organization for Economic Cooperation and Development (OECD) constitute not only a caucus or interest group. These states also exercise considerable military, economic, and diplomatic power. They constitute the current motor to a process that has been going on for several centuries: the westernization of international relations.[15] In general, these states and the non-governmental actors based within them have been introducing human rights into world affairs, especially since 1945. The globalization of the western version of liberalism has been going on for some time, especially when one understands that globalization pertains to social as well as economic issues.

If the Axis powers had won World War II or if the communist alliance had won the Cold War, international relations would be different than it is today – and much less supportive of human rights. In broader retrospective, if conservative Islamic actors had proved dominant over the past four centuries and not western ones, human rights would not have fared so well. I do not mean that each liberal democracy has been genuinely supportive of every human rights issue that arose in international relations. Clearly that was not the case. France and the United States, the two western states most prone to present themselves to the rest of the world as a universal model for human rights, have compiled a quite mixed record on the practice of human rights in international relations. France actively supported various repressive regimes within its former African colonies, even in the 1990s after the demise of

---

[14] David P. Forsythe, "The United Nations and Human Rights at Fifty: An Incremental but Incomplete Revolution," *Global Governance*, 1, 3 (September 1995), 297–318.

[15] Theodore H. Von Laue, *The World Revolution of Westernization: The Twentieth Century in Global Perspective* (New York: Oxford University Press, 1987).

Soviet-led communism. During the Algerian war of 1954–1962 it operated a torture bureau as part of its military structure. The United States, to put it kindly, did not always interest itself in various individual freedoms in Central America during much of the Cold War. In places like Guatemala, Nicaragua, and El Salvador Washington was indirectly responsible for many political killings and other forms of repression. It is quite clear that during the Cold War, the democratic West, to protect its own human rights, supported the denial of many human rights in many parts of the world many times. It has proved all too possible for liberal democracies at home to manifest less than liberal foreign policies abroad.

But a larger point remains valid. Dominant international norms and central international organizations reflect to a large extent the values of the most powerful members of the international community. The OECD coalition has been the most powerful, and particularly in terms of basic norms and diplomatic practices, OECD states, along with certain other actors, have made a liberal imprint on international relations. At least in this one sense, and for limited purposes, it is correct to view international relations sometimes as a clash of civilizations.[16] For all their domestic imperfections and imperialistic foreign policies, the liberal democracies have advanced the notion of the equal autonomy of and respect for the individual. History does not move in straight lines, but certain ideas do advance. Should an authoritarian China come to dominate international relations, the place of human rights in world affairs would change.

However, the economic and military increase in China's power and the concomitant decline in US economic clout and military effect raise troubling questions about the long-term future of human rights – if China remains authoritarian and if the United States does not make needed adjustments to its power base. Other troubling factors can also be briefly noted – e.g., repressive trends in Russia, the growing power of authoritarian Iran, Pakistan's inability to suppress illiberal Islamist movements, India's colonial experience and hence its distaste for western-inspired review of national policies (not to mention its highly repressive control of Kashmir), and so on. In short, the westernization of international relations may come to an end by 2050 if not before.[17]

Third, there is a more intriguing but debatable explanation for the staying power of human rights in world affairs, beyond these first two and

---

[16] Samuel P. Huntington, "The Clash of Civilizations," *Foreign Affairs*, 72, 3 (Summer 1993), 22–49; Huntington, *The Clash of Civilizations and the Remaking of World Order* (New York: Simon & Schuster, 1996).

[17] See especially Stephen Hopgood, *The Endtimes of Human Rights* (Ithaca and London: Cornell University Press, 2013). He considers state-sponsored human rights efforts to be a form of Western cultural imperialism. Recall also Moyn, *The Last Utopia*.

related factors: the weight of international institutions (meaning the cumulative weight of international law and organizations), and the political influence of powerful states. This third factor pertains to political theory and personal values. Francis Fukuyama argued that all persons have a drive to be respected, and that the ultimate form of personal respect finds satisfaction in the idea of human rights.[18] Stated differently, Fukuyama argued that the process of history drives persons toward acknowledgment of human rights, since the *ideal* of human rights (rather than its imperfect practice) constitutes the most perfect form of contribution to human dignity.

In this Hegelian interpretation of purposeful or teleological world history, at least intellectual history, liberal democracies have been instrumental to the institutionalization of human rights less because of their military and economic power, and more because they have adopted an ideology of human respect that cannot be improved upon. Or, liberal democracies exert influence for human rights because they reflect an appealing way to legitimate power. Liberal democracies stipulate that power must be exercised in conformity with, primarily, individual civil and political rights. Other states, such as Sukarno's Indonesia or Khomeini's Iran, may temporarily achieve popular goals such as economic growth or conformity with fundamentalist religious principles. But in the long run they suffer a crisis of legitimacy, because they have an inferior way of trying to justify their power. In Fukuyama's view, accepting human rights is the best way to legitimate power. Thus human rights becomes a hegemonic idea with staying power because of its theoretical or ideational supremacy. We have the "end of history" and have seen the "last political man" because the formal-legal triumph of human rights cannot be improved upon as a legitimating ideal. Never mind for now that human practice fails to fully implement the theoretical ideal.

Some have seen a smug self-satisfaction and triumphalism in Fukuyama's argument – which was presented after the demise of European communism. They are inclined to argue that in particular the US model of human rights is overly individualistic, causing great damage to a sense of community and perhaps even to order. This view is sometimes

---

[18] Francis Fukuyama, *The End of History and the Last Man* (New York: The Free Press, 1992). Fukuyama has not changed his views, except to say that if medical psychology could change the nature of man, his theory would have to be revisited. See Fukuyama, "Second Thoughts: The Last Man in a Bottle," *The National Interest*, 56 (Summer 1999). But see his "At the 'End of History' Still Stands Democracy," *Wall Street Journal* (June 6, 2014), www.wsj.com/articles/at-the-end-of-history-still-stands-democracy-1402080661, arguing that there are indeed competing sources of political legitimacy, but liberal democracy based on human rights should triumph in the long run.

presented in the form of the superiority of certain Asian values.[19] Several western observers are also critical of the extent of individual rights found especially in the United States.[20] Some critics argue there is too much western emphasis on civil and political rights, and not enough emphasis on the economic, social, and cultural aspects of human dignity, which after all is the commonly agreed end product. Others argue that Fukuyama's view of human rights is too secular as well as too universal, and thus too demeaning to local cultures and religions that give fundamental meaning to many people.[21] Some observers saw early on a socioeconomic globalization giving rise to a particularistic and fundamentalist backlash that was the antithesis of the triumph of the idea of universal human rights.[22] Even many pragmatic liberals said that human rights is only one means, and not necessarily always the most significant one, for achieving human dignity.[23] There was, for example, considerable attention to the idea of human security, a notion that might or might not be compatible with the human rights discourse.

It seems clear enough that there are various means to try to legitimate power: achieve impressive economic growth (e.g., China), obtain the endorsement of religious authorities (e.g., Iran), restore national power (e.g., Russia), provide stability after disruption (e.g., al-Sisi in Egypt), incorporate familiar traditions from past regimes (e.g., Putin in Russia often emulates the Tzars), and so on. A sense of correctness might evolve from each of these factors.

Still, Fukuyama may be proven correct when he notes that as of the end of the twentieth century liberal democratic state capitalism as grounded in human rights ideas has proved broadly appealing. One sees this appeal in the Arab Spring of 2011 in which broad grassroots activism demanded more democracy and human rights as traditionally

[19] See further among many sources Joanne R. Bauer and Daniel A. Bell, eds., *The East Asian Challenge for Human Rights* (New York: Cambridge University Press, 1999).

[20] Michael Hunt writes of those critics of the USA who worried about its "aggressive and asocial individualism," in *Ideology and US Foreign Policy* (New Haven: Yale University Press, 1987), 44 and *passim*. Rhoda Howard, *Human Rights and the Search for Community* (Boulder: Westview, 1995), believes that the US version of human rights has undermined a sense of community but suggests that Canada's version has not.

[21] Michael J. Perry in *The Idea of Human Rights: Four Inquiries* (New York: Oxford University Press, 1998) argues that religion is a necessary base for human rights.

[22] Benjamin R. Barber, *Jihad v. McWorld* (New York: Ballantyne Publishing Group, 1995).

[23] See further Herbert C. Kelman, "The Conditions, Criteria, and Dialectics of Human Dignity: A Transnational Perspective," *International Studies Quarterly*, 21, 3 (September 1977), 529–552; and Harold K. Jacobson, "The Global System and the Realization of Human Dignity and Justice," *International Studies Quarterly*, 26, 3 (September 1982), 315–332; and see below, especially Chapter 4.

understood (in part because they were seen as leading to more economic opportunity).

Moreover, one has only to compare the number of migrants (including refugees) seeking entrance to OECD states with those seeking to enter various illiberal or repressive states. This is not to say that the OECD states do not present problems of material consumption, ecological overload, democratic deficits, mismanagement of economics and finances, and a host of other problems. The perfect society has yet to manifest itself. Nevertheless, liberal democratic state capitalism is associated with a broadly appealing series of human rights centering on civil and political rights, including a right to private property. Most OECD states other than the USA have added the conception of economic and social human rights to their view of the fundamental entitlements of the individual in society. This OECD model has indeed proved broadly attractive even beyond the western world. Many "have nots" in places like Asia, the Arab world, Africa, etc. do indeed accept the superiority of the idea of respect for human rights, and they are active in organizing groups to pursue that goal. Some non-western elites, too, have endorsed the human rights model in places like Japan and South Korea.

Just as the originally western notion of state sovereignty has been widely accepted, so the once western notion of human rights has found broad acceptance especially during the past fifty years of world history. This stems in part from western military and economic achievements. But it also stems in part from an intellectual or ethical hegemony as outlined by Fukuyama. The *idea* of individual human rights has proved broadly appealing. As Michael Ignatieff has noted, human rights can be seen as a form of "idolatry," of worshiping the human being, and naturally enough this vision has proven attractive to lots of human beings.[24] Even those like Stalin, who denied most human rights in practice, wrote liberal constitutions and organized (controlled) elections so as to pretend to recognize human rights.

Is Fukuyama guilty of triumphalism, of overstating the appeal of western-style democracy after NATO's victory in the Cold War? It is difficult to fully separate basic political theory from the net results of the practice associated with theory. If all liberal democracies had compiled the practical record of Weimar Germany, or more recently Greece and Argentina, the theory of liberal democracy would be dead today. Probably the greatest challenge to the fundamental ideas of democratic state capitalism (based on human rights) comes from authoritarian capitalism

---

[24] Michael Ignatieff, *Human Rights as Politics and Idolatry* (Princeton: Princeton University Press, 2001).

along the lines of China or Singapore. While these two states do not overtly reject the fundamental notion of human rights leading to liberal democracy, their practice indicates that their core political theory is really authoritarian capitalism. (In China's case it is certainly not Marxism-Leninism, and never was for Singapore.)

In the past thirty years China has overcome instability and poverty to grow at an annual average of 9–10 percent. It is the most impressive record of sustained national economic growth in history. In approximately the same period Singapore has moved from being a poor colony in the British Empire to surpassing the British in per capita gross national product. This politically illiberal model of national development is appealing to some. Much remains to be seen as to how attractive the Chinese/Singapore model proves. China in particular has much uneven development and many pockets of discontent. It is not at all clear that China can continue to encourage considerable personal freedom in economic matters but deny significant individual freedom in the political system. Moreover, in many authoritarian states beyond China and Singapore there is even more corruption and much less impressive development. One has only to look at Egypt at the time of writing to conclude that authoritarianism can lead to considerable socioeconomic problems and instability.

It is premature to say that Fukuyama is definitely either correct or incorrect regarding the superiority of legitimating ideologies based on civil-political rights. As Chinese foreign minister Chou En-lai supposedly said to Henry Kissinger in the 1970s with regard to an evaluation of the French revolution of 1789 made in the name of the "rights of man," it is too soon to say. If China disintegrates into renewed instability because of bad decisions made by its authoritarian elite, the human rights promises of the French revolution will look more attractive.[25]

It bears stressing that Fukuyama's argument in support of human rights is mostly about political theory and not about democratic practice. One of the points emphasized in this book is that western states, including the USA, can greatly benefit from a more serious consideration of how internationally recognized human rights might improve their societies.[26] Ultra-nationalists like the late US senator Jesse Helms resist

---

[25] For a short discussion of the power and problems of China with its projected status as the largest economy in the world by 2030, see Gideon Rachman, "American Decline: This Time It's for Real," http://foreignpolicy.com/2011/01/03/think-again-american-decline/.

[26] See further David P. Forsythe, *Global Human Rights and American Exceptionalism* (Lincoln: University of Nebraska, University Professor Distinguished Lecture, 1999); and Forsythe, ed., *The United States and Human Rights: Looking Inward and Outward* (Lincoln: University of Nebraska Press, 1999).

international review of the racist strains and other imperfections in American society, as shown especially in Chapters 4 and 6 of the present volume. A certain intellectual isolationism persists among some US policy makers and voters. They easily accept the notion that because the US Constitution is revered, and because the United States manifests an independent and powerful judicial system, American society has no need of international standards or international review of human rights practices. Their intellectual or cultural isolationism causes them to overlook much pertinent evidence about the utility of international review of democratic violations of human rights.

During the Cold War the Council of Europe was made up of only liberal democracies (excepting Greek and Turkish governments during certain periods). Yet human rights violations by these liberal democracies, under the European Convention on Human Rights, as reviewed by the European Commission on Human Rights and the European Court of Human Rights, were not few. As will be noted in Chapter 5, the case load at the European Court of Human Rights was such that procedures had to be changed to accommodate the large and growing number of cases. Against this background, it is difficult to sustain the view that the US Constitution and Bill of Rights emphasizing the American version of human rights could not benefit from further international review. It is perfectly clear that even well-intentioned democracies violate some human rights, both at home and through their foreign policies.[27] Fukuyama's argument was not that western democracies are perfect or cannot be improved, only that they institutionalize a superior political theory for legitimating power (that they helped transfer to international relations from 1945). This mode of legitimating power is the theory of protecting human rights.

For the immediate future, the international law of human rights exists, for whatever reason. Hence the primary issue about human rights in international relations is not whether we should acknowledge them as fundamental norms. Rather, the primary issue is when and how to implement human rights in particular situations. A central dilemma has always been, and remains, how to guarantee personal rights when the community itself, or its major interests, is threatened. Thus, what is the proper protection of human rights when the order or security of the nation-state is at risk, or its major economic interests are challenged?

---

[27] Donald W. Jackson, *The United Kingdom Confronts the European Convention on Human Rights* (Gainesville: University Press of Florida, 1997).

Human rights as soft law

Hard law is "black letter law," the exact law as specified in court decisions. Soft law comes in two forms. There are legal rules that are not the subject of court decisions, but which nevertheless influence extra-judicial policy making. For example, some influential treaties are never or rarely adjudicated in court. They achieve their impact on policy and behavior by being interpreted by non-judicial bodies such as the legal office of the foreign ministry. Additionally there are norms that do not meet the procedural test of being law, but which nevertheless influence policy making as if they were law. For example, some UN resolutions become accepted as authoritative guidelines even while remaining, legally speaking, non-binding recommendations.

One of the official long-term goals of many actors in international relations is to institute the rule of law on behalf of human rights. This means not only that world affairs would be characterized by human rights standards, but also that these general norms would lead regularly to international and national court cases to protect human rights. Court cases would transform international legal principles into specific rules providing concrete protection. In this vision the international law of human rights would become hard law. This is an admirable goal, already partially realized.

For example, within the Council of Europe, and under the European Convention on Human Rights, we already have hard law. As will be shown primarily in Chapter 5, we have not just legal principles on behalf of civil and political rights. We also have hard or black letter law: we have court cases comprising specific judgments about what is legal and illegal in particular situations. The European states party to this legal system, which created, *inter alia*, a supranational court to issue binding judgments in human rights matters under this multilateral treaty, have thus far largely complied with all judgments of the European Court of Human Rights. There is nothing in the nature of the international law of human rights that prevents it from becoming hard law, even reasonably effective hard law. (The subject of national compliance with international court judgments is complex. For example, some states will pay reparations to wronged individuals as ordered by courts, but fail to make changes in national law so as to prevent future violations. So there is the matter of partial compliance.)

This book, however, is not a case book for law students. While covering considerable traditional legal materials, it stresses the importance, perhaps sometimes even the superiority, of soft law on human rights. The primary form of soft law covered is the attention given to international human rights standards through non-judicial means such as state foreign policy, the action of non-profit non-governmental organizations (NGOs) like Amnesty International, the action of for-profit corporations, and the actions of private individuals. When these actors pursue human rights standards through their various actions, sometimes they can have greater impact than through court cases.

Apartheid was not ended in South Africa by a court case. Communism was not ended in Europe by a court case. Torture was not terminated in the Shah's Iran by a court case. Death squads were not suppressed in El Salvador by a court case. In all these examples, considerable progress was made on human rights through non-judicial action. This book emphasizes the reality of action on human rights through soft law – the implementation of human rights norms via public policy, reflecting the interplay of governments, intergovernmental organizations (IGOs), NGOs, corporations, and even individuals.

Two further examples can be cited to make the same point. If important strides are to be made on the problem of child soldiers, we need not only legal rules backed by court cases prohibiting child soldiers, but also a multifaceted approach to society's structures that lead to the recruitment of child soldiers.[28] Similarly one might recall the Danish cartoon controversy from 2006 in which there was a negative reaction (managed by certain actors leading to violent events with fatalities) to cartoons published in Copenhagen making fun of the prophet Mohamed. Certainly a court case will not resolve the problem. When the practice of freedom of speech and freedom of the press led to charges of defaming a religion, that clash was resolved, to the extent that it was, by diplomacy and cross-cultural communication.[29] Hence on these subjects, as on most others, we need soft law in addition to hard law.

Global international relations would be much improved if it approximated the regional international law of Western Europe with its inter-

---

[28] Scott Gates and Simon Reich, eds., *Child Soldiers in the Age of Fractured States* (Pittsburgh: University of Pittsburgh Press, 2010).

[29] For background, see David Keane, "Cartoon Violence and Freedom of Expression," *Human Rights Quarterly*, 30, 4 (November 2008), 845–875. In the UN Human Rights Council during the spring of 2011, a resolution was adopted that dropped language about defaming Islam. This language had been pushed for years by certain Arab and other Islamic actors. It had been strongly resisted by Denmark and other liberal states. Contributing to events was the assassination of Pakistani officials for supposedly defaming Islam. The resolution reaffirmed freedom of speech but opposed incitement to imminent violence. See Patrick Goodenough, "UN Human Rights Council Moves Away from 'Dangerous' Defamation of Religion Concept," March 25, 2011, www.cnsnews.com/news/article/un-human-rights-council-moves-away-dangerous-defamation-religion-concept.

locking human rights standards as specified by the European Court of Human Rights and European Court of Justice – the latter court ruling on certain human rights questions although it is supposedly and primarily a court for economic issues. When US courts have ruled on certain human rights issues affecting foreign relations, at least some symbolic victories have been achieved on such matters as prosecution of alien torturers.[30]

But one can make advances on human rights apart from courts and hard law. Armed conflict is a clear case in point. Since 1864 there have been a number of treaties codifying various legal protections for persons not active in armed conflict. What is now called international humanitarian law, or the law for the protection of victims of war, or the law of human rights in armed conflict, manifests a rich normative history. Numerous books, and even a few libraries, focus on these legal standards. We do not lack for lawyers in the various national military establishments. However, the number of important or influential national and international court cases adjudicating this international law, and the national laws derived from it, over the past 140 years is minuscule by any means of calculation. The relative paucity of court cases (excepting Germany after World War II) pertaining to the international law of human rights in armed conflict does not mean that the law is irrelevant to armed conflict. Rather, this law is brought to bear (to the extent that it is) mostly by military and political decisions, and by the private efforts of groups like the International Committee of the Red Cross. (This macro-evaluation remains valid even though one can point to the occasional important court case dealing with international humanitarian law, such as the US Supreme Court's Hamdan judgment of 2006 holding that a provision of the 1949 Geneva Conventions applied to the US military prison at Guantanamo Bay on the island of Cuba.)

In the complicated armed conflicts that characterized much of the territory of the former Yugoslavia between 1992 and 1995, eventually it proved possible to reduce the violations of international humanitarian law. This was achieved primarily by political means, chief of which was the negotiation of the 1995 Dayton accords. Systematic rape as a weapon of war, the killing and mistreatment of prisoners, and attacks on – and evictions of – civilians were all reduced over time, but not through court

---

[30] US federal courts have asserted jurisdiction over alien torts that violate the law of nations. Thus certain foreign or alien torturers who enter the United States have been successfully prosecuted for violations of international human rights. Monetary judgments have rarely been collected, but international travel has been restricted for those convicted. See further Henry J. Steiner and Philip Alton, *International Human Rights in Context: Law, Politics, Morals* (New York: Oxford University Press, 1996), 779–810. This subject is updated later in the text.

cases. Indeed, Chapter 4 in particular addresses the thorny question of whether attempts at war crimes trials during or immediately after an armed conflict always comprise a preferred course of action. Suffice it to say at this point that the Clinton administration, with widespread support among European governments, decided not to vigorously pursue certain of those indicted as war criminals circa 1995, making the political judgment that pursuit of peace in former Yugoslavia – and with it the reduction of abuses of civilians and prisoners – overruled pursuit of legal justice at least for certain persons for certain times.[31] This book emphasizes those types of policy decisions in relation to international human rights, rather than hard law emerging from courts. (The creation in 1993 of the International Criminal Tribunal for the former Yugoslavia did not alter the fact that it was US mediation at the Dayton conference in 1995 that greatly reduced atrocities mainly in Bosnia, in the context of broader political and military developments. The first Balkan war of 1991–1995, and its series of atrocities, was not ended by court cases.)

One of the basic functions of all law, international law included, is to educate in an informal sense. To the extent that the international law of human rights informs military training, foreign policy decisions, and the actions of private groups, *inter alia*, it has achieved one of its primary purposes. It is not necessary to have court cases for the law to exert influence – and sometimes broad influence. It is commonplace to have legal obedience or compliance without legal enforcement. Indeed, the optimum situation is for legal standards to be internalized by individuals to such an extent that court cases are unnecessary. Effective law is usually that law which is internalized successfully, with court cases attempting to sanction a few violators. When violations are widespread, they overwhelm the justice system and usually lead to the collapse of the law. The ineffective laws in the USA making alcoholic drinks illegal during the era of prohibition classically demonstrate this point.

A number of lawyers active on human rights issues always argue for more hard law on human rights. From one point of view that is a laudable objective. The OECD states endorse the principle that all individuals are equal before the law. All those who violate the law should be prosecuted without regard to "political" considerations. From another point of view, however, the pursuit of international human rights standards through mostly hard law decisions is not likely to transpire with any regularity in the coming century – nor should it in all situations. The USA tried to

---

[31] See Richard Holbrooke, *To End a War* (New York: Random House, 1999), who says that in mediating the Dayton accords his mandate was to obtain peace and not to pursue legal justice.

arrest one of the more powerful warlords in Somalia during the early 1990s, holding him personally responsible for a number of violations of international law. The result was a firefight in downtown Mogadishu in October of 1993 that killed eighteen US soldiers and many more Somalis, led to the withdrawal of US troops from that failed state, and contributed to the reluctance of the USA to have the UN decisively engage to stop massive genocide in Rwanda during 1994. There is no doubt in retrospect that the pursuit of legal justice in Somalia led to a hell of good intentions, and that it would have been better, for Somalia and for the entire Great Lakes region of Africa, if the USA and other actors had defined their objectives in less criminal terms.

At the end of the Desert Storm campaign in early 1991, the USA and its coalition partners decided not to follow up on all their talk about war crimes committed by the Iraqi leadership. Such a pursuit would have entailed a continuation of the war, as the Allied Coalition would have had to launch a ground attack on Baghdad in order to try to capture Saddam Hussein and his commanders. That attack would have cost many Coalition lives and entailed much "collateral damage" to civilians in Baghdad. It is highly doubtful if American public opinion would have sustained such an operation at that time, based on pursuit of legal justice. To expect the first President Bush and his military staff to ignore such political calculations and look only at human rights violations and other violations of international law is to joust with windmills in the tradition of Don Quixote. Putting human rights violators in the dock is, after all, only one human rights strategy.[32]

After the US invasion of Iraq in 2003, with prolonged instability that cost more than 4,425 US military deaths by 2016, and tens of thousands of Iraqi deaths, mostly civilian, debate grew about the wisdom of decisions by George W. Bush to pursue a radical solution to the problem of Saddam Hussein – especially since weapons of mass destruction were never found. One of the outcomes from the US invasion was the increased power of the Shi'ite government of Iran next door, a government that was brutally repressive and anti-USA. And the trial and execution of Hussein after his overthrow and capture proved not to be a decisive factor in the evolution of Iraqi and regional politics. The decision to remove by force a gross violator of human rights such as Saddam Hussein can be fraught with complexity, especially since the "law of unintended consequences" often comes into play.

---

[32] Paul Hunt, *Reclaiming Social Rights: International and Comparative Perspectives* (Aldershot: Dartmouth, 1997), 41.

When it became clear that the Saddam regime had not been a clear and present danger to US society, American opinion turned against the invasion and the administration that had produced it – especially when the follow-on occupation and transition were badly managed for several years. This in turn contributed to American fatigue with foreign interventions and hence a reluctance to get deeply involved in the Syrian internationalized civil war next door. So just as one saw the "Somalia syndrome" from 1993 impede opposition to the Rwandan genocide in 1994, so one saw an Iraqi syndrome impeding measures to stop the humanitarian disaster in Syria.

Moreover, the US invasion of Iraq in 2003 and the follow-on mismanaged occupation helped create the vicious Islamic State group. Much of its leadership and core support were made up of Iraqi Sunnis who had been imprisoned during the war, but later released into an Iraq dominated by a narrowly partisan Shia elite. Feeling strangers in their own country, they became radicalized against Shia, the USA, and even moderate Sunni Muslims. The result was horrific: torture and murder of prisoners, beheadings, systematic rape and sexual slavery, and a host of other atrocities. This was all rationalized as the will of Allah, as the Islamic State Group created for a time a brutally repressive and exploitative "caliphate" in parts of Iraq and Syria. The US take-down of the brutal Saddam and the hope for a democratic Middle East led instead to a series of horrors constituting one of the worst human rights situations in the world circa 2015.

In El Salvador by the early 1990s, the USA, the UN, and others decided that human dignity would be best advanced by avoiding the question of legal justice for those on both sides of the civil war who had murdered civilians or engaged in other violations of human rights. Human rights concerns were addressed through various political and administrative steps, but prosecutions of past crimes associated with the political struggle were not attempted. Likewise in the Republic of South Africa after the era of apartheid, the government of Nelson Mandela decided to emphasize a national Truth and Reconciliation Commission that had the authority to pardon those on either side who had violated human rights during the long and brutal conflict over apartheid, provided they were truthful and publicly took full responsibility for their actions.

The South African experience in turn affected developments in Colombia by 2016. The government and its main armed opposition, FARC, negotiated a peace accord that avoided most criminal responsibility for war crimes in the long-running insurgency. This negotiated agreement was then opposed both by certain political and social circles in the country who had borne the brunt of FARC abuses, and by Human Rights Watch which wanted more criminal responsibility for abuses on both sides. A popular referendum rejected the peace agreement by a narrow margin. The government then negotiated a modified agreement by FARC which was approved by the legislature. It also did not emphasize full criminal justice.

Whether international courts are created, whether they are supported with adequate political and material resources, and whether national courts are to be encouraged to take up human rights issues on sensitive questions are all considerations that policy makers face. Whether and how far human rights issues should be pushed at the expense of traditional security and economic concerns is a classic dilemma in soft law decisions. This is the clash of liberalism and realism. Foreign policy is inescapably about the management of contradictions.[33] This fact means that policy makers will frequently find it necessary to strike compromises between the advancement of human rights through criminal prosecutions and that of another perceived public good such as physical security and/or economic welfare. Moreover, peace accords that by-pass or delay or limit prosecution for human rights violations also reduce human rights violations by terminating the conflict. This was true of the 1995 Dayton accords in Bosnia, and will be true of the 2016 modified accord in Colombia.

Even after a "third wave" of democratization in the world,[34] many governments remain authoritarian and without serious interest in advancing democratic and other rights. This was certainly true of China and Russia under Presidents Xi and Putin. Moreover, public and especially corporate opinion in the liberal democracies does not always or easily endorse national cost in order to advance the rights of foreigners. The US Supreme Court, in the 2013 Kiobel judgment, made it more difficult for foreign plaintiffs to use US courts to sue corporations for complicity in human rights abuses abroad.[35] As one scholar has written, even in the 1990s there were many "structural" constraints faced by those interested in international human rights.[36] Policy makers, including those in the

---

[33] Stanley Hoffmann, "The Hell of Good Intentions," *Foreign Policy*, 29 (1977–1978), 3–26.

[34] Samuel P. Huntington, *The Third Wave: Democratization in the Late Twentieth Century* (Norman: University of Oklahoma Press, 1991). Twenty-five years later, this third wave had dissipated. There was an uptick in autocratic rule.

[35] See David P. Forsythe and Patrice C. McMahon, *American Exceptionalism Reconsidered: US Foreign Policy, Human Rights, and World Order* (London and New York: Routledge, 2016), ch. 5.

[36] Jack Donnelly, *International Human Rights*, 2nd edn. (Boulder: Westview, 1997).

OECD states, operate in this context, in which there can be genuine debate about how best to advance human dignity, and what can be attempted with reasonable prospect of success. This book focuses on those debates and dilemmas in soft law decisions – while not omitting the contributions of hard law to the place of international human rights in the modern world.

This orientation leads to an emphasis on politics in the form of power and policy choice, not just legal judgments. In both national and international societies, it is politics that determines the content of the law. All law is made in a legislative process, and the legislative process always involves policy choice and calculations of power.[37]

With regard to applying the law, even in the OECD states a political decision frequently affects judicial or administrative application of the law. If a federal or state attorney-general in the USA decides to make the prosecution of a certain category of crime – or a particular defendant – a high priority, this is in essence a policy choice; no legal rule tells an attorney-general that he/she must have certain priorities. If the US Environmental Protection Agency or an equivalent agency in one of the states decides to prosecute an entity for violation of environmental laws, as opposed to seeking a negotiated solution outside court, that decision is in essence a policy one, not controlled by a rule of law. Prosecutorial discretion is not tightly regulated by legal rules. So even in the OECD states characterized by the rule of law in general, the law does not make itself or apply itself. Political decisions based on policy choice and calculations of power are intertwined in various ways with decisions mandated by legal rules. Within states, chief executive officers and their legal staff make political decisions all the time about whether and how to apply the law in particular situations. International relations presents this same basic situation, but with much greater emphasis on political decisions in a soft law process, and relatively less emphasis on hard law emerging from judges in adjudication.

Because my approach does not simply ask, "What is the law, and how can we get courts to adjudicate it?," in Chapter 2 I explain the difference between classical liberals (who emphasize hard law for personal rights), pragmatic liberals (who emphasize both hard law and various soft law decisions for personal welfare, not just for rights), and realists (who emphasize national interest and power).

---

[37] See further Werner Levi, *Law and Politics in the International Society* (Beverly Hills: Sage Publications, 1976).

Non-governmental actors

Under the Westphalian system of international relations, in place more or less since the middle of the seventeenth century, it is states that make the basic rules of the game. It is states that are full legal subjects, or have full legal personality, under the international law which is fashioned on the basis of state consent – explicit consent via treaty law, implicit consent via international customary law. As noted above, states can fulfill their duties and exercise their rights through judicial action, but even more so by their extra-judicial foreign policies. But this traditional and somewhat legalistic view of international relations has great difficulty in accommodating the sometimes important role played by various nongovernmental actors. This book seeks to expand the usual state-centric focus by paying considerable attention to non-profit and for-profit private actors. Whether or not the state has actually lost control of many important foreign policy decisions to a variety of non-state actors is a matter of considerable debate.[38] It is reasonably clear that on many issues in international relations, including those pertaining to human rights, the state *shares* decisions with important non-state actors – especially from a political rather than strictly legal perspective. (The issue of armed non-state actors is a separate subject.)

It should be noted here that some observers view human rights NGOs as the real motor to the process of growing attention to international human rights. In this view, it is the relatively well known transnational human rights organizations (e.g., Amnesty International, Human Rights Watch, the International Commission of Jurists, the International Federation for Human Rights, etc.) and their less well known colleagues (e.g., Africa Rights, Lawyer's Committee for International Human Rights, now renamed Human Rights First, etc.) that push states into giving attention to rights issues. Without the sum total of human rights NGOs, it is said, contemporary international relations would be far less supportive of human rights.

A related view is that it is not human rights NGOs *per se* that account for much transnational influence on behalf of human rights, but rather these groups acting in tandem with other actors, the sum total of which is a human rights network or movement.[39] It is said that various human

---

[38] See further Robert H. Jackson and Alan James, eds., *States in a Changing World: A Contemporary Analysis* (New York: Oxford University Press, 1993).
[39] See especially Kathryn Sikkink, "Human Rights, Principled Issue-Networks, and Sovereignty in Latin America," *International Organization*, 47, 3 (Summer 1993), 411–442.

rights actors, the international communications media, the Catholic Church, the Inter-American Commission on Human Rights, etc. all brought effective pressure to bear on certain countries in the Western Hemisphere leading to an improved human rights situation. In this view, state foreign policy was relatively unimportant in improving the human rights situation in places like Mexico, because it was an essentially non-governmental network that generated most of the effective pressure. Also in this view, the Arab Spring in Egypt circa 2011 was propelled mostly by individuals with smartphones making up a movement who teamed with various NGOs to enlist media coverage and some outside governmental support to at least oust the ruling dictator Hosni Mubarak.[40]

It follows from the above that if important for-profit actors such as multinational corporations join this transnational human rights network, or act parallel to it, even more pressure can be generated for human rights – whatever the position taken by states through their official foreign policies. Some believe it was a series of private decisions by for-profit actors that helped convince white supremacists in the Republic of South Africa that apartheid, and with it minority rule, had to be abandoned. When western investors judged the future of South Africa too risky and otherwise problematical for safe and productive investments, in this view progressive change was accelerated. In other situations for-profit actors have taken clear human rights decisions in fashioning their various market strategies, as will be noted especially in Chapter 8. Pepsico refused to expand operations into Burma/Myanmar under military rule there, with related rights violations of various types. Levi Strauss refused to make blue jeans in China between 1993 and 1998 because of certain violations of labor rights.[41] A coalition of sporting goods companies, including Nike and Reebok, will only produce soccer balls in Pakistan and elsewhere if they can certify that child labor is not involved.

At the same time, if important corporations refuse to engage for the advancement of human rights, but rather take the view that profits and not human rights are their proper concern, then that is a factor of considerable importance. In the 1990s there was considerable debate about the role of the Royal Dutch Shell oil company in Nigeria, where authoritarian government, human rights violations, and ecological damage led some states to consider various types of sanctions.

---

[40] See further Mahmood Monshipouri, ed., *Information Politics, Protests, and Human Rights in the Digital Age* (Cambridge: Cambridge University Press, 2016).
[41] Mark Landler, "Levi Strauss Going Back to China Market," *International Herald Tribune*, April 9, 1998, 1.

The central debate for present purposes concerns the precise role played, and influence generated, by all these non-governmental actors, relative to governments and their intergovernmental organizations. This is a longstanding and complex debate, similar to the debate about national politics and the role and influence of interest groups. Some observers and policy makers are not convinced that governments have been so relatively unimportant in international human rights developments. Two examples suffice to make the point. One author believes that officials in the Truman administration, not the representatives of private groups (or Latin American states), were primarily responsible for the human rights language that eventually appeared in the UN Charter.[42] Also, Donald Fraser, who organized a series of hearings on human rights and foreign policy when he was a member of Congress in 1974, and who is generally regarded as having been instrumental in the placing of human rights on the agenda of US foreign policy from that time, indicated that he was not pushed into that action by any human rights NGO.[43] His account is that the basic idea of renewed attention to human rights in US foreign policy was his, and that he then subsequently invited the rights groups to testify in order to support his objectives. (A contrary view expressed by some NGOs is that it was their action that created the context within which Fraser decided to hold hearings on rights.)

This latter situation typifies the problems for social science analysis in this regard. Private action for human rights is frequently merged, or dovetails, with public action (governmental and intergovernmental), making it extremely difficult to separate the lines of influence that went into a decision or impacted a situation. Was US foreign policy, bilaterally and through NAFTA, really unimportant for rights in Mexico, relative to an essentially private and transnational network at play? How can we be sure, since we cannot hold one line of influence constant or even remove it, while we replay history with only the other line of influence at play?

Fortunately we do not need to be so precise about who generated what exact influence in what exact situation. For some questions, it is enough to know that the combined weight of public and private actors for human rights led to definite developments. We know, for example, that both representatives of Amnesty International and the Dutch government, *inter alia*, combined to help negotiate the UN Convention against

---

[42] Cathal Nolan, *Principled Diplomacy: Security and Rights in US Foreign Policy* (Westport: Greenwood, 1993).
[43] David P. Forsythe, *US Foreign Policy and Human Rights: Congress Reconsidered* (Gainesville: University Press of Florida, 1989).

Torture.[44] We know that various public and private actors combined to negotiate the UN Convention on the Rights of the Child.[45] We know that various types of actors combined to help create the new post of UN High Commissioner for Human Rights in 1993.

Because of such cumulative effects of non-governmental *and* governmental actors on human rights matters, we know that there have been considerable changes in international relations.

Changing state sovereignty

This book treats the notion of state sovereignty as a social construct.[46] It is an idea devised by social beings. It can change along with changing circumstances. Like the concept of human rights itself, the idea of state sovereignty is a claim relating to proper exercise of public authority, a claim to be evaluated by the rest of the international community. Thus state sovereignty is not some immutable principle decreed in fixed form once and for all time, but rather an argument about state authority whose meaning and scope are constantly subject to re-evaluation. Just as the nature of "states' rights" can change over time in a federal political-legal system, ebbing and flowing with political tides, so the notion of state sovereignty can change in international relations.

Prior to 1945, the relation between an individual and the state controlling "its" citizens was a matter for that state alone. The state was sovereign in an almost absolute sense, exercising supreme legal authority within its jurisdiction. International law existed primarily to keep states apart, and thus prevent conflicts, by confirming separate national jurisdictions.[47] Prior to 1945 there were four exceptions to the basic rule that individual rights were a matter of national rather than international concern.[48] In war, or international armed conflict, from the 1860s belligerent states were obligated to allow neutral medical assistance to the sick and wounded under their control, and from the 1920s a humanitarian quarantine to prisoners of war. In peace, foreigners residing in a state, called legal aliens, were granted some minimum civil rights. Also in

---

[44] Peter R. Baehr, "Negotiating the Convention on Torture," in David P. Forsythe, ed., *The United Nations in the World Political Economy* (London: Macmillan, 1989), 36–53.

[45] Lawrence J. LeBlanc, *The Convention on the Rights of the Child: United Nations Lawmaking on Human Rights* (Lincoln: University of Nebraska Press, 1995).

[46] Thomas J. Biersteker and Cynthia Weber, eds., *State Sovereignty as Social Construct* (Cambridge: Cambridge University Press, 1996).

[47] Among many sources, see C. Wilfred Jenks, *The Common Law of Mankind* (London: Stevens, 1958).

[48] See in general David P. Forsythe, *Human Rights and World Politics*, 2nd rev. edn. (Lincoln: University of Nebraska Press, 1989).

peace, from 1920, laborers might be legally protected under conventions developed and supervised by the International Labour Organization. Finally, in what passed for peace in the European interwar years of 1919–1939, certain minorities in some of the defeated states were officially afforded certain international rights as supervised by the League of Nations. Furthermore, certain of the European Great Powers claimed a right to act in foreign states when events shocked public morality. As noted below, these claims to "humanitarian intervention" were never collectively approved, and most European interventions for supposedly humanitarian purposes were heavily affected by political calculations.[49] Otherwise, while European states and private actors might debate human rights, they remained a matter of national rather than international law and policy.[50]

The situation summarized above represents the basic legal view. Rules for organizing international relations and centering on the central notion of state sovereignty (with few restrictions) were always "organized hypocrisy," because states often violated in practice the rules that they endorsed in theory.[51] Nevertheless, international relations were indeed affected by the notion derived from state sovereignty, that states should not intervene in the domestic affairs of other states; and while this norm was violated, it also exerted considerable influence.[52]

International human rights trends since 1945, summarized in the first paragraph of this chapter, have, in tandem with certain other developments in international relations, caused some to see a radical reformulation of state sovereignty. Javier Perez de Cuellar, UN Secretary-General 1981–1991, saw "an irresistible shift in public attitudes toward the belief that the defense of the oppressed in the name of morality should prevail over frontiers and legal documents."[53] This statement was made during the high tide of multilateral optimism immediately after the end of the Cold War. His successor during 1992–1996, Boutros Boutros-Ghali, believed that, "The time of absolute and exclusive sovereignty . . . has passed."[54] Because of aggression against Kuwait

---

[49] See especially Gary J. Bass, *Freedom's Battle: The Origins of Humanitarian Intervention* (New York: Vintage, 2008).
[50] Herman Burgers, "The Road to San Francisco: The Revival of the Human Rights Idea in the Twentieth Century," *Human Rights Quarterly*, 14, 4 (November 1992), 447–477.
[51] Stephen D. Krasner, *Sovereignty: Organized Hypocrisy* (Princeton: Princeton University Press, 1999).
[52] R. J. Vincent, *Human Rights and International Relations* (Cambridge: Cambridge University Press, 1986).
[53] Quoted in Thomas G. Weiss, ed., *Collective Security in a Changing World* (Boulder: Lynne Rienner, 1993), 14.
[54] "Agenda for Peace," A/47/277 and S/24111, June 17, 1992, para. 17.

and subsequently renewed abuse of Iraqi citizens, Iraq was placed in a kind of "receivership" by the international community and denied the normal perks of state sovereignty during 1991–2003. Baghdad was not allowed to develop weapons of mass destruction, to engage in full trade with others, or even to have full control of parts of its territory. Because of Milosevic's repression of the Albanian Kosovars in 1999, other western states overrode his claims to state sovereignty and tried to coerce him into a change of policy.

Outside Europe, one should not overstate, however, the importance of various "humanitarian interventions" in international relations after the Cold War.[55] As suggested above, international law had never codified a clear right of humanitarian intervention for the benefit of nationals oppressed by their own government. Particularly developing countries, fearful of the action of the most powerful states, and ever mindful of their colonial experience, remained opposed during the 1990s to any such effort at codification. Even developed countries such as the USA and UK resisted international review of national policy in the name of human rights when the issue was something like racial discrimination in the application of the death penalty or UN debate on Northern Ireland. In fact, these western states were not eager to have their national decisions reviewed by international bodies. One of the reasons for the Brexit vote in 2016, by which the British decided to withdraw from the European Union, was that regional governance had become too intrusive in national affairs.

By 2005, however, as already briefly noted, states agreed on the abstract notion of an international responsibility to protect (R2P): that if a sovereign state failed to exercise its primary responsibility to prevent gross violations of human rights, being unable or unwilling to do so, outside states inherited a responsibility to act. But, as also already noted, norms do not implement themselves. Thus the question arose after 2005 of the political will to make the principle of R2P meaningful in the real world of failed, failing, and weak states. In some cases, e.g. Sudan (Darfur) and Democratic Republic of Congo (Ituri province), political will to decisively end atrocities was lacking despite some international involvement. The endorsement of R2P at a UN meeting in New York was not the first time that progressive principles had been agreed to, only to find subsequently that state enthusiasm for the agreed norm waned in the face of complex situations and disagreeable estimates of

---

[55] Kelly Kate Pease and David P. Forsythe, "Human Rights, Humanitarian Intervention, and World Politics," *Human Rights Quarterly*, 15, 2 (May 1993), 290–314.

the costs of implementation.[56] But in other cases, e.g. Kenya wracked by ethnic tensions in 2008, timely diplomacy and various actions by the International Criminal Court, *inter alia*, brought the country back from the brink of major instability-cum-human rights violations. This was true in the interim despite the fact that the Kenyan case eventually collapsed at the ICC because of effective maneuvering by the targeted elites, along with lack of effective support of the Court from important outside states. The long-term effect of diplomatic agreement on R2P was not yet clear.

By comparison especially with the statement of Perez de Cuellar above, a more analytical view was that the nature of state sovereignty had indeed changed, but that the "reality of state power and authority cannot be ignored."[57] So the principle of R2P was almost always joined by outside states' calculations about expending blood or treasure to protect the rights of "others."

More generally, state consent was still a bedrock principle of international law. But increasingly states were using their sovereign consent to create international institutions that restricted the subsequent operation of state sovereignty. Almost all of the states of Eastern Europe emerged from the control of the Soviet empire only to stand in line to join the Council of Europe, the European Union, and NATO. Each of these international organizations would reduce the operational independence of the state. Even the USA, the one superpower on the planet, chose to use its sovereign authority to join international institutions like NAFTA and the World Trade Organization that restricted its subsequent freedom of choice. In general, virtually all states felt the necessity to choose to participate in international legal regimes that "enmeshed" the state in international governing arrangements.[58] International arrangements concerning human rights constituted an important part of this trend.

States came to share jurisdiction over human rights issues with various international organizations and even foreign governments. Routinized

---

[56] For a discussion of R2P and the literature it has generated, see Jennifer Welsh, "Implementing the Responsibility to Protect: Where Expectations Meet Reality," *Ethics & International Affairs*, 24, 4 (Winter 2010). For a discussion of how Winston Churchill joined with FDR in issuing the Atlantic Charter in 1941 promising broad human rights guarantees, then later tried to preserve the British Empire by saying the promises of the Atlantic Charter did not pertain to India, Nigeria, etc., see Richard Toye, *Churchill's Empire: The World that Made Him and the World He Made* (New York: Henry Holt, 2010), 212–216.

[57] Oscar Schachter, "Sovereignty and Threats to Peace," in Weiss, ed., *Collective Security*, 20.

[58] Mark Zacher, "The Decaying Pillars of the Westphalian Temple: Implications for International Order and Governance," in Rosenau and Czempiel, eds., *Governance Without Government*, 58–101.

international diplomacy confirmed the legality and legitimacy of state and IGO discussion of almost all human rights issues. This debate, and resulting forms of diplomatic pressure, constituted an international attempt at *indirect* protection of human rights. IGOs, and also NGOs, tried to get states to meet their responsibilities under international rights standards. Emerging practice suggested that if a state failed to meet its responsibility to protect internationally recognized human rights, then the UN Security Council or some other entity might override traditional notions of state sovereignty and try international *direct* protection of rights. Where political will was adequate, the UN Security Council might declare large-scale human rights violations to constitute a threat to, or breach of, international peace and security, permitting authoritative action under Chapter VII of the UN Charter. The Council, using Cold War precedents stemming from Rhodesia and South Africa, had done so after the Cold War in places like Iraq, Somalia, the former Yugoslavia, and Haiti. The result might be military coercion, economic coercion, or the creation of international courts entailing mandatory cooperation, etc.[59]

While some observers had been predicting the decline of the territorial state for a considerable time,[60] international relations on the eve of the twenty-first century remained a modified state system. The territorial state and its claim to sovereignty remained important features of this international political system. But increasingly the territorial state was obliged to share the international stage with other actors. On some issues the state might retain supreme or ultimate authority. But in Western Europe on migration issues the national executives became intermediate authorities, sandwiched between individual claims on the one hand and the rulings of courts about international law on the other.[61] On still other issues the state might be legally superseded by another organization such as the European Court of Human Rights, the European Court of Justice, the UN Security Council, a dispute resolution panel of the World Trade Organization, etc. It was states themselves that found it desirable to create these processes that some called supranational. Others referred to "pooled sovereignty." States themselves recognized that state independence might need to be restricted for the achievement of other public

---

[59] See further Oliver Ramsbotham and Tom Woodhouse, *Humanitarian Intervention in Contemporary Conflict* (Cambridge: Polity Press, 1996), on the various forms of international involvement in conflict situations.

[60] John Herz, *The Nation-State and the Crises of World Politics* (New York: D. McKay, 1976).

[61] David Jacobson, *Rights Across Borders: Immigration and the Decline of Citizenship* (Baltimore: Johns Hopkins University Press, 1995).

goods such as prosperity, security, or human rights. Once these international organs that transcended state sovereignty were created, they might in certain cases override the particular wishes of a particular state. This was the price paid for orderly and beneficial international relations, a situation long recognized in most national societies. As President Eisenhower remarked about binding international decisions, "It is better to lose a point now and then in an international tribunal and gain a world in which everyone lives at peace under the rule of law."[62] (Ike's view might be seen as heresy if not treason to later Republican presidents such as Ronald Reagan and George W. Bush.)

The changing nature of state sovereignty, and along with it the changing nature of international norms and organizations, was produced by many causes. Science and technology had produced both terribly destructive wars and globalized markets. Following in the wake of each was a process of social globalization, with human rights as the cutting edge. The Geneva Convention of 1864, mandating neutral medical assistance to the sick and wounded in war, came about in part because improved communications allowed news of the wounded to reach the home front more quickly. European governments realized they had to do more for the wounded, in an era in which armies had more veterinarians to care for horses than doctors to care for the wounded,[63] in order to preserve support for the war back home.[64] Especially by 1945 there was a widespread moral revulsion against large-scale industrialized warfare,[65] and the idea took hold that internationalizing the concept of human rights might help erect barriers against the destruction so evident in the two world wars.[66] By about 2000, globally integrated markets had also led to increased emphasis on the plight of workers worldwide, such as the estimated 250 million child laborers.

In sum, science and technology had produced changing material and psychological conditions so that state sovereignty was no longer what it once was. Reference to the idea of state sovereignty no longer provided an automatic and impenetrable shield against international action on issues once regarded as essentially domestic. But then, human rights was also not

---

[62] Quoted in David P. Forsythe, *The Politics of International Law: US Foreign Policy Reconsidered* (Boulder: Lynne Rienner, 1990), 55.

[63] François Bugnion, *Le Comité International de la Croix-Rouge et la Protection des Victimes de la Guerre* (Geneva: ICRC, 1994). An English edition was published subsequently.

[64] John Hutchinson, *Champions of Charity: War and the Rise of the Red Cross* (Boulder: Westview, 1996).

[65] John Mueller, *Retreat from Doomsday: The Obsolescence of Major War* (New York: Basic Books, 1989).

[66] Nolan, *Principled Diplomacy*.

what it had been. Human rights was essentially a western concept, first put into widespread political and legal practice by western states.[67] But over time and for various reasons human rights had become internationalized.[68] Modern war, modern markets, modern repression all presented similar threats to human dignity. Human rights was widely seen as a useful means to help achieve human dignity in contemporary international relations.

However, by 2016 it was evident there was a pervasive push back against international regimes and a resurgence of nativist nationalism and desire for more state sovereignty. We already mentioned the Brexit vote in the UK, supported in large part by the belief that the EU principle of freedom of labor movement was producing undesirable changes particularly in more rural England.[69] Similarly, states like Hungary and Poland were adamant about not wanting to accept more Muslim refugees fleeing Middle Eastern crises, even when urged to do so by the EU, Council of Europe, and UN. European developments paralleled the surprising success of Donald Trump as Republican presidential candidate in the USA. Many of his white supporters with less than a college education felt aggrieved by economic globalization and the loss of manufacturing jobs abroad under the rules of the World Trade Organization. All of these political developments in the West reflected a dislike for changes that were occurring under the forces of economic globalization, international integration, and multiculturalism.[70] As such, these Western political factors dovetailed with strong nativist nationalism in China, Russia, and most of the post-colonial states. A backlash against the existing international structure, sometimes referred to as American hegemony and/or liberal world order, had been noted some time ago.[71]

Conclusion

As we look at global, regional, national, and sub-national actors for international human rights, we will see time and time again that liberal norms have indeed been injected into international relations, and that:

[67] See especially Burns Weston, "Human Rights," in Richard P. Claude and Burns Weston, eds., *Human Rights in the World Community*, 2nd rev. edn. (Philadelphia: University of Pennsylvania Press, 1992), 14–30; and also Jack Donnelly, *Universal Human Rights in Theory and Practice* (Ithaca: Cornell University Press, 1989).

[68] David P. Forsythe, *The Internationalization of Human Rights* (Lexington: Lexington Books, 1991).

[69] See http://lordashcroftpolls.com/2016/06/how-the-united-kingdom-voted-and-why/.

[70] See http://blogs.timesofindia.indiatimes.com/just-graffiti/nativist-dog-whistles-hyper-nationalism-threatens-the-idea-of-liberal-democracy-in-both-india-and-the-us/.

[71] Thomas L. Friedman, in *The Lexus and the Olive Tree: Understanding Globalization* (New York: Picador, 1999), noted that globalization was accompanied by resentment and a reassertion of traditional cultures, whether real or imagined.

(1) the notion of human rights is here to stay in international relations –
    certainly for the immediate future,
(2) human rights as soft law is important and pervasive – which is not to
    denigrate the role of hard law through court cases,
(3) private actors – not just public ones – play a very large role, and
(4) state sovereignty is not what it used to be. Because of these changes,
    one can be guardedly optimistic about the future of human rights in
    international relations – of liberalism in a realist world. However,
    insecurities fueled by economic dislocation, terrorism, and cultural
    change make evident that history does not move in straight lines or in
    a teleological direction. No particular future is guaranteed.

Case study: from humanitarian intervention to the responsibility to protect

It is generally agreed that the territorial state system of international
relations began to emerge from the middle of the seventeenth century
with its central notions of state sovereignty and domestic jurisdiction. It
is also generally agreed that after the great destruction from the "Great
War" of 1914–1918 there was a concerted effort to restrict state use of
force to self-defense and to outlaw the aggressive first use of force. This
left open the question of the use of force for other purposes, such as to
protect human rights within the domestic jurisdiction of another
sovereign state.

Already in the nineteenth century, improvements in communications
technology made possible the rather rapid knowledge of atrocities in
foreign states. In Britain and France, two of the leading powers at this
time, governments faced the question of whether to take action to stop
atrocities in places such as Greece and Bulgaria, the western Balkans,
and the eastern Mediterranean. The Ottoman Empire was in decline and
a humane order was not guaranteed. In Britain and France foreign policy
realists were mostly in key positions. They therefore tended to be reluctant to use military force for humanitarian reasons, preferring to concentrate on power struggles and other disputes among leading states. Yet
these realist national officials faced such domestic and international
pressures that they wound up authorizing military action to stop what
today we would call gross violations of human rights.

These interventions were obviously carried out by the stronger against
the weaker, with no centralized approval from any international organization (there not being any of a general political nature), and with many
other atrocities being ignored (as in the case of, somewhat later, the
fate of Christian Armenians under Ottoman control). And no state

intervened to stop, for example, British atrocities in colonial India. Still, it was clear that, at least sometimes, leading states could be pressured to deal with mass killings in foreign lands. Liberal transnational activism was relatively effective, at least sometimes – as shown by the British and French interventions mentioned earlier.

Subsequent events for a time only accentuated the tension between, on one hand, state power and authority and, on the other, the fate of individuals inside states. The German Holocaust certainly gave sovereignty a bad name. German Jews and other German outcasts were not protected by the international law of that time and were, legally speaking, at the mercy of Nazi persecution and murder. Yet in 1945 the UN Charter codified traditional thinking, namely that the organization was prohibited from intervening in matters that were "essentially within the domestic jurisdiction" of member states (Article 2 [7]). While the UN Security Council was given the authority to take action, including forceful action, in order to guarantee international peace and security, it was not at all clear from 1945 that outside parties, whether states or the UN Security Council, could "intervene" (whatever that meant) regarding human rights violations *per se*, particularly those not seen as affecting *international* peace and security. The 1948 UN Convention against Genocide obligated ratifying states to take action to prevent and correct genocide, but without specifying any precise action. And what about human rights violations falling short of genocide?

It was NATO's intervention against Serbia over the issue of Kosovo in 1999 that brought some new normative developments concerning humanitarian intervention. European and North American governments had not been persistently decisive, to put it mildly, in their responses to mass starvation in Somalia in the early 1990s, to genocide in Rwanda in 1994, and to various atrocities in the first Balkan wars of 1991–1995 with the epicenter of distress being in Bosnia. But when Serbia escalated the persecution of ethnic Albanians in the Kosovo region, the United States led a delicately unified NATO into a bombing campaign with the ostensible purpose of compelling Belgrade and Slobodan Milosevic to stop the policy of ethnic cleansing or forced displacement. NATO did not claim self-defense nor did it have the advance approval of the UN Security Council, China and Russia possessing the veto and being opposed to NATO's role. NATO "won ugly" in the sense of compelling a shift in Serb policy, but only with much controversy, damage to civilians and civilian structures, and help from Russian quiet diplomacy. The status of, and conditions within, Kosovo at the time of writing cannot be treated here.

For present purposes the point to be emphasized is this: given a widespread view in the West that the NATO operation in Serbia/ Kosovo was "technically" illegal but morally justified, some parties tried to clarify the status of the idea of humanitarian intervention. They sought to close the gap between legality and legitimacy. In particular, the Canadian government appointed a panel of private eminent persons to consider the issues. This process led to the influential report (2001) of the International Commission on Intervention and State Sovereignty (ICISS). This report gave a renewed push to the notion of the permissibility of outside involvement to deal with gross violations of human rights.

The ICISS report in turn led to new developments at the UN. "Norm entrepreneurs" such as Gareth Evans from Australia and Francis Deng from Sudan, among others, argued that what was really at issue was not outside punishment of recalcitrant states. Such a formulation tended to conjure up visions of powerful western states imposing their will in a neocolonial process. Rather, so it was argued, what was involved was a broad and largely diplomatic process to guarantee responsible sovereignty. Hence, what was at issue was not an attack on sovereignty, but a broad, largely diplomatic process to redefine sovereignty to ensure it was compatible with human rights. It was this approach that led in 2005 to consensus endorsement at the UN of the idea of R2P, a responsibility to protect. Concerning genocide, crimes against humanity, war crimes, and ethnic cleansing, states had the primary responsibility to prevent such mass atrocities – as they did for other human rights. But if a state was unwilling or unable to handle this responsibility, the undefined "international community" had a responsibility to become involved concerning gross violations.

One could reasonably be cautious about the importance of this apparent agreement. The Outcome Document of the 2005 UN Summit consisted of 178 paragraphs. Two paragraphs, nos. 138 and 139, made up the principle of R2P. Other paragraphs reaffirmed virtually all ideas normally endorsed at the UN every year: peace, security, international law, human security, etc. This sort of ritual lip service often means very little.

It was evident this 2005 UN document did not lead to a radically transformed international relations and certainly not in the field of human rights. In fact, more or less as soon as the ink was dry on the summit outcome document, various delegations at the UN tried to undermine the apparent agreement. There was certainly only a little increased determination by outsiders to stop gross violations of human rights in Sudan (e.g., Darfur) or in Democratic Republic of Congo (e.g.,

Ituri province). These situations were terribly complex, the USA and much of the West were preoccupied with Islamist militants not to mention being overstretched in military commitments and having a weakened economic foundation, and those carrying out the atrocities were both brutal and persistent.

Still, once the language was in the UN summit outcome document, various state and non-state personnel made reference to it as they sought to improve the fate of individuals in places such as Burma (Myanmar), Kenya, Ivory Coast, and elsewhere. Those jousting for power in various national settings did not do so in a vacuum. They had to anticipate the possibility of various international involvements and pressures. One needs only to recall Libya in 2011 to realize the upper range of an international duty to protect that might come into play.

What are the lessons to be drawn from this case study? One conclusion is that decisive improvement for human rights in international relations is difficult, takes time, and is affected by the history of the subject. Another conclusion is that ideas matter, and once there is formal agreement on an idea, that new principle can be appealed to by a variety of actors interested in protecting human rights. Yet another conclusion runs in a somewhat different direction, namely that power matters. It is important to note whether powerful states are willing to take action for human rights abroad, whether one speaks of NATO and Serbia or Libya, or France and Ivory Coast, or South Africa regarding the Mugabe government in Zimbabwe, etc.

Discussion questions

- Is support for international human rights a form of western imperialism? Is Francis Fukuyama correct that history shows no better way to legitimize and limit government's power aside from human rights? Did the Arab Spring of 2011 confirm the accuracy of Fukuyama's views? Is it not true that those supporting "Asian values" are correct in pointing out excessive individualism and legalism and too much litigation in the West? How can human rights be a good thing when the western liberal democracies, based on human rights, show so many problems?
- Which is more important, hard law or soft law? How do we know when to pursue hard law options, viz., litigation, as opposed to soft law options, viz., extra-judicial policy? Is it sufficient for law to educate over time, as opposed to providing legal rules for litigation? Whatever our conclusions about sufficiency, is soft law a necessity much of the time in international relations?

- Are human rights statements by private advocacy groups more reliable than governmental statements? Does it depend on which group is under discussion? Are private human rights groups too rigid and one-dimensional in their focus? How do we separate out the influence of private groups compared to public authorities in the evolution of human rights?
- Is state sovereignty a good thing or a bad thing? Should the international community disregard claims to state sovereignty when gross violations of human rights are at issue? Is any subject essentially or totally within the sovereign domestic affairs of states? Is it not true that state power, state authority, and citizen loyalty to the nation-state are still very strong in modern international relations? Is it not true that the nation-state and state sovereignty will be with us for some time? But in what precise form?

SUGGESTIONS FOR FURTHER READING

Barber, Benjamin R., *Jihad v. McWorld* (New York: Ballantyne Publishing Group, 1995). Sees the world as a contest between universal secularism (human rights fits here) and romantic particularism such as renewed assertions of virulent nationalism as in the Balkans, Iran, and other places.

Bass, Gary J., *Freedom's Battle: The Origins of Humanitarian Intervention* (New York: Vintage, 2008). A highly readable account of how domestic public opinion, as led by liberal activists, compelled realists in high positions in Britain and France to take action to protect human rights in foreign countries during the nineteenth century.

Burgers, Jan Herman, "The Road to San Francisco: The Revival of the Human Rights Idea in the Twentieth Century," *Human Rights Quarterly*, 14, 4 (November 1992), 447–477. The best short treatment of the origins of human rights as practical politics and diplomacy in the twentieth century.

Carey, Sabine, Mark Gibney, and Steven Poe, *The Politics of Human Rights: The Quest for Dignity* (Cambridge and New York: Cambridge University Press, 2010). A clear introduction to the subject focusing on selected subject matter and based on much empirical information.

Donnelly, Jack, *Universal Human Rights in Theory and Practice* (Ithaca: Cornell University Press, 2013). One of the best advanced treatments of human rights in international context.

International Human Rights (Boulder: Westview, 2012). A sound introduction by a leading scholar on the subject. Strong on theory.

Evans, Gareth, *The Responsibility to Protect: Ending Mass Atrocity Crimes Once and for All* (Washington: Brookings Institution Press, 2008). An excellent discussion of the attempted move from the discourse on humanitarian intervention to that on the responsibility to protect. This involved an attempt to redefine state sovereignty as the primary responsibility of states to avoid gross violations of human rights, and the permissibility of outsiders to act when states were unwilling or unable to fulfill this responsibility.

Forsythe, David P. and Patrice C. McMahon, *American Exceptionalism Reconsidered: US Foreign Policy, Human Rights, and World Order* (London and New York: Routledge, 2016). Argues that the USA has not been as committed to human rights abroad as the language of American exceptionalism would suggest, but that the contempory world order established by US leadership will prove better on human rights than any world dominated by the BRICs (Brazil, Russia, India, China).

Freeman, Michael, *Human Rights* (Cambridge: Polity, 2017). A very good introductory overview, strong on political theory.

Fukuyama, Francis, *The End of History and the Last Man* (New York: Free Press, 1992). A former US foreign service officer and leading conservative intellectual argues that the highest stage of history reflects recognition of human rights as the superior way to legitimize the exercise of power.

Hoffmann, Stanley, *Duties Beyond Borders: On the Limits and Possibilities of Ethical International Politics* (Syracuse: Syracuse University Press, 1981). The late Harvard professor of United States foreign policy and international relations examines international ethics from a liberal perspective.

Hopgood, Stephen, *The Endtimes of Human Rights* (Ithaca and London: Cornell University Press, 2013). A very critical account of human rights as Western cultural imperialism. Sees the power decline of the West as signaling a much weaker human rights push by states at the UN.

Ignatieff, Michael, *Human Rights as Politics and Idolatry* (Princeton: Princeton University Press, 2001). A short, provocative treatment, stressing the social construction of human rights and emphasizing the value of the individual.

Ishay, Micheline R., *The History of Human Rights: From Ancient Times to the Globalization Era* (Berkeley: University of California Press, 2004). A thematic, conceptually interesting, and provocative history of human rights.

Krasner, Stephen D., *Sovereignty: Organized Hypocrisy* (Princeton: Princeton University Press, 1999). An analytical look at the theory and practice of this central concept. The author is a realist analyst who continues to emphasize the power of states and to suggest that all the ideas and diplomacy and laws about human rights, among other subjects, have not altered traditional understandings of world affairs very much.

Moyn, Samuel, *The Last Utopia: Human Rights In History* (Cambridge, MA: Belknap for Harvard University Press, 2012). Criticizes the push for human rights in the world as being contingent on politics circa 1970 and destined to fail in the long term, as did communism and national liberation movements. Provocative argument but with many critics.

Rosenau, James N., and Ernst-Otto Czempiel, eds., *Governance Without Government: Order and Change in World Politics* (Cambridge: Cambridge University Press, 1992). An excellent collection showing the extensive efforts to collectively manage problems in international relations, with a good chapter by Marc Zacher pertaining to human rights.

Singer, Max, and Aaron Wildavsky, *The Real World Order: Zones of Peace, Zones of Turmoil*, 2nd edn. (Chatham, NJ: Chatham House Publishers, 1996).

Two conservatives indicate why they are optimistic about the future of international relations, believing that current authoritarian and failed states will learn the proper lessons about the benefits of democratic capitalism.

Vincent, R. J., *Human Rights and International Relations* (Cambridge: Cambridge University Press, 1986). A somewhat dated introduction, but still good on basic philosophical and legal points.

2 Establishing human rights standards

It is quite remarkable that the notion of human rights has played such a large role in western history, and now in international relations since 1945, and yet no one has been able to definitively settle questions about the origins and "true" nature of these rights. Despite continuing debate over such philosophical matters, the international community – mostly through the United Nations – has agreed on a modern version of human rights. States, the most important actors in that community, who supposedly follow "realist" principles of harsh self-interest, have used international law and organization to adopt "liberal" standards requiring attention to individual and collective human rights.[1] Internationally recognized human rights, as social construct, are a fact of international relations.

A philosophy of rights?

We do not lack for differing theories about human rights.[2] Even among western philosophers there is great variation. For Edmund Burke, the concept of human rights was a monstrous fiction.[3] For Jeremy Bentham, it was absurd to base human rights on natural rights, because *"Natural rights is simple nonsense ... nonsense upon stilts."*[4] The contemporary

[1] David P. Forsythe, "Human Rights and US Foreign Policy: Two Levels, Two Worlds," in David Beetham, ed., *Politics and Human Rights* (Oxford: Blackwell, 1995), 111–130.

[2] In a voluminous literature see further David P. Forsythe, *Human Rights and World Politics*, rev. 2nd edn. (Lincoln: University of Nebraska Press, 1989), ch. 7; Morton E. Winston, ed., *The Philosophy of Human Rights* (Belmont: Wadsworth, 1989); part I of Tim Dunne and Nicholas J. Wheeler, eds., *Human Rights in Global Politics* (Cambridge: Cambridge University Press, 1999); James Nickel, *Making Sense of Human Rights*, rev. 2nd edn. (Malden, MA: Blackwell, 2007); and Charles R. Beitz, *The Idea of Human Rights* (New York and Oxford: Oxford University Press, 2009). For a concise overview, see Michael Freeman, "Philosophy," in David P. Forsythe, ed., *Encyclopedia of Human Rights* (New York: Oxford University Press, 2009), vol. IV, 228–238.

[3] Jeremy Waldron, ed., *Nonsense upon Stilts: Bentham, Burke and Marx on the Rights of Man* (London: Methuen, 1987).

[4] Quoted ibid., 53.

philosopher Alasdair MacIntyre tells us there are no such things as human rights; they are similar to witches and unicorns and other figments of the imagination.[5] Karl Marx, for that matter, was not born in Beijing. He too was western, both by birth and by principal area of concern. At the risk of oversimplifying his many and not always consistent writings, one can say that he regarded many civil rights as inherently good and tactically helpful in achieving socialism, while regarding property rights as contributing to the social ills of the modern world.[6]

John Locke has been subjected to many interpretations. In a dominant strain of western political philosophy, he seems to say that natural law provides human rights as property rights – owned by each individual. Human rights are moral rights that no public authority can transgress. Individuals, in his liberal view, are equal and autonomous beings whose natural rights predate national and international laws. A primary purpose of public authority is to secure these rights in legal practice. Attracta Ingram tells us, on the other hand, that human rights are not property rights that derive from natural law.[7] They are constructed in a political process featuring self-government, not discovery of metaphysical principles. There are other constructivist or analytical theories of human rights.[8]

Ingram goes on to argue for the legitimacy of economic and social rights in addition to civil and political rights. She emphasizes the importance of the positive rights featuring entitlements to minimal standards of food, clothing, shelter, and health care. On the other hand, Maurice Cranston argues that human rights can only be civil-political, not economic-social.[9] He ends his list of fundamental personal rights with the so-called negative rights that block governmental interference into the private domain. Morris Abrams agrees,[10] but Donnelly disagrees – supporting Ingram on the validity of economic and social rights.[11]

---

[5] Alasdair MacIntyre, *After Virtue* (Notre Dame: University of Notre Dame Press, 1981), 61–69. See also Susan Mendus, "Human Rights in Political Theory," in Beetham, ed., *Politics and Human Rights*, 10–24.
[6] I am indebted to Professor Jack Donnelly for much of this formulation.
[7] Attracta Ingram, *A Political Theory of Rights* (New York: Oxford University Press, 1994).
[8] See especially Michael Ignatieff, *Human Rights as Politics and Idolatry* (Princeton: Princeton University Press, 2001).
[9] Maurice Cranston, "Human Rights, Real and Supposed," in D. D. Raphael, ed., *Political Theory and the Rights of Man* (Bloomington: Indiana University Press, 1967), 43–53; also Cranston, *What Are Human Rights?* (New York: Basic Books, 1964).
[10] Morris Abrams, "The United Nations, the United States, and International Human Rights," in Roger A. Coate, ed., *US Policy and the Future of the United Nations* (New York: Twentieth Century Fund Press, 1994), 113–138.
[11] Jack Donnelly, *Universal Human Rights in Theory and Practice* (Ithaca: Cornell University Press, 1989). See also Nobel laureate Amartya Sen, *Development as Freedom* (New York:

Henry Shue and John Vincent argue for the primacy of subsistence rights (mostly but not entirely socioeconomic) over procedural rights (which are civil and political).[12] Donnelly in turn says that human rights can only be individual, not collective. William Felice disagrees, arguing for the legitimacy of group rights.[13] Some go beyond the first generation of negative rights (said to be of the first generation because they were recognized first), and the second generation of positive rights, to a third generation of synthetic rights: the rights to peace, a healthy environment, development, and perhaps humanitarian assistance.[14]

One could continue with arguments and citations, but almost every notion put forward in regard to foundational arguments about human rights has become what political scientists like to call a "contested concept." Ingram notes that "propositions of rights are a pervasive and contested feature of our political practice."[15] Chris Brown writes that "Virtually everything encompassed by the notion of 'human rights' is the subject of controversy."[16] Belden Fields, in an excellent review of differing theoretical justifications for human rights, notes that none are perfect and that all have strong and weak points; he then puts forward his own grounding and justification, centering on development of the human personality.[17] Especially given the lack of intellectual agreement on the sources and nature of fundamental personal rights, and the fact that foundational theories continue to be published all the time, one might well agree with Vincent "that the list of objections to the idea of human rights seems formidable."[18]

In so far as the notion of human rights is associated with the West (and it is only western scholars that have been cited above), the unity and

Anchor Books, 1999), on the importance of socioeconomic rights in order to eliminate various "unfreedoms" that impede human development.

[12] Henry Shue, *Basic Rights: Subsistence, Affluence, and US Foreign Policy*, 2nd edn. (Princeton: Princeton University Press, 1997); John Vincent, *Human Rights and International Relations* (Cambridge: Cambridge University Press, 1986).

[13] William Felice, *Taking Suffering Seriously: The Importance of Collective Human Rights* (Albany: SUNY Press, 1996). See further A. Belden Fields, "Collective/Group Rights," in *Encyclopedia of Human Rights*, vol. I, 345–353; and also Gene M. Lyons and James Mayall, eds., *International Human Rights in the 21st Century: Protecting the Rights of Groups* (London: Rowman & Littlefield, 2003).

[14] See, e.g., William F. Felice, "Right to Development," in *Encyclopedia of Human Rights*, vol. II, 21–31.

[15] Ingram, *Political Theory of Rights*.

[16] Chris Brown, "Universal Human Rights: A Critique," in Dunne and Wheeler, eds., *Human Rights in Global Politics*, 103.

[17] A. Belden Fields, *Rethinking Human Rights for the New Millennium* (New York: Palgrave Macmillan, 2003). See also Michael Freeman, *Human Rights*, 2nd edn. (Cambridge: Polity, 2010), for a good introduction with much attention to political theory.

[18] Vincent, *Human Rights and International Relations*, 35.

coherence of western civilization on the rights question have been greatly overstated. It remains true, however, that the dominant western view of rights comprises some version of liberalism. Individuals, at least, are said to have rights that public authority must respect. They are to be written into law and defended via independent courts. Debate then ensues over which individuals should have recognized rights (women, racial minorities, gays, members of certain political groups?), who besides individuals have rights (animals, human groups, which groups?), whether rights should go beyond traditional civil and political rights (socioeconomic rights, cultural rights, solidarity rights to peace, or economic development, or a healthy environment?), where rights originate (God, natural law, human construction?), and what is the best way to implement them (courts, extra-judicial policy, private action, education?).[19]

Despite these disagreements, human rights as intellectual construct and as widespread political-legal practice was indeed first associated with the West. Other regions or cultures displayed moral principles and movements in favor of some version of human dignity, but they were not grounded in a rights discourse.[20] It was in the West that individuals were first said to be entitled to fundamental personal rights, giving rise to institutionalized claims that public authority had to respect them. Britain pioneered the development of constitutionalism, in this case monarchical government limited by the rights of other elites. France and the USA began to practice a type of democratic politics based on individual rights from the 1780s – at least for white males. In most non-western cultures individuals were still dependent on rulers to recognize abstract principles of good governance; individuals were not seen as having personal rights and the means (such as access to independent courts) to compel rulers to respect them.

Thus western states, some earlier and some later, became associated with a set of liberal principles: personal rights matter, the vulnerable and marginalized should be accorded special attention, public authority should respect personal autonomy and preferences, reason should

---

[19] See further Rhoda E. Howard-Hassmann, *Compassionate Canadians: Civic Leaders Discuss Human Rights* (Toronto: University of Toronto Press, 2003). This work, based on interviews with civic leaders in Hamilton, Ontario, Canada, shows, among other things, that it is possible to have a conception of human rights and a sense of community at the same time.

[20] Jack Donnelly, "Human Rights and Human Dignity: An Analytic Critique of Non-Western Human Rights Conceptions," *American Political Science Review*, 76, 2 (June 1982), 433–449. For a different view, see Paul Gordon Lauren, *The Evolution of International Human Rights: Visions Seen* (Philadelphia: University of Pennsylvania Press, 1998); and Micheline Ishay, ed., *The Human Rights Reader: Major Political Essays, Speeches, and Documents from the Bible to the Present* (London: Routledge, 1997).

prevail over emotionalism, violence should give way to negotiated arrangements, progress is possible.[21]

For present purposes, as stated in the previous chapter, and consistent with John Locke, I consider liberalism to connote above all attention to the essential moral and legal rights of the person. These fundamental rights, these human rights, are supposed to be trumps in that public policies must respect them.

Also for present purposes, I want to distinguish a modern version of classical political liberals from pragmatic liberals. The former emphasize peaceful and rational discussion to the point that sometimes they become judicial romantics and opposed to forceful action to stop human rights violations. They overemphasize the role of adjudication by courts, either national or international, and they overemphasize as well what diplomacy can achieve when divorced from considerations of coercion.

A pragmatic liberal, by comparison, while starting from the same assumption that human rights in general are a good thing, recognizes that there is morality or ethics beyond the human rights discourse. Thus a pragmatic liberal believes there are forms of justice apart from criminal justice, and is therefore sometimes prepared to suspend court action on behalf of personal rights for other values such as peace or reconciliation. A pragmatic liberal also believes that, while one of the important goals of international relations should remain peaceful and rational diplomacy, at times the only realistic way to end some calculated human rights violations by evil persons is through coercion.

The discourses on "human security" and/or "complex humanitarian emergency" can be noted here. They came into usage partly as diplomatic devices to try to do good for individuals in situations when reference to specific human rights and humanitarian law might in fact impede human dignity. If, for example, UN officials and state representatives referred to a situation as one of internal war and implied the possibility of war crimes, this would necessarily suggest that the government in question had lost much control of national territory and faced serious challenge. Many if not most governments are hesitant to admit this, or to invoke specific rules about what could and could not be done. But if one referred to a concern for "human security" and/or a "complex humanitarian emergency," it might be possible to obtain governmental cooperation for remedial action through international efforts. The same logic might prevail where a weak, ineffective government confronted situations

---

[21] In addition to the fine synthesis of liberalism by Michael Doyle cited in Chapter 1, see further Andrew Moravcsik, "Taking Preferences Seriously: A Liberal Theory of International Politics," *International Organization*, 51, 4 (Winter 1997), 513–554.

such as serious drought and/or plague. If a government resisted the notion of socioeconomic rights, it might be moved to progressive action by reference to the ideas of human security or humanitarian emergency. Bypassing individual responsibility and threat of legal action for war crimes or crimes against humanity might actually improve the lives of large numbers of persons in certain circumstances.

On the other hand, if the fuzzy, imprecise, a-legal language was used frequently, it might undercut the long struggle to develop clear human rights and humanitarian legal standards under which officials could be held responsible for doing – or allowing – evil. Like most policy options, reference to the language of human security, complex emergency, or even human rights held the potential for positive or negative effect. Recall the effort to label militia leader General Mohamed Farrah Aideed in Somalia a war criminal. This led to more violence, the withdrawal of various outside actors from that complicated situation, and then a reluctance by various outsiders to intervene decisively in the subsequent genocide in Rwanda. Policy decisions have to be evaluated in particular context, with "bounded rationality" or lack of certainty about what the future holds. Use of the discourse on human rights with attendant notions of violation of law and criminal responsibility may or may not be superior to other efforts to do good in particular circumstances.[22]

While there are many varieties of liberalism and liberals, the classical idea of liberalism remains centered on respect for personal moral rights, based above all on the equal worth of the individual, whose preferences should be followed in the public domain. Classical liberals emphasize above all legal rights derived from political morality, independent court judgments, and peaceful policy making.[23] Pragmatic liberals, depending on context, may emphasize the importance of other values *in addition to human rights*, other modes of conduct *in addition to rational discourse*, and

---

[22] For a concise introduction, see Gerd Oberleitner, "Human Security," in *Encyclopedia of Human Rights*, vol. II, 486–493. For a discussion of the relationship between the notions of human security and human rights, see Rhoda E. Howard-Hassmann, "Working Paper: Human Security," *Human Rights and Human Welfare*, January 2011, on-line via hrhw@du.edu. See also Tom Farer, "Human Security: Defining the Elephant and Imagining Its Tasks," *Asian Journal of International Law*, 1, 1 (Fall 2010), 43–55, who confirms the imprecise notion of human security and discusses its links to human rights. See further Edward Newman and Oliver P. Richmond, eds., *The United Nations and Human Security* (New York: Palgrave, 2001). For a discussion of the idea of complex humanitarian emergency, see E. Wayne Nafziger, et al., eds., *War, Hunger, and Disease: The Origins of Complex Humanitarian Emergencies* (New York and Oxford: Oxford University Press, 2000).

[23] It is true that Locke argued for a right of rebellion as a last resort in the face of tyranny, but short of persistent and systematic gross violations of human rights, Locke emphasizes the role of independent courts to protect human rights.

wind up recognizing the necessity of difficult choices in the context of how to better human dignity and social justice. In the face of human rights violations the classical liberal almost always looks to the rule of law and court decisions, whereas the pragmatic liberal may well favor diplomatic compromises and other extra-judicial action. For both the classical and the pragmatic liberal, the good or welfare of the person remains their touchstone for policy making.[24] Realists remain focused on the power of the state as their primary concern.

Bringing some closure to this brief synopsis about especially a liberal philosophy of rights, Susan Mendus correctly observes that the more philosophers find theories of rights to be wanting, the more public authorities proceed to codify human rights in public law.[25] There is a remarkable lack of connection between philosophical or theoretical debate on the one hand, and, on the other, considerable agreement on behalf of internationally recognized human rights – "one of the twentieth century's most powerful ideas."[26] According to Zbigniew Brzezinski, who was national security advisor to President Jimmy Carter, "Human rights is the single most magnetic political idea of the contemporary time."[27] Whether he has changed his view after the end of the Cold War saw the rise of Islamist terrorism and tough counterterrorism policies is an interesting question. However, broad-based opposition movements against longstanding autocrats in places such as Tunisia in 2011 indicated that the idea of human rights still had broad appeal, even in areas long dominated by illiberal forces.

The American lawyer Cass R. Sunstein, when noting agreement on the 1948 Universal Declaration of Human Rights, quotes Jacques Maritain's explanation: "Yes, we agree about the rights but on condition that no one

---

[24] My concern is with liberalism as a political (and legal) philosophy. Liberalism applied to economics is mostly a separate subject, except that political liberalism suggests the right to personal property, which may have some role in also producing limited (constitutional) government. Liberalism and economics form an important subject, but it is not necessary for my primary purposes to go into it in great detail here. It can be added, however, that when many scholars speak about a liberal world order, they write mostly about private corporations, private markets, and free trade. They write comparatively little about individual civil and political rights. And, liberal economics may be detrimental to liberal politics, to the extent that the profit motive leads to the repression and exploitation of persons. One has to be careful not to automatically conflate economic and political dimensions of liberalism.

[25] Mendus, "Human Rights in Political Theory."

[26] Tony Evans, *US Hegemony and the Project of Universal Human Rights* (New York: St. Martin's Press, 1996), 41.

[27] Zbigniew Brzezinski, *The Grand Failure: The Birth and Death of Communism in the Twentieth Century* (New York: Collier Books, 1990), 256.

asks us why."[28] Sunstein then notes that "A nation's constitutional rights are often respected without anything like agreement about what best justifies them."[29] The Canadian Michael Ignatieff provides a good reason why: historical awareness. "Our grounds for believing that the spread of human rights represent moral progress ... are pragmatic and historical. We know from historical experience that when human beings have defensible rights ... they are less likely to be abused and oppressed."[30]

So we have in the notion of human rights perhaps a matter of secular religion, something which is metaphysical and cannot be proved but often taken on faith, or different versions of faith. But by reading history, we can see and study the results of that belief, that human beings are usually more secure, free, and prosperous when they exist in a society that takes human rights seriously.[31] After all, other ideas, like Locke's social contract, cannot be proven to exist independently of belief. But when believed, such ideas often have affected behavioral reality and have bettered lives. Still, context matters. Had all efforts to devise liberal laws and protect human rights ended up like Weimar Germany certainly in the 1930s, with great economic distress and political instability, we would not sing the praises of human rights quite so much. Or maybe we would, seeing the Nazi regime that followed Weimar.[32]

An international politics of rights

As discussed in Chapter 1, western power has been dominant in international relations for about two centuries, which means for present purposes that powerful western states have been in a central position to advance or retard ideas about the human being in world affairs.[33] From more or less the middle of the nineteenth century, western transnational moralism made itself felt in international public policy. Nineteenth- and early twentieth-century action occurred against slavery and the slave trade, on behalf of war-wounded, for the protection of industrialized labor, and on behalf of legal aliens. Most of this western-based moralism

---

[28] Cass R. Sunstein, *The Second Billl of Rights: FDR's Unfinished Revolution and Why We Need It More than Ever* (New York: Basic Books, 2004).
[29] Ibid., 177.   [30] Ignatieff, *Human Rights as Politics and Idolatry*, 4.
[31] For an examination of the idea that practicing human rights contributes to secure societies and peaceful international relations, see David P. Forsythe, "Peace and Human Rights," in *Encyclopedia of Human Rights*, vol. IV, 187–196.
[32] See Deborah E. Kipstadt, "Holocaust," ibid., vol. II, 412–423.
[33] See further Glenda Sluga, *Internationalism in the Age of Nationalism* (Philadelphia: University of Pennsylvania Press, 2013); and Eivind Hovden and Edward Keene, eds., *The Globalization of Liberalism* (New York: Palgrave, 2002).

was of a liberal nature, focusing on downtrodden individuals and seeking to legally require changes in public policy.

Even Marxism can be seen as part of this western-based international moralism.[34] Marx's concern for the industrialized laborer under crude capitalism occurred at more or less the same time as Henry Dunant's concern for victims of war and the start of the Red Cross, as well as widespread western concern about slavery and the African slave trade.

Within western states, it was accepted that the legitimate purposes of public authority extended beyond defense against external threat and maintenance of minimal public order. Such a libertarian or "night watchman" view was superseded everywhere, to varying degrees, by the view that the state should advance the health and welfare, defined rather broadly, of its citizens. This same expansive view about public authority, which led to the welfare state everywhere in the West, but again to varying degrees, has produced similar developments in international relations. For example, the magnitude of refugee and disaster problems outstripped private charitable efforts, leading to expanding public policies.[35] Other regions of the world also displayed moral principles and movements,[36] but they were not in a position to influence the western states that dominated world affairs.

Curiously enough, the discourse of human rights was largely absent from western-inspired transnational moral developments during roughly 1845–1945.[37] Private groups such as the Anti-Slavery Society in London or what became the International Committee of the Red Cross in Geneva pushed western states to adopt treaties obligating governments to correct injustices (stop the slave trade from Africa, provide neutral medical assistance to the sick and wounded in war). The International Labour Organization was created. But for the most part personal human rights were bypassed. In the anti-slavery movement, some took the approach of Christian charity toward the less fortunate and not the approach of

---

[34] See especially John Hutchinson, "Rethinking the Origins of the Red Cross," *Bulletin of the History of Medicine*, 63 (1989), 557–578.

[35] David P. Forsythe, "Humanitarian Assistance in US Foreign Policy, 1947–1987," in Bruce Nichols and Gil Loescher, eds., *The Moral Nation: Humanitarianism and US Foreign Policy Today* (Notre Dame: University of Notre Dame Press, 1989), 63–90.

[36] Donnelly, "Human Rights and Human Dignity."

[37] Jan Herman Burgers, "The Road to San Francisco: The Revival of the Human Rights Idea in the Twentieth Century," *Human Rights Quarterly*, 14, 4 (November 1992), 447–477. For the argument that certain Catholic intellectuals and political parties were important in stressing human rights as a means to human dignity in the 1930s and 1940s, see Samuel Moyn, *Christian Human Rights* (Philadelphia: University of Pennsylvania Press, 2015).

human rights based on equality of persons.[38] Human rights as such remained largely a national rather than international matter. The most notable exception pertained to the minority treaties and declarations in Central and Eastern Europe after World War I, in which individuals from minority groups were afforded certain rights of petition to international bodies in order to hopefully offset any prospect of discrimination by a tyranny of the national majority.[39] The League of Nations did guarantee, with deployment of military force, a democratic election in the Saar in 1934, and did allow individual petitions to the Mandates Commission which "supervised" certain territories not deemed ready for legal independence or statehood.[40] Some efforts would have transformed moral concern for individuals into internationally recognized human rights. A few European non-governmental organizations were active in this regard, as were a few states, during the 1920s and 1930s. Poland and Haiti, for example, were advocates of universal human rights during the League era. Britain and the United States had tried to write the principle of individual religious freedom into the Versailles Peace Treaty and League of Nations Covenant, but withdrew the proposal in order to block Japan from advancing the principle of racial equality.[41] Thus the League was largely silent about human rights, although it later developed social agencies and programs dealing with refugees, slave-like practices, etc.

Key developments that were to lead to the international recognition of human rights occurred when Franklin D. Roosevelt and others drew the conclusion that human rights might, at least sometimes, be connected to international peace and security. It cannot be stressed too strongly, because the point has not been sufficiently emphasized, that human rights as such became a formal part of international relations when important states were willing to allow that universal human rights might sometimes affect their own self-interests. The human rights language that was written into the United Nations Charter had less to do with a western moral crusade to do good for others than with the expediential concerns of particularly the United States. It is not by accident that the UN Charter's Article 55 reads: "*With a view to the creation of conditions of stability and well-being which are necessary for peaceful and friendly relations*

---

[38] Adam Hochschild, *Bury the Chains: Prophets and Rebels in the Fight to Free an Empire's Slaves* (Boston and New York: Mariner Books, for Houghton Mifflin, 2005, 2006).
[39] See especially Inis L. Claude, Jr., *National Minorities* (Cambridge, MA: Harvard University Press, 1955).
[40] See Neta Crawford, *Argument and Change in World Politics: Ethics, Decolonization, and Humanitarian Intervention* (Cambridge: Cambridge University Press, 2002).
[41] Burgers, "The Road to San Francisco," 449.

among nations, based on respect for the principle of equal rights and self-determination of peoples, the United Nations shall promote ... universal respect for, and observance of, human rights and fundamental freedoms for all without distinction as to race, sex, language, or religion" (emphasis added).

President Roosevelt was familiar with the British intellectual H. G. Wells and his proposals for an international code of human rights.[42] In the summer of 1941 FDR and Winston Churchill issued the Atlantic Charter in order to contest fascism and militarism. This document stressed, among various topics, political freedom and national self-determination.[43] Then in late 1941 FDR made his famous "four freedoms" speech in which he tried to give both an ideological framework for US participation in World War II and a blueprint for the post-war peace. The four freedoms (freedom of speech, of religion, from want, and from fear) were to presage much of the International Bill of Rights. In the early 1940s US planning moved ahead with regard to a post-war international organization, with continuing attention to human rights. Roosevelt, along with Truman after him, was convinced that attention to a broad range of human rights in international relations was needed in order to help forestall a repeat of the kind of aggression witnessed in the 1930s from Japan, Germany, and Italy. In this view the United Nations was needed not just to coordinate traditional interstate diplomacy, but to adopt social and economic programs in order to deal with the national conditions that led to dictators and military governments – and eventually to world wars. Roosevelt believed strongly that aggression grew out of deprivation and persecution.[44] International attention to universal

---

[42] Ibid., *passim*.

[43] There is reason to argue that FDR truly believed in the Atlantic Charter, especially given his persistent opposition to colonialism and other factors. On the other hand, Churchill probably would have signed on to any document getting the USA involved in the defense of the beleaguered UK at that stage. He clearly tried to continue with the British Empire and was not in favor of equal rights for persons in India, Kenya, etc. In general, he believed in the superiority of the English-speaking "races" rather than most versions of international equal rights.

[44] In the context of American politics in the 1990s, and in particular in the context of attacks from the American right wing stating that the UN was somehow injurious to US security, two authors present FDR as a classic power politician who saw the UN as part of his realist plans to keep the peace after 1945. FDR saw the UN Security Council as a great power club necessary for policing global order, and parts of the UN Charter authorized the Security Council to override even treaty commitments if necessary for security. There are indeed realist elements to FDR's thinking, especially since he was highly pragmatic, believed in juggling competing ideas and personalities, and was not wedded to any one simple philosophy. But he and Truman saw the UN as also advancing peace by attacking human rights violations and poverty. See further Townsend Hoopes and Douglas Brinkley, *FDR and the Creation of the UN*

human rights was in the security interests of the USA, western states, and everyone else. So much the better if self-interest dovetailed with political morality.

The US Executive, aware of racists and ultra-nationalists at home, a skeptical United Kingdom still interested in maintaining colonialism, and a brutally repressive Soviet Union, abandoned plans for writing into international law immediately binding human rights language of a specific nature. Human rights proposals were extremely modest at Dumbarton Oaks and other Allied conferences during the war. Eventually the USA led a coalition at the San Francisco conference, which created the United Nations, that was in favor of general human rights language in the Charter.[45] This general language was slightly expanded by several western NGOs and Latin American states that were, nevertheless, unable to get the USA to agree to specific commitments to protect rights in the here and now.

Here we see a basic and still incompletely resolved contradiction about international human rights. Violations of human rights domestically may lead to aggression abroad. But if you establish a global rule of law to deal with the human rights violations of others, you will restrict your own freedom of maneuver and highlight your own defects. Roosevelt and Truman were convinced that the origins of World War II lay in Germany's internal policies of the 1930s. But if they created precise international law with strong enforcement mechanisms, these arrangements would reduce US freedom of choice in the making of public policy at home. A strong international legal regime for human rights costs something in national discretion. In fact, FDR had not been a vigorous advocate for civil rights at home primarily because he wanted the cooperation of Southern senators, in whose states persecution of African-Americans was still rampant, for his New Deal approach to economic recovery. And Harry Truman knew, in similar fashion, that robust language on human rights in the UN Charter would undermine its chances of obtaining Senate advice and consent, owing to the key position of those same Southern senators in the mid-1940s. Both presidents saw internationally recognized human rights as important, but both adjusted their policies to the realities of domestic politics.[46]

(New Haven: Yale University Press, 1997). Compare Ruth B. Russell, *A History of the UN Charter: The Role of the US 1940–1945* (Washington: Brookings, 1958).

[45] Antonio Cassese, "The General Assembly: Historical Perspective 1945–1989," in Philip Alston, ed., *The United Nations and Human Rights: A Critical Appraisal* (New York: Oxford University Press, 1992), 25–54. See also Cathal Nolan, *Principled Diplomacy: Security and Rights in US Foreign Policy* (Westport: Greenwood Press, 1993), 181–206.

[46] David P. Forsythe, "Human Rights and Humanitarian Intervention," in David Coates, ed., *The Oxford Companion to American Politics* (New York: Oxford University Press, in

The compromises were frustrating to many human rights advocates at the time but laid the foundations for important developments later. Despite contradictions, the UN Charter came to be the first treaty in world history to recognize universal human rights. Yet no Great Power proposed a radical restructuring of international relations to benefit individuals after the two immensely destructive world wars of the twentieth century. Human rights were vaguely endorsed, but they were to be pursued by traditional state diplomacy. The theory of rights was revolutionary: all individuals manifested them, and even sovereign states had to respect them. But neither the United Nations nor any other international organization in 1945 was given clear supranational authority to ensure their respect. The UN Charter allowed the Security Council to take binding decisions on security questions, but not on social questions. The Charter also contained a prohibition on UN interference in national domestic affairs. The International Court of Justice, the so-called World Court that was technically part of the UN system, could address only those cases that states chose to submit to it. Much of world politics in subsequent years was to deal with this contradiction between the affirmation of universal human rights and the reaffirmation of state sovereignty over domestic social issues.

At about the same time the UN Charter was adopted, the victorious states in World War II organized the Nuremberg and Tokyo international criminal tribunals for the prosecution of some German and Japanese leaders. International prosecutions for war crimes and crimes against peace solidified the notion that individuals could be held legally responsible for violating the laws of war and for waging aggressive war. But the idea of a "crime against humanity," while somewhat new and thus raising questions about due process, implied that individual leaders could be held responsible for violating certain human rights of their own citizens.[47] Certain gross violations of human rights, such as murder,

press). See also Carol Anderson, "United States: Race Relations in the 1940s and 1950s and International Human Rights," in *Encyclopedia of Human Rights*, vol. V, 224–233. It should be stressed again that the Democratic Party during the FDR and Truman eras was made up mostly of New Dealers, interested in helping the poor, and Southern racists, interested in repressing African-Americans whether poor or not.

[47] The notion of a crime against humanity was articulated by the British after World War I with regard to the Ottoman Empire and its atrocities against the Armenian community of that empire. But since the defeated Ottomans, or Turks, still held some British prisoners of war, Britain dropped the subject of crimes against humanity by the Turks in order to secure the release of its POWs. During World War II, no treaty covered crimes against humanity, nor was this latter legal notion part of international customary law. Yet some German leaders were prosecuted for violating this "rule" nevertheless. See further Gary Jonathan Bass, *Stay the Hand of Vengeance: The Politics of War Crimes Tribunals* (Princeton: Princeton University Press, 2000), 114–146. See also Peter

enslavement, deportation, and pseudo-medical experiments, when practiced on a mass scale, could lead to prosecution, conviction, and even the
death penalty. These two international criminal proceedings were not
free from well-founded charges of bias and "victor's justice," but they did
further the idea that all individuals had fundamental rights in both peace
and war.[48]

One dimension to the Nuremberg tale is important but not very well
known. While the USA was an early champion of international criminal
justice at the end of World War II, it eventually changed course. Many
Germans saw those trials as more political than legal, particularly since
the USA, UK, and USSR had also committed war crimes but did not
have to answer to an international proceeding. Thus much West German
opinion was not entirely supportive of German politicians associated with
the USA. So in the context of the Cold War, to get the pro-western
Konrad Adenauer elected as Chancellor of a West Germany firmly
integrated into NATO, the USA led the way in abandoning the
Nuremberg process and its results. Various convicted Germans were
released and new rounds of trials were suspended. The United States
engaged in "strategic legalism," pushing criminal justice when it seemed
a good idea and abandoning it when it interfered with larger foreign
policy goals. Abandoning Nuremberg was not simply to secure West
Germany as a reliable NATO ally, but also to lock in genuine democracy,
thereby undercutting extremists.[49] Once again, context mattered in a
calculation of complicated trade-offs. Norms mattered, as did the rule of
law and independent courts, but when to push them, and how hard, was
a complex policy decision.

Balakian, "Armenians in the Ottoman Empire," in *Encyclopedia of Human Rights*, vol. I,
92–103.

[48] Christian Tomuschat, "International Criminal Prosecution: The Precedent of
Nuremberg Confirmed," *Criminal Law Forum*, 5, 2–3 (1994), 237–248. Hersh
Lauterpact, who was born in east-central Europe, was highly influential in the
development of the concept of crime against humanity as a British law professor and
governmental advisor. He was disappointed that such crimes were not made clearly
enforceable by the UN in 1945 and thereafter. He disliked the notion of genocide since it
referred to group rights, whereas he emphasized individual rights. Rafael Lemkin, also
born in east-central Europe, was highly influential in the development of the concept of
genocide. He was disappointed that such crimes were not made part of the Nuremburg
proceedings and not made automatically enforceable under the 1948 convention
prohibiting genocide. Both their families were decimated by the Nazis. See especially
Philippe Sands, *East West Street: On the Origins of "Genocide" and "Crimes against
Humanity"* (New York: Knopf, 2016).

[49] Peter McGuire, *Law and War: An American Story*, rev. edn. (New York: Columbia
University Press, 2010).

An international bill of rights

Because the Charter made references to universal human rights but did not specify them, early UN diplomacy sought to fill that void. On December 10, 1948, the General Assembly adopted the Universal Declaration of Human Rights, which was, according to Eleanor Roosevelt, then chair of the UN Human Rights Commission, a statement of aspirations.[50] Its thirty principles covered the same range of rights long endorsed by many western leaders and private parties: rights of political participation and of civic freedom; rights to freedom from want in the form of entitlements to adequate food, clothing, shelter, and health care; and rights to freedom from fear in the form of a pursuit of an international order in which all other rights could be realized. Even this Declaration, which in international law was not immediately binding, proved too much for Saudi Arabia, South Africa, and the Soviet Union and five of its allies – all of which abstained. (All successor governments excepting Saudi Arabia publicly disavowed their abstentions later.)

For the remaining forty-six members of the UN in 1948, the Declaration could be negotiated rather rapidly by international standards, although there were many specific points of controversy.[51] Most of the General Assembly members represented governments that were comfortable with the notion of individual fundamental rights in the abstract and who did not object to their elaboration in this general way. During 1946–1948 there was relatively little acrimonious debate about universalism versus relativism, or about various generations of rights. Especially the West European democracies were comfortable with the values found in the Universal Declaration, as it closely paralleled the domestic policies they wanted to pursue. Moreover, it cannot be stressed too much that in the mid-1940s the US Executive was in favor of socioeconomic as well as civil-political rights. The Democratic Party, through its long control of the White House, had coped with economic depression after 1932 via broad governmental programming that responded to the failures of capitalist markets to provide for the people (and, it must be noted, with participation in World War II which finally conquered high unemployment). Roosevelt had proposed an economic bill of rights in 1944.[52]

[50] Mary Ann Glendon, *A World Made New: Eleanor Roosevelt and the Universal Declaration of Human Rights* (New York: Random House, 2001).
[51] See further Johannes Morsink, *The Universal Declaration of Human Rights: Origins, Drafting, and Intent* (Philadelphia: University of Pennsylvania Press, 1998).
[52] Bertram Gross, "The Human Rights Paradox," in Peter Juviler, Bertram Gross, et al., eds., *Human Rights for the 21st Century: Foundations for Responsible Hope* (Armonk: M. E. Sharpe, 1993), 128.

Truman strongly advocated a right to national health care, although he was never able to get his proposals approved by Congress. (Members of the Democratic Party from the states of the former Confederacy, however, were mostly opposed to internationally recognized human rights.)

Women's organizations were highly active in negotiating the Declaration and achieved a number of semantical changes to their liking.[53] The Indian representative in the Human Rights Commission, Hansa Mehta, was highly assertive on substantive matters, unlike Eleanor Roosevelt who made her contributions mainly through procedural diplomacy and liaison with officials in Washington. Feminist critiques of mainstream UN human rights developments were largely absent. With a female as chair of the Human Rights Commission, and with the creation of the UN Commission on the Status of Women, dominant opinion within the UN believed that sufficient attention was being paid to gender issues – especially since the UN Charter spoke of equality without regard to sex.

The negotiating process entailed a broad range of views, not just western ones, although Africa and Asia were underrepresented.[54] Beyond Western Europe and North America, Latin American political elites were essentially western. Their governments reflected Iberian, and hence western, values in the abstract, rather than indigenous Indian values.[55] The Latin American social democrats, working with the Canadian social democrat John Humphrey, who was a UN international civil servant, were largely responsible for the wording on socioeconomic rights. This language was not the product of the communist states.[56] Lebanon was also strongly in favor of international human rights, being greatly affected by French influence. The same was true for the Philippines, being affected by American influence. The relatively easy adoption of the 1948 Universal Declaration, a "mere" General Assembly nonbinding recommendation, was to prove a major step in the evolving attention to internationally recognized human rights. According to one source, it is "the essential document, the touchstone, the creed of humanity that surely sums up all other creeds directing human behavior."[57] This most basic statement of international ethics is liberal

---

[53] Morsink, *Universal Declaration*, ch. 3 and *passim*.   [54] Ibid., *passim*.
[55] On the compatibility of abstract Latin American Iberian values with international human rights standards, the many violations of these rights notwithstanding, see David P. Forsythe, "Human Rights, the United States and the Organization of American States," *Human Rights Quarterly*, 13, 1 (February 1991), 66–98; and see below, Chapter 5.
[56] Morsink, *Universal Declaration*, chs. 5, 6, and *passim*.
[57] Nadine Gordimer, "Reflections by Nobel Laureates," in Yeal Danieli, Elsa Stamatopoulou, and Clarence J. Dias, eds., *The Universal Declaration of Human Rights: Fifty Years and Beyond* (Amityville, NY: Baywood, 1998).

in tone and content. In late 1948 the Cold War had not fully emerged, and so the Universal Declaration was approved. Had it been delayed for any reason beyond December 1948, it might never have passed the General Assembly. The Cold War soon deeply divided that body.

There is reason to compare the 1948 Universal Declaration with Magna Carta from 1215. Both documents are often cited. Magna Carta is said to be the touchstone for subsequent developments pertaining to the national rule of law, constitutional law, and checks on Executive authority. The Universal Declaration is said to be the touchstone for the considerable law and diplomacy of human rights since its adoption at the UN. Magna Carta has had a checkered history, sometimes revised, often forgotten, suffering eras of slight impact.[58] Likewise, the 1948 Declaration has had its ups and downs, being ignored when its contents clashed with other deeply held views. Magna Carta always re-emerged at some point as a major reference document. The same seems to be true thus far for the Universal Declaration.[59]

It proved quite time-consuming and controversial to translate the Universal Declaration into supposedly enforceable treaties. The Great Powers were preoccupied by the Cold War. It was to take from 1948 to 1966 to accomplish the task of producing the International Covenant on Civil and Political Rights, and also the International Covenant on Economic, Social, and Cultural Rights. These two treaties, discussed in Chapter 3, together with the Universal Declaration, against the background of the UN Charter, make up the International Bill of Rights. Despite the fact that substantive negotiations for the two treaties were completed by 1966, it took another decade for the required number of legal adherences to be obtained in order to bring the treaties into legal force for full parties. This indicated a certain caution by states in moving from general principles to specific treaty provisions that might prove to limit their freedom of choice in foreign and domestic policy – or what had been domestic policy prior to international legislation.[60]

The negotiations after 1948 were complicated by several factors.[61] The USA was in no hurry to move things forward, since the Executive Branch

---

[58] Jill Lepore, "The Meaning of Magna Carta," *The New Yorker*, April 20, 2015, pp. 83–88.

[59] Magna Carta is not directly a human rights document. It does not address the rights of all those living in England. Rather, it codifies limits on the English king in dealings with noblemen. It says nothing directly about the rights of peasants, merchants, etc.

[60] See further Stephen James, *Universal Human Rights: Origins and Development* (El Paso: LFB Scholarly, 2007). It is perfectly clear that the slaughter and atrocities of World War II, including the Holocaust, did *not* shock governments into approving a revolutionary new international law of human rights that would immediately curtail the workings of state sovereignty.

[61] See further Evans, *US Hegemony*.

was under attack by certain powerful domestic groups fearful of international pressures to change the existing American way of life. The Executive was sometimes seen as in favor of a domineering federal government that would introduce foreign and excessively permissive principles and thus destroy the existing *status quo* as protected by the US Constitution and state/provincial governments. The Soviet bloc and the developing countries seized the opportunity to push for economic and social rights in ways, and to an extent, that troubled the western bloc. The western group finally accepted socioeconomic rights in treaty form only as realized gradually over time, and when two separate Covenants were drafted – with different supervisory mechanisms.[62] The developing countries, supported by the communist coalition, pressed hard for rewriting the principle of national self-determination as a collective human right. The western states finally accepted political reality and agreed to a common Article 1 in the two Covenants focusing on a highly ambiguous right to collective self-determination. It has never been clear in international law as to what exactly comprises a people entitled to self-determination, what form self-determination should take, or who can pronounce authoritatively on these controversies.[63] There was also controversy about whether ratification of the Covenants obligated a colonial state to apply human rights provisions in dependent territories. Thus many of the disputes between the East and West, between the North and South, played themselves out in UN debates about human rights.

It bears emphasizing that the General Assembly changed in composition, especially from the mid-1950s. Many non-western states were added to UN membership. This complicated negotiations concerning human rights compared with 1948. Most of these newer states were not only non-western, but also non-affluent and non-democratic. They were

---

[62] It should be stressed that many western societies had long accepted socioeconomic rights in their domestic arrangements, although this was more controversial in the USA. See further Daniel J. Whelan and Jack Donnelly, "The West, Economic and Social Rights, and the Global Human Rights Regime: Setting the Record Straight," *Human Rights Quarterly*, 29, 4 (November 2007), 908–949. In that journal the reader can follow a subsequent debate over several issues about this article.

[63] From a vast literature, see especially Hurst Hannum, *Autonomy, Sovereignty, and Self-Determination: The Accommodation of Conflicting Rights* (Philadelphia: University of Pennsylvania Press, 1992); and Morton H. Halperin and David J. Scheffer, with Patricia L. Small, *Self-Determination in the New World Order* (Washington: Carnegie Endowment, 1992). The UN Charter endorses human rights in the name of promotion of international peace and security. But in writing the national self-determination of peoples into subsequent human rights legal instruments, the international community endorsed a principle of collective human rights that has caused much mischief and no little instability in both national and international politics.

therefore not hesitant in expressing concern about an emphasis on democratic rights and a civic society replete with many civil rights, or in emphasizing economic rights to an extent that troubled particularly the USA.[64] These developments were welcomed by the Soviet Union and its allies. Moreover, as noted above, a number of states were hesitant to place themselves under specific international legal obligation in the field of human rights, even though they had voted for the Universal Declaration – and even though a UN human rights court had not been created. The Covenants always entailed weak supervisory or enforcement mechanisms, as we will see. Many states sought to preserve considerable independence in policy making, even as they found it prudent to be vaguely associated with the notion of human rights.

Be all that as it may, by 2016 many states had become parties to the International Covenant on Civil and Political Rights (168), and also to the International Covenant on Economic, Social, and Cultural Rights (164). With UN membership at 193 states in 2016, it is apparent that approximately 85 percent of states found it desirable to at least give formal endorsement to the liberal notion of universal human rights. There is something about the idea of human rights that has proved widely attractive, as Francis Fukuyama predicted, even as endorsement has not always been followed by compliance. As we will see, many states, including liberal ones like the USA, wish to have it both ways. They wish to identify with support for human rights, but they wish to maintain national independence in policy making both at home and abroad – which may lead to violation of human rights.

Legal regimes without hegemonic leadership

One of the central problems in the development of international human rights law at the United Nations was that the USA was compelled by domestic politics to abandon a position of clear leadership in the setting of international human rights standards.[65] FDR had led on human rights, up to a point. But Truman, Eisenhower, and other presidents were severely constrained by American domestic politics. The start of the Cold War between the USA and the USSR caused some members of Congress to view socioeconomic rights as a form of creeping socialism on the road to communism. The conservative and fanatical movement known as McCarthyism made rational congressional discourse about

---

[64] See further Upendra Baxi, "North–South Views on Human Rights," in *Encyclopedia of Human Rights*, vol. IV, 131–136.

[65] Evans, *US Hegemony*.

international rights difficult if not impossible; that movement only allowed in Washington's policy debates a mindless defense of a chauvinistic version of American moral superiority and security. Racists took courage from the overall situation and demanded an end to international developments in support of racial equality and freedom from racial discrimination. Nationalists championed the supremacy of the US Constitution compared with treaty law. The American Bar Association acted irresponsibly, manufacturing and exaggerating problems supposedly entailed in US adherence to the International Bill of Rights. When the Bricker movement in Congress sought to undermine the Executive's authority to negotiate and ratify self-implementing treaties (with the advice and consent of a supermajority in the Senate), the Eisenhower Administration agreed to back away from open support for human rights treaties. In this way the Executive preserved its overall position in tugs of war with Congress, but at the sacrifice of leadership on international human rights matters. UN human rights developments were left without the full support of the most powerful state in the world, despite the US penchant for seeing itself as a human rights model for others.[66]

In other parts or issue-areas of international relations, a hegemonic power had taken the lead in the construction of norms and organizations to manage important issues.[67] For example, the USA had taken the lead in both Western Europe and the Western Hemisphere to construct security arrangements for the defense of multilateral interests. NATO and the workings of the InterAmerican system reflected broad deference to, or cooperation with, US views on security. The USA did not have to coerce other states into compliance with its views (Cuba excepted after 1959) but rather exercised hegemonic leadership through a series of initiatives, burdens, payments, etc.

But with regard to global human rights, the USA was not able to play this role of hegemon, not so much because of clear Executive disagreement with the course of UN human rights developments. Rather, congressional and public views relegated the Executive Branch, under both Republicans and Democrats, to a background and low-profile role regarding international rights. From Dwight Eisenhower

---

[66] In addition to Evans, US Hegemony, and Forsythe, "Human Rights and US Foreign Policy," see Natalie Hevener Kaufman, Human Rights Treaties and the Senate: A History of Opposition (Chapel Hill: University of North Carolina Press, 1990); and Lawrence J. LeBlanc, The United States and the Genocide Convention (Durham: Duke University Press, 1991).

[67] See especially Stephen D. Krasner, ed., International Regimes (Ithaca: Cornell University Press, 1983); Volker Rittberger and Peter Mayer, eds., Regime Theory and International Relations (New York: Oxford University Press, 1993).

through Gerald Ford, the USA did not emphasize international human rights in its foreign policy, and this orientation certainly was evident in UN proceedings. It was only when Congress shifted position in the mid-1970s, and began to stress what it had rejected in the 1940s, namely an emphasis on human rights in foreign policy, that presidents like Jimmy Carter felt free to make human rights a more salient issue in world politics.[68] Even after 1976 and Carter's election, the USA did not ratify the International Covenant on Economic, Social, and Cultural Rights or the Convention on the Rights of the Child or the Convention on the Elimination of Discrimination against Women; it ratified other human rights treaties only with restrictive conditions; still manifested evident and widespread problems of racism; and utilized the death penalty for common, non-political crime far more than any other industrialized democracy. Thus the USA still found it difficult to play the role of hegemonic leader at the UN on human rights issues, although from 1977 it tried to a greater extent than during 1953–1976.

Beyond the International Bill of Rights

Despite the absence of hegemonic leadership from the USA, other states, international civil servants, and non-governmental organizations combined their efforts to provide at the UN a relatively large body of treaties and declarations about universal human rights. Through the UN General Assembly, in 1948 states adopted the Convention on the Prevention and Punishment of the Crime of Genocide, making individuals responsible for prosecution if they intend to destroy a national, ethnic, religious, or racial group, in whole or in part. Only four groups fall under this treaty, and the very notion of genocide is vaguely defined.[69] Nevertheless, the convention represents some progress in humane matters. The Assembly adopted a treaty regulating prostitution in 1949, and in 1951 it adopted the Convention Relating to the Status of Refugees, adding a protocol in 1967. The central rule in international refugee law obliges states to give temporary asylum to those who have fled their homeland because of a well-founded fear of persecution. In 1953 the Assembly amended the 1926 Slavery Convention. In the same year it adopted the Convention on the Political Rights of Women, and the following year the Convention Relating to the Status of Stateless

---

[68] See further David P. Forsythe, *Human Rights and US Foreign Policy: Congress Reconsidered* (Gainesville: University Press of Florida, 1988).
[69] See further William A. Schabas, "Genocide," in *Encyclopedia of Human Rights*, vol. II, 294–304.

Persons. In 1956 the Assembly approved the Convention on the Abolition of Slavery, the Slave Trade, and Institutions and Practices Similar to Slavery, thus supplementing earlier treaties and protocols on this subject. The treaty on the Reduction of Statelessness was adopted in 1961. Reflecting the impact of many new non-western member states, the General Assembly in 1965 adopted the Convention on Racial Discrimination. This was followed in 1973 by the Convention against Apartheid, referring to legal racial segregation primarily as then practiced by the Republic of South Africa. In 1979 the Assembly adopted the Convention on General Discrimination against Women and the UN Convention against Torture was approved in 1984. In a highly popular move, the Assembly in 1989 adopted the Convention on the Rights of the Child.

During this same era, the International Labour Organization, a carry-over from the League of Nations period but after 1945 technically part of the UN system, adopted a series of treaties dealing with such subjects as freedom of association (1948), the right of labor movements to engage in collective bargaining (1949), freedom from forced labor (1957), freedom from social discrimination (1958), and the protection of indigenous peoples (1989). The United Nations Educational, Scientific, and Cultural Organization adopted a convention in 1960 dealing with discrimination in education.

Outside the United Nations, but still concerning universal standards, states agreed to further develop international humanitarian law – sometimes also referred to as international law for human rights in armed conflict.[70] In 1949 they adopted the interlocking four Geneva Conventions of August 12 for Protection of Victims of War. In a subsequent diplomatic conference during 1974–1977, also called by the Swiss government, the depository state for humanitarian law since 1864, two protocols were added to the 1949 law. The first protocol increased humanitarian regulation of international armed conflict. The second provided a mini-convention, the first ever, on internal armed conflict, sometimes called civil war. In 1980 many states agreed to a framework convention on conventional weapons that might cause indiscriminate or unnecessary suffering. The sum total of this Geneva law or Red Cross law, so named because of the supporting role played by the Geneva-based International Committee of the Red Cross (ICRC), an independent component of the International Red Cross and Red Crescent Movement, focused on victims of war.

---

[70] See Hans-Peter Gasser, "Humanitarian Law," ibid., vol. II, 462–472.

The thrust of international humanitarian law was nothing less than to humanize war, in the sense of trying to protect and assist those fighters held as prisoners or otherwise inactive through sickness or wounds; civilians; those in occupied territory; those separated from and without information about family members; those in a war zone and in need of food, clothing, shelter, and medical care; and those victimized by certain weaponry – among other subject matter.[71] A fundamental point is that even in war, international or civil, fighting parties are not legally free to engage in wanton destruction, but rather must direct military action only to permissible targets in an effort to minimize human misery. This general principle is formally accepted by all professional military establishments, even as many civilians still wonder how there can be a humane law of war in the midst of intentional killing.

Much has been written about the relationship between the international law for human rights in peacetime, and international humanitarian law for situations of international and non-international armed conflict. The essential and non-legalistic point is that these two bodies of international law share the objective of creating minimal standards designed to protect human dignity in different situations.[72] Human rights law is general law, and the law of armed conflict is specialized law. However, some parts of human rights law apply in situations of armed conflict. For example, the prohibition on torture applies both in peace and war. The United Nations, which historically dealt with human rights in peace, has increasingly developed policies and programs for

---

[71] From a vast literature which frequently focuses on strictly legal aspects, see especially the following: Geoffrey Best, *War and Law Since 1945* (Oxford: Clarendon Press, 1994); Caroline Morehead, *Dunant's Dream: War, Switzerland, and the History of the Red Cross* (New York: St. Martin's Press, 1998); Francois Bugnion, *The International Committee of the Red Cross and the Protection of War Victims* (Geneva: ICRC, 2003); John Hutchinson, *Champions of Charity: War and the Rise of the Red Cross* (Boulder: Westview, 1996); Stephen C. Neff, *War and the Law of Nations: A General History* (Cambridge: Cambridge University Press, 2005); Gary D. Solis, *The Law of Armed Conflict: International Humanitarian Law in War* (Cambridge: Cambridge University Press, 2010); David P. Forsythe, *Humanitarian Politics: The International Committee of the Red Cross* (Baltimore: Johns Hopkins University Press, 1977); Forsythe, *The Internationalization of Human Rights* (Lexington: Lexington Books for D. C. Heath, 1991), ch. 6; and Forsythe, *The Humanitarians: The International Committee of the Red Cross* (Cambridge: Cambridge University Press, 2005).

[72] It has never been clear how international law can obligate non-state parties in a non-international armed conflict. International law is state-centric. The rebel side in a civil war did not participate in the drafting of the laws of war, and cannot deposit a signature of adherence with the depository agent giving its consent to be bound. Nevertheless, a number of rebel movements have promised to abide by humanitarian law, whatever their subsequent behavior. It is not legal technicalities but political calculation that is important. If a rebel side seeks recognition as a responsible party, it frequently is an asset to have a reputation for humane conduct.

humanitarian action in war. The ICRC, the theoretical coordinator for the private Red Cross Movement in wartime, increasingly interacts with UN bodies (and other actors) about its humanitarian action. Legal distinctions should not be allowed to obscure common objectives and cooperation in programs.[73]

If one adds together the human rights and humanitarian treaties negotiated through the UN General Assembly, the ILO, UNESCO, and the diplomatic conferences called by Switzerland in consultation with the ICRC, it is clear we do not lack global or universal humane standards in both peace and war. One could add to the list certain declarations and other forms of soft law adopted by various international organizations on these same subjects. States clearly wish to picture themselves as standing for something besides harsh realist principles of narrow self-interest. Many non-western and non-democratic states have become legal parties to human rights treaties. Actual behavior in concrete situations will be examined later. Enough was said at the start of Chapter 1 to suggest a yawning chasm between statements of noble principle and the reality of political action under the pressures of winning and losing power struggles – or perhaps under the weight of sheer indifference to human suffering. It bears repeating what David Rieff wrote, namely that the twentieth century displayed the best principles and the worst realities.[74] Still, human rights standards are indeed a liberal fact of international relations, and the possibility of their actually generating some beneficial influence on behalf of human dignity cannot be discounted out of hand. As has been said of the United Nations, so it can be said of international human rights standards: their purpose is not to get us to heaven, but to save us from hell.[75]

Continuing debates

It was clear at the 1993 UN Vienna Conference on Human Rights that a number of states harbored serious reservations about internationally recognized human rights as codified and interpreted up to that time. In

---

[73] See further David P. Forsythe, "The International Committee of the Red Cross and Humanitarian Assistance: A Policy Analysis," *International Review of the Red Cross*, 314 (September–October 1996), 512–531; Larry Minear and Thomas G. Weiss, *Mercy Under Fire: War and the Global Humanitarian Community* (Boulder: Westview, 1995); and Thomas G. Weiss, David P. Forsythe, and Roger Coate, *The United Nations and Changing World Politics*, 2nd edn. (Boulder: Westview, 1997), ch. 5.

[74] David Rieff, *A Bed for the Night: Humanitarianism in Crisis* (New York: Simon & Schuster, 2002), 70.

[75] Weiss, et al., *The United Nations*, 282.

the view of the USA, which took the lead in an effort to reaffirm universal human rights, a number of states tried to say at Vienna that international human rights were essentially western and therefore inappropriate to other societies. In this group of states at that time were China, Cuba, Syria, Iran, Vietnam, Pakistan, Malaysia, Singapore, Yemen, and Indonesia.[76] From Singapore's view,[77] it was legitimate to note that certain Asian countries were so crowded as to call into question the wisdom of pursuing a highly individualistic human rights orientation that might jeopardize the welfare of the community as a whole.[78] Moreover, Asian societies had long emphasized precisely that emphasis on collective welfare that seems notably lacking in the West. Some western observers found it hypocritical that the USA should push for universal human rights in international relations while itself refusing to fully endorse socioeconomic rights as approved by the international community, continuing to employ the death penalty for common crime despite considerable opposition from the rest of the democratic community, and violating refugee rights when convenient – as in dealing with Haitians in the late 1980s and early 1990s.[79] As noted above, the USA intentionally abused some detainees in its "war on terrorism" after September 11, 2001, having made them "ghost detainees" by adopting a policy of enforced disappearances.

As so often happens in international conferences, basic differences were not fully resolved. The Vienna Final Declaration reaffirmed "universal respect for, and observance of, human rights and fundamental freedoms for all ... The universal nature of these rights and freedoms is beyond question." But the Declaration also stated, "While the significance of national and regional particularities and various historical, cultural and religious backgrounds must be borne in mind, it is the duty of states, regardless of their political, economic and cultural systems, to promote and protect all human rights and fundamental freedoms." This latter language gave some "wiggle room" to the Singapores of the world

---

[76] *New York Times*, June 14, 1993, A3.
[77] For a concise overview, see Ian Neary, "East Asian Values," in *Encyclopedia of Human Rights*, vol. II, 73–77. See further Mark Hong, "Convergence and Divergence in Human Rights," in David P. Forsythe, ed., *The United States and Human Rights: Looking Inward and Outward* (Lincoln: University of Nebraska Press, 1999); Fareed Zakaria, "A Conversation with Lee Kuan Yew," *Foreign Affairs*, 73, 2 (March/April 1994), 109–127; Bilahari Kausikan, "Asia's Different Standard," *Foreign Policy*, 92 (Fall 1993), 24–41. In general see Joanne R. Bauer and Daniel A. Bell, eds., *The East Asian Challenge for Human Rights* (Cambridge: Cambridge University Press, 1999).
[78] See further Brian Orend, "Communitarianism and Community," in *Encyclopedia of Human Rights*, vol. I, 377–386.
[79] Beth Stephens, "Hypocrisy on Rights," *New York Times*, June 24, 1993, A13.

who claimed they were not in fact authoritarian but had devised a successful and regionally particular Asian-style democracy, built on a shortened version of genuine human rights.

It cannot be denied, however, that those in favor of universal human rights, with only a weak form of particularism allowed, constituted a majority at the end of the Vienna meeting, even if that position did not fully convert those on the other side of the question.[80] The dominant view was that universal human rights responded to universal problems such as governmental repression and harsh capitalistic markets. This was recognized by any number of non-western observers.[81] Persons need protection from these problems regardless of civilization, region, or nation. States might well differ, for example, on whether presidential or parliamentary models best implemented the right to political participation in policy making, but they were obligated to provide a genuine and not bogus right to democratic governance. It was a historical fact that the human rights discourse arose in the West, but so did the discourse about state sovereignty. Just as the idea of state sovereignty had found broad acceptance in the non-western world, it was argued, so should the notion of human rights. Like state sovereignty, there was nothing in the history of human rights that made it *ipso facto* inappropriate to non-western societies. A simple analogy might not be out of place: whether the bicycle was invented in France ca. 1790 or Germany ca. 1815, that European origin did not mean the bicycle was inappropriate in other parts of the world.

There were other critiques of the International Bill of Rights toward the close of the twentieth century. In the final chapter I discuss a number of these further – especially feminist perspectives. For the moment it suffices to note that the most important critique of liberalism has come from the realists.

Contemporary realists like former National Security Advisor and Secretary of State Henry Kissinger regard international human rights as mostly an unfortunate and sentimental intrusion into the real stuff of international relations – interstate power calculations. Realists barely tolerate diplomacy for human rights because they know states like the USA or the Netherlands will insist sometimes on attention to democracy and hence civil and political rights, but they still think an emphasis on

---

[80] On combining universal principles with weak cultural relativism, or some particular/local variation in how the principles are implemented, see especially Jack Donnelly, *Universal Human Rights in Theory and Practice* (Ithaca: Cornell University Press, 1989), part III.

[81] See the clear exposition by Onuma Yasuaki, *In Quest of Intercivilizational Human Rights: "Universal" vs. "Relative" Human Rights Viewed from an Asian Perspective*, Occasional Paper No. 2, Center for Asian Pacific Affairs, the Asia Foundation (March 1996), 15.

such things is unwise. Rational states in anarchic international relations concentrate on the power relations that can protect their existence and domestic values. Unique and sentimental states, above all the USA, unwisely try to project their domestic values and conditions into international relations, where the situation of anarchy and lack of moral and political consensus means a very different context.[82]

A widely cited version of this realist position regarded international action to stop gross violations of internationally recognized human rights as "social work" more properly in the domain of the late Mother Teresa, known for her charitable works with the poor in India.[83] In this view, United States' and others' actions to stop mass misery in Somalia or misrule in Haiti and Kosovo were not things that rational states did. Such action was supposedly best left to private social agencies, not rational great powers. States needed to keep their powder dry and their military forces prepared for traditional wars involving traditional vital national interests, and not dissipate their power in what the Pentagon called "operations other than war." If this realist approach meant ineffective policies to cope with human suffering abroad, this might be unfortunate. But the wise policy maker or diplomat was not moved by sentiment, only by hard-headed calculations of power and security. The touchstone for realist policy was narrow and expedient national interest, not personal welfare and certainly not universal human rights. Condoleezza Rice, National Security Advisor to President George W. Bush, reflected this realist tradition when she wrote that the USA should focus on transcendent national interests; by implication she was suggesting that the Clinton Administration had wrongly used the US military for nation-building in the Balkans and other diversions from true national interests.[84]

It does not go too far to say that a central problem of contemporary international relations is how to reconcile the liberal framework of international human rights law with the widespread practice of realist foreign policy based on the fact that in anarchic international relations each state must provide for its own security and economic welfare. International law and organization demand liberalism, but traditional international

---

[82] See especially Henry Kissinger, *Diplomacy* (New York: Simon & Schuster, 1994).

[83] Michael Mandelbaum, "Foreign Policy as Social Work," *Foreign Affairs*, 75, 1 (January/February 1996), 16–32. See the rejoinder by Stanley Hoffmann in the same journal, "In Defense of Mother Teresa," 75, 2 (March/April 1996), 172–176.

[84] Condoleezza Rice, "Promoting the National Interest," *Foreign Affairs*, 79, 1 (January/February 2000), 45–62. Ironically, when the Bush administration failed to adopt effective policies of nation-building in Iraq after ousting Saddam Hussein in 2003, starting with bungled occupation and transition policies, various horrors ensued which negatively affected US interests as well as many Iraqi lives.

relations has often produced realism. The nation-state system of inter-national relations produces insecurities and sometimes even paranoia, resulting in states sometimes adopting brutal self-centered policies.

In the dialectical clash of liberalism and realism, questions of human rights remain central. The liberal concept of human rights is a malleable and evolving notion. Without doubt new human rights norms would be adopted and new meanings read into existing documents, as new threats to human dignity emerged. When science made the cloning of animals possible, it gave rise to a new debate on the ethics of cloning, with laws sure to follow. When science made possible the freezing of sperm and delayed *in vitro* fertilization of the human egg, it produced both ethical debate and new legislation. Threats to human dignity change with time and place. International human rights standards, as means to ensure minimal standards of human dignity, change as well. It is a normal, even necessary, process to debate universal human rights in an effort to retain what is still sound and valid, and to make changes as moral and political judgment dictate. But how to protect human rights, however defined, in the state system of international relations remains a perplexing question.

Case study: more on crimes against humanity

There is no treaty specifically focused on crimes against humanity as there is, for example, on genocide or torture. Yet the crime exists in international law. Both international and national prosecutions have found individuals guilty of a crime against humanity. The history of the subject shows that international norms to protect against abuses of the individual or of individuals can evolve in various ways over considerable time.

In the more distant history of international relations one finds seman-tics about crimes against humanity, violations of the laws of humanity, enemies of the human family, crime against the whole world, and similar phrases. By 1907 and the Hague Regulations on the laws and customs of war, one can find reference to customary international law and crimes against humanity. But the particular act or acts said to make up this crime were not specified. The "law of humanity" remained vague, as well as the customs that gave rise to it. Sporadically there was moral outrage at certain acts, but translating this moral intuition into clear law was not quick or easy.

After World War I, the victorious powers discussed proceedings against the defeated Ottoman leadership for crimes against humanity as represented by the deaths, deportations, and other atrocities inflicted on ethnic Armenians particularly during that war. But no institutionalized measures resulted as other concerns took priority – from the return of prisoners of war to coping with the massive dislocations and epidemics that followed the war.

After World War II again the victors took aim at the losers, and this time the Nuremberg and Tokyo criminal courts addressed German and Japanese crimes against humanity in more specific terms. In the wake of the German Holocaust and Japanese atrocities particularly against Chinese and Koreans, both panels dealt with acts such as murder, extermination, enslavement, pseudo-medical experiments, deportation, and more. At this time it was fairly clear that the victors had in mind acts just before or during the war that were directed against the civilian population, whether domestic or foreign. The notion of war crimes did not clearly cover all of this subject matter, and the concept of genocide had not yet been codified.

Whatever the merits and demerits of these two examples of international criminal courts, the new United Nations General Assembly endorsed the broad outlines of these developments. But the entire subject of international criminal justice, with crimes against humanity as a subset, went into the deep freeze because of the Cold War. A thaw first occurred in 1993 with the creation of the International Criminal Tribunal for the former Yugoslavia (ICTY), followed the next year by the International Criminal Tribunal for Rwanda (ICTR). Both courts were created by the UN Security Council and were mandated to deal with genocide, war crimes, and crimes against humanity. Thus the two international criminal courts from 1945, warts and all, led to proceedings that were more procedurally correct some fifty years later. The ICTY and the ICTR demonstrated less victor's justice and more careful attention to due process than previously was the case.

The rules, regulations, and case law of these and subsequent international proceedings changed somewhat the notion of crimes against humanity. Torture and rape were added to the list of acts that could, in some contexts, constitute such crimes. Other treaties also expanded the definition; for example, enforced disappearance was added to the list of proscribed actions. Civilians remained the main target of protection, but some experts held that military personnel could also be victims. It came to be accepted that the crime could be committed in peacetime as well as during war, in internal as well as international armed conflict. How systematic and pervasive the act or acts had to be remained a matter of some dispute. Reports from the Office of the UN Secretary-General and from private organizations might or might not clarify changes as compared to muddying the definitional waters.

During the 1980s and 1990s there were also national laws, proceedings, and convictions for crimes against humanity in states such as Canada and France. These national judgments added complexity to definitions, as the wordings chosen by a set of judges did not always prove consistent with international or other national documents. In some states such as the United States, there were no statutory or judicial developments pertaining to the concept of a crime against humanity. What Washington endorsed in international relations was not translated into US domestic law. What Washington pursued in 1945–46 at Nuremberg it tended to downplay in later years.

In 1998 states, pushed by various advocacy groups, met in Rome to negotiate a permanent or standing International Criminal Court (ICC). This was in large part to eliminate the "transition costs" involved in creating various *ad hoc* criminal courts, which entailed considerable time, money, and diplomatic or political "capital." The resulting ICC again was delegated by states the task of addressing genocide, war crimes, and crimes against humanity. (These legal concepts could overlap; depending on facts, a defendant might be found guilty of all three for the same or similar actions.) States retained the primary responsibility for action in this domain, but when they proved unable or unwilling to discharge their responsibility through proper investigation and, when warranted, prosecution, the ICC was to be brought off the shelf and into action.

The treaty called the Rome Statute that created the ICC contained a modern formulation for the core notion of crimes against humanity. According to the Rome Statute, crimes against humanity entailed "particularly odious offences in that they constitute a serious attack on human dignity or grave humiliation or a degradation of one or more human beings. They are not isolated or sporadic events, but are part either of a government policy (although the perpetrators need not identify themselves with this policy) or of a wide practice of atrocities tolerated or condoned by a government or a *de facto* authority. Murder; extermination; torture; rape; political, racial, or religious persecution; and other inhumane acts reach the threshold of crimes against humanity only if they are part of a widespread or systematic practice."

Some experts maintained that the idea of crimes against humanity as found in customary international law was broader than that found in the Rome Statute. Nevertheless, from 1907 if not before, one found an intermittent political and legal process that spasmodically advanced and refined the idea of crimes against humanity.

In the ICTY the Serbian leader Slobodan Milosevic faced charges not only of war crimes and genocide but also of crimes against humanity.

(He died of natural causes in UN custody before the completion of his trial.) The ICC public prosecutor brought charges against the Sudanese leader Omar Hassan al-Bashir not only of war crimes and genocide but also of crimes against humanity. (The ultimate effect of this indictment and a subsequent arrest warrant was not clear at the end of 2016.) These and other developments in the early twenty-first century were very different from the vague reference to a law of humanity found in the 1907 Hague Convention. The concept of crimes against humanity had been greatly improved in specificity, even if not fully agreed upon, and both international and national courts sometimes carried out fair and independent proceedings to enforce this aspect of criminal justice. The core objective was to punish for, and hopefully deter against, certain gross violations of human rights. Certain individuals had made a difference in trying to develop law over time in order to protect human dignity against a background of atrocious policy by the likes of the Nazis.[85]

Discussion questions

• Do human rights derive from basic humane principles that are found in various societies around the world, as Professor Lauren argues, or do human rights derive from western liberal principles as Professor Donnelly argues? Should we expect non-western societies, without a long history of exposure to liberalism, to accept and protect human rights on a par with industrialized western democracies? Is it philosophical tradition that matters for the protection of human rights, or economic development? Where does India fit in this debate? South Korea? Botswana?

• Given the lack of connection between philosophical argument on the one hand, and on the other the widespread acceptance of human rights treaties, is the philosophy of human rights irrelevant to the practice of human rights? Or do we have great problems in applying human rights standards because we do not sufficiently understand the difference between liberalism and other "isms" like conservatism, communitarianism, and realism?

• What is the significance of widespread formal acceptance by states of the international law of human rights? When states consent to human rights treaties and diplomatic practice, is this realist hypocrisy? Is it sincere commitment to liberalism that they are sometimes unable to implement in specific situations? Why do states that practice liberalism

[85] See further Sands, *East West Street.*

and human rights at home sometimes find it difficult to advance human rights in international relations?

- Do international organizations (IOs) always reflect the policies of their most powerful members? Can international civil servants, less powerful states, and private organizations advance human rights through these IOs, even if the major states are not always in favor?
- Do we have human rights in the UN Charter because of a concern for the human dignity of persons, that is because of some sort of liberal crusade; or because of a concern for the security of states, that is because of realist concerns? Is it possible that human rights contribute to security? Is liberalism sometimes compatible with realism? And sometimes not?
- Do human rights properly encompass only civil and political rights, as Professor Cranston (and the USA) argues, or also economic and social rights as Professor Shue (and most of the rest of the world) argues? Should we recognize a third generation of solidarity rights including rights to development, peace, and a healthy or safe environment? Should we have a moratorium on further internationally recognized human rights until we can better implement the ones already recognized?

SUGGESTIONS FOR FURTHER READING

Best, Geoffrey, *War and Law Since 1945* (Oxford: Clarendon Press, 1994). A readable account of the modern development of international humanitarian law, its content, and efforts to apply it.

Brownlie, Ian, ed., *Basic Documents on Human Rights*, 3rd edn. (New York: Oxford University Press, 1992). An extensive and useful collection.

Claude, Inis L., Jr., *National Minorities* (Cambridge, MA: Harvard University Press, 1955). A classic study of the effort to use international law to protect minority rights in Europe in the interwar years, and of the causes of failure.

Cook, Rebecca J., *Human Rights of Women: National and International Perspectives* (Philadelphia: University of Pennsylvania Press, 1994). An excellent overview of a subject of growing importance.

Cranston, Maurice, "Human Rights, Real and Supposed," in D. D. Raphael, ed., *Political Theory and the Rights of Man* (Bloomington: Indiana University Press, 1967). A classic defense of civil and political rights, especially as utilitarian to state stability and security, and an attack on economic and social rights. Other chapters in this book are useful as well.

Crawford, Neta, *Argument and Change in World Politics: Ethics, Decolonization, and Humanitarian Intervention* (Cambridge: Cambridge University Press, 2002). A good study of the impact of ideas and arguments over time to delegitimize colonialism and other violations of human rights. In the last analysis, she is vague about the exact interaction of ideas, military power, and economic resources.

Donnelly, Jack, "Human Rights and Human Dignity: An Analytic Critique of Non-Western Human Rights Conceptions," *American Political Science*

Review, 76, 2 (June 1982), 433–449. A seminal article noting the distinction between human rights and other means to advance human dignity. Argues that human rights in history was an essentially Western construct.

Dunne, Tim, and Nicholas J. Wheeler, eds., *Human Rights in Global Politics* (Cambridge: Cambridge University Press, 1999). Advanced discussions of the conceptual bases of human rights and their relations to different cultures and societies. Addresses the question of whether human rights are violated because there is something fundamentally wrong with the concept of human rights in international relations.

Evans, Tony, *US Hegemony and the Project of Universal Human Rights* (New York: St. Martin's Press, 1996). A European academic takes a critical look at the US role in the evolution of international human rights standards, stressing the nefarious impact of American domestic politics on international developments.

ed., *Human Rights Fifty Years On: A Reappraisal* (Manchester: University of Manchester Press, 1998). A critical, even hypercritical, evaluation of international human rights fifty years after the adoption of the 1948 Universal Declaration of Human Rights.

Fields, A. Belden, *Rethinking Human Rights for the New Millennium* (New York: Palgrave Macmillan, 2003). A good introduction to the theory of human rights. A review of major thinkers is followed by Belden's own attempt at justification, centering on what is needed for proper development of the human personality.

Glendon, Mary Ann, *A World Made New: Eleanor Roosevelt and the Universal Declaration of Human Rights* (New York: Random House, 2001). A readable history showing how Roosevelt made her contributions through social diplomacy rather than engaging on the substantive wording of different articles in the Declaration.

Hannum, Hurst, *Autonomy, Sovereignty, and Self-Determination: The Accommodation of Conflicting Rights* (Philadelphia: University of Pennsylvania Press, 1992). A lawyer provides a sound review, with case studies, of how various claims to the collective human right of national self-determination have been handled in different parts of the world. A good blend of general legal principles with knowledge of specific problems.

Hunt, Paul, *Reclaiming Social Rights: International and Comparative Perspectives* (Aldershot: Dartmouth, 1996). One of the earlier books to give serious and in-depth treatment to economic and social rights, arguing that they are important, and some of them can be adjudicated.

Hutchinson, John F., *Champions of Charity: War and the Rise of the Red Cross* (Boulder: Westview, 1996). Takes a critical look at the International Red Cross and Red Crescent Movement from its origins in about 1859 to just after World War I. Stresses the strength of nationalism and militarism in the face of private efforts for victims of war.

Ignatieff, Michael, *Human Rights as Politics and Idolatry* (Princeton: Princeton University Press, 2001). Two short but provocative essays by a prolific Canadian thinker. He defends civil and political rights on the basis of historical pragmatism. He also sees human rights as individuals "worshipping" their own worth and agency.

Krasner, Stephen D., ed., *International Regimes* (Ithaca: Cornell University Press, 1983). Reprint of a special issue of the journal *International Organization* dealing with the concept of international regimes. Useful background for discussion of one or more international human rights regimes, a popular concept among social scientists.

Lauren, Paul Gordon, *The Evolution of International Human Rights: Visions Seen* (Philadelphia: University of Pennsylvania Press, 1998). Emphasizes the role of private organizations and individuals, including non-western ones, in advancing human rights over time in international relations. Argues that the human rights idea is not a strictly western one.

Maguire, Peter, *Law and War: An American Story*, rev. edn. (New York: Columbia University Press, 2010). An eye-opening account of the Nuremberg trials and their aftermath, showing that the USA was not fully committed to international criminal justice over time, making the complex judgment that there were other ways to advance pro-western democracy in West Germany.

Morsink, Johannes, *The Universal Declaration of Human Rights: Origins, Drafting, and Intent* (Philadelphia: University of Pennsylvania Press, 1998). The definitive treatment, fifteen years in the making, about this legislative process.

Moyn, Samuel, *The Last Utopia: Human Rights in History* (Cambridge, MA: Belknap for Harvard University Press, 2010). Against considerable evidence, argues that universal human rights were started about 1970 because of particular factors and had little connection to the 1930s and 1940s, much less any deeper roots.

Sands, Philippe, *East West Street: On the Origins of "Genocide" and "Crimes against Humanity"* (New York: Simon & Schuster, 2016). A readable and personalized history of the role of Hersh Lauterpact and Rafael Lemkin in developing important legal concepts in the 1940s. Both were Jewish and deeply affected by Nazi policies.

Sen, Amartya, *Development as Freedom* (New York: Anchor, 1999). A Nobel laureate in economics argues, like FDR, that persons in socioeconomic need are not free persons. Thus for him a certain socioeconomic development, especially in education and health care, is necessary for real freedom.

Shue, Henry, *Basic Rights: Subsistence, Affluence, and US Foreign Policy*, 2nd edn. (Princeton: Princeton University Press, 1997). An influential book arguing that the most important human rights cut across traditional categories, thus including some civil rights such as the right to life in the form of freedom from summary execution, and the right to life in the form of adequate food, clothing, and shelter. In his view, some economic and social rights are fundamental, being necessary for the enjoyment of certain other rights.

Sunstein, Cass R., *The Second Bill of Rights: FDR's Unfinished Revolution and Why We Need It More than Ever* (New York: Basic Books, 2004). An argument, grounded in American history, for socioeconomic rights, at least as "constitutive principles" if not as full-fledged constitutional or international law.

Winston, Morton, ed., *The Philosophy of Human Rights* (Belmont: Wadsworth, 1989). A sound overview.

Part II

Implementing human rights standards

3   Global application of human rights norms

In this chapter we examine more closely the evolving process for applying universal human rights standards on a global basis. We inquire whether there is now more commitment to liberalism, as shown through institutionalized procedures to protect human rights.

International law has traditionally been clearer about "What?" than "Who?"[1] The law has emphasized what legal rules apply in different situations. It has frequently not explicitly addressed who is authorized to make authoritative judgments about legal compliance. By default this means that states remain judge and jury in conflicts involving themselves – a principle accepted by no well-ordered society. Certainly the global law on human rights and humanitarian affairs has traditionally been characterized by decentralized decision making leading to much ambiguity about compliance. As this author concluded some time ago, "Most states, in negotiating human rights agreements, do not want authoritative international means of protection."[2] Many states have asserted an apparently liberal commitment to internationally recognized human rights (including humanitarian law for armed conflicts). But states have often elevated national independence, particularly the supremacy of national policy making, over the realization of universal human rights. States have wanted to retain the authority to delay or opt out of human rights commitments, for whatever reason.

Is this conventional wisdom still valid? This chapter will show that, first, global enforcement of human rights, in the form of international court judgments and other forms of direct international responsibility for the application of human rights standards, is still a relatively rare event. Direct protection by international agencies exists, but not often. Neither the International Court of Justice, nor other international courts, nor the

---

[1] David P. Forsythe, "Who Guards the Guardians: Third Parties and the Law of Armed Conflict," *American Journal of International Law*, 70, 2 (January 1976), 41–61.
[2] David P. Forsythe, *Human Rights and World Politics*, 2nd rev. edn. (Lincoln: University of Nebraska Press, 1989), 46.

UN Security Council frequently assumes direct responsibility in seeing that universal human rights norms prevail over competing values. This is so especially outside Europe. There may be some change under way on this point in the early twenty-first century, particularly for smaller or weaker states. But the generalization still holds, especially for the more powerful. The global international community does not often frontally and flagrantly override state sovereignty in the name of human rights despite the 2005 norm of an international responsibility to protect (R2P).

At the same time, states generally find themselves enmeshed in global governance.[3] By their own consent, they find themselves part of international legal regimes that generate diplomatic pressure to conform to human rights standards. While direct international protection or enforcement of human rights is mostly absent, attempts at indirect international implementation of human rights are frequently present. There still is no world government to systematically override state sovereignty. But there are arrangements for global governance to restrict and redefine state sovereignty. The effectiveness of these many implementation efforts, which still fall short of direct enforcement, is a matter requiring careful analysis.[4] (The matter of human rights treaties leading to compliance with their norms because of domestic politics is addressed later in this chapter and in Chapter 6.)

State sovereignty is not likely to disappear from world affairs any time soon, but it is being restricted and revised in a continuing and complex process.[5] Human rights norms are often at the core of this historical evolution. States may use their sovereignty to restrict their sovereignty in the name of human rights. In broad historical terms, the importance of internationally recognized human rights is increasing, and the value placed on full national independence decreasing. Liberalism is relatively more important in international relations than it used to be. But realism, especially in times of insecurity, is still a potent force. Moreover, at the

---

[3] Mark W. Zacher, "The Decaying Pillars of the Westphalian Temple: Implications for International Order and Governance," in James N. Rosenau and Ernst-Otto Czempiel, eds., *Governance Without Government: Order and Change in World Politics* (Cambridge: Cambridge University Press, 1992), 58–101. See further Thomas G. Weiss and Rorden Wilkinson, eds., *International Organization and Global Governance* (New York: Routledge, 2014); and Karen Alter, *The New Terrain of International Law* (Princeton: Princeton University Press, 2014).

[4] See further B. G. Ramcharan, *The Concept and Present Status of the International Protection of Human Rights* (Dordrecht: Martinus Nijhoff, 1989), 37 and *passim*.

[5] The realist Stephen Krasner, in *Sovereignty: Organized Hypocrisy* (Princeton: Princeton University Press, 1999), reminds us states have long endorsed state sovereignty and violated that norm when power allowed. See also his *Problematic Sovereignty* (New York: Columbia University Press, 2001).

time of writing there was a populist and nativist push back against many international trends including norms on refugees. This was not classical realism constructed on strategic thinking, but rather an emotional nationalism seeking to recreate a glorified national past.

Principal UN organs

The Security Council

A fair reading of the UN Charter, as it was drawn up in 1945, indicates that the Security Council was given primary responsibility for the maintenance of international peace and security, which meant issues of peace and war. On security issues the Council could take legally binding decisions under Chapter VII of the Charter pertaining to enforcement action. In addition, there were economic, social, cultural, and humanitarian issues. On these issues the Council, like the General Assembly, could make recommendations under Chapter VI. Presumably human rights fell into one of the categories other than security – such as social or humanitarian.

But the Council was authorized by the Charter to take action to remove threats to the peace. Logically, threats to the peace could arise from violations of human rights. In political fact, early in the life of the Security Council some states did attempt to bring human rights issues before it, precisely on grounds of a relationship to security. The early Council responded to these human rights issues in an inconsistent fashion,[6] being greatly affected by the Cold War. From about 1960 to the end of the Cold War, the Council began to deal more systematically with human rights issues as linked to four subjects: racism giving rise to violence – especially in southern Africa; human rights in armed conflict; armed intervention across international boundaries; and armed supervision of elections and plebiscites.[7] During this era the Council sometimes asserted a link between human rights issues and transnational violence. All of this is to say that the dividing line between security and human rights issues is sometimes unclear, and the history of the UN Security Council reflects this messy fact of life.

After the Cold War the Security Council, building on some of these earlier decisions, especially those pertaining to Southern Rhodesia and

---

[6] Sydney D. Bailey, "The Security Council," in Philip Alston, ed., *The United Nations and Human Rights: A Critical Appraisal* (Oxford: Clarendon Press, 1995), 304–336. The second edition, with Frederic Megret as second editor, is forthcoming.
[7] Ibid.

the Republic of South Africa, expanded the notion of international peace and security.[8] The line dividing security issues from human rights issues was often blurred. In these developments the Council was aware that, when dealing with especially internal conflicts, it was difficult to wind down the violence without addressing the human rights violations that drove much of the rebellion.[9] The Council thus expanded the range of Chapter VII enforcement action and stated, much more often compared with the past, that human rights violations were linked to international peace and security, thus permitting invocation of Chapter VII and even leading to an occasional enforcement action. In the process the Council shrank the scope of domestic jurisdiction protected by state sovereignty. In so doing, the Council implied more than once that security could refer to the security of persons within states, based on their human rights, and not just to traditional military violence across international frontiers. All these developments, mostly during the 1990s, held out the potential of increasing the UN Security Council's systematic action for human rights, based on pooled or collective sovereignty, relative to autonomous state sovereignty.

Five summary points deserve emphasis. First, there were numerous situations of violence in world affairs around the close of the Cold War; the UN Security Council did not address all of them. Vicious wars in places like Chechnya, Sri Lanka, and Algeria never drew systematic Council attention, much less bold assertions of international authority. Realist principles still mattered; if major states, especially the United States, did not see their narrow interests threatened, or believed a conflict resided in another's sphere of influence, the Council might not be activated.

Second, on occasion the Council has continued to say that human rights violations inside states can threaten international peace and security, at least implying the possibility of enforcement action under Chapter VII to correct the violations. In early 1992 a Council summit meeting of heads of state issued a very expansive statement indicating that threats to

---

[8] The Council invoked Chapter VII in the mid-1960s in dealing with the situation in Southern Rhodesia (now Zimbabwe) without making clear whether the central issue was illegal secession from the United Kingdom, racism and other violations of human rights including denial of national self-determination and majority rule, or fighting between the Patriotic Front and the Ian Smith government. The Council invoked Chapter VII in the late 1970s in dealing with the situation in the Republic of South Africa without making clear whether the issue was denial of majority rule or political violence and instability. For political reasons, the Council sometimes acts in ways that make life difficult for professors of international law.

[9] Thomas G. Weiss, "United Nations Security Council," in David P. Forsythe, ed., *Encyclopedia of Human Rights* (New York: Oxford University Press, 2009), vol. V, 204–209.

security could arise from economic, ecological, and social causes, not just traditional military ones.[10] Now, for example, there is growing concern about how environmental refugees, fleeing extreme-climate-induced geographical situations, might destabilize states.

Third, the Council sometimes made bold pronouncements on behalf of Council authority, but then proceeded to seek extensive consent from the parties to a conflict. Sometimes, as in dealing with Iraq in the spring of 1991, there were enough votes in the Council to declare the consequences of repression a matter that threatened international peace and security, but not enough votes to proceed to an explicit authorization to take collective military action. Sometimes, as in dealing with Somalia during 1992–1994, or Cambodia 1993–1996, or Bosnia in 1992–1995, the Council would adopt a bold stand in New York, asserting broad international authority, but in the field UN officials made every effort to obtain local consent for what the Council had mandated.[11]

Fourth, the Council has frequently deployed lightly armed forces in "peacekeeping operations" under Chapter VI, with the consent of the parties, to help ensure not just simple peace based on the constellation of military forces, but a more complex liberal democratic peace based on civil and political rights.[12]

Fifth, the Council has asserted the authority under Chapter VII to create *ad hoc* criminal courts, to prosecute and try those engaging in war crimes, crimes against humanity, and genocide. In this last regard the Council has asserted that all member states of the UN are legally obligated to cooperate with the *ad hoc* courts in order to pursue those who have committed certain gross violations of internationally recognized human rights. These courts are reviewed in Chapter 4. Other uses of Chapter VII are discussed below.

Other sources provide detailed information on the Security Council's invocation of Chapters VI and VII to deal with putative security issues since the end of the Cold War.[13] Aside from Iraq's invasion of Kuwait in

---

[10] S/23500, January 31, 1992, "Note by the President of the Security Council."

[11] On Somalia, see Mohamed Sahnoun, *Somalia: The Missed Opportunities* (Washington: US Institute for Peace Press, 1994). On Cambodia, see Steven J. Ratner, *The New UN Peacekeeping* (New York: St. Martin's Press, 1995).

[12] In addition to Ratner, *The New UN Peacekeeping*, see Ramesh Thakur and Carlyle A. Thayer, eds., *A Crisis of Expectations: UN Peacekeeping in the 1990s* (Boulder: Westview, 1995); Paul F. Diehl, *International Peacekeeping* (Baltimore: Johns Hopkins University Press, 1993); William J. Durch, *The Evolution of UN Peacekeeping: Case Studies and Comparative Analysis* (New York: St. Martin's Press, 1993).

[13] Lori Fisler Damrosch, ed., *Enforcing Restraint: Collective Intervention in Internal Conflicts* (New York: Council on Foreign Relations Press, 1993); James Mayall, ed., *The New Interventionism: United Nations Experience in Cambodia, Former Yugoslavia, and Somalia*

1990, and South Africa's involvement in Namibia, most of these situations drew international attention because of the death and debilitation of civilians inside states. The Security Council, no longer paralyzed by Cold War divisions, responded in various ways to instability and violence, mostly in the global south but also in the Western Balkans.

To cite just two examples, the Council manifested prolonged engagement in both with the Democratic Republic of the Congo (DRC), where more persons had been killed in political conflict than any other place on the planet during a five-year period since 1945,[14] and Sudan, where millions were affected by displacement, rape, disease and malnutrition, and political killing in the western province of Darfur. At one point the USA labeled the situation in the latter case as genocide.[15] Moreover, the creation of the new state of South Sudan in 2011 was followed by vicious internal struggles for power and another complex UN security operation. On the one hand the Council authorized a security force to try to protect civilians. On the other hand the Council lacked the political will to try to impose a cessation of hostilities. And so the conflict dragged on like in the DRC and Darfur.

With due respect to the continuing importance of interstate conflict in places such as Afghanistan and Iraq when invaded by the USA, nevertheless the most striking feature about Security Council action after the Cold War was its willingness to deal with conflicts whose origins were essentially national rather than international. The central issues of conflict revolved around "who governs" and "how humanely." For example, this was precisely the issue in Ivory Coast in 2011, where a UN security field mission was caught up in disputes about free and fair elections and who should rule the country. The UN mission was trapped between demands that it leave from the politician trying to cling to power, and instructions from the Security Council that it stay in order to contribute to legitimate order and good governance.

In a few of these situations there were indeed international dimensions to the conflict that pushed the Council into action. Iraqi flight into Iran and Turkey, Haitian flight to the United States, Rwandan flight into

---

(Cambridge: Cambridge University Press, 1996). See also Richard M. Price and Mark W. Zacher, eds., *The United Nations and Global Security* (New York: Palgrave, 2005); and Michael J. Matheson, *Council Unbound: The Growth of UN Decision Making on Conflict and Postconflict Issues After the Cold War* (Washington: US Institute of Peace, 2006). Finally, see Vaughan Lowe, et al., eds., *The United Nations Security Council and War: The Evolution of Thought and Practice Since 1945* (New York: Oxford University Press, 2008), for an encyclopedic overview.

[14] See further Emizet F. Kisangani, "Democratic Republic of the Congo," in *Encyclopedia of Human Rights*, vol. II, 12–20.

[15] See further Linda Bishai, "Darfur," in *Encyclopedia of Human Rights*, vol. I, 470–480.

Tanzania and eastern Zaire, for example, did call for an international response. The Syrian internationalized civil war affected a number of neighboring counties and much of Europe as well, primarily because of sizable refugee flows. The protracted political instability of the DRC invited unauthorized military intervention by a handful of neighboring states, interested either in natural resources or eliminating sanctuaries for enemies. In places like El Salvador and Bosnia, among others, there was real concern that the violence might expand to engulf nearby states. Yet in places like Somalia, Cambodia, and Guatemala, the international dimensions were originally not so pressing. In Ivory Coast there was some movement of fighters across borders and some transnational flight of civilians. The really core issues, however, remained those pertaining to effective and democratic and humane governance – which inherently raised questions about human rights.

Syria presented the ultimate challenge – and ultimate failure – at the time of writing. When peaceful demands for the removal of the autocratic Bashar al-Assad government was met by savage repression in 2011, the United States had been fighting in Afghanistan since late 2001 and in Iraq since 2003. The Obama Administration was trying to extract itself from deep involvement in the Middle East in order to shift its primary attention to Asia. Moreover, more than one armed group challenging Assad was anti-Western and no friend of universal human rights. Still further, Russia under President Putin increasingly intervened on the side of Assad, apparently convinced that the USA was trying to impose its will on the world, including encircling and undermining Russia as during the Cold War. The worsening relations between Washington and Moscow, as in the Cold War, made decisive action by the Council impossible on Syria and some other issues.

The Council's response in Libya had complicated matters. The Council authorized a no-fly zone in order to protect civilians threatened by Kaddafi's forces in 2011. Russia and China abstained on the vote, despite knowing that it would be some NATO states plus a few pro-Western Arab states enforcing the Council's resolution. Those NATO states then used their military power not just to protect civilians but to support armed groups trying to depose the long-standing but isolated dictator. His capture and death no more brought stability and rights to Libya than Saddam's capture and death stabilized a liberal Iraq. In both cases, the dictator's downfall was followed by much violence and misery. In Libya from 2012 there was not only instability, terrorism, and unregulated migration, but hard feelings by China and Russia who felt the United States and its allies had played fast and loose with the intent of Council resolutions. On the ground many Libyans opposed the type of prolonged UN involvement that had characterized Bosnia and the western Balkans. But they lacked the agreement and capability to replace Kaddafi with a responsible government. So intervention authorized by the UNSC led to a hell of good intentions.

One bright aspect of this general picture was the willingness of the Council to expand the notions of both security and Chapter VII to try to improve the personal security of citizens inside various states by improving attention to their human rights. "Human security" became a new buzzword at the United Nations.[16]

A related development was the UN General Assembly's declaration of R2P: the Responsibility to Protect. This 2005 statement asserted that if a state was "unwilling or unable" to properly exercise its national sovereignty so as to preclude atrocities, outside parties had a duty to get involved in keeping with international law. The authors of this idea of R2P tried to stress diplomatic involvement in order to deal with festering problems. If the internal difficulties could be managed, outside coercive intervention would be forestalled. Timely attention to potential genocide, crimes against humanity (including ethnic cleansing), and major war crimes would obviate the need for "humanitarian intervention" through military force. The intent was not to frontally override national sovereignty but to help in its proper exercise.[17] A follow-on UN report stressed steps that could be taken within a nation to stop any drift toward atrocities.[18]

The not-so-bright aspect of this big picture was the gap between the blizzard of Council resolutions endorsing human rights and even making reference to Chapter VII enforcement actions, and the paucity of political will to take the costly steps necessary to make Council resolutions effective on the ground. In Somalia in the early 1990s, the Council declared that to interfere with the delivery of humanitarian assistance was a war crime. But when certain Somalis not only continued to interfere with relief, but killed eighteen US Rangers in one incident, the USA removed most of its military personnel from the country. Extensive starvation was eventually checked in Somalia, but national reconciliation and humane

---

[16] Lloyd Axworthy, "Human Security: An Opening for UN Reform," in Richard M. Price and Mark W. Zacher, eds., *The United Nations and Global Security* (New York: Palgrave, 2004), 245–260. See also Edward Newman and Oliver P. Richmond, *The United Nations and Human Security* (New York: Palgrave, 2001). The discourse on human security might or might not be expressly linked to human rights as noted in Chapter 2.

[17] Gareth Evans, *The Responsibility to Protect: Ending Mass Atrocity Crimes Once and for All* (Washington: Brookings, 2008).

[18] Stephen McLoughlin, "From Reaction to Resilience in Mass Atrocity Prevention: An Analysis of the 2013 UN Report," *Global Governance*, 22, 4 (Fall, 2016), 473–490.

governance were not quickly established. US casualties in Somalia caused Washington to block deployment of a significant UN force in Rwanda, despite clear and massive genocide.[19] It was one thing for diplomats in New York to say the right words. It was another thing for nations to accept costs when protecting the rights of "others" when not seen as involving their vital national interests.

In former Yugoslavia 1992–1995, the Council focused in large part on human rights and humanitarian issues in order to avoid tough decisions about self-determination of peoples and later collective security for Bosnia. When the Council did authorize strong measures particularly against Bosnian Serbs and their supporters, and when the Serbs responded in tough ways, such as by taking UN personnel hostage, the Council generally backed down. The Council was willing to declare "safe areas" within Bosnia, but then it refused to provide the military forces necessary to effectively defend them, which again set the stage for massacres at Srebrenica and elsewhere.[20] The key states on the Council, meaning the USA, France, and Britain, had no stomach for decisive but costly action in places like Bosnia and Cambodia, Somalia and Rwanda.[21]

In the DRC, the UN Security Council only put a small contingent of blue helmets on the ground, policing just a small area of that very large state. A later expansion of this force was much less than what the Secretary-General recommended. In Sudan, to cope with massive misery in the area of western Darfur, the Council tried to mobilize troops through the African Union (formerly the Organization of African States). But the process proceeded slowly, with much foot-dragging by the government in Khartoum and various other parties not tremendously concerned about death and destruction in the African part of that tormented country. A joint UN-AU field operation lacked the military muscle and diplomatic backing to be fully effective.

This trend of limited and indecisive action by the international community to guarantee human security made NATO's intervention in Kosovo in 1999 all the more remarkable. With the western states bypassing the Security Council because of Chinese and Russian opposition to what the West wanted to do, NATO and particularly the United States

---

[19] The ethics of non-intervention in Rwanda are well discussed in Michael A. Barnett, *Eyewitness to a Genocide: The United Nations and Rwanda* (Ithaca: Cornell University Press, 2002).

[20] Srebrenica represented the worst massacre in Europe since World War II. See David Rohde, *End Game: The Betrayal and Fall of Srebrenica* (Boulder: Westview, 1997).

[21] Edward Luttwak, "Where Are the Great Powers?," *Foreign Affairs*, 73, 4 (July/August, 1994), 23–29.

expended considerable treasure and prestige to try to stop and then reverse the repression, ethnic cleansing, and other violations of human rights being visited upon ethnic Albanians by the Serbian-dominated government of Yugoslavia.[22] In a portentous development, members of NATO declared that the absence of liberal democracy in Yugoslavia – especially in the internal province of Kosovo – constituted a vital interest, justifying the use of military force despite the absence of explicit Security Council authorization. Eventually Kosovo's declaration of independence was recognized by western states, which was sometimes cited by Russian authorities as precedent when they detached by force the Crimea from Ukraine in 2014.

Yet the main problem for most situations of human insecurity remained lack of humanitarian intervention, not too much of it. NATO's intervention in Kosovo – and then Libya in 2011 – remained the exceptions that proved the general rule. The international community normally did not intervene decisively and quickly in response to gross violations of human rights. This was true in Burma/Myanmar, Sri Lanka, and other places – above all in Syria from 2011. Transnational morality remained thin or weak. Often, third parties with the military muscle to make a difference perceived no vital interest at risk in the situation. Sometimes former colonial powers roused themselves to action, as did the British in Sierra Leone and the French in Ivory Coast. At other times the former colonial power was part of the problem, as were the French in Rwanda with their support for militant Hutus. The USA's President Obama was very clear and consistent in his views about not intervening decisively in Syria from 2011: the Middle East would have to sort out its own problems over time; one had to be hard-headed about what was doable at reasonable cost.[23]

Despite the inconsistency of state policies which drove Council proceedings, some improvements were achieved. A study by the Rand Corporation showed that when the UN undertook moderately challenging field operations directed to establishing humane governance after violent conflict, the organization used its experience and soft power to manage matters reasonably well, although some problems were evident – such as delay in the arrival of resources and inconsistency in quality of personnel loaned by states.[24] This study concluded that the UN record

---

[22] A good inside look at the details of the process can be found in Wesley Clark, *Waging Modern War* (New York: Perseus, 2002).

[23] Jeffrey Goldberg, "The Obama Doctrine," *The Atlantic Magazine*, April 2016, www.theatlantic.com/magazine/archive/2016/04/the-obama-doctrine/471525/.

[24] James Dobbins, et al., *The UN's Role in Nation-Building: From the Congo to Iraq* (Santa Monica, CA: Rand, 2005).

in deployment of force was not inferior to that of the USA, although the latter took on tougher situations in places like Afghanistan and Iraq from about 2002–2003.

The overall record of the Council on human rights issues after the Cold War was complex, defying simple summation. Clearly the Council was more extensively involved in trying to help apply human rights standards than ever before. It had demonstrated on a number of occasions that human rights protections could be intertwined with considerations of peace and security. It had certainly blurred the outer boundaries of state sovereignty and its corollary, domestic jurisdiction. If it lacked the collective political will to make effective on the ground some of its bolder pronouncements from New York, it had nevertheless expanded second-generation peacekeeping to encompass more attention to a rather broad range of human rights.[25] The Council also increased its references not just to human rights but also to humanitarian affairs.[26]

A continuing problem was the inconsistent record of the Permanent Five (P-5) members of the Security Council when dealing with human rights and conflict. This was certainly true of the USA, which took much more interest in Kosovo than in almost all problems in Africa (even before it became preoccupied with Afghanistan and Iraq after September 11, 2001). Britain and France had not been on the front lines of those pressing for action in Rwanda and Sudan. Yet they did press for military action under a UN mandate in Libya in 2011. Russia and China were consistently hesitant about using the UNSC to endorse military action to protect human rights, yet they too were inconsistent – threatening to veto action to protect the Kosovars but abstaining on the resolution authorizing all necessary means to protect civilians in Libya. Clearly the Council was a political as well as legal institution.

Office of the Secretary-General

Although relatively little has been published about the Office of the UN Secretary-General and human rights, it appears that two factors explain a great deal about the evolution of events in this area. On the one hand, as human rights have become more institutionalized in UN affairs,

[25] For an overview of UN second-generation peacekeeping and human rights, see David P. Forsythe, "Human Rights and International Security: United Nations Field Operations Redux," in Monique Castermans-Holleman, et al., eds., *The Role of the Nation-State in the 21st Century* (The Hague: Kluwer, 1998), 265–276.
[26] Weiss, "UN Security Council." See further George Nolte, "The Different Functions of the Security Council with Respect to Humanitarian Law," in Lowe, et al., eds., *UN Security Council and War*, 519–534.

Secretaries-General have spoken out more frequently and been generally more active in this domain.[27] There is almost a straight-line progression on increasing action by Secretaries-General on human rights over time. Second, while all Secretaries-General have given priority to trying to resolve issues of international peace and security, increasingly they have found human rights intertwined with security. In so far as security issues can be separated from human rights, rights issues tended to be either downgraded or dealt with by quiet diplomacy – because UN officials, to be effective, have to avoid a rupture with major states.[28] If U Thant had been outspoken in condemning communist violations of human rights, it is doubtful he would have been acceptable to the Soviet Union for sensitive mediation in the 1962 Cuban missile crisis. In contemporary times, with human rights increasingly institutionalized within the UN and meshed with many security concerns, a Secretary-General like Kofi Annan appeared to be more willing to take firm stands for the protection of human rights. The fate of his nomination of Mary Robinson, former President of Ireland, to be the second High Commissioner for Human Rights, however, indicates that all executive authority in the UN, as an intergovernmental system, remains fragile – as explained below.

From the earliest days of the UN there were Secretariat officials active in the promotion of human rights through setting of standards, even if they were not able to achieve a great deal in specific protection efforts.[29] At the highest level, however, neither Trygve Lie nor Dag Hammarskjöld showed much direct and clear interest in internationally recognized human rights. Lie became ineffective and eventually resigned because of his clear opposition to the communist invasion of South Korea, and there is no reason to think the result would have been any different had he strongly opposed communist violations of human rights. During the Cold War, forthright and public stands on any major issue were likely to make any Secretary-General *persona non grata* to one coalition or the other. Hammarskjöld was, surprisingly enough given his Swedish nation-ality and overall dynamism and creativity, not to mention his religious

---

[27] David P. Forsythe, "The UN Secretary-General and Human Rights: The Question of Leadership in a Changing Context," in Benjamin Rivlin and Leon Gordenker, eds., *The Challenging Role of the UN Secretary-General: Making "The Most Impossible Job in the World" Possible* (Westport: Praeger, 1993), 211–232. See also Kent J. Kille, ed., *The UN Secretary-General and Moral Authority: Ethics and Religion in International Leadership* (Washington: Georgetown University Press, 2007).

[28] In addition to Forsythe, "The UN Secretary-General and Human Rights," see Theo van Boven, "The Role of the United Nations Secretariat," in Alston, ed., *United Nations and Human Rights*, 549–579.

[29] John P. Humphrey, *Human Rights and the United Nations: A Great Adventure* (Dobbs Ferry: Transnational, 1984).

mysticism, not much interested in human rights at the UN. While he was willing to take a strong stand on security issues in the Belgian Congo (now Zaire), even to the point of serious friction with both the Soviet Union and France, he never devoted much effort to more than a handful of rights issues via quiet diplomacy.

After U Thant, a transitional figure for present purposes, both Kurt Waldheim and Perez de Cuellar showed relatively more interest in the protection of human rights. Given the personal histories of the two men, this trend is partly explained by the institutionalization factor. The Austrian Waldheim had been in the Nazi army and had consistently misrepresented that part of his past. De Cuellar had been a traditional Peruvian diplomat well versed in diplomacy based on state sovereignty, whose first major act as Secretary-General was to decide not to renew the contract of the then activist UN Director of Human Rights – the Dutchman Theo van Boven.[30] Van Boven had proved an irritant to both the military junta in Argentina and the Reagan Administration in Washington, then aligned with Buenos Aires. Yet both Waldheim and de Cuellar turned out to be more active in the protection of human rights than their predecessors, clearly so in de Cuellar's case.[31] Particularly in dealing with Central America, de Cuellar came to realize that peace and security in places like Nicaragua and El Salvador depended on progress in human rights. He therefore helped arrange deeply intrusive rights agreements, especially in El Salvador, and persistently acted to rein in death squads and other gross violators of human rights through his mediation and other diplomatic actions.[32] By the end of his second term, de Cuellar held quite different views on the importance of human rights, compared with when he entered office and got rid of van Boven.[33]

Boutros Boutros-Ghali was the most outspoken Secretary-General on human rights up to that time, making a strong case in particular for democracy. His *Agenda for Development* strongly advocated democratic

---

[30] See further Theo van Boven, *People Matter: Views on International Human Rights Policy* (Amsterdam: Beulenhoff Netherlands, 1982).

[31] De Cuellar listed human rights second in importance only to disarmament among pressing issues. See his "The Role of the UN Secretary-General," in Adam Roberts and Benedict Kingsbury, eds., *United Nations, Divided World: The UN's Roles in International Relations*, 2nd edn. (Oxford: Clarendon, 1993), 125 and *passim*. See also Barbara Ann J. Rieffer-Flanagan and David P. Forsythe, "Religion, Ethics, and Reality: A Study of Javier-Perez de Cuellar," in Kille, ed., *UN Secretary-General*, 229–264.

[32] See the details in David P. Forsythe, "The United Nations, Democracy, and the Americas," in Tom J. Farer, ed., *Beyond Sovereignty: Collectively Defending Democracy in the Americas* (Baltimore: Johns Hopkins University Press, 1996), 107–131.

[33] This argument, already expressed in print, I recently reconfirmed via interviews with some of those close to de Cuellar during his time in New York and with the former Secretary-General himself in interviews in Paris.

development, based on civil and political rights, at a time when the General Assembly and the World Bank were, to put it kindly, less than clear in their support for civil and political rights.[34] He thus sought to correct what had been a major deficiency in human rights programming at the UN, the lack of integration between human rights and development activities.[35] A human rights dimension was present in a number of his decisions in places such as Somalia (seeing militia leader Aideed as a war criminal) and Rwanda (expressing regret that he did not persuade the USA to take more action), but this dimension was not so evident in certain other decisions.[36]

As for Kofi Annan, he may have displayed the strongest commitment to human dignity of any of the UN Secretaries-General, and he once suggested that action for human rights should generally override state sovereignty.[37] Yet like the other UN Secretaries-General, his options and policy positions were constrained by member states and their interests. And so Annan was necessarily implicated in the UN's lack of decisive action for human rights in places such as the Balkans and Rwanda, among other situations. As noted below, he responded to US pressures by getting rid of Mary Robinson when she was UN High Commissioner for Human Rights, similar to de Cuellar's sidelining of van Boven. Still, both because of his own personal values and because human rights were institutionalized in UN affairs by the time of his tenure, Annan is generally associated with as strong a support for human rights as his political context allowed. Certainly by comparison to his successor, Ban Ki-moon, Annan was widely seen as having compiled a reasonable record on human rights overall.

Secretary-General Ban, certainly in comparison with Annan, was lacking in a kind of quiet charisma. Like many office holders, he grew into the job and became more outspoken about rights toward the end of his two terms. During his last months in office he strongly castigated various governments for their narrow nationalism and pursuit of

---

[34] A/48/935 (1994). See further David P. Forsythe, "The United Nations, Human Rights, and Development," *Human Rights Quarterly*, 19, 2 (May 1997), 334–349. See further Anthony F. Lang, Jr., "A Realist in the Utopian City: Boutros Boutros-Ghali's Ethical Framework and Its Impact," in Kille, ed., *UN Secretary-General*, 265–298.

[35] Theo van Boven, "Human Rights and Development: The UN Experience," in David P. Forsythe, ed., *Human Rights and Development: International Views* (London: Macmillan, 1989), 121–136. Compare James Gustave Speth, "Poverty: A Denial of Human Rights," *Journal of International Affairs*, 52, 1 (Fall 1998), 277–292.

[36] See Lang, "Realist in the Utopian City."

[37] Courtney B. Smith, "Politics and Values at the United Nations: Kofi Annan's Balancing Act," in Kille, ed., *UN Secretary-General*, 299–336.

narrow national interests at the expense of universal values and international cooperation.[38]

The Secretary-General appoints the UN High Commissioner for Human Rights, a post created by the UN General Assembly in 1993, subject to the (*pro forma*) approval of that body.[39] Boutros-Ghali appointed the Ecuadoran, José Ayala Lasso, as the first UN High Commissioner for Human Rights, probably hoping to assuage the fears of developing countries that the new post would be used only to hammer them on issues of civil and political rights. Thus the Secretary-General probably hoped to encourage acceptance by developing countries over time of this new and somewhat controversial post. The new High Commissioner had been a foreign minister in a previous military government in Quito.[40] Upon Ayala Lasso's resignation to return to Ecuadoran politics, Secretary-General Annan turned to Mary Robinson, a lawyer with a record of dynamism especially on issues affecting women and the less fortunate in Ireland, which gave the promise of more dynamism on rights issues. The Cold War was over, human rights had been integrated with many UN security concerns, and much of the powerful West was demanding more vigorous UN diplomacy for human rights. The USA, the most important of the P-5, was very happy with the nomination of Robinson and her subsequent approval by the General Assembly.

One of the reasons for having a UN High Commissioner for Human Rights was to free the Secretary-General in public diplomacy to concentrate on security issues. A dynamic High Commissioner might play the role that van Boven tried to play as Director of the UN Human Rights Program. But since the Director was nominated by the Secretary-General, and without an independent power base, disaffected countries like Argentina under military rule could bring pressure on him through having a patron – in this case the Reagan Administration – lobby the Secretary-General to rein in or get rid of a human rights official like van Boven causing a state embarrassment.[41]

---

[38] See www.huffingtonpost.com/entry/ban-ki-moon-donald-trump-refugees_us_58010892 e4b06e0475947895.

[39] For a concise overview of this office, see Theo van Boven, "United Nations High Commissioner for Human Rights," in *Encyclopedia of Human Rights*, vol. V, 173–182. For a very good overview, see Gelice D. Gaer and Christen L. Broecker, eds., *The United Nations High Commissioner for Human Rights: Conscience for the World* (Leiden and Boston: Martinus Nijhoff, 2014).

[40] Ayala Lasso did originate the operation of UN field offices for human rights, generating grassroots activities for human rights within consenting countries. See further Alfred de Zayas, "Jose Ayala Lasso," in *Encyclopedia of Human Rights*, vol. I, 130–132.

[41] See further Iain Guest, *Behind the Disappearances: Argentina's Dirty War Against Human Rights and the United Nations* (Philadelphia: University of Pennsylvania Press, 1990).

In theory, an independent High Commissioner, once appointed in a higher-profile position created by the General Assembly, had slightly more protection from such pressures. But the fate of Robinson, the second High Commissioner for Human Rights, suggested that things had not progressed much beyond the era of de Cuellar and van Boven. Robinson was so outspoken about rights violations in places such as China, Israel, and Russia – and also by the USA regarding treatment of enemy prisoners after 9/11 – that she raised questions about whether her activism was matched by enough diplomatic acumen. Especially after a UN conference at Durban, South Africa on the subject of racism and xenophobia, in which the USA and Israel walked out after repeated speeches denouncing Israel, Washington became deeply dissatisfied with Robinson. The George W. Bush Administration leaned on the Secretary-General, Kofi Annan, not to renew her contract. He finally did as Washington desired, although Robinson wanted to continue.[42] The critique of Robinson for being too outspoken in defense of human rights was somewhat ironic, given that the first High Commissioner, Ayala Lasso of Ecuador, had been criticized by a number of human rights advocacy groups for being too diplomatic and not assertive enough. This indicates the crosspressures that UN officials have to manage.

After Robinson, the Secretary-General then nominated, and the General Assembly approved, Sergio de Mello of Brazil, who was an experienced diplomat with a career in the UN refugee office. But he was killed by an insurgent bombing in Iraq, and so Louise Arbour of Canada became the UN High Commissioner for Human Rights. She was a jurist, formerly the prosecutor for the UN *ad hoc* criminal court for Yugoslavia (covered in Chapter 4). She was widely respected and had more of a "judicial temperament" than Robinson. Seeing what had happened to Robinson, early on she relied more on quiet diplomacy than public criticism. Yet over time she, too, spoke out on a number of issues and also was criticized by, in particular, the George W. Bush Administration in the USA.[43]

Arbour was followed by Navi Pillay, a female jurist of Asian descent from South Africa. Pillay proved dynamic and assertive, did not hesitate to speak out on a variety of rights issues including gay rights, but managed not to consistently offend the major governments of her time. She combined the personal commitment of Mary Robinson with the

---

[42] See David P. Forsythe, "Mary Robinson," in *Encyclopedia of Human Rights*, vol. IV, 347–349.
[43] See further William A. Schabas, "Louise Arbour," ibid., vol. II, 88–91.

strategizing of Louise Arbour, setting an exemplary record for that difficult office.

She in turn was followed by Zeid Ra'ad al-Hussein of Jordan. Al-Hussein had held many positions for Jordan and also for the United Nations. The first Muslim to hold the position, he had been highly active in the creation of the International Criminal Court. He did not hesitate to publicly criticize a number of governments as well as the Islamic State group. On occasion he noted defects in the rights policies of the United States despite Jordan's close ties to Washington and London.

In sum, the Office of the Secretary-General, including after 1993 the related office of the UN High Commissioner for Human Rights, represented the purposes of the organization as found in the Charter. Among these purposes was international cooperation on human rights. Yet most important decisions taken in the name of the UN were taken by states, and the Secretary-General, while independent, was also given instructions by states acting collectively through UN organs. Moreover, he (or she in the future) could only be effective when he retained the confidence of the more important states. Thus there was room for action on human rights, which Secretaries-General had progressively exercised as human rights became more and more a regular part of international and UN affairs. The Secretary-General's protective action, beyond promotional activities, consisted mostly of reasoning in quiet diplomacy.

But there were also major constraints imposed by states – such as lack of real commitment to international human rights, lack of consensus on priorities, and lack of adequate funding. Even as states endorsed human rights norms, they still did not like being criticized in public on human rights issues, as especially Theo van Boven and Mary Robinson discovered when they were eased out of office. It was certainly ironic that the USA, which often presented itself to the world as a model on human rights, undercut both van Boven and Robinson when an ally – military government in Argentina or Israel as occupying power – was publicly criticized by the UN High Commissioner for Human Rights. Particularly the George W. Bush Administration, with its strong unilateralist tendencies at times, did not take kindly to public criticisms of its detention and interrogation policies at Guantanamo and other places by Robinson and Arbour.

Other main organs: the General Assembly, ECOSOC, and the ICJ

The GA The UN General Assembly has been instrumental in the promotion of human rights, approving some two dozen treaties and adopting a number of "motherhood" resolutions endorsing various human rights in general. It was the Assembly that adopted the norm of R2P. The Assembly has played a much less important role in the protection of specific human rights in specific situations, although much ambiguity inheres in this subject. The Assembly has mandated a number of new UN offices to deal with human rights.

One can take a minimalist approach and note that the General Assembly did not try to reverse certain decisions taken in the Economic and Social Council (ECOSOC) and the UN Human Rights Commission that were directed to specific protection attempts (see below).[44] Furthermore, since many of the treaty monitoring mechanisms report to the Assembly, the same can be said for the Assembly's review of those bodies (see below). More optimistically, after the Cold War as before, the Assembly adopted a number of specific resolutions condemning human rights violations in various countries.[45] During the Cold War, it is likely that repeated Assembly condemnation of Israeli and South African policies had little immediate remedial effect on those two target states, as they viewed the Assembly as inherently biased against them. This was certainly the case when the Assembly declared Zionism to be a form of racism in 1975, a resolution eventually rescinded in 1991. (Some of the standard arguments about Zionism as racism, however, were renewed at the Durban I conference of 2001 mentioned above. They did not figure prominently at Durban II in 2009.)[46] It is possible that repeated Assembly attacks on apartheid policies in South Africa contributed to an international normative climate in which powerful states eventually brought pressure to bear on racist South Africa.[47] How ideas as expressed in Assembly resolutions affect states' definitions of their national interests remains a murky matter.[48] In any event the Assembly shrank the realm of state sovereignty by demonstrating clearly that

[44] John Quinn, "The General Assembly into the 1990s," in Alston, ed., United Nations and Human Rights, 55–106.

[45] Soo Yeon Kim and Bruce Russett, "The New Politics of Voting Alignments in the United Nations General Assembly," International Organization, 50, 4 (Autumn 1996), 629–652.

[46] On the politics of victimhood as it relates to struggles over legitimacy, see Pierre Hazan, Judging War, Judging History: Behind Truth and Reconciliation (Stanford: Stanford University Press, 2007). Israel has sought to bolster its legitimacy by reference to its hosting victims of the Holocaust, while some developing countries present themselves as the victims of imperialism and colonialism, picturing Israel as part of those processes. These views played out in various UN meetings.

[47] See further Audie Klotz, "Norms Reconstituting Interests: Global Racial Equality and US Sanctions Against South Africa," International Organization, 49, 3 (Summer 1995), 451–478.

[48] See further Judith Goldstein and Robert O. Keohane, eds., Ideas and Foreign Policy: Beliefs, Institutions and Political Change (Ithaca: Cornell University Press, 1993); and

diplomatic discussion of specific human rights situations in specific countries was indeed part of routinized international relations, even if the Assembly displayed a tendency to adopt paper solutions to complex and controversial subjects.[49] As one expert noted, the UN General Assembly did not invent the politicization of human rights, as political debates are inherent in construction and interpretation of the concept. So it should come as no surprise that the Assembly was the scene of different disputes as state members from a diverse world contested meanings, priorities, and targets of action.[50] As suggested above, it was clear that states did not like to be criticized in the Assembly on human rights, as this criticism was seen as affecting their sense of legitimacy – which was a perceptual matter.

ECOSOC ECOSOC, officially one of the UN's principal organs, very rapidly became little more than a mailbox between the Assembly and various bodies subsidiary to ECOSOC, transmitting or reaffirming instructions from the Assembly to a proliferation of social and economic agencies. ECOSOC is not, and has never been, a major actor for human rights.[51] The states elected to ECOSOC have taken three decisions of importance since 1945 regarding human rights, one essentially negative and two positive. First, ECOSOC decided that the members of the UN Human Rights Commission should be state representatives and not independent experts. This decision put the foxes inside the hen house. Later ECOSOC adopted its resolution 1235, permitting the Commission to take up specific complaints about specific countries. Resolution 1503 was also eventually adopted, permitting the Commission to deal with private petitions indicating a systematic pattern of gross violations of internationally recognized human rights. While ECOSOC resolutions 1235 and 1503 affected considerable diplomacy, they did not lead to sure protection of human rights on the ground.

In addition, ECOSOC maintains a committee that decides which nongovernmental organizations (NGOs) will be given which category of consultative status with the UN system. The highest status allows NGOs to attend UN meetings and submit documents. Both before and after the Cold War, this committee was the scene of various struggles

Albert S. Yee, "The Causal Effects of Ideas on Politics," *International Organization*, 50, 1 (Winter 1996), 69–108.
[49] Antonio Cassese, "The General Assembly: Historical Perspective 1945–1989," in Alston, ed., *United Nations and Human Rights*, 25–54.
[50] M. J. Peterson, "United Nations General Assembly," in *Encyclopedia of Human Rights*, vol. V, 165–172.
[51] Declan O'Donovan, "The Economic and Social Council," in Alston, ed., *United Nations and Human Rights*, 107–125.

over human rights NGOs. Certain states that were defensive about human rights matters tried, with periodic success, to deny full status, or sometimes any status, to legitimate human rights NGOs. These problems diminished by the end of the twentieth century. Still, in the late 1990s, a western-based NGO that had antagonized the Sudanese government and engaged in a controversial policy of buying back hostages taken in Sudan's longrunning civil war (such a policy provided money to the fighting parties and led to the retaking of sometimes the same hostages) was denied consultative status.

Finally, ECOSOC officially supervises a number of UN agencies such as the UN Development Program (UNDP). UNDP remains primarily a development agency but clearly it has increased its activities pertaining to human rights associated with democracy and the status of women. Its Human Development Reports are widely cited; they chart indicators of sustainable human development – a broad concept that overlaps with human rights. Most of these initiatives came from UNDP itself and not from ECOSOC.[52]

The ICJ The International Court of Justice (ICJ), technically a principal UN organ but highly independent once its judges are elected by the Security Council and General Assembly, has not made a major imprint on the protection of international human rights.[53] This is primarily because only states have standing before the Court in binding cases, and states have demonstrated for a long time a reluctance to either sue or be sued – especially on human rights matters – in international tribunals.[54] As long as individuals lack legal standing, the ICJ's case load on human rights is highly likely to remain light.

From time to time the Court is presented with the opportunity to rule on issues of international human rights and humanitarian law. In 1986 in *Nicaragua v. the United States* it reaffirmed some points about both human rights and international humanitarian law while dealing primarily with security issues such as what activity constitutes an armed attack giving rise to a right of self-defense.

In the Belgian arrest warrant judgment of 2002, the ICJ held that an individual state (in this case Belgium) could not on its own exercise the

---

[52] See further Elizabeth A. Mandeville, "United Nations Development Programme," in *Encyclopedia of Human Rights*, vol. V, 50–157. Compare Carmen Huckel Schneider, "World Health Organization (WHO)," ibid., vol. V, 388–394.

[53] For a concise introduction with mention of several cases, see Ralph G. Steinhardt, "International Court of Justice," ibid., vol. III, 103–112.

[54] A. S. Muller, D. Raic, and J. M. Thuranszky, eds., *The International Court of Justice: Its Future Role After Fifty Years* (The Hague: Martinus Nijhoff, 1997), especially the chapter by Mark Janis.

principle of universal jurisdiction and pursue legal charges for gross violations of human rights against a sitting state official (in this case the foreign minister of Democratic Congo). In the Court's view such sitting officials were protected by the principle of sovereign immunity, which should be respected in the interests of orderly international relations. On the other hand, one might conclude from other developments that, if a centralized body like the UN Security Council, and/or its derivative agencies, sought similar legal proceedings, they might continue. One could note that Slobodan Milosevic, when an official of Serbia, and Omar Hassan al-Bashir, when an official of Sudan, were both required to answer to legal proceedings about human rights violations (in the first instance via the International Criminal Tribunal for the former Yugoslavia, and in the second via the International Criminal Court).[55]

In 2004 in the Avena judgment, the ICJ handed down a ruling ostensibly about a treaty on consular relations but in substance about the death penalty in the USA. Under the 1963 Vienna Convention on Consular Relations, a state party is obligated, when detaining aliens charged with a capital offense, to notify defendants of a right to contact their consular officials in order to guarantee adequate defense counsel. This the state of Texas did not do with regard to several defendants from Mexico. Mexico sued the USA at the ICJ, particularly since the death penalty was facing a number of its nationals detained in the USA. By overwhelming majority the ICJ held the USA in violation of its treaty obligations. A central problem for the USA was its federalism and the fact that the Mexican prisoners had been prosecuted in state, not federal, courts. A subsequent US Supreme Court decision, the Medellin judgment, held that US authorities in Washington had no authority under the US Constitution to instruct Texas courts as to proper procedure. José Medellin was eventually executed in Texas for murder, the USA remained in violation of its obligations under international law, and some states such as California, but not Texas,

---

[55] Pieter H. H. Bekker, "World Court Orders Belgium to Cancel an Arrest Warrant Issued Against the Congolese Foreign Minister," *ASIL Insights* (February 2002), www.asil.org/insights/volume/7/issue/2/world-court-orders-belgium-cancel-arrest-warrant-issued-agai nst-congolese. In the 1999 Pinochet case in the UK, not involving the ICJ but involving this same subject matter, the British court held that Pinochet, as a *former* head of state, could indeed be extradited to Spain to stand trial for allegations of past torture in Chile under Spain's exercise of universal jurisdiction. Britain eventually returned Pinochet to Chile on supposedly humanitarian grounds (ill health) but probably because he had been a staunch anti-communist ally of Britain during the Cold War. The legal principle about prosecution for torture remained, even if Pinochet died without having to stand trial for his actions.

changed their state law to provide the requirement of notification required via the Vienna Consular Convention.[56]

Also in 2004 the ICJ gave an advisory opinion on the legality of Israel's new security wall, part of which was built on territory beyond "the green line" or Israel's *de facto* borders in 1949. In this case the ICJ showed evident concern for the fate of Palestinians adversely affected by the wall, with the Court paying much attention to the Fourth Geneva Convention of 1949 dealing with occupied territory. (The ICJ is allowed to give advisory as well as binding judgments; such advisory rulings might become binding over time, dependent on whether they enter customary international law.)[57]

In 2007 the ICJ made a ruling on genocide in the Balkans that satisfied very few analysts. In responding to a petition from Bosnia against Serbia, the Court held on the one hand that it could not find evidence of genocide by Serbia. On the other hand it found that Serbia had failed in its legal obligations to prevent genocide in cases such as the Srebrenica massacre of 1995. This complex judgment, obviously a compromise, did little to improve the situation in the Balkans or to enhance the status of the Court.[58] In sum, the Bosnian Serb massacre at Srebrenica was held to be genocide, Serb authorities in Belgrade were held not to be responsible, but those same authorities were held liable for not preventing the genocidal massacre by whomever might have been directly responsible.

In general, while the ICJ's case load has increased on average from two or three cases per year to ten or eleven after the Cold War, it is still rare for the Court to make a major pronouncement on human rights. States still generally regard human rights as too important a subject to entrust to some fifteen independent judges of various nationalities who make their judgments with reference to rules of law rather than national interest or public opinion. Thus, for example, while the 1948 Genocide Convention contains an article providing for compulsory jurisdiction for the ICJ in resolving disputes under this treaty, states like the USA reserved against this article when ratifying the treaty.

---

[56] William J. Aceves, "Consular Notification and the Death Penalty: The ICJ's Judgment in *Avena*," *ASIL Insights* (April 2004), www.asil.org/insights/volume/8/issue/6/consular-notification-and-death-penalty-icjs-judgment-avena; *Medellín v. Texas*, 552 U.S. 491 (2008).

[57] For a variety of reactions to the ICJ advisory ruling on Israel's security wall, see *American Journal of International Law*, 99, 1 (January 2005), 1–141.

[58] For a short overview see Jason Morgan-Foster and Pierre-Olivier Savoie, "World Court Finds Serbia Responsible for Breaches of Genocide Convention, but Not Liable for Committing Genocide," *ASIL Insights* (April 2007), www.asil.org/insights/volume/11/issue/9/world-court-finds-serbia-responsible-breaches-genocide-convention-not.

Under the Court's statute, states can give a blanket jurisdiction to the ICJ to rule on all or some legal issues, but few states have done so in unambiguous fashion. In this respect the end of the Cold War has made no difference. State defense of sovereignty still trumps interest in orderly and humane international relations, at least in so far as the ICJ is concerned. The ICJ case load shows that realism is alive and well, as states protect their claims to sovereign decision making so as to pursue their national interests as they define them. In general, states, certainly most major military powers, are still reluctant to place the ICJ in a supranational position and do not often give it legal authority to have the final say on human rights issues. Recent cases at the ICJ pertain mostly to border disputes in the global south and other jurisdictional issues. There were no major human rights cases in recent years.

Major subsidiary bodies

In addition to the principal UN organs, there are several subsidiary bodies that concern themselves with the application of human rights standards. The focus here is on the UN Human Rights Council (formerly the Human Rights Commission), the International Labour Organization, and the Office of the UN High Commissioner for Refugees. The Sub-Commission on Prevention of Discrimination and Protection of Minorities, first renamed the UN Sub-Commission on Human Rights, and since 2006 recast again as the Human Rights Advisory Committee, has been active but reports to the Council. Space constraints oblige its omission. The Commission on the Status of Women has been primarily engaged in promotional and assistance activities rather than protection efforts.[59] The two *ad hoc* criminal courts are addressed in Chapter 4. UNESCO can be mentioned in passing. Its activities too are primarily promotional rather than protective.[60]

The Human Rights Commission, now Council

It used to be said of the UN Human Rights Commission that it was the organization's premier body, or diplomatic hub, for human rights issues. After the Cold War this was no longer completely the case. If the Security

[59] Stephanie Farrior, "United Nations Commission on the Status of Women," in *Encyclopedia of Human Rights*, vol. V, 142–149.
[60] Roger A. Coate, "United Nations Educational, Scientific, and Cultural Organization (UNESCO)," ibid., vol. V, 158–164; and David Weissbrodt and Rose Farley, "The UNESCO Human Rights Procedure: An Evaluation," *Human Rights Quarterly*, 16, 2 (May 1994), 391–414.

Council establishes a connection between human rights and international peace and security, then the Council becomes the most important, certainly the most authoritative, UN forum for human rights – as discussed above. What can be said is that until 2005 the Commission remained the center for traditional or routine human rights diplomacy, in addition to the Secretary-General's office, and in loose tandem with the UN High Commissioner for Human Rights. The UN system has never been known for tight organization and streamlined, clear chains of command.

The Commission for Human Rights was anticipated from the very beginning of the UN and first served as a drafting body for the International Bill of Rights and many other international instruments on human rights.[61] As noted above, it was composed of representatives of states, elected by ECOSOC, itself composed of states. Because of its composition as well as its focus on drafting legal standards, for its first twenty years the Commission avoided specific inquiries about specific rights in specific countries. In one wonderful phrase, it demonstrated a "fierce commitment to inoffensiveness."[62] Contributing to this situation was the fact that both the East and West during the Cold War knew that if they raised specific human rights issues, such inquiries could be turned against them. The West controlled the Commission in its early days, but its own record on racism and discrimination suggested prudence in the face of any desire to hammer the communists on their evident violations of civil and political rights. In any event, Cold War debates about human rights violations occurred in the UN General Assembly, and, it might be noted, without any notable effects on improving the actual practice of human rights on either side of the Cold War divide.

Beginning in about 1967 the Commission began to stumble toward more protection activities rather than just promotional ones. This change was made possible primarily by the greater number of developing countries in the organization. They were determined to do something about racism in southern Africa and what they saw as neo-imperialism and racism via the Zionist movement in the Middle East. They did not apparently anticipate how a focus on specific rights in specific places could also be turned against them in the future. Some western governments, pushed by western-based non-governmental organizations, then struck a deal with the developing countries in the newly expanded

---

[61] This and many other points about the Commission are drawn from Alston, ed., *United Nations and Human Rights*, 126–210.

[62] Tom J. Farer, "The UN and Human Rights: More than a Whimper, Less than a Roar," in Roberts and Kingsbury, eds., *United Nations, Divided World*, 23.

ECOSOC and Commission, agreeing to debates about Israel and South Africa in return for similar attention to countries like Haiti and Greece, both then under authoritarian rule. The door was thus opened for attempts under the Charter to monitor and supervise all state behavior relative to international rights standards, using the Universal Declaration of Human Rights as the central guide.[63]

ECOSOC's Resolutions 1235 and 1503, mentioned above, authorized specific review of state behavior on rights, and a Commission response to private petitions alleging a pattern of gross violations of rights, respectively. In theory, both procedures represented a constriction of absolute and expansive state sovereignty. In practice, neither procedure resulted in systematic, sure, and impressive protections of specific rights for specific persons in specific countries. Lawyers sometimes got excited about the new procedures, but victims of rights violations were much less impressed. Mostly because of the 1235 procedure allowing a debate and resolutions on particular states, the Commission sometimes used "Special Procedures" and appointed country investigators, by whatever name, to continue investigations and keep the diplomatic spotlight on certain states, thus continuing the politics of embarrassment. This step, too, while sometimes bringing some limited improvement to a rights situation, failed to provide systematic and sure protection. The 1503 procedure on private petitions, triggered by NGOs as well as by individuals, took too long to transpire and was mostly shielded from publicity by its confidential nature. Somewhat more effective was the Commission's use of *thematic* investigators or working groups, such as on forced disappearances. These developed the techniques of "urgent action" and "prompt intervention." The Commission also started the practice of holding emergency sessions to give prominence to a subject. Yet if at the end of emergency sessions, and reports by the country, thematic, or emergency investigators, member states were not prepared to take further action, Commission proceedings still failed to generate the necessary impact on violative states.

Summarizing the protective role of the Commission has never been easy.[64] If one looks at what transpires inside Commission meetings, there

---

[63] Samuel Moyn, in *The Last Utopia: Human Rights in History* (Cambridge, MA: Belknap for Harvard, 2010) is correct in writing that concentrated action for global human rights protection started about 1970 and not in 1945. But he is wrong in asserting that this human rights diplomacy started *de novo* at that time and had no connections with past human rights developments in the 1940s. On when the USA became more interested in active diplomacy on human rights, and whether it was in the 1940s or 1970s, see Mark Philip Bradley, *The World Reimagined: Americans and Human Rights in the Twentieth Century* (Cambridge: Cambridge University Press, 2016).

[64] See further Howard Tolley, Jr., *The UN Commission on Human Rights* (Boulder: Westview, 1987). See also the relevant essays in Gudmundur Alredsson, et al.,

was clear progress after about 1967 in attempts by this UN agency to pressure states into complying with internationally recognized human rights. States mostly took Commission proceedings seriously. They did not like to have the Commission focus on their deficiencies. Many went to great efforts to block, delay, or weaken criticism by the Commission and its agents. This was true, for example, of Argentina in the 1980s and China in the 1990s. Despite these obstructionist efforts, at first a fairly balanced list of states was publicly put in the diplomatic dock via the Commission. Careful scholarship established that the actual record of the Commission over time in attempted protection was not as poor as often suggested, with much appropriate diplomacy directed at precisely those states with poor human rights records.[65]

The Commission, however, suffered a decline in reputation. The main reason for this was state foreign policy, since the Commission was made up of states. In the geographical caucuses of the UN, where many real decisions about the UN are made, member states elevated certain concerns like equitable geographical representation over concern for serious and impartial protection of human rights. Thus the Latin American caucus elected Cuba to the UN Human Rights Commission, despite its poor record on civil and political rights. Thus the African and Arab caucuses combined to ensure the election of repressive Libya as President of the Commission at one point. Also debilitating in the Commission were persistent double standards in rights debates, especially by the major countries. The P-5 countries were always elected to the Commission by tradition (with the USA denied a seat only one time in a controversial vote in its caucuses group). China, for example, was certainly not committed to systematic protection of human rights, going to great lengths, including use of foreign assistance, to try to ensure that its rights record was not the target of a critical resolution. The USA, for example, spent much time in focusing on the rights record of adversaries like Cuba, while remaining silent on egregious human rights violations in allies like Saudi Arabia. African and other developing countries were reluctant to address the rights violations of their compatriots in places

eds., *International Human Rights Monitoring Mechanisms* (The Hague: Martinus Nijhoff, 2001).

[65] J. H. Lebovic and E. Voeten, "The Politics of Shame: The Condemnation of Country Human Rights Practices in the UNCHR," *International Studies Quarterly*, 50, 3 (2006), 861–888. Note that this study was not published until after the Commission gave way to the Council. See the follow-on study by David P. Forsythe with Baekkwan Park, "Turbulent Transition: From the UN Human Rights Commission to the Council," in Scott Kaufman and Alissa Warters, eds., *The United Nations: Past, Present and Future* (Haupagge, NY: Nova Science Publishers, 2009), 85–110.

like Zimbabwe, preferring to focus on Israeli policies in the occupied territories. So, given the very messy political process of the body, the Commission lost legitimacy in the eyes of many.

If one looks at the Commission in broad context, it is clear that many states were prepared to continue with rights violations, even if this brought various forms of criticism and condemnation. In places like the former Yugoslavia or the Great Lakes region of Africa, numerous parties were prepared to go on killing and maiming in the name of ethnic group or political power, regardless of words spoken or written in Geneva where the Commission was based. Russia was the only P-5 country to be the target of a resolution of criticism in the Commission, but this did not change to any appreciable extent its brutal policies in the secessionist region of Chechnya.[66] In the last analysis the Commission was divorced from control of military, economic, and the more important diplomatic sanctions. If the Commission's special procedures (such as Rapporteurs and Working Groups) on forced disappearances and other subjects could provide some protection to perhaps 40 percent of its persons of concern, this was considered a very good relative figure of success.[67] Diplomatic pressure conducted with weak resources stood little chance of cracking the hard nut of intentional and systematic, rather than accidental and episodic, violations of human rights.

Such was the dissatisfaction with the UN Human Rights Commission, whether carefully considered or not, that during 2005 Secretary-General Kofi Annan proposed the dissolution of the Commission and its replacement by a Human Rights Council as a major organ of the UN. This change in fact transpired, with the new Council reporting to the General Assembly.[68] But changes turned out to be more superficial than substantive.

From 2006 the new Human Rights Council looked more or less like, and acted more or less like, the old Commission. While the western-style democracies and the non-western developing countries might agree on dissolution of the old Commission, for different reasons as it turned out, they could not agree on new arrangements that would guarantee improved protection of human rights. The new Council was still

---

[66] See further Catherine Osgood, "Chechnya," in *Encyclopedia of Human Rights*, vol. I, 290–299.
[67] Ted Piconne, *The Future of the United Nations Special Procedures* (Washington: Brookings Institution, 2014).
[68] In addition to Forsythe and Park, "Turbulent Transition," see Paul Gordon Lauren, "To Preserve and Build on Its Achievements and to Redress Its Shortcomings: The Journey from the Commission on Human Rights to the Human Rights Council," *Human Rights Quarterly*, 29, 2 (May 2007), 307–345.

dominated by the numerous African and Asian states. As lobbied especially by the Arab League and Conference of Islamic States, the Council continued to vote disproportionate criticism of Israel compared to similar or greater human rights violations in various developing countries. The USA changed from a policy of boycott (under the George W. Bush Administration) to one of engagement (under the Obama Administration). But this did not much change the double standards and other weaknesses of the Council. The Council remained a politicized talking shop of minor importance relative to many other developments concerning internationally recognized human rights. On occasion, but not consistently, it took a principled decision, as when it suspended Kaddafi's Libya from membership in 2011.

The change from Commission to Council amounted to a repackaging of old wine in a new bottle, although some held out hope for progress over time. There was a new Universal Periodic Review in which all states that were members of the Council had to defend their human rights records, but the input from the UN High Commissioner for Human Rights was meager. And the so-called Special Procedures continued (Rapporteurs and Working Groups) which allowed relatively independent and non-politicized diplomacy on behalf of certain human rights problems.[69] But often the Council paid scant attention to their reports. It was mildly encouraging that the Council often appointed independent persons to carry out investigations. These fact-finding missions might indeed delay the politicization of an issue for a time. But the reports still went back to state members of the Council who often manifested less than impartial views based on political alignment and ideological preference. If the Council, like the Commission, was engaged in a long-term effort to educate or socialize about human rights, this process might eventually bear some fruit. But serious and evident protection of human rights through the Council in the short run remained elusive. The Security Council was much more important, if also inconsistent as noted earlier.

International Labour Organization

The ILO has long been concerned with labor rights, first as a parallel organization to the League of Nations, then as a specialized agency of the UN system. It has developed several complicated procedures for

---

[69] Surya P. Subedi, "Protection of Human Rights Through the Mechanism of UN Special Rapporteurs," *Human Rights Quarterly*, 33, 1 (February 2011), 201–228. And recall Piconne, op. cit.

monitoring state behavior in the area of labor rights. In general, certain differences aside, its record on helping apply international labor rights is similar to that of the UN Human Rights Commission, now the Council, in two respects: it proceeds according to indirect implementation efforts falling short of direct enforcement; and its exact influence is difficult to specify.[70]

Of the more than 170 treaties developed through and supervised by the ILO, a handful are considered oriented toward basic human rights such as the freedom to associate in trade unions, the freedom to bargain collectively, and the right to be free from forced labor. States consenting to these treaties are obligated to submit reports to the ILO, indicating steps they have taken to apply treaty provisions. These reports are reviewed first by a committee of experts, then by a larger and more political body. Specialized ILO secretariat personnel assist the review committees. At both stages, workers' organizations participate actively. Other participants come from owners' organizations, and states. This tripartite membership of the ILO at least reduces or delays some of the problems inherent in the UN Human Rights Commission, such as states' political obstruction that makes serious review difficult. Nevertheless, at the end of the day the ILO regular review process centers on polite if persistent diplomacy devoid of more stringent sanctions beyond public criticism. Some issues remain under review for years. States may not enjoy multilateral criticism, but they learn to live with it as the price of continued political power or economic transactions.

All member states of the ILO are subject to a special review procedure on the key subject of freedom of association, regardless of their consent to various ILO treaties. Despite procedural differences, the outcome of these special procedures is not very different from the regular review. Workers' organizations are more active than owner and state representatives, and public criticism of state malfeasance must be repeated because amelioration comes slowly. Indeed, a study of freedom of association and the ILO during the Cold War concluded that those states most violative

[70] For a positive overview see Lee Swepston, "International Labor Organization," in *Encyclopedia of Human Rights*, vol. III, 144–150. Along similar lines, see Virginia A. Leary, "Lessons from the Experience of the International Labor Organization," in Alston, ed., *United Nations and Human Rights*, 580–619. Compare Hector G. Bartolomei de la Cruz, Geraldo von Potobsky, and Lee Swepston, *The International Labor Organization: The International Standards System and Basic Human Rights* (Boulder: Westview, 1996); and Nicolas Valticos, "The International Labor Organization," in Karel Vasak, ed., *The International Dimensions of Human Rights*, edited for the English edition by Philip Alston (Westport: Greenwood, for UNESCO, 1982). For a historical treatment and optimistic evaluation, see Gerry Rodgers, et al., *The ILO and the Quest for Social Justice, 1919–2009* (Ithaca: Cornell University Press, 2009).

of freedom of association were also most resistant to ILO pressures for change.[71] There are procedures for "urgent cases," but these sometimes take months to unfold. If a Chile under Pinochet or a Poland under Jaruzelski was determined to suppress independent labor movements, the ILO was unable to protect them – at least in the short term.

There are still further actions the ILO can take in defense of labor rights, such as sending special representatives of the Director-General for contact with offending governments. Moreover, the ILO is not the only UN agency concerned with labor rights. UNICEF, for example, is much concerned with child labor, arguing in early 1997 that some 250 million child laborers were being harshly exploited.[72]

All the ILO diplomacy for labor rights no doubt has an educational effect over time and constitutes a certain nuisance factor for states interested in their reputations in international circles. It remains true, however, that some states regard cheap and disorganized labor as part of their "comparative advantage" in international markets, and therefore useful in pursuit of economic growth for the nation as a whole. Suppressed labor organizations may also prove convenient to ruling elites. While some see labor rights as an essential part of human rights, others see labor rights as disguised claims to privileges or special benefits.[73] There are those who see the western emphasis on labor rights as part of neo-imperialism, designed to hamstring developing countries' drive for economic growth by saddling them with labor standards that the more developed countries never met in their "takeoff" stage of "crude capitalism" in the earlier years of the industrial revolution. The contrary view was that international labor rights were necessary to protect labor even in the developing countries, by mandating equal competition and a level playing field in global economic matters.

Then there was the very real problem of black market labor associated with human trafficking, certainly recognized by the ILO. Organized crime, both large and small, moved illegal labor across state borders for coerced prostitution, for compelled servitude as domestic servants,

---

[71] Ernst B. Haas, *Human Rights and International Action: The Case of Freedom of Association* (Stanford: Stanford University Press, 1970).

[72] UNICEF helped develop the Convention on the Rights of the Child, which contains provisions relevant to child labor. See Lawrence J. LeBlanc, *The Convention on the Rights of the Child: United Nations Lawmaking on Human Rights* (Lincoln: University of Nebraska Press, 1995).

[73] See further Lance A. Compa and Stephen F. Diamond, *Human Rights, Labor Rights, and International Trade* (Philadelphia: University of Pennsylvania Press, 1996). Note that in the USA in the state of Wisconsin and other internal states in 2011, political conservatives thought labor unions for public workers had negotiated contracts for "elevated" benefits that were unsustainable in a time of economic difficulties.

for indebted workers for migrant agricultural labor, and more. Given that often significant money could be made by those who controlled the trafficking (illegal human trafficking across the Mexican–USA border was worth about $6 billion annually), this proved a growing problem that both the ILO and its member states found difficult to deal with. A modern form of slavery, human trafficking belied the legal prohibitions on slavery established in the nineteenth and twentieth centuries.[74]

At the start of the twenty-first century, with more global markets than ever before, labor issues remained one of the more controversial features of global efforts to apply human rights standards. I return to this subject in Chapter 8, dealing with transnational corporations.

The High Commissioner for Refugees

After World War II, such was the naïvety of the international community that it was thought the problem of refugees was a small residue of that war and would be cleared up rather quickly.[75] Over half a century later, refugees and similarly displaced persons who found themselves in a refugee-like situation had become an enduring problem. The UN Office of the High Commissioner for Refugees (UNHCR) had become a permanent organization with an annual budget of over $1 billion.[76] Some 2 million persons fled genocide in the Great Lakes region of Africa in 1994–1995. Some 800,000 ethnic Albanians were forced out of Yugoslavia's Kosovo area in 1999. At the time of writing, driven by events such as the war in Syria, the number of persons uprooted by persecution and conflict around the world had risen to about 60 million – the highest number since the Second World War. About 20 million of these were refugees and 40 million internally displaced.

International law provided for legal refugees – those individuals crossing an international boundary on the basis of a well-founded fear of

---

[74] See the concise but analytical coverage by Howard B. Tolley, Jr., "Human Trafficking," in *Encyclopedia of Human Rights*, vol. II, 494–502; Joel Quirk, "Slavery and the Slave Trade," ibid., vol. IV, 462–471. See also Kevin Bales, ed., *Understanding Global Slavery: A Reader* (Berkeley: University of California Press, 2005). See further Jorge Heine and Ramesh Thakur, eds., *The Dark Side of Globalization* (Tokyo: United Nations University Press, 2011). The latter note that labor rights are relatively poorly regulated on a global basis, accurately contesting some of the optimistic evaluations of the ILO.

[75] On this and subsequent points, see in particular Gil Loescher, *Beyond Charity: International Cooperation and the Global Refugee Crisis* (New York: Oxford University Press, 1993, for the Twentieth Century Fund). See also his excellent overview, *The UNHCR and World Politics: A Perilous Path* (Oxford: Oxford University Press, 2001).

[76] See Geoff Gilbert, "United Nations High Commissioner for Refugees," in *Encyclopedia of Human Rights*, vol. V, 183–190; Joel R. Charny, "Internally Displaced Persons," ibid., vol. III, 70–79.

persecution (also called social, political, or convention refugees). Such persons had the legal right not to be returned to a threatening situation, and thus were to be granted at least temporary asylum in states of first sanctuary. But in addition, many persons fled disorder without being individually singled out for persecution, and others found themselves displaced but still within their country of habitual residence (and thus internally displaced persons, or IDPs). Others needed international protection after returning to their original state ("returnees"). After the Cold War virtually all of the traditional states of asylum, historically speaking, adopted more restrictive policies regarding refugees and asylum seekers. Being protective of traditional national values and numbers, these western states feared being overwhelmed with outsiders in an era of easier transportation, not to mention an era of international organized crime and human trafficking.

The UNHCR started out primarily as a protective agency that sought to represent legal refugees diplomatically and legally. States retained final authority as to who was recognized as a legal refugee and thus who was to be granted temporary or permanent entrance to the country. Hence the early role of the UNHCR was primarily to contact states' legal authorities and/or foreign ministries on behalf of those exiles with a well-founded fear of persecution. Increasingly the UNHCR was drawn into the relief business, to such an extent that some observers believed it was no longer able to adequately protect refugees because its time, personnel, and budgets were consumed by relief operations. In its relief, the UNHCR felt compelled by moral concerns to disregard most distinctions between legal refugees, war refugees, and internally displaced persons. They were all in humanitarian need. This approach was approved by the General Assembly. Given that repatriation rather than resettlement became increasingly the only hope for a durable solution to refugee problems, the UNHCR increasingly addressed itself to the human rights problems causing flight in the first place. Thus the UNHCR became less and less a strictly humanitarian actor, and more and more a human rights actor dealing with the root causes of refugee problems.[77] In 1999, for example, High Commissioner Sadako Ogata testified to the UN Security Council that the primary cause of flight from Kosovo was not NATO bombing but mass persecution and terror by the Serbian authorities in Yugoslavia.

---

[77] See further Gil Loescher, "Refugees: A Global Human Rights and Security Crisis," in Tim Dunne and Nicholas J. Wheeler, eds., *Human Rights in Global Politics* (Cambridge: Cambridge University Press, 1999), 233–258. More generally see Emma Haddad, *The Refugee in International Society: Between Sovereigns* (Cambridge: Cambridge University Press, 2008).

The UNHCR faced numerous and complex issues while trying to provide protection and relief to those who had broken normal relations with their governments. In Bosnia in the early 1990s the UNHCR found itself contributing to ethnic cleansing by moving persons out of harm's way in accordance with the desires of certain fighting parties, but it was morally preferable to do so rather than see the persons killed. In effect in the Balkans in the early 1990s, important states "hid behind" the UNHCR, insisting it stay on the scene to give the impression that "the international community" was doing something. In reality, these states wanted to avoid decisive military involvement that might prove unpopular at home; for this cynical reason the UNHCR (and Red Cross agencies) proved politically useful. But their humanitarian missions became compromised.

In the Great Lakes region of Africa after the Rwandan genocide, armed militia were mixed with civilian refugees. The UNHCR had no authority or power to police refugee areas, and thus faced the dilemma of whether to provide relief to all or to withdraw in protest against the presence of armed groups interested in continuing the violence. While some private relief agencies pulled out, the UNHCR stayed – and tried to arrange the proper policing of refugee camps by security forces from certain local states. State members of the UN Security Council were clearly briefed as to the situation but refused to take the necessary steps to clear the brutal militias out of the refugee camps.[78]

Despite some evidence of poor accounting and other mismanagement, and charges that its bureaucracy in Geneva was not as committed to the needs of refugees as it could be, the UNHCR was often seen as one of the more respected UN agencies. It became one of the more important UN relief agencies, it was trying to re-establish a sound record of protection, and its legal staff had been a pioneer in addressing the special problems of female refugees.[79]

By 2016 the internationalized civil war in Syria had produced some 5 million refugees and about 7 million internally displaced persons (out of a national population of about 17 million). The threats to civilians were so dire in that country that many risked dangerous flight, with

---

[78] See Sadako Ogata, *The Turbulent Decade: Confronting the Refugee Crises of the 1990s* (New York: Norton, 2005).

[79] Unfortunately some of its local personnel in East Africa were implicated in the sexual harassment of women and girls, in that special attention was offered in return for sexual favors. The problem also sometimes occurred in UN peacekeeping operations. A principal problem especially in peacekeeping was that the UN Secretariat lacked the authority to properly train, and in some cases ensure the punishment of, personnel loaned by states.

subsequent loss of life. Despite the humanitarian catastrophe in Syria, more than one European country resisted this influx of persons in need of safe sanctuary. Even the United States, with few asylum seekers able to reach its jurisdiction from the Middle East, manifested considerable anti-foreigner feeling. In fact for some decades, it had been clear that Western countries would agree to fund UNHCR relief programs through volun-tary donations as long as refugees were kept "over there" in developing countries close to areas of instability and conflict.[80] As for the Syrian situation, it was Jordan, Lebanon, and Turkey who wound up with large numbers of refugees, while particularly European democracies for the most part erected legal and physical barriers to entry. Governments like the Merkel government in Germany, which sought to be welcoming, faced a critical public opinion and had to change course. The UNHCR did what it could to champion the plight of the forcibly displaced but was unable to alter many Western governmental policies of resistance to asylum and resettlement.

Treaty-specific bodies

The United Nations is a decentralized and poorly coordinated system. Since states are unwilling thus far to create a human rights court to centralize the juridical protection of internationally recognized human rights, each human rights treaty may (or may not) provide its own monitoring mechanism. (The 1948 Genocide Convention, with 143 parties as of 2016, refers unresolved disputes to the International Court of Justice.) Since obviously the UN Human Rights Council, the ILO, and the UNHCR have not resolved all or even most human rights problems, the tendency is to respond to pressing problems via a special-ized treaty with an additional supervisory system. States keep adopting human rights standards, but avoiding the hard issue of effective enforce-ment. The result is a proliferation of weak implementation agencies and a further lack of coordination. The heads of the treaty monitoring mech-anisms, however, have started meeting together to exchange views. Sometimes human rights independent experts also try concerted or pooled diplomacy, as when in 2004–2005 they compiled a joint report about, and asked to visit, the US detention center at Guantanamo Bay. The existence of the post of UN High Commissioner for Human Rights since 1993 may eventually improve coordination in relative terms. (There is also the international criminal court, analyzed in Chapter 4.)

---

[80] Phil Orchard, *A Right to Flee: Refugees, States, and the Construction of International Cooperation* (Cambridge: Cambridge University Press, 2014).

Here we cover the two monitoring mechanisms under the two basic Covenants, then make quick reference to other treaty-based bodies.

The Human Rights Committee

The International Covenant on Civil and Political Rights, with 168 parties as of 2016, provides for a Human Rights Committee with two basic protective functions. Composed of individual experts nominated and elected by states that are party to the Covenant, the Committee reviews and comments on obligatory state reports. The Committee also processes individual petitions alleging violations of rights under the Covenant, from those states consenting to an optional protocol. As of 2016, 115 states had provided that specialized consent. There is also a procedure for state-to-state complaints, but it has never been activated.

A second protocol forbidding the death penalty has fewer ratifications (83), and has had no clear influence yet on states such as the USA, Japan, China, and Iran, *inter alia*, that widely use the death penalty for common crime (as compared to political crime like treason). In the case of the USA, it defends its position on use of the death penalty by arguing in human rights forums that: (1) it is not forbidden by general international law; (2) it is established by democratic process reflecting majority opinion and independent court judgments; (3) it is not much used by federal courts, but under US federalism it is up to state (provincial) authorities over which federal authorities have no control. Nevertheless, the USA does have to take into account opposition to the death penalty particularly in extradition matters, where the USA often has to agree to forgo capital charges in order to secure the return of a fugitive. There are scholars who believe the USA is on the way to eliminating the death penalty, in part because of international criticism.[81] The actual use of the death penalty in US state courts is on the decline, with the exception of a few states like Texas, Florida, and Georgia.

States are obligated to report on measures they have taken to make national law and practice compatible with their obligations under the Covenant. The Committee, however, was divided during the Cold War on its proper role. A minimalist view, articulated mostly by individuals from the European socialist states, maintained that the Committee was only to facilitate dialogue among sovereign states. A maximalist view was that the Committee was to pronounce both on whether a state had reported correctly, and on whether that state was in compliance with its

---

[81] See further William Schabas, *The Abolition of the Death Penalty in International Law*, 3rd edn. (Cambridge: Cambridge University Press, 2002).

legal obligations. Since the end of the Cold War the Committee has been freer to adopt the maximalist view.[82] But once again we see that the Committee could not proceed beyond some public criticism of the states that were found to be wanting in one respect or another via their reports. The volume of Committee proceedings and comments appeared to be in inverse proportion to the actual protection of civil and political rights in violative states.[83] Some states, mostly western democracies, did make changes in their national law and practice in the wake of Committee questions. The USA, however, proved more recalcitrant. During an earlier era the US Senate Foreign Relations Committee, ironically identifying with the old European communist position, challenged the right of the Committee to pass judgment on US reservations, understandings, and comments concerning the Covenant.[84]

Committee practice has evolved so that it makes summary comments about a state's compliance report, and general comments about the meaning of the Covenant. The former provides an authoritative agenda for any state seeking to improve its record on civil and political rights. The latter may affect the evolution of legal standards, as when the Committee's comments on how to interpret the prohibition on torture fed into the drafting of the 1984 UN Convention against Torture and Cruel, Inhuman, and Degrading Treatment.[85] As might be expected, states sometimes challenge the validity of both the summary comments and the general comments.

When individuals bring complaints under the Optional Protocol, having exhausted national remedies, the situation is not so very different. The Committee, when justified, will make public its views, frequently holding states to be in violation of their obligations. The range of countries found to be in violation is rather broad, ranging from one case of technical deficiencies (Canada) to numerous cases of gross violations (Uruguay). It remains uncertain in how many of these cases ameliorative steps were taken by offending governments, and whether such steps, if

---

[82] An optimistic account is found in Ineke Boerfijn, "Towards a Strong System of Supervision," *Human Rights Quarterly*, 17, 4 (November 1995), 766–793.

[83] Dominic McGoldrick, *The Human Rights Committee* (Oxford: Clarendon, 1991); Manfred Nowak, *UN Covenant on Civil and Political Rights: CCPR Comments* (Arlington: Engel, 1993).

[84] William A. Schabas, "Spare the RUD or Spoil the Treaty: The United States Challenges the Human Rights Committee on the Subject of Reservations," in David P. Forsythe, ed., *The United States and Human Rights: Looking Inward and Outward* (Lincoln: University of Nebraska Press, 2000).

[85] David Weissbrodt, "International Covenant on Civil and Political Rights," in *Encyclopedia of Human Rights*, vol. I, 339–344. For more substance on the specific interpretations of this monitoring mechanism, consult the index to the *Encyclopedia*.

taken, were due strictly to the Committee. Uruguay eventually moved away from massive repression, because of which at one time it had more political prisoners per capita than any other country in the world. Whether progressive change was due to the Committee, to any great extent, is dubious. One expert believes that most states comply with Committee recommendations concerning private petitions,[86] which may be true of this non-public process since the more repressive and/or contentious states do not accept this optional protocol to begin with.

The Committee on Economic, Social, and Cultural Rights

The International Covenant on Economic, Social, and Cultural Rights, despite 164 adherences by 2016, has always been the stepchild of the international human rights movement. Certain states, when speaking in the General Assembly or another political forum, may give it some prominence in order to deflect attention away from violations of civil and political rights. But few states have paid serious and sustained attention to this convention. The same is true for the question of its application.

After the E/S/C Covenant came into legal force in 1976, it took a full two years for any monitoring mechanism to be put in place. This first body, a working group of states derived from ECOSOC, compiled a truly miserable record of incompetence and was replaced in 1986 by an independent Committee of Experts. This Committee has shown considerable dynamism in confronting some daunting tasks: imprecision of the Covenant's terms; lack of jurisprudence to clarify obligations; lack of broad and sustained governmental interest in the subject matter; paucity of national and transnational private organizations interested in socioeconomic and cultural rights as rights and not as aspects of development; and lack of, *inter alia*, relevant information for arriving at judgments.[87]

The Committee has struggled first with the problem of states failing to submit even an initial report on compliance, although legally required. This problem is widespread across the UN system of human rights reporting, but it is a pronounced problem under this Covenant. It has also faced the usual problem that many states' reports, even when submitted, are more designed to meet formal obligations than to give a full and frank picture of the true situation of E/S/C rights in the country. The Committee has persisted in trying to serve as an effective catalyst for

---

[86] Weissbrodt, "International Covenant."
[87] Philip Alston, "The Committee on Economic, Social, and Cultural Rights," in Alston, ed., *United Nations and Human Rights*, 473–508.

serious national policy making in this domain, and has tried mostly to establish minimum base lines for national requirements – rather than universal rules – regarding economic, social, and cultural rights.[88] Some argue that socioeconomic rights are receiving more attention now than in the past, and that a new monitoring mechanism is in order.[89]

In 2008 state members of the UN approved an optional protocol to the socioeconomic covenant allowing for private communications, similar to the civil-political covenant. By 2016 a total of 20 states had ratified this instrument. The Protocol did show a continuing effort to make socio-economic rights more important, but clearly there were more noteworthy developments concerning civil-political rights, which had always been the case since the 1940s.[90]

On the one hand it could be shown that many if not most of the members of the influential coalition of western-style democracies had long accepted the notion of socioeconomic rights as a matter of public policy.[91] On the other hand these and other states showed some reluctance to have third parties require the enforcement of socioeconomic rights in the short term. For example, even in Europe where social democracy and large welfare states were the norm, regional arrangements for protecting human rights were weaker for socioeconomic rights than for civil-political rights. This is covered in Chapter 5 on regional developments. Nevertheless, in various states such as India and South Africa one could indeed find court cases on socioeconomic rights.

Other treaty-based mechanisms

As of 2016, compliance committees exist under these major conventions: the Rights of the Child (196 state parties), Racial Discrimination (196 parties), Torture (159 parties), and Discrimination Against Women (189 parties). Similar committees exist or will exist regarding treaties on

---

[88] See further Robert E. Robertson, "Measuring State Compliance with the Obligation to Devote the 'Maximum Available Resources' to Realizing Economic, Social, and Cultural Rights," *Human Rights Quarterly*, 16, 4 (November 1994), 693–714.

[89] Mario Gomez, "Social Economic Rights and Human Rights Commissions," *Human Rights Quarterly*, 17, 1 (February 1995), 155–169.

[90] See further Shareen Hertel and Lanse Minkler, eds., *Economic Rights: Conceptual, Measurement, and Policy Issues* (Cambridge: Cambridge University Press, 2007); and Rhoda E. Howard-Hassmann and Claude E. Welch, Jr., eds., *Economic Rights in Canada and the United States* (Philadelphia: University of Pennsylvania Press, 2006).

[91] Jack Donnelly, "The West and Economic Rights," in Hertel and Minkler, eds., *Economic Rights*, 37–55; Daniel J. Whelan and Jack Donnelly, "The West, Economic and Social Rights, and the Global Human Rights Regime: Setting the Record Straight," *Human Rights Quarterly*, 29, 4 (November 2007), 908–949. See the follow-on debate on this subject in that journal.

Migrant Workers, Persons with Disabilities, and Enforced Disappearances.[92]

State endorsement of international human rights in these areas is generally not matched by timely and fulsome reporting by the state, nor by a willingness to respond affirmatively and quickly to critical comments by the control committees – which are composed of individual experts. As with other human rights treaties discussed above, UN Secretariat assistance is meager owing to budgetary problems. Some NGOs do give special attention to one or more of these treaties. For example, Amnesty International gives considerable support to the Committee Against Torture.[93] But the Committee Against Racial Discrimination has adopted restrictive decisions about the use of NGO information, as has the Committee on Discrimination Against Women.[94] This latter committee operates under a treaty that does not allow individual petitions, in part because the UN Commission on the Status of Women does.[95] Most of these treaties contain a provision on interstate complaints, but these provisions have remained dormant. States do not like to petition other states about human rights, because of the boomerang effect on themselves. The Committee Against Torture exercises a right of automatic investigation unless a state expressly reserves against that article; relatively few parties have. But as of 2016 UN prison inspections had yet to become systematic, because of the lack of large numbers of ratifications of this legal instrument. The Committee on the Rights of the Child has functioned for such a short time that its influence cannot be judged. There has been some effort to improve the coordination of all of these treaty-based monitoring mechanisms, but one cannot yet discern any greater influence in the short term generated by the sum of the parts, or the separate parts themselves.

From one view, the international regimes that center on these human rights treaties and their monitoring mechanisms constitute weak regimes that have not been able to make a significant dent thus far in violations of various human rights on a global scale.[96] The control committees do

---

[92] Some totals exceed UN membership because some political entities, recognized by some states, are allowed to deposit documents of consent to treaties – such as Abkhazia, Kosovo, Republic of China.

[93] See further Howard B. Tolley, Jr., "Torture: Convention Against Torture," in *Encyclopedia of Human Rights*, vol. V, 51–59; Nigel S. Rodley, "Torture: International Law," ibid., vol. V, 65–80.

[94] See Marsha A. Freeman, "Women: Convention on the Elimination of Discrimination Against Women," ibid., vol. V, 331–340.

[95] See further Stephanie Farrior, "United Nations Commission on the Status of Women," ibid., vol. V, 142–149.

[96] Jack Donnelly, *Universal Human Rights in Theory and Practice* (Ithaca: Cornell University Press, 1989), ch. 11.

make their contribution to long-term promotion via socialization or informal and practical education for human rights.[97] States have to report and subject themselves to various forms of review. Their sovereignty is not absolute but restricted. At the end of the day, however, it is not these regimes, but the Security Council and the Secretary-General – and perhaps the High Commissioner for Human Rights – that are best positioned among UN actors to effectively press states to improve their human rights records in the short term.

From another view, one that focuses on related national developments, it is possible that some of these treaties may sometimes give rise to important changes despite the weak legal authority of international agencies.[98] Once ratified, a treaty may change the nature of national legislation and politics if influential persons and organizations pursue the norms found in the treaty. In these cases, it is not so much the official international review that generates impact for human rights, but rather those in national politics who appeal successfully to treaty standards. According to the leading scholar on this matter: "Human rights treaties matter most where they have domestic political and legal traction ... [D]omestic mechanisms [may allow] a treaty to effect elite-initiated agendas, to support litigation, and to spark political mobilization."[99] In her view, human rights treaties usually have the greatest impact in unstable or transitional polities where views on human rights are not fully institutionalized. The foundational point is that no treaty implements itself. Some political actor with clout, or at least determined persistence, needs to "adopt" the treaty and "run with it." A transnational focus, with due attention to national politics, seems required for full understanding.[100] (See further the case study at the end of this chapter.)

The World Bank and International Monetary Fund The World Bank (International Bank for Reconstruction and Development, IBRD) and the International Monetary Fund (IMF) are the major agencies of the Bretton Woods institutions and are officially part of the UN system, but historically they have operated in a highly independent manner with their

---

[97] David P. Forsythe, "The United Nations and Human Rights 1945–1985," *Political Science Quarterly*, 100 (Summer 1985), 249–269; and Forsythe, "The UN and Human Rights at Fifty: An Incremental but Incomplete Revolution," *Global Governance*, 1, 3 (September–December 1995), 297–318.

[98] See especially Beth A. Simmons, *Mobilizing for Human Rights: International Law in Domestic Politics* (Cambridge: Cambridge University Press, 2009).

[99] Ibid., *passim*. See also Heather Smith-Cannoy, *Insincere Commitments: Human Rights Treaties, Abusive States, and Citizen Activism* (Washington: Georgetown University Press, 2012).

[100] See further an earlier study by David P. Forsythe, *The Politics of International Law: US Foreign Policy Reconsidered* (Boulder: Lynne Rienner, 1990).

own governing boards and constituent legal instruments. Voting by member states in each agency is greatly affected by financial contributions, which makes them different from other parts of the UN system. This arrangement obviously gives great weight to developed as compared to developing states. In recent years the Bank, but not so much the IMF, has become more closely linked to other UN agencies, such as via the Global Environment Facility in quest of better funded ecological programs. Likewise the Bank, but not so much the IMF, has made halting steps to pay more attention to human rights. The Bank, which makes loans for development, has declared that "creating the conditions for the attainment of human rights is a central and irreducible goal of development."[101]

As the Bank funded a number of large infrastructure projects such as dams to generate energy, local populations were adversely affected. In response the Bank created an Inspection Panel to which various stakeholders had access under certain rules. This was, therefore, an effort to increase participation in decision making by community-based organizations (CBOs) and the NGOs who often worked with them. Over time a number of local and international human rights groups played a larger role in Bank processes. Yet formal power and authority still resided with national governments on the Bank governing board, in interaction with Bank staff headed by a president (who is always an American, named by the US government).

Likewise controversial were Bank structural adjustment programs (SAPs), again often pitting the quest for national economic development against the welfare of local populations. In return for Bank loans, governments often had to agree to specific conditions intended to restructure national economic programs. Typically the SAPs required reduced governmental spending on programs such as aid or subsidies to the poor, in quest of greater earnings through exports and other revenue-enhancing measures. The formula of the so-called Washington consensus was more economic liberalization or privatization or expanded "free markets" and less governmental spending. This formula normally disadvantaged, at least in the short term, the most needy in a country. Not surprisingly, research showed that SAPs correlated negatively with protection or fulfillment of socioeconomic human rights.[102] That same

---

[101] Quoted in Marc Darrow, "World Bank and International Monetary Fund," in *Encyclopedia of Human Rights*, vol. V, at 374. See further Joel E. Oestreich, *Power and Principle: Human Rights Programming in International Organizations* (Washington: Georgetown University Press, 2007), ch. 3.

[102] See, e.g., M. Rodwan Abouharb and David Cingranelli, *Human Rights and Structural Adjustment* (Cambridge: Cambridge University Press, 2007).

research also concluded that SAPs negatively impacted civil and political rights in many cases, since some repression was required to implement painful conditionality.

In 2006 the legal counsel of the Bank issued a report entitled "Legal Opinion on Human Rights and the Work of the World Bank." While asserting that under the Bank's Articles of Agreement the agency had the legal duty to take into account the human rights implications of its work, in subsequent years the specifics of this duty were not completely clarified. A major review of Bank policies did not end the confusion and debate by 2016. On the one hand, new rules seemed to pay more attention to labor rights and rights of communities affected by Bank projects. On the other hand, some observers still found the Bank averse to firm and clear rules consistent with many human rights. The President of the Bank professed commitment to human rights in general, but some of the Bank's 189 member states were clearly skeptical of binding human rights guidelines. Complicating the big picture was that authoritarian China had created an Asian Infrastructure and Investment Bank that competed with the World Bank in providing development loans. This latter bank, reflecting Chinese governmental policies, paid scant attention to human rights.[103]

In certain situations the state members of the Bank have pushed the agency into an active and open human rights posture, as when the Bank was utilized to bring economic pressure on Serbia to cooperate with the International Criminal Tribunal for the former Yugoslavia, or to likewise hold up loans to Ivory Coast until the results of a free and fair election were honored. But this type of open support for criminal justice or democratic elections has not been pursued consistently. Thus the Bank has sometimes served as the means to implement the political objectives of the moment by the wealthy countries rather than manifesting a consistent and carefully considered human rights program by the Bank as an independent international organization.

The Bank evolved a concern with "good government" but this was generally intended to focus on transparency and proper accounting, and other matters related to sound economic decisions, rather than on fidelity to democratic and other human rights standards. Bank loans have certainly flowed at times to various authoritarian governments, even those committing or allowing atrocities. Pinochet in Chile was a case in point. To cite a more recent example, Bank loans have gone to authoritarian but pro-western Ethiopia.

---

[103] See www.wsj.com/articles/world-bank-revamps-lending-rules-mindful-of-human-rights-abuses-1470346831.

In general the IMF (which has been always headed by a European) more than the Bank adhered to the position that it was a technical organization focused on currency and balance of payments problems within the domain of international monetary policy. Not being officially a development organization, the IMF mostly maintained the position that it was independent from human rights norms and obligations.[104]

International humanitarian law

If states have been generally slow to enforce global human rights norms in peace, or what passes for peace in modern international relations, it is not surprising to find that they have been even more reluctant to engage in broad and systematic enforcement of international humanitarian law.[105] In all states, including liberal democracies, it is politically difficult to put the national military in harm's way and then prosecute its members or their civilian superiors for violating parts of the laws of war pertaining to humane values. Even prosecuting the enemy for war crimes can also prove difficult. Often one has control of neither the guilty person nor the documentary evidence that would stand judicial scrutiny. Obtaining such persons or evidence may require more combat, with more death and destruction. This is a main reason the USA did not move on Baghdad in 1991 at the end of major combat to force the Iraqi army out of Kuwait. Trying to gain custody of Saddam Hussein and his supporting cast of commanders for war crimes trials was judged to be not politically sustainable at that time. Also, attempting to prosecute enemy personnel may give rise to further steps against one's own interests, especially if the other side has certain leverage points. One can recall that after World War I the British gave up on plans to prosecute Turkish/ Ottoman officials for crimes against humanity related to their treatment of Armenians. The Turks held a number of British POWs and would not release them until the idea of prosecutions was dropped. Given difficulties of enforcement via judicial action, or various forms of collectively organized sanctions, once again interested parties must look primarily to diplomacy or other means of political application of humanitarian norms.

Under the Geneva Conventions of 1949 and Additional Protocol I of 1977 pertaining to international armed conflict, fighting states are supposed to appoint a neutral state as a Protecting Power to oversee

---

[104] See further Bahram Ghazi, *The IMF, the World Bank Group, and the Question of Human Rights* (Leiden: Brill, 2005).

[105] Among many sources see Hazel Fox and Michael A. Meyer, eds., *Effecting Compliance* (London: British Institute of International and Comparative Law, 1993).

application of appropriate international rules. Few Protecting Powers have been appointed since World War II. This situation leaves the International Committee of the Red Cross, a private Swiss agency, to do what it can to encourage states to see that captured, wounded, and sick military personnel benefit from international legal provisions as written, and that civilians in occupied territory and other war zones likewise benefit from protective norms.

There is also the matter of reciprocity among fighting parties, and such considerations played a role in World War II. Allied POWs in German hands and German POWs under Allied control were, in general and for the most part, treated according to the terms of the 1929 POW Convention. Such was definitely not the case for Soviet POWs in German hands and vice versa, where death rates were appalling, as neither was legally bound to the other under that same Geneva Convention. In this regard it is difficult to say whether the driving force was legal factors backed by positive reciprocity, for good treatment, or racial views, for ill-treatment. German and non-Soviet Allied prisoners were mostly of the same ethnic and racial stock, whereas particularly the "Aryan" Germans looked down upon the Soviets as inferior Slavs. Between Germans and Soviets there was negative reciprocity, as each side abused and killed many of the other's prisoners. The workings of positive reciprocity are particularly problematic in asymmetric warfare, since the weaker party fighting via guerrilla tactics and terrorism usually controls little fixed territory for safe detention and generally does not pay much attention to the laws of war.[106]

The overall record of applying humanitarian law is not an altogether happy one, especially in internal armed conflicts where the rules are more lenient and some of the fighting parties usually woefully uninformed about humanitarian standards.[107] Even in international armed conflict perhaps a minimalist approach is in order, as when one expert remarked that, if it were not legally wrong to bomb hospitals, they would be bombed all of the time instead of only some of the time. Occasionally, as in the Falklands/Malvinas war of 1982, states like Argentina and the United Kingdom engage in combat more or less according to humanitarian law. Even in places like the former Yugoslavia during 1992–1995, perhaps more civilians benefited from humanitarian protection and

---

[106] From a vast literature, see David P. Forsythe, *The Politics of Prisoner Abuse: US Policy Toward Enemy Prisoners After 9/11* (Cambridge: Cambridge University Press, 2011); and Mark Osiel, *The End of Reciprocity: Terror, Torture, and the Law of War* (Cambridge: Cambridge University Press, 2009).

[107] A useful overview is Larry Minear and Thomas G. Weiss, *Mercy Under Fire: War and the Global Humanitarian Community* (Boulder: Westview, 1995).

assistance than were intentionally shot, raped, tortured, maimed, or otherwise attacked and persecuted. It is a difficult comparison and judgment to make. Never before in world history have civilians constituted such a high percentage of the casualties in armed conflicts. But never have there been so many rules and actors trying to humanize war.[108] I will continue this subject in Chapter 4, when I address criminal prosecution in more detail.

Conclusion

If one compares the United Nations and the League of Nations with regard to setting human rights and humanitarian standards and trying to apply them, one can clearly see the increased commitment to liberal values centering on personal human rights in international relations, both in peace and war. But one can also see that much of this commitment is *pro forma*, which is to say, insincere. The members of the United Nations are states, and they still express considerable interest in their independence and freedom from authoritative international supervision on rights issues. Yet gradually, as subsequent chapters will also demonstrate, they are beginning to redefine their national interests to include more attention to human rights and humanitarian values, even if realist concerns with independent power and a tough pursuit of narrow national interests have not vanished.

Case study: human rights and humanitarian law at Guantanamo

After the Al Qaeda terrorist attacks on the US homeland on 9/11/2001, the George W. Bush Administration responded with military and CIA operations in Afghanistan and other places. The Al Qaeda core leadership was then in Afghanistan, in liaison with the Taliban government of Mullah Omar. As a result of military and paramilitary operations in conjunction with the local Northern Alliance militia, the US military began to detain a number of prisoners, especially in Afghanistan. Local detention arrangements were inadequate and sometimes insecure. Also, the highest levels of the Bush Administration decided that the terrorist threat was significant enough that it was unwise to observe the normal legal rules pertaining to the treatment of enemy or security prisoners.

---

[108] David P. Forsythe, "The International Committee of the Red Cross and Humanitarian Assistance: A Policy Analysis," *International Review of the Red Cross*, 314 (September–October 1996), 512–531.

It therefore opened a military detention center on the island of Guantanamo, leased in perpetuity from Cuba. The facility was secure, and Bush officials hoped it would be a legal black hole, immune from US judicial oversight given their claim that it was foreign territory. The Administration claimed that detainees there were "unlawful enemy combatants" who had no rights under international humanitarian law.

Bush officials were concerned above all with two human rights or humanitarian treaties to which the US was a full party, having ratified them without crippling reservations: the 1984 UN Convention against Torture and Cruel, Inhuman, and Degrading Treatment; and the 1949 Geneva Conventions for situations of armed conflict, which prohibited torture, cruel treatment, and humiliation. The United States had also ratified the International Covenant on Civil and Political Rights, which also prohibited major abuse of prisoners. But at the time of ratification the United States had submitted reservations which prevented its use in courts in the USA. From the beginning the Administration was worried about domestic review of its planned abusive policies toward prisoners.

As 2002 progressed, the US Department of Defense Under Secretary Donald Rumsfeld moved in fits and starts toward abusive interrogation of probably about 15–20 percent of the detainees at Guantanamo (or GTMO, or Gitmo in military parlance). In the winter of 2002–2003, for example, a suspected potential hijacker by the name of Mohammed al-Qahtani was subjected to an interrogation process that a US official later characterized as torture.

The United States continued to submit periodic reports to the CAT, the Committee against Torture, which is the monitoring mechanism under the Torture Convention. The United States, because of convoluted events, also wound up with the International Committee of the Red Cross having a permanent presence at GTMO. The ICRC is mandated under the 1949 Geneva Conventions (referred to as "Geneva" in military parlance) to visit all detainees in international armed conflict, and is also often given permission to visit detainees in internal war and domestic troubles and tensions. From January 2002 the ICRC did its usual prison visits at GTMO and as usual submitted its confidential reports to the detaining authority. So two normal review processes were in place regarding the treatment of what can be factually called enemy prisoners, regardless of debate over legal categories or labels.

Domestically the US Congress, being under Republican Party control and sympathetic to the claims of a Republican Administration, did not at first much involve itself in matters pertaining to GTMO. Congress had passed an AUMF (authorization to use military force) under which the Bush Administration claimed it had the authority to set prisoner policy.

Congress deferred to that Executive claim for a time. It was only in 2005 that Congress mustered the effort to deal with policy toward enemy prisoners, after the release of unauthorized photos from the Abu Ghraib prison in Iraq showing horrific US treatment of Iraqi and other prisoners there. From 2005 under the Detainee Treatment Act (DTA), Congress required the US military to return to the treatment of detainees specified in the US Army Field Manual which was based on the 1949 Geneva Conventions, especially concerning the interrogation of prisoners under military control. Certain Republican senators with an interest in military honor and military law, and traditional American values, took the lead in this legislative effort, which gave political cover to Democratic members of Congress also interested in curtailing abuse of prisoners. The DTA passed by such margins that a presidential veto was not in play, and so the Bush Administration formally accepted this congressional restriction on its prisoner policy.

In parallel fashion, the US Supreme Court wound up making a number of judgments that had been initiated by American human rights advocacy groups, working with detainees, based on international as well as US law. In particular, the US Supreme Court in 2006 ruled in the Hamdan case that part of the 1949 Geneva Conventions (Common Article 3) applied to all detainees at GTMO. While the case dealt with the subject of military commissions for the trial of detainees, the judgment clearly implied that no torture or cruel treatment could legally obtain at GTMO.

Therefore from 2005–2006 both Congress and the courts pushed back against Bush policies of abusive treatment of certain detainees at GTMO in ways that cemented a change in Bush policies. The significant push back, as far as the present analysis is concerned, came from human rights and humanitarian treaties "gaining traction" in American legislative and judicial processes, not simply from international actors reviewing the US record in Geneva or New York or other centers of international diplomacy. The process was transnational, with international law merging with national law and politics.

One might observe that all of this took time, and without doubt from 2002 until 2005–2006 a number of GTMO prisoners were subjected to torture and/or cruel treatment while in US military custody. Nevertheless the abusive policies were eventually rolled back because of national decisions in the framework of international law. One can also observe that still other prisoner policies were debated in the context of inter-national human rights and humanitarian law, such as what kind of due process in the military commissions satisfied the requirements of the 1949 Geneva Conventions and their Additional Protocol I which had been added in 1977. Finally, one should observe that Bush policies toward prisoners under CIA control comprise an additional and somewhat separate subject, too lengthy for coverage here.

Discussion questions

- Can a decentralized or Westphalian system of international law and diplomacy, in which equal sovereign states apply human rights norms, be fully effective? To what extent have contemporary states moved away from this Westphalian system for the purpose of using the United Nations to protect internationally recognized human rights?
- Can one always draw a clear distinction between security issues and human rights issues? Can a putative human rights issue also be a genuine security issue? Is it ever proper for the UN Security Council to invoke Charter Chapter VII, thus permitting legally binding enforcement decisions, when dealing with violations of human rights?
- Is it ever proper for a state, or a collection of states, to use coercion in another state to protect human rights, without the explicit and advance approval of the UN Security Council? What lessons should be drawn from NATO's action in Kosovo? Is this a form of humanitarian intervention that should be approved and repeated by the international community?
- What is the difference between international and internal (civil) armed conflicts, from the standpoint of law, and from the standpoint of practical action, when it comes to protecting human rights in such conflicts?
- Beyond the Security Council, which parts of the UN system, if any, have compiled a noteworthy record in applying human rights standards? Is this because of direct protection, indirect protection, or long-term education? Is it possible to generalize about the UN and protecting human rights under Charter Chapter VI and peaceful or quasi-peaceful diplomacy? What is the relationship between human rights and UN complex peacekeeping?
- What is the relationship between the international law of human rights and international humanitarian law concerning practical action to advance human dignity in "failed states" and "complex emergencies"?

SUGGESTIONS FOR FURTHER READING

Alston, Philip, ed., *The United Nations and Human Rights: A Critical Appraisal* (Oxford: Clarendon Press, 1995). A broad and excellent survey by experts on the subject; indispensable. A second edition with Frederic Megret as second editor is forthcoming in 2017.

Cohen, Roberta, and Francis M. Deng, eds., *The Forsaken People: Case Studies of the Internally Displaced* (Washington: Brookings, 1998). An authoritative look at a growing human rights problem, as displaced persons do not always benefit from the protection and assistance given to official refugees.

Dobbins, James, Seth G. Jones, Keith Crane, et al., *The UN's Role in Nation-Building: From the Congo to Iraq* (Santa Monica, CA: Rand, 2005). A good analytical overview, noting several positive contributions.

Evans, Gareth. *The Responsibility to Protect: Ending Mass Atrocity Crimes Once and for All* (Washington: Brookings, 2009). The definitive treatment of original intentions by one of the authors of this norm.

Forsythe, David, *The Politics of Prisoner Abuse: US Policy Toward Enemy Prisoners After 9/11* (Cambridge: Cambridge University Press, 2011). An overview of how the George W. Bush Administration sought to obtain information via abusive interrogation after 9/11/2001, despite the human rights and humanitarian treaties to which it was a party.

Gaer, Felice, and Christen L. Broecker, eds., *The United Nations High Commissioner for Human Rights: Conscience for the World* (Leiden and Boston: Martinus Nijhoff, 2014). A variety of experts examine the office from different perspectives. Substantive and informative.

Guest, Iain, *Behind the Disappearances: Argentina's Dirty War Against Human Rights and the United Nations* (Philadelphia: University of Pennsylvania Press, 1990). A journalist uncovers Argentina's extensive efforts, supported by the Reagan Administration in Washington, to block UN investigation into its brutal policies during military rule in the 1980s.

Humphrey, John P., *Human Rights and the United Nations: A Great Adventure* (Dobbs Ferry: Transnational, 1984). The first Director of the Human Rights Division in the UN Secretariat reflects on his experiences. Humphrey, a Canadian social democrat, was influential behind the scenes in the drafting of the Universal Declaration of Human Rights, although others like the Frenchman René Casin were often given more credit in public.

Kille, Kent, ed., *The UN Secretary-General and Moral Authority: Ethics and Religion in International Leadership* (Washington: Georgetown University Press, 2007). The best overview of the UN Secretaries-General with regard to personal values. Thus a study of the interplay of commitment to human rights, international law, and ethics, but in the context of state power and policy.

Lebovic, J. H., and E. Voeten, "The Politics of Shame: The Condemnation of Country Human Rights Practices in the UNCHR," *International Studies Quarterly*, 50, 3 (2006), 861–888. An important study showing that the UN Human Rights Commission was not as politicized as often pictured.

Loescher, Gil, *The UNHCR and World Politics: A Perilous Path* (New York and Oxford: Oxford University Press, 2001). The best comprehensive treatment of the UN Refugee Office (UNHCR). His proposals for change in the future are well considered but stand little chance of being adopted by states.

Matheson, Michael J., *Council Unbound: The Growth of UN Decision Making on Conflict and Postconflict Issues After the Cold War* (Washington: US Institute of Peace, 2006). A former State Department lawyer examines the UNSC's expanding role in conflicts, with some attention to human rights.

Mertus, Julie, *The United Nations and Human Rights* (New York: Routledge, 2005). A basic survey of the different agents in the UN system, intended for students.

Ogata, Sadako, *Turbulent Decade: Confronting the Refugee Crises of the 1990s* (New York: Norton, 2005). Account by the former head of the UNHCR about the problems she faced in places like Bosnia and the Great Lakes region of Africa.

Orchard, Phil, *A Right to Flee: Refugees, States, and the Construction of International Cooperation* (Cambridge: Cambridge University Press, 2014). A very good overview of the history of international cooperation in dealing with refugees, including contemporary developments.

Roberts, Adam, and Benedict Kingsbury, eds., *United Nations, Divided World: The UN's Roles in International Relations*, 2nd edn. (Oxford: Clarendon, 1993). A good collection of essays, mostly by legal experts, with considerable attention to human rights. The chapter centering on human rights by Tom Farer and Felice Gaer was one of the best short analyses that existed at that time.

Simmons, Beth, *Mobilizing for Human Rights: International Law in Domestic Politics* (Cambridge: Cambridge University Press, 2009). An outstanding analysis of why states ratify human rights treaties and why some of the treaty norms come to be taken seriously by states – mainly because of certain developments in the domestic politics of transitional states rather than the international monitoring process.

Tolley, Howard, Jr., *The UN Commission on Human Rights* (Boulder: Westview, 1987). While this book is now dated, it remains the definitive treatment for its time. No one has written a comparable sequel.

Tyagi, Yogesh, *The UN Human Rights Committee: Practice and Procedure* (Cambridge: Cambridge University Press, 2011). A comprehensive legal treatise.

Weiss, Thomas G., David P. Forsythe, and Roger A. Coate, *The United Nations and Changing World Politics*, 8th edn. (Boulder: Westview, for Perseus, 2017). A widely used text devotes Part II to human rights and humanitarian affairs.

4 Transitional justice: criminal courts and alternatives

After gross violations of human rights, what is one to do? This is the subject of transitional justice, a growth industry for intellectuals and policy makers after the Cold War. Should one prosecute individuals in international courts, or in hybrid or special courts, or in national courts? Should one avoid courts and rely on truth commissions, or bar violators from public office, or just move on to concentrate on building a rights-protective state in the future rather than looking back via criminal prosecution? There are many complexities facing those interested in international criminal justice – meaning those interested in whether to prosecute individuals against the background of international human rights and humanitarian norms. Beyond punishment of evildoers, one needs to keep in mind other possible goals of transitional justice: deterring future atrocities, bringing psychological closure to victims and/or relatives, producing reconciliation among divided communities, building a rights-protective polity in the future, adjusting to the lingering power of elements of the old regime.

In the last decade of the twentieth century the United Nations created two international criminal courts, the first in almost fifty years. Moreover a new International Criminal Court (ICC) came into legal existence in July 2002. Furthermore, special courts were created in the aftermath of atrocities in Sierra Leone, East Timor, Kosovo, and Cambodia, while a new court was created by the interim government of Iraq after the US invasion and occupation of 2003 to try Saddam Hussein and his lieutenants. The United Kingdom agreed that the former dictator of Chile, Augusto Pinochet, could be extradited to Spain to stand trial there for torture. The Security Council authorized a special court in response to a political assassination in Lebanon, although that was more political theatre than expectation of effective criminal justice.

In the abstract it is hard to disagree with the proposition that those who commit gross violations of internationally recognized standards pertaining to genocide, war crimes, and crimes against humanity should face criminal justice. The principle of R2P, already noted as adopted by the UN in 2005, adds ethnic cleansing to this list of major violations (but without changing the subject matter jurisdiction of existing courts).[1] If we had reliable criminal justice on a global scale, we could punish individual criminals with more certainty, bring some catharsis to victims and/or their relatives, try to break the vicious circle of group violence, and hope to deter similar future acts.

In international relations as it continues to exist in the early twenty-first century, however, while there may be an embryonic trend toward "legalization" and more use of adjudication,[2] many policy makers are obviously reluctant to pursue criminal justice – especially through international tribunals. Sometimes this hesitancy is the product of realist attitudes and/or chauvinistic nationalism. But sometimes these policies of hesitation are characterized by careful reasoning and serious liberal argument.

Hesitancy about international criminal justice is thus not always a reaction by those who wish to elevate repressive privilege over protection of international human rights. Caution is also sometimes evidenced by persons of relatively liberal persuasion who by definition are motivated by considerable concern for human dignity. In general they are in favor of human rights, but on occasion they find it both politically prudent and morally defensible to bypass the enforcement of human rights through criminal justice. I term this position pragmatic liberalism. This view can be contrasted with judicial romanticism, which brushes aside such political and diplomatic concerns in the belief that criminal justice is a panacea for violations of human rights, and that "impunity" for those violations ought never be allowed. Judicial romantics overestimate what courts can achieve and underestimate the role of soft law and essentially political approaches to advancing human rights and humanitarian norms.

Like Martha Minow, this chapter suggests that in the wake of atrocities there is no single response that is always appropriate everywhere, but rather a menu of choice in which the proper selection depends upon political context.[3] Like Richard J. Goldstone, the first ICTY prosecutor,

---

[1] See further Jennifer Jackson Preece, "Ethnic Cleansing," in David P. Forsythe, ed., *Encyclopedia of Human Rights* (New York: Oxford University Press, 2009), vol. II, 163–168.

[2] See the special issue of the journal *International Organization* on "Legalization and World Politics," March 2001. See also Mary L. Volcansek, *Law Above Nations: Supranational Courts and the Legalization of Politics* (Gainesville: University Press of Florida, 1997).

[3] Martha Minow, in *Between Vengeance and Forgiveness: Facing History After Genocide and Mass Violence* (Boston: Beacon Press, 1998), argues that neither trials nor truth

this chapter argues that considerations of peace and justice have to be carefully calculated, and that pursuit of justice does not always require criminal justice as compared to social and political forms of justice.[4]

Historical background to 1991: few trials, small impact

The history of criminal prosecution – both international and national – related to international events is reasonably well known, at least to some scholars.[5] Since books have been written on the subject, here I seek merely to highlight several important points. Even a cursory retrospective shows that many policy makers have found ample reason to avoid international trials, with a few exceptions. As is usually the case, political calculation precedes reference to legal rules. As Werner Levi has written, "[P]olitics decides who the lawmaker and what the formulation of the law shall be; law formalizes these decisions and makes them binding. This distribution of functions makes law dependent upon politics."[6]

International trials

While there was some discussion of criminal prosecution of German (and Turkish) leaders after World War I, movement in that direction was aborted.[7] It was only after World War II that the first international criminal proceedings transpired, with well-known defects.[8] For a time Allied leaders leaned toward summary execution of high German policy makers, but eventually concluded a treaty creating the Nuremberg tribunal. The stated objectives were lofty enough, but the taint of victor's justice was pervasive. At Nuremberg (and Tokyo) only the losing leaders

commissions are always the most appropriate option. Compare Andrew Rigby, *Justice and Reconciliation: After the Violence* (Boulder: Lynne Rienner, 2001), and Ruti G. Teitel, *Transitional Justice* (New York: Oxford University Press, 2002). Teitel provides a concise overview in "Transitional Justice," in *Encyclopedia of Human Rights*, vol. V, 81–86. See further the various articles in the journal *International Transitional Justice*.

[4] "Bringing War Criminals to Justice During an Ongoing War," in Jonathan Moore, ed., *Hard Choices: Moral Dilemmas in Humanitarian Intervention* (Lanham: Rowman & Littlefield, 1998), 195–210.

[5] Steven R. Ratner and Jason S. Abrams, *Accountability for Human Rights Atrocities in International Law: Beyond the Nuremberg Legacy*, 3rd edn. (Oxford: Clarendon Press, 2009; 1st edn., 1997; 2nd edn., 2001). See further Ramesh Thakur and Peter Malcontent, eds., *From Sovereign Impunity to International Accountability: The Search for Justice in a World of States* (Tokyo: United Nations University Press, 2004).

[6] Werner Levi, *Law and Politics in the International Society* (Beverly Hills: Sage, 1976), 31.

[7] James F. Willis, *Prologue to Nuremberg: The Politics and Diplomacy of Punishing War Criminals of the First World War* (Westport: Greenwood, 1982).

[8] A vast bibliography is recorded in Telford Taylor, *The Anatomy of the Nuremberg Tribunal: A Personal Memoir* (New York: Knopf, 1992).

were tried, even though Allied leaders had engaged in such acts as attacking cities through conventional, incendiary, and atomic bombings, thus failing to distinguish between combatants and civilians – a cardinal principle of international humanitarian law (viz., that part of the law of war oriented to the protection of victims of war, especially now the 1949 Geneva Conventions). Soviet military personnel committed perhaps 100,000 rapes in Berlin after the defeat of the Nazis. Rapes were systematic practice, yet no commanding officers, much less lower-ranking soldiers, were ever held accountable. The Soviet Union then sat in judgment of Germans at Nuremberg.[9]

There was also some prosecution and conviction via *ex post facto* laws (laws created after the act in question). The concept of individual responsibility for war crimes was reasonably well established through national laws by 1939. But crimes against peace and crimes against humanity were concepts that had never been the subject of precise legislation or prosecution until 1946. Also, procedural guarantees of a fair trial could have been improved.[10]

Twenty-two German leaders were prosecuted at Nuremberg in the first round of trials, nineteen of whom were convicted, with twelve of these being executed. Other individual German cases occurred, in both international and national courts. Similar proceedings were held at Tokyo for Japanese leaders, through fiat of the US military command.[11] A pronounced defect of especially the Tokyo tribunal was the total ignoring of gender crimes, despite a broad policy of sexual slavery carried out by Japanese officials.[12]

The effect of these trials on subsequent thinking in Germany and Japan remains a matter of conjecture. Did the Nuremberg and Tokyo trials, through emphasis on individual criminal responsibility, force those nations to confront the past and face up to the individual moral choices that existed? There is widespread agreement that Germany more than Japan has tried to come to terms with the atrocities of the past – although

---

[9] Anonymous, *A Woman in Berlin* (Boston: Henry Holt, 2005).
[10] Michael P. Scharf, *Balkan Justice: The Story Behind the First International War Crimes Trial Since Nuremberg* (Durham: Carolina Academic Press, 1997).
[11] Arnold Brackman, *The Other Nuremberg: The Untold Story of the Tokyo War Crimes Trials* (New York: Morrow, 1987). Compare Richard Minear, *Victor's Justice: The Tokyo War Crimes Trial* (Princeton: Princeton University Press, 1971). For a further comparison of the Nuremberg and Tokyo trials see Gerry Simpson, "Nuremberg and Tokyo Trials," in *Encyclopedia of Human Rights*, vol. IV, 137–144.
[12] For a concise review see Kelly D. Askin, "A Decade of the Development of Gender Crimes in International Courts and Tribunals: 1993 to 2003," in *Human Rights Brief*, American University, Center for Human Rights and Humanitarian Law, 11, 3 (Spring 2004), 16–19.

Japan has made increased gestures in that direction in recent years. Yet both nations experienced similar international criminal tribunals. A researcher for the *Congressional Quarterly* wrote that "The tribunals were viewed as illegitimate by the defendants and by much, perhaps most, of the German and Japanese publics."[13]

Archival research shows that the Nuremberg process was deeply unpopular in Germany through the 1950s, and that the USA backed away from it in order to get Konrad Adenauer elected Chancellor in West Germany and also to get that new state integrated into NATO. As noted earlier, the USA thus engaged in "strategic legalism" concerning German war crimes trials, pushing them as long as they did not interfere with other foreign policy objectives but abandoning them when judged expedient.[14] It is possible but not certain that later, when the West Germans themselves pursued criminal prosecutions for Nazi crimes, in conjunction with transnational pressures to never forget the Holocaust, this combined process had some considerable impact on evolving German political culture – with developments in Japan being quite different.[15]

Since Nuremberg and Tokyo were not followed by other international tribunals for almost fifty years, it is clear that the international trials of the 1940s did little to deter other atrocities through credible threat of sure prosecution. The two tribunals certainly did clarify relevant facts, perhaps providing some catharsis and relief. Most clearly, the trials provided punishment for some national leaders. The trials also expressed the West's aspirations for a liberal world order based on rule of law and accountability for human rights violations.

---

[13] "War Crimes," *CQ Researcher*, 5, 25 (July 5, 1995), 589. See further Wilbourn E. Benton and Georg Grimm, eds., *Nuremberg: German Views of the War Trials* (Dallas: Southern Methodist University Press, 1955).

[14] Peter Maguire, *Law and War: An American Story* (New York: Columbia University Press, 2000).

[15] David P. Forsythe, "Human Rights and Mass Atrocities: Revisiting Transitional Justice," *International Studies Review*, 13, 1 (March 2011), 85–95. I think it likely that the Nuremberg tribunal, especially when followed up later by German courts, combined with other reminders of the German past such as a widespread and persistent socialization project about the Holocaust, has caused Germany to be highly sensitive to most human rights issues today. Similar western pressure on Japan has been less, providing one major reason why Japan has been more reluctant to come to terms with its past. The Tokyo trial was less well known in the West, Japanese atrocities such as the rape of Nanking were less well known, and there has been no western-based project like that of remembering the Holocaust which is comparable in the Japanese case. Nuremberg is part of a much broader campaign to remind Germans of their history during 1933–1945, making it difficult to factor out the singular impact of international criminal justice.

Yet realist concerns were not absent. Particularly regarding Germany but also Japan, the USA shielded certain officials, especially scientists, from criminal prosecution and brought them to the USA for work in weapons development – given the start of the Cold War with the Soviet Union. In Japan, the USA shielded the Emperor from prosecution, judging him useful in democratic state-building after the war.[16]

In numerous situations between the end of World War II and the end of the Cold War international criminal proceedings were not practical. As in the Korean War, most international armed conflicts ended inconclusively, and certainly without unconditional surrender, thus preventing the trial of those not in custody who were suspected of violations of international law. (And in the Korean War, US and South Korean forces had fired indiscriminately into civilians, fearing that enemy agents were hiding among those fleeing.[17] So raising the issue of war crimes by the enemy might point embarrassing fingers toward one's own side.)

Those wars like the 1991 Persian Gulf War that ended in decisive military defeat still did not result in unconditional surrender and the victors gaining control over the losers. The George H. W. Bush Administration made the judgment, among other considerations, that pursuit of prosecution for Iraqi war crimes was not worth the continued death, injury, and destruction that would have been involved in the attempted capture of the Iraqi leadership. This was a reasoned policy, not devoid of moral considerations. It was almost universally accepted at that time as the proper policy. Later the US House of Representatives voted overwhelmingly in favor of Iraqi trials for war crimes. But based on congressional reactions to American casualties in both Lebanon in the 1980s and Somalia in the 1990s, that body would have been among the first to heatedly criticize a costly ground war designed to apprehend the Iraqi leadership had such been launched by the senior Bush or his successor. By 2005, a majority of the American public gave the George W. Bush Administration very low marks for its 2003 invasion of Iraq. Even though that Administration could point to the capture and forthcoming trial of Saddam Hussein (and others), the public was primarily concerned with American casualties and lack of a clear exit strategy.

In other situations international tribunals could have been organized but for the strength of nationalism. Decisive outcomes produced by such

[16] See further Dapo Akande, "International Law Immunities and the International Criminal Court," *American Journal of International Law*, 98, 3 (July 2004), 417; and Timothy Brook, "The Tokyo Judgment and the Rape of Nanking," *Journal of Asian Studies*, 60, 3 (August 2001), 673–700.

[17] See, e.g., Robert L. Bateman, III, *No Gun Ri: A Military History of the Korean War Incident* (Mechanicsburg: Stackpole Books, 2002).

as the Soviet intervention in Hungary or the US intervention in Grenada did not result in international trials since the victors did not want an international tribunal to closely examine embarrassing aspects of the use of force. Clearly the preferred value was not impartial application of human rights, humanitarian law, or criminal justice but rather protection of the national record and safeguarding unfettered decision making in the future.[18]

Some war crimes usually occur during any use of force. This was made clear, *inter alia*, by eventual disclosure that Israelis had massacred a number of Egyptian prisoners of war during the 1956 Middle East War.[19] Either by design, in the context of what is judged to be pressing military necessity, or by loss of control, even personnel of democracies commit war crimes. I have already noted US involvement in massacres in the Korean War.

National trials

As for crimes against humanity, before the 1990s only the French and Israelis held national trials involving this concept. Britain, France, the Soviet Union, and the United States were willing enough to apply this concept *ex post facto* to Nazi Germany and Imperial Japan, but of these only France developed the concept (slightly) in its own national law. French and Israeli cases were exceedingly few in number, and, with the exception of the Eichmann trial in Jerusalem, pursued with considerable domestic political difficulties. This was especially so in France, as charges against French citizens for aiding in the Holocaust through crimes against humanity resurrected a painful episode in French history. Officials of the Vichy government administered half of France during World War II. Some of its French officials displayed a vicious anti-Semitism.

---

[18] After the USA deposed the Panamanian strongman Manuel Noriega in 1989 through military invasion, he was tried and convicted in a US federal court for drug-smuggling and racketeering, not for war crimes or human rights violations. His history of being on the CIA payroll did not save him from US regime change and prosecution. The USA then extradited him to France for further prosecution. All of this was dependent on political factors, namely his falling out of favor with western states. The same was true for Saddam Hussein, who had received US and other western support for his containment of revolutionary Iran, before he became the target of US regime change and US-supported Iraqi prosecution.

[19] Barton Gellman, "Confronting History," *Washington Post*, National Weekly Edition, August 28–September 3, 1995, 12; Serge Schmemann, "After a General Tells of Killing POWs in 1956, Israelis Argue Over Ethics of War," *New York Times*, August 21, 1995, A1.

As for genocide, until the mid-1990s and events in Bosnia and Rwanda, no procedurally correct national trials were held entailing this concept, only procedurally suspect trials in places like Equatorial Guinea. Germany, being the temporary home of a number of refugees from the fighting in the former Yugoslavia, found itself the site of at least one national trial pertaining to both war crimes and genocide in the 1990s.[20] Rwandan national courts were to pursue this subject in numerous cases.

By far the most numerous national trials for gross violations of human rights connected to international events concern war crimes, although they are not always technically called that when prosecuted under national military law. For the most part these trials involve western liberal democracies applying the laws of war to their own military personnel. Very rarely, a country such as Denmark, Switzerland, or Germany will hold a war crimes trial concerning a foreigner, usually pertaining to events in the former Yugoslavia. National war crimes trials have not been without problems. As noted above, the military personnel even of democracies do commit war crimes, for those democracies that have used force abroad have not lacked for courts martial for violations of the laws of war. This, for example, the Americans discovered at My Lai and other places in Vietnam, the Israelis discovered in Arab territory occupied since 1967, and the Canadians and Italians discovered in Somalia during the 1990s.

Even when such national trials are held in liberal democracies, it has not always proved easy to apply the full force of national military law (which is derived from international law). No US senior officers were ever held responsible for the massacre at My Lai in Vietnam in the late 1960s. Moreover, President Richard Nixon felt compelled by public opinion to reduce the punishment for Lt. Calley who was held responsible for the deaths of between twenty and seventy "Oriental" civilians at My Lai. At the time of writing US officials have moved mostly against low-ranking soldiers for prisoner abuse connected to Washington's "war on terrorism." The Israeli authorities have been quite lenient in punishing their military personnel for violations of various human rights and humanitarian norms in disputed territory. The Canadians have found it difficult to come to full terms with the actions of some of their troops in Somalia. Only the Italians moved rapidly and vigorously against some of

---

[20] In re Jorgic, regarding the Bosnian Serb convicted in Germany for atrocities committed in Bosnia during 1992–1993 (Alan Cowell, "German Court Sentences Serb to Life for Genocide in Bosnia," *New York Times*, September 27, 1997, www.nytimes.com/1997/09/27/world/german-court-sentences-serb-to-life-for-genocide-in-bosnia.html).

their soldiers who had abused Somalis. Rome concluded that the incidents in question were the result of a few "bad apples" and not part of a systematic or structural problem.

In Israel, even a video of an Israeli soldier shooting a wounded and unresisting Palestinian who had been involved in a knife attack led not to swift and sure legal sanction, but to a national debate. While certain Israeli officials insisted on application of the laws of war, others – and many in the public – rallied to the soldier's defense on emotive nationalistic grounds. The Israeli sergeant was convicted, but widespread and high-level pleas in his behalf continued. It was reminiscent of how much American public opinion had rallied to the defense of Lt. Calley despite his murderous and rapacious role in the My Lai massacre in Vietnam.[21] The laws of war when applied to one's own often were undermined by emotive nationalism.

More than anything else this national record suggests the continuing power of nationalism, rather than any carefully reasoned and morally compelling argument about national criminal justice associated with war. That is to say that no compelling political or moral argument explains why the US military justice system mostly failed in its handling of the My Lai massacre.[22] (First, the military attempted to suppress the facts. Then the military establishment focused the spotlight of inquiry at platoon level, mostly ignoring the training and orders given to foot soldiers by superior commanders. There was never punishment that fitted the extent of the crime.) A defensive and emotional nationalism has frequently overwhelmed aspects of proper criminal justice. If this is true in national trials, it indicates much difficulty for the prospects of international criminal justice. If national governments have trouble prosecuting their own, particularly those who authorized or allowed the wrongdoing, how much more difficult it will be for them to turn over their own for trial by others. Serbia and the United States are not so different in this regard, except in the power of the USA to resist the kind of pressures that caused Serbia to grudgingly cooperate in matters of international criminal justice. When Ratko Mladic was finally arrested in 2011 for his role in the genocidal massacre at Srebrenica in 1995 and earlier attacks on Bosnian civilians in

[21] See www.washingtonpost.com/world/middle_east/the-military-trial-thats-tearing-israel-apart/2016/11/01/7f0d203c-9b93-11e6-b552-b1f85e484086_story.html; and www.washingtonpost.com/world/israeli-court-convicts-soldier-of-shooting-dead-wounded-palestinian-assailant/2017/01/04/b766ecdc-d1d6-11e6-9651-54a0154cf5b3_story.html?postshare=7361483571823527&tid=ss_mail&utm_term=.c26e574056d1.

[22] Joseph Goldstein, Burke Marshall, and Jack Schwartz, eds., *The My Lai Massacre and Its Cover-Up: Beyond the Reach of Law?* (New York: Free Press, 1976).

Sarajevo, thousands of Serbs demonstrated in his support, seeing him as a national war hero.

In sum, international criminal proceedings were very rare before the end of the Cold War, and thus we do not know very much about their effects. Rare also have been national proceedings for crimes against humanity and genocide. Only national trials for war crimes have occurred with any regularity, and these – mostly in democracies – have been frequently constricted by the continuing strength of an emotional nationalism.

International criminal justice since 1991

After the Cold War and the demise of European communism, international relations saw the creation of two UN *ad hoc* criminal courts, several special hybrid criminal courts, and for the first time in history a standing – which is to say permanent – International Criminal Court. There were also important national developments in criminal justice linked to international human rights and humanitarian law. Paradoxically, this movement toward increased international criminal justice only intensified the debate about other forms of transitional justice – and whether some forms of justice might be preferred that downplayed criminal justice in favor of social or political justice. Some spoke of the difference between retributive and restorative justice.

The ICTY

At first glance, the creation of the International Criminal Tribunal for the former Yugoslavia (ICTY) in 1993 by the UN Security Council seemed to usher in a new age in international criminal justice.[23] The Security Council voted to create a balanced and mostly procedurally correct international tribunal while the fighting and atrocities still raged, and legally required all UN member states to cooperate with the tribunal by invoking Chapter VII of the Charter. Those who committed war crimes, crimes against humanity, and genocide in that particular situation were to be prosecuted. The emphasis was on commanders who authorized or allowed the crimes.

---

[23] A useful compilation of documents about the creation of the ICTY can be found in Virginia Morris and Michael Scharf, *An Insider's Guide to the International Criminal Tribunal for the Former Yugoslavia* (Irvington-on-Hudson: Transnational Publishers, 1995).

Several commentators tried to create the impression that pursuit of criminal justice in the former Yugoslavia was a clear and simple matter. David Scheffer, soon to become head of a new office in the State Department for war crimes, wrote of the creation of the ICTY: "The Council recognized the enforcement of international law as an immediate priority, subordinate to neither political nor military imperatives."[24] A United Nations lawyer, Payam Akhavan, wrote: "there was a political consensus on the complementary interrelationship between the establishment of the Tribunal and the restoration of peace and security in the former Yugoslavia."[25] To critics, these quotes might reflect a continuation of legalistic-moralistic reasoning that characterized exaggerated hopes for the arbitration treaties of the 1920s.[26] To critics, this was judicial romanticism *par excellence*. Public documents (and public posturing) notwithstanding, the tribunal was created in large part because of realist reasoning, not because of moral or legal commitment to human rights standards.[27] States like the USA were under pressure to act to stop the atrocities being reported by the communications media. The USA and some other Security Council members did not want to engage in a decisive intervention that could prove costly in terms of blood and treasure. They saw no self-interest in a complicated intervention. As James Baker, Secretary of State during the George H. W. Bush Administration, was reported to have said, "We have no dog in that fight." But they felt the need to do something. So the Clinton Administration helped create the tribunal in a short-term, public relations maneuver, leaving various contradictions to sort themselves out later.

---

[24] David Scheffer, "International Judicial Intervention," *Foreign Policy*, 102 (Spring 1996), 38.

[25] Payam Akhavan, "The Yugoslav Tribunal at a Crossroads: The Dayton Peace Agreement and Beyond," *Human Rights Quarterly*, 18, 2 (May 1996), 267. See also his views in "Justice in The Hague, Peace in the Former Yugoslavia?," *Human Rights Quarterly*, 20, 4 (November 1998), 737–816. In this latter article he refers to me as a "realist," and acknowledges "judicial romanticism" while saying the latter concept does not apply to him. I am not a realist of either the classical (Hans Morgenthau) or structural (Kenneth Walz) variety, but a pragmatic liberal. I am in favor of attention to human dignity, frequently via human rights, but recognize the pervasive power and interests of the territorial state. See further Forsythe, "International Criminal Courts: A Political View," *Netherlands Quarterly of Human Rights*, 15, 1 (March 1997), 5–19.

[26] See further George Kennan, *American Diplomacy 1900–1950* (Chicago: University of Chicago Press, 1951).

[27] I lay out the evidence in "Politics and the International Tribunal for the Former Yugoslavia," *Criminal Law Forum*, 5, 2–3 (Spring 1994), 401–422; also in Robert S. Clark and Madeleine Sann, eds., *The Prosecution of International Crimes* (New Brunswick: Transaction Publishers, 1996), 185–206.

From the creation of the tribunal in 1993 to the conclusion of the Dayton peace agreement in 1995, many policy makers and observers found fault with the very existence of the ICTY for possibly impeding diplomatic peacemaking.[28] The logic was clear enough. Would one prolong the fighting, with accompanying atrocities, by requiring that the principal fighting parties make a just peace – after which their responsible officials would be subjected to criminal justice? Would they not prefer to fight on, rather than cooperate in a peace agreement that would make their arrest and trial more likely?

This classic dilemma between peace and justice, between stability and punishment, became pronounced with the creation of the new court. Thus particularly the British during the John Major government played a hypocritical double game, voting for the tribunal but operating behind the scenes to hamper its work. London preferred the diplomatic to the juridical track, arguing in private that diplomacy was a better path to peace and human security. Public posturing aside, Major's approach was a pragmatic liberal strategy, hopeful of ending atrocities via diplomacy, but not one that gave more than cosmetic support to adjudication. Even Scheffer, before he entered the State Department, perhaps with El Salvador or South Africa in mind where criminal justice had been bypassed or minimized, wrote that "Despite the hard hits human rights standards take in these [unspecified] cases and the risk of never breaking the cycle of retribution and violence, the choice of 'peace over justice' is sometimes the most effective means of reconciliation."[29] It can be a serious matter to question the wisdom of international criminal justice in certain cases, and whether its pursuit in those situations reflects judicial romanticism.

Even Judge Goldstone, the first prosecutor for the ICTY, noted that truth commissions had certain advantages over criminal trials as far as establishing facts in a form broadly understandable and thus in providing education and catharsis. He advocated both trials and truth commissions.[30]

---

[28] See further Anthony D'Amato, "Peace v. Accountability in Bosnia," *American Journal of International Law*, 88, 3 (July 1994), 500–506; and Anonymous, "Human Rights in Peace Negotiations," *Human Rights Quarterly*, 18, 2 (May 1996), 249–258.

[29] Scheffer, "International Judicial Intervention," 37.

[30] "Ethnic Reconciliation Needs the Help of a Truth Commission," *International Herald Tribune*, October 24, 1998, 6. See also Goldstone, "Bringing War Criminals to Justice During an Ongoing War." Given the difficulty of educating the public via technical trials, Mark Osiel proposes liberal show trials in *Mass Atrocity, Collective Memory, and the Law* (New Brunswick: Transaction Publishers, 1997). But liberal show trials are inherently contradictory, as Samantha Power notes in *New Republic*, March 2, 1998, 32–38.

The Dayton agreement showed that at least superficially or on paper one could have both relative peace and some criminal justice – one could end most of the combat and reduce much of the multifaceted victimization of individuals while at least promising criminal justice for those who had engaged in war crimes, crimes against humanity, and genocide.[31] However, one could secure the cooperation of Slobodan Milosevic, and the Serb-dominated Yugoslavian army that he controlled, only by an evident deal at Dayton exempting him from prosecution – at least for a time. At that time there was no public indictment against Milosevic who, more than any other single individual, was responsible for the breakup of former Yugoslavia and no doubt the Serbian strategy of ethnic cleansing. As far as we know from the public record and the logic of the situation, in Milosevic's case one had to trade away in 1995 criminal justice for diplomatic peacemaking, although lawyers for the ICTY argued that they simply did not have a good legal case against him. It seemed to be a fact that western states did not make a serious effort to go after certain individuals who were guilty of atrocities such as Milosevic, Ratko Mladic, and Radovan Karadzic until later – when the Dayton agreement was more secure.

The same dilemma resurfaced regarding Kosovo. Milosevic was both the arsonist and the firefighter in that situation, as in Bosnia earlier. He undertook repressive policies and forced expulsions in Kosovo, a province in new Yugoslavia (later Serbia), that inflamed discontent among the ethnic Albanians who made up 90 percent of the local population. But the West had to deal with him, since he possessed the authority and power to restrain the Yugoslav forces (of Serbian ethnicity) who were engaged in hostilities in the province. How could one solicit his cooperation in reducing human rights and humanitarian violations if one threatened him with criminal justice? The US Congress, on record earlier as in favor of prosecuting Iraqi war criminals, voted to urge the Clinton Administration to offer Milosevic a deal – sanctuary in a friendly country in return for his abdication of power within new Yugoslavia. The prosecutor's office of the ICTY finally indicted Milosevic and several of his high-ranking colleagues in Belgrade for ordering criminal acts in

---

[31] See further Richard Holbrooke, *To End a War* (New York: Random House, 1998). Holbrooke was the key mediator at Dayton. He wrote that his mandate was to secure peace, not pursue criminal justice. This indirectly confirms that Milosevic did not face any threat of criminal justice from US diplomatic officials. No doubt Milosevic could at least infer a *de facto* trade-off: if he signed the Dayton accord US officials would not go after him for human rights violations. Whether there were secret and/or explicit assurances is not known.

Kosovo, but this was after hope was lost for a negotiated deal with Milosevic, à la Bosnia, to end the atrocities in Kosovo.

Immediately after Dayton, the fear of doing more harm than good via criminal justice resurfaced in still other forms. One fear was that pursuit of indicted suspects would cause the fragile commitment to the Dayton accord to collapse. In early 1996 certain Bosnian Serb military officers wandered into areas controlled by the Bosnian Muslims by error and were arrested on suspicion of war crimes. Bosnian Serb parties then refused to cooperate with talks on continued military disengagement called for under the peace agreements and supervised by IFOR (the NATO implementation force). A political crisis resulted, entailing high-level mediation by US diplomats. The Serbian officers were eventually returned to Serbia rather than transferred to The Hague for trial. It was a vivid if small demonstration of how pursuit of legal justice could endanger the broader political agreements that had ended both the combat and related human rights violations.

A similar fear was that pursuit of criminal justice in Bosnia would produce another Somalia. In that East African country in 1993, the attempt to arrest one of the warlords, General Aideed, leading as it did to the deaths of eighteen US soldiers and the wounding of many more, produced an early US withdrawal from that country and more generally a US reluctance to support other UN-approved deployments of force in places like Rwanda the following year. The goal of national reconciliation with liberal democracy was never achieved by the international community in Somalia, arguably at least in part because of the defection of the USA from the international effort in 1994. The companion fear in Bosnia was that similar US casualties would force a premature withdrawal of NATO forces (via IFOR and SFOR – the latter being the stabilization force) and a collapse of the effort to make the Dayton agreement work. European contributors to NATO deployments made it clear that if the USA pulled out, they would also.

After a passive policy of non-arrests by NATO forces during 1993–1995, some arrests were made after 1995. But for a considerable time NATO did not seek to arrest the Serbian leaders who had devised and commanded the policies of ethnic cleansing of Muslims in Bosnia. They were well connected and well protected. In Washington especially, it was feared that a costly shoot-out would undermine the shaky congressional tolerance of American military personnel on the ground in the Balkans. It was only later, when the Dayton agreement seemed more secure, as enforced by a sizable contingent of first NATO and then EU troops on the ground, that a more vigorous pursuit of Milosevic, Ratko Mladic, and Radovan Karadzic took place. Eventually, particularly because of US financial pressure, a newly elected Serbian government detained Milosevic in spring of 2001 and transferred him to The Hague for trial in the ICTY. Thus in 1995 the USA negotiated with Milosevic at Dayton, but by 2001 the USA was demanding his arrest and trial. Either policy might prove justified, taking into account the broader political context of the Balkans. Later Karadzic, the Bosnian Serb inflammatory leader, was arrested and sent to The Hague. Still later Mladic, immediate author of the Serb massacre of Bosnian Muslim males at Srebrenica in 1995, was finally arrested by Serb authorities after more than fifteen years of evasion – sometimes with Belgrade's connivance. Under persistent pressure from the western network backing the ICTY, the highest Serb authorities knew that their chances of joining the European Union would be greatly affected by such arrests.

What we see with regard to the ICTY is an early tension between pragmatic liberalism and classical liberalism in the form of international criminal justice, a tension that was resolved only with the negotiated Dayton peace agreement for Bosnia, plus NATO intervention regarding Kosovo. It was only after these political events that there was serious pursuit of various Serbian leaders (and some Croat and Bosnian Muslim officials) in order to hold them personally accountable for certain crimes. What we also see in the example of the ICTY is the creation of the Court for essentially realist reasons, but then the transformation of the Court into a serious enterprise of criminal justice largely through the office of its prosecutor, supported by many non-governmental organizations and a few states. In this history one also sees the sequencing of criminal justice – delaying it during peace negotiations, then pursuing it later.

The USA, which had led in the creation of the Court for cosmetic and self-serving reasons, then became the key backer of the Court. Having authored the Court, along with the French, Washington felt it had to make it a success. Until 1999 and the NATO bombing of Serbia because of Kosovo, Washington could support the ICTY as criminal justice for others, the Court's jurisdiction being limited to behavior within the boundaries of the former Yugoslavia. But with the 1999 NATO bombing, NATO personnel became subject to the jurisdiction of the Court. (The jurisdiction of the Court pertained to allegations of certain crimes committed in the territory of the former Yugoslavia – or in the air space above it. So in carrying out bombing raids on Serb targets, NATO put itself under the Court's jurisdiction. NATO states did not contest this logic.) The ICTY prosecutor declined, on the basis of a staff investigation, to pursue charges of war crimes articulated against certain NATO personnel. Some observers thought this was a political decision, it being difficult for NATO to carry out military actions over several months without questionable decisions about, for example, bombing targets. (Serbia also pursued a legal complaint in the International Court of Justice against certain NATO states for violations of international law in the bombing campaign, but this legal action also came to naught. There was also a case filed with the European Court of Human Rights against certain European states that were members of NATO, but this litigation also failed.)

Out of these complicated origins, the ICTY compiled a complicated record. Without question the Court was able to punish a number of persons, including some high officials; it also helped develop international law in important ways.

As of 2016 the ICTY had convicted eighty-three persons (some via plea bargains and some via full trials). Those who pled guilty got about two years' less jail time than those convicted. There is no death penalty, the longest available punishment being life in prison. The average sentence handed down was about fifteen years' detention. Incarceration occurred in certain states that contracted with the ICC at The Hague.

The Court in various cases held that: the 1995 massacre at Srebrenica constituted genocide, in that there was an intentional attempt to destroy a substantial part of the Bosnian Muslim people through the killing of over 7,000 men and boys; that individuals could be held responsible for crimes committed in internal war, not just international war; that a detention camp commander was responsible for crimes, including sex crimes, that occurred under his command, whether committed against men or women; that rape crimes could constitute war crimes or crimes against humanity, not just individual illegal acts; that someone who did not participate directly in rapes could be convicted of rape for allowing or encouraging it to happen, and that rape was also a form of torture and discrimination. It can be seen that the ICTY was especially attentive to various gender issues, certainly by comparison to the Nuremberg and Tokyo tribunals.

The most important case, that of Milosevic, ended prematurely with the death of the defendant from natural causes. The Serb leader had insisted on defending himself. This fact prolonged the trial, both because of health-related delays and time he devoted to histrionics. There were also disputes between the defendant and his court-appointed lawyers. It took some two years for the prosecution to present its case, with the defense phase also prolonged. Much of the trial centered on proof of Milosevic's role in various war crimes, crimes against humanity, and genocide. The latter seemed the most difficult to prove, given that any commands reflecting an intent to destroy a national, ethnic, religious, or racial people were not likely to be found in written documents or clear and uncontested statements. This case was one of several in different courts that raised serious questions about the time and costs associated with international criminal justice, especially when defendants were given rather wide latitude to request repeated delays and make long speeches of dubious relevance.[32] It was not only Milosevic but other defendants in other courts that used their trial as a political platform. Karadzic played the game the same way, as did Mladic.

It was difficult to say whether the Court achieved goals beyond punishment and legal development, which is not to denigrate gains in those categories, since it was hard to gauge its effect on regional reconciliation and stability, and on closure for affected individuals.[33] The Court early on did not have a good outreach program, explaining its actions to parties in the Balkans. Certainly in much of Serbia and the Serb part of Bosnia, the ICTY was widely seen as anti-Serb. This was partially because of the large number of Serbs indicted, arrested, and made defendants. Also, the third prosecutor, Carla del Ponte of Switzerland, often had pointed things to say about the lack of Serb and Bosnian Serb cooperation with the Court.[34] On the one hand some analysts thought Serb cooperation was secured only in direct response to outside pressures; when those pressures waned, so did Serb cooperation.[35] On the other hand a few analysts saw some genuine improvement in human rights matters in various Balkan states because of the ICTY.[36]

It was certainly difficult for the ICTY to promote reconciliation among Bosnian Muslims, Serbs of various sorts, and Croats, when the Dayton agreement itself had recognized largely autonomous Serb, Croat, and Muslim sectors within Bosnia.[37] As of 2016 there was clearly substantial

[32] See further William Schabas, "Balancing the Rights of the Accused with the Imperatives of Accountability," in Thakur and Malcontent, eds., *Sovereign Impunity*.
[33] David Tolbert, "The Criminal Tribunal for the Former Yugoslavia: Unforeseen Successes and Unforeseeable Shortcomings," *Fletcher Forum of World Affairs*, 26, 2 (Summer/Fall, 2002).
[34] Misha Glenny, "The Prosecutor Muddies Serbian Waters," *International Herald Tribune*, February 17, 2004, as quoted in Kingsley Chiedu Moghalu, *Global Justice: The Politics of War Crimes Trials* (Westport, CT and London: Praeger, 2006), ch. 3, n. 77. See further Heikelina Verrijn Stuart, "Carla Del Ponte," in *Encyclopedia of Human Rights*, vol. I, 481–486.
[35] Patrice McMahon and David P. Forsythe, "The ICTY's Impact on Serbia: Judicial Romanticism Meets Network Politics," *Human Rights Quarterly*, 30, 2 (May 2008), 412–435. See also Jelena Subotic, *Hijacked Justice: Dealing with the Past in the Balkans* (Ithaca: Cornell University Press, 2009); and Christopher K. Lamont, *International Criminal Justice and the Politics of Cooperation* (Farnham: Ashgate, 2010).
[36] See, e.g., Diane Orentlicher, *Shrinking the Space for Denial: The Impact of the ICTY in Serbia* (New York: Open Society Initiative, 2008).
[37] See further Patrice McMahon and Jon Western, "The Death of Dayton: How to Stop Bosnia from Falling Apart," *Foreign Affairs*, 88, 5 (September–October 2009), 69–83.

antagonism remaining among the various communities in the Balkans, with a rather fragile peace being mainly the result of interposition and enforcement by NATO and EU states, under UN aegis, rather than because of genuine intercommunal reconciliation. Despite various Court judgments, Muslim refugees and displaced persons had trouble returning to their homes in Serb portions of Bosnia. Tensions also remained high in Kosovo between the Serbs and Albanians. Croats often did not fully cooperate with the ICTY, it usually being difficult for any nation to prosecute those claiming to defend the nation from insidious opponents.

The ICTY, costing around $275 million per year, had been asked to finish its trials (but not appeals) by 2014. This was later extended. The existence of the Court did contribute to the move to create a permanent international criminal court, as noted below. According to one summary evaluation that stressed once again not political but legal achievements: "The Tribunal's accomplishments are many. It established that an international tribunal could conduct trials according to law ... It has also established a large number of important legal and institutional precedents, notably those clarifying the elements of international crimes, affirming the applicability of international humanitarian law to internal armed conflict [and covering] sexual violence in wartime ... the ICTY made a unique and major contribution to the development of international criminal law and practice."[38]

The Rwandan court

The reasons for the creation of a second *ad hoc* UN criminal court were similar to the first. States on the Security Council, principally the United States, did not want to incur the costs of a decisive intervention in Rwanda in 1994 to stop the longstanding conflict between Hutu and Tutsi communities which resulted in a genocide with perhaps 500,000–800,000 deaths.[39] They saw no vital self-interests in

---

[38] Bartram S. Brown, "International Criminal Tribunal for the Former Yugoslavia (ICTY)," in *Encyclopedia of Human Rights*, vol. III, 137. See further James Gow, Rachel Kerr, and Zoran Pajic, *Prosecuting War Crimes: Lessons and Legacies of the International Criminal Tribunal for the Former Yugoslavia* (London and New York: Routledge, 2014).

[39] The difference between Hutus and Tutsis had been codified by Belgium when a colonial power and was originally more a class than biological or blood distinction. By the time of Rwandan independence the distinction had been solidified, and it had great political significance – as those identifying as Hutu made up a large majority of the country, controlling the outcome of elections. By 1994 the Hutu community was divided between militants advocating Hutu power to the detriment of Tutsis, and moderates interested in

such action. Somalia in 1993 had shown that international intervention in a situation where persons of ill will engaged in brutal and inhumane power struggles could be a dangerous venture. The USA and others were eventually willing to pay billions of dollars for the care of those fleeing genocide in Rwanda. But loss of western life, even in a professional and volunteer military establishment, was another matter. This was certainly true of Belgium, a former colonial power in Rwanda, which, when faced with ten deaths in its peacekeeping unit there, was in favor of the withdrawal, not the expansion, of those forces. Feeling nevertheless the impulse to do something, states on the Council created a second criminal court with similar jurisdiction and authority. Thus, as in former Yugoslavia, it was not consistent attention to moral norms and legal rules that drove the Security Council to action. Rather, it was a search for a tolerable expedient that resulted in attention to criminal justice. The best that can be said for the USA and the Security Council was that evident unease at the absence of moral and legal consistency across roughly similar cases produced at least some action on the question of prosecution for atrocities via ethnic/tribal slaughter in Rwanda.

As was true for the ICTY, so for the ICTR, it fell to the prosecutor's office, supporting NGOs, and a few concerned states to turn a venture based on guilt and public relations into something more substantive. The prosecutor's position proved problematic. The initial shared prosecutor showed more interest in former Yugoslavia than in Rwanda, and a later prosecutor, del Ponte, developed major frictions with the Rwanda government (Tutsi-controlled) that had triumphed in the fighting of 1994. So eventually a separate prosecutor was established for the ICTR in 2003.

The Court early on was hamstrung by petty corruption, mismanagement, lack of adequate support, and not-so-veiled hostility on the part of more than one Rwandan.[40] Despite all this, by 2015 when the court wrapped up its work after 21 years, it had issued ninety-three indictments, made fifty-five preliminary judgments, and forty-five appellate

power-sharing. By contrast to the perhaps 800,000 killed in Rwanda in 1994, eighteen US soldiers were killed in one day in Mogadishu, among a total of some thirty-five US military deaths in Somalia in the early 1990s overall. This is a modest cost for a "great power" or superpower in relative terms. The USA suffered nine deaths in one military air crash off South Africa in September 1997, but the media did not emphasize it and commentators did not call for a change of policy there. See further Edward N. Luttwak, "Where Are the Great Powers?," *Foreign Affairs*, 73, 4 (July/August 1994), 23–29.

[40] For a brief summary see Paul Lewis, "UN Report Comes Down Hard on Rwandan Genocide Tribunal," *New York Times*, February 13, 1997, A9.

rulings.[41] Several high officials had been convicted, including a prime minister and a mayor. The ICTR produced the first conviction for genocide ever recorded in a proper court of law. This was the Akayesu case, in which, in the view of the trial chamber, the mayor of the Taba Commune "had reason to know and in fact knew that sexual violence was taking place ... and that women were being taken away ... and sexually violated."[42] In this same judgment, rape of women was seen as part of genocide and crimes against humanity.

A summary evaluation seems accurate. "The ICTR punished only Hutu[s], as Rwanda effectively blocked the indictment of Tutsi[s] ... officers who [President] Kagame feared would stage a coup rather than submit to prosecution ... The ICTR did succeed in bringing to justice the major leaders of Rwanda's genocide and in creating an irrefutable historic record of their crimes ... Over half of the extremist regime's cabinet ministers, a significant number of military commanders, business leaders, and local administrators were convicted in fair trials."[43]

Ironically, high Hutu officials convicted of genocide and/or crimes against humanity in the ICTR received only a maximum sentence of life imprisonment, whereas lower Hutu officials or citizens convicted in Rwanda national courts – mostly staffed by Tutsis – could receive the death penalty.

In Rwanda after 2002 one also found Gacaca or community courts designed in part to ease the intense overcrowding in Rwanda prisons and backlog of defendants. Controversial because of the lack of trained judges and full judicial process, the Gacaca courts nevertheless went forward with mixed results.[44] They were scheduled for termination at the time of writing.

Beyond punishment of individuals and development of legal concepts, the ICTR merits further discussion. It was highly unlikely that an

---

[41] Early on one could find positive assessments of the ICTR. See Payam Akhavan, "Justice and Reconciliation in the Great Lakes Region of Africa: The Contribution of the International Criminal Tribunal for Rwanda," *Duke Journal of Comparative and International Law*, 7 (1997), 325–348. For an official final overview, see http://unictr.unmict.org/en/news/address-united-nations-security-council-final-report-comple tion-strategy-international-criminal. See further Nicola Palmer, *Courts in Conflict: Interpreting the Layers of Justice in Post-Genocide Rwanda* (New York: Oxford University Press, 2015).

[42] *Prosecutor v. Akayesu*, Judgment, Case No. 96-4-T (September 2, 1998).

[43] Howard Tolley, "International Criminal Tribunal for Rwanda (ICTR)," in *Encyclopedia of Human Rights*, vol. III, 127–128.

[44] Erin Daly, "Between Punitive and Reconstructive Justice: The Gacaca Courts in Rwanda," *New York University Journal of International Law and Politics*, 34 (2002), 355–396; and Christopher J. Le Mon, "Rwanda's Troubled Gacaca Courts," *Human Rights Brief*, 14, 2 (Winter 2007), 16–20.

international tribunal prosecuting Hutus during a time of Tutsi control
of Rwanda could interject a decisive break in the cycle of ethnic violence
that had long characterized that country. True, militant Hutus had
planned, organized, and executed the wave of killing in 1994. But consider the parallels with former Yugoslavia. By most accounts, Serbs had
committed the greatest number of atrocities during 1992–1995, even
though Croats and Bosnian Muslims did not have clean hands. And
Serbs had certainly persecuted ethnic Albanians in Kosovo. But when
the prosecutor brought indictments mostly against Serbs, many in this
latter ethnic group claimed bias by the ICTY.[45] Thus the early pattern of
indictments and convictions did little to break down group allegiance
and group hostility. In similar fashion, it was unlikely that many Rwandan Hutus would be led to re-evaluate their prejudices by trials focusing
only on Hutus, especially when some Tutsi violence had not been met
with international prosecution.[46] So one might punish leading Hutu
criminals, but using the tribunal to break the cycle of ethnic violence
was a tougher nut to crack. It was fairly clear, unfortunately, that the
ICTR had not contributed to regional stability.

During the life of the ICTR ethnic violence continued on a large scale
in the Great Lakes region of Africa, with only relative decline compared
with 1994. There was mounting evidence that Tutsis had massacred
Hutus in eastern Zaire during the struggle for control of that country.
That is precisely why the late President Kabila in the new Congo, who
owed his position to Tutsi support, among other factors, consistently
tried to block a United Nations investigation into the reported massacre.
Tutsis and Hutus continued to fight in both the Democratic Republic of
the Congo and Burundi, as well as in Rwanda. Murder and torture
continued to be practiced by both sides. Could one realistically expect
one international court, with a lack of full respect and support from either
ethnic group, to make any great difference in the evolution of events – at
least in the foreseeable future?

The International Criminal Court

On July 17, 1998, a diplomatic conference meeting in Rome, relying
heavily on the experience of the ICTY and ICTR, approved the statute of

---

[45] For a critique of the pattern of indictments by the office of the independent prosecutor,
see Cedric Thornberry, "Saving the War Crimes Tribunal," *Foreign Policy*, 104 (Fall
1996), 72–86.
[46] See further Leo J. DeSouza, "Assigning Blame in Rwanda," *Washington Monthly*, 29, 9
(September 1997), 40–43.

a permanent criminal court to be loosely associated with the United Nations. The statute consists of 128 articles and is longer than the UN Charter.[47] Subject matter jurisdiction covers genocide, crimes against humanity, war crimes, and aggression (crimes against peace) when international law presents a sufficiently precise definition – which was said not to be the case in July 1998 and was still not the case at the time of writing. Judges are elected by the states that are parties to the statute; these judges sit in their individual capacity and not as state representatives. An independent prosecutor is attached to the Court. The final vote was 120 in favor, 7 opposed (the USA, Israel, China, Iraq, Sudan, Yemen, Libya), and the rest abstaining.

The Court became operational as of July 1, 2002, sixty ratifications being obtained, on the basis of complementarity. This means that the Court does not function unless a state in question is unable or unwilling to investigate and, if warranted, prosecute for one of the covered crimes. Thus, whereas the ICTY and ICTR had primary jurisdiction and could supersede state action, the ICC only has complementary jurisdiction. It is a backup system, designed to encourage states to exercise their primary jurisdiction and authority in responsible ways. The prosecutor can go forward with a case if the state where the crime has been committed is a party to the statute, or is the state of the defendant. But the prosecutor must obtain approval of a pre-trial chamber of the Court, whose decision to approve prosecution is subject to appeal to another chamber. This is designed to prevent political or other improper action by the prosecutor, who is also elected by state parties to the statute. The UN Security Council can also refer cases to the Court, or can delay proceedings for up to a year, renewable. This latter provision is to allow for diplomacy to trump prosecution – to allow pragmatic liberalism to trump classical liberalism in the form of criminal justice.

In the final analysis the ICC was the product of a group of "like-minded" states, led periodically by Canada, and a swarm of NGOs. They, as in Ottawa a year earlier with regard to a treaty banning anti-personnel landmines,[48] decided to move ahead despite belated but clear opposition from the USA. Ironically, part of the momentum for a standing criminal court had come from the latter. But in Rome the USA made very clear that it did not intend to have its nationals appear before the

---

[47] See especially Benjamin Schiff, *Building the International Criminal Court* (Cambridge: Cambridge University Press, 2008). See further Robert C. Johansen, "International Criminal Court," in *Encyclopedia of Human Rights*, vol. III, 113–120.

[48] Among many sources see further Richard A. Mathew, Bryan McDonald, and Kenneth R. Rutherford, eds., *Landmines and Human Security: International Politics and War's Hidden Legacy* (Albany: State University of New York Press, 2004).

tribunal. According to David Scheffer, Ambassador at Large for War Crimes Issues:

There is a reality, and the reality is that the United States is a global military power and presence. Other countries are not. We are. Our military forces are often called upon to engage overseas in conflict situations, for purposes of humanitarian intervention, to rescue hostages, to bring out American citizens from threatening environments, to deal with terrorists. We have to be extremely careful that this proposal [for a standing court] does not limit the capacity of our armed forces to legitimately operate internationally. We have to be careful that it does not open up opportunities for endless frivolous complaints to be lodged against the United States as a global military power.[49]

This was largely a smokescreen argument. The rule of complementarity meant that if US personnel were suspected of having committed an international crime, a proper investigation by the USA and, if warranted, prosecution would keep the new court from functioning. A prosecutor who wanted to bring charges against Americans would need to secure approval from the pre-trial chamber, whose approval could be appealed to a different chamber. By simple majority vote, the UN Security Council could delay proceedings, renewable, against the USA. Yet the Clinton Administration was unyielding in opposition. This was largely in deference to the Pentagon, and to the ultra-nationalists in the Congress. Senator Jesse Helms, the Chair of the Senate Foreign Relations Committee at that time, declared the treaty would be dead on arrival should it ever be submitted to the Senate.

For a country that saw itself as a leader for human rights, and that had led the effort to create two *ad hoc* criminal tribunals with jurisdiction over others, its posture at Rome was not a policy designed to appeal to many states. The double standards were too evident. (The French did successfully insist on a seven-year grace period for war crimes proceedings against adhering states, apparently to give it some wiggle room in the event of investigations into its African policies.)[50]

The George W. Bush Administration "unsigned" the Clinton signature on the Rome Statute, sought through bilateral diplomacy to persuade or pressure other states into exempting US personnel from the coverage of the ICC, delayed UN peacekeeping deployments until the Security Council exempted any participating US personnel from any

---

[49] *New York Times*, August 13, 1997, A8.

[50] The British, in breaking with the USA over this issue, issued the following statement: "we and other major NATO allies are satisfied that the safeguards that are built in to the International Criminal Court will protect our servicemen against malicious or politically motivated prosecution" (British Information Services, Press Release 214/98, July 20, 1998).

review by the ICC, and in almost every way imaginable tried to undermine the ICC. In 2005, however, the USA abstained on a UN Security Council resolution that authorized the ICC prosecutor to open investigations about possibly indicting certain Sudanese leaders for atrocities in the Darfur region of that country. In effect, the Bush Administration prioritized action on Darfur over trying to kill the ICC. The USA, however, never seriously considered becoming a member of the Court.

The follow-on Administration of Barack Obama was more sympathetic to the Court in quiet ways, but without any movement toward seeking the Senate's advice and consent for ratification of the Rome Statute. Obtaining such consent was perceived as a bruising and uphill battle. Since the Senate refused to give its consent to a mild treaty patterned on US law enhancing the rights of disabled persons in 2012, despite pleas from some Republican leaders for endorsement, it seemed quite unrealistic to expect the USA to formally join the Court. Such was the nature of particularly the Republican Party in contemporary times that almost all treaties were suspect, particularly those on human rights.

In the Libyan crisis of 2011, as NATO states tried to coax Muammar Kaddafi from power in the face of significant rebellion, a majority in the UN Security Council voted to refer the question of human rights violations to the prosecutor's office for further investigation. This move was debated. If one wanted to facilitate Kaddafi's departure after many years of dictatorial rule, as was true of Saddam Hussein in Iraq and Slobodan Milosevic in Serbia, promising prosecution after stepping down created a dubious incentive. On the other hand, would not impunity after gross violation of human rights encourage other national leaders to engage in brutal repression?

Despite some shift in US policies of periodic support, the ICC was certainly not free from controversy. As all of the early investigations and cases involved African defendants, some African states began to rethink their support for the Court. True, African states such as Democratic Congo, Central African Republic, and Uganda had all referred cases to the Court. In effect, these governments were asking the Court to help suppress various opposition figures. But when, in particular, the ICC prosecutor began to consider indictments against Kenyan and Sudanese political figures, some African state opinion began to shift to a more critical stance. Moreover, in Uganda the prosecutor became entangled in a dispute about the wisdom of criminal justice for Joseph Kony, leader of the so-called Lord's Resistance Army, as compared to seeking a diplomatic solution to the longrunning violent conflict there.[51]

---

[51] See further Susan Dicklitch, "Uganda," in *Encyclopedia of Human Rights*, vol. V, 109–114.

Also, it was alleged that human rights violations had been committed by the government side as well, thus raising issues about the scope of ICC investigations. In general, after about a decade of the Court's existence, there were many debates about the exercise of prosecutorial discretion, as well as the conduct of the few trials that actually got under way. A broad review of the ICC's record in DRC, Uganda, and Kenya in 2011 by the Open Society Foundations showed just how complicated matters could be.[52]

By late 2016, the ICC was in a weakened position. Burundi and South Africa had announced plans to withdraw from Court membership, as had the Gambia. The case against Kenyans Uhuru Kenyatta and William Ruto had failed due primarily to determined obstructionism by those defendants. The case against Omar al-Bashir of the Sudan was near collapse, with China and other states openly flouting the arrest warrant issued by the Court. It was widely thought that the first prosecutor, Louis Gabriel Moreno Ocampo, had made numerous mistakes during his tenure. His successor, Fatou Bensouda of Gambia, had been unable to make up all the lost ground with regard to the ICC's image and effectiveness.[53] It was certainly debatable whether the Court could offset increased criticism from African states by considering investigations into possible war crimes by Russian troops in the past armed conflict with Georgia, or by US troops in Afghanistan. Triggering the wrath of powerful states that had never ratified the Rome Statute did not seem a clever strategy for ensuring the success of the Court.

Hybrid courts

After atrocities in Bosnia, Kosovo, East Timor, Sierra Leone, and Cambodia, special courts or their equivalent were created that might be called hybrid or transnational.[54] Their composition and applicable law reflected a blend of the domestic and the international. Two will be highlighted here as examples. Perhaps the most successful was the one created for Sierra Leone in 2002. The government that emerged from a

---

[52] Kelly Askin, for Open Society Foundations, "Putting Complementarity into Practice: Domestic Justice for International Crimes in DRC, Uganda, and Kenya," www.opensocietyfoundations.org/reports/putting-complementarity-practice.

[53] See, for example, James Verini, "The Prosecutor and the President," *New York Times Magazine*, June 26, 2016, www.nytimes.com/2016/06/26/magazine/international-criminal-court-moreno-ocampo-the-prosecutor-and-the-president.html.

[54] For further basic information, with the exception of Cambodia, see Laura A. Dickinson, "The Promise of Hybrid Courts," *American Journal of International Law*, 97, 2 (April 2003), 295–310.

brutal internal armed conflict signed an agreement with the United Nations to create a special criminal court. Local authorities wanted some hand in trials, but not total responsibility. This court operated outside, and had legal primacy over, local courts. There were two international judges and one local judge in each case, and they used a mixture of local and international law. Judgments were handed down in nine cases, and there were convictions against both pro-government individuals as well as against rebel commanders.

In a special chamber of this hybrid court, Charles Taylor, the former President of neighboring Liberia, was indicted in 2003. Taylor, given temporary asylum and immunity in Nigeria, was eventually extradited to The Hague where he was put on trial in 2006. The special chamber sat at The Hague because of fears of unrest from Taylor's supporters in West Africa. So, similar to Milosevic in Serbia, this national leader was first dealt with gingerly, then made subject to criminal justice in a different political context. Taylor's slow-moving trial was full of histrionics and controversies, with a conviction handed down in 2012. Taylor is serving his 50-year prison sentence in the UK.

The special court for Sierra Leone finished its work in 2013. Its record was enhanced by the fact that: the national government was committed to proper criminal justice; Taylor and other defendants had lost power and wound up in captivity; and both the UK and the USA supported the court with voluntary personnel and funds. They also may have leaned on Nigeria to curtail the asylum initially offered to Taylor.

Among rulings of the broader Sierra Leone special court was a noteworthy judgment that the recruitment of child soldiers constituted a war crime. In Sierra Leone there was also a truth commission to establish past facts, completely apart from considerations of criminal justice.[55]

The special criminal court in Cambodia, created in 2004 long after the agrarian communists known as the Khmer Rouge had killed about two million persons during 1975–1979, proved much less satisfying. The government of Hun Sen, who himself had been a low-level member of the Khmer Rouge, was ambivalent about criminal justice in keeping with international standards, but finally agreed to panels entailing two local and one international judge. There were co-prosecutors, one local and one international. This arrangement, against the background of a very weak local judicial system, prompted criticism by international human rights advocacy groups, as well as from the UN Secretary-General.

---

[55] See further William A. Schabas, "The Relationship Between Truth Commissions and International Courts: The Case of Sierra Leone," *Human Rights Quarterly*, 25, 4 (November 2003), 1035–1066.

Many officials in the Hun Sen regime had manifested connections to the Khmer Rouge.

But certain circles of opinion thought that imperfect legal justice was better than no legal justice, particularly since the senior Khmer Rouge leadership was rapidly dying off. So legal proceedings finally got under way some thirty years after the horrific Khmer Rouge reign of terror.[56] Three aged Khmer Rouge officials received a life sentence, but the trial of others got bogged down. Some others who were indicted either died or were judged unfit to stand trial. In still other cases, certain individuals were indicted (that is, were the targets of arrest warrants), but were never pursued by the proper authorities. Some of the international personnel, either prosecutors or judges, either spoke out or resigned because of the lack of dynamism in the judicial process.

At the time of writing, the Cambodian special court continued its slow pace, had spent several hundreds of millions of dollars (contributed mostly by UN member states), and was as mired in controversy as before. Some cases inched forward, while others seemed blocked by political interference. Contemporary Cambodian politics showed many violations of human rights and many troubling developments, so it was clear that the hybrid criminal court had not ushered in a new wave of liberalism in Cambodian affairs. True, the facts of the auto-genocide of the 1970s had been revisited and certain horrific acts denounced. A few perpetrators had received prison time. But a transition to a clearly rights-oriented and rule-of-law polity was yet to occur.[57]

One reason for having the ICC is to reduce the "transaction costs" so evident in the creation of the two UN *ad hoc* courts and these hybrid courts. It takes much time to negotiate the composition, jurisdiction, authority, and rules of the court – and sometimes the details of the related prosecutor's office. Moreover, these hybrid courts do not produce a uniform jurisprudence, as their rules of procedure and substantive judgments do not always follow similar tracks.[58]

---

[56] For an informative website that is periodically updated on recent developments, see www.globalpolicy.org/international-justice.html.

[57] For the changing situation, see www.ijmonitor.org/2016/09/the-extraordinary-chambers-in-the-courts-in-cambodia-lessons-in-human-rights-ignored-by-cambodian-government/.

[58] Brief mention can be made of the special court created by the UN Security Council after the assassination of a Lebanese prime minister in 2005. Evidence mounted of Hezbollah responsibility. Hezbollah, having a Lebanese parliamentary faction, withdrew its support from the governing coalition, thus creating a political crisis in that country. Once again international juridical proceedings failed to constitute an easy and effective response to events. It was not clear how concerned parties should respond to violent events affecting Lebanese democracy and stability, especially given the probable involvement of Iran and its

National courts

It should not be forgotten that most international law, to the extent that it is adjudicated at all, is treated in national courts. Moreover, under the principles that undergird the ICC and also the norm of R2P (the responsibility to protect), it is the territorial state that has the primary responsibility to protect internationally recognized human rights. That being so, it is impossible here to review over 190 national legal systems and their treatment of major violations of international human rights and humanitarian law. Two points began to deal with the tip of this large iceberg.

First, after atrocities, particularly during and after war, real or metaphorical, it is often difficult for national courts to provide independent and impartial due process, leading to substantive judgments widely regarded as legitimate forms of criminal justice. After the fall of communism in Poland, for example, the subsequent trial of General Jaruzelski turned into a comical show trial, with numerous irregularities. At one point in his trial the presiding official said that "The hearings will continue, and the accusations will be formulated later."[59] Victor's justice is often easy to identify.

Against this background, the new criminal court created by the Interim Government in Iraq after the fall of the Saddam Hussein regime raised questions about proper criminal justice. Given the political instability of that situation after the US-led invasion and occupation, juridical problems were evident: the newness and transitory nature of the ruling authorities, the weakness of the embryonic Iraqi judicial system – if there was a real system, the lack of due process already evident in the

non-state proxies such as Hezbollah. Council action, pushed by Western states, seemed to give the appearance of doing something, but in reality this creation of a special court had little chance of success given the power configuration in the area. See further David P. Forsythe, "The UN Security Council and Response to Atrocities: International Criminal Law and the P-5," *Human Rights Quarterly*, 34, 3 (August 2012), 840–863.

[59] Tina Rosenberg, *The Haunted Land: Facing Europe's Ghosts After Communism* (New York: Vintage Books, 1996), 254. She argues that criminal trials were inappropriate for the violations of human rights committed under European communism. In passing she suggests that trials were more appropriate in Latin America for human rights violations under military regimes. But it was precisely in some Latin American situations that the military remained strong, and a threat to democracy, after the end of formal military rule. See also David Pion-Berlin, "To Prosecute or Pardon: Human Rights Decisions in the Latin American Southern Cone," *Human Rights Quarterly*, 15, 1 (Winter 1993), 105–130, who tries to explain different policies in Argentina, Chile, and Uruguay regarding investigations and trials for human rights violations. See further the special issue "Accountability for International Crime and Serious Violations of Fundamental Human Rights," *Law and Contemporary Problems*, 59, 4 (Autumn 1996). Most of the authors are lawyers who predictably endorse legal proceedings and oppose impunity. But see the articles by Stephan Landsman, Naomi Roht-Arriaza, and Neil J. Kritz.

interrogation of defendants, and so on. Thus it was hardly surprising that the UN Secretary-General and many international human rights advocacy groups were critical of the process. The execution process was highly irregular. Yet the USA, quite influential in such matters, was so opposed to the ICC and many international forms of criminal justice that it and its Iraqi allies pushed ahead with national legal measures that were sure to remain controversial in historical perspective. In Iraq it might have been better to proceed with a hybrid court, with some international judges and international standards of due process, in order to enhance independence, impartiality, and ultimately legitimacy.

Second, the principle of universal jurisdiction has had something of a renaissance, stimulated by the Pinochet case. But states like Britain and Belgium found the subject perplexing.

The concept of universal jurisdiction attaches to certain crimes like torture, genocide, and crimes against humanity – and also to serious violations of the Geneva Conventions of August 12, 1949, pertaining to victims of war.[60] Thus the principle of universal jurisdiction permits national authorities to pursue foreign as well as domestic suspects. Certain crimes are seen as so heinous that national prosecution is allowed regardless of the place of the crime or the nationality of the defendant. In general, however, states remain reluctant to exercise extensive universal jurisdiction. They remain reluctant to open Pandora's box by establishing themselves as a global judge that would complicate relations with other states by legally judging their citizens.

In 1998, a Spanish legal official presented British authorities with a request to extradite the visiting former Chilean dictator to Spain, to stand trial for genocide, terrorism, and torture.[61] Britain arrested Augusto Pinochet, and in complicated and confusing rulings finally decided that the former head of state was indeed extraditable, since Britain had ratified, and incorporated into British law, the UN Torture Convention. This treaty recognized that universal jurisdiction was appropriate in the case of charges of torture.

While the British ruling technically was a matter of interpreting British law, it held among other things that Pinochet's status as former head of

---

[60] Darren Hawkins, "Universal Jurisdiction for Human Rights: From Legal Principle to Limited Reality," *Global Governance*, 9, 3 (July–Sept., 2003), 347–366; and Stephen Macedo, ed., *Universal Jurisdiction: National Courts and the Prosecution of Serious Crimes Under International Law* (Philadelphia: University of Pennsylvania Press, 2004). For a concise overview, see Gabor Rona, "Universal Jurisdiction," in *Encyclopedia of Human Rights*, vol. V, 253–260; and Beth Stephens, "National Courts," ibid., vol. IV, 41–49.

[61] See further Darren Hawkins, "Chile in the Pinochet Era," in *Encyclopedia of Human Rights*, vol. I, 309–320.

state offered him no immunity from Spanish charges. Indeed, Slobodan Milosevic had been indicted by the prosecutor of the ICTY while he was a sitting high Serbian official. And Charles Taylor had been indicted by the special court in Sierra Leone despite his being a high former official of Liberia. Moreover, the British ruling made clear that it made no difference that the victims of Pinochet's alleged abuses were Spanish or otherwise. For heinous crimes like torture, the nationality of the victims or the defendant is not a relevant factor.

It is true that under intense pressure from former Prime Minister Margaret Thatcher and other British arch-conservatives, who were admirers of the staunch anti-communist Pinochet, British Executive authorities released Pinochet to Chile on grounds of alleged poor health. Thus he was in fact not extradited to Spain to face charges. But the importance of the Pinochet ruling was that he legally could have been extradited to Spain, that as a legal matter claims to sovereign immunity did not trump valid attention to gross violations of human rights, and that other high officials in other situations might indeed have to face accountability for deeds done in office. There were other ripple effects from the British ruling in Chile, Argentina, and other places.[62]

As for Belgium, in 1993 its parliament passed a broad law opening the door to many suits in Belgian courts based on universal jurisdiction.[63] While the legislative history of this Belgian statute showed an intent to allow cases in Belgium stemming originally from Rwanda, very quickly enterprising lawyers filed cases against a variety of public officials including Ariel Sharon of Israel, Yasir Arafat of the Palestinian Authority, George H. W. Bush of the USA, and so on. The Belgian Executive was certainly not happy about that country being involved in so many controversial matters, and so successfully worked for a much narrower statute requiring some Belgian connection to charges. The USA brought heavy pressure on Belgium, including discussing the relocation of NATO headquarters from Brussels, to alter the broad assertion of Belgian judicial authority.

---

[62] Stacie Jonas, "The Ripple Effect of the Pinochet Case," in *Human Rights Brief*, 36–38. See also Richard Falk, "Assessing the Pinochet Litigation," in Macedo, ed., *Universal Jurisdiction*, 97–120. In *Torture Team: Rumsfeld's Memo and the Betrayal of American Values* (New York: Palgrave Macmillan, 2008), Philippe Sands argues that high officials of the George W. Bush administration will be subject to universal jurisdiction because of having authorized torture. The practical problem with this argument is that most states do not want to go after Rumsfeld and others if it means intense conflict with the powerful USA.

[63] Richard Bernstein, "Belgium Rethinks Its Prosecutorial Zeal," *New York Times*, April 1, 2003, A8.

In both the British and Belgian examples above, it is clear that many Executive Branch officials are highly reluctant to see criminal justice proceedings interfere with good relations with other states. And the activation of the principle of universal jurisdiction, by an investigative judge like Baltasar Garzon of Spain, can certainly generate frictions that many national authorities, especially in Foreign Offices, would prefer to avoid. Noting this situation is not an argument for amnesty, immunity, or tolerance for heinous crimes like torture, genocide, crimes against humanity, or major breaches of international humanitarian law. It is only to note that political difficulties often arise in exercising universal jurisdiction in contemporary international relations.

It is not well known, but until recently the USA endorsed universal jurisdiction in civil matters concerning human rights. The above discussion focuses on universal jurisdiction in criminal law – that is, individual responsibility for atrocious violation of public international law in charges brought by a public prosecutor representing a state or states. In the USA, from 1789 there was a congressional statute opening US courts to private plaintiffs seeking redress from individuals who had violated the law of nations. This was the Alien Tort Statute (ATS), under which, say, a Frenchman victimized by piracy could use US courts to sue for the wrong done by the pirate – should the pirate be found within the USA. From 1980, it was settled law that, for example, a Paraguayan whose relative had been tortured to death in Paraguay by another Paraguayan could sue for damages in US federal courts if the torturer or his property had been found in the USA. The key court held that the torturer had the same status as the pirate, and thus universal civil jurisdiction was appropriate according to US law as related to international law. The controlling view was that the USA should not be a safe haven for gross violators of human rights.

The US Supreme Court held in 2013, however, that plaintiffs could not use ATS to sue for human rights torts or private damages under international law unless certain conditions were met. The tort had to be a violation of a clear and precisely defined part of international law, that part of the law had to be widely accepted, and there had to be some US connection to events. The Kiobel case,[64] which triggered this ruling, involved actions by the Royal Dutch Shell oil company operating in Nigeria. And so the Court held that the ATS should not govern this case, even though Shell has offices in the USA and was charged by a group of Nigerians with complicity in human rights violations by

---

[64] *Kiobel v. Royal Dutch Petroleum Co.*, 133 S.Ct. 1659 (2013).

Nigerian security forces protecting its property in the Nigerian delta. All the US Supreme Court judges held that events did not "touch and concern" the USA sufficiently. This was similar to the Belgian shift of law when it found itself involved in various cases of criminal law without a major Belgian connection. In the Kiobel case, it was not irrelevant that plaintiffs were suing a major corporation, and that the Roberts court was known to be sympathetic to minimizing legal restrictions on corporations.[65]

Kiobel made it difficult but not impossible for private plaintiffs to use US courts in order to sue corporations for aiding and abetting in human rights violations around the world. It remains to be seen what actions sufficiently "touch and concern" the USA in order for a case to go forward under the ATS. It also remains to be seen what happens when the defendant is a natural individual like a police official and not a legally constructed person like a corporation.[66]

Alternatives to criminal justice

A large number of human rights activists, like Aryeh Neier, argue for consistent implementation of criminal justice and decry any amnesty or immunity offered to those who have committed atrocities.[67] But our discussion above of criminal justice in places like Bosnia, Somalia, Rwanda, Sierra Leone, Poland, Iraq, etc. has already suggested that criminal justice might interfere with, or fail to make a contribution to, other desirable goals such as peace, stability, reconciliation, consolidation of liberal democracy, or full closure for affected individuals.

Criminal justice is not the only way to advance human rights, and the human rights discourse is not the only way to advance human dignity in international relations. Well-considered diplomatic/political steps also have their role to play in advancing a liberal international order beneficial to individuals.[68]

---

[65] On the Roberts Court and protecting corporate interests, see James Surowiecki, "Courting Business," *The New Yorker*, March 7, 2016, p. 21.

[66] See David P. Forsythe and Patrice C. McMahon, *American Exceptionalism Reconsidered: US Foreign Policy, Human Rights, and World Order* (London and New York: Routledge, 2016), ch. 5.

[67] Aryeh Neier, "The New Double Standard," *Foreign Policy*, 105 (Winter 1996–1997), 91–101. See further Aryeh Neier's book extolling the virtues of criminal justice: *War Crimes: Brutality, Genocide, Terror, and the Struggle for Justice* (New York: Times Books, 1998).

[68] See further Jeffrey E. Garten, "Comment: The Need for Pragmatism," *Foreign Policy*, 105 (Winter 1996–1997), 103–106. This is a rebuttal to the Neier argument for consistent implementation of criminal justice.

No less than Nelson Mandela, supported by others with impeccable liberal and human rights credentials like Bishop Desmond Tutu, thought that in the Republic of South Africa after the apartheid era, the best way to build a multiracial rights-protective society there was to avoid criminal justice as much as possible. They opted for a truth and reconciliation commission with apologies and reparations as the preferred course of action. If those responsible for political violence, on both the government and rebel sides, would acknowledge what they had done and express remorse, trials would be avoided and reparations paid to victims or their families. After all, trials focus on the past and often stir up animosities. Complicated rules of evidence can sometimes make it difficult to get the truth out in a clear and simple way. Truth commissions may be better than courts at getting to the "macro-truth" – the big social and political picture of why atrocities took place.[69] Since criminal courts focus on individual responsibility for particular acts, the larger context with its group responsibility may escape examination in judicial proceedings and remain in place to impede "social repair."[70] Certainly the relatives of some victims of white minority rule in South Africa are not happy that the perpetrators of foul deeds have gone unpunished. A full accounting of the pluses and minuses of the South African T&R Commission is still in progress. But the South African model for dealing with transitional justice, which downplays criminal justice, is an interesting one – especially since the new South Africa features all-race elections and the attempted protection of many human rights.[71]

In other places like El Salvador after protracted civil war, again trials were avoided. Leading suspects in criminal behavior were eased out of public office and sometimes eased out of the country altogether. Two commissions made their reports. In this case, as in some other cases like Chile and Argentina, the continuing power of the supporters of the old

---

[69] See Audrey R. Chapman and Patrick Ball, "The Truth of Truth Commissions: Comparative Lessons from Haiti, South Africa, and Guatemala," *Human Rights Quarterly*, 23, 1 (February 2001), 1–43. See especially Audrey Chapman and Hugo van der Merwe, eds., *Truth and Reconciliation in South Africa: Did the TRC Deliver?* (Philadelphia: University of Pennsylvania Press, 2008).

[70] Laurel E. Fletcher and Harvey M. Weinstein, "Violence and Social Repair: Rethinking the Contribution of Justice to Reconciliation," *Human Rights Quarterly*, 24, 3 (August 2002), 573–639.

[71] Priscilla B. Hayner, *Unspeakable Truths: Facing the Challenge of Truth Commissions*, 2nd edn. (New York: Routledge, 2010; 1st edn., 2002). She places the South African experience in the context of some twenty other truth commissions dealing with human rights, concluding that there is no one way to create a model truth commission. She also deals with the relationship between such commissions and criminal justice. See further the substantive book review of the Hayner volume by Juan E. Mendez and Javier Mariezcurrena in *Human Rights Quarterly*, 25, 1 (February 2003), 237–256.

regime made full and fair criminal justice exceedingly difficult in the short run. El Salvador is another country that has made progress toward stable liberal democracy without a prominent role for criminal justice after atrocities.[72] Still other countries like Spain and Portugal moved from dictatorships to stable liberal democracy without either criminal trials for past political behavior or even truth commissions. But not all countries can be like Spain and Portugal and join regional organizations like the Council of Europe and the European Union that strongly insist on liberal democracy in member states.

What is now the Czech Republic implemented a policy of barring former high communist officials from public office after the fall of communism in that country. Yet controversy and hard feelings were still evident long after 1989. A former judge in the communist era, not a party member but one who had supported the old regime with repressive rulings, was elevated to the Constitutional Court, as confirmed by the democratic Senate. This provoked outrage on the part of some, but not on the part of others who felt the democratic state needed experienced judges.[73]

Through an act of Congress, the USA apologized for, and paid reparations for, the internment of Japanese-Americans during World War II. Since that time there has been considerable debate in the USA over an apology and reparations to African-Americans for slavery and racial discrimination in that country.[74]

Democracy was at least encouraged in Haiti by offering the high officials of the Cedras autocratic regime a pleasant amnesty abroad, a

---

[72] I note in passing that not all relatives of victims were satisfied with the absence of criminal justice related to the past civil war. Some Salvadorans have pursued legal action in US courts under provisions allowing civil suits for aliens claiming violation of international law. Under the US 1879 Alien Tort Statute, as discussed above, these Salvadorans sought monetary compensation from former Salvadoran security officials now residing in the USA. So while avoidance of public criminal justice was part of the political deal to end fighting and atrocities in El Salvador, some civil litigation went forward in US courts. For a journalistic summary, see David Gonzalez, "Victim Links Retired General to Torture in El Salvador War," *New York Times*, June 25, 2002. In 2015, a former Defense Minister of El Salvador was deported from the USA. An immigration judge found him responsible for human rights violations in the 1980s. Political deals and de facto amnesties may not bar eventual legal proceedings. See www.nytimes.com/2015/04/09/us/us-deports-salvadoran-general-accused-in-80s-killings .html.

[73] Matt Reynolds, "A Top Judicial Posting Stirs Anger in Prague," *International Herald Tribune*, August 22, 2005.

[74] See further Mark Gibney and Erik Roxstrom, "The Status of State Apologies," *Human Rights Quarterly*, 23, 4 (November 2001), 911–939; and Max du Plessis, "Historical Injustice and International Law: An Exploratory Discussion of Reparation for Slavery," *Human Rights Quarterly*, 25, 3 (August 2003), 624–659.

diplomatic move by the USA and others that managed to restore an elected President Aristide there without major bloodshed. Likewise, George W. Bush offered Saddam Hussein safe passage out of Iraq in 2003. In this latter case, more than four thousand American lives, and no doubt tens of thousands of Iraqi lives, along with much injury and destruction, would have been saved had Saddam accepted the offer of asylum. True, criminal trials would not have been held for him and his equally despicable colleagues. But what price to human life and dignity did those trials entail, and did such trials – particularly given their irregular aspects – really contribute to liberal democracy and intercommunal reconciliation in Iraq? Avoiding war is also a liberal value.

In Uganda, the government sought the aid of the International Criminal Court in order to prosecute leaders of the vicious rebel movement known as the Lord's Resistance Army. Yet a number of traditional Ugandans preferred traditional rituals emphasizing forgiveness, rather than criminal prosecution.[75]

Conclusion

The creative thinker David Rieff seems to mostly argue not for various forms of transitional justice, but for forgetting and forgiving.[76] In his mostly pessimistic reflections, he argues that when persons opt for apologies, reparations, and memorials to past evil, they are demonstrating power and prejudice. In his view, nationalism almost always blocks truth, so we wind up with a distorted view when we have organized efforts to look back. He is deeply skeptical of serious attention to universal human rights, which he thinks is a "pipedream" and a form of "bogus universality." He prefers to "commit to the hard work of forgiveness." But then he argues that "if a practical possibility exists not only of establishing an honest record of what was done but also of bringing the perpetrators to justice, in principle it should be done." Hence this intriguing exploration of approaches to past atrocities in the context of human limitations and frailties seems to suggest a priority to criminal justice, a willingness to look at other options, and a default position of forgive and forget.

Suffice it to say that transitional justice can take, and has taken, many forms. None are perfect. All are controversial in that they entail pluses and minuses.

---

[75] Mark Lacey, "Victims of Uganda Atrocities Follow a Path of Forgiveness," *New York Times*, April 18, 2005, A1.

[76] David Rieff, *In Praise of Forgetting: Historical Memory and Its Ironies* (New Haven: Yale University Press, 2016).

Pursuit of an effective rule of law in international relations is a noble quest. International criminal justice has manifested a renaissance in international law.[77] In general and from a liberal perspective this is probably a good thing. But criminal justice in relation to international events is no simple matter. A morally pure and consistent approach to the subject as advocated by the distinguished human rights activist Aryeh Neier is inadequate for both policy making and general understanding. Judicial romanticism is not an adequate policy; it is a moral posture. As such, it is widely endorsed by many private lawyers and human rights activists, but evaluated more carefully by most policy makers.

There are ways of doing good for individuals, and maybe even advancing certain human rights over time, through delaying or bypassing criminal justice. As noted in Chapter 1, litigation is only one human rights strategy. The liberal West did not try to shun or isolate Stalin for his various crimes, but actively supported him during World War II in order to defeat fascism. The liberal West brought a great reduction in violence to the former Yugoslavia by giving a temporary de facto immunity from prosecution to Slobodan Milosevic.[78] The liberal West supported legal impunity in South Africa, El Salvador and the Czech Republic and many other places with adequate if not perfect results. One does not always advance human welfare and human rights by criminalizing behavior, as the attempted arrest of General Aideed in Somalia shows. There is much to be said for pragmatic liberalism at times as one approach to international human rights, however morally mixed the outcome.[79]

The process of making complicated contextual analyses leads to competing judgments because of the inability of the legal and policy sciences, or of policy makers, to accurately predict the future. Will provisions on criminal justice impede peacemaking? Can suspects be arrested without undermining the limited peace already achieved? Will court judgments against gross violators of human rights really have any major impact concerning ongoing patterns of violence or future atrocities? Would more good be achieved, with less bad, via truth commissions rather than

---

[77] M. Cherif Bassiouni, *International Criminal Law* (Leiden: Brill Publishers, 2008, 3 vols.).
[78] The question can fairly be raised, however, of whether NATO would have bombed Yugoslavia in 1999 over Kosovo had Milosevic been indicted and arrested for his role in Bosnia. Then again, would NATO have had to fight in Bosnia if Milosevic had not cooperated in producing the Dayton peace agreement?
[79] See further Mahmood Monshipouri and Claude E. Welch, "The Search for International Human Rights and Justice: Coming to Terms with the New Global Realities," *Human Rights Quarterly*, 23, 2 (May 2001), 370–401.

criminal proceedings? These are important questions, to which no one's crystal ball has adequate answers thus far.

Social science research is examining the above questions with considerable energy and determination. Results at the time of writing are not fully consistent. Some authors find that criminal justice at both international and national levels contributes to democracy and improved human rights protection. Other authors find that liberal progress can be made when trials are combined with amnesties. Still other authors find that truth commissions alone correlate *negatively* with consolidation of democracy and human rights protections. So there is a vigorous search for macro-patterns, which may or may not shed light on particular situations. What is clear is that the issue of transitional justice – viz., what to do after gross violations of human rights – will be with us for some time. Given that states and their intergovernmental organizations will face this issue as a policy matter, they can be expected to ask researchers if there is an empirically grounded science of transitional justice. An epistemic community (group of experts) now exists for this subject matter; its findings in the future merit serious attention.[80] Included in this debate is whether sufficient attention in transitional justice has been given to women's concerns.[81]

Case study: the ICC and Uganda

In 1986 Yoweri Museveni seized power in Uganda, after a series of authoritarian governments, and remained in office at the time of writing. His rise to power, based on the support of various ethnic groups mostly in the southern parts of the country, was met with armed resistance by various factions, the most notorious of which was the Lord's Resistance Army (LRA), led by Joseph Kony. The LRA was based in the northern regions populated mostly by the Acholi people. To maintain its numbers and political prospects, the LRA engaged in intimidation including via murder, rape, and disfigurement. It relied heavily on the forced recruitment of children for use as fighters, sexual slaves, and other forced labor. The tactics of Kony's movement belied its claims to be a religious faction intending to create a benign theocracy in Uganda.

---

[80] See the overview in David P. Forsythe, "Responding to Mass Atrocities: Revisiting Transitional Justice," *International Studies Review*, 13, 1 (March 2011), 85–95.
[81] See further for a critical view, Fionnuala Ni Aolain, "Women, Security, and the Patriarchy of Internationalized Transitional Justice," *Human Rights Quarterly*, 31, 4 (November 2009), 1055–1085.

As instability and fighting continued, the government side was also accused of gross violations of human rights mainly through the actions of the army, the Ugandan Public Defense Force (UPDF), but also by a rapid-reaction division of the central police. Numerous reports accused Museveni of being indifferent to various abuses against those Acholi who had fled to supposedly secure relocation camps, as well as allowing various abuses against others – including active campaigners for gay, lesbian, transgendered, and bisexual rights. In UPDF actions against the LRA, there were numerous reports of "collateral damage" among civilians. The situation was further complicated by international terrorist attacks, which – as is often the case – led to harsh responses by government forces.

In 2000 the Ugandan parliament passed an amnesty law promising impunity to those of the LRA who laid down their weapons and gave up the rebellion. In 2003, however, the Museveni government, having ratified the Rome Statute of the International Criminal Court, which began to function in 2002, asked the ICC prosecutor, Luis Moreno Ocampo, to open an investigation of the LRA leadership with a view to criminal prosecutions. In 2005 Moreno Ocampo unsealed indictments against Kony and his top assistants.

The indictments met with both praise and criticism. Those supporting the indictments talked of moving toward the rule of law, ending impunity for gross human rights violations, and increasing pressure on the LRA to reach a peaceful settlement perhaps in return for the suspension of criminal proceedings. Those criticizing the indictments talked about undermining the prospects for a negotiated end to violence and turning a blind eye to violations of human rights by the government side. It appears that a peace agreement was almost reached between the LRA and the government in 2008, but negotiations collapsed at the last moment.

It was reported that the LRA was receiving some support from the government of Omar al-Bashir in Sudan, in the context of allegations that the Museveni government was encouraging a rebellion in the south of Sudan by the South Sudanese Liberation Movement. It appears to be the case that, as international pressures increased against al-Bashir for his policies mainly in the Sudanese western region of Darfur, he curtailed his support for the LRA. Whatever the facts of various motivations and maneuvers, Kony and some of his colleagues, under relentless military pressure from the UPDF, with assistance from its allies, moved their base of operations to other countries such as the Central African Republic. Violence and atrocities were reduced over time, but without a definitive end to the conflict.

At the time of writing, the ICC indictments had not been effectuated, Kony remaining elusive and not under arrest by any government. The ICC prosecutor remained in the center of controversy particularly for not having brought any indictments against those in the Ugandan government or military. Moreno Ocampo continued to defend his focus on bringing to trial the leadership of the LRA rather than on a negotiated end to the violence, while arguing that his office lacked credible and admissible evidence of wrongdoing by Museveni authorities (the ICC lacks jurisdiction over certain gross violations of human rights transpiring before summer 2002). A 2011 report by Human Rights Watch, documenting governmental violations of human rights including torture and summary execution, tended to dilute a singular focus on the LRA.

One LRA commander, who had himself been a child soldier, turned himself in and was set to be a defendant at the ICC in The Hague. Some argued that he and his similar colleagues should not be prosecuted, but should be allowed to re-enter society as husbands and fathers in order to take care of their families. So there was the argument for social justice broadly defined rather than an individualized legal justice through prosecution.[82]

Discussion questions

- Did the Nuremberg and Tokyo trials make a positive contribution to the evolution of human rights in international relations, despite their procedural and substantive errors, not to mention their use of the death penalty?
- Was the indictment and perhaps arrest of certain persons in the Balkans during 1992–1999 an impediment to peace, or compatible with peace? Would the indictment and perhaps arrest of Saddam Hussein in Iraq after his invasion of Kuwait have been an impediment to peace, or compatible with peace?
- What explains the US opposition to the 1998 statute of the International Criminal Court, when US democratic allies like Britain, Italy, Canada, France, etc. all voted to approve the statute?
- What impact, if any, has the International Criminal Tribunal for Rwanda made on the politics of the Great Lakes region of Africa?

---

[82] For a discussion of different conceptions of international justice, comparing legal justice with other forms, see Patrick Keyzer, Vesselin Popovski, and Charles Sampford, eds., *Access to International Justice* (London and New York: Routledge, 2015).

- In South Africa after apartheid and El Salvador after civil war, among other places, there was considerable national reconciliation, and more liberal democracy, at least relatively speaking, while avoiding criminal prosecution for most political acts of the past. Is this a useful model for the future?
- What are the purported advantages and disadvantages of truth commissions as compared with judicial proceedings, concerning past gross violations of human rights?
- Given that international and hybrid criminal courts all manifest a public prosecutor, how have these persons exercised their prosecutorial discretion in conducting investigations and bringing charges, and is that evaluation strictly legal or also political?

SUGGESTIONS FOR FURTHER READING

Bass, Gary Jonathan, *Stay the Hand of Vengeance: The Politics of War Crimes Tribunals* (Princeton: Princeton University Press, 2000). An excellent historical overview of the political decisions preceding the establishment of, or in some cases the failure to establish, international criminal courts.

Cobban, Helena, *Amnesty After Atrocity: Healing Nations After Genocide and War Crimes* (Boulder: Paradigm, 2007). A sympathetic look at the option of avoiding prosecutions, with an emphasis on reconciliation, and with several good case studies out of Africa.

Garten, Jeffrey, "Comment: The Need for Pragmatism," *Foreign Policy*, 105 (Winter 1996–1997), 103–106. Criticizes consistent emphasis on legal punishment in international relations; emphasizes other ways of doing good for persons and improving the environment for human rights besides judicial action.

Goldstein, Joseph, William R. Peers, Burke Marshall, Jack Schwartz, and US Department of the Army, eds., *The My Lai Massacre and Its Cover-Up: Beyond the Reach of Law?* (New York: The Free Press, 1976). Excellent collection about an American military unit that committed a massacre in Vietnam, but whose members never were subjected to appropriate punishment because of the Pentagon's maneuvering and nationalist American public opinion.

Holbrooke, Richard, *To End a War* (New York: Random House, 1998). By the principal mediator at Dayton on dealing with Milosevic to end the war in Bosnia. Holbrooke was also influential in the West's dealing with Kosovo four years later. Upon his nomination to be US ambassador at the United Nations, at his Senate confirmation hearings Holbrooke said his job in 1995 was to end the war, not pass judgment on various leaders.

Malcontent, Peter, ed., *Facing the Past: Amending Historical Injustices through Instruments of Transitional Justice* (Cambridge: Intersentia, 2016). European and North American scholars reflect on transitional justice.

Minow, Martha, *Between Vengeance and Forgiveness: Facing History After Genocide and Mass Violence* (Boston: Beacon Press, 1998). Careful reflection about whether there is any particular policy response that is always appropriate after atrocities, suggesting that debates over peace v. justice and reconciliation v. punishment have to be resolved case by case.

Neier, Aryeh, "The New Double Standard," *Foreign Policy*, 105 (Winter 1996–1997), 91–101. A short form of the following book.

War Crimes: Brutality, Genocide, Terror, and the Struggle for Justice (New York: Times Books, 1998). Passionate but one-sided advocacy for criminal justice in all situations.

Olsen, Tricia D., Leigh A. Payne, and Andrew G. Reiter, *Transitional Justice in Balance: Comparing Processes, Weighing Efficacy* (Washington: United States Institute of Peace Press, 2010). An empirical study arguing for a combination of trials and amnesties. Contradicts some other research findings that argue for trials alone. Indicative of many timely studies of an empirical nature focused on the scientific examination of the impact of transitional justice options.

Ratner, Steven R., and Jason S. Abrams, *Accountability for Human Rights Atrocities in International Law: Beyond the Nuremberg Legacy*, 3rd edn. (Oxford: Clarendon Press, 2009; 1st edn., 1997; 2nd edn., 2001). An overview of legal developments about international criminal justice in contemporary times.

Rieff, David, *In Praise of Forgetting: Historical Memory and Its Ironies* (New Haven and London: Yale University Press, 2016). An intriguing but not simple exploration of transitional justice, with an emphasis on forgive and forget.

Roht-Arriaza, Naomi, and Javier Mariezcurrena, eds., *Transitional Justice in the Twenty-First Century: Beyond Truth Versus Justice* (Cambridge: Cambridge University Press, 2006). A group of experts delves into particular situations and issues associated with transitional justice. Evaluations vary about measures adopted in Africa, Latin America, and elsewhere, which is characteristic of the field.

Rosenberg, Tina, *The Haunted Land: Facing Europe's Ghosts After Communism* (New York: Vintage Books, 1996). A journalist gives a fascinating account of her travels and interviews on the subject of how to respond to communist violations of human rights in Europe after 1991, but her conclusions based on quick comparisons with Latin America are not fully persuasive.

Scheffer, David, *All the Missing Souls: A Personal History of the War Crimes Tribunals* (Princeton: Princeton University Press, 2012). A former State Department official, Scheffer argues for criminal justice, but suggests in passing that there are some situations in which national peace and reconciliation may hinge on bypassing it.

Thakur, Ramesh, and Peter Malcontent, eds., *From Sovereign Impunity to International Accountability: The Search for Justice in a World of States* (Tokyo: United Nations University Press, 2004). A group of experts present views on international criminal justice and other forms of international accountability for gross violations of human rights.

Visscher, Charles de, *Theory and Reality in Public International Law* (Princeton: Princeton University Press, 1957). Classic treatment of, among other subjects, peace v. justice in international relations.

5 Regional application of human rights norms

The world may be a smaller place in the light of communication and travel technology, but it is still a large planet when it comes to effective international governance. Given the approximately 6 billion persons and the more than 190 states that existed at the turn of the twenty-first century, and given the weakness of global organizations like the United Nations, it was both logical and sometimes politically feasible to look to regional organizations for the advancement of human rights. This chapter will show that regional developments for human rights were truly remarkable for a time in Europe, delicately progressive in the Western Hemisphere, embryonic in Africa, and otherwise weak. The key to the effective regional protection of human rights is not legal drafting, but underlying political culture, political will, and political acumen. One sees this clearly in the light of Brexit, the 2016 British decision to leave the European Union, in large part because of resentment about the deep intrusion of regional authority into traditional national affairs. In Europe where there are considerable cases and other regional human rights decisions to analyze, I provide a summary analysis. In the Western Hemisphere with substantial case law and other important regional decisions only recently, I provide mostly political analysis of underlying conditions but some attention to legal factors. I treat Africa briefly because of lack of major impact through regional arrangements.

Europe

After World War II, significant US foreign aid to Europe in the form of the Marshall Plan encouraged regional cooperation, especially of an economic nature. Most West European elites endorsed this approach at least to some degree, both in pursuit of economic recovery and to defend traditional western values in the face of Soviet-led communism. One result was the creation of the Council of Europe (CE) with its strong focus on human rights. Separately, owing to reluctance of the UK to integrate fully with the rest of Western Europe, one had the development of the European Communities, which more or less evolved into the European Union (EU). By the start of the twenty-first century it was evident that this bifurcation, while it had "worked" to a considerable degree, was not a completely happy situation. As European international integration proceeded, the contradictions of bifurcation were salient as never before. In addition to the EU and the CE, there was also the Organization for Security and Co-operation in Europe (OSCE), not to mention the North Atlantic Treaty Organization (NATO).[1] While trans-Atlantic, they had substantial European membership. The combined effect of all these regional arrangements produced a populist, nativist, and narrow nationalistic push back across Europe, especially in parts of England.

Council of Europe

European Convention on Human Rights

From the very beginning of European regionalism in the 1940s, West European governments made it clear that promotion and protection of civil and political rights lay at the core of these regional developments.[2] They created the Council of Europe in the late 1940s to coordinate social policies (originally it was supposed to coordinate economic policies as well); the centerpiece of the CE's efforts was the European Convention on Human Rights and Fundamental Freedoms (hereafter the Convention).[3] This legal instrument was approved in 1950 and took legal effect in 1953. It covered only fundamental civil and political rights. (The Convention covers property rights and rights to education, both of which are sometimes viewed as civil rights.) Slightly later these same governments negotiated the European Social Charter to deal with social and economic rights. Attention to labor rights lay at the center of this development. The CE, whose governing organs are entirely separate from the EU's, eventually produced still other human rights documents including

---

[1] For the sake of completeness one can also mention other European regional organizations, such as the Western European Union (WEU, now defunct), a strictly European military arrangement, and the European Free Trade Agreement (EFTA). They had little impact on human rights.

[2] Mark Janis, Richard Kay, and Anthony Bradly, *European Human Rights Law* (New York: Oxford University Press, 1995), 3.

[3] Donald W. Jackson, "European Convention on Human Rights and Fundamental Freedoms," in David P. Forsythe, ed., *Encyclopedia of Human Rights* (New York: Oxford University Press, 2009), vol. II, 175.

a 1986 convention for the prevention of torture, and a 1995 framework convention for the protection of national minorities. The 1950 Human Rights Convention remains the principal achievement of the CE. It does not go too far to say that it comprises a quasi-constitutional regional bill of rights for Europe which has led to a declaration of fundamental human rights by the European Union. The Convention is the foundation for the "most successful system of international law for the protection of human rights."[4] The influence of the Convention in European public law is "immense."[5] Precisely because of the impact of regional norms and agencies, champions of traditional national arrangements sought a limit to, or escape from, growing regional authority.

Given especially Europe's history of fascism, anti-Semitism, and the wars derived therefrom, one theory holds that European states wanted to lock in to strong regional human rights protections to prevent any backsliding into repressive policies – with consolidated democracies such as Britain facilitating the process.[6] If valid, this view still has to acknowledge that state sovereignty was not restricted easily or quickly but rather in fits and starts over time. By 2016, it was clear that many in various European nations had not learned a central lesson from 1945 – namely that powerful regional arrangements were needed to control a dangerous nationalism that had produced two world wars and intense persecution in the twentieth century.

The Convention specifies a series of mostly negative or blocking rights familiar to western liberals. These rights are designed to block public interference with the citizen's private domain; to block the government from overstepping its rightful authority when the citizen encounters public authority through arrest, detention, and trial; and to guarantee citizen participation in public affairs. Of course governmental positive steps are required to make these negative rights effective. Public monies have to be spent to supervise and sometimes correct governmental policies; to run police departments, prisons, and courts; and to hold free and fair elections. The state may need to take positive action to ensure the dignity of children born outside marriage and to prevent discrimination against them. None of this is very new to liberalism, except that in Europe these norms are articulated on a regional basis in addition to national norms.

---

[4] Janis, et al., *European Human Rights Law*, 3.
[5] R. Beddard, *Human Rights and Europe*, 3rd edn. (Cambridge: Grotius Publications, 1993), 6–7.
[6] Andrew Moravscik, "Explaining International Human Rights Regimes: Liberal Theory and Western Europe," *European Journal of International Relations*, 1, 2 (Summer 1995), 157–189.

The really interesting aspect to the CE's work on human rights concerns methods to ensure compliance with the norms. In this regard under the Convention, the CE proceeded cautiously. Despite general agreement on the desirability of international norms on civil and political rights, the original ratifying states differed over how much state sovereignty should be restricted by regional international organizations. Under the Convention and additional protocols, therefore, early ratifying states had the option of accepting or not the jurisdiction and supranational authority of the European Court of Human Rights. States also had the option of allowing private petitions to the separate European Commission of Human Rights. This latter body was a screening commission of first recourse, as well as a fact-finding and conciliation commission. Thus complaints about violations could be brought by one ratifying state against another, with the Commission taking its findings to the Committee of Ministers if a state involved had not yet accepted the jurisdiction of the Court. Pending the consent of ratifying states, complaints could also be brought by private parties whether individuals, nongovernmental organizations, or associations of persons. Again the Commission had the option of taking its conclusions to the Committee of Ministers or to the Court (the state involved also could pursue several avenues). Originally private parties had no legal standing before the Court, being dependent on representation by the Commission. But under Protocol 9, additional to the Convention, if the Commission ruled in favor of a private petition, the private party then appeared before a special chamber of the larger Court for a further hearing. Thus private parties gained rights of action in an international court.

Lest one become lost in legal technicalities, it is important to stay focused on summary developments. First, over time the number of states adhering to the Convention increased. This was particularly evident after the Cold War, when Central and East European states, having recovered their operational sovereignty from Soviet control, sought membership in the CE and legal adherence to the Convention. Such adherence was a sign of being European, as well as a stepping stone to possible membership in the EU. CE membership reached forty-seven states, with all of these (except Monaco) ratifying the Convention. Belarus remained outside the CE; it applied for membership but its poor human rights record, including lack of what the CE called pluralist democracy, blocked admission.

Second, over time all of these states accepted the right of private petition, as well as the jurisdiction in all complaints of the European Court of Human Rights. Thus particularly the former communist states of Eastern Europe recovered their sovereignty only to immediately trade aspects of it away for enhanced international protection of human rights. It was also noteworthy that highly nationalistic states like France, with a long history of national discourse about human rights, finally also accepted the need for private petitions and binding adjudication at the regional level. Equally noteworthy was the decision by Turkey to accept the right of private petitions and the presumed supranational role of the Court, despite evident human rights problems – historically associated with the Kurdish question in that state. Turkey manifested additional human rights controversies after a failed coup in 2016 and resultant governmental crackdown on presumed critics and dissidents. Again, some state motivation can be attributed as much to the desire to be considered for membership in the EU, with its projected economic benefits, as to a simpler or purer commitment to civil and political rights *per se*. Politically speaking, the Council of Europe, with the Human Rights Convention required for membership, became an ante-chamber leading to the doorway of the EU.[7] By 1998 the CE had decided that private petitions and acceptance of the Court were no longer options, but had to be part of a state's adherence to the Convention. From a cautious beginning the CE had developed rigorous standards for human rights protection. The newly independent states of Eastern Europe were immediately held to standards that the West European states were allowed to accept over time. As we will see, judicial enforcement existed on a regular basis.

Third, the Convention system has always been cautious about accepting private complaints for further action. The Commission, before it was replaced by a revised procedure, usually threw out around 90 percent of the private petitions filed in support of an alleged violation of the Convention as being ill-founded. From 1955 to 1994, the Commission accepted only 8 percent of the petitions submitted. In 2010, the new procedures resulted in similar figures: only 6 percent of private petitions were advanced to the next stage of consideration (362 out of 5,954, with 5,592 rejected). For the period 1999–2010, of 61,300 private petitions submitted, only 8,400 were advanced, an acceptance rate of about 14 percent. Some of these were later declared inadmissible, thus reducing the final acceptance rate to usual levels. (It might be noted by comparison that the US Supreme Court is petitioned to take up cases about 10,000 times per year, out of which it usually accepts about 100 cases.)

Fourth, despite the rejection rate, the overall number of such private petitions has been growing consistently. In 1955, the Commission had

---

[7] Hugo Storey, "Human Rights and the New Europe: Experience and Experiment," in David Beetham, ed., *Politics and Human Rights* (Oxford: Blackwell, 1995), 131–151.

received a total of 138 private petitions. In 1997, it received 4,750. From 1999 to 2010, complaints increased significantly; during this time, it should be observed, CE membership expanded considerably, given the demise of the Soviet empire in Eastern Europe. Or, in a different summary indicating the same trend, as of 1991 the Commission had dealt with 19,000 petitions, all but 8 of which (13 if you count the same case presented in different forms) were triggered by private petitions. Of the 19,000 petitions, 3,000 were discussed seriously further, and 1,000 pursued by either the Commission, the Court, and/or the Committee of Ministers.

This trend manifested itself despite the fact that ratifying states were all either liberal democracies or aspired to be. Clearly, before 1991, the evident fact was that consolidated pluralist democracy at the national level did not guarantee that there would be no further violations of human rights. Indeed, the early history of the CE and Convention indicated just the opposite: that even with liberal democracy at the national level, there was still a need for regional monitoring of human rights – there being evident violations by national authorities.

It bears emphasizing that contributing to the great number of petitions more recently was the presence in the CE after the Cold War of highly problematic states such as Romania, the Russian Federation, Ukraine, and a few others. Their human rights records were inferior to those of many older CE members and generated numerous complaints. The human rights NGO Freedom House, based in New York, for example, downgraded the Russian Federation to "unfree," its lowest category, by 2016 – which indicated problems with free and fair elections, suppression of dissent, and other important human rights issues. The longer Vladimir Putin remained the central figure in Russian politics, the greater the human rights defects in that increasingly autocratic polity.

One sees the pattern when one looks at cases pending as of 2010 in the European Court of Human Rights regarding particular states: Russia, 28.4 percent of cases; Turkey, 10.7; Romania, 8.7; Ukraine, 7.5; Italy, 7.5; Poland, 4.8; Serbia, 2.8; Moldova, 2.7; Bulgaria, 2.4; Slovenia, 2.4. With the exception of Turkey and Italy, it was some former communist states that seemed to have trouble adjusting to European human rights standards. This was perfectly clear in the Russian case where Putin, a former secret service agent for the Soviet Union, spoke with nostalgia of that highly repressive era, while dismissing many internationally endorsed rights as the product of a decadent West. Rather than becoming a "normal" Western state, Putin saw Russia as presenting an alternative to Western trends.

At the same time, we can note that some former communist states in Europe seemed flexible in adjusting to the regional human rights regime. If for the period 1999–2010 we look at states that, in the face of accepted private petitions, reached a friendly settlement or other national accommodation, and thus did not insist on Court adjudication, we find that Hungary settled almost 40 percent of the time, Croatia almost 75 percent of the time. But by 2016, both Hungary and Poland manifested some national developments that ran counter to standard interpretations about human rights in the CE. At the time of writing, Poland as dominated by the Law and Justice Party was the locus of considerable controversy about judicial independence, while Hungary seemed to be drifting in an autocratic direction under Prime Minister Viktor Orban. Both governments were clearly hostile to accepting Muslim refugees from conflict areas like Syria.

Fifth, public confidence in the system was high in general. Whether one looks at consolidated pluralist democracies that made up early CE membership or later members from the communist zone of Europe, the trend line for private petitions was upward. This was even true in states long known for commitment to human rights such as Denmark, the Netherlands, or Switzerland, to take just three examples. It was clear that many persons within the jurisdiction of the CE thought their international rights were being violated, that they increasingly looked to the regional "machinery" of the CE for relief, and that they were not deterred by the evident "conservatism" of the procedures which screened out the overwhelming number of petitions at the very first stage of review.

Sixth, one could not rely on state action to consistently protect human rights in another state. If one moves from private to interstate complaints, the numbers change dramatically. Without doubt, private petitions, and within these, individual complaints, drive the work of the Commission and Court. Even in Europe, states do not like to petition each other about human rights. Under the principle of reciprocity, my complaint about you today may lead you to complain about me tomorrow. States normally put a premium on good relations, especially among trading partners and security allies. There have been only nine state-to-state complaints up to the time of writing, not counting second and third phases of the same dispute. Several of these occurred in the context of already strained relations: Greece v. the UK over Cyprus (twice), Ireland v. the UK (twice), Cyprus v. Turkey (four times), Georgia v. Russia (twice). Military government in Greece in 1967–1974 produced two complaints by a group made up of Denmark, Norway, Sweden, and the Netherlands. The same group plus France brought a complaint against

Turkey. Denmark alone also brought a case against Turkey.[8] But these are small numbers over the life of the Convention. Between 1959 and 1985 the Court handled 100 cases; 98 of these started with private petitions.[9] This pattern has profound relevance for other efforts to apply human rights standards relying on state complaints. Two interstate cases involved Georgia v. Russia in 2007 and 2008. The two states engaged in a brief armed conflict during late summer 2008. In 2014, Ukraine lodged a complaint against Russia regarding Crimea, and in 2016 Slovenia lodged a complaint against Croatia regarding banking regulations. The latter case is the only one thus far between two EU member states.

Seventh, if one can get a private petition cleared for admissibility in the first stage of technical review, one stands a rather good chance of prevailing on substance. One of the reasons that private petitions continue to mount is that if one's petition is declared admissible, if a friendly settlement cannot be achieved between petitioner and state, and if the matter goes to the Court of Human Rights, the petitioner stands a very good chance of winning the case. For many states, the success rate of complaints against it is over 50 percent. As of 2004, the Court had found at least one violation in 11 of 15 cases against Belgium; for France, 59 out of 75; for Greece, 32 out of 40; for Italy, 36 out of 47; for the Netherlands, 6 out of 10; for the UK, 19 out of 23. The total was 589 violations (at a minimum) out of 719 admitted petitions. When one includes multiple violations, it appears that petitioners usually win about two-thirds of their claims.[10]

These are good odds for the petitioner across all types of European states, including some of those with the best general reputations for serious attention to civil and political rights. The judges of the European Court of Human Rights, sitting in their personal capacity through election by the CE's European Parliamentary Assembly, were not hesitant to find fault with governmental policy. They had once been cautious about

---

[8] Turkey might be considered a special case by European standards. The military was highly influential, taking over the government on several occasions and conducting, by almost all accounts, a brutal suppression of the Kurdish separatist movement. NGOs were reporting torture and other gross violations of human rights, especially in connection with the Kurdish question. But many in the Turkish elite believed that some Christian European political circles were using the human rights issue in an effort to block Muslim Turkey's entrance into the EU. It was said that these Christian circles feared the free movement of Muslim Turks as labor within the EU.

[9] Janis, et al., *European Human Rights Law*, 70.

[10] See https://fullfact.org/news/does-uk-lose-three-out-four-european-human-rights-cases/. This press report focuses on British cases at the Court, but provides an overview of all cases, showing that in over 80 percent of substantive cases, the Court found at least one claimed violation was correct.

ruling against states, in order to build state support for the CE system. It took the Court ten years to make its first ruling against a state.[11] But things have changed.

Eighth, the Court was overburdened with cases. It took thirty years to decide its first 200 cases; it only took three years to decide the next 200.[12] During its lifetime, the European Court of Human Rights has decided more than twenty times the cases handled by the World Court – the International Court of Justice at The Hague, to which only states have access for legally binding cases.[13] The case load for the Court, and delays in reaching it, had become of such concern that a protocol (number 11) to the Convention that would expedite proceedings went into legal force during the fall of 1998. All details of that change need not concern us here, but Protocol 11 eliminated the Commission, created a chamber of the Court made up of several judges to take over the screening functions, and utilized other chambers of several judges in order to process more cases at once. The full Court still sat to hear certain cases, including all state-to-state complaints. Thus, far from withering away because of national commitment to civil and political rights, the European Court of Human Rights was trying to figure out how to accommodate increased demand for its services. In 2010 the Court issued 1,499 judgments (some involving combined cases). In that same year there was a backlog of 139,650 cases pending.

Given this backlog, which had been building for several years, to further improve the efficiency of the Court, Protocol 14 to the Convention was put into effect as of June 2010. The Protocol, with complicated wording, seeks to provide the Court with the procedural flexibility and means to expeditiously process cases. Particularly when a state has failed to comply with the decision of the Court, the Committee of Ministers will be able to bring the state more quickly to the Court for non-compliance. Still, despite various procedures to expedite the Court's functioning, by early 2013 there were some 70,000 cases accepted and waiting to be heard.

One can note the number of "high importance" cases. These have no set subject matter but can include cases of non-compliance. In 1999 there were 105 high importance cases; in 2010 there were 1,012. Thus in 1999 high importance cases made up 60 percent of the Court workload, whereas the numbers had grown to 83 percent in 2010. The backlog

---

[11] Janis, et al., *European Human Rights Law*, 71.
[12] D. J. Harris, M. O'Boyle, and C. Warbrick, *The Law of the European Convention on Human Rights* (London: Butterworths, 1995), 35–36.
[13] Janis, et al., *European Human Rights Law*, 71.

presented something of a crisis for the system. At present rates of processing, it would take an expanded Court with more judges years and years to catch up to the number of validly filed complaints.[14]

It should be noted that before 1991 most breaches of the Convention did not concern what are sometimes called gross and systematic violations. (The question of torture is covered below.) Most CE states were genuinely sympathetic to civil and political rights. But where the CE faced a government that was non-cooperative and determined to engage in gross and systematic violations, the CE functioned in a way not dissimilar to the United Nations or the Organization of American States. This is shown by the Greek case of 1967–1974, and also by Turkish policy in Cyprus. The CE system for protecting civil and political rights did not prevent or easily correct violations in those situations, because the target government was basically non-cooperative. Liberal democracies might sometimes violate civil and political rights here and there, perhaps inadvertently, or due to delay or personal malfeasance, and therefore be in need of regional monitoring. But the presence of genuine liberal democracy at the national level was a *sine qua non* for an effective regional protective system.[15] The situation has changed somewhat with the admission to CE membership of states that Freedom House regards as only "partially free" rather than "free." According to some analysts, a number of experts who followed details closely always thought the Convention would not work well regarding Russia. Its human rights problems were seen as fundamental and the attitude of the elites basically non-cooperative. In this view, major West European policy makers agreed to have Russia join the CE and be eligible to ratify the Human Rights Convention because it would be politically awkward to block Russian membership. But the legal experts were not surprised that Russian full compliance with Court judgments has been problematic. It seems clear enough that an autocratic or "unfree" Russia, as under Putin, cannot be effectively brought back into compliance with human rights standards by the European Court of Human Rights. The Court by itself is too weak to counter strong political forces of an autocratic nature.

As for Turkey, leading legal experts there such as Isil Karakas (a judge on the European Court of Human Rights) openly acknowledged that

---

[14] See further Spyridon Flogaitis, Tom Zwart, and Julie Fraser, eds., *The European Court of Human Rights and Its Discontents: Turning Criticism into Strengths* (Cheltenham: Edward Elgar, 2013).

[15] Menno T. Kamminga, "Is the European Convention on Human Rights Sufficiently Equipped to Cope with Gross and Systematic Violations?," *Netherlands Human Rights Quarterly*, 12, 2 (1994), 153–164.

Turkey's political culture was not as supportive of basic democratic values as was the case elsewhere in western Europe. Consequently, Turkey was still trying to improve its legal record on such fundamental rights as right to life, freedom from torture and inhuman treatment, and freedom of expression, *inter alia*. The crackdown by President Erdogan after the failed coup of 2016 further distanced Turkey from compliance with European human rights standards. In general, Turkey under Erdogan seemed to drift further and further toward autocratic rule and toward alignment with non-Western powers.

As for the Court's important jurisprudence, it covered, among other subjects, treatment while detained, freedom of expression, respect for private and family life, the right to liberty and security of person, the right to fair and public hearing, and the effect of the Convention in national law.[16] According to one summary, the Court is one of the most important international organizations yet created, has made numerous rulings of major importance to even established democracies such as Britain and Sweden, and routinely secures at least partial compliance with its decisions.[17]

A special consideration was the "margin of appreciation" afforded to states in applying the Convention. For example, Article 15 allowed states to derogate from many provisions of the Convention in "public emergencies threatening the life of the nation." A democratic state did have the right to defend itself. On the other hand, certain articles could never be legally abridged, such as those prohibiting torture. States had to formally declare such emergencies and subject them to authoritative review. In the matter of the seizure of the government by the Greek military in 1967, the Commission held that such action was not justified under Article 15. The Committee of Ministers, however, was not able to take corrective action. (The junta collapsed of its own ineffectiveness in 1974.) But in general, under Article 15 and others, the review organs tend to give some leeway to states – a margin of appreciation – in highly controversial interpretations of the Convention. The Court did so in upholding invocation of Article 15 by the UK regarding Northern Ireland. "Margin of appreciation," perhaps like "executive privilege"

---

[16] Ibid. More traditional legal analysis covers the details of actual cases. That is not my intent here, and space does not allow it. For a short summary of some of the leading cases, see Jackson, "European Convention on Human Rights and Fundamental Freedoms."

[17] Darrin Hawkins and Wade Jacoby, "Agent Permeability, Principal Delegation, and the European Court of Human Rights," *Review of International Organization*, 3, 1 (2008), 1–28.

in US constitutional law, was a matter of great complexity and continuing case law.[18]

In general, there are three measures open to the Court and Committee of Ministers: just satisfaction (e.g., payment of compensation), individual measures (e.g., revocation of a deportation order), or general measures (e.g., adopt new legislation). The Court can order the first and the Committee can utilize the other two. It is up to the Committee of Ministers to supervise the implementation of Court judgments. Early on, compliance was not a great problem, as most states complied with most judgments most of the time.

Before 1991, and thus before the expansion of state parties to the Court, Britain and Italy had been found in violation of the Convention more times than any other of the thirty-eight states then subject to its terms. In Britain it is said that this is because of its unwritten constitution and lack of judicial review.[19] But these factors, if true, do not explain Italy's record. The slowness of Italian judicial procedures seems to account for a considerable number of Italian violations of the Convention. Over time, states such as Britain and Italy did eventually comply with European Court judgments. By 2005, however, the bulk of the findings of violations were against Turkey, rising from 18 in 1999 to 154 in 2004.[20] As the CE has expanded its membership over time, it has also expanded the number of highly problematic members. Illiberal trends in Russia, Turkey, Hungary, and Poland mean great challenges for regional enforcement of human rights. The matter of compliance merits further commentary. In the Russian case, for example, the government may agree to pay compensation to individuals whose rights have been violated as per Court interpretation, but it may fail to make legislative and other structural changes ensuring that such violations are not repeated. Thus there may be partial compliance by a state. The growing number of repeat cases on the same legal subject within a country is an indicator of the lack of fundamental, structural, or systematic change.

In general, given the changed CE membership after 1991, with states such as Russia and Romania in the mix, along with Turkey, the Court's record of securing compliance was not quite as stellar as in previous years. Ultimate responsibility then devolved to the Committee of

---

[18] Yutaka Arat, "The Margin of Appreciation Doctrine in the Jurisprudence of Article 8 of the European Convention on Human Rights," *Netherlands Human Rights Quarterly,* 16, 1 (1998), 41–56.

[19] Donald W. Jackson, *The United Kingdom Confronts the European Convention on Human Rights* (Gainesville: University Press of Florida, 1997).

[20] See further Arthur Bonner, "Turkey, the European Union and Paradigm Shifts," *Middle East Policy,* 7, 1 (2005), 44–71.

Ministers in the tough cases. It was clear in the Russian situation, for example, that such major violations of human rights as fatal attacks on investigative journalists and arbitrary detention for those challenging the primacy of the existing elite were tough nuts to crack. It did not help that, during a certain era, some desires for progressive developments by President Dmitry Medvedev were undercut by the actions of Prime Minister Vladimir Putin.[21] Then over time, Putin resumed the Presidency and the somewhat more liberal Medvedev was pushed into the background.

In the past, the role of the Committee of Ministers has been generally underappreciated in human rights matters. When the Commission reached a decision on a petition, and could not advance the matter to the Court because of lack of state consent, its decision was only intermediate – with the final decision up to the Committee of Ministers. At least one observer holds that the Committee, made up of state representatives, was overly "statist" in its orientation by comparison with the Commission made up of independent experts.[22] All states have now accepted the Court's jurisdiction, and all new ratifiers of the Convention must do the same. Under Protocol 11, the Commission is eliminated, the Court will judge all well-founded petitions, and the role of the Committee will remain solely that of supervising the execution of Court judgments.

In all CE states the guarantees of the Convention can be invoked before the domestic courts, once the petitioner has exhausted local remedies (meaning, has tried national and sub-national norms and procedures first). There was a cottage industry for lawyers and law professors deciding on the exact legal effects of the Convention at the national level, either via direct effects or via domestic legislation. Yet almost fifty European states remain bound by the Convention and subject to the rulings by the Court, however the legal specifics might play out in national courts and other national public bodies.

Repeatedly, controversies have arisen about whether the European Court of Human Rights is always supreme over national constitutional courts. In general, it can be said that the more assertive of the latter type of courts, as in Germany and Italy, have satisfied themselves that the European Court protects human rights sufficiently so that the national

---

[21] See in general Amnesty International, "Russian Federation Human Rights," www.amnestyusa.org/all-countries/russian-federation/page.do?id=1011228.

[22] Adam Tomkins, "Civil Liberties in the Council of Europe: A Critical Survey," in C. Gearty, ed., *European Civil Liberties and the European Convention on Human Rights* (The Hague: Martinus Nijhoff, 1977), 1–52.

authorities can properly defer to regional law. But there is the possibility of a different ruling in some future case.[23]

Clearly, the European Convention had evolved in impressive ways, fueled by the underlying political agreement among national policy makers that protection of civil and political rights was central to their self-identification and self-image. This commitment was so strong that significant elements of state sovereignty were to be yielded in order to achieve it. Because of CE norms and judgments, the United Kingdom felt compelled to introduce a written bill of rights despite its long history of having an unwritten constitution. To be sure there was some grumbling in many states, certainly in the UK, about the intrusiveness of regional norms and the assertiveness of the Court.

For a time, it seemed clear that national decisions about human rights would be authoritatively reviewed by the European Court of Human Rights. This is now less clear, as there has been a renaissance across Europe of populist, nativist, and nationalist movements – triggered in part by resentment against refugees and migrants. Then there is the matter of the domestic popularity of repressive autocrats like Putin. So the future of European regional arrangements was not as clear as had apparently been the case. In some places, national commitment to a rights-protective society was weaker, which meant problems for enforcement of human rights. It had been widely hoped that material interdependence through economics would produce moral interdependence and hence a strong commitment to European regional norms and institutions. This hope was greatly undercut by Brexit and the anti-refugee sentiment so clear in 2016 – the latter leading to bitter disputes among different governments about burden-sharing. The idea of being European was weak, and traditional national identities seemed as strong as ever.

One question for the future, in addition to how to maintain a good record of compliance with Court judgments, was how these decisions could be coordinated with other human rights judgments handed down by the EU's supranational court, the European Court of Justice. As of the time of writing, twenty-seven European states were subject to a potential double human rights review by supranational courts – once in the CE and once in the EU when human rights controversies fell within the purview of both organizations.

---

[23] See further Machiko Kanetake and Andre Nollkaemper, eds., *The Rule of Law at the National and International Levels: Contestations and Deference* (Oxford and Portland, OR: Bloomsbury, 2016).

CE Social Charter

This 1961 legal instrument covers social and economic rights, originally workers' rights in and out of the work environment.[24] As of 1996 it had been comprehensively revised into a new document, and there was talk in the advisory European Assembly of converting some of its ideas into a new protocol that would be added to the European Convention on Human Rights, and thus made subject to the authoritative review of the European Court of Human Rights.[25] But this had not transpired at the time of writing. Thus there was increased attention to social (and economic) rights in Europe, and some effort was being made to deal with their secondary or inferior status. Still, it remained clear that even in Europe, with much social democracy and relatively large welfare states, socioeconomic rights received less attention, and less vigorous enforcement, than civil-political rights.

By 2016, forty-three states had consented to be bound by various versions of the European Social Charter. (States that accepted an earlier version remained bound by it, if they did not accept the 1996 version.) There was no court dealing with economic and social rights, but a European Committee of Social Rights, composed of independent experts, made recommendations to superior intergovernmental bodies about application of the Charter. This Committee was advised by the International Labour Organization. It frequently found states to be in violation of their reporting obligations under the Charter. It lacked the authority, however, to compel a change in policy by the states in violation. Its superior bodies also pursued the path of persuasion over time, rather than punitive enforcement.

A 1995 protocol adding a right of collective private petition, by trade unions and certain human rights groups, for alleged Charter violations had been accepted by only thirteen states. The Monitoring Committee, acting on the basis of state reports as well as these non-governmental petitions, has found states in violation in a diversity of areas: child labor in Portugal, forced labor in Greece, right to organize in Sweden, discrimination on basis of disability in France, and protection of children against corporal punishment in Ireland and Belgium among others.

The revised Charter specified a number of new rights in addition to existing labor rights: the right to protection against poverty and social exclusion, to housing, to protection in case of termination of

---

[24] See www.coe.int/en/web/turin-european-social-charter.
[25] See further Catherine Barnard, et al., eds., *Cambridge Yearbook of European Legal Studies* (Oxford and Portland, OR: Hart, 2013), vol. 15, 171–174.

employment, to protection against sexual harassment and victimization, etc. Certain existing economic and social rights were revised: reinforcement of the principle of non-discrimination, increased equality between genders, better maternity protection and social protection for mothers, increased protection for children and disabled persons. Some rights were designated core or non-core rights (in non-legal terms), owing to the different levels of economic development in a CE of more than forty-five states. The non-core rights seem to be the ones considered more expensive to implement, such as fair remuneration. Unlike some other socio-economic treaties, the rights codified are to be implemented immediately upon ratification and not over time depending on economic factors.

Still, even under the 1996 revisions of the Social Charter, the highest control mechanisms remained unchanged. That caused the Parliamentary Assembly of the CE in 1999 to call for a new protocol to the European Convention on Human Rights covering certain economic and social rights. Outside experts had agreed that some economic and social rights could be adjudicated, being not very different in some substantive respects from civil rights.[26] Should such a protocol to the European Convention be adopted, the question of subject matter jurisdiction between the European Court of Human Rights and the European Court of Justice (part of the EU system) would be brought into bold relief. Both would be dealing more with labor rights and economic matters. But a number of experts thought such a protocol was unlikely to be accepted by very many member states, and events thus far have borne out this skepticism.

As of 2016 one could not say what the effect of the revised Social Charter might be in the long run. In general, it was still true to say that European states were not prepared to subject themselves to the same type of authoritative third-party review concerning economic and social rights as they had accepted for civil and political rights. On the other hand, they were experimenting with procedures of application that might direct more attention to labor rights, the right to housing, and various forms of social security. Unlike the USA, most European states, including those in Central and Eastern Europe, were social democracies that believed in extensive economic and social rights, as well as civil and political ones – even if European states were hesitant to encourage binding adjudication in this subject area. One expert believed that the Charter in its various versions had had "pervasive, though not spectacular impact," as many European states made small changes to their socioeconomic legislation to

---

[26] Paul Hunt, *Reclaiming Social Rights: International and Comparative Perspectives* (Aldershot: Dartmouth, 1996).

conform to its norms. The Charter seemed to have had some impact in the newly independent states of Eastern Europe after the demise of communism there.[27] Given the highly nationalistic mood across Europe in 2016, it was highly unlikely that dramatic changes to strengthen the European Social Charter system would occur in the near future.

CE Prevention of Torture

All of the states that ratified the European Convention on Human Rights and Fundamental Freedoms also ratified the European Convention for the Prevention of Torture (CPT). Under this treaty a committee of uninstructed persons had the right to regularly visit ratifying states to inquire into measures and conditions pertaining to torture and inhuman or degrading treatment. The committee could also make *ad hoc* visits with minimal advance notification. The committee initially operated on the basis of confidentiality. Similar to the detention visits of the International Committee of the Red Cross, if a state did not show adequate progress over time in meeting the norms of the Convention, the committee might publicize its conclusions. However, in practice most states ask the CPT to release its report after a visit. A few states, most prominently the Russian Federation, have declined to follow this practice, with the result that outsiders assume major problems exist. At times the CPT has itself taken the initiative to publish its findings in the context of clear non-cooperation by a state. This situation obtained in places such as Turkey (1992, 1996) and Russia/Chechnya (2001, 2003, 2007).[28] Over time the committee interpreted its mandate broadly, so that general prison conditions, and not just torture and cruel treatment, were reviewed. The committee also developed the tradition of making very specific recommendations to governments. One could read, for example, the executive summary of reports on Armenia and Kosovo as of late 2016, inter alia.

Some might assume that this treaty was made possible by the absence of torture in Europe. Such an assumption might be mistaken for several reasons, partially evident in the above paragraphs. First, older CE member states such as Britain, when dealing with perceived public emergencies such as Northern Ireland, had been known to engage in controversial interrogation techniques. Whether these techniques should be properly labeled torture, inhuman mistreatment, or something else

[27] Robin Churchill, "European Social Charter," in *Encyclopedia of Human Rights*, vol. II, 181–185.
[28] Malcolm D. Evans, "Torture: European Convention on Prevention of Torture," ibid., vol. V, 60–63.

was for review bodies to determine.[29] In the summer of 1999 France, having abused a suspected drug dealer while detained, was found guilty of torture by the European Court of Human Rights. Second, some of the newer members of the CE, especially the former communist states, displayed a history that was not free of a pattern of controversial interrogation techniques. Third, Turkey, and also Russia, which ratified the European Torture Convention, were regularly charged with using torture as public policy by various human rights groups, as well as the media.

CE Protection of Minorities

The European Convention on Human Rights and Fundamental Freedoms deals explicitly only with individual civil and political rights. Likewise, the European Social Charter does not mention national minorities. Given the changing membership of the CE, and the historical importance to public order of national minorities not only in Central and Eastern Europe, but also in West European states such as Spain, the CE in 1995 concluded a Framework Convention for the Protection of National Minorities. The question of the protection of national minorities within nation-states has long bedeviled world affairs, starting with problems of definition, so it is no surprise that many problems are evident in European approaches to this subject. The UN Sub-Commission on Protection of Minorities, when it existed, also encountered many problems in its work for minority protection.

The CE Convention on Minorities entered into force in 1998 and had been ratified by thirty-nine states as of late 2016. Four others have signed but not ratified. Four more have done neither. It contains no special monitoring mechanisms aside from an unspecified role for the CE's Committee of Ministers. The Committee of Ministers has, however, created an Advisory Committee of eighteen independent experts to assist in the monitoring of state compliance. The Advisory Committee examines state reports and gives an Opinion on the measures taken by the reporting state. The Advisory Committee had also introduced country visits as part of its monitoring mandate. It is the Committee of Ministers, however, that adopts Conclusions and issues Recommendations to

---

[29] At one point the European Commission on Human Rights held that the UK had employed torture in dealing with Northern Ireland, whereas the European Court of Human Rights held only that the UK had engaged in mistreatment. In any event, because of domestic as well as international criticism, the British government presumably altered the interrogation techniques in question – at least officially in that particular controversy.

states. It has also started the practice of issuing commentaries on particular themes such as education or participation.

The treaty, rather than endorsing assimilation of all groups into one homogeneous society, endorses the preservation of national minorities. It urges governments to accommodate national minorities, although they are not defined in the treaty, through public policies on language, state services, etc. Parts of the treaty repeat non-discrimination norms found in other international human rights instruments. Other parts mandate states to enable individual members of national minorities to maintain their language, religion, and culture. These provisions give rise to questions such as whether the state, in public documents and processes, must accommodate minority languages.

France and Turkey are strongly opposed to the treaty in general, having neither signed nor ratified it. France thinks it unwise to focus on minorities at the expense of national unity; Turkey has long been concerned with its ethnic (national?) Kurdish minority in its southeastern region. The lack of definition has allowed individual states to pick and choose which groups are covered by the treaty. Estonia tends to see its Russian minority as a potential Trojan horse put at the service of the neighboring Russian Federation and thus labels that group as linguistic and not national. Germany has excluded Turkish residents from treaty coverage. A number of states watch Belgium with dismay, as elements in the north, Flemish-speaking, talk of secession which is opposed by most French speakers in the south of that state. Are these linguistic groups to be properly viewed as national minorities? Despite the treaty, Roma are often discriminated against in both West and East European states.[30]

Despite these problems and more, some experts believe the treaty and its supervisory mechanism have political utility, even with their legal difficulties, in focusing on a troublesome subject and encouraging a dialogue designed to reduce frictions and misunderstandings.[31]

European Union

In the treaties during the 1950s that lay at the origin of the present EU, there was no mention of human rights. This anomaly was formally corrected in the 1992 Maastricht Treaty transforming the Communities

---

[30] Geoff Gilbert, "The Council of Europe and Minority Rights," *Human Rights Quarterly*, 18, 1 (Winter 1996), 160–189. See further Safia Swimelar, "Roma in Europe," in *Encyclopedia of Human Rights*, vol. IV, 350–360.
[31] Tove H. Malloy, "Minority Rights: European Framework Convention," in *Encyclopedia of Human Rights*, vol. IV, 1–5.

into the EU, whereby it was stipulated (in Article F.2) that "the Union shall respect fundamental rights, as guaranteed by the European Convention for the Protection of Human Rights and Fundamental Freedoms ... and as they result from the constitutional traditions common to the Member States, as general principles of Community law." This treaty provision codified important human rights developments that had already been occurring in the EU.

The European Court of Justice (ECJ), the supranational court of the EU, had been encouraging European integration by, among other things, declaring the supremacy of Community law compared with national law. German and Italian courts, against the background of their countries' experience with fascism, balked at supranational economic integration without explicit protections of human rights.[32] These and eventually other national bodies feared that national bills of rights and other national protections of human rights – primarily civil and political rights – would be washed away by Community law geared to purely economic considerations. The ECJ, therefore, began to address human rights issues as they related to economic decisions by Community institutions – the Commission (the collective executive), the Council of Ministers (officially a meeting of cabinet ministers of the member states), and the Parliament (a mostly advisory body). Later the Council, a meeting of heads of state, came into being.

All of these other EU organs eventually took up human rights subjects. EU bodies addressed human rights issues from the late 1960s, and in 1977 the European Commission, Council, and Parliament issued a joint declaration saying what Article F.2 was to say in 1992 – namely that human rights were to be protected as found in the European Convention on Human Rights and in the constitutional traditions of member states. In 1989 the European Parliament proposed a European declaration of human rights. This was not immediately acted upon by the Commission and Council, but the proposal did contribute to later developments noted below.

Indeed, by 1992 the EU aspired not only to protecting human rights within its jurisdiction but also in a "common foreign and security policy" (Article J.1[2]).[33] The EU pledged to "develop and consolidate democracy and the rule of law, and respect for human rights and fundamental

---

[32] See especially Nanette A. Neuwahl, "The Treaty on European Union: A Step Forward in the Protection of Human Rights?," in Neuwahl and Allan Rosas, eds., *The European Union and Human Rights* (The Hague: Martinus Nijhoff, 1995), 1–22.

[33] Daniela Napoli, "The European Union's Foreign Policy and Human Rights," ibid., 297–312.

freedoms" in its dealings with other states. EU resources are devoted to this objective, as the EU is the largest donor of international development assistance and also a major donor of international humanitarian assistance in emergency situations. References to human rights and particularly democracy are included in treaties with other developing countries. Occasionally development assistance was suspended on human rights grounds. The EU instituted an arms embargo after the Chinese massacre in Tiananmen Square in 1989. The EU has helped supervise elections in numerous countries. It was a major player in efforts to deal with human rights violations in the western Balkans throughout the 1990s. The EU Council sometimes tries to coordinate the foreign policies of its member states at the United Nations Human Rights Commission, now the Human Rights Council, and General Assembly, but without total success. For example, EU member states split badly on how to deal with China at the UN Commission in 1997.[34] EU unity is not always evident in the new UN Human Rights Council from 2006.

Clearly the EU emphasis on human rights affects aspiring members. Slovakia was delayed admission until certain human rights changes were effectuated. Turkey has yet to gain membership in part because of human rights controversies. In the case of Turkey, observers debate whether that state's difficulty in entering the EU is genuinely because of human rights issues, or whether certain European states use the subject of human rights to block admission of a largely Islamic nation. Does France really want more Islamic workers to have open access to the French labor market? With President Erdogan showing repressive tendencies after the failed coup of 2016, the barriers to Turkey's joining the EU mounted. There was much commentary about how Erdogan no longer aspired for Turkey to be a European nation.

It was the ECJ that had led the way in interjecting human rights into EU proceedings, and some observers – but certainly not all – thought the Court might rule on foreign policy decisions in the future. Some case law by the ECJ suggests that human rights values must be respected not only by EU organs but also by member states when taking decisions within the EU framework.[35]

In Europe at the beginning of the twenty-first century there were two supranational courts making judgments on regional human rights law – the EU's ECJ and the CE's Court of Human Rights. There was no

---

[34] See further Marine Fouwels, "The European Union's Common Foreign and Security Policy and Human Rights," *Netherlands Quarterly of Human Rights*, 15, 3 (September 1997), 291–324.

[35] Neuwahl, "The Treaty on European Union," 9.

explicit coordination between the two. The latter worked from an explicit human rights treaty containing specified human rights. The former did not, at least early on, but rather worked from "principles" vaguely derived from other sources, including the CE treaty. The potential for conflict and confusion was considerable between the CE's Strasbourg court and the EU's Luxemburg court. The Strasbourg court was staffed by human rights specialists. The Luxemburg court was staffed by judges primarily interested in economic law, but they had shown remarkable flexibility and creativity in adapting EU law to broad concerns – including human rights.[36]

For some time there has been discussion about whether the EC, as it then was, and which has some legal personality in international law, should try to formally adhere to the European Convention on Human Rights. The CE/EU Commission was in favor, but the ECJ held that under current law this was not possible, as the European Convention was open only to states and the CE did not have comparable legal personality. The state members of the CE/EU declined to change the appropriate law to make such an adherence possible, perhaps fearing the further loss of influence for national constitutions as the cost of Community law. The continued bifurcation in Europe between economic and social institutions no doubt would demand sorting out in the future, especially if there is ever to be a "United States of Europe." This latter prospect seems more remote than ever through the lens of regional politics in 2016, given the resurgence of nativist nationalism in many places.

By 2005 events had progressed to the point that an EU Charter of Fundamental Rights was negotiated by the leaders of the then-25 EU member nations as part of the projected EU Constitution. This Charter represented a further integration among the member states, as well as providing the most detailed legal obligations yet in the area of human rights. In effect, the Charter moved the members further toward what was in reality an EU bill of rights.[37] As it turned out, some of the nations of Europe were not completely sold on the constitutional project, and voters in both France and the Netherlands refused to accept the Charter in referenda. Since approval by all states was required, the movement for a more tightly unified Europe was thrown into turmoil.

---

[36] G. Federico Manchini, "The Making of a Constitution for Europe," in Robert O. Keohane and Stanley Hoffmann, eds., *The New European Community: Decisionmaking and Institutional Change* (Boulder: Westview Press, 1991), 177–194.

[37] See further Victor Bojkov, "National Identity, Political Interest and Human Rights in Europe: The Charter of Fundamental Rights of the European Union," *Nationalities Papers*, 32, 2 (2004), 323–353.

As for the Charter of Fundamental Rights, it has already been separately accepted as a stand-alone document in 2000 and had been applied from time to time by the European Court of Justice as part of "the general principles of Community law." The Charter is one of the most extensive and innovative human rights documents anywhere, with most of its provisions pertaining to all individuals within the EU zone. Some political norms pertain only to nationals of EU member states. Increasingly the Charter, which is now legally binding within the EU, has affected juridical and legislative developments.[38]

After the no vote in France and the Netherlands, the *status quo ante* prevailed. This meant that the EU, while not fully integrating its member states, was still an actor for human rights both within its own jurisdiction and through its emerging but often disjointed foreign policy.[39] In general the EU joined the Council of Europe in being a major actor for human rights both in the region and in the larger world. But this certainly did not mean that all human rights issues had been resolved within the EU, whether pertaining to immigration, discrimination against minorities (e.g., the Roma), detention and interrogation of terrorism suspects, or other subject matter. The EU was still primarily an economic organization, but greater attention to human rights had changed its identity over time.[40]

The 2016 referendum in the United Kingdom on whether to exit or remain in the EU led to a surprising outcome – Brexit, or the British decision to exit. Britain was one of the Big Four in the EU along with Germany, France, and Italy. The close popular vote to leave, strongest in rural England, cast the future of both the EU and the UK itself into uncharted waters. (Voters in Scotland and Northern Ireland voted to stay.) Explanations of the vote varied, but clearly non-urban voters in England felt that various international arrangements had not benefitted them, and that free movement of labor plus more refugees had changed traditional English society in undesired ways. This combination of economic malaise and social/cultural discontent drove the exit vote. This same combination of socio-economic factors could be seen in nativist movements in the rest of the Western democratic world including in

---

[38] See further Mielle Bulterman, "European Union Charter of Fundamental Rights," in *Encyclopedia of Human Rights*, vol. II, 195–199.

[39] See further Andrew Williams, *EU Human Rights Policies: A Study in Irony* (Oxford: Oxford University Press, 2004).

[40] See Frederic Megret, "European Union," in *Encyclopedia of Human Rights*, vol. II, 186–194. See also Sonia Morano-Foadi and Lucy Vickers, eds., *Fundamental Rights in the EU: A Matter for Two Courts* (Oxford and Portland, OR: Bloomsbury, 2015); and Sybe de Vries, Ulf Bernitz, and Stephen Weatherill, eds., *The EU Charter of Fundamental Rights as a Binding Instrument* (Oxford and Portland, OR: Bloomsbury, 2015).

the USA. More than a few voters believed that international arrangements benefitted only the elites, and that those same elites gave prefer-
ential treatment to foreign workers, refugees, and various minorities.
Those older and less-educated voters, usually members of a past dominant group, who felt they were no longer central to the national society as
it had been in the past, voted for major change to counter existing trends.

Organization for Security and Co-operation in Europe

The diplomatic process known during the Cold War as the CSCE – the
Conference on Security and Co-operation in Europe – became an organization, and hence OSCE, after the Cold War.[41] From 1973 to 1974, the
communist East sought security and economic objectives vis-à-vis the
democratic West. The West responded with an insistence that certain
principles of human rights and humanitarian affairs be respected by all.
The Helsinki Accord of 1975, plus various follow-up conferences, generated considerable pressure on European communist regimes to respect
the principles they had formally endorsed. Individuals and private groups
in the East, backed by western governments and private human rights
groups, became more assertive in demanding respect for rights. The
short-term response by communist party-state regimes was more repression, but the long-term outcome was to further undermine an increasingly discredited communist framework in Europe.

It is impossible to scientifically prove the exact role of the CSCE in the
decline of European communism and the disintegration of the Soviet
Union. As John J. Maresca, a high US diplomat, remarked, "It is a puzzle
to analyze Helsinki's accomplishments, because it is impossible to establish what resulted from Helsinki and what was simply the result of history
moving on."[42] Stefan Lehne, a high Austrian diplomat, argued that the
primary factors leading to dramatic change in European communism were
the internal contradictions of the system of political economy, combined
with Mikhail Gorbachev's refusal to defend the status quo with force. But
he goes on to argue that the CSCE process played a significant if secondary
role.[43] This view was seconded by a number of other observers.[44]

[41] See Patrice C. McMahon, "Helsinki Accord and CSCE/OSCE," ibid., vol. II, 377–383.
[42] Quoted in David P. Forsythe, "Human Rights and Multilateral Institutions in the New
Europe," in Forsythe, ed., Human Rights in the New Europe: Problems and Progress
(Lincoln: University of Nebraska Press, 1994), 176.
[43] Stefan Lehne, The Vienna Meetings of the Conference on Security and Cooperation in Europe,
1986–1989: A Turning Point in East–West Relations (Boulder: Westview, 1991).
[44] See, e.g., William Korey, The Promises We Keep: Human Rights, the Helsinki Process, and
American Foreign Policy (New York: St. Martin's Press, 1993). Korey gives pride of place

After the Cold War the new OSCE increased its membership from thirty-five to fifty-seven states, which broadened its jurisdiction but weakened its capability. A number of the new states emerging from the old Soviet Union lacked early and firm commitment to human rights as well as the real capability to resolve human rights problems. Some states such as the former Yugoslavia descended into murderous armed conflict, about which the OSCE could do little since it had no enforcement authority and no military power, aside from suspending Belgrade from the organization. The OSCE operated as a diplomatic framework to try to advance internationally recognized human rights, especially the civil and political rights associated with liberal democracy. To the extent that it manifested a strong point or area of expertise, it lay in the area of minority rights, about which the Council of Europe had been mostly silent.[45] The first OSCE High Commissioner for National Minorities, the Dutchman Max van der Stoel, was widely respected. He operated through quiet diplomacy to try to prevent and resolve conflicts over national minorities. It was difficult to document his success, in part because successful prevention of disputes left very little to document, and in part because not all minority problems could be resolved. He concentrated mostly on Central and Eastern European affairs, there being political opposition to his taking on minority problems in certain West European states.[46] His office became a focal point for diplomacy on minority issues in Europe, effectively if informally coordinating other IGO and NGO efforts so as to try to make a concentrated impact regarding minority rights.[47]

NATO

While historically NATO had been a traditional military alliance, and not a "regional organization" as per the terms of the UN Charter,

to the US Congress and private interest groups, especially Jewish ones, in generating influence on European communists. See further Sandra L. Gubin, "Between Regimes and Realism – Transnational Agenda Setting: Soviet Compliance with CSCE Human Rights Norms," *Human Rights Quarterly*, 17, 2 (May 1995), 278–302, who argues it was a combination of international and domestic politics in the West that brought effective pressure on the USSR with regard to Jewish emigration.

[45] Jane Wright, "The OSCE and the Protection of Minority Rights," *Human Rights Quarterly*, 18, 1 (Winter 1996), 190–205. See above for coverage of the European Framework Convention on Minority Rights which was developed in weak legal form after the fall of European communism.

[46] Rob Zagman and Joanne Thorburn, *The Role of the High Commission on National Minorities in OSCE Conflict Prevention* (The Hague: Foundation for Inter-Ethnic Relations, 1997). See further Nigel Rodley, "Conception Problems in the Protection of Minorities: International Legal Developments," *Human Rights Quarterly*, 17, 1 (February 1995), 48–71.

[47] See further McMahon, "Helsinki Accord and CSCE/OSCE."

increasingly after the Cold War it took on human rights duties – such as trying to lay the groundwork for liberal democracy in the former Yugoslavia, including the roles of arresting indicted war crimes suspects and ensuring the safe return of refugees and the internally displaced. Indeed, one of the reasons advanced for the 1998 expansion of NATO to include the Czech Republic, Hungary, and Poland was to provide an additional, military framework for reinforcing liberal democracy in those three formerly communist states. As already noted, in 1999 NATO undertook military force "out of area" in order to try to coerce the Milosevic government in modern Yugoslavia to stop its persecution and expulsion of ethnic Albanians in Kosovo. In fact, regardless of legal argument, NATO became an agent of humanitarian intervention and enforcer of liberal democracy in Europe. This trend was confirmed and expanded when NATO took military action in Libya in 2011, officially designed to stop the Kaddafi government from committing atrocities against its civilians. (That NATO was active in combatting piracy "east of Suez" showed that the organization was much more than a defensive alliance for the North Atlantic area.)

A number of realists objected to this orientation, arguing that situations like Bosnia and Kosovo in the 1990s, and then Libya, did not engage the vital interests of the West and should not lead to tying down NATO through air campaigns and sometimes a presence on the ground. They argued that NATO military action should remain focused on traditional state security issues involving Russia, China, state-supported terrorism, and oil in the Middle East. They objected to military commitment to "minor" problems linked to self-determination and humanitarian assistance, as pushed by the communications media and private human rights groups.[48] For realists, priorities remained centered on individual and collective national interests traditionally defined in geopolitical terms, not on alleviating human misery and distress in non-member states.

The different versions of realism have never been very precise about how states define their vital interests. Realist authors basically *assume* that states define their interests in terms of independent power, and then move on to emphasize competition that supposedly affects the "balance of power." In the third volume of his memoirs, Henry Kissinger refers repeatedly to the US "national interest."[49] He argues that his congressional critics (precisely because they were sentimental McGovernites)

[48] See, e.g., the special section on NATO at fifty, in *Foreign Affairs*, 78, 3 (May/June 1999), 163–210, especially the articles by Robert E. Hunter and Michael E. Brown.
[49] Henry Kissinger, *Years of Renewal* (New York: Simon & Schuster, 1999).

were not always interested in US national interests, rather than acknowledging that they had a *different* conception of the national interest. For Kissinger national interest centered on a geo-political power struggle with the old Soviet Union. But it is not self-evident that the USA should have expended blood and treasure in a place like Angola or the Horn of Africa during the Cold War, or that the Congress was in error in trying to block national involvement in such places. After all, if the Soviets wanted to collect a handful of "basket cases" as allies, it is not self-evident that such expansion threatened US security. Thus there is room for reasonable persons to differ over what constitutes national interest, and within that, vital interests.

In Kosovo in 1999, NATO member states defined their vital interests to include a liberal democratic "neighborhood" in Europe. Just as European states had considered human rights important enough to merit two supranational regional courts that restricted state sovereignty in the name of human rights, so they, plus Canada and the USA, considered repression of ethnic Albanians in Kosovo important enough to merit military intervention – having come to feel highly uncomfortable with *not* undertaking military intervention in Bosnia during 1992–1994.

Regarding Libya in 2011, many of these same arguments resurfaced. Did the USA and NATO have an interest in intervening to pre-empt a possible slaughter of rebelling citizens, as Kaddafi seemed to promise? What would happen to NATO soft power in the event of non-intervention and atrocities? But should NATO have intervened in Libya and not in neighboring rebellions in Syria, Bahrain, Yemen, and other places? Would standing aside in Libya encourage repression by other autocrats? Was such a posture in the long-term interests of western states? Was it in the long-term interest of NATO states to be on the side of democratic change in the Arab world, and not just a matter of western "values"? US Secretary of Defense Robert Gates was opposed to the Libyan intervention on grounds that US vital interests were not affected, regardless of what might happen to Libyan civilians.

Serious debate about national interest and human rights could be perplexing. Was it correct to push NATO membership eastward after 1991 toward the borders of the Russian Federation in the name of helping to consolidate democratic capitalism in the states of east-central Europe? Or did such a push inflame Russian fears of encirclement by an aggressive and ill-intentioned West? Given a distrustful Putin government with an evident desire to dominate its near abroad (immediately neighboring countries), could NATO be a force for better protection of human rights in places like Ukraine and Georgia, not to mention in the

Baltic states of Estonia, Latvia, and Lithuania – the latter three being already members of NATO?

After the Cold War, a relaxation of tensions among the great powers had allowed more liberalism in the form of human rights to be interjected into foreign policy through such instruments as NATO.[50] Realist thinking was not *passé*, but it did share the agenda more with a liberal conception of the national interest. The Al Qaeda attacks on the USA in 2001 supposedly brought a tough realism back to the fore, with a diminished interest in human rights. But for a time NATO increasingly played a larger role in efforts to "secure" or "pacify" Afghanistan with an emphasis on democracy and broader human rights – including women's rights. So even in "an age of terrorism" or "an age of insecurity," the subject of human rights displayed considerable staying power. In post-combat situations, NATO was often expected to contribute to democratic nation-building and protection of human rights. Yet over time in Afghanistan, US policy shifted, bringing NATO with it. Rather than seeking full nation-building with the goal of liberal democracy, that policy became more oriented to the lesser goal of counter-terrorism. One sought to keep Afghanistan from being used as a base to launch attacks on the West, whatever the fate internally for women's rights and other human rights considerations.

The Western Hemisphere

By comparison with Europe, a major paradox exists with regard to regional organization and human rights in the Western Hemisphere. There we find, similar to Europe, an international organization, the Organization of American States (OAS), with human rights programs, a regional convention for the protection of human rights, and a commission and court to move beyond passive standards to active implementation. Yet we also find in that Hemisphere during much of the past fifty years an abundance of gross and systematic violations of human rights by OAS member states. How can it be that the states which are members of the Organization of American States engaged both in the repeated endorsement of well-known human rights standards, and at the same time, for much of the time during the Cold War, in their repeated violation? The answer is to be found most fundamentally in a regional conflicted political culture.[51]

---

[50] Ryan Hendrickson, "North Atlantic Treaty Organization," in *Encyclopedia of Human Rights*, vol. IV, 119–123.

[51] This section is drawn from a revision of David P. Forsythe, "Human Rights, the United States, and the Organization of American States," *Human Rights Quarterly*, 13, 2 (Spring 1991), 66–98.

Supportive factors

Three hemispheric political values largely account for the creation and continued functioning of this regional regime for the promotion and protection of human rights. The first of these is widespread but abstract agreement that the legitimate state is the liberal democratic state. This is not a newly articulated value; most hemispheric states professed political liberalism from the time of their independence. More recent developments since 1945 mostly reaffirmed what had been preached if not practiced consistently since the early nineteenth century – namely that hemispheric republics aspired to be liberal democracies along the lines of the models in Europe and North America. The American Declaration on the Rights and Duties of Man, from 1948, and the Inter-American Convention on Human Rights, from 1969, were but modern manifestations of this longstanding tradition of lip service to political liberalism. (One can note in passing that, whereas Europe developed its main human rights treaty in 1950, in legal force from 1953, the OAS took until 1969.)

A second widespread political value that undergirds regional developments in favor of human rights has been moral leadership for rights by OAS agencies and a shifting coalition of hemispheric states. A key player in this regard since the mid-1950s has been the InterAmerican Commission on Human Rights, now a principal organ of the OAS, and a persistent leader for human rights. This uninstructed body, charged with an active program of reporting, investigating, and diplomacy for human rights, also has duties under the InterAmerican Convention. The dynamism of this body has been supported by a variety of states with active and progressive human rights policies – although the composition of this group of states changes according to the government in power. Costa Rica and other states have been part of this pro-human rights coalition from time to time.

A third supporting factor has been erratic influence for human rights by the United States. Very little happens in the OAS that is strongly opposed by the USA. More positively, the USA on occasion has used the OAS to push for such things as the American Declaration, diplomatic pressure against particular rights-violating governments at particular times, and OAS supervision of elections in places like Central America. US support for regional human rights standards and action has been highly selective, which is to say inconsistent, as I will note below. Nevertheless, periodic support by the USA for certain human rights developments via the OAS has been important – whether one speaks of efforts to rid Nicaragua of the Somoza dynasty, or efforts on behalf of a diplomacy generally supportive of liberal democracy in the 1990s.

Blocking factors

On the other side of the fence, however, three factors have historically constrained regional human rights developments in the Western Hemisphere. The first of these has been the historical trend on the part of Latin and Caribbean states to emphasize the principle of state sovereignty in the wake of repeated US interventions into their domestic affairs. This widespread endorsement of broad and traditional notions of state sovereignty was articulated to block OAS authority as well as US power, since the former (viz., OAS authority) was seen by many in the region to reflect the latter (viz., US power). By the turn of the twenty-first century there had been some movement away from historical patterns in this regard.

In 1991 the OAS declared unanimously, apart from Cuba, through its Santiago Declaration, that the question of democratic government within any state was an international and not strictly a domestic matter. But at approximately the same time the OAS continued to resist authorizing the use of force to create, recreate, or protect democratic government, as in Haiti, since such an authorization meant authorizing predominantly US use of force. In the latter situation, the USA had to turn to the United Nations Security Council for authorization of deployment of force to restore the elected government of Father Aristide in Haiti in the face of military usurpation. Thus the OAS remained unreliable for the direct protection of human rights in the Hemisphere, due to lingering widespread fears about US power.

This tension resurfaced over Venezuela in 2005, when the OAS refused to lend its name to a US plan to monitor democracy in the Hemisphere. Important OAS member states feared the plan was nothing more than a scheme to undermine the government of Hugo Chavez, whose left-of-center elected government in Caracas had incurred considerable criticism from Washington.[52]

A second limiting factor on regional action for human rights in the Western Hemisphere stems from the fact that many national elites, while identifying with political liberalism in the abstract, have not really been able to bring themselves to practice liberal democracy when it meant recognizing human rights for indigenous peoples, the lower classes (the two are not mutually exclusive), those on the political left (the three are not mutually exclusive), etc. Military and other governments in the hemisphere have often found it "desirable" to emphasize a "national

---

[52] Joel Brinkley, "Latin Nations Resist Plan for Monitor of Democracy," *New York Times*, June 6, 2005, A9.

security state" and other departures from liberal democracy in order to save the nation from itself – viz., to save the state from control by some element deemed undesirable by the traditional elites made up of the military, the aristocracy, and conservative elements in the Catholic Church. Thus the abstract endorsement of liberal democracy has been frequently joined by the practice of authoritarian government, and even authoritarian government with a very brutal face, as a "necessary and exceptional" measure when the traditional elites have feared "subversive" movements. This was particularly the case in the Southern Cone of South America during the Cold War years of the 1970s and 1980s.[53]

Given the difficulties of securing agreement on equitable development in the Hemisphere, which has led to both polarized societies and radical movements, a backlash emerged against the "Washington consensus" and the pursuit of economic growth by relatively unregulated global capitalism from about 1980. The development course laid out by the Reagan Administration, the World Bank, and the IMF seemed to perpetually exclude from prosperity many on the lower rungs of society, particularly the indigenous Indian groups. Therefore in the early twenty-first century a leftist populism emerged (or in some cases re-emerged) in places such as Venezuela, Bolivia, Ecuador, and Nicaragua. This Latin American populism manifested at times certain authoritarian tendencies, as had been true, for example, in the populism of Huey Long in Louisiana in the USA.[54]

(There was also the problem of murderous narco-trafficking in states such as Colombia and Mexico, states where elected governments did not have full control over national territory and where the pursuit of the lucrative illegal drug trade entailed many human rights violations and even atrocities.)

A third and last limiting factor on human rights norms and practice was the preoccupation of the USA with containing if not rolling back Soviet-led communism during the Cold War. This orientation, a modern version of the Monroe Doctrine designed to keep the Hemisphere free from the influence of any external power, caused the USA to repeatedly emphasize national and regional freedom from communism as compared with individual freedom from non-communist repression. Until the Carter Administration of 1977–1981, the USA repeatedly aligned with

---

[53] See further Jack Donnelly, *International Human Rights*, 2nd edn. (Boulder: Westview, 1998), ch. 3; and Rebecca Evans, "South American Southern Cone: National Security State, 1970s–1980s," in *Encyclopedia of Human Rights*, vol. IV, 492–504.
[54] Francisco Lopez-Bermudez, "Latin American Populism," in *Encyclopedia of Human Rights*, vol. III, 400–411.

repressive but non-communist governments in the Hemisphere. The goal may have been to protect human rights in the USA (along with the power of the USA in international relations), but the means entailed opposition to human rights developments in places like Guatemala in 1954 where the USA organized the overthrow of the elected Arbenz government. The murderous military governments that followed were propped up by Washington. After the Cold War this type of situation has obviously changed, and the USA has become less opposed to OAS actions for human rights in the Hemisphere. Cuba aside, there are no fully authoritarian governments and none consistently aligned with an external hostile power. (True, Chavez in Venezuela occasionally flirted with making a diplomatic alliance with the Iranian clerics but this was not seen by any government in Washington as posing a major security threat. After Chavez, Venezuela under Maduro also manifested autocratic tendencies.)

After the Cold War, the USA remained staunchly unilateralist on human rights matters, refusing to accept the jurisdiction of the InterAmerican Court of Human Rights and going its own way on certain other human rights matters (see the case study that concludes this chapter). But it did not insist that others copy its unilateralism.

Synthesis

The interplay of these three supporting factors (general commitment to liberal democracy, moral leadership for human rights by various actors, inconsistent leadership for human rights by the USA) and three limiting factors (fondness for traditional notions of state sovereignty, widespread if periodic practice of authoritarianism particularly of a brutal sort, US security concerns during the Cold War) meant that until about the end of the Cold War one found an ambitious regional human rights program that was mostly ineffective in the actual protection of human rights in most places most of the time. Human rights activities constituted the bright spot of the OAS, compared with security, economic, and environmental matters. At the same time regional action for human rights did not prevent or correct gross violations of human rights in many places between the 1940s and the 1990s. After the Cold War matters have been moving in a relatively progressive direction, but without radical change since the USA and Canada (and a few other states) remain outside the jurisdiction of the regional human rights court, the English-speaking nations not having accepted the InterAmerican Convention on Human Rights.

Details

The American Declaration was voted into being (even before the UN Universal Declaration of Human Rights, and before the European regional instruments), and the InterAmerican Convention was eventually adhered to by up to twenty-five of the OAS thirty-five member states (Cuba being the thirty-sixth but suspended between 1962 and 2009). Twenty of these accepted the supranational jurisdiction of the InterAmerican Court.

The InterAmerican Commission basically tried to "referee the game of politics" in the Hemisphere by "blowing the whistle" on violations of human rights. But, to continue the analogy, the game continued in brutal fashion in many places as if that referee did not exist. To change the analogy, the InterAmerican Commission generated modest influence as a liberal ombudsman in the region.[55] Until the end of the Cold War, however, only sixteen (now twenty) of thirty-five states consented to supranational adjudication by the InterAmerican Court of Human Rights, which had come into being in 1979. Its caseload remains less than those of the two European courts. Part of the reason for this low case-load for the Court is the fact that only the InterAmerican Commission and states can present cases to the InterAmerican Court. In a sense, therefore, the Commission operates almost as a court of first instance handling a multitude of cases since its creation.[56] No state so far has lodged a case at the Court. The USA continued to object to the Court's authority and jurisdiction, and to argue that the American Declaration had not passed into international customary law in whole or in part. In Europe, by contrast, all major states were supportive of most CE and EU human rights developments, at least until Brexit in 2016.

It is a measure of the positive evolution of the InterAmerican system, however, that after the Cold War regionally important states like Brazil and Mexico accepted the Court's jurisdiction. Moreover, the countries that have accepted the jurisdiction of the InterAmerican Court have demonstrated a surprising willingness to comply with its decisions, when in the past they have often ignored the decisions of the Commission.[57] However, while states have been more prepared to pay monetary

---

[55] See, e.g., Cecilia Medina, "The Role of Country Reports in the Inter-American System of Human Rights," *Netherlands Quarterly of Human Rights*, 15, 4 (December 1997), 457–473.
[56] Christina M. Cerna, "The Inter-American System for the Protection of Human Rights," *Florida Journal of International Law*, 16, 195 (2004), 195–212.
[57] See further Courtney Hillebrecht, *Domestic Politics and International Human Rights Treaties: The Problem of Compliance* (Cambridge: Cambridge University Press, 2014).

damages to plaintiffs, they have been less willing to make further investigations and punish perpetrators.[58] After the Cold War it could be said that OAS developments pertaining to human rights were somewhat improved, with some of the Court's jurisprudence beginning to have broad effect particularly in Latin America.[59] The overall record remained mixed, with Mexico more impacted by regional human rights norms and institutions, but Brazil showing more resistance to such developments.

The Commission reported in the past that states had complied fully with its recommendations 12.5 percent of the time, partially 69.5 percent, and not at all in 18 percent. The Commission was overstretched, trying to process many complaints but with insufficient staff and budgets.[60] As for the Court, as of 2016, states under the Court's jurisdiction had agreed, as ordered by the Court, to: pay reparations to victims about 55 percent of the time; issue apologies or make other symbolic gestures about 58 percent of the time; adopt new legislation and take other structural measures to ensure non-repetition of violations about 23 percent of the time; etc. Commission and Court conclusions often became enmeshed in domestic politics, with the Executive often trying to signal to the Legislature and domestic groups its commitment to human rights.[61]

Resistance to the Court still remains, as attested by the withdrawal of Trinidad and Tobago from the InterAmerican Convention in 1999 to shield its death penalty regime from the Court's scrutiny – and Peru's short-lived intended withdrawal in the same year. Venezuela withdrew in 2012. Further, it is correct to generalize that while Latin American states have accepted the authority of the Court and the Commission (with the exception of Cuba), the English-speaking states of the hemisphere have only partially embraced the system.[62]

Overall, one found in the Western Hemisphere a regional system for the promotion and protection of human rights that resembled the European system on paper, but did not completely resemble it in reality.[63] For example, in both systems one found a right of private petition about

---

[58] Cerna, "The Inter-American System," 203.
[59] Jo M. Pasqualucci and Christina M. Cerna, "Organization of American States," in *Encyclopedia of Human Rights*, vol. IV, 145–153.
[60] Robert K. Goldman, "History and Action: The Inter-American Human Rights System and the Role of the Inter-American Commission of Human Rights," *Human Rights Quarterly*, 31, 4 (November 2009), 856–887.
[61] See further Hillebrecht, *Domestic Politics*.
[62] Cerna, "The Inter-American System for the Protection of Human Rights," 203.
[63] See further Tom J. Farer, "The Rise of the Inter-American Human Rights Regime: No Longer a Unicorn, Not Yet an Ox," *Human Rights Quarterly*, 19, 3 (August 1997), 510–546.

human rights violations. But the results of such petitions in Europe provided consistent and real restraints on state policy, even in major states, through binding court judgments, whereas the results in the Americas were different and relatively inferior. Since the Cold War, the Hemispheric system showed real progress, but without the full support of the USA, Brazil, and certain other states.[64] But for some states like Chile, one could show that the regional system for human rights had indeed changed Chilean law and practice on certain human rights issues.[65]

Africa

African states, seared by the experience of colonialism and plagued by numerous problems of political instability, first used the Organization of African Unity (OAU), which was created in 1963, primarily to reinforce traditional notions of state sovereignty and domestic jurisdiction. The OAU Charter mentioned human rights. But for the OAU, concern with human rights was restricted to questions of racial discrimination by Whites against Blacks as in Rhodesia, South Africa, and the then remaining Portuguese colonies of Angola, Guinea-Bissau, and Mozambique. Even the most egregious violations of human rights in Idi Amin's Uganda or "Emperor" Jean-Bedel Bokassa's Central African "Empire" were met with a deafening silence from the OAU.

This embarrassing double standard contributed eventually to adoption of the African Charter on Human and Peoples' Rights – the so-called Banjul Charter – in 1981.[66] It received a sufficient number of ratifications to enter into legal force in 1986, at which time perhaps three states in Africa might be considered something relatively close to a liberal democracy and thus showing national commitment to civil and political rights. In brief summary, the Banjul Charter encompassed: an absolute endorsement of certain civil and political rights familiar to the liberal West; a conditional endorsement of other civil and political rights that were limited by "claw back" clauses permitting deviation from international standards on the basis of national laws; mention of fundamental economic and social rights requiring considerable material resources for their application; a list of individual duties; and a list of "people's" rights

---

[64] See further Par Engstrom and Courtney Hillebrecht, "Institutional Change and the Inter-American Human Rights System: Introduction to a Special Issue," *International Journal of Human Rights*, forthcoming.

[65] Karinna Fernandez, Sebastián Smart, and Cristián Peña, *Chile and the Inter-American Human Rights System* (Washington: Brookings, 2017).

[66] U. Oji Umozurike, *The African Charter on Human and Peoples' Rights* (The Hague: Martinus Nijhoff, 1997).

such as to existence, self-determination, and disposal of natural resources.[67] These regional developments mirrored an emphasis by developing states at the United Nations on, among other principles, the collective right to development and the collective right to freely dispose of national resources.

It was said by some that especially individual duties and people's rights reflected uniquely African approaches to internationally recognized human rights.[68] It was also said that since the Banjul Charter eschewed an African human rights court and established only an advisory African Human Rights Commission to oversee application of the Charter, this approach reflected African preferences for discussion and conciliation rather than adversarial adjudication. The fact remains that during the early stages of post-colonial Africa, political liberalism was in short supply on that continent. It would have been inconceivable for the OAU in the 1980s to adopt a human rights convention that was normatively strong and clear on behalf of individual rights, and subject to enforcement by a supranational regional court. Whether this was because of "African culture" or the political self-interests of those who ruled African states can be left to the historians and anthropologists.

What is undeniable, and entirely predictable, was that the Banjul Charter had only slight impact on anyone's behavior in the fifty-three states making up the OAU during the first ten years after 1986. As was true in general in other regions, African states did not avail themselves of the opportunity to petition other states about human rights violations. The only state petition lodged during this time was a bogus one: Libya petitioned against the United States. Since the latter was not a member of the OAU, the petition was properly dismissed. Moreover, African states were tardy at best, and frequently negligent, in submitting reports to the Commission about how they were applying the Charter. The Commission had neither the authority nor the power to correct the situation. When the Commission raised questions about the reports that were submitted, states tended toward silence. Likewise, when private communications were submitted to the Commission claiming a violation of the

---

[67] See further Rachel Murray, "African Union: Banjul Charter," in *Encyclopedia of Human Rights*, vol. I, 12–18.

[68] In addition to Umozurike, *The African Charter on Human and Peoples' Rights*, ch. 8, see Rhoda Howard, *Human Rights in Commonwealth Africa* (Totowa, NJ: Rowman & Littlefield, 1986), ch. 2; Timothy Fernyhough, "Human Rights and Precolonial Africa," in Ronald Cohen, Goran Hyden, and Winston P. Nagan, eds., *Human Rights and Governance in Africa* (Gainesville: University Press of Florida, 1993), ch. 2; and Abdullah Ahmed An-Na'im and Francis M. Deng, eds., *Human Rights in Africa: Cross-Cultural Perspectives* (Washington: Brookings, 1990).

Charter, as best we can tell during the early days (the Commission at that time interpreted its mandate as requiring full confidentiality), states tended to disregard the entire process of inquiry and friendly settlement that the Commission was trying to conduct.[69] It was well known that after 1986, as before, there were many gross and systematic violations of internationally recognized human rights throughout Africa, not to mention more mundane or quotidian violations, and that both types went uncorrected by regional (and other) arrangements.

Early on the Commission was poorly funded, its support staff or secretariat was weak, human rights non-governmental organizations in Africa were neither numerous nor well prepared for interaction with the Commission, and the imposition of confidentiality made the Commission's promotion and protection work exceedingly difficult.[70] Yet by the late 1990s the Commission, with the help of a number of European public and private parties, had managed to escape from some of the confidentiality restrictions, had improved both its staff and the quality of its decisions, had carried out several in-country investigations with the consent of the appropriate state, had taken some initiatives without waiting for petitions, and was in relative terms drawing slightly more support and praise.[71] Over time the Commission clearly became more active and assertive. The result was a determined socialization process by the agency, as it pronounced on various private petitions (there was only one state to state complaint) and in various ways tried to advance attention to human rights in Africa.[72]

In June 1998 the OAU adopted a protocol to the Banjul Charter approving the creation of an African human rights court.[73] The Protocol creating the court entered into force in 2004. As of early 2016, thirty states had consented to the court, and it had handled some two dozen cases. Early judgments found Tanzania and Burkina Faso to be in violation of their obligations regarding voting and protection of journalists

[69] Evelyn A. Ankumah, *The African Commission on Human and Peoples' Rights: Practice and Procedures* (The Hague: Martinus Nijhoff, 1996).
[70] Claude E. Welch, "The African Commission on Human and Peoples' Rights: A Five-Year Report and Assessment," *Human Rights Quarterly*, 14, 1 (February 1992), 43–61.
[71] Chidi Anselm Odinkalu and Camilla Christensen, "The African Commission on Human and Peoples' Rights: The Development of its Non-State Communication Procedures," *Human Rights Quarterly*, 20, 2 (May 1998), 235–280. See also Claude E. Welch, *Protecting Human Rights in Africa* (Philadelphia: University of Pennsylvania Press, 1995), especially ch. 5, on the interaction between the International Commission of Jurists, the NGO based in Geneva, and the African Commission.
[72] Rachel Murray, "African Union: Commission and Court on Human Rights," in *Encyclopedia of Human Rights*, vol. I, 19–25.
[73] Makau Mutua, "The African Human Rights Court: A Two-Legged Stool?," *Human Rights Quarterly*, 21, 2 (May 1999), 342–363.

respectively. African states mostly did not accept the optional protocol allowing individual petitions to the court, but through other means – for example, referrals from the African Human Rights Commission – the court was reasonably assertive. There was discussion of merging this human rights court with a future African Court of Justice that would have broad subject-matter jurisdiction.

In 2001 the African Union (AU) had succeeded the old OAU. Its Constitutive Act gave a central place to human rights, including a right of humanitarian intervention in cases of genocide, war crimes, and crimes against humanity.[74] Yet authoritarianism, persistent political instability, violation of many basic civil rights, and even mass atrocities remained a feature of much of Africa. In this context, not to mention ongoing underdevelopment of the most dire economic sort, it would take a great deal of optimism to believe that a regional human rights court could make a major difference. The AU did participate with the UN in a security operation in the Darfur region of Sudan, in an effort to improve the human rights situation there. But the lightly armed military forces were too few in number and too poorly equipped to completely control the situation. In West Africa it was not the AU that either intervened or threatened to do so to stop atrocities in places such as Liberia, Sierra Leone, and Ivory Coast, but rather ECOWAS (Economic Community of West African States) under the leadership of Nigeria. It was British military intervention, however, that finally stopped atrocities in Sierra Leone, and French military action that stabilized Ivory Coast.[75] It was again the French who, under UN mandate, deployed forces to try to quell instability and human rights violations in both Mali and the Central African Republic. It was the UN that undertook various security operations in Democratic Congo in the context of numerous and repeated human rights violations.

Regarding both Europe and the Western Hemisphere, I have already noted in this chapter that, when regional human rights arrangements confront governments unsympathetic to human rights, the regional machinery is not very effective in its protection efforts. One cannot have robust regional protection of human rights without the necessary building blocks, which means a supportive national political culture and leadership genuinely committed to protecting the rights of nationals.

---

[74] Article 4 (h) and (j), Constitutive Act of the African Union.
[75] In places such as Ivory Coast and Democratic Republic of Congo, it was not the AU but the UN which put military forces on the ground in part to deal with gross violations of human rights. Sometimes the field missions had an enforcement mandate under UN Charter Chapter VII, and not just a more limited peacekeeping mandate.

Regarding international criminal courts, I have already noted the phenomenon of "judicial romanticism." If the International Criminal Tribunal for Rwanda has not made much of an impact on the Great Lakes region of Africa, and if the International Criminal Court has not quickly and easily made its mark in places such as Uganda, Sudan, Kenya, and elsewhere, as we saw in Chapter 4, surely there is not much reason to believe the impact of an African human rights court would be different – unless there were profoundly progressive changes in its context.

A particular and pervasive problem was the failure of various authorities to protect the LGBT community (lesbians, gays, bisexuals, and transgendered persons) from persecution and even physical attacks. Across most of Africa, referring to the rights of sexually diverse persons as human rights proved highly divisive, tending to discredit the very notion of human rights.[76] In many African countries such as Uganda, but also in many Middle Eastern and Asian countries, the LGBT community was at risk of much abuse, even fatal attacks. The possibilities for ameliorative dialogue and action were quite small. It can be recalled, however, that in Europe and the Western Hemisphere where one saw the most progress in protecting the LGBT community, it was not so long ago that some of this sexual identity was considered a mental illness. Change was possible, but on the basis of reasoned discussion over time and not via outside pressure.

That said, all was not gloom and doom regarding human rights in the African region. The context for regional human rights actors was decidedly mixed. For example, Nigeria displayed a continuing commitment to electoral democracy even as it struggled to protect a variety of rights – especially in the northeastern regions where the radical Islamic movement Boko Haram wreaked much havoc. States like Ghana saw peaceful changes of top offices several times, with sophisticated procedures for internal verification of free and fair voting. Various actors across sub-Saharan Africa struggled to reduce child marriage and female genital mutilation, along with promoting empowerment of women.

Conclusions

The Arab League's Human Rights Commission has mostly contented itself with one-sided attention to Israel's policies in territories controlled since 1967, while ignoring gross and systematic violations in many Arab

---

[76] See the excellent book by Dennis Altman and Jonathan Symons, *Queer Wars* (Cambridge: Polity Press, 2016).

countries. Only in 2011 did the Arab League's political organs confront authoritarianism and atrocity in Kaddafi's Libya, calling for outside intervention against his policies, and some observers thought this was because Kaddafi had uniquely managed to antagonize even the rest of the Arab League membership. The organization remained largely ineffectual regarding denial of many human rights in many other Arab states. The impact of the League and its human rights agency having been mostly negligible over the years, despite a few human rights developments, it does not merit analysis here.[77]

Asia, being large and extremely diverse, not to mention being the locus of much criticism of western models of political liberalism, manifests no intergovernmental organizations for human rights. However, ASEAN (Association of Southeast Asian Nations) did inch toward some human rights activity, but not very much.[78]

Regional developments especially in Europe, the Western Hemisphere, and Africa make clear the paradox that in the absence of national commitment to political liberalism including human rights, it is impossible to build a regional system for protecting human rights that is genuinely effective. Where you have illiberal governments of various types, you lack the building blocks for effective regional intergovernmental action for rights. Conversely, however, the experience of particularly Europe shows clearly that just because you have liberal democracy at the national level, that does not mean that you do not need regional systems for review of state policies. Liberal democracy at the national level, meaning above all a commitment to civil and political rights, is a necessary but not entirely sufficient condition for achieving a truly rights-protective society. One needs regional review – and perhaps global action as well.

Case study: the OAS, democracy, and Honduras

Honduras is a small country of some eight million persons situated in Central America, bordered by Nicaragua on the south and by Guatemala

---

[77] See further details in David P. Forsythe, "The Arab League," in *Encyclopedia of Human Rights*, vol. III, 312–316.

[78] See further Kenneth Christie, "Association of Southeast Asian Nations (ASEAN)," ibid., vol. I, 119–125. Some Asian (and African) states were members of the Commonwealth of Nations, formerly the British Commonwealth. This transnational organization, while not a regional one, was not a global one either. The point here is that the Commonwealth, under British influence, did have a human rights program and thus did involve its member states, as former British colonies, in various human rights questions, such as the suspension of the Robert Mugabe government in Zimbabwe for serious violations of rights. See Timothy Shaw, "Commonwealth of Nations," ibid., vol. I, 372–376. For a similar organization under French influence, also with a human rights program, see Emmanuel Decaux, "La Francophonie," ibid., vol. II, 261–265.

and El Salvador on the north and northwest. An independent republic since the 1840s, it has experienced much multiparty democracy despite its persistent poverty. But it has also known periods of autocratic rule and is associated in some circles with the origin of the phrase "banana republic." From the 1980s pluralist democracy seemed increasingly stable under two dominant parties, human rights violations by the military were reduced, and the democratic constitution of 1987 seemed more durable than many others in the country's turbulent political history. The dominant political culture of this time seemed basically conservative, being pro-business and friendly to transnational corporations, with some analysts seeing the two dominant political parties as historically center-right.

Honduras was a founding member of the Organization of American States. That organization has long endorsed a regional version of human rights that was generally compatible with UN norms. OAS activities for human rights were more notable than in the domains of economics, security, and environment. In 2001 the OAS adopted the InterAmerican Democratic Charter, followed in 2003 by a resolution that became known as the Santiago Declaration. These steps made clear that all OAS members had to maintain genuine, liberal, pluralist, or constitutional democracy. These democratic norms were similar to other standards in the Council of Europe, European Union, Commonwealth of Nations, and about a dozen other intergovernmental organizations. Thus organizational "democracy clauses" were a prevalent feature of international relations.

In June 2009 the elected Honduran President, Manuel Zelaya of the Liberal Party, in office since 2006, was deposed by military coup. He had offended important sectors of the conservative elites of the country by several maneuvers including failure to enforce certain Supreme Court judgments and planning a referendum for a new constitutional convention that some thought might pave the way to his extended rule. As Honduran politics polarized, many conservatives feared that Zelaya was "moving left" and was positioning himself to become another Hugo Chavez in Venezuela – a relatively more authoritarian populist of the left, appealing to the poor while cracking down on dissent and opposition.

From the summer of 2009 Honduras was governed by a *de facto* administration of Roberto Micheletti of the National Party who had been speaker of the House in the Congress. His administration was endorsed by both the Honduran Congress and Supreme Court. In November of that year national elections saw the transfer of power from Micheletti to Porfirio Lobo, also of the National Party. A number of analysts noted that access to the media was restricted for those supporting Zelaya, and independent criticism of the Micheletti faction had become dangerous.

The international response to the events of June 2009 was at first remarkably uniform, vigorous, and opposed to the interruption of the 1987 Honduran Constitution. This was, after all, the first military coup in the region in several decades. The OAS suspended Honduras from membership by unanimous vote (the vote suspending Cuba had been split), and the OAS Secretary-General tried to persuade the Micheletti faction to change course. The InterAmerican Commission on Human Rights, having conducted an in-country investigation, condemned what it called a coup, then detailed a sizable list of human rights violations. The European Union imposed economic sanctions. The UN General Assembly also condemned the unconstitutional transfer of power, and various units of the UN system ceased dealing with Honduras. Most states withdrew their ambassadors from Tegucigalpa. The USA opposed the coup and imposed some sanctions, although it did not withdraw its ambassador and slightly later it tried to mediate a compromise solution to the crisis.

However, despite the inconvenience of economic and diplomatic sanctions, those opposed to Zelaya had a strategy of holding a firm course until the November 2010 elections. This was a broad coalition including elements of the Liberal Party, some state officials under Zelaya, most of the military, most of the Supreme Court, and much of the Congress. Their calculations proved to be a winning strategy, not only because economic sanctions take time to have full effect, but also and more importantly because the international coalition opposed to the extra-constitutional transfer of power fractured. With the election of Lobo, the USA, Colombia, Costa Rica, Guatemala, Panama, and Peru all recognized him as the legitimate head of state. Other OAS members continued their opposition, treating the Lobo Administration as a pariah government. Honduran membership in the OAS had not been restored at the time of writing but was foreseen, with Zelaya being allowed to return under a governmental promise of no prosecution.

It was not as if the removal of Zelaya had led to military government as in Chile in 1973 or in Argentina in 1976. Rather, by November 2010 one found in Honduras that one elected president had been replaced by another elected president, after about six months of interim civilian rule. This sequence made it difficult to hold the international line against interruption of the 1987 constitution, especially since a number of actors feared that Zelaya himself would not prove faithful to that constitution. In the view of some, however, in Honduras under the Lobo presidency one found illiberal democracy: elections had resulted in rule supported by the majority voting, but with many human rights violations directed at dissidents, independent journalists, etc. In this view Lobo was similar to Milosevic in Serbia: locally popular but using the state to stifle opposition and criticism, thus falling far short of genuine democracy.

In the USA several conservative Republican senators had taken an interest in the situation, had visited Honduras against the wishes of the Obama Administration, had supported the coup in the name of economic freedom and fear of another Chavez, and held up several Obama appointments to foreign policy positions dealing with the Hemisphere. These developments made it doubly difficult for the USA either to achieve some negotiated solution (since the Micheletti faction was encouraged to hold firm because of its support in US right-wing circles), or to help hold together the international efforts to support the principle of constitutional democracy without military interference. Critics charged that the Obama Administration did a deal with conservative senators in order to get its nominees secured in office, at the expense of a robust defense of constitutional democracy in Latin America.

One sees in this case first of all the workings of transnational politics, or the blending of domestic politics with foreign policy and international relations. One also sees the continuing importance of the USA in hemispheric affairs; absent Republican senatorial pressures, it is likely that Obama policy would have remained more closely aligned with OAS positions. Finally, the outcome raised questions about the effect of OAS norms in favor of constitutional democracy. If the OAS could not reverse the coup in Honduras, a small and weak country, what precedent would this set for the future? On the other hand, a regional military coup strongly opposed by the USA might evolve according to different dynamics.

Discussion questions

• What explains the quality of regional protection of human rights in Europe, compared with the Western Hemisphere and Africa? Is it likely that the latter two regions will evolve so as to duplicate the European record?

• Is any one of these three regions seriously interested in the protection of economic and social rights? Can economic and social rights be adjudicated? Is there always a clear distinction between civil rights and economic or social rights?

• With regard to human rights, what is the relationship between the Council of Europe and the European Union? Have the OSCE and

NATO carved out a special role for themselves regarding the protection of human rights in Europe?
• Does the United States have a reasonable and coherent policy toward the regional mechanisms for the protection of human rights in the Western Hemisphere? Is the Hemisphere evolving the political context in which the OAS can improve the regional protection of human rights?
• Is it likely that the projected African Court of Human Rights could function so as to make a major difference in the regional protection of human rights on that continent?

SUGGESTIONS FOR FURTHER READING

Ankumah, Evelyn A., *The African Commission on Human and Peoples' Rights: Practice and Procedures* (The Hague: Martinus Nijhoff, 1996). A generally sympathetic overview of historical developments, but with appropriate criticism. Some sections are mainly of use to practicing lawyers who want to use OAU regional procedures.

An-Na'im, Ahmed, and Francis M. Deng, eds., *Human Rights in Africa: Cross-Cultural Perspectives* (Washington: Brookings, 1990). A stimulating collection about universalism and cultural relativism with regard to Africa. Deals broadly and intelligently with the cultural context within which the OAU human rights initiatives occur.

Aziz, Miriam, *The Impact of European Rights on National Legal Cultures* (Oxford: Hart Publishing Ltd., 2004). A study of the interplay of regional and national standards on human rights in Europe.

Bartels, Lorand, *Human Rights Conditionality and EU External Relations* (Oxford: Oxford University Press, 2005). A sound treatment on a subject of growing importance.

Beddard, R., *Human Rights and Europe*, 3rd edn. (Cambridge: Grotius Publications, 1993). A good overview, but now dated, widely used in specialized classes.

Cardenas, Sonia, *Human Rights in Latin America: The Politics of Terror and Hope* (Philadelphia: University of Pennsylvania Press, 2009). A very good survey of regional developments.

Davidson, Scott, *The Inter-American Human Rights System* (Aldershot: Dartmouth, 1997). A traditional legal overview.

Farer, Tom, "The Rise of the Inter-American Human Rights Regime: No Longer a Unicorn, Not Yet an Ox," *Human Rights Quarterly*, 19, 3 (August 1997), 510–546. One of the best short historical overviews.

Hillebrecht, Courtney, *Domestic Politics and International Human Rights Tribunals: The Problem of Compliance* (Cambridge: Cambridge University Press, 2014). A comparison of European and Hemispheric Courts, with an emphasis on national executive concern for reputation.

Jackson, Donald W., *The United Kingdom Confronts the European Convention on Human Rights* (Gainesville: University Press of Florida, 1997). A thorough look at why Britain has encountered so much difficulty after becoming a party to the European Convention on Civil and Political Rights. A good reminder that even those Anglo-Saxon states with a long commitment to liberal democracy still violate international human rights and are in need of international (in this case, regional) review. Good background for the Brexit vote.

Janis, Mark, Richard Kay, and Anthony Bradly, *European Human Rights Law* (New York: Oxford University Press, 2008). A broad and analytical overview.

Kissinger, Henry, *Years of Renewal* (New York: Simon & Schuster, 1999). The former National Security Advisor and Secretary of State warmly endorses human rights in the CSCE process (for which he was not responsible) since it helped to generate problems for the Soviet empire, but generally, and explicitly in his African and Latin American diplomacy, he regarded human rights as frequently an unwelcome addition to his realist orientation. What caused him to work actively for majority rule in southern Africa was the appearance of Soviet and Cuban military personnel in Angola.

Korey, William, *The Promises We Keep: Human Rights, the Helsinki Process, and American Foreign Policy* (New York: St. Martin's Press, 1993). A favorable overview of the CSCE process that helped to de-legitimize European communism. Emphasizes the roles of the US Congress and private human rights groups, especially Jewish ones.

Neuwahl, Nanette A., and Allan Rosas, eds., *The European Union and Human Rights* (The Hague: Martinus Nijhoff, 1995). A solid reminder that the EU has a human rights dimension in addition to its economic activities.

Umozurike, U. Oji, *The African Charter on Human and Peoples' Rights* (The Hague: Martinus Nijhoff, 1997). A direct and to-the-point overview, with sensible interpretations.

Williams, Andrew, *EU Human Rights Policies: A Study in Irony* (Oxford: Oxford University Press, 2004). A study of the discrepancy between internal and external EU standards on human rights.

6 Human rights and foreign policy in comparative perspective

While intergovernmental agencies and private transnational groups deal-ing with human rights proliferate, one central key to progressive developments remains states and their foreign policies.[1] As we have already seen, IGOs, from the UN through the OAS to the Organization for Security and Cooperation in Europe, have extensive human rights programs. Independent international officials for these organizations generate some influence. But it is usually state members of these IGOs that take the most important decisions, and it is primarily states that are the targets of reform efforts. Likewise, as we will see in Chapter 7, NGOs such as Amnesty International, Human Rights Watch, and Physicians for Human Rights, among others, are highly active in human rights matters and generate some influence. But, still, it is states that approve treaties and their monitoring mechanisms, states that sometimes manipulate foreign assistance in relation to rights, states that (may or may not) arrest war criminals – either singly or via international organizations such as NATO. NGOs mainly pressure *states* to do the right thing.

This chapter looks at human rights and state foreign policy in com-parative perspective. It begins with a short discussion of three prominent mechanisms states can and do – at least sometimes – employ to influence another government's human rights policies: diplomatic, economic, and

[1] The views in this chapter are my own, but I gratefully acknowledge the contributions of others who worked on a research project on this subject funded by the United Nations University: Peter Baehr (Netherlands), Sally Morphet (United Kingdom), Chiyuki Aoi and Yozo Yokota (Japan), Gabor Kardos (Central Europe), Sergei Chugrov (Russia), Sanjoy Banerjee (India), Cristina Eguizabal (Latin America), Tiyanjana Maluwa (South Africa), and Zachary Karabell (Iran). Jack Donnelly also participated in this project and wrote the final chapter in D. Forsythe, ed., *Human Rights and Comparative Foreign Policy* (Tokyo: United Nations University Press, 2000). An earlier version of this chapter was published in the *International Journal* (Canada), 53, 1 (Winter 1997–1998), 113–132. I am grateful to the editors for their helpful suggestions.
    An introduction can be found in Peter R. Baehr, "Foreign Policy," in David P. Forsythe, ed., *Encyclopedia of Human Rights* (New York: Oxford University Press, 2009), vol. II, 237–247.

military means. Different approaches may be taken in different situations, as states usually calculate the instruments available, the expected effect of the action taken, anticipated reactions – and above all the costs to themselves of trying to advance human rights abroad.[2] This is followed by a focus on the United States, the most important actor in international relations early in the twenty-first century. I show that the USA has a particular slant to its foreign policy on rights, and that Washington is often more prone to preach to others than to take international rights standards very seriously in its own policies. Clearly, the USA is highly selective when and how it pushes for rights abroad. The chapter then provides a comparative analysis of human rights in the foreign policies of some other states that either are liberal democracies or aspire to be so. I show that most differ from the US approach in one way or another, due to a varying combination of history and political culture, geo-political position, and perceived national interests.

While the structure of international relations, and in particular the modified nation-state system and its security dilemmas, pushes states to emphasize factors other than human rights in foreign policy, agency still matters. It matters that Donald Trump was elected to replace Barack Obama, or that Obama replaced George W. Bush, or that Vladimir Putin replaced Boris Yeltsin, and so on. There is still room to maneuver in favor of human rights or to undercut them. Foreign policy leaders still matter, even if various structures (or contextual factors) also matter, whether they might be national public opinion or influence of for-profit corporations.

Policy instruments

In the past, states have often proven reluctant to speak out on human rights violations by others, fearing interruption of "business as usual" – not only on business but also on other important matters like security cooperation. As indicated in Chapter 4, it is very clear that states do not like to sue each other about human rights in the International Court of Justice, and the number of cases on human rights is very small. As shown in Chapter 5, even within the Council of Europe, neighboring states with numerous common concerns do not often sue each other in the European Court of Human Rights, the overwhelming number of cases being triggered by private rather than state complaint. The same pattern

[2] Peter R. Baehr and Monique Castermans-Holleman, *The Role of Human Rights in Foreign Policy*, 3rd edn. (New York: Palgrave Macmillan, 2004), 69.

is evident with regard to the InterAmerican Court of Human Rights. Nevertheless, many states do address human rights issues in other states short of judicial proceedings. Sometimes this public diplomacy on human rights is primarily to embarrass enemies, as was true of East–West debates in the UN General Assembly during the Cold War. And sometimes taking a public position on human rights abroad is designed for domestic consumption, as was true of Henry Kissinger's public comments about the importance of human rights in South America – even as he was committing the USA to quiet support for repressive regimes. But sometimes states are genuinely interested in advancing rights abroad; and then they seriously think about ends and means.

Diplomatic means

There are a number of ways a state may utilize diplomacy to try to influence the policies of states violating human rights. The traditional, classical method has been that of "quiet" diplomacy, that is, to hold a confidential discussion behind closed doors and away from public view. Emissaries may meet with foreign officials to discuss a particular human rights situation or to request a halt to certain actions. This is sometimes a useful way to bring objections and matters of concern to the offending party without risk of widespread controversy or public outcry. Sometimes a target government will prove flexible if it can avoid the public appearance of caving in to foreign pressure. Quiet diplomacy is of course hard to track and evaluate, precisely because it may be some years before outsiders know what has transpired.

From time to time private diplomacy for human rights is then followed by public statements, as when President George W. Bush met with Russian president Vladimir Putin in early 2005. President Bush, having devoted his second inaugural address to the theme of freedom, could hardly not raise the subject of Russian policies at home and abroad that touched on human rights. And by all accounts there was some private attention to human rights in places like Chechnya and the Ukraine during this presidential summit.

But when the dialogue moves to the public arena, states undertaking a human rights discourse frequently meet "blowback" or negative reactions. State leaders who are subjected to public criticism often become defensive and inflexible in the name of national pride, state sovereignty, or because they have domestic elements who are "hardliners" about resisting foreign pressure. When in the 1970s the US Congress passed the Jackson–Vanik Amendment publicly requiring greater emigration (freedom of movement) from Romania, the Soviet Union, and other

European communist countries, the numbers of those allowed out actually dropped in the short term, as the target governments did not want to
be seen caving in to US public pressure.

On the other hand, sometimes some public pressure can be productive, and the human rights NGOs that engage in the "naming and
shaming" game can cite a number of situations in which public pressure
brought some progressive gains over time. European state pressure on
Turkey to improve its human rights record, in the context of the debate
over Turkey's admission to the European Union, clearly had some
beneficial effect – at least for a time.

Other essentially diplomatic steps can be undertaken, such as cancel-
lation or postponement of ministerial visits or recall of ambassadors. This
is likely to draw attention to the issue at hand, particularly when done by
prominent states. In early February 2005, in the wake of the assassination
of a former Lebanese prime minister, the United States recalled its
ambassador to Syria, believing that state bore at least some measure of
responsibility. The USA used the opportunity to criticize Syria for its lax
border-control policies, its anti-democratic domestic practices, and what
it felt was an unnecessary Syrian military presence in Lebanon. While
Syria condemned the assassination and denied involvement, greater
international attention was being paid to its policies, including human
rights policies.[3] We mentioned previously that Western states pushed for
the UN Security Council to create an international criminal tribunal in
response to this assassination, even if the court represented an example of
judicial romanticism and political theatre. Such moves did highlight the
killing that had taken place.

The large number of intergovernmental agencies dealing with human
rights means that member states are confronted almost daily about taking
a diplomatic position on some human rights question. This is certainly
true in the sprawling UN system, but also true in more limited IGOs like
the OSCE, Council of Europe, and OAS. Even in the Commonwealth of
Nations, formerly the British Commonwealth, there are occasions for
voting on human rights issues pertaining, for example, to governmental
violation of rights in Zimbabwe.[4] Former British colonies in Asia, a
region with no human rights intergovernmental organization, are

---

[3] See Steve R. Weissman, "Bush Considers Syria 'Out of Step' with Democracy,"
International Herald Tribune, February 19, 2005, www.theguardian.com/world/2005/feb/
21/eu.usa1.
[4] See further Rhoda Howard-Hassmann, "Zimbabwe," in *Encyclopedia of Human Rights*,
vol. V, 399–406; and see her longer analysis in "Mugabe's Zimbabwe, 2000–2009:
Massive Human Rights Violations and the Failure to Protect," *Human Rights Quarterly*,
32, 4 (November 2010), 898–920.

compelled to address human rights issues through the Commonwealth. Canada, for example, suspended funding to the Commonwealth to protest the role of Sri Lanka in the organization; Ottawa believed Sri Lanka was not responding properly to charges of war crimes during its internal armed conflict with the Tamil Tigers.

Often less influential, though undeniably symbolic, are various cultural or sports-related embargoes enacted by states. For example, many states refused to participate in sporting events with South Africa under white minority rule to protest the country's policy of apartheid. These actions were generally supported by apartheid's victims and often found favor with public opinion in criticizing states – in part because one could take a stand for human rights without paying much price in national blood or treasure. While these sports and cultural boycotts did not by themselves lead to the end of apartheid, such policies made their contribution to the broader effort to delegitimize repressive minority rule. Given white South Africa's love of sports such as rugby and soccer (often called football outside the USA), etc., some effective pressure from sports diplomacy could not be discounted even if it could not be scientifically documented. (How is one to measure the impact of John McEnroe refusing to play tennis in South Africa during apartheid?)

The diplomatic methods discussed above are used to protest or draw attention to particular human rights violations. It can be noted, too, that not all diplomatic techniques are negative in nature. States may offer ministerial visits or invite foreign diplomats or heads of state to visit in an effort to support a country's human rights policies. Governments may be invited to participate in international conferences or to join international organizations, such as the Council of Europe or the European Union, in order to influence human rights policy. Organizations like the EU do note the domestic human rights policies of member states. One of the reasons for expanding NATO membership was to integrate militarily certain former authoritarian states into an alliance for constitutional democracies. The Commonwealth readmitted several states to membership after the end of military rule and return to electoral democracy.

While diplomatic means may or may not be effective by themselves, they can be linked to other steps.

Economic means

Governments are often reluctant to undertake economic sanctions against another state – whether for human rights or other reasons – as they may hurt themselves. One of the reasons Switzerland did not join the United Nations until 2004 was that the economic sanctions it had imposed on Mussolini's Italy as voted by the League of Nations damaged the Swiss economy as well as proving highly unpopular in Italian-speaking Switzerland. One of the reasons that the USA violated mandatory trade sanctions on the breakaway white minority government of Ian Smith in Rhodesia, now Zimbabwe, was the damage otherwise done to American businesses, particularly Union Carbide. Economic sanctions mostly cut both ways.

States, however, do sometimes suspend full trade, and also development aid or other types of foreign assistance. This may be done for lack of other appealing options – e.g., diplomacy alone has proven ineffective but military action is not desired. But this type of sanctioning can have unintended or unwanted effects.[5] Former UN Secretary-General Boutros Boutros-Ghali expressed this concern succinctly: "[Economic sanctions] raise the ethical question of whether suffering inflicted on vulnerable groups in the target country is a legitimate means of exerting pressure on political leaders whose behavior is unlikely to be affected by the plight of their subjects."[6] Indeed, virulent debate ensued during the 1990s regarding sanctions imposed on the people of Iraq, as authorized by the UN Security Council. Supporters of the sanctions pointed to their efficacy in making life difficult for Saddam Hussein's abusive regime, while critics stressed their destructive effects on the people of Iraq, notably children.[7] Eventually the UNSC voted to allow Iraq to sell some oil, using the proceeds supposedly to purchase goods necessary for the civilian population. But the Council failed to supervise the program effectively. Money was siphoned off to the Hussein regime, and other problems manifested themselves.[8] The sanctions were generally ineffective in compelling more moderate policies from Saddam's brutal regime. We now know, however, that Saddam altered his policies on weapons of mass destruction. It is not clear whether this change stemmed from the UN-mandated weapons inspections system, as compared to economic and military pressures, or some combination of the three.[9]

---

[5] Boutros Boutros-Ghali, quoted in Baehr and Castermans-Holleman, *The Role of Human Rights*, 74.

[6] Ibid.

[7] David P. Forsythe, *The Humanitarians: The International Committee of the Red Cross* (Cambridge: Cambridge University Press, 2005). The private ICRC was the first to raise the alarm, followed by UN agencies such as UNICEF and WHO.

[8] While much commentary focused on "UN" failures and corruption, the main difficulty was that western states turned a blind eye to such things as black market trade and profiteering, since western allies Jordan and Turkey were the main beneficiaries.

[9] Jean Krasno and James S. Sutterlin, *The United Nations and Iraq: Defanging the Viper* (New York: Praeger, 2003).

Most general economic sanctions undoubtedly do not decisively affect the elite in the short term, because the rulers and associated social circles are well positioned to avoid inconvenience. Such sanctions have never brought down a repressive regime, and the overall success rate of general economic sanctions, according to various measures, has been estimated at about 33 percent or lower.[10] On the other hand, "smart sanctions" have been tried on occasion in an effort to affect target governments while avoiding harm to civilian populations. In Haiti, for example, after general sanctions had been tried with predictable results, smart sanctions were applied to the military elite associated with Lt.-General Raoul Cedras, that group then blocking the return of the elected president, Father Aristide. These smart sanctions, closing off elite bank accounts and freedom to travel, contributed to the departure of Cedras and his entourage – along with promises of safe passage and comfortable life in exile. Smart sanctions have been either debated or adopted regarding other situations, for example with regard to the Sudanese government because of its policies pertaining to the Darfur region in 2005. They were applied to leaders of the Kaddafi regime in Libya during 2011 – and then relaxed for some of those who defected. The West has imposed targeted sanctions on a number of individuals in Russia close to President Putin, in response to Russian policies in Ukraine.

One overview of economic sanctions and human rights concludes that: (1) multilateral rather than unilateral sanctions are to be preferred; (2) negative punishment should be combined with positive inducements; (3) even smart sanctions usually fail to produce complete compliance with demands; (4) economic sanctions that last more than two years are rarely effective; (5) economic measures should probably be combined with military threats; and (6) both ends and means should be clear.[11]

As with diplomatic means, economic steps do not have to be negative in nature. States may often provide loans or credits to governments who are willing to adopt measures conducive to human rights protection. Most liberal democracies, as well as the IGOs that they influence, manifest democracy promotion programs in order to provide economic and technical assistance to certain transitional states. The funding is used to sponsor and supervise free and fair elections, state-building (for example, the construction of vigorous parliaments and independent courts), and nation-building (for example, encouraging an active and

---

[10] George Lopez, "Economic Sanctions," in *Encyclopedia of Human Rights*, vol. II, 82–87.
[11] Ibid.

rights-supportive civil society). Particularly Western states were undertaking unilateral and multilateral democracy promotion and other
rights-protective policies costing hundreds of millions of dollars in
foreign assistance.

Military means

Finally, there is a range of military steps available at least to those states
with effective military establishments. The most dramatic measure is that
of coercive military action. When undertaken without UN Security
Council approval, such action is highly controversial, as seen by NATO's
bombing of Serbia in 1999 to try to stop violent persecution and forced
displacement of the ethnic Albanians constituting a majority of the
Kosovars.

There is certainly the longstanding problem that states may claim to be
engaged in "humanitarian intervention" whereas in reality they have
other primary motives. The US-initiated war in Iraq from 2003, though
it may have produced some positive long-term consequences for human
rights there, along with many human rights problems, should not be
defined as a humanitarian intervention. True, by 2005 the George
W. Bush Administration's main justification for the war was advancing
democracy. But the foundations for the war were steeped in the rhetoric
of national security. At the time of the US invasion Washington argued
that Iraq had ties to terrorist groups such as Al Qaeda, that it possessed
illegal weapons of mass destruction, and that the Hussein regime needed
to be removed because of future security problems. As Peter Baehr and
Monique Castermans-Holleman note, however, "This regime had for a
number of years been guilty of human rights violations, but to put an end
to these violations was not [initially] mentioned as a main objective of
military action."[12]

There have been numerous cases of "mixed motives" regarding the use
of force in other states without UN approval. In 1971 India used force to
stop Pakistan's Punjabi-dominated elites from slaughtering Bengalis, and
in the process took the opportunity to weaken rival Pakistan by creating
Bangladesh. In 1979 Tanzania used force to drive out the murderous Idi
Amin from Uganda, after he had made a military incursion into Tanzania, which resulted in rule by the equally dictatorial but relatively more
moderate Milton Obote. Also in 1979 Vietnam used force to topple
the genocidal regime of the Khmer Rouge in Cambodia, then installed

---

[12] Baehr and Castermans-Holleman, *The Role of Human Rights*, 80.

the pro-Vietnamese and anti-Chinese Hun Sen as leader. It is not just various western interventions over the years (by the Americans, British, and French, for example) that have made claims to humanitarian intervention so controversial.

There have not been many clear-cut cases of "humanitarian war." Most states have been reluctant to spill national blood for the protection of the rights of "others," and it is especially hard to justify such uses of force at home when loss of life by the intervening state(s) is not linked to traditional notions of security. Moreover, humanitarian intervention almost always makes the situation worse in terms of human costs in the short run. NATO's bombing of Serbia in 1999 was initially met with Belgrade's expanded persecution and displacement of Albanian Kosovars.

Less controversial, at least initially, than unauthorized state military action in the name of human rights protection is state military support for a UN Security Council resolution designed to alleviate human rights problems. As discussed in earlier chapters, this may take the form of an enforcement or peacekeeping field operation. As already noted in Chapter 3, after the Cold War these multilateral security missions almost always entailed a human rights dimension. Whether these field operations were designed to be coercive, evolved into coercion, or remained mostly a matter of armed diplomacy, states were at the center of action. It was states in the UN Security Council that authorized the deployment, states that contributed the troops, and often states that pressed for termination of mission when difficulties occurred. In 2011 member states of the UN Security Council passed Resolution 1973 authorizing states to take "all necessary measures" to protect civilians in Libya: it was then states which chose the strategy and tactics of military action that implemented this vague resolution, which as usual contained no measure of follow-on supervision by any UN body. "The UN" had acted, but it was states that controlled developments. Furthermore, it was states that were responsible to see that military personnel were trained in international humanitarian law, and states that (perhaps) prosecuted military personnel who engaged in sex trafficking or other crimes.

As with diplomatic and economic means, there was a positive side to military options. I have already mentioned one reason for expansion of NATO membership, namely to shore up transitional democracies by linking them to more established democracies. Bilaterally, states may choose to expand military assistance to reward another state for democratic and rights reform. In 2005 the USA expanded military assistance to Guatemala, partly in response to some rights-protective reforms in that state. (At the same time the USA reduced military assistance to some states supportive of the ICC, thus using military assistance to try to undercut certain judicial developments.)

US foreign policy and human rights

To a great extent a state's foreign policy on human rights is bound up with its version of nationalism, which is to say with a nation's collective self-image, which is to say with its informal ideology. Since many nations in the past have thought well of themselves, many states' policies on human rights reflect the conviction that the state has some virtuous point to teach others. As Britain, France, Russia, and others extended their power in the nineteenth century, through formal colonialism or otherwise, they saw themselves as doing God's work in bringing a superior civilization to the inferior (and non-white) peoples of the world. As a matter of fact, this spreading of a "superior" civilization supposedly featuring freedom and the rule of law was accompanied by various atrocities.[13] When local attitudes were not very appreciative of the "benefits" of outside rule, the western response was not exactly charitable, but periodically vindictive toward the "unruly natives." In this sense we can understand why it has been written that American exceptionalism is not so exceptional: others, too, have seen themselves as exceptionally good and hence superior to others.

American exceptionalism

In the case of the United States, to understand the place of human rights in foreign policy it is initially important to understand that many in the elite and mass public view the USA as a beacon of freedom to the world. The notion of American exceptionalism is well known, but its precise application in public policy is open to various constructions.[14]

---

[13] See, e.g., Peter Hopkirk, *The Great Game: The Struggle for Empire in Central Asia* (New York: Kodansha International, 1990, 1992). See also Juan Cole, *Napoleon's Egypt: Invading the Middle East* (Basingstroke: Palgrave Macmillan, 2007). See further Casper W. Erichsen, "Namibia: Germany's Colonial Wars Against the Herero and Nama," in *Encyclopedia of Human Rights*, vol. IV, 17–27.

[14] See especially David P. Forsythe and Patrice C. McMahon, *American Exceptionalism Reconsidered: US Foreign Policy, Human Rights, and World Order* (New York and London: Routledge, 2016). See also Michael Ignatieff, ed., *American Exceptionalism and Human Rights* (Princeton: Princeton University Press, 2005); and Tony Smith, *America's Mission: The Worldwide Struggle for Democracy in the Twentieth Century* (Princeton: Princeton University Press, 1995).

Human rights in foreign policy is often a matter of Washington pressing others to improve personal and political freedom.[15] Particularly for American ultra-nationalists, a powerful force in modern American politics since about 1980, human rights was equated with personal freedom as found in the US Bill of Rights appended to its constitution, and not with the broader and more complex conception found in the International Bill of Rights (as indicated, this means the Universal Declaration, and the 1966 International Covenants on Civil-Political and Socio-Economic-Cultural Rights). Particularly the Ronald Reagan and George W. Bush Administrations – whether one calls them romantic nationalists, chauvinist nationalists, providential nationalists, Jacksonian nationalists, militant American exceptionalists, crusading neo-conservatives, nativists, or some other label – certainly did not try to use internationally recognized human rights to improve US policies. Being disdainful of international law, they often preferred a strictly American conception of human rights in order to bypass many international rights standards and implementing agencies.[16] The election of Donald Trump in 2016 presaged more of this orientation.

More generally, from the early settlers in New England to the powerful Goldwater–Reagan–George W. Bush wing of the Republican Party in contemporary times, important political circles have seen the USA not as an ordinary nation but as a great experiment in personal liberty that has implications for the planet.[17] Well-known defects in American society such as ethnic cleansing of Native Americans, a history of slavery, segregation, racist immigration laws, anti-Semitism, religious and other bigotry, gender discrimination, and grinding poverty have failed to alter this dominant self-image. American exceptionalism, the belief in the exceptional freedom and goodness of the American people, is the core of the dominant American political culture.[18]

The continuing strength of American exceptionalism should not necessarily be equated with an automatic crusade for human rights in US foreign policy. The belief in American greatness, as linked to personal freedom, can lead to involvement or isolationism. Two underlying

---

[15] See further David P. Forsythe, "Human Rights and US Foreign Policy: Situating Obama," *Human Rights Quarterly* 33, 3 (August 2011), 767–789.

[16] See further David P. Forsythe, *The Politics of Prisoner Abuse: The US and Enemy Prisoners After 9/11* (Cambridge: Cambridge University Press, 2011), ch. 2.

[17] T. Davis and S. Lynn-Jones, "City upon a Hill," *Foreign Policy*, 66 (1987), 20–38.

[18] See further David P. Forsythe, *American Exceptionalism and Global Human Rights* (Lincoln: University of Nebraska Distinguished Lecture Series, 1999); and Forsythe, "Human Rights and US Foreign Policy: Two Levels, Two Worlds," in David Beetham, ed., *Politics and Human Rights* (Oxford: Blackwell, 1995), 111–130.

schools of thought have long competed for control of US foreign policy. The first, associated with Washington, Jefferson, and Patrick Buchanan, would perfect American society at home and thus provide international leadership mainly by indirect example. This school was clearly dominant in the Congress in the 1930s. The second, associated with Hamilton and most presidents since Woodrow Wilson, would have the USA actively involved in world affairs – on the assumption that US impact would be for the better.[19] All modern presidents have manifested an activist foreign policy, including on human rights (to varying degrees). This activist stance leaves open the question of the general nature of decisions: realist, liberal, or "neo-con."

American exceptionalism does not so much guarantee specific foreign policy initiatives as it predisposes Washington to talk about freedom and democracy and to assume it can make a difference for the better when and if it gets involved. The American public and Congress were deferential if not supportive in 1992 when President George H. W. Bush deployed military force to guarantee the secure delivery of humanitarian assistance in Somalia. But after difficulties there, especially in 1993, the American public and Congress were content not only to withdraw from Somalia but also to avoid military intervention during the genocide in Rwanda during 1994. The Vietnam syndrome, now supplemented by Somalia, and further buttressed by the long and inconclusive engagements in Afghanistan and Iraq, occasionally or inconsistently puts a brake on direct US military intervention by reminding of the complexity of deep involvement abroad. Military operations for advancement of human rights in places such as Haiti, Bosnia, and Kosovo could only be sustained because combat casualties were avoided. But the more fundamental faith in American greatness as a symbol of freedom is alive and reasonably well, as shown by President Barack Obama's views (covered below). Donald Trump got elected in 2016 under the slogan of "Make America Great Again."

Events in Serbian Kosovo, for example, can be understood against this background. The United States felt the moral obligation to oppose the 1999 repression and expulsion of ethnic Albanians, a Serbian policy that also contested NATO's hegemony and somewhat destabilized other European states, but fear of casualties caused the Clinton Administration and NATO to adopt the military strategy of high-altitude air strikes without ground troops. This approach failed to protect the Albanian Kosovars in the short term, contributed to continuing

---

[19] See Michael H. Hunt, *Ideology and US Foreign Policy* (New Haven: Yale University Press, 1987).

destabilizing pressures on neighboring states, and solidified Serb opinion behind the Milosevic government. But, in the long term, as noted in Chapter 5, the United States and NATO weakened Milosevic's ability to persecute the Albanian Kosovars, and weakened his power in Belgrade. In a quite remarkable if controversial military operation, Washington led NATO in using military force to protect human rights. But the USA was careful not to suffer more casualties (and civilian damage abroad) than domestic opinion would tolerate. (In fact, no NATO pilots were killed or captured during eleven weeks of bombings.) It was a delicate balancing act: to proceed militarily primarily for human rights abroad but maintain domestic support for an operation not linked to traditional security concerns. (Congress never voted yea or nay on the military venture.)[20]

US foreign policy toward Libya in 2011 fits well with themes discussed here. President Obama appealed to American exceptionalism in his televised national address on March 28, saying that, while other nations might be able to stand aside if Kaddafi threatened atrocities, the USA could not.[21] Bill Clinton's failure to stop the Rwandan genocide in 1994 was a dark cloud in Obama's White House. But Obama then noted that military action, presumably to protect Libyan civilians, was occurring under UN mandate. American exceptionalism was thus combined with multilateral approval, hence presumably doubly legitimate. Actual military operations, whether led by the USA or NATO, were conducted with considerable prudence, both to avoid casualties and to avoid public responsibility for post-conflict events and hence a possible long and costly involvement. The "real" policy was indeed regime change, with western states trying to induce defections from the Kaddafi inner circle and hence the collapse of the regime. But the only way to get a UN mandate for military intervention (even with China, Russia, Germany, India, and Brazil abstaining in the Security Council vote) was to argue that the military operation was only to protect civilians. Of course, some apparent civilians were, in reality, fighters for the rebellion, so outside involvement to protect civilians inherently worked to enhance armed opposition to the government.

In sum to this point, one finds in US foreign policy on human rights much rhetoric about American exceptionalism – about a special US role to be active on human rights and democracy. But this periodic rhetoric does not always guarantee action (recall Rwanda) nor does it mean that

---

[20] Ryan C. Hendrickson, *The Clinton Wars: The Constitution, Congress, and War Powers* (Nashville: Vanderbilt University Press, 2002).

[21] See https://obamawhitehouse.archives.gov/the-press-office/2011/03/28/remarks-president-address-nation-libya.

the attentive public and elites in Washington are prepared to easily incur costs to protect the rights of others.[22] (The pattern of liberal rhetoric but realist hesitations is prevalent among liberal democracies. When Belgium suffered a few casualties in the early days of the 1994 Rwandan tragedy [about the same number as the USA suffered in Somalia in 1993], that state withdrew its remaining personnel and did not directly contest the genocide. When the Netherlands suffered one military fatality prior to the massacre at Srebrenica, Bosnia, in 1995, it withdrew its remaining personnel from a UN field operation and did not directly contest the ensuing genocide.)

More on bold rhetoric but limited measures

Even before the Libyan intervention, current public opinion on rights in US foreign policy indicated a blend of liberalism and realism – of universal concern for others and narrow self-interest. Polls showed that the general public as well as opinion leaders did indeed list "promoting and defending human rights in other countries," as well as "helping to bring a democratic form of government to other nations" as "very important" goals of US foreign policy. But in 1995 these goals were in thirteenth and fourteenth place, respectively, with only 34 percent and 25 percent of the general public listing them as very important. Eighty percent or more of the general public listed "stopping the flow of illegal drugs into the USA," "protecting the jobs of American workers," and "preventing the spread of nuclear weapons" as much more important. Analysts concluded that there was considerable American popular support for pragmatic internationalism, but not a great deal of support for moral internationalism.[23] If human rights could be linked to self-interest, or if human rights do not interfere with self-interest, one could build a political coalition for action. But if one made only moral and altruistic arguments, it was difficult to sustain a principled foreign policy centering on rights. With regard to Kosovo, American public opinion was permissive as long as significant numbers of American casualties were avoided.

---

[22] See further Julie A. Mertus, *Bait and Switch: Human Rights and US Foreign Policy* (New York and London: Routledge, 2004). See also Eric A. Heinze, "The Rhetoric of Genocide and US Foreign Policy: Rwanda and Darfur Compared," *Political Science Quarterly* 122, 3 (2007), 359–383. The George W. Bush Administration, having come to the conclusion of genocide in Darfur, still found reasons to avoid direct and major action in response.

[23] Ole Holsti, "Public Opinion on Human Rights in American Foreign Policy," in David P. Forsythe, ed., *The United States and Human Rights: Looking Inward and Outward* (Lincoln: University of Nebraska Press, 2000).

But in the spring of 1999 polls showed that almost two-thirds of the public were in favor of early negotiations to end the NATO air strikes.

Public opinion polls showed that in general or in the abstract, American public support for military means to advance democracy abroad was relatively low. It seemed very clear that had the George W. Bush Administration gone to the public and Congress in 2003 and asked for a mandate to use force to advance democracy in Iraq, that would have been a hard sell for the president. The actual rationale for that war was national security – Iraq's supposed links to terrorism, its presumed weapons of mass destruction, and general US security fears for the future. It was only after clarification of facts – no substantive Hussein links to Al Qaeda, no weapons of mass destruction, and hence no clear and present security danger – that the Bush Administration stressed the role of advancing democracy in Iraq. Movement toward democracy in Iraq and Saddam Hussein being on trial and executed did not save George W. Bush from very low public approval at home regarding his Iraq policy during the last few years of his presidency.

Washington is full of private groups that lobby for some version of human rights abroad.[24] This subject is treated in detail in Chapter 7. The national communications media also report on international human rights issues with some regularity. But many of the human rights NGOs often bemoaned their inability to stimulate more action, and more consistent action, for rights in US foreign policy.[25] The polls cited above indicate why. There is no grassroots movement supportive of a costly crusade for human rights abroad. While "the CNN factor" was given some credit for pushing the USA into action in both northern Iraq (the flight of Kurds) and Somalia (domestic starvation and disorder), both Rwanda in 1994 and what was then Zaire (now Democratic Congo) in 1997, showed that Washington was not always moved to action by media coverage of human rights violations and humanitarian hardship. With regard to Kosovo, media pictures of trainloads of ethnic Albanians being forced from their homes, and other reports of refugee hardships,

---

[24] The USA manifests no national institute of human rights, as do several European states, to serve as a transmission belt between international norms and national policies on human rights. It has a Civil Rights Commission, but that body rarely takes an international approach to its limited subject. See further Julie Mertus, *Human Rights Matters: Local Politics and National Human Rights Institutions* (Stanford: Stanford University Press, 2009). See also Thomas Pegrane, "Diffusion Across Political Systems: The Global Spread of National Human Rights Institutions," *Human Rights Quarterly*, 32, 3 (August 2010), 471–501.

[25] Aryeh Neier, "The New Double Standard," *Foreign Policy*, 105 (1996–1997), 91–102; and Ellen Dorsey, "US Foreign Policy and the Human Rights Movement," in Forsythe, ed., *The United States and Human Rights*.

probably had something to do with western support for air strikes on Serbia despite mistakes and collateral damage. But those pictures did not cause a public demand for ground troops and costly humanitarian intervention in terms of soldiers' lives.

Similar commentary could be made about "the Arab Spring" or the "Arab awakening" in early 2011. Street protests in the name of human rights and democracy (and better economic opportunity) resulted in much media coverage, with Arab (and Iranian) repressive elites trying to shut off television and social media coverage. The Obama foreign policy team selectively and inconsistently aligned the USA with democratic change in places such as Tunisia and Egypt and belatedly Yemen (but not so clearly in Bahrain or Syria). In Libya, as noted, western military opposition to Kaddafi's policies was careful in trying not to entail western casualties and prolonged responsibilities. Obama faced fractured domestic opinion: some supported limited involvement, some wanted more open pursuit of regime change, some were critical of further military operations in the wake of fighting in Afghanistan and Iraq (and budget deficits at home). As per Rwanda, American media reported on atrocities in Syria, but the domestic pressure to intervene there was slight, partially because of military involvements elsewhere.

As for Syria, after 2010, the communications media of various types regularly reported on the humanitarian disaster that emerged from the internationalized civil war (see further Chapter 9). But President Obama was determined to avoid major military intervention, as we have already noted several times. This policy choice meant injury or death to many during the fight for control of Syria.

Samantha Power, who as US Ambassador to the UN reportedly had some influence on Obama's decision to intervene in Libya, but was ineffective in advocating more UN involvement in Syria, has shown that throughout its modern history, when the USA has faced situations of genocide or near-genocide abroad, there has never been a powerful domestic push from public opinion or Congress forcing the president into a decisive involvement. Presidents have felt free to pursue mostly realist policies of narrow self-interest, rather than liberal policies of protecting the rights of others.[26] When involvements have occurred more recently largely for human rights reasons in places such as Somalia (1992), Kosovo (1999), and Libya (2011), care has been taken to try to limit US casualties and other costs, as noted. As Obama mentioned in his television address on Libya, US involvement in Iraq from 2003 had cost

---

[26] Samantha Power, *"A Problem From Hell": America and the Age of Genocide* (New York: Basic Books, 2002).

at least one trillion dollars and many American and Iraqi lives. Hence Obama's intervention in Libya was no crusade to be pursued regardless of cost. Moreover, the Obama team, like the British government, tried to cast the Libyan intervention sometimes in self-interested terms – that it was in the national interest to be on the side of democratic change in the Arab world.

To take one further concrete example, the matter of religious persecution abroad is instructive regarding US foreign policy and human rights – and the blending of ethical consideration with self-interest. The subject of religious freedom has a nice ring to it in American society, founded partly as it was to secure freedom from religious bigotry in Europe. In the 1990s, especially social conservatives pushed hard to elevate the subject of religious freedom in US foreign policy. But a number of pragmatic conservatives, as well as some international liberals, objected to the bills introduced in Congress. These bills called for automatic sanctions against countries engaging in, or tolerating, religious persecution. As such, these bills would have created sanctions on such US allies as Saudi Arabia, Israel, Greece, Pakistan, etc. Only when the bills were weakened so as to give the president considerable discretion in dealing with religious persecution abroad did a law finally pass. So there was more attention to religious freedom in US foreign policy, and a new office for such was created in the State Department. But there was also concern not to interfere very much with traditional US economic and strategic interests.[27] Some religious conservatives had teamed with some secular liberals to produce more attention to religious freedom and religious persecution, but traditional self-interest in economic and secur-ity matters was hardly absent.[28]

Recent administrations

There is much more to say about modern diplomatic history pertaining to the USA and human rights. Space limitations impose considerable brevity. First of all, presidents do not have a free hand on this issue; Congress asserts itself periodically. It was Congress during the early Eisenhower Administration that forced the USA to abandon a high-profile posture on internationally recognized human rights,

---

[27] See further Eric Schmitt, "Bill to Punish Nations Limiting Religious Beliefs Passes Senate," *New York Times*, October 10, 1998, A3.

[28] See further Allen D. Hertzke, *Freeing God's Children: The Unlikely Alliance for Global Human Rights* (New York: Rowman & Littlefield, 2004); and Felice Gaer, "Religious Freedom," in *Encyclopedia of Human Rights*, vol. IV, 323–329, where one also finds brief discussion of US foreign policy on this issue.

a conservative Congress being caught up in the hysteria of McCarthyism and seeing universal human rights as a subversive foreign influence. It was then Congress toward the end of the Nixon Administration that reintroduced human rights into the US foreign policy agenda, a Democratic Congress wanting to characterize the Nixon–Kissinger period as lacking in ethical values.[29] It was Congress, not Jimmy Carter, that first insisted on more attention to human rights abroad in the 1970s, and it was Congress, not Carter, that created a new human rights bureau in the State Department.

Second, particularly since the mid-1970s all presidents have had to fashion some sort of policy on human rights in world affairs, that subject being institutionalized at the UN and other international organizations, and Congress often being inclined to track developments – if only for partisan reasons.[30] Jimmy Carter (President 1977–1981), building on congressional developments, promised to make human rights the cornerstone of his foreign policy, a promise he largely abandoned after the Soviet invasion of Afghanistan in 1979. For his part Ronald Reagan (1981–1989) first attempted to collapse his human rights policy into his anti-communist orientation, but wound up reaching compromise with the Democrats on a bipartisan approach to democracy promotion, and on backing away from full support of anti-communist dictators such as Marcos in the Philippines and Pinochet in Chile.[31]

Giving somewhat more detailed treatment to later developments, we find that President Clinton's rhetoric on foreign policy, although spasmodically delivered, was squarely within the activist tradition of American exceptionalism. Enlarging the global democratic community was supposedly one of the basic pillars of his foreign policy. The semantic emphasis was on personal freedom and democracy. He justified US troops in Bosnia by saying Washington must lead, must hold the feet of the European allies to the fire, must make a difference for a liberal democratic peace with human rights in the Balkans. The 1995 Dayton agreement was not just about peace, but about liberal democracy and human rights. There was strong Clinton talk in support of human

---

[29] See further David P. Forsythe, *Human Rights and US Foreign Policy: Congress Reconsidered* (Gainesville: University Press of Florida, 1988).

[30] Once the USA became a party to treaties on human rights and humanitarian affairs, the domestic political process was altered to some extent, with various domestic groups making appeal to the treaties' provisions both in Congress and in the courts. See further Beth A. Simmons, *Mobilizing for Human Rights: International Law in Domestic Politics* (Cambridge: Cambridge University Press, 2009).

[31] A short summary can be found in Forsythe, "Human Rights and US Foreign Policy: Two Levels, Two Worlds."

rights: for universal rights at the UN Vienna Conference on Human Rights in 1993, which created the post of UN High Commissioner for Human Rights; for criminal prosecutions at The Hague in the International Criminal Tribunal for the former Yugoslavia; for containment of repressive states such as Sudan, Iraq, and Iran; for sanctions on Burma/Myanmar. As long as one did not have to pay a high national price, in blood or treasure, to advance human rights, the Clinton Administration was certainly for them – at least for the civil and political rights congruent with the American self-image. These were the rights stressed in Clinton's 1998 visit to China.

Self-interested economic and strategic concerns, however, were hardly absent from US foreign policy during the Clinton era. His first Assistant Secretary of State for human rights, John Shattuck, contemplated resigning several times in frustration over the lack of systematic commitment to human rights.[32] Not only did the Clinton Administration not intervene to stop genocide in Rwanda in 1994, after strong domestic criticism concerning loss of American life in Somalia, but also that administration delinked trading privileges from basic civil and political rights in China. Clinton's argument on that issue, not without reason, was that a strong defensive nationalism prevailed in China, and thus the only route to progress on human rights lay in economic growth and a larger middle class over time. Presumably, when that middle class had met its basic needs, it would then demand more personal and political freedoms. By 2016, that evolution had not happened, but that is not to say that it might not happen in the future.

President George W. Bush's foreign policy also stressed American exceptionalism as its guiding principle, but in a way very different from the Clinton era. Rhetoric promoting American ideals – namely freedom and liberty – was omnipresent in his speeches, especially his second inaugural address.[33] Despite the originally declared justifications for invading Iraq in 2003, which had little to do with human rights and much to do with claims to national security, the president's post-war language was replete with references to democracy and personal freedom. Whereas during his first term George W. Bush paid hardly any discernible attention to the decline of democracy in Russia, during the second term Bush himself laid great public and private stress on precisely that topic. Increasingly George W. Bush went beyond Clinton's

---

[32] John Shattuck, *Freedom on Fire: Human Rights Wars and America's Response* (Cambridge, MA: Harvard University Press, 2003).
[33] See georgewbush-whitehouse.archives.gov/news/releases/2005/01/images/20050120-1_ p44289.

rhetorical but sporadic forays into the human rights domain. Increasingly the Republican Bush took on the political coloring of a Jimmy Carter or a Woodrow Wilson to stress the advancement of democracy, and its civil and political rights, as a central pillar of his foreign policy.

A year after the September 11 terrorist attacks, the Bush Administration had presented its National Security Strategy statement, outlining a foreign policy with much semantic attention to personal rights. "Human rights" was not a privileged phrase, but freedom and democracy were. While the first major section of the outline declared an intention to "Champion Aspirations for Human Dignity," it was also the strategy's shortest portion, other than its initial outline.[34] References to "human rights" can be found sparsely strung about the document, but even more apparent were references to "human dignity." Throughout the document, "human rights" was offered as a vague matter to be dealt with by other states, while "human dignity" was outlined in substantial detail: "the rule of law; limits on the absolute power of the state; free speech; freedom of worship; equal justice; respect for women; religious and ethnic tolerance; and respect for private property."[35] Norms such as free speech, freedom of worship, and respect for private property are all values firmly embedded in American political discourse. "Human rights" abroad inevitably gets one into the domain of international law and organization, and in general this is not what the Bush Administration wanted to emphasize. The Bush team, much more so than the Clinton team, was in favor of unilateral assertions of hard power, as many commentators recognized.

Like all administrations, Bush foreign policy gave rhetorical emphasis to a freedom agenda and democracy promotion. And there was some substance behind the words. But also like other administrations, the Bush team continued close relations with a number of autocrats, notably the long-time dictator, Hosni Mubarak, in Egypt. Thus on the one hand Bush foreign policy claimed to be using the invasion of Iraq to start falling dominoes in favor of democracy in the Middle East. On the other hand the Bush team did not pressure Mubarak and other authoritarian allies to liberalize their political systems, much less to move toward genuine democracy. That would only come from the Arab street in 2011, an indigenous and largely secular regional movement at the start that almost never mentioned developments in Iraq.

---

[34] See "The National Security Strategy," https://georgewbush-whitehouse.archives.gov/nsc/nss/2002/.
[35] See further Mertus, *Bait and Switch*, 59.

As for the Obama Administration, there was both continuity and change on human rights compared to the Bush II years. In the electoral campaign of 2008, human rights in foreign policy was not a leading issue, the country prioritizing concerns about economic recession. Candidate Obama did criticize the Republican Administration for sacrificing American values on the altar of national security.

As for change, President Obama undertook a high-profile stance to disassociate the USA from torture and cruel treatment of security prisoners. The Bush team, led by Vice President Richard Cheney, had gone to the "dark side" after 9/11 on grounds of national security, engaging in policies in CIA secret prisons that the International Committee of the Red Cross termed torture and inhuman treatment. At the Guantanamo prison facility on the island of Cuba, under military jurisdiction, and at other military prisons, there had also been torture and inhuman treatment, so characterized by some US military and legal officials.[36] On other issues one could also see some change, as in the Obama decision to rejoin (stand for election to) the UN Human Rights Council, boycotted by the previous Administration for its lack of even-handed policies (mainly concerning Israel). The matter of new US policies concerning the Arab Spring of 2011 has already been noted, as Obama did slowly align the USA with democratic change for a time in certain countries but not in others.

But there was much continuity as well. Some continuity was compelled by Congress despite Obama's wishes, such as in the continued operation of the Guantanamo prison for security prisoners, and the use of military commissions and administrative detention there as well. Some continuity came from the Obama team itself, as in efforts to keep courts from reviewing various prisoner claims of mistreatment. Initially the Obama Administration downplayed human rights issues in China, until NGO criticism and media coverage required increasing attention to rights there. Also regarding Russia, the Obama emphasis primarily was on securing Moscow's cooperation on a variety of issues such as Iranian nuclear weapons, not on its backsliding on human rights in Russian domestic and foreign policy. When the Obama team moved to apply targeted sanctions to certain individuals close to Putin, it was largely because of Russia's use of force to detach Crimea from Ukraine.

The fact was that across various administrations, with all being non-isolationist in foreign policy, and regardless of aspirations to being realist or liberal or some version of ultra-nationalist, the balance sheet regarding

---

[36] For overviews, see James P. Pfiffner, *Torture as Public Policy: Restoring US Credibility on the World Stage* (Boulder: Paradigm, 2010); and Forsythe, *Politics of Prisoner Abuse.*

human rights was normally very mixed with much inconsistency and muddling through. This was inherent in the subject, with many internationally recognized human rights, many countries and organizations on the US foreign policy agenda, many different conceptions of US interests, and much shifting domestic concern and pressure. Nixon and Bush I were not consistently realist, Clinton and Obama were not consistently liberal, and Reagan and Bush II were not consistently neo-conservative.[37] Some distinctions held up over time. For example, liberals gave greater weight to international law and organization, compared to realists and neo-cons. The latter were more unilateralists, on balance.

Obama in 2016 gave a candid interview to a journalist from *The Atlantic* magazine.[38] The President acknowledged an inconsistent, case-by-case approach to human rights in foreign policy.[39] The determining factor, he said, was cost to the USA. One had to be hard-headed in a tough world, and some action for human rights was not doable. Presumably the Syrian internationalized civil war fell into this category. In other situations, the USA could act, various costs being low. Presumably the rescue of Iraqi Yazidi from the murderous and rapacious Islamic State group fell into this category. So, in the Obama approach, the international law of human rights was implemented or not depending on US factors such as cost and domestic politics. Even so, Obama believed that on balance the USA was a force for good in the world, which fits with the idea of American exceptionalism.

Further observations

Further analysis reveals a major soft spot in the contemporary US approach to human rights, regardless of changing administrations. The USA, unlike all other developed democracies, refuses to accept cultural, economic, and social rights as real human rights. When the USA talks about its support for the Universal Declaration of Human Rights, it simply omits reference to those articles endorsing fundamental rights to adequate standards of food, clothing, shelter, health care, and social security. It has never ratified the International Covenant on Economic, Social, and Cultural Rights. Federal laws, and most internal state laws,

---

[37] See further Forsythe, "Situating Obama." On inconsistent US policies in Latin America, see Kathryn Sikkink, *Mixed Signals: US Human Rights Policy and Latin America* (Ithaca: Cornell University Press, for the Century Foundation, 2004).

[38] Jeffrey Goldberg, "The Obama Doctrine," *The Atlantic*, March 10, 2016, www.theatlantic.com/press-releases/archive/2016/03/the-obama-doctrine-the-atlantics-exclusive-report-on-presidents-hardest-foreign-policy-decisions/473151/.

[39] See above, note 15.

do not provide for socioeconomic fundamental entitlements, as compared with optional benefits. There is no recognized right to health care, much less a recognized right to adequate food, clothing, and shelter. The USA is one of two states not to adhere to the UN Convention on the Rights of the Child. The Convention appears to make encroachments on family privacy, arguably protected by the US Constitution. The Clinton Administration did rhetorically accept the right to development at the 1998 UN Vienna Conference on Human Rights, but this posture has been of no practical consequence.

The USA continues to exclusively emphasize civil and political rights, including the civil right to private property. But even on this subject the US support for international standards is highly qualified. The Senate has added many reservations, declarations, and understandings to its 1992 consent to the International Covenant on Civil and Political Rights (as well as failing to accept the Optional Protocol that would allow individual complaints about violations). It is clear the USA continues to emphasize a narrower national law rather than a broader international law of human rights. Even some of its international partners, like the Netherlands, have criticized this US orientation. It is well known that a number of Canadians view the US version of market democracy as unnecessarily harsh, overly individualized, and lacking in a sense of community.[40] Nevertheless, a powerful segment of the American political class remains strongly opposed to the "European nanny state." The phrase "social democracy" is a pejorative term in those circles of opinion. In the Republican Party in particular, the rhetorical emphasis continued to be on personal liberty and shrinking government, even if in reality both Reagan and Bush II expanded federal programs and federal deficit spending – while the latter Administration favored government bailouts to big investment banks in the major recession of 2008. Despite the prominent role of Senator Bernie Sanders in the 2016 Presidential campaign, who was a proud democratic socialist, the USA remained much more libertarian than most other democracies. The emphasis was on a negative liberty rather than positive freedom. One needed rights to block interference from outsiders, rather than rights to develop full personhood.

There are three strong points to recent US foreign policy on rights abroad. First, as noted in Chapter 3, all US administrations after the Cold War have led – albeit inconsistently – in expanding the scope of Chapter VII of the UN Charter, involving matters on which the Council

[40] Rhoda E. Howard, *Human Rights and the Search for Community* (Boulder: Westview, 1995).

can take a binding decision. As a result of US policy in the UN Security Council when dealing with northern Iraq, Somalia, Bosnia, Haiti, Rwanda, Angola, and Libya in 2011, the Council has effectively decided that the security of persons inside states can constitute a threat to international peace and security, leading to authoritative protection attempts by the international community. Deployments of military force, limited combat, economic sanctions, and deeply intrusive diplomacy have all occurred in recent years in relation to human rights issues under Chapter VII. International law still provides no doctrine of humanitarian intervention, although from 2005 one has the vague endorsement of R2P, as already noted, but the concept of international peace and security has been expanded to substitute for this lack.

The USA has led in shrinking the domain of exclusive domestic jurisdiction, and in expanding the realm of authoritative decisions by the Council – at least for others but not for itself. This is a somewhat promising trend, at least in theory, for the international protection of human rights. In terms of sequence, UNSC decisions as they evolved after the Cold War in the 1990s laid the foundation for the adoption of R2P in 2005 – the responsibility to protect by outsiders, if a state proved unwilling or unable to protect the rights of its citizens. This was the diplomatic (and legal) background for events during 2011 in places like Libya and Ivory Coast where outside parties did indeed take forceful action to advance human rights concerns under UN mandate.

Second, also noted in Chapter 3, the USA has also led in expanding the notion of peacekeeping so as to provide complex or second-generation peacekeeping with human rights dimensions. In places like Namibia, El Salvador, Cambodia, Guatemala, Bosnia, and Sudan, *inter alia*, the USA has encouraged UN and other field missions under Chapter VI of the Charter not simply to oversee a cease-fire or other military agreement, but more broadly to try to establish and consolidate a liberal democratic peace. As might be expected, the actual record of results is mixed. There has been more success in Namibia and El Salvador than in Cambodia and Bosnia. Nevertheless, Washington has been a leader in these developments particularly where the local protagonists show signs of good-faith efforts to reach and implement international agreements.[41] The trend continued in 2005, with the US encouraging a UN security operation in Sudan, long wracked by violence and instability and atrocities in the Darfur region, once it became clear

---

[41] See further David P. Forsythe, "Human Rights and International Security: United Nations Field Operations Redux," in M. Castermans, et al., eds., *The Role of the Nation State in the 21st Century* (Dordrecht: Kluwer, 1998), 265–276.

that the African Union would not be able to decisively improve the situation. There was also a small UN security operation in the Democratic Republic of the Congo. The USA was supportive of a UN security operation in South Sudan when civilians were seriously endangered by factional violence in that new and impoverished state. The same was generally true in Democratic Congo and some other conflict situations.

Third, as noted in Chapter 4, the USA led in the resurrection of the idea of international criminal courts, dormant since the 1940s at Nuremberg and Tokyo. True, as we saw in an earlier chapter, when the US-led Security Council created the 1993 *ad hoc* court for former Yugoslavia and the 1995 *ad hoc* court for Rwanda, it was searching for action that would not entail costly military intervention. The two courts were as much the product of escape from responsibility as of commitment to legal justice for gross violations of human rights such as grave breaches of the laws of war, crimes against humanity, and genocide. Be that as it may, the USA has contributed more money and personnel to particularly the Yugoslav court than any other state.

US support for an independent and authoritative standing UN criminal court, however, is an entirely different matter. Whereas President Clinton had signed the Rome Statute to keep the USA engaged in various negotiations about the ICC, President George W. Bush's opposition to the new court was so strong that he took the unprecedented step of "unsigning" that legal document. The Bush II Administration, like the Reagan Administration before it, was very clear in its hostility to many international agreements, including human rights agreements. For the most part it was highly skeptical of supranational authority and international adjudication. Only on trade matters, centered on the WTO, did US governments allow an international organization to authoritatively review US policies. In 2005, however, the US did allow the UN Security Council to pass a resolution allowing the ICC prosecutor to conduct investigations of individual criminal responsibility by Sudanese leaders for atrocities in the Darfur region. Rather then vetoing that resolution the USA abstained. This action suggested that Washington might tolerate the ICC as long as US nationals were exempted from its jurisdiction. The Obama Administration followed up this shift in Bush II policies by continuing quiet cooperation with the ICC as long as there was no likelihood of Americans being defendants in that court. These and other developments caused the Obama team to back away from using the pressure of military assistance agreements to undermine the ICC.

Overall, and consistent with the analysis above, US foreign policy on human rights after the Cold War reflects a number of contradictions.

The USA rhetorically supports universal human rights with great enthusiasm, but reserves to itself the practice of national particularism (eleva-
tion of national over international law, no socioeconomic rights, rejection
of the treaty on rights of the child which is virtually unanimously
endorsed, relative lack of legal protections for minors and the develop-
mentally challenged in the criminal justice system, harsh prison conditions for common criminals, much injustice for security prisoners after
9/11, etc.).[42] Washington endorses development according to liberal
democracy, but has extensive economic relations with numerous authoritarian states, from China to Kuwait, from Saudi Arabia to Ethiopia. The
USA led in creating new *ad hoc* international criminal tribunals to
respond to gross violations of human rights in certain states, but opposes
the ICC having jurisdiction over Americans. Washington led in
expanding the notions of enforcement action under Chapter VII of the
Charter and of complex peacekeeping under Chapter VI, but blocked
any significant UN deployments of force to protect persons in Rwanda.
It then engaged in prolonged intervention in Yugoslavia on behalf of
Kosovar Albanians and in Libya in 2011. US leaders spoke out against
torture, even while engaging in abuse of prisoners that on occasion was
tantamount to torture, and even while turning prisoners over to countries
that had a long history of torture. Whether other states have compiled a
better or more consistent record in their foreign policy on rights abroad is
an interesting question. If we think of international relations after 1991 as
a Pax Americana with the USA as the hegemonic power, the fate of
human rights around the world was not all that good; but if the USA
declined and the BRICs replaced it as the dominant power center, the
human rights record would probably be worse.[43]

Other states

Virtually all other liberal democracies and polities that strive to be liberal
democracies display increasingly active policies on international human
rights.[44] Like the USA, they take various initiatives on human rights

---

[42] See further Amnesty International, *United States of America: Rights for All* (London:
Amnesty International Publications, 1998); and David P. Forsythe, "Human Rights
Policy: Change and Continuity," in Randall B. Ripley and James M. Lindsay, eds., *US
Foreign Policy After the Cold War* (Pittsburgh: University of Pittsburgh Press, 1997),
257–282.
[43] See Forsythe and McMahon, *American Exceptionalism Reconsidered*. BRICs refer to
Brazil, Russia, India, and China.
[44] See further Alison Brysk, *Global Good Samaritans: Human Rights as Foreign Policy*
(Oxford and New York: Oxford University Press, 2009).

abroad. Like the USA, they give a particular national slant to their policies. Like the USA, their general orientation to international human rights reflects their national political culture. Like the USA, most ascribe virtue to themselves in their orientation to internationally recognized human rights. Some, like Britain, are very similar to the USA in their rights policies abroad. Some, like Japan, are quite different. All evaluate action for human rights in foreign policy in terms of national costs and benefits. At the risk of superficiality, one can provide a brief summary of more thorough inquiries.

The Netherlands for most of the time under review liked to picture itself as highly international and cosmopolitan.[45] It was the home of Grotius, the father of international law; it was a great trading nation; it was and is a country interested in world peace, for normal trade requires peace; and now it prides itself as a country highly active on human rights. This last orientation is affected both by its Protestant missionary tradition, and in some circles by a certain guilt about its colonial record and especially its handling of claims to independence by Indonesia in the 1940s. Both historical elements push the Dutch into activism on human rights. Thus Dutch governments engage in a friendly competition with like-minded states, perhaps especially Denmark and Norway, about who is the most progressive in foreign policy. The Dutch political classes see themselves as making a special contribution through their development assistance policies, perhaps because they know that the USA has one of the lowest ratios between gross domestic product and official development assistance of any western democracy (less than one-quarter of one percent). During the Cold War, if the USA had to sacrifice some attention to human rights in order to lead on security issues, some in The Hague wanted to fill that gap.

Because of the Dutch self-image and considerable Dutch activism at the United Nations on both human rights and peacekeeping issues, the Dutch role in the Srebrenica massacre in the former Yugoslavia in July 1995 proved to be a national trauma – perhaps roughly similar to Canadian reactions to charges of human rights violations against some of their military forces in Somalia. A lightly armed Dutch contingent in UNPROFOR, supposedly guaranteeing Srebrenica as a "safe area," was

---

[45] See further David Gillies, *Between Principle and Practice: Human Rights in North–South Relations* (Montreal: McGill-Queen's University Press, 1996); Peter R. Baehr, "The Netherlands and the United Nations: The Future Lies in the Past," in Chadwick F. Alger, Gene M. Lyons, and John E. Trent, eds., *The United Nations System: The Policies of Member States* (Tokyo: United Nations University Press, 1995), 271–328; and Baehr, "Problems of Aid Conditionality: The Netherlands and Indonesia," *Third World Quarterly*, 18, 2 (June 1997), 363–376.

withdrawn – after which a massacre by Serbian partisans of thousands of remaining Muslim males occurred.

Also problematic, but not so traumatic, was the Dutch effort to combine development assistance with protection of human rights – especially civil and political ones. The Netherlands was inclined to assist poorer countries, and regularly was among the leading countries in amount of the gross domestic product contributed to official development assistance as a percentage of national economic productivity. But aid was not offered to some countries because of human rights problems. To other countries aid was offered but suspended for a time, for the same reason. Indonesia has posed a special case for Dutch governments, given the history involved and Jakarta's poor human rights record during times of authoritarian government. Certain Dutch statements led Indonesia in 1992 to indicate it would no longer accept foreign assistance from the Netherlands. So the aid relationship was terminated, leaving The Hague with no leverage on human rights developments in East Timor and other places controlled by Indonesia. Similar difficulties arose in relations with Suriname after a coup in that South American former colony, with the Dutch finally deciding to suspend assistance. Thus the Dutch, like the USA, have found it difficult to establish a consistent and principled policy on rights abroad, not only because of being entangled with other states via international organizations, but also because of wanting to pursue conflicting "public goods" – e.g., economic growth in poorer countries but with respect for civil and political rights.

British history, too, affects London's modern orientation to international human rights.[46] Political classes there strongly identify with civil and political rights and are proud of such early documents as the Magna Carta of 1215, the English Bill of Rights of 1689, laws on freedom of the press from 1695, etc. British leaders tend to see themselves as having generated great influence on subsequent developments for human rights in places like France and the USA, not to mention later developments in places like India. Like the USA, the UK prides itself on a strong legal culture emphasizing constitutionalism or limited government. Britain, like other colonial powers, tended to see its rule over foreign lands as benign and enlightening, rather than repressive and oppressive. Once it ended its colonial period, it became even more supportive of international human rights instruments – not having to be defensive about

---

[46] See further *Human Rights in Foreign Policy*, Foreign Policy Document No. 268 (London: Foreign and Commonwealth Office, July 1996); *Foreign Policy and Human Rights, Vol. 1*, House of Commons Sessions 1998–9, Foreign Affairs Committee (London: The Stationery Office, December 1998).

claims to national self-determination as a collective human right, or about the issue of individual petitions claiming rights violations in overseas territories.

Various British governments, unlike the USA, have not only accepted the full International Bill of Rights, along with European legal instruments, but also have undertaken concrete policies for specific situations – engaging in quiet diplomacy for the release of some Indonesian detainees, suspending foreign assistance to states like Chile and Uganda for human rights violations, supporting arms embargoes against South Africa and Chile, and so forth. It fought the Falklands/Malvinas war with Argentina with considerable attention to international humanitarian law. Like the USA, however, London has muted its criticism of some important states, such as Saudi Arabia which provides the British with important arms sales. On the other hand, Britain did join the USA in trying to have the UN Human Rights Commission adopt a resolution critical of China in 1997.

Some observers believe British governments are not as influenced by domestic human rights groups and media coverage as US policy, given the British tradition of parliamentary sovereignty, but not necessarily popular sovereignty and radical interpretations of individual rights. Britain still does not have a written constitution or practice judicial review of parliamentary acts. On the other hand it has found its rights policies at home and abroad increasingly affected by its membership of the Council of Europe and the European Union. Britain has been far more affected by regional rights standards than the USA. These domestic and foreign factors interact to produce a foreign policy on rights somewhat similar to those of other European states – increasingly active and complicated, but inconsistent due to its variety of interests in international relations. In striking contrast to the USA, British governments support the ICC, even though Britain has sent its troops abroad in places like Iraq and Sierra Leone.

Britain, along with France, pushed hard for the use of force in Libya in 2011 to head off attacks on civilians by the Kaddafi regime. As usual European states found it impossible to present to the world a unified foreign and security policy, with Germany in particular unable to support the UN Security Council resolution providing a legal basis for attacks on Kaddafi's assets. Nevertheless the David Cameron coalition government in London framed the issue as a matter not just of humanitarianism but also of national interests – to be on the right side of history with new Arab governments and to deter further repression by other Arab trading partners, arguments which seemed to have had some effect on the Obama Administration.

However, as already noted, among the factors affecting Brexit in 2016 was the view in parts of England (not so much in the rest of Britain) that not just the European Union but also the Council of Europe and its human rights court had intruded too deeply into domestic affairs. Regional attention to the rights of migrant workers and refugees had contributed to the controlling view that the UK should leave the EU. Similar antagonistic views toward EU and CE human rights decisions were evident in parts of the Netherlands and most other European countries. This was part of the "New Nationalism" of nativist nature that was pushing back against many forms of international governance.

Japan, by contrast, readily admits that the concept of human rights was not indigenous but was introduced from the West in the nineteenth century.[47] Obviously in a country with a history of imperial and military government, and with an era of atrocities during World War II, the notion of human rights did not take firm hold until the modern constitution was imposed during a time of military defeat and foreign occupation. Even so, and despite the existence of some indigenous "liberal" groups, Japan has still struggled at home with issues of equality or fairness for women, other races, and various ethnic and national groups. Given this history, it is not so surprising that Japan during the Cold War was a liberal democracy aligned with the other western liberal democracies, but was more passive than active on international human rights issues. In 1992, long after the US Congress put human rights back on the foreign policy agenda in Washington in the mid-1970s, Japan issued a white paper saying that human rights and democracy could be factors that affected foreign assistance and investment. But in general, and certainly in dealings with Peru which had a president of Japanese descent, human rights considerations did not appear to be a major factor in Japanese foreign policy.

As Japan has sought to show the world that it deserves a permanent seat in the UN Security Council, that it is more than an appendage of the USA, and that it has put its darker past behind it, Tokyo has become more active on rights issues abroad. Japan played a leading role, a far larger role than Washington, in trying to produce a liberal democratic peace with human rights in Cambodia. But it remains much less active in general on rights abroad than most other western-style liberal

---

[47] See further John Peek, "Japan, the United Nations, and Human Rights," *Asian Survey*, 32, 3 (March 1992); Seiichiro Takagi, "Japan's Policy Towards China After Tiananmen," in James T. H. Tang, ed., *Human Rights and International Relations in the Asia Pacific* (London: Pinter, 1995); and Yasuhiro Ueki, "Japan's New Diplomacy: Sources of Passivism and Activism," in Gerard Curtis, ed., *Japan's Foreign Policy After the Cold War: Coping with Change* (New York: M. E. Sharpe, 1997).

democracies. Tokyo has not pressed the human rights issue in its economic relations with other Asian states in particular, although it did suspend economic dealings for a time with China after the Tiananmen Square massacre of 1989. Tokyo has been more reluctant than Washington to press the rights issues in Myanmar (Burma). Given the history of Japanese relations with the Asian mainland during the 1930s and 1940s, it would be quite difficult for Japan to play a leading role on rights matters. This history reinforces those public officials who would like to concentrate primarily on Japanese economic interests. Likewise, Japan has not been one of the members of the World Bank that seeks to link loans with human rights performance, including democratic governance. Japan has, however, mostly voted with the western group at the UN on various rights matters in such bodies as the General Assembly and the Human Rights Commission and Council.

With regards to Japan's official development assistance (ODA) program, recent years have seen telling trends in Japanese policy making. While human rights have not been inextricably linked to foreign assistance, they are far from absent. In 2003, Japan reformed its ODA charter, citing domestic and international debate over its development policies and practices. The reformed document declares that its bedrock objective is "to contribute to the peace and development of the international community, and thereby to help ensure Japan's own security and prosperity." It even goes so far as to list paying "adequate attention to . . . the situation regarding the protection of basic human rights and freedoms" as one of four ODA principles of implementation, albeit behind such principles as environmental conservation and attention to military expenditures and WMD.[48] Later, in March 2005, Japan announced its Initiative on Gender Development, a new push to integrate gender concerns with other ODA considerations.[49]

Japan pressed North Korea on nuclear proliferation, but also on its human rights record, particularly with regard to its involvement in the abduction of up to fifteen Japanese nationals during the 1970s and 1980s. Japan threatened to withdraw food aid, and even considered sanctions against Kim Jong Il's regime.[50] It brought the issue to the United Nations Commission on Human Rights, helping to draft a resolution that dealt with North Korea's abduction of foreign nationals,

---

[48] See "Overview: Circumstances Surrounding Japan's Official Development Assistance (ODA) and Revision of the ODA Charter," www.mofa.go.jp/policy/other/bluebook/ 2004/chap3-d.pdf.
[49] See www.mofa.go.jp/policy/oda/category/wid/gad.html.
[50] See David Pilling and Jung a Song, "Tokyo Seeks Facts about Abducted Japanese," *Financial Times* (London), November 9, 2004, Asia edn.: Asia-Pacific, 2.

among other human rights concerns.[51] But even as Japan sought to induce change in one of the world's most brutal regimes, it was forced to face its own tarnished past. While Tokyo was pressing Pyongyang to come clean on abductions, South Korea was demanding Japan follow Germany's example and apologize more completely for its wartime atrocities.[52]

Like most democracies, Japan has manifested a resurgent ultra-nationalist or nativist movement little inclined to emphasize international human rights. Rather, this far-right movement has tended to try to explain away past national atrocities and glorify past eras of power and expansion. This global resurgence of narrow – even chauvinistic – nationalism is not the monopoly of democracies, as developments show in some former communist states.

States like Hungary and Russia, to choose two almost at random, are now also active on international human rights issues – but not necessarily in a positive sense.[53] Hungary after 1991 wanted to be like any other European state on these issues, although its relationship to ethnic Hungarians abroad generates clear differences. The Russian Federation is much more critical about the place of human rights in foreign policy, although it too is propelled to considerable extent by concern for the protection of compatriots abroad. Both of these states stress minority rights in foreign policy much more than Washington.

Hungary presents an interesting situation in terms of foreign policy and human rights. Its history is mostly one of authoritarian rule, whether as part of the Austro-Hungarian empire or Soviet-imposed communism. Yet certain liberal tendencies were present, such as considerable respect for private property and a certain affinity for legal rules. Many politically active Hungarians considered themselves to be liberal and a part of the West. Considerable resistance to Leninist or Stalinist repression was much in evidence in the 1956 uprising, as was also the case at different times in what was then the German Democratic Republic, Poland, and

---

[51] For an overview of this long-running issue, see Michael Astor, "Japan Seeks to Keep Pressure on N. Korea over Abductions," *Associated Press*, December 2, 2016, http://bigstory.ap.org/article/64585c8de41542de9af4af1b9adf7c2c/japan-seeks-keep-pressure-nkorea-over-abductions; and www.mofa.go.jp/policy/other/bluebook/2004/chap3-c.pdf.

[52] Richard Lloyd Parry, "Seoul Searching for Japanese War Apology," *The Australian*, March 3, 2005, All-Around Country edn.: World 8.

[53] See further Bruce D. Porter and Carol R. Saivets, "The Once and Future Empire: Russia and the 'Near Abroad,'" *Washington Quarterly*, 17, 3 (1994), 75–76; Alexei Arbatov, "Russian Foreign Policy Thinking in Transition," in Vladimir Baranovsky, ed., *Russia and Europe: The Emerging Security Agenda* (Oxford: Oxford University Press, 1997); and Istvan Pogany, ed., *Human Rights in Eastern Europe* (Aldershot: Edward Elgar, 1995).

what is now the Czech Republic. Many in these areas would have chosen western-style liberalism had free choice been allowed. It was thus not very surprising that when the Soviet Union allowed Eastern Europe to go its own way in the late 1980s, Hungary embraced international human rights. This orientation came about not only because of a need to prove that it belonged in the Council of Europe, and perhaps the European Union and NATO, but also because of genuine domestic preferences.

Hungary has given special attention to minority rights in its foreign policy after the Cold War, given the number of ethnic Hungarians who reside in Romania, Slovakia, and Ukraine. Even while still officially communist, Hungary criticized its fellow communist neighbor, Romania, for its treatment of the Hungarian minority. Hungary thus broke the unwritten rule that European communist regimes did not criticize each other on human rights issues. Since adopting liberal democracy, Budapest has continued to make the relationship with ethnic Hungarians abroad the centerpiece of its foreign policy. This has led to periodic friction with especially Romania, which fears too much local autonomy, if not separatism, for the sizable Hungarian minority. Budapest has found more satisfactory relations on this issue with Ukraine and Slovakia. On other human rights issues Hungary generally behaved for a time as any other European state, voting with the western group at the UN and accepting regional human rights obligations through the Council of Europe.

With the election of Viktor Orban in 2010, however, one saw a new attack on many liberal values and an open defense of certain illiberal values. Nationalism and religion were emphasized, refugee flows and European regional authorities were criticized. German Chancellor Merkel and her early welcoming policy toward Muslim refugees were denigrated. Nice things were said about autocrats like Putin in Russia and Erdogan in Turkey. This orientation played well in the less-urban and less-educated parts of the nation. Thus the Hungarian voters put in power the equivalent of Donald Trump in the USA or Marine le Pen in France. A type of illiberal democracy manifested itself. Foreign policy was largely devoted to narrow self-interests and promotion of national identity and prestige.

Russia presents a fascinating study of human rights and foreign policy. Whether as Russia or the Soviet Union, this area has long manifested a conflicted political culture. The dominant aspect was and is authoritarian, illiberal, Slavic, and suspicious of the West. The tradition of legal rights, especially individual rights, was very weak – especially in the *mir* as a rural, organic community in which law and individualism were insignificant. But at least from the time of Peter the Great there was a weaker, more liberal aspect to Russian culture. These liberal tendencies were encouraged in the Gorbachev and Yeltsin eras, yet one does not change the dominant culture by simply issuing legal documents and making proclamations. Russian policies, for example, directed toward suppression of a separatist movement in Chechnya were clearly brutal. Russia under Putin has undermined an independent media. The legislature and the courts do not provide any meaningful checks and balances on him. Critics have been jailed, their property confiscated, and sometimes killed.

There is a part of the Russian political class that longs for the Stalinist days of order and superpower status, and believes that human rights equates with pornography, criminality, and foreign religious sects. Putin is now part of this faction. There is another part of the political class that is more sympathetic to human rights,[54] but believes the West has not treated the new Russia with proper sensitivity and respect. In the view of this circle, Russia struggles to determine whether it should follow the US lead on certain human rights issues, align with a different European position, or strike out on its own. Like Hungary, Russia has given special attention to minority rights in foreign policy. Given the large number of ethnic Russians and Russian speakers in its "near abroad," and given its own problems with separatist movements, Russian foreign policy has been highly active on ethno-territorial-linguistic disputes in many former areas of Soviet control.

Like Orban in Hungary, Putin now stresses religion (the Orthodox Russian Church) and national achievements (whether under the Tzars or communism). He sees Western democracies and their international organizations as inimical to Russia. He does not hesitate to align with reactionary foreign elements (Assad in Syria or Russian-speaking separatists in eastern Ukraine). Despite repressive policies at home and abroad, he sees himself and Russia as providing a moral third way in world affairs between the decadent West and an emerging Asia led by China.

Interestingly, Putin was not especially anti-USA or anti-West circa 1991 – despite having been a routine agent in the Soviet secret security force. For a time, he was on the staff of the elected mayor of Saint Petersburg (formerly Petrograd), and worked to arrange foreign investment from Western nations. He was elevated to high office by the elected Boris Yeltsin who regarded him as (a) dependable and (b) not likely to

---

[54] See further Anatoly L. Adamishin and Richard Schifter, *Human Rights, Perestroika, and the End of the Cold War* (Washington: United States Institute of Peace, 2009). This book is the joint effort of two diplomats, the first in Moscow and the second in Washington, who negotiated human rights issues toward the end of the USSR.

probe into possible corruption by Yeltsin's family and associates. But with NATO expanding its membership eastward and engaging in regime change in Libya, and with the USA backing anti-Russian leaders in Georgia and Ukraine, Putin clearly shifted to a more antagonistic view of the West and its human rights rhetoric.

One could look at any number of other states and their foreign policies on human rights, from India to South Africa, from Canada to Costa Rica. Most such inquiries prove intriguing. France, origin of the 1789 Declaration on the Rights of Man and the state most like the USA in seeing itself as a universal model for human rights, presents a long history of support for corrupt and authoritarian rulers in Africa, not to mention a policy of torture and summary execution during the Algerian war of 1954–1962. Costa Rica, with some similarity to the USA, sees itself made up of an exceptionally good and peaceful people who therefore have a special and progressive role to play particularly in hemispheric affairs. However, the moralizing of Oscar Arias, like that of Jimmy Carter, was not always well received by other Latin American heads of state.

India, the most populous democracy, has become much more defensive and low-key about international human rights matters.[55] This is so despite the fact that India was one of the first states to challenge apartheid in South Africa, India having many nationals there. In part Indian skepticism about international action stems from an awareness of certain domestic problems – including brutal treatment of terror suspects involved in the disputed region of Kashmir. Also, the collapse of the Soviet Union, its major strategic partner, reduced its standing in international relations. Its foray into Sri Lankan ethnic struggles under Rajiv Gandhi, by way of an Indian "peacekeeping" force which itself engaged in atrocities, proved disastrous, both personally and politically speaking, contributing to the current Indian low profile.

In general, India now tends to favor the principle of state sovereignty when in conflict with international action for human rights, believing that the US-led Security Council has intervened too much in the affairs of the governments of the global south. The election of a clearly nationalistic government in 1998 intensified these trends. In 2011 it was still the case that India, given its colonial experience, was very sensitive about the USA or any other state engaging in public criticism of its human rights record. Some analysts were not at all surprised that India abstained on the UN Security Council vote regarding use of force in Libya in 2011.

---

[55] See further R. Suresh, *Foreign Policy and Human Rights: An Indian Perspective* (Guragon: Madhav Books, 2009).

The election of Narendra Modi in 2014 did not lead to any change in the downgrading of human rights in Indian foreign policy. Rather, Modi himself had been denied a visa to enter the USA because of his role in Hindu pogroms against Muslims. He was associated with a Hindu chauvinistic political movement that sought to center Indian national identity on Hinduism, which predictably was rejected by Muslims and secularists, among other non-Hindus. He emphasized economic reform and growth rather than highlighting attempts to deal with the myriad human rights problems in India. India remained a vibrant democracy with fundamental civil and political rights, but para-doxically that did not mean an absence of pressing human rights prob-lems of varying natures.[56]

Governments in South Africa emerging from all-race elections have identified strongly with international human rights, and – along with El Salvador – have pioneered official "truth commissions" to reveal the facts of past repression but without criminal prosecution for political crime. The Mandela government, however, was heavily involved in fairly disas-trous gun-running in the Great Lakes region of Africa, and also defied UN sanctions on dictatorial Libya in order to repay Libyan support for the anti-apartheid movement. The Thabo Mbeki government that followed Mandela was certainly not at the forefront of the struggle against HIV/AIDS, even though that affliction was debilitating many African nations. The Mbeki team also was reluctant to press hard for decisive change in neighboring Zimbabwe where an aging Robert Mugabe was running the country into the ground with major human rights abuses over considerable time. It seems South African policy was based on fear of increased refugee flows into the country if Mugabe fell. Then the Jacob Zuma government seemed wildly inconsistent in its international human rights policies.

Canadian foreign policy has been generally progressive on rights abroad.[57] It is well known that Ottawa has long prided itself on its record especially in UN peacekeeping – including second-generation or com-plex peacekeeping that includes human rights dimensions. Canada, for example, joined the USA in practical efforts to bring liberal democracy to Haiti, no easy task given the history and impoverishment of that country. Canada has also been a leader in regard to a ban on anti-personnel landmines, and the creation of a UN criminal court. Limitations of space, however, compel us to move on.

---

[56] For a concise overview, see www.hrw.org/world-report/2016/country-chapters/india.
[57] The standard work in this area is Robert O. Mathews and R. C. Pratt, eds., *Human Rights and Canadian Foreign Policy* (Montreal: McGill-Queen's Press, 1988).

Conclusions

During the era of the League of Nations, this chapter could not have been written. The League Covenant did not mention universal human rights, and states did not often address human rights in their foreign policies. There was some international humanitarian law for armed conflicts, and states did sometimes display humanitarian policies dealing with refugees, the nature of rule in colonies (via the League Mandates Commission), and other social subjects. But as late as 1944 human rights remained essentially a national rather than international matter (with the exception of the minority treaties for some Central European states in the interwar years, and international law governing aliens).

Increasingly all states, whatever their political character, have to deal with internationally recognized human rights. International relations or world politics is not what it once was. Much of international law codifies liberal principles of human rights. But in addressing human rights, states bring with them their national history, character, self-image, and nationalism. These national traits cause states to be more or less active on human rights issues, more or less confident and assertive, more or less defensive. This history, plus their contemporary situation and how they define their interests, causes states to take different slants or emphases on rights in foreign policy. When addressing human rights, the USA, for example, consistent with its national tradition, does not focus on socio-economic rights but rather on personal freedom. The Netherlands tries especially hard to link development assistance with rights behavior, and has a special focus on Indonesia. The Hungarians and Russians tend to emphasize minority rights for their ethnic and/or linguistic compatriots abroad, even as they play fast and loose with many human rights at home. And so on.

It is significant that even states without a strong rights tradition or legal culture have been propelled to direct more attention to rights in foreign policy. This is true, for example, for both Japan and Russia. Even Iran, if it wishes to be accepted as a full or normal member of the international community, has found that it needs to respond to international criticism by addressing defects in Iranian society, even if it does so under the cover of a discussion of religious law rather than the secular law of international human rights.

Without downplaying the importance of international organizations, private non-profit groups, and even multinational corporations, it is still state foreign policy that plays a very large role in the promotion and protection of international human rights. So with regard to universal human rights and state foreign policy, it is both true and false to say: *la plus ça change, la plus c'est la même chose* (the more things change, the more they remain the same). True, because despite the fact that we have change in favor of human rights norms in international relations, we still have to deal with nationalism and national interests. False, because we do have real changes in foreign policy concerning human rights; there is much more attention to international human rights in 2017 compared with the foreign policies of 1897, 1907, or 1937.

Case study: French foreign policy, Ivory Coast, and human rights

Ivory Coast is a West African state of about 22 million persons that is rich in natural resources such as cocoa, coffee, and palm oil. It was a French colony from the 1890s until independence in 1960. For the first thirty years of independence the country was ruled by the strongman Felix Houphouet-Boigny, in close cooperation with France. The latter maintained a military base in the country, the nation being the hub of economic and political activity for French-speaking West Africa. Some analysts thought independence in 1960 brought little change in substance, such was the continuing influence of France.

The retirement and then death in 1993 of Houphouet-Boigny was followed by movement toward multiparty democracy, interspersed by coups and autocratic rule. As in other places, in Ivory Coast political parties and political leaders were frequently associated with particular ethnic and sectarian groups. By the late 1990s, as political leaders developed identity politics in order to mobilize voters and attract donor support, the country could be superficially seen as politically split between the largely Islamic north (perhaps 35–40 percent of the population) and the largely Christian south (of approximately the same percentage of the population), with other local beliefs covering the rest of the people. There were perhaps sixty ethnic groups in the country. Some analysts believe that sectarian divisions do not run deep and that a strong element of economic pragmatism and political opportunism are strong factors in public life.

In the widespread political violence that erupted in 2002 in the wake of disputed elections and various politico-legal maneuvers, France beefed up its military forces in the country in order to act as a stabilizing force. These French forces acted in tandem with first the troops, largely Nigerian, from ECOWAS (Economic Community of West African States), and then later from the United Nations. As of 2004 the UN field operation was given a Chapter VII mandate under the UN Charter, meaning that it was not just a peacekeeping force engaging in armed

diplomacy, but rather was authorized to take enforcement action pursu-
ant to a variety of goals pertaining to human rights as well as security.
French troops acted as a rapid reaction force, taking on the more difficult
military missions that the UN forces had difficulty handling alone.

A period of uneasy but relative calm from about 2003 was undermined
by a disputed election in late 2010. The then President, Laurent Gbagbo,
whose political base was largely in the south, refused to leave office after
international election monitors agreed that his opponent, Alassane
Ouattara, a Muslim from the north, had won the 2010 election. With
remarkable international consensus running against Gbagbo, various
public and private intermediaries tried to resolve the dispute. They
appealed to the principle of R2P, the responsibility to protect, arguing
that, if a national government was unable or unwilling to protect
the human rights of the nation, outside parties had a duty to become
involved.

Despite all the international activity, during early 2011 Ivory Coast was
once again caught up in widespread violence. Both the forces loyal to
Gbagbo and those supporting Ouattara were reported to have committed
atrocities. There were many more political deaths in 2011 than had been
the case in 2002.

In this violent context French military forces teamed with the UN
forces to bring intense military pressure on Gbagbo, hunkered down in
the presidential residence in Abidjan. The French government of Nicolas
Sarkozy (teaming with Nigeria) had successfully pushed the UN Security
Council to adopt a mandate (SC Resolution 1975) authorizing states and
UN units to utilize "all necessary measures" to protect civilians in Ivory
Coast. This was similar to French policy in Liberia at approximately the
same time, in which French (and British) leadership resulted in Security
Council approval for a limited if unclear military action in Libya. In both
Libya and Ivory Coast, a UN enforcement mandate was worded in
humanitarian terms but was applied for political purposes – namely to
affect the central government. In both cases Russia and some other states
protested how France and others interpreted UNSC resolutions. In the
case of Ivory Coast, the combined effect of actions by UN and French
troops, and militias loyal to Ouattara, led to the capture of Gbagbo and
the tenuous control of the state apparatus by the Ouattara movement.

This case demonstrates above all the difficulty of establishing firm
generalizations and expectations about western democratic foreign policy
and democracy abroad. France's important role in supporting the duly
elected Ouattara was at variance with its past support for many autocratic
factions in Africa including the genocidal militant Hutus in Rwanda. The
Sarkozy team continued to defer to autocrats in half a dozen African

states even after its forceful role in Ivory Coast. But this inconsistency was not significantly different from the United Kingdom or the United States, *inter alia*, who continued close relations with (and arms sales to) Saudi Arabia and other autocratic regimes, even as they supported democratic change in Egypt and Tunisia. Local pressures for democratic change varied, as did media coverage of those pressures, as did state conception of its national interests. Consequently these factors, plus others such as historical relations, caused all states' foreign policy to be inconsistent but often important regarding democracy promotion.

Discussion questions

- Is there a theoretical or otherwise systematic reason why different states come up with different emphases and interpretations of international human rights standards? Even among liberal democratic states of the OECD, such as the United States, Britain, the Netherlands, and Japan, there are major differences in their approaches to international human rights: why is this?
- In general, are states paying more or less attention to human rights through foreign policy? Why? What does it mean for human rights that a "new nationalism" is spreading around the world?
- Why is it that democracies like India and the United Kingdom take very different approaches to questions of international human rights?
- Why is it that countries like France and the United States, which have a long national history of attention to human rights, repeatedly find it so difficult to apply international standards to themselves – even though the West has had great influence on the evolution of international human rights, both regional and global?
- Which non-Western states have a relatively good record on human rights in foreign policy, and why?
- Is human rights in foreign policy primarily a matter of the executive branch, or do legislatures (and public opinion, with interest groups) play an important role?

SUGGESTIONS FOR FURTHER READING

Baehr, Peter, and Monique Castermans-Holleman, *The Role of Human Rights in Foreign Policy* (New York: Palgrave Macmillan, 2004). Thorough text examining the various aspects of the role human rights plays in state foreign policy, with particular attention to US and Dutch foreign policy.

Brysk, Alison, *Global Good Samaritans: Human Rights as Foreign Policy* (Oxford and New York: Oxford University Press, 2009). A very good study of the foreign policies of Sweden, Canada, Costa Rica, the Netherlands, Japan, and South Africa on the subject of human rights.

Carothers, Thomas, *Assessing Democracy: The Case of Romania* (Washington: Carnegie Endowment, 1996). Shows how difficult it is to evaluate US foreign policy and democracy assistance, even in one country.

Curtis, Gerard, ed., *Japan's Foreign Policy After the Cold War: Coping with Change* (New York: M. E. Sharpe, 1997). Shows the changing nature of Japanese foreign policy, with some attention to human rights.

Egeland, Jan, *Impotent Large State – Potent Small State: Potentialities and Limitations of Human Rights Objectives in the Foreign Policies of the United States* (Oslo: Norwegian University Press, 1988). Argues that during the Cold War Norway had more room to maneuver for human rights in foreign policy than the United States, mainly because of US security obligations.

Forsythe, David, *The Politics of Prisoner Abuse: The US and Enemy Prisoners After 9/11* (Cambridge: Cambridge University Press, 2011). An overview of the policy by the George W. Bush Administration to gain intelligence by abuse of prisoners, and how the policy spun out of control because of poor design and weak oversight. Also covers the similarities and differences by the Obama Administration on this subject.

Forsythe, David, and Patrice McMahon, *American Exceptionalism Reconsidered: US Foreign Policy, Human Rights, and World Order* (New York and London: Routledge, 2016). A critique of a central concept in much US foreign policy decision making, with attention to both elite decisions and public opinion. Compares the US record to that of the BRICs.

Gillies, David, *Between Principle and Practice: Human Rights in North–South Relations* (Montreal: McGill-Queen's University Press, 1996). A good comparative study of the role of human rights in foreign policy among several developed countries, when dealing with certain less developed countries. Shows how difficult it is to construct a principled foreign policy when trying to blend human rights and support for development.

Goldberg, Jeffrey, "The Obama Doctrine," *The Atlantic* (April 2016), www.theatlantic.com/magazine/archive/2016/04/the-obama-doctrine/471525/. A candid interview with the President, who defends a case-by-case approach to international problems, along with selective attention to human rights.

Hunt, Michael H., *Ideology and US Foreign Policy* (New Haven: Yale University Press, 1987). Argues that while the United States sees itself as an exceptionally good nation, it has done a great deal of harm in the world through its racism and commitment to the *status quo*. Argues for a reduced US role in the world, even at the cost of less attention to liberal causes like international human rights.

Kissinger, Henry, *Diplomacy* (New York: Simon & Schuster, 1994). As in his other modern works, Kissinger is critical of liberal views of foreign policy and international relations, which he calls Wilsonianism, and argues that the United States must beware of liberal crusades that go beyond American power and wisdom. He is suspicious of the validity of universal standards pertaining to democracy and human rights, believing them to have evolved in special western circumstances. But he says pure realism is not sustainable in American foreign policy.

Mathews, Robert O., and R. C. Pratt, eds., *Human Rights and Canadian Foreign Policy* (Montreal: McGill-Queen's Press, 1988). The definitive work for its time.

McGovern, Mike, *Making War in Cote d'Ivoire* (London: Hurst Publishing, 2010). An extremely well-researched study by a former member of the International Crisis Group dealing with Ivory Coast.

Mertus, Julie, *Bait and Switch: Human Rights and US Foreign Policy* (New York: Routledge, 2004). Based on interviews with numerous current and former US officials, the author finds that international human rights norms predispose Washington to talk about human rights, while human rights considerations remain frequently absent from US foreign policy.

Power, Samantha, *"A Problem From Hell": America and the Age of Genocide* (New York: Basic Books, 2002). Examines the United States' response to genocide throughout the twentieth century, concluding that America's record has been consistently poor.

Renouard, Joe, *Human Rights in American Foreign Policy: From the 1960s to the Soviet Collapse* (Philadelphia: University of Pennsylvania Press, 2016). An accurate and detailed history of the subject. More narrative than creatively conceptual.

Sikkink, Kathryn, *Mixed Signals: U.S. Human Rights Policy and Latin America* (New York: Century Foundation, 2004). A scholarly overview of US human rights policy in most of the Western Hemisphere, stressing the mixed record emanating from Washington. Much rights talk is not always followed by consistent influence on behalf of that rhetoric.

Vogelgesang, Sandy, *American Dream, Global Nightmare: The Dilemma of US Human Rights Policy* (New York: Norton, 1980). One of the first studies of human rights and US foreign policy suggests the difficulty of establishing a foreign policy that is both principled and consistent.

Zakaria, Fareed, "The Rise of Illiberal Democracy," *Foreign Affairs*, 76, 6 (November–December 1997), 22–43. An important article noting the difference between liberal and illiberal democracy. Certain genuinely elected governments then engage in tyranny by, *inter alia*, persecuting minorities. Liberal democracies by contrast are characterized not just by free and fair elections, but by rule of law, independent courts, and limits on majority rule.

7 Non-governmental organizations and human rights

By now it should be clear that states, acting frequently through international organizations and/or diplomatic conferences, produce the international law of human rights by concluding treaties and developing customary law. The resulting law obligates states, primarily. In Chapter 6 we examined state foreign policy against the background of the international law of human rights. But private actors can be important at both ends of this process, affecting legislation and implementation.[1]

This chapter starts with an analysis of non-governmental organizations and their advocacy of human rights ideas, which is directed both to the creation and application of human rights norms. Probably the best known of these groups is Amnesty International, but which over time may have lost some of its former status. This analysis is eventually set within the confines of social movements. Such actors push for more liberalism in the form of human rights protection in international relations. The chapter then turns to those private groups that are mostly called relief or development agencies, or sometimes PVOs (private voluntary agencies) or VOLAGs (voluntary agencies). A classic example is Oxfam. These private actors are crucial especially for grass-roots action that directly or indirectly attends to social and economic rights. Most can be said to be liberal or pragmatic liberal actors, in that they emphasize policies for the betterment of individuals under legal norms, rather than emphasizing the collective national interests of states as pursued through the application of power. Chapter 8 addresses private for-profit actors, commonly called multinational or transnational corporations when they act across national borders.

---

[1] For an introductory overview, see Ann Marie Clark, "Nongovernmental Organizations: Overview," in David P. Forsythe, ed., *Encyclopedia of Human Rights* (New York: Oxford University Press, 2009), vol. IV, 87–96. See also William Korey, *NGOs and the Universal Declaration of Human Rights: "A Curious Grapevine"* (New York: St. Martin's Press, 1998). See further Claude E. Welch, Jr., *NGOs and Human Rights: Promise and Performance* (Philadelphia: University of Pennsylvania Press, 2001).

Private advocacy for human rights

There are perhaps 250 private organizations consistently active across borders that take as their reason for being (*raison d'être*) the advocacy of some part of the international law of human rights and/or humanitarian affairs on a global basis.[2] From this group a handful have the requisite budget, contacts, expertise, and reputation to get the global traditional media and major governments to pay them at least periodic attention across a range of issues and situations: Amnesty International (AI), Human Rights Watch (HRW), the International Commission of Jurists, the International Federation for Human Rights, the International Committee of the Red Cross, Human Rights First, Lawyers Without Borders, Doctors Without Borders, Physicians for Human Rights, Anti-Slavery International, PEN (Poets, Essayists, Novelists), Article 19 (devoted to freedom of expression), etc. When there is an international meeting touching on human rights, private groups that identify themselves as working primarily for international law, peace, world order, and women's issues, etc. may swell the numbers of active advocacy groups to several hundred – 200 to 800 might be an expected range. The core advocacy groups are usually called NGOs or INGOS – non-governmental organizations or international non-governmental organizations. A related phenomenon is a governmentally created, quasi-private human rights organization, or GONGO. Some GONGOs have been surprisingly active and independent, as in Indonesia and Mexico.

The oldest and best-funded human rights NGOs are based in the West and concern themselves primarily with civil and political rights in peacetime and international humanitarian law in war or similar situations. Western societies have manifested the civil rights, private wealth, leisure time and value structures that allow for the successful operation of major human rights NGOs. To advocate human rights via a truly independent and dynamic NGO, there must be respect for civil rights and a civic society to start with. With the spread of liberal democracy and more open societies after the Cold War, the number of NGOs at least spasmodically active on some human rights issues has greatly increased. But the percentage of human rights groups, relative to the total number of NGOs active in international relations, has remained rather stable.[3]

---

[2] Jackie Smith and Ron Pagnucco with George A. Lopez, "Globalizing Human Rights: The Work of Transnational Human Rights NGOs in the 1990s," *Human Rights Quarterly*, 20, 2 (May 1998), 379–412.

[3] Margaret E. Keck and Kathryn Sikkink, *Activists Beyond Borders: Advocacy Networks in International Politics* (Ithaca: Cornell University Press, 1998), 11.

Here we should note the important role of private foundations in their financial support of NGOs, individuals, and programs active for internationally recognized human rights. According to one important source, in 2013 there were 806 funders across forty-six nations, which gave a total of $2.3 billion for various human rights causes.[4] The Open Society and the Ford Foundation, both located in the USA, ranked first and second in money contributed. Funders were concentrated in the North Atlantic area, but 18 percent were headquartered outside this area. Contrary to some expectations, funds were directed to a wide variety of human rights and not just to civil and political legal rights. Women's rights and general health and well-being rights fared well. For a variety of reasons, many grants were expended in North America rather than in the global south.

Many NGOs based in the global south manifest a different agenda from those based in the north or northwest. The former tend to emphasize the right to development and many socioeconomic rights, without neglecting entirely civil and political rights. Some of the better-known NGOs based in the richer countries, like AI and HRW, have adopted mission statements that now pay some attention to socioeconomic rights, on the argument that they do indeed impinge on civil and political rights. But for these latter, their emphasis remains on civil-political rights and humanitarian affairs (including humanitarian relief).[5]

Complicating the analysis is the fact that other private groups that exist for secular or religious purposes may become international human rights actors at particular times and for particular causes. The Catholic Church in its various manifestations and the World Council of Churches, *inter alia*, are examples of religious groups that fit this mold.[6] As noted in the previous chapter, some faith-based groups, for example, teamed with some secular human rights groups to help achieve greater attention to the right to religious freedom and the right to be free from religious

---

[4] See http://humanrightsfunding.org/report-2016/.
[5] For a discussion of the lack of effective lobbying by NGOs such as HRW regarding socioeconomic rights, see David P. Forsythe and Eric Heinze, "On the Margins of the Human Rights Discourse: International Welfare Rights and Foreign Policy," in Rhoda Howard-Hassmann and Claude E. Welch, Jr., eds., *Economic Rights in Canada and the United States: Sleeping Under Bridges* (Philadelphia: University of Pennsylvania Press, 2006). Aryeh Neier, long-time Executive Director of Human Rights Watch, was strongly opposed to broadening the focus of HRW so as to include socioeconomic rights. See Aryeh Neier, *Taking Liberties: Four Decades in the Struggle for Rights* (New York: Public Affairs, 2003), introduction, xxx. For a discussion about NGOs and socioeconomic rights, see *Human Rights Quarterly*, 26, 4 (November, 2004), 866–881.
[6] See further Claude E. Welch, Jr., "Mobilizing Morality: The World Council of Churches and Its Program to Combat Racism, 1969–1994," *Human Rights Quarterly*, 23, 4 (November 2001), 863–910.

discrimination in the recent past, at least in US foreign policy.[7] Labor unions that normally focus on domestic "bread and butter" issues, like the AFL-CIO in the United States, may – and increasingly do – have a private foreign policy on rights questions. Labor unions, in order to try to protect labor wages and benefits in their home country, may find it necessary to address labor rights in foreign countries. "Ethnic lobbies" such as "the Greek lobby" or "the China lobby" may and occasionally do take up human rights issues of concern. There are numerous national civil rights groups, such as the American Civil Liberties Union or the Center for Constitutional Rights in the United States, that occasionally turn to international rights issues under the 1949 Geneva Conventions or the 1984 Convention against Torture. Given the existence of transnational issues, or the penetration of international relations into domestic affairs, it is increasingly difficult to separate national from international human rights groups. A good example was the ACLU interest in US policy toward "enemy detainees" during the George W. Bush Administrations, leading to a focus on international humanitarian law (aka laws of war) among other concerns.

Increasingly this amalgam of private actors is referred to as civic action groups, or as making up civil society. In global civil society, there was a great variety of private, non-profit groups, some of them clearly opposed to internationally recognized human rights.[8] Some of these groups seemed to generate so much influence on certain issues that some observers saw a "power shift" in international relations, with governments becoming less important and private groups decidedly more important.[9] On various issues the human rights NGOs could sometimes be influential, without doubt. Under CEDAW (Convention on the Elimination of Discrimination against Women), when governments submitted the required report about national implementation, the International Women's Rights Action Watch submitted a "shadow report" usually providing a more honest evaluation of the situation. This shadow report was then used in subsequent deliberations in the review process.

Along with the growing numbers, salience, and maybe even influence of civil society organizations came growing criticism. If one wanted to contest the activism of Human Rights Watch, one might say that it was

---

[7] Allen D. Hertzke, *Freeing God's Children: The Unlikely Alliance for Global Human Rights* (London and New York: Rowman & Littlefield, 2004).
[8] See especially A. Florini, *The Third Force: The Rise of Transnational Civil Society* (Washington: Carnegie Endowment, 2000); and Michael Edwards, *Civil Society* (Cambridge: Polity, 2004). In general, see the *Global Civil Society Yearbook*, published by the London School of Economics and Political Science.
[9] Jessica Tuchman Mathews, "Power Shift," *Foreign Affairs*, 76, 1 (Jan.–Feb. 1997), 50–66.

elitist, non-democratic, non-transparent, and unaccountable. It was true that aside from AI, most human rights NGOs were not mass-membership organizations and held no elections for their leaders. They were indeed self-appointed.

On the other hand, there was the view that arguments about democracy and accountability for governments were inappropriate for human rights NGOs.[10] Human rights NGOs might be perceived as legitimate, or playing a correct role, if they impartially and neutrally worked in a non-partisan way to advance norms that had been approved by states. And they might be considered accountable if they were transparent about the sources and uses of their funds, and how they reached their advocacy positions. It was illogical to argue that NGOs were illegitimate when they were approved to attend UN and other IGO meetings. The International Committee of the Red Cross, technically a private Swiss civic association, was even recognized – and given rights and duties – in the international humanitarian law approved by states.

Because traditional international human rights groups may indeed join with a variety of other actors to deal with particular human rights situations or issues, some prefer to speak of movements, coalitions, or networks rather than separate organizations.[11] Thus it was said that there was a movement to ban landmines, or a movement in support of an international criminal court. According to Keck and Sikkink, such movements may include NGOs, local social movements, foundations, the media, churches, trade unions, consumer organizations, intellectuals, parts of intergovernmental organizations, and parts of national or sub-national governments.[12] Hence it was said sometimes that the movement in support of a UN criminal court was made up of "like-minded states" plus over 200 human rights NGOs plus elements of the communications media, along with individuals. The foreign minister of Canada, in his efforts to achieve a strong international criminal court, wrote in 1998: "With lessons learned from the successful campaign for a treaty banning land mines, we are engaging not only political leaders but also

---

[10] For background, see M. Edwards, *NGO Rights and Responsibilities: A New Deal for Global Governance* (London: Foreign Policy Center, 2000).

[11] See, e.g., Jackie Smith, Charles Chatfield, and Ron Pagnucco, eds., *Transnational Social Movements and Global Politics: Solidarity Beyond the State* (Syracuse: Syracuse University Press, 1997); and Keck and Sikkink, *Activists Beyond Borders*.

[12] On the important but little-studied matter of funding of NGOs by charitable foundations, see Jay Ovsiovitch, "Feeding the Watchdogs: Philanthropic Support for Human Rights NGOs," *Buffalo Human Rights Law Review*, 4 (1998), 341–364.

nongovernmental organizations, media and citizens around the world."[13] Such movements or coalitions were indeed made up of diverse partners.[14]

Increasingly individuals or organizations that operate websites on the internet may be part of a coalition active on one or more human rights issues. The collection and spreading of information about human rights on the internet was a relatively new development in the 1990s that had the potential for considerable impact. For example, the International Monitor Institute started documenting human rights violations in the Balkans, moved to providing information on war crimes trials from the former Yugoslavia, and then created the Rwanda Archive.[15] This and other relevant electronic activity fed into the Rome diplomatic conference of July 1998 that approved a statute for an international criminal court.

In the so-called Arab Spring of 2011, in which grassroots demonstrations broke out across the Arab world and Iran demanding more democracy and human rights, social networking and social media utilizing instruments such as Facebook and Twitter were central. A number of local and international NGOs were active, and the response of governments was crucial. But much networked activism arose through previously unknown informal groups. An individual in Tunisia set himself ablaze in frustrated reaction to economic distress in the context of repressive governmental policies. This incident was transmitted widely among individuals not only in Tunisia but then in Egypt. Demonstrations in Egypt then affected other protests in Bahrain, Libya, Syria, Jordan, Yemen, Morocco, and elsewhere. As far away as China, the nervous government cracked down on dissidents, human rights activists, journalists, and others, fearing that knowledge of street protests in the Middle East would generate similar demands for liberalization in China. The so-called mainstream media also transmitted images and played a role in helping to set the policy agenda of various governments. But in Egypt, for example, some of the early protests were led and organized by

---

[13] Lloyd Axworthy, "Without Justice, No Security for Ordinary People," *International Herald Tribune*, June 16, 1998, 6. See further Benjamin N. Schiff, *Building the International Criminal Court* (Cambridge: Cambridge University Press, 2008), for a good analysis of the interaction of states and NGOs.

[14] See further Henry J. Steiner, *Diverse Partners: Non Governmental Organizations and the Human Rights Movement* (Cambridge, MA: Harvard Law College, 1991, for the Harvard Law School Human Rights Program and the Human Rights Internet). See also Laurie Wiseberg, "Human Rights Non-Governmental Organizations," in *The Role of Non-Governmental Organizations in the Promotion and Protection of Human Rights* (Leiden: Stichting NJCM-Boekerig, 1989); and Keck and Sikkink, *Activists Beyond Borders*.

[15] See http://library.duke.edu/rubenstein/findingaids/imi/.

secular liberals utilizing the internet and cell phones, who then had to face competition from certain highly organized private groups such as the Muslim Brotherhood for control and direction of the movement. A key organizer of the early demonstrations was an employee of Google "on leave" from his job. The Arab street, loosely linked by social media, forced governmental change in Tunisia and Egypt, destabilized Yemen, Syria, and Bahrain, threatened the *status quo* in Jordan and Morocco, and led to civil war in Libya with major outside intervention by NATO and various states.[16]

The process

If we focus on the advocacy of traditional human rights organizations, either as separate entities or part of a network or movement, it is reasonably clear what these groups do.[17] First, the bedrock of all their activity is the collection of accurate information and its timely dissemination. For a group to generate influence on governments and other public authorities like the UN Human Rights Council, it must manifest a reputation for accurate reporting and dissemination of information. States do not exist primarily to report the truth. They exist primarily to exercise power on behalf of national interests as they see them. Relevant is the old maxim about the role of ambassadors: they are sent abroad to lie for their country. Private human rights groups, on the other hand, do not fare very well if they do not develop a reputation for accurate reporting of human rights information.

Amnesty International has developed a general reputation since its founding in 1961 for accurate reporting primarily about prisoners of conscience – those imprisoned for their political and social views expressed mostly non-violently – and about torture and the death penalty, *inter alia*.[18] It has a research staff in London of about 320 persons

---

[16] See Sydney G. Tarrow, *Power in Movement: Social Movements and Contentious Politics*, 3rd edn. (Cambridge: Cambridge University Press, 2011). For further background see John Lannon, Steven F. Hick, and Edward F. Halpin, "Internet," in *Encyclopedia of Human Rights*, vol. III, 182–194. See further Chapter 9, this volume, covering the media and the Arab Spring.

[17] For a different approach, see Howard J. Tolley, Jr., *The International Commission of Jurists: Global Advocates for Human Rights* (Philadelphia: University of Pennsylvania Press, 1994).

[18] AI has manifested internal debate about its proper focus. Traditionalists want it to concentrate on a narrow range of civil rights, while others want it to broaden its focus and activities. The basic identity of the organization has been the subject of disagreement. See especially Stephen Hopgood, *Keepers of the Flame: Understanding Amnesty International* (Ithaca: Cornell University Press, 2006).

(plus about 100 volunteers) that is much larger than the staff of the UN Human Rights Centre in Geneva.[19] AI's record is not perfect regarding accuracy, and in several instances it has had to retract public statements and reports, as when it got caught up in Kuwaiti propaganda in 1990 and erroneously repeated the story that invading Iraqi forces had torn incubators from premature Kuwaiti babies. But in general, AI is known for reliable reporting. One study found that AI's reporting was affected not just by the severity of human rights violations in a nation, but also by such factors as: the nation's links to US military assistance and prominence in the global media; and AI's opportunities to maximize advocacy, chance to shape norms, desire to raise its own profile, and other factors.[20]

The International Committee of the Red Cross (ICRC) has built up a reputation since 1863 for meticulously careful statements about prisoners of war and other victims of armed conflict and complex emergencies. Its staff of some 800 in Geneva, plus another 1,200 or so in the field (including those seconded from national Red Cross/Red Crescent societies but not counting those hired locally), is extremely hesitant to comment unless its delegates in the field can directly verify what has transpired. This author could find few examples in the ICRC's long history of false public statements about factual conditions. When they occurred, they arose from repeating information that had been obtained from other organizations but without sufficient verification. There seemed to be no examples in contemporary international relations of ICRC delegates misrepresenting what they had directly observed in conflict situations.[21]

While various actors may disagree with some of the policies that human rights NGOs advocate, very few scholars and responsible public officials challenge the record of accurate reporting over time by the most salient NGOs. The actors that do attack their veracity usually have

---

[19] For details about AI, see its News Service Release 108/99, March 1999.

[20] James Ron, et al., "Transnational Information Politics: NGO Human Rights Reporting, 1986–2000," *International Studies Quarterly*, 49, 3 (September 2005), 557–588. Some of the findings pertain to HRW as well as to AI.

[21] See further David P. Forsythe, *The Humanitarians: The International Committee of the Red Cross* (Cambridge: Cambridge University Press, 2005); and Forsythe and Barbara Ann J. Rieffer-Flanagan, *The International Committee of the Red Cross* (London and New York: Routledge, 2008; 2nd edn. 2016). This is not to say that the ICRC was never involved in controversy about public statements, only that its public statements were almost never shown to be at variance with facts "on the ground." If one goes back in history, however, say to the ICRC's involvement in the Italian invasion of what is now Ethiopia, it seems the ICRC had direct knowledge of Italian attacks on Red Cross hospitals, but chose not to speak about the matter and otherwise tilted toward Italy. See Ranier Baudendistel, *Between Bombs and Good Intentions: The International Committee of the Red Cross and the Italo-Ethiopian War, 1935–1936* (New York and Oxford: Berghahn Books, 2005).

something to hide. This was true of the Reagan Administration in the 1980s, which supported gross violations of human rights by its clients in Central America while trying to roll back what it saw as communism in especially El Salvador and Nicaragua. Reagan officials therefore attacked the veracity of AI, when it reported on brutal US clients, precisely because they found its reports – which were eventually proved accurate – irritating and embarrassing.[22] The George W. Bush Administration attacked the veracity and impartiality of AI when the latter criticized US politics toward enemy detainees after 9/11, but at the same time used AI reports to try to highlight the brutality of Saddam Hussein in Iraq. Israel has at times charged AI and Human Rights Watch with being biased against the Jewish state. So even democracies will at times seek to try to discredit the human rights organizations presenting critical reports.

Disturbingly, some democracies have tried to impede the work of human rights NGOs which receive donations from foreign sources. Israel has done so, requiring certain human rights groups to engage in onerous disclosure and reporting requirements if at least half of their funding comes from foreign governments. Several Palestinian human rights NGOs are affected that monitor Israeli policies in Occupied Territory, as their funding comes from European democracies. At the same time, the law is worded so that foreign donors who support Zionist settlement activity on the West Bank are exempt from the disclosure and reporting requirements.[23] In India, human rights groups must obtain a state license to receive foreign funds, and in 2016 this license was denied to twenty-five groups, including some human rights groups, on the vague grounds of "national interest." Human Rights Watch and Amnesty International protested.[24] Earlier we noted the idea of illiberal democracy, in which free and fair elections can lead to broad-scale violations of human rights and interference with their defenders.

One might expect this kind of restriction on human rights NGOs from autocratic Russia or Egypt, *inter alia*, and this type of interference has indeed transpired in those states. China also has been very active in blocking websites and otherwise restricting the efforts of various human rights groups. (Extensive attention is given to the internet and social media in Chapter 9.)

---

[22] See further David P. Forsythe, "Human Rights and US Foreign Policy: Two Levels, Two Worlds," in David Beetham, ed., *Politics and Human Rights* (Oxford: Blackwell, 1995), 111–130, especially 120.
[23] See www.hrw.org/news/2016/07/13/israel-law-targets-human-rights-groups.
[24] See www.hrw.org/news/2016/11/08/india-foreign-funding-law-used-harass-25-groups.

Disturbingly, by 2016, some seventy countries had created legal and other barriers to transnational NGO activity. Thus various private groups advocating for human rights and democracy were adversely affected. There seemed to be two causes of this shrinking space. One had illiberal governments intentionally trying to block liberal groups. But one also had a response to international terrorism which tried to shut off funding to civil society groups that might be seen as fronts helping to channel money to militants.[25]

Second, the human rights advocacy NGOs, on the basis of their analysis and dissemination of information, try to persuade public authorities to adopt new human rights standards or apply those already adopted. This activity can fairly be termed lobbying, but in order to preserve their non-political and tax-free status in most western societies, the groups tend to refer to this action as education.[26] The techniques are well known to students of politics. One can organize letter-writing campaigns, meet face-to-face with officials, arrange briefing sessions for staff assistants, submit editorials or "op ed" pieces to the print media, become a "talking head" on television, and so forth. A mass organization like AI will frequently combine a letter-writing campaign with elite contact. An organization like Human Rights Watch or the International Commission of Jurists, lacking a mass membership, eschews grassroots letter-writing and other grassroots lobbying and concentrates on reporting and then contact by the professional staff with public officials. The point is to press one's point of view, and of course its reasonableness under law, until it becomes controlling policy.

In this process prominent NGOs such as AI and HRW can be considered part of the "gatekeepers" who determine what claims are to be considered human rights claims, and with what prominence.[27] The HIV/AIDS pandemic was once considered strictly a public health issue. Water was once considered an economic or geographical issue.

---

[25] Thomas Carothers, "Closing Space for International Democracy and Human Rights Support," *Journal of Human Rights Practice*, 8, 3 (2016), 358–377.

[26] Claude E. Welch, Jr., makes the argument that human rights NGOs are not interest groups because they are altruistic rather than self-centered actors seeking interests for themselves. This is not persuasive. There are public interest groups, like Common Cause in the USA, that are similar to the international human rights NGOs. They lobby in traditional ways for values that benefit society in general, and particular persons or groups of persons along the way. Common Cause is a public interest group, and so is Amnesty International. They are both interest groups. Compare Welch, *Protecting Human Rights in Africa: Strategies and Roles of Non-Governmental Organizations* (Philadelphia: University of Pennsylvania Press, 1995), 44 and *passim*.

[27] See Clifford Bob, ed., *The International Struggle for New Human Rights* (Philadelphia: University of Pennsylvania Press, 2008).

Both, among other issues, were transformed into human rights issues, at least partially, by the decisions and actions of various agencies and personalities – including human rights NGOs. Also in this process one has to think carefully about whether it is always wise to press a concern as a human rights issue. If one does this with regard to gay rights (or LGBT rights) in many parts of the global south, one may wind up producing a backlash not just against gays, but against the very concept of internationally recognized human rights.[28] According to one study that focused on basic civil rights called rights to personal integrity (made up of the right to life, to freedom from forced disappearances and summary execution, and freedom from torture and inhumane treatment), international NGOs worked with domestic groups both to protect the space for action of the domestic groups and to bring about change in the policy of the target government.[29]

A danger for human rights NGOs is that in their single-minded pursuit of the issue of human rights, and with a concern for moral consistency, they may come across to public officials as moralistic, rigid, and politically naive.[30] Top foreign policy officials are challenged to manage the contradictions inherent in the effort to blend security, economic, ecological, and human rights concerns into one overall policy.[31] I noted in Chapter 6 how difficult it was for any state with multiple goals and interests, which means all of them, to present a consistent record on human rights issues. An NGO quest for perfect moral consistency may strike many foreign policy professionals as utopian. Only 11 percent of surveyed NGOs reported success in achieving policy change in favor of the human rights positions they advocated.[32]

The other side of the coin, however, is that many movements that seemed moralistic and utopian at the outset achieved changed policies and situations over time. Slavery, jousting, foot-binding, denial of the vote to women, and many other ideas were firmly institutionalized in

[28] Dennis Altman and Jonathan Symons, *Queer Wars: The New Global Polarization over Gay Rights* (Cambridge: Polity, 2016).

[29] Thomas Risse, et al., *The Power of Human Rights* (Cambridge: Cambridge University Press, 1999).

[30] See the debate in *Foreign Policy*, 105 (Winter 1996–1997), 91–106, between Aryeh Neier, formerly of Human Rights Watch, who stresses the importance of moral consistency for human rights NGOs ("The New Double Standard"), and Jeffrey Garten, a former US official, who stresses the many roads to progress and the necessity for flexible judgment in context – and by implication the tolerance of inconsistency ("Comment: The Need for Pragmatism"). This debate was covered in detail in Chapter 4.

[31] On foreign policy as the inherent management of contradictions, see Stanley Hoffmann, "The Hell of Good Intentions," *Foreign Policy*, 29 (Winter 1977–1978), 3–26.

[32] Smith, et al., "Globalizing Human Rights," 392.

many societies in the past. Being ideas, they were all subject to change, and all did change under relentless pressure over time.[33] What was utopian became practical. What was firmly entrenched, even central, became anachronistic. In the 1980s there were not many foreign policy officials, or human rights advocates for that matter, who thought a standing international criminal court was likely. By 1998–2002, it became a reality, although its future was uncertain.

Even agreement between governments and NGOs on general or long-term goals may lead to disputes about immediate tactics. In the 1990s, many human rights NGOs pressed for immediate action to arrest those indicted for gross violations of human rights in former Yugoslavia. Many US officials, supportive of international criminal prosecution in principle, but concerned about neo-isolationistic impulses within the public and Congress should there be US casualties, chose a policy on arrest that was more cautious than most human rights NGOs desired. Likewise during the 1990s, many human rights NGOs pressed for immediate sanctions on China in the context of continued systematic repression. Many US officials, desiring China's cooperation on a range of security, economic, and ecological issues, chose a policy on human rights in China that was more cautious and long term than many human rights NGOs desired. The broad responsibilities of top state officials even in liberal democracies guaranteed that from time to time their views of the best course of action would differ from those of human rights NGOs.

During 1999 AI bitterly denounced the brief and *pro forma* meeting that had been called to discuss the application of the Fourth Geneva Convention of 1949 to the territories occupied through war by Israel in the Middle East.[34] AI wanted a longer and more substantive meeting to deal with such questions as interrogation methods used by Israel on Palestinian detainees. But the Palestinian Authority, the United States, Israel, and finally most other participants decided that after the election of the Barak government in Israel, restarting a general peace process took precedence over criticizing Israel about issues in the territories. AI emphasized human rights issues in Israeli-controlled areas, whereas the key public authorities thought that peace and stable relations between the Israelis and Palestinians constituted the top priority, after which one could make better progress on other issues.

---

[33] On the role of ideas in international relations, see especially John Mueller, *Quiet Cataclysm: Reflections on the Recent Transformation of World Politics* (New York: Basic Books, 1995); and Judith Goldstein and Robert O. Keohane, eds., *Ideas and Foreign Policy: Beliefs, Institutions, and Political Change* (Ithaca: Cornell University Press, 1993).

[34] News Service Release 135/99, July 15, 1999.

In Syria in 2011, as the Arab Spring spread street protests demanding more democracy and attention to human rights in a state dictatorially ruled by the same family for some four decades, the US government deplored the killing of protestors. But, despite ample NGO and media reports about the extent of repression, it did not move decisively and quickly against the Assad regime. The Obama team worried about what governing arrangements might follow the fall of Assad and the implications particularly for Turkey, its NATO ally (which, like Syria, had an important Kurdish minority), and Israel (Assad in fact had not made much direct trouble for Israel for quite some time). So as deaths mounted primarily at the hands of the government's security forces, the Obama team did not intervene militarily or push NATO to do so, as had been the case in Libya where the US complicating concerns were fewer. It was also the case that, by the time of increasing street protests and fatalities in Syria, the USA was militarily bogged down in Libya whether acting unilaterally or via NATO under UN general mandate. Human rights NGOs maintained their singular focus on human rights in Syria, but as usual various governments including Israel looked at the situation with much concern for their version of national interest. (The Netanyahu government in Israel was not, in general, a strong advocate for more democracy and human rights in the Arab world. It knew that some of the dictators, such as Mubarak in Egypt, had been quiet friends, and that more genuinely democratic governments in the Arab world might result in more sympathy, at a minimum, for the plight of Palestinians in the West Bank and Gaza, and thus more difficulties for the Jewish state. Israel had good relations with the new strong man, al Sisi, whose regime was more repressive than Mubarak's.)

Traditional human rights NGOs cannot utilize two basic resources of many successful interest groups when dealing with public officials, because human rights NGOs possess neither the large or concentrated membership to threaten electoral punishment, nor the budgets to threaten the withholding of significant financial contributions. In the absence of these two resources, these NGOs fall back on accurate information and energetic lobbying by whatever name. These are combined with knowledge of the timing of key public policy decisions (easier in the legislative rather than the executive process of decision making), and the development of access to key policy makers and media outlets.

Third, traditional human rights NGOs publish information in the hopes of long-term education. This blends with the objective of influencing policy in the short term through dissemination. Today's education may become the context for tomorrow's policy making. Those educated today may be the policy makers of tomorrow. Virtually all of the traditional human rights NGOs manifest an active and extensive publishing program. Human Rights Watch has a publishing agreement with Yale University Press. Most of the human rights NGOs have a line in their budget for publishing books, brochures, reports, etc. They all make use of the internet to disseminate their information. They wish to raise the consciousness of both policy makers and the attentive public, so as to provide a better environment for their lobbying efforts.

The issue of publication to create and maintain a supportive political environment for human rights policy is crucial, whether one pictures it as part of grassroots lobbying or long-term education. We have already noted that in the USA in the 1990s, American public opinion in general tended to support pragmatic internationalism but not so much moral internationalism.[35] That is to say, American public opinion was supportive of an active foreign policy on trade and other issues such as interdicting illegal drugs from abroad, as long as some direct connection could be shown to the betterment of American society. But where projected foreign policies seemed to be based on morality divorced from self-interest, as was the case with ending starvation in Somalia, or contesting genocide in Rwanda, American public opinion was not so supportive if perceived national interests had to be sacrificed – e.g., the deaths of American soldiers. In this type of political environment, private human rights groups regularly bemoaned their lack of ability to significantly and consistently influence foreign policy and international relations.[36] This type of pragmatic context worked to the advantage of those business and labor organizations that advocated business as usual and the downgrading of human rights concerns to the extent that they interfered with international trade. Self-interest being the strong factor that it was, the Executive Director of AI-USA wrote a book about why American citizens should be concerned about human rights in other countries. He based his arguments on American self-interest, not transnational morality.[37]

Symptomatic of the situation in the USA was a growing consensus in both the executive and legislative branches that general and unilateral

---

[35] Ole Holsti, "Public Opinion and Human Rights in American Foreign Policy," in David P. Forsythe, ed., *The United States and Human Rights: Looking Inward and Outward* (Lincoln: University of Nebraska Press, 1999), ch. 7. This point was covered in Chapter 6 of the present volume.

[36] In addition to Neier, "The New Double Standard," see Ellen Dorsey, "US Foreign Policy and the Human Rights Movement: New Strategies for a Global Era," in Forsythe, ed., *The United States and Human Rights*, ch. 8.

[37] William F. Schulz, *In Our Own Best Interest: How Defending Human Rights Benefits Us All* (Boston: Beacon Press, 2001).

economic sanctions interfered with trade objectives, caused friction with allies, and were not very effective.[38] General economic sanctions in support of human rights goals were not very popular. Policy makers in Washington knew that they would not be subjected to mass public pressure in support of most human rights situations abroad. They knew that if foreign policy exceeded a certain permissive range and began to incur costs divorced from evident self-interest, that policy would be in trouble – as in Somalia from late fall 1993. As already noted, this attitudinal environment helps explain the NATO policy of relatively high-altitude air strikes on Yugoslavia in 1999 and the reluctance to commit ground troops in Kosovo. It also partially explains the reluctance of most western states to put troops on the ground in the Libyan civil war of 2011. This general political environment, in which many citizens in many countries were unwilling to sacrifice for the rights of others, undercut much effort by private human rights groups. All of this did not rule out, however, "smart" sanctions against particular repressive elites, allowing some normal relations to continue to the nation while targeting the ruling elites' travel and banking. In this regard, we can cite the US Magnitsky Act of 2012, applying various targeted sanctions on some elites within Russia as a protest against the death in custody of the dissident lawyer Sergei Magnitsky. (Russia responded by blocking the adoption of Russian children by Americans.)

A pragmatic rather than moralistic political culture, as a general political environment, did not mean that no advances could be made on behalf of internationally recognized human rights. Some private human rights groups teamed up with the Black Caucus in Congress to successfully direct attention to the situation in repressive Haiti in the mid-1990s. The Clinton Administration, which had from its beginnings manifested some officials also interested in doing something about repressive rule in Haiti, was able to undertake a military operation in support of democracy there and essentially end Haitian illegal emigration to the USA – but only as long as "significant" amounts of American blood and treasure were not sacrificed. Had Clinton's Haitian policy incurred the same costs as that in Somalia, namely the combat deaths of a dozen or so soldiers, it is highly likely the Haitian policy would have resulted in the same fate as the US's Somali policy – the withdrawal of congressional and public support.

---

[38] Eric Schmitt, "US Backs Off Sanctions, Seeing Poor Effect Abroad," *New York Times*, July 31, 1998, 1. But in 1999 the Clinton Administration announced unilateral economic sanctions against the Taliban government in Afghanistan, primarily in reaction to alleged state-supported terrorism, but also because of discrimination against women. Congress and the American public quietly deferred.

The same analysis could be applied to the deployment of US troops in Bosnia and their arrest of indicted war criminals. The Executive could advance human rights abroad as long as no costs arose that important political circles might deem "significant." But if perceived major costs arose, especially human costs, the public would expect the Executive to show a direct connection to expediential US concerns. (All of the examples noted above involve congressional influence, as much as NGO influence, along with the influence of the media.) Whether NGO human rights education could make transnational political culture more sensitive to, and supportive of, human rights concerns was an important question.[39]

At least in the USA after the terrorist attacks of September 11, 2001, if one wanted to do something about violations of human rights and lack of democracy in a failed state such as Somalia, one was more likely to get a sympathetic hearing in Congress and the public if one stressed US self-interests in closing down a safe haven for terrorists, rather than stressing the need for better rights for foreigners. Even so, in that situation the USA worked very hard to involve Kenya, Ethiopia, the African Union, and the United Nations, so as to reduce the need for direct and public US intervention.

Fourth and finally, some human rights advocacy groups also provide direct services to those victimized by human rights violations. They may engage in "judicial lobbying" or legal advocacy by participating in court cases. They may advise litigants or submit friendly briefs (*amicus curiae* briefs) in an effort to get courts to make rulings favorable to human rights standards. They may advise asylum seekers about how to present their claims to refugee status under international law. They may observe trials in the hopes of deterring a miscarriage of justice. A unique (*sui generis*) organization like the ICRC engages both in detention visits to help ensure humanitarian conditions of detention (and sometimes the release of the detainee on humanitarian grounds), and in multifaceted relief efforts for both prisoners and other victims of war and political conflict.

In sum to this point, the number of advocacy groups for various human rights causes grew dramatically in the last quarter of the twentieth century, even if the core group with a global focus and a link strictly to the international law of human rights and humanitarian affairs has

---

[39] NGO human rights education was joined by formal human rights education at all levels of learning, and by human rights education in professional associations. See further George J. Andreopoulos and Richard Pierre Claude, eds., *Human Rights Education for the Twenty-First Century* (Philadelphia: University of Pennsylvania Press, 1997); and Sia Spiliopoulou Akermark, *Human Rights Education: Achievements and Challenges* (Turku/ Abo, Finland: Institute for Human Rights, Abo Akademi University, 1998).

remained relatively small. At the 1993 UN Conference on Human Rights at Vienna, the UN officially reported that 841 NGOs attended.[40] Particularly remarkable has been the number of groups advocating greater attention to women's rights as human rights. Their presence was felt both at Vienna and at the 1991 UN Conference on Women at Beijing. These and other UN conferences were sometimes criticized as nothing more than talking shops or debating societies. Hardly ever did states drastically change their policies immediately after these meetings. But the conferences provided focal points for NGO organizing and networking. And at least for a time they raised the world's consciousness about human rights in general or particular rights questions.[41] In the early twenty-first century there were more private reports being issued on more human rights topics than ever before in world history. Women's rights, children's rights, prisoner's rights, etc. all drew extensive NGO attention. True, biases continued. Social and economic rights continued to be the step-children or illegitimate offspring of the human rights movement, especially on the part of NGOs based in the West. Nevertheless, an international civic society was emerging in which human rights advocacy groups and their shifting partners were highly active.

Influence?

The most important question was not so much what the human rights groups did, and how; that was reasonably clear to close observers. Rather, the challenging question was how to specify, then generalize about, their influence.[42] It had long proved difficult to precisely analyze the influence of any interest group or coalition in any political system over time.[43] Why was it that in the USA the "tobacco lobby" seemed so powerful, only to suddenly be placed on the defensive in the 1990s and lose a series of votes in the US Congress that produced tougher laws on tobacco advertising and use? Why was it that the "Israeli lobby," generally thought to be one of the more powerful in American politics, seemed

---

[40] UN Doc.: A/conf.157/24 (Report of the World Conference on Human Rights), October 13, 1993, Part I, 9.

[41] In general see Michael Schechter, *UN Global Conferences* (London and New York: Routledge, 2005).

[42] See further Don Hubert, "Inferring Influence: Gauging the Impact of NGOs," in Charlotte Ku and Thomas G. Weiss, eds., *Toward Understanding Global Governance: The International Law and International Relations Toolbox* (Providence, RI: ACUNS Reports and Papers, No. 2, 1998), 27–54.

[43] Bernard C. Cohen, *The Public's Impact on Foreign Policy* (Boston: Little, Brown, 1973). In general see David P. Forsythe, *Human Rights and World Politics*, 2nd edn. (Lincoln: University of Nebraska Press, 1989), ch. 6.

to weaken in the 1990s and was certainly unable to block a whole series of arms sales to Arab states? Why was the "China lobby," presumably strong in Washington during the Cold War, unable to block a rapprochement between Washington and Beijing? These and other questions about the influence of lobbies in general, or in relation to foreign policy, are not easy to answer. It was often said that "special interests" dominated modern politics, but proving the precise influence of these "special interests" became more difficult the more one probed into specifics.

A pervasive difficulty in analyzing NGO influence centered around the concept of success. If one or more NGOs succeeded in helping a UN Security Council resolution creating a criminal court for Rwanda to be adopted, but the *ad hoc* court turned out to have little impact on the Great Lakes region of Africa, could that be considered a success for NGO influence? But if later the *ad hoc* court contributed to the creation of a standing international criminal court at the UN, would the criteria for success change? If Amnesty International or the International Committee of the Red Cross prevented some instances of torture, how would one prove that success since the violation of human rights never occurred? If in Bosnia in the 1990s actors such as the ICRC and UNHCR helped reduce political rape and murder, but in so doing, by moving vulnerable civilians out of the path of enemy forces, they thereby contributed to ethnic cleansing and the basic political objective of a fighting party, was that a success?

In dealing with the sometimes elusive notion of success or achievement, sometimes it helped to distinguish among the following: success in getting an item or subject on the agenda for discussion, success in achieving serious discussion, success in getting procedural or institutional change, and finally success in achieving substantive policy change that clearly ameliorated or eliminated the problem. In the early stages of campaigns against slavery or female genital mutilation, it could be considered remarkable success just to get high state officials to think about the subject as an important problem.[44] In addressing gay rights in certain Muslim or African nations, it might be a mark of success just to get reasonable public debate.

Relatedly, one of the most helpful contributions that a human rights NGO or movement could obtain was the supportive finding of an epistemic community. Epistemic communities are networks of scientists or "thinkers" who deal in "truth" as demonstrated by cause and effect. To the extent that there is widespread agreement on scientific truth, public

---

[44] Keck and Sikkink, *Activists Beyond Borders*.

policy tends to follow accordingly – albeit with a time lag during which advocacy or lobbying comes into play. If the scientific evidence of the harmful effects of "second-hand smoke" had been stronger sooner, those campaigning against smoking in public and indoor places would have had an easier time of it. When medical personnel can show conclusively that female genital mutilation presents clear risks to those undergoing this ritual cutting in much of Africa and other places, the reporting and dissemination of this scientific truth aids those human rights groups trying to eliminate the practice.[45] If the science of global warming led to clearer conclusions now, effectuating policy change would be easier. Unfortunately, most decisions in support of international human rights involved political and moral choice rather than scientific truth. However, there are always those who have vested interests in the status quo and block out empirical findings that contradict their preferences. The danger of cognitive dissonance, of rejecting facts that do not fit with established preferences, is well known.

The greatest obstacle to proving the influence of human rights NGOs was that in most situations their influence was merged with the influence of public officials in the context of other factors such as media coverage or foreign events. In social science jargon, this is the agent–structure problem: agents, or actors, operate in a particular context (structure). Even using the same tactics, sometimes an agent is successful and sometimes not.[46]

Private human rights groups had long urged the creation of a United Nations High Commissioner for Human Rights, and the post was voted into being in 1993. This was two years after the implosion of the Soviet Union and the discrediting of European communism. Many private groups wanted to claim credit, but many governments had also been active in support of this cause. Salient personalities like former President Carter had campaigned vigorously for the creation of the post. And much media coverage was at work as well. Given that it was governments representing states that voted to create the office, it was difficult if not impossible to specify the exact influence of human rights advocacy groups.

---

[45] See further Ernst Haas, *When Knowledge Is Power: Three Models of Change in International Organizations* (Berkeley: University of California Press, 1990); and Peter Haas, "Introduction: Epistemic Communities and International Policy Coordination," *International Organization*, 46, 3 (Winter 1992), 1–36.

[46] Adam Hochschild, *Bury the Chains: Prophets and Rebels in the Fight to Free an Empire's Slaves* (Boston and New York: Houghton Mifflin, 2005, 2006). Sometimes the Anti-Slavery Society met with success and sometimes not, depending on the context in Britain and the larger world.

Likewise, human rights NGOs like Helsinki Watch (which evolved into Human Rights Watch) certainly pressured the European communists during the Cold War, acting in tandem with private individuals and groups inside those communist states. But western states were also active on human rights issues through the CSCE process. When European communism fell, it was impossible to say scientifically what was the exact impact of the human rights NGOs compared with state pressures, or for that matter compared with the economic difficulties of the European communists themselves (as noted in Chapter 4).

Most events have multiple causes, and it is often impossible to factor out in a precise way the exact impact of a human rights NGO or even a movement or coalition. In 1975 a relatively unknown member of the lower house of the US Congress, Donald Fraser, decided to hold hearings on human rights in US foreign policy. As chair of a sub-committee in the House of Representatives, Fraser had the authority to take such a decision by himself.[47] The Fraser hearings led to the reintroduction of the issue of human rights into US foreign policy after an absence of some two decades. But NGOs had some impact on these events in three ways.

Various anti-war NGOs and movements, which were the forerunners of several human rights NGOs in the USA, helped set the stage for the Fraser hearings.[48] It was growing domestic opposition to US policies in Vietnam, and a growing sense that US foreign policy had become amoral if not immoral, that contributed to the political climate in the USA in which Fraser acted. NGOs and social movements helped create that climate of opinion. Second, once scheduled, the Fraser hearings were the scene of testimony on human rights issues by AI-USA and other human rights NGOs. Third, Fraser's principal staff person on foreign policy, John Salzburg, had worked for an NGO and still shared the values of a number of those in the NGO community in Washington. So although there is no clear evidence that NGOs pressed Fraser to take the momentous course of action he did, NGOs did have some influence, probably of rather high significance, in combining with Fraser and other public officials to emphasize human rights in US foreign policy.

Niall McDermot, an experienced staff member of the International Commission of Jurists, wrote accurately: "NGOs create the conditions in

---

[47] See further Donald M. Fraser, "Freedom and Foreign Policy," *Foreign Policy*, 26 (Spring 1977), 140–156; and John Salzburg, "A View from the Hill: US Legislation and Human Rights," in David D. Newsom, ed., *The Diplomacy of Human Rights* (Lanham: University Press of America, 1986), 13–20.

[48] Lowell W. Livezey, *Non-Governmental Organizations and the Idea of Human Rights* (Princeton: Princeton University Center for International Studies, 1988).

which governmental pressure can be effective."[49] It is in the synergy or interplay of public and private action that one normally understands the full role of human rights NGOs and their coalitions. Thus influence by private human rights groups is normally exercised in a quasi-private, quasi-public way. Just as much policy making is now transnational or interdomestic, involving both international and domestic players, so that policy making is also both public and private at one and the same time. Public officials may join with NGOs and the media, etc. to effectuate change. This is precisely why a focus on movements or coalitions or networks has come into vogue, although it is still challenging to try to determine which actor in the movement exercised crucial influence at crucial times.

In some situations it is relatively clear that human rights NGOs, or a coalition of them and their allies, have had direct impact on what might be termed a human rights decision. Several authors have shown that one can trace the release of one or more prisoners of conscience to action by AI.[50] One can also show that NGOs made significant contributions to the negotiation of human rights standards in certain treaties.[51] A strong case can be made that human rights NGOs, in combination with other actors such as media representatives, *inter alia*, have helped transform the political culture of Mexico, Argentina, and other states in the Western Hemisphere which now show more sensitivity to human rights issues.[52] Many if not most of the UN monitoring mechanisms, from review committees to Special Rapporteurs, rely on NGO information in conducting their activities. When critical questions are raised, or critical conclusions reached, it is frequently on the basis, at least in part, of NGO information. The reduction of state funding for certain UN activities has increased the impact of NGOs in the human rights domain; the UN offices lack the resources to conduct their own extensive inquiries, and thus fall back on information from the human rights NGOs.[53]

---

[49] N. McDermot, "The Role of NGOs in the Promotion and Protection of Human Rights," in *The Role of Non-Governmental Organizations*, 45–52.

[50] Jonathan Power, *Amnesty International: The Human Rights Story* (New York: McGraw-Hill, 1981); Egon Larsen, *A Flame in Barbed Wire: The Story of Amnesty International* (London: F. Muller, 1978). See also Jane Connors, "Amnesty International at the United Nations," in Peter Willetts, ed., *"The Conscience of the World": The Influence of Non-Governmental Organizations in the UN System* (Washington: Brookings, 1996).

[51] Peter R. Baehr, "The General Assembly: Negotiating the Convention on Torture," in David P. Forsythe, ed., *The United Nations in the World Political Economy* (London: Macmillan, 1989), 36–53; Lawrence J. LeBlanc, *The Convention on the Rights of the Child: United Nations Lawmaking on Human Rights* (Lincoln: University of Nebraska Press, 1995), ch. 2.

[52] Keck and Sikkink, *Activists Beyond Borders*, 3.

[53] P. H. Kooijmans, "The Non-Governmental Organizations and the Monitoring Activities of the United Nations in the Field of Human Rights," in *The Role of*

From time to time certain states have tried to block some human rights NGOs from receiving or renewing their consultative status with the UN system. This is a status that allows NGOs to circulate documents and speak in certain UN meetings. If NGOs had no influence, and never proved embarrassing to states, the latter would not be so interested in blocking the activities of the former. State opposition to, and criticism of, NGOs is a reasonably clear indication that states, meaning the governments that speak for them, pay some attention to human rights NGOs and worry about what they say. It is obvious that most states care about their reputations in international relations, and go to great efforts to try to counter critical commentary.[54]

During 1999, the UN Committee on Non-Governmental Organizations, which reports to ECOSOC, withdrew consultative status for Christian Solidarity International, based in Zurich. That controversial NGO had antagonized the government of Sudan in several ways. Likewise the committee refused to approve the credentials of Human Rights in China, based in New York, which had offended the government in Beijing.[55] So even after the Cold War, and despite the immense influence of western states in the UN system, mainly the states of the global south continued to try to limit the role of some human rights advocacy groups in UN proceedings.

It cannot be scientifically proved, but a null hypothesis is certainly interesting: if human rights NGOs had not existed during the past thirty-five years, human rights would have a much less salient position in international relations. Serious, even grave, human rights violations in Cambodia in the 1970s and Mexico in the late 1960s did not lead to international attention and pressure because local and international NGOs were not in place to report on and act against those violations.[56] More positively, what began as action by the Anti-Slavery Society in London in the early nineteenth century triggered a successful movement against slavery and the slave trade over about a century. It is quite clear as

---

Non-Governmental Organizations, 15–22; Peter R. Baehr and Leon Gordenker, United Nations University Public Forum on Human Rights and Non-Governmental Organizations (Tokyo: United Nations University Lectures, September 14, 15, 18, 1996).

[54] A classic case in point is the effort by the Argentine junta in the 1980s to try to block criticism of its human rights record in the UN Human Rights Commission, as recorded by Iain Guest in Behind the Disappearances: Argentina's Dirty War Against Human Rights and the United Nations (Philadelphia: University of Pennsylvania Press, 1990).

[55] Paul Lewis, "UN Committee, Under Pressure, Limits Rights Groups," New York Times, June 22, 1999, A3.

[56] On Mexico, see Keck and Sikkink, Activists Beyond Borders. On Cambodia, I refer to genocide on a massive scale after most foreign observers had been kicked out by the Khmer Rouge.

well that since 1863, what is now called the International Committee of the Red Cross has advanced the cause of international humanitarian law, or the law of human rights in armed conflict. These are clear examples of NGOs that have had a broad impact on international relations, even if they frequently acted, or act today, in conjunction with public authorities.

Public officials may take the decision to adopt human rights standards or seek certain forms of implementation. But they may act in an environment ("structure") created to a considerable extent by human rights NGOs or human rights coalitions. Much of this influence is amorphous and remains difficult to specify. In the future it might prove possible to further elaborate the conditions under which a human rights NGO or movement might expect to be successful – e.g., where leaders of a state targeted for pressure are on record as favoring human rights in principle, where such leaders do not regard the human rights violation as crucial to their hold on power or to the security of their state, where a target state is not a pivotal or vital state to others in strategic or economic terms, etc.

In the meantime, human rights NGOs have helped create a climate of opinion in international relations sympathetic to human rights – although this impact varies according to time and place. In this regard these NGOs have helped restrict and thus transform the idea of state sovereignty. It can be stated in general that the responsible exercise of state sovereignty entails respect for at least certain internationally recognized human rights. Recall the norm of R2P, approved in 2005 at the UN: when a state is unwilling or unable to protect against genocide, crimes against humanity, major war crimes, and/or ethnic cleansing, outside parties have a duty to become involved. States, like Saddam Hussein's Iraq, that engage in gross and systematic violation of the most elemental human rights are not afforded the normal prerogatives that stem from the principle of state sovereignty. During the 1990s Iraq was put into *de facto* receivership under United Nations supervision. This was because of the misuse of sovereignty via violations of human rights in Iraq and Kuwait, combined with aggression against Kuwait. A similar analysis could be made about Milosevic in Yugoslavia or Kaddafi in Libya. It is still valid to say, as Francis Fukuyama wrote, that in dominant international political theory, the most fully legitimate state is the liberal democratic state that respects civil and political rights.[57] Advocacy groups for human rights play the basic role of reminding everyone of human rights performance,

---

[57] Francis Fukuyama, *The End of History and the Last Man* (New York: Free Press, 1992). Of course there is a gap between the political theory of legitimate states and the practice of international relations. In practice, persons and public authorities may grant

and particularly when gross and systematic violations occur that call into existence the basic legitimacy of a government to act for the state. This is why governments pay human rights NGOs so much attention, including sometimes trying to undermine and restrict what they do.

It remains true, however, that important actors have counter-narratives to the importance of human rights. These actors take definite steps to undercut human rights NGOs. Elites in places like China, Russia, and at the time of writing in the Philippines, sometimes argue that human rights are a strictly Western notion inappropriate for their nations. At home and in foreign policy, they seek to restrict NGO actions seeking to advance human rights.

Private action for relief and development

As we have seen, the International Bill of Rights contains economic and social rights such as the rights to adequate food, clothing, shelter, and medical care in peacetime. International humanitarian law contains non-combatant rights to emergency assistance – referring to similar food, clothing, shelter, and medical care – in armed conflict.[58] United Nations resolutions have extended these same rights to "complex emergencies," an imprecise term meant to cover situations in which the relevant authority denies that there is an armed conflict covered by international humanitarian law, but in which civilians are in need and public order disrupted. In a tradition that defies legal logic, private groups working to implement these socioeconomic rights in peace and war are not normally referred to as human rights groups but as relief (or humanitarian) and development agencies. This semantic tradition may exist because many agencies were working for relief and development before the discourse on human rights became so salient. These groups may or may not reference human rights in their fieldwork.

Whatever the semantic traditions, there are complicated international systems for both relief and development, and neither would function without private agencies. At the same time, the private groups are

legitimacy, meaning a sense of correct rule, on the basis of tradition, alliances, and/or effective exercise of power, and not just human rights performance. See David P. Forsythe, *Human Rights and Peace: International and National Views* (Lincoln: University of Nebraska Press, 1993), ch. 3. Compare Jack Donnelly, "Human Rights: A New Standard of Civilization?," *International Affairs*, 74, 1 (1998), 1–24.

[58] Legal obligations in this regard under the 1949 Geneva Conventions, and 1977 Additional Protocols, for victims of armed conflicts have been analyzed by numerous commentators, including Monika Sandvik-Nylund, *Caught in Conflicts: Civilian Victims, Humanitarian Assistance and International Law* (Turku/Abo, Finland: Institute for Human Rights of Abo Akademi University, 1998).

frequently supported by state donations of one type or another, and frequently act in conjunction with intergovernmental organizations. As with advocacy groups, so with relief and development agencies, the resulting process is both private and public at the same time. In both relief and development, the United States and the states of the European Union provide most of the resources.[59] In both, UN agencies are heavily involved – UNICEF, the WHO, the World Food Program, the UN Development Program, etc. But in both, private grassroots action is, to a very great extent, essential to whether persons on the ground get the food, clothing, shelter, and medical care which international law guarantees on paper. It is the private groups that turn the law on the books into the law in action. It is the private groups that condition and sometimes transform the operation of state sovereignty.

Relief

Because of international humanitarian law, the relief system in armed conflict and complex emergencies is somewhat different from that in peacetime. The norms supposedly guiding action are different, and some of the actors are different. For reasons of space, only relief in wars and complex emergencies is covered here.[60]

In so-called man-made disasters, the private International Committee of the Red Cross usually plays a central role because of its long association with victims of war and international humanitarian law. It was ultimately, for example, the best-positioned relief actor in Somalia in the early 1990s, and remained so even after the arrival of tens of thousands of US military personnel. The ICRC does not monopolize relief in these situations, however. In Bosnia in the first half of the 1990s, it was the Office of the UN High Commissioner for Refugees that ran the largest civilian relief program, followed by the ICRC. In Cambodia in the late 1980s, the UNHCR and the ICRC were essentially co-lead agencies for international relief. In Sudan during the 1970s and 1980s, UNICEF and the ICRC carried out important roles. But in these and similar situations, numerous private agencies are active in relief: World Vision, Church World Service, Caritas, Oxfam, Save the Children,

---

[59] See further Alexander Natsios, *US Foreign Policy and the Four Horsemen of the Apocalypse: Humanitarian Relief in Complex Emergencies* (Westport: Praeger, 1997).

[60] Relief in natural disasters such as floods, earthquakes, typhoons, volcanic eruptions, etc. is analyzed in many sources, including by the late expert Frederick Cuny in *Disasters and Development* (New York: Oxford University Press, 1983). See also Peter Walker and Daniel G. Maxwell, *Shaping the Humanitarian World* (New York and London: Routledge, 2009).

Doctors Without Borders, etc. It was not unusual to find several hundred private relief agencies active in a conflict situation like Rwanda and its environs in the mid-1990s, or in Syria and South Sudan circa 2015.

Relief: process

One can summarize the challenges facing all these private relief agencies (aka socioeconomic human rights groups).[61]

(1) *They must negotiate access to those in need.* One may speak of guaranteed rights, even a right to assistance. And in the 1990s there was much discussion about a right to humanitarian intervention. But as a practical matter, one must reach agreement with those who have the guns on the ground in order to provide relief/assistance in armed conflict and complex emergencies. Even if there is some general agreement between public authorities (*de jure* and *de facto*) and relief agencies on providing relief, specifics have to be agreed upon for particular times and places. Negotiating conditions of access can be a tricky business, as fighting parties may seek to divert relief for military and political objectives, even as relief agencies may insist on impartiality and neutrality. With numerous relief agencies vying for a piece of the action, Machiavellian political actors may play one off against another. Some of the smaller, less-experienced agencies have proved themselves subject to political manipulation.

(2) *Relief agencies must provide an accurate assessment of need.* Relief must be tailored to local conditions, and there should be control for redundant or unneeded goods and services. The use of systematic rape as a weapon of war, terror, and ethnic cleansing has meant the need for gynecological and psychiatric services for many women.

(3) *The private groups must mobilize relief in a timely and effective way.* Here the ICRC has certain advantages, as it is well known and respected by most states, and has links to national Red Cross or Red Crescent societies in over 185 states. But other private agencies have their own means of mobilization, being able to tap into well-established religious or secular networks.

(4) *Of obvious importance is the ability of a private group to actually deliver the assistance in a timely and cost-effective way.* Here again the ICRC presents certain advantages, as it is smaller and less bureaucratic than some UN bodies; has regional, country, and intra-country offices in

---

[61] The following is drawn from David P. Forsythe, "The International Committee of the Red Cross and Humanitarian Assistance: A Policy Analysis," *International Review of the Red Cross*, 314 (September–October 1996), 512–531.

many places around the world (in addition to the national Red Cross/ Red Crescent societies); and since the 1970s has built up experience in the delivery of relief in ongoing conflicts and occupied territory. Its reputation for effectiveness on the ground was particularly outstanding in Somalia in the early 1990s. But other agencies, particularly the UNHCR, have been accumulating experience as well. And often the sheer size of a relief problem can be too great for the ICRC. In Rwanda in 1994 and thereafter, where as many as two million persons fled genocidal ethnic conflict and civil war, the ICRC concentrated its activities inside Rwanda and left to other actors the matter of relief in neighboring countries. The same was true in the Syrian internationalized civil war from 2011.

(5) *All relief agencies have to engage in evaluation of past action and planning for the future.* All of the major relief players do this, but some of the smaller, less-experienced, and more *ad hoc* groups do not.

The international system, movement, or coalition for relief in man-made disasters faces no shortage of pressing issues.

(1) *Should there be more coordination?* There has been much talk about more coordination, but none of the major players wants to be dominated by any other actor. Legally speaking, the ICRC is a Swiss private agency whose statutes give policy-making authority to an all-Swiss assembly that co-opts members from Swiss society only. It resists control by any United Nations body, any other Red Cross agency, or any state. Also, the UNHCR, UNICEF, the WHO, and the WFP all have independent budgets, executive heads, governing bodies, and mandates. Each resists control by any UN principal organ or by the UN Emergency Relief Coordinator (now the Under Secretary-General for Humanitarian Assistance) who reports to the Secretary-General. The latter UN office lacked the legal, political, and budgetary clout to bring the other actors under its control. Politically speaking, the major donors, the USA and the EU, have not insisted on more formal coordination. There are advantages to the present system. The UNHCR may be best positioned in one conflict, UNICEF or the ICRC in another. And there was *de facto* cooperation among many of the relief actors much of the time, with processes for voluntary coordination both in New York and Geneva. More importantly, there was considerable cooperation among agencies in the field. Yet duplication and conflicts occurred with regularity; there was certainly room for improvement.

(2) *Should one try to separate politics from humanitarian action?* Particularly the ICRC argued in favor of strict adherence to the principles of

impartiality and neutrality, and preferred to keep its distance from "political" decisions which involved coercion or any official preference for one side over another in armed conflict and complex emergencies. But even the ICRC had to operate under military protection in Somalia to deliver relief effectively (and had to accept military protection for released prisoners on occasion in Bosnia). In Bosnia, much of the fighting was about civilians – their location and sustenance. The UNHCR's relief program became "politicized" in the sense of intertwined with carrots and sticks provided in relation to diplomacy and peacemaking. There was disagreement about the wisdom of this course of action. But it was clear that once the UN authorized use of force in places like Bosnia to coerce a change in Serbian policy, then UN civilian (and military) personnel on the ground became subject to hostage-taking by antagonized Serb combatants. It was clear that the idea of a neutral Red Cross or UN presence for relief purposes was not widely respected in almost all of the armed conflicts and complex emergencies after the Cold War. Relief workers from various organizations were killed in places like Chechnya, Bosnia, Rwanda, Burundi, Liberia, Somalia, Afghanistan, etc. Other relief workers were taken hostage for ransom. Sometimes armed relief, even "humanitarian war," seemed the only feasible option, but others disagreed.[62]

(3) *Could one change the situation through new legislation and/or better dissemination of norms?* It was evident from the Soviet Union to communist Yugoslavia, to take just two clear examples, that former states had not taken fully seriously their obligation to teach international humanitarian law to military personnel, despite the strictures of especially the 1949 Geneva Conventions and additional 1977 Protocols for the protection of victims of war. After especially the French failed to have codified new laws on humanitarian intervention in the 1990s, action turned to international criminal justice and the creation of international tribunals to try those individuals accused of war crimes, genocide, and crimes against humanity.

NGOs lobbied vigorously for these new norms and agencies to enforce them, as I have already noted in Chapter 4. But much violence was

---

[62] Adam Roberts, "Humanitarian War: Military Intervention and Human Rights," *International Affairs*, 69, 3 (July, 1993), 429f. See further Jonathan Moore, ed., *Hard Choices: Moral Dilemmas in Humanitarian Intervention* (Lanham: Rowman & Littlefield, 1998); and Thomas G. Weiss, "The Humanitarian Identity Crisis," in *Ethics & International Affairs*, 13 (1999), 1–22, with associated commentary.

carried out by private armies such as rebel or secessionist groups, clans, and organized mobs. Relief workers more than once faced child soldiers on drugs armed with automatic weapons. How to make international norms, whether new or old, effective on such combatants was a tough nut to crack. It was said of Somalia, only in slight exaggeration, that no one with a weapon had ever heard of the Geneva Conventions.[63] At least many of the relief agencies agreed on a code of conduct for themselves, which approximated but did not exactly replicate the core principles of the Geneva Conventions. In the internationalized civil war in Yemen, the fighting parties were reported to have regularly bombed civilian and medical targets. Various private human rights actors protested, but states often had priorities that downgraded attention to human rights and humanitarian law – such as affecting the regional power struggle between Sunni Saudi Arabia and Shia Iran.

Relief: influence?

There is no question but that private actors have considerable if amorphous influence or impact in the matter of international relief in "man-made" conflicts. The ICRC was a major player in Somalia 1991–1995, the UNHCR and its private partners were a major player in Bosnia 1992–1995. The UNHCR does not so much deliver relief itself as contract with private agencies for that task. The UNHCR manages, supervises, and coordinates, but private actors like Doctors Without Borders do much of the grassroots relief. To use a negative example of influence, if several private groups disagree with a policy decision taken by the UNHCR and decide to operate differently, the UNHCR is constrained in what it can do. The same is even more true for the World Food Program, which has a very limited capacity to operate in the field by itself. The ICRC, as should be clear by now, is a private actor whose norms and accomplishments often affect the other players, directly or indirectly.

Having noted this NGO independent position, one must still recognize that states and intergovernmental organizations are the major sources for material resources directed to humanitarian assistance in wars and complex emergencies. It is states, directly or through IGOs, that provide the physical security that relief NGOs need for their

---

[63] Jennifer Learning, "When the System Doesn't Work: Somalia, 1992," in Kevin M. Cahill, ed., *Framework for Survival: Health, Human Rights, and Humanitarian Assistance in Conflicts and Disasters* (New York: Basic Books, for the Council on Foreign Relations, 1993), 112.

grassroots operations – at least in territory that these states control. (These NGOs may prefer to rely on their own reputation for security of operations, but if that fails, they have to rely on the hard power of states.) Influence is a complex two-way street. Public authorities need the NGOs, which opens up possibilities for subtle influence on the part of the latter. But the NGOs need the support and cooperation of the public authorities. If NGOs pull out of a relief operation and develop the image of unreasonable non-cooperation, they will: (1) cut themselves out of operations that constitute their reason for being, (2) perhaps get bad publicity, and (3) make it more difficult to raise money. Once again, as with traditional advocacy for human rights, we find that the movement to provide relief is both private and public at the same time, and that influence among the disparate elements is difficult to pinpoint in general.

The challenge facing relief/humanitarian agencies in armed conflict is probably even greater than that facing more traditional human rights advocacy groups. The former are dealing with states and other primary protagonists that have resorted to violence in pursuit of their goals. The issues at stake have already been deemed worth fighting over. In this context of armed conflict or complex emergency, it is exceedingly difficult to get the protagonists to elevate assistance to civilians to a rank of the first order. Moreover, in all too many conflicts, especially after the Cold War, intentional attacks on civilians, and their brutal manipulation otherwise, became part of the grand strategy of one or more of the fighting parties. It was therefore difficult if not impossible to fully neutralize and humanize civilian relief.[64] In Syria from 2011, whatever the law on the books might say, denying civilian relief was sometimes used as a tactic of war, employed to pressure opponents into withdrawal or surrender. It was often difficult to negotiate humanitarian truces in order to allow delivery of humanitarian relief.

Development: process

As in relief, the development process on an international scale presents a mixture of public and private actors. If we focus just on the PVOs based in the North Atlantic area we find they are exceedingly numerous – perhaps now up to about 5,000 in number – and quite varied in their

---

[64] See further Michael Barnett and Thomas G. Weiss, eds., *Humanitarianism in Question: Politics, Power, Ethics* (Ithaca and London: Cornell University Press, 2008); and Richard A. Wilson and Richard D. Brown, *Humanitarianism and Suffering: The Mobilization of Empathy* (Cambridge and New York: Cambridge University Press, 2009).

orientations.[65] While some of these PVOs or VOLAGs reject state funding to protect their independence, and consequently wind up frequently on the margins of the development process, most act otherwise and serve as conduits for public monies and public policies. PVOs themselves provide only about 10 percent of development assistance in a typical year.

Private development agencies, like Oxfam, that cooperate with public authorities and operate consistently across international borders are a crucial part of the public–private development process. These development NGOs provide values and services often lacking in the public sector: "smallness, good contacts at the local level, freedom from political manipulation, a labor (rather than capital) intensive orientation, innovativeness, and flexibility in administration."[66]

The OECD states find "mainstream" NGOs useful in implementing their goals while reducing suspicions of neo-imperialism or other unwanted intrusions in the affairs of developing states. Other public authorities seem to be coming around to this same view. Major intergovernmental actors are the World Bank (officially the International Bank for Reconstruction and Development), other development banks on a regional basis, and the United Nations Development Program (UNDP). The International Monetary Fund (IMF) is not, strictly speaking, a development institution. It frequently functions, however, in conjunction with the World Bank in making loans (affording drawing rights) to stabilize currency transactions or correct balance of payments problems.

Increasingly the World Bank officially endorses the participation of NGOs and community-based organizations (CBOs) in establishing development programs.[67] Theory and practice are not always the same, and historically relations between the Bank and development NGOs have been less than perfectly smooth. Many development NGOs have criticized the Bank for being insensitive to the needs of especially the rural poor, and within that group especially indigenous peoples, who did not benefit so clearly from the past industrial schemes of the Bank, and who may have been forced out of their traditional homes by development projects funded by the Bank.

The UNDP also officially endorses the bringing together of NGOs and CBOs to provide grassroots participation in development projects.

---

[65] *Directory of Non-Governmental Organisations Active in Sustainable Development* (Paris: OECD, 1996).

[66] Brian H. Smith, *More than Altruism: The Politics of Private Foreign Aid* (Princeton: Princeton University Press, 1990), 6.

[67] See further David P. Forsythe, "The United Nations, Human Rights, and Development," *Human Rights Quarterly*, 19, 2 (May 1997), 334–349.

If practiced seriously, this type of micro- or economic democracy would combine *de facto* attention to civil and political rights, as the rights of participation, with social and economic rights. Endorsement of NGO and CBO participation in the development process by the Bank, UNDP, and OECD states comprised part of the mantra of "sustainable human development" at the turn of the century. As theory, it was an improvement over the top-down massive infrastructure projects devised in Washington and New York in the 1960s and 1970s.

Development: influence?

Private development agencies faced no lack of problems in trying to help achieve sustainable human development in keeping with internationally recognized human rights. A new barrier in the 1990s was that the prevalence of ethnic conflict and other forms of internal armed conflict and political instability caused public authorities to channel vast amounts of resources into relief. Consequently, fewer funds and less attention went to development. Moreover, from about 1980 and especially after 1990, western donor governments put great emphasis on "market solutions" and the role of direct foreign investment by transnational corporations, rather than official development assistance (ODA) by governments.

A historical problem was that PVOs and VOLAGs did not always think of development in relation to human rights,[68] although with time there was a shift toward focusing on empowerment – which was a synonym for participatory rights.[69] This shift was certainly welcomed by those development NGOs that had long expressed concern about authoritarian rather than democratic development.[70] I noted above how the theory of the World Bank, UNDP, and OECD states all accepted participation in decision making by NGOs and CBOs. There was also a considerable shift toward integrating women's rights with development strategies.[71] Much less pronounced historically was any shift toward emphasizing socioeconomic rights in the development process. But since at the UN,

[68] Theo van Boven, "Human Rights and Development: The UN Experience," in David P. Forsythe, ed., *Human Rights and Development: International Views* (London: Macmillan, 1989), 121–135.
[69] Julie Fisher, *Non-Governments: NGOs and the Political Development of the Third World* (West Hartford: Kumarian Press, 1998).
[70] Smith, *More than Altruism*, 72.
[71] See, e.g., Sue Ellen M. Charlton and Jana Everett, eds., *NGOs and Grassroots in Development Work in South India: Elizabeth Moen Mathiot* (Lanham: University Press of America, 1998).

in the era of Boutros Boutros-Ghali and Kofi Annan, there was an effort to "mainstream human rights" in the development process, this approach affected the private development agencies. This rights-based approach (RBA) to development certainly affected the rhetoric and semantics of both public and private development agencies, and maybe even some of the substance.[72]

Development NGOs, much like traditional advocacy NGOs for human rights, had trouble in precisely specifying their influence in the development process vis-à-vis other actors.[73] As with the advocacy groups, many leaders of development NGOs were active out of moral commitment and would continue with their ideas and objectives whether or not they were able to change public programs to their liking. As with advocacy groups, the real influence of development NGOs was to be found in their amorphous contribution to a wider movement, network, or coalition interested in sustainable *human* development. While true that public authorities provide most of the capital for development projects, some influence flows from the NGOs back toward public authorities – especially through the give and take over different approaches to development. Public authorities have no monopoly over ideas related to development, and some of the ideas that prove controlling over time originate with NGOs. If the point of the human rights discourse was to allow human beings to maximize their full potential as rational and autonomous beings worthy of dignity, this was essentially compatible with the notion of sustainable human development.

Conclusion

NGOs that advocate for human rights ideas, that implement the right to humanitarian assistance for those in dire straits, and that contribute to the human rights inherent in sustainable human development have impacted both public authorities and private individuals in numerous ways. They have advanced some form of liberalism in international relations through their emphasis on individuals and law, as compared with state interests and power. Advocacy groups provide much of the information that allows the rights agencies of international organizations to function, while challenging or validating the facts and policies put

---

[72] See further Joel Oestreich, *Power and Principle: Human Rights Programming in International Organizations* (Washington: Georgetown University Press, 2007).
[73] Michael Edwards and David Hulme, eds., *Beyond the Magic Bullet: NGO Performance and Accountability in the Post-Cold War World* (West Hartford: Kumarian Press, in cooperation with Save the Children Fund, 1996).

forward by states. It is difficult to believe the making and implementing of human rights standards would operate in the same way without these advocacy groups. The international relief system would simply not be able to get humanitarian assistance to those in need in most situations without the private relief agencies. The development process would be seriously hampered without the private development organizations to serve as intermediaries between the public authorities that provide most of the resources and the individuals and indigenous groups that implement, and benefit from, the development programs at the grassroots level.

States and their intergovernmental organizations are thus dependent on these NGOs. States share the stage of international relations with these NGOs, which is to say that state sovereignty is at times restricted by the activity of these NGOs that work for civil and political, social and economic rights. A restricted sovereignty is a transformed sovereignty, no longer absolute.

As much as NGOs need states – to arrest war criminals, to provide food and tents and sometimes physical protection for relief, to provide capital and guidelines for development – states need NGOs for a variety of ideas and services. Thus the stage is set for the subtle interplay of influence between the two types of actors on behalf of human rights, relief, and sustainable *human* development.

Case study: women's NGOs and mobilizing women voters in Ghana

In sub-Saharan Africa, decolonization and national independence produced much autocracy of a patriarchal nature in the 1960s and 1970s.[74] This was true in Ghana, which until 1957 was a British colony manifesting at times elections to a restricted local parliament. During the Nkrumah era (1957–1966), politics evolved into one-party rule. He gave some attention to women's concerns and even instituted some gender quotas in certain offices. But over time many women's interests were often excluded from public policy matters, and women's civic society organizations of various sorts were mostly underdeveloped.

After much political instability, a coup in 1981 by Flight Lt. Jerry Rawlings proved to be a major event as he retained power for nineteen

[74] Author's adaption from Kathleen M. Fallon, "Getting Out the Vote: Women's Democratic Political Mobilization in Ghana," *Mobilization: An International Journal*, 8, 3 (2003), 273–296.

years until 2000: first as strong man, then as winner of clearly flawed elections, and finally as winner of elections generally judged to be reasonably fair and free. He oversaw a peaceful transition to a genuinely elected successor in 2001. The latter part of his rule can thus be considered a transition to genuine democracy, and during this time of political opening women's civic society organizations became more active – with some demonstrable impact on women's participation in the political process. This exercise of their civil and political rights is our focus here.

A combination of international and internal pressures led Rawlings to try to legitimize his power via elections in 1992. Not only foreign governments providing foreign assistance and western-based NGOs interested in democracy and human rights pushed in this direction, but also so did a wide variety of Ghanaian civic society organizations such as trade unions, student groups, and lawyers' associations. While autocratic, the Ghanaian state was not totalitarian.

For women's groups seeking influence in public affairs, a particular problem was that Rawlings had created the 31st December Women's Movement (later headed by his wife). This GONGO (governmentally organized non-governmental organization) existed primarily to enlist women's support for the regime. With governmental support and resources, the 31st December Movement constricted the political space for genuinely independent groups to mobilize and have effect.

Research that was focused on groups such as the Christian Council Women's and Children's Desk, Christian Mothers Association, CUSAASA, Ghana Association of Women Entrepreneurs, the International Association for the Advancement of Women in Africa, International Association for Women Lawyers, the United Women's Front, Women in Law and Development in Africa, and the Young Women's Christian Association indicated that these organizations had an impact on women's political thinking and action. Members of these groups, and other women having some contact with these groups, were more likely to vote in the 1996 elections than other women. (Other factors also correlated with voting, such as living with a husband and having a larger number of children, but not as strongly as membership in these civic society organizations.) Shortly after the 1996 elections women took to the streets to demonstrate for more governmental attention to their concerns, and in the context of physical attacks on women, sometimes fatal, they formed Sisters' Keepers which had demonstrable effect in replacing certain officials and improving female physical security – certainly in the capital city of Accra. By 2010, Ghana scored better than the average for sub-Saharan Africa on the Human Development Index as adjusted for gender issues.[75] This brief study does not directly emphasize the international norms codifying the right to participate in the public policy process, nor the states and human rights advocacy groups that made reference to those norms in trying to push the Ghanaian government to respect those standards. No doubt this combined public and private human rights pressure helped set the stage for the political opening or liberalization in Ghana in the 1990s during the Rawlings regime. It was true that some who were politically active in Ghana saw this foreign commentary (pressure?) as a neo-colonial or neo-imperial intrusion into domestic affairs. Nevertheless, Rawlings did progressively move toward genuine multiparty elections.

What this study does emphasize, during the transition to genuine democracy, is the effect of a wide variety of grassroots civic society organizations. The latter did indeed mobilize women to greater political participation. This reflects commitment not just to the political right to vote, but also to the necessary civil rights inherent in that process such as freedom of thought, speech, and association. The women in Ghana then used their newly found political awareness to advance various public policies of interest to them.

The exercise of women's civil and political rights in Ghana, and in sub-Saharan Africa more generally, can be compared to women's political participation in Latin America (and elsewhere, of course). There are variations in patterns and sequences. Women's civic action groups do not always operate according to the same dynamic or metric in every country and region. But Ghana shows that women's grassroots organizations, sometimes called community-based organizations (CBOs), can be a potent force to advance women's interests, starting with political participation. A key structural factor is that the electoral regime must be relatively free and fair, and the political contestants have to abide by its outcome, which is often encouraged by international pressure – both public and private.

---

[75] See hdrstats.undp.org/en/countries/profiles/GHA.html. The UN Human Development Index (HDI), compiled by UNDP, the UN Development Program, is based on three core factors: literacy rates as a reflection of education; longevity as a reflection of nutrition and health care; and per capita GDP as a reflection of income or economic well-being. It also produces a gendered HDI paying special attention to factors affecting women.

Discussion questions

- Is it more helpful for understanding to focus on separate or distinct private human rights organizations, or to focus on networks or movements? Can one understand a movement without understanding the precise actors that make up that movement? Can public officials be part of a human rights or humanitarian movement?
- Are western-based private human rights organizations part of western cultural imperialism? To what extent does an organization like Amnesty International have broad support in the non-western world?
- Are the better-known private human rights organizations moralistic and legalistic, in that they fail to consistently understand and appreciate the political context within which governments take decisions that impact human rights? Do they unreasonably discount other values and policies that governments and their publics consider legitimate – such as peace, security, economic growth? Or are the private groups absolutely vital to shaking governments and mass public opinion out of their set ways regarding the death penalty, gay rights, the continuing prevalence of torture, excessive spending on the military compared with basic human needs, etc.?
- What practical steps can be taken to improve the delivery of food, clothing, shelter, and medical care to civilians in armed conflicts and complex emergencies? Do these steps involve private actors such as the International Committee of the Red Cross, Doctors Without Borders, etc.? Given that a number of fighting parties *intentionally* attack and abuse civilians, should humanitarian action be left to NATO or the US Department of Defense in place of private relief organizations? After all, national military establishments (at least the major ones) have tremendous logistical capacity. Paradoxes aside, should humanitarian action be nationalized and militarized?
- Is the global pursuit of "development" sufficiently attentive to "sustainable *human* development" and human rights? How important is the role of private actors like Oxfam in this development process? Do public authorities like the World Bank, the UN Development Program, and the US Agency for International Development approve of a large role for private organizations and human-oriented development? Is this orientation perhaps theory and not practice? How would practical policies change if human rights were genuinely incorporated into the "development" process?

SUGGESTIONS FOR FURTHER READING

Bob, Clifford, ed., *The International Struggle for New Human Rights*, Pennsylvania Studies in Human Rights Series (Philadelphia: University of Pennsylvania Press, 2008). A study of how NGOs and other actors serve as "gatekeepers," endorsing some claims as new human rights while failing to endorse others and thus denying prominence.

Carothers, Thomas, "Closing Space for International Democracy and Human Rights Support," *Journal of Human Rights Practice*, 8, 3 (2016), 358–377. A leading authority on democracy promotion documents the broad effort by many governments to block international connections supporting NGOs active on human rights and democracy.

Edwards, Michael, and David Hulme, eds., *Beyond the Magic Bullet: NGO Performance and Accountability in the Post-Cold War World* (West Hartford: Kumarian Press, in cooperation with Save the Children Fund, 1996). Deals with the central question of how democratic, accountable, and open NGOs really are, even though they claim to represent "the people."

Fisher, Julie, *Non-Governments: NGOs and the Political Development of the Third World* (West Hartford: Kumarian Press, 1998). A critical look at the impact of human rights and development NGOs in the global south.

Florini, A., *The Third Force: The Rise of Transnational Civil Society* (Washington: Carnegie Endowment, 2000). An excellent overview of the global spread of NGOs in all their variety.

Hochschild, Adam, *Bury the Chains: Prophets and Rebels in the Fight to Free an Empire's Slaves* (Boston and New York: Houghton Mifflin, 2005, 2006). A very readable study of the organizations and personalities active in the anti-slave trade and anti-slavery movements in the nineteenth century.

Hopgood, Stephen, *Keepers of the Flame: Understanding Amnesty International* (Ithaca: Cornell University Press, 2006). A creative study of the internal dynamics of AI and concentrating on a clash over the organization's proper mandate and programs.

Keck, Margaret E., and Kathryn Sikkink, *Activists Beyond Borders: Advocacy Networks in International Politics* (Ithaca: Cornell University Press, 1998). An outstanding example of using the concept of "movement" to try to analyze essentially private action for human rights, although the authors conceive of certain public officials as part of a movement.

Korey, William, *NGOs and the Universal Declaration of Human Rights: "A Curious Grapevine"* (New York: St. Martin's Press, 1998). A personalized and disjointed account, but containing much useful information for introductory purposes. Places great weight on NGO action, especially by Jewish groups, in the evolution of modern human rights.

Mathews, Jessica Tuchman, "Power Shift," *Foreign Affairs*, 76, 1 (January–February 1997), 50–66. A sweeping argument and highly optimistic view about the growing influence of all sorts of NGOs in international relations. The other side of her coin is the declining influence of the territorial state.

Moore, Jonathan, ed., *Hard Choices: Moral Dilemmas in Humanitarian Intervention* (Lanham: Rowman & Littlefield, 1998). A good collection by practitioners and theorists about different views toward, and experiences with, humanitarian assistance.

Natsios, Alexander, *US Foreign Policy and the Four Horsemen of the Apocalypse: Humanitarian Relief in Complex Emergencies* (Westport: Praeger, 1997). The author, who was at different times both a US official and a key player for World Vision, a church-related private relief organization, focuses on the USA but stresses the interactions of governments, international organizations, and private actors like the ICRC.

Smith, Brian H., *More than Altruism: The Politics of Private Foreign Aid* (Princeton: Princeton University Press, 1990). A sharp look at private development and relief organizations.

Smith, Jackie, Charles Chatfield, and Ron Pagnucco, eds., *Transnational Social Movements and Global Politics: Solidarity Beyond the State* (Syracuse: Syracuse University Press, 1997). A good collection of case studies featuring private networks and their impact on human rights.

Smith, Jackie, and Ron Pagnucco, with George A. Lopez, "Globalizing Human Rights: The Work of Transnational Human Rights NGOs in the 1990s," *Human Rights Quarterly*, 20, 2 (May 1998), 379–412. An essential if largely descriptive overview.

Steiner, Henry J., *Diverse Partners: Non-Governmental Organizations and the Human Rights Movement* (Cambridge, MA: Harvard Law College, 1991, for the Harvard Law School Human Rights Program and the Human Rights Internet). A short analysis of the different types of private actors working on human rights issues.

Tolley, Howard J., Jr., *The International Commission of Jurists: Global Advocates for Human Rights* (Philadelphia: University of Pennsylvania Press, 1994). A careful look at a well-known, Geneva-based human rights NGO with a legal focus. Also an attempt to blend political history with social science theory.

Weiss, Thomas G., "The Humanitarian Identity Crisis," *Ethics & International Affairs*, 13 (1999), 1–22. A leading scholar of humanitarian affairs nicely summarizes much debate, while advocating major changes in international action. Accompanied by other views on the same topic in the same journal.

Weiss, Thomas G., and Leon Gordenker, eds., *NGOs, the UN, and Global Governance* (Boulder: Lynne Rienner, 1996). An examination of how private actors intersect with UN bodies, with attention to human rights, humanitarian affairs, and women's rights.

Welch, Claude E., *Protecting Human Rights in Africa: Strategies and Roles of Non-Governmental Organizations* (Philadelphia: University of Pennsylvania Press, 1995). A good overview of this subject, with a generally favorable view of African NGOs and their impact over time, despite a hostile environment.

NGOs and Human Rights: Promise and Performance (Philadelphia: University of Pennsylvania Press, 2001). A solid overview.

Willetts, Peter, ed., *"The Conscience of the World": The Influence of Non-Governmental Organizations in the UN System* (Washington: Brookings, 1996). An excellent collection with a very good chapter on Amnesty International and human rights by Jane Connors.

8   Transnational corporations and human rights

We saw in Chapter 7 that the international law of human rights was directed mainly to public authorities like states and their governments, but that private non-profit actors like human rights advocacy groups helped shape the rights discourse and action. In this chapter I will show that for-profit private actors like transnational corporations have a tremendous effect on persons in the modern world, for good or ill. For the first fifty years after the adoption of the United Nations Charter and Universal Declaration of Human Rights, these business enterprises mostly fell outside the mainstream debate about the promotion and protection of internationally recognized human rights. This was so despite the fact that the leaders of the German firm I. G. Farben and other business leaders had faced legal justice at the Nuremberg Trials (second round, US jurisdiction) for their role in criminal behavior.

This general situation was changing in the early twenty-first century. Attention to transnational corporations and human rights constitutes an important dimension in the international discourse on human rights.[1] Non-profit human rights groups, along with the media and particularly consumer organizations and movements, are targeting the corporations. The result is renewed pressure on public authorities, especially states, to adopt norms and policies ensuring that business practices contribute to, rather than contradict, internationally recognized human rights. The corporations themselves are under considerable pressure to pay attention to human rights, although there remain formidable obstacles to a broad corporate social responsibility that includes human rights.[2]

---

[1] Jedrzej George Frynas and Scott Pegg, eds., *Transnational Corporations and Human Rights* (London: Palgrave Macmillan, 2003); Michael K. Addo, *Human Rights Standards and the Responsibility of Transnational Corporations* (The Hague: Kluwer Law International, 1999); S. Rees, ed., *Human Rights, Corporate Responsibility: A Dialogue* (Sydney: Allen and Unwin, 2000).
[2] See Mahmood Monshipouri, Claude E. Welch, Jr., and Evan T. Kennedy, "Multinational Corporations and the Ethics of Global Responsibility: Problems and

295

Enormous impact

It has been long recognized that business enterprises that operate across national boundaries have an enormous impact on the modern world. If we compare the revenues of the twenty-five largest transnational corporations (TNCs) with revenues of states, as in Table 8.1, we see that economic significance.

The world's 200 largest TNCs are incorporated in just ten states, as shown in Table 8.2, above all in the United States and Japan. This means, of course, that if one could affect the national policies of these TNCs in this small number of states, one could greatly affect TNCs' global impact.

Beyond macro-statistics, it is clear that with regard to the internationally recognized right to health, and if we take the case of the HIV/AIDS pandemic in Africa and other places, the role of drug companies (often claiming intellectual property rights) is central. The willingness of these companies, under pressure of course, to contribute to managing the crisis through such policies as helping with lower-priced generic drugs is highly important.[3]

Debate continues as to whether TNCs, because of their enormous economic power, which can sometimes be translated into political power, are beyond the effective control of national governments. A classic study concluded that TNCs were not, in general, beyond the reach of the "sovereign" state.[4] At the same time, however, most observers today agree that it is difficult for a given state to effectively regulate "its" corporations abroad for a variety of reasons. Business enterprises move resources, especially capital, rapidly around the globe, and it is only with some difficulty and a time lag that national governments know what TNCs are doing. Also, TNCs normally have considerable influence in national political systems, especially through pro-business political parties. Furthermore, if a home state tightly regulates corporations incorporated there, the business has the option of moving its headquarters to a different state where taxes and other rules are less burdensome.

Moreover, it is difficult for one state to act alone in this regard. International law has not historically encouraged states to try to project

Possibilities," *Human Rights Quarterly*, 25, 4 (November 2004), 965–989. They argue against MNC self-policing and for some combination of external pressures.

[3] See, e.g., Nana K. Polu and Alan Whiteside, eds., *Political Economy of AIDS in Africa* (Aldershot: Ashgate, 2004).

[4] Raymond Vernon, *Sovereignty at Bay: The Multinational Spread of US Enterprises* (New York: Basic Books, 1971).

Table 8.1 *States and TNCs compared*

Rank	Country/corporation	GDP/revenue $ millions
1	United States	11,667,515
2	Japan	4,623,398
3	Germany	2,714,418
4	United Kingdom	2,140,898
5	France	2,002,582
6	Italy	1,672,302
7	China	1,649,329
8	Spain	991,442
9	Canada	979,764
10	India	691,876
11	Korea, Rep.	679,674
12	Mexico	676,497
13	Australia	631,256
14	Brazil	604,855
15	Russian Federation	582,395
16	Netherlands	577,260
17	Switzerland	359,465
18	Belgium	349,830
19	Sweden	346,404
20	Turkey	301,950
21	Austria	290,109
22	Wal-Mart Stores	287,989
23	BP	285,059
24	Exxon Mobil	270,772
25	Royal Dutch Shell Group	268,690
26	Indonesia	257,641
27	Saudi Arabia	250,557
28	Norway	250,168
29	Denmark	243,043
30	Poland	241,833
31	South Africa	212,777
32	Greece	203,401
33	General Motors	193,517
34	Finland	186,597
35	Ireland	183,560
36	DaimlerChrysler	176,688
37	Toyota Motor	172,616
38	Ford Motor	172,233
39	Portugal	168,281
40	Thailand	163,491
41	Hong Kong, China	163,005
42	Iran, Islamic Rep.	162,709
43	General Electric	152,866
44	Total	152,610
45	Argentina	151,501

(*cont.*)

Table 8.1 (*cont.*)

Rank	Country/corporation	GDP/revenue $ millions
46	Chevron	147,967
47	ConocoPhillips	121,663
48	AXA	121,606
49	Allianz	118,937
50	Malaysia	117,776
51	Israel	117,548
52	Volkswagen	110,649
53	Venezuela, RB	109,322
54	Citigroup	108,276
55	Czech Republic	107,047
56	Singapore	106,818
57	ING Group	105,886
58	Nippon Telegraph & Telephone	100,545
59	Hungary	99,712
60	New Zealand	99,687

Source: news.mongabay.com/2005/0718-worlds_largest.html.

Table 8.2 *Top world companies 2008: most profitable*

		Profits: return on revenues		
Rank	Company	Global 500 rank	2008 profits ($ millions)	Profits % change from 2007
1	Exxon Mobil	2	45,220.0	11.4
2	Gazprom	22	29,864.1	16.1
3	Royal Dutch Shell	1	26,277.0	−16.1
4	Chevron	5	23,931.0	28.1
5	BP	4	21,157.0	1.5
6	Petrobras	34	18,879.0	43.7
7	Microsoft	117	17,681.0	25.7
8	General Electric	12	17,410.0	−21.6
9	Nestlé	48	16,669.6	87.8
10	Industrial & Commercial Bank of China	92	15,948.5	48.8
11	Total	6	15,500.4	−14.1
12	BHP Billiton	120	15,390.0	14.7
13	Petronas	80	15,308.9	−15.5
14	Wal-Mart Stores	3	13,400.0	5.3
15	China Construction Bank	125	13,323.7	46.8
16	CVRD	205	13,218.0	11.8
17	Banco Santander	35	12,992.3	4.8

Table 8.2 (*cont.*)

		Profits: return on revenues		
Rank	Company	Global 500 rank	2008 profits ($ millions)	Profits % change from 2007
18	Johnson & Johnson	103	12,949.0	22.4
19	ENI	17	12,917.0	−5.7
20	AT&T	29	12,867.0	7.7
21	International Business Machines	45	12,334.0	18.4
22	Procter & Gamble	68	12,075.0	16.8
23	China Mobile Communications	99	11,442.0	35.8
24	Rosneft Oil	158	11,120.0	−13.5
25	Telefónica	66	11,112.3	−8.8
26	China National Petroleum	13	10,270.8	−31.2
27	ArcelorMittal	28	9,399.0	−9.3
28	Bank of China	145	9,260.5	25.2
29	Lukoil	65	9,144.0	−3.9
30	Siemens	30	8,595.1	69.8
31	GlaxoSmithKline	168	8,438.6	−19.1
32	Hewlett-Packard	32	8,329.0	14.7
33	Roche Group	171	8,288.1	1.9
34	Novartis	183	8,195.0	−31.4
35	Pfizer	152	8,104.0	−0.5
36	Cisco Systems	191	8,052.0	9.8
37	Barclays	83	8,035.2	−9.1
38	Merck	378	7,808.4	138.4
39	Enel	62	7,747.3	42.3
40	Statoil Hydro	36	7,664.2	1.8
41	PDVSA	27	7,451.0	38.7
42	Agricultural Bank of China	155	7,406.4	28.7
43	Unilever	121	7,357.9	38.3
44	Banco Bilbao Vizcaya Argentaria	113	7,347.7	−12.4
45	GDF Suez	53	7,109.3	110.1
46	Volkswagen	14	6,956.9	23.4
47	Philip Morris International	345	6,890.0	N.A.
48	Occidental Petroleum	365	6,857.0	27.0
49	Verizon Communications	55	6,428.0	16.4
50	TNK-BP Holding	234	6,384.0	11.4

Source: money.cnn.com/magazines/fortune/global500/ . . . /profits/.
Note: Rankings of corporations in Tables 8.1 and 8.2 vary slightly because data are for different years.

extra-territorial jurisdiction in economic matters.[5] And if the state did so, it might restrict "its" corporations in global competition so that the state received fewer economic benefits and competitors more. When in 1977 the USA passed anti-corruption legislation (the Foreign Corrupt Practices Act) making it illegal for corporations registered in the country to pay bribes to get contracts from foreign parties, this put those firms at a competitive disadvantage in global competition. It was only in 1998 that the USA could persuade its partners in the Organization for Economic Cooperation and Development to level the playing field by adopting a multilateral convention, implemented through national legislation, on the subject.[6] The logic of cooperation under conditions of anarchy, or in this case relatively unregulated market competition, is an important subject. Particularly social regulation is weak – viz., regulation for social rather than economic purposes.

The central question is not so much the power of TNCs, or the difficulty of their regulation. Both points are readily agreed to. The more complex question is what, on balance, the impact of TNCs is on persons and their human rights in the modern world. On this there is considerable debate. It follows that there is also a lively exchange on whether there should be more public regulation of TNCs in the name of human rights. On the one hand are the traditional economists who argue that the business of business is business, and human rights have no place in this paradigm. On the other hand are those who believe that TNCs are powerful organizations which should not only do no harm but also actively advance internationally recognized rights.[7]

A critical view

Few persons other than Social Darwinists look with favor on the early stages of the capitalist industrial revolution. There was a certain national economic advance that was achieved via basically unregulated capitalism, and certainly the property owners and money managers benefited. But now there is almost universal rejection of the human conditions (not to

---

[5] But see Mark Gibney and David R. Emerick, "The Extraterritorial Application of United States Law and the Protection of Human Rights: Holding Multinational Corporations to Domestic and International Standards," *Temple International and Comparative Law Journal*, 10, 1 (Spring 1996), 123–145.

[6] AP, "Congress Passes Bill to Curb International Business Bribery," *New York Times*, October 22, 1998, A5.

[7] See Florian Wettstein, *Multinational Corporations and Global Justice: Human Rights Obligations of a Quasi-Governmental Institution* (Stanford: Stanford Business Books, 2009). He addresses the traditional view while advocating active human rights policies by TNCs.

mention environmental damage) of that early industrial capitalism, illustrated by the novels of Charles Dickens. No western market democracy,
and no capitalist state in any developed country, now endorses pure
laissez-faire economics.

A first basic point is that a sophisticated view of modern markets
recognizes they are a social construct, with deep governmental intrusion.[8] Markets are actually created by governments, and extensively
regulated by them, for reasons of economic effectiveness. Markets have
rules and supervisors to promote investor confidence and minimize
inhibiting factors like corruption, fraud, and theft. Modern national
markets do not exist in nature, as it were, but as the result of governmental action. Even so-called *laissez-faire* economics results from governmental action, not a state of nature.

A second basic point is that in contemporary market democracies,
even so-called political conservatives such as Ronald Reagan and Margaret Thatcher endorsed certain aspects of regulated and welfare state
capitalism (Thatcher was a strong defender, for example, of the British
National Health Service). Socially responsible pro-business persons recognize that capitalism is a harsh system, that not all persons benefit, that
some persons require the protection of the state for a life with dignity
under an economic system based on the right to private property.[9] It has
never proved persuasive to argue that both the poor and the rich have the
same freedom to sleep under the bridges as they wish.[10] And so all
modern market democracies regulate national markets for social as well
as economic reasons. All use tax and other policies to limit the harshness
of crude capitalism. At the national level, all western democratic polities
try in different ways to create capitalism with a human face.[11]

This brief reference to historical patterns and basic realities is an
important critique of unregulated business. If left to itself, even in

---

[8] See especially Cass Sunstein, *The Second Bill of Rights: FDR's Unfinished Revolution and Why We Need It More than Ever* (New York: Basic Books, 2004), especially ch. 2.

[9] See Michael Novak and Leslie Lenkowsky, "Economic Growth Won't End Poverty," *New York Times*, July 24, 1985, A19. The authors were associated with the American Enterprise Institute, a conservative, pro-business think tank in Washington.

[10] See further Rhoda Howard-Hassmann and Claude E. Welch, Jr., eds., *Economic Rights in Canada and the United States* (Philadelphia: University of Pennsylvania Press, 2006).

[11] Those unfamiliar with the history of the Cold War may not fully appreciate this irony of semantics. In events leading up to 1968, particularly reform communists in what was then Czechoslovakia tried to create what was called communism with a human face. The attempt was to create a communism that was less harsh and repressive, that blended a new socialism with certain civil and political rights. This move was endorsed by western market democracies, even as it was crushed by a pre-Gorbachev Soviet Union. In the early twenty-first century it was the western-led economic globalization that was often said to be in need of a human face.

western countries that manifested so much concern for the individual that they evolved into liberal and/or social democracies, unregulated business has often exploited, crushed, de-humanized, and affronted human dignity. Once the bonds of community, found in rural and agricultural settings, were replaced by the urban and more impersonal conditions of industrial and technocratic capitalism, the have-nots were clearly in need of protection from the power of the haves. Whatever the difficulties of the political process, relatively humane national regulation of the for-profit system was achieved (at least relative to Dickens' England). The intervention of the state was used to limit the enormous power of the Henry Fords and Andrew Carnegies and the other "robber barons" of early industrial capitalism.[12] One of the great problems immediately after the Cold War in places like Russia and Albania, *inter alia*, was that this regulation of the robber barons had yet to be made effective. This is why the successful financier, investor, and philanthropist George Soros wrote that the greatest threat to democracy in the former communist lands of the Soviet Union and Eastern Europe is precisely capitalism.[13] As one who understands capitalism well, Soros knows that crude capitalism is so harsh and unfair that it is not sustainable when citizens have the freedom to accept or reject it.

What has not been tolerated in the national political economies of the West for about a century, namely unregulated capitalism, has been allowed to proceed in international relations – at least until recently. And while one can chart growing international law in the domain of economics, most of that regulation is designed to encourage free trade and commercial activity, certainly not to restrict it in the name of human rights. That regulation is for economic, not social, reasons. The General Agreement on Tariffs and Trade (GATT) and the World Trade Organization (WTO) are primarily designed to encourage international capitalism, not regulate it according to social values. This was also the main thrust of NAFTA (North American Free Trade Agreement), with provisions on ecology and labor rights added only as afterthoughts when demanded by American unions and others. There is a disconnect between much of the normative framework for *national* capitalism (to prevent gross exploitation) and the main concern of regulation of *international* capitalism (to stabilize capitalism regardless of exploitation).

---

[12] On the political system as a counterweight to business power in the West, see especially E. E. Schattschneider, *The Semi-Sovereign People: A Realist's View of Democracy in America* (New York: Holt, Rinehart and Winston, 1960).

[13] George Soros, "The Capitalist Threat," *Atlantic Monthly*, 279, 2 (February 1997), 45 and *passim*.

Given these factors, it should not be surprising that by 2016 there was a pushback in many nations against globalized economics. Across most wealthy democracies, and in other states too, there was a broadly shared belief that various trade agreements and international economic organizations had benefited elites rather than the so-called working class. In Brexit (as already explained), there was a vote in the UK to leave the EU rather than reform it. In the USA after the election of Donald Trump, the TPP (Trans-Pacific Partnership trade deal) was DOA (dead on arrival).

Thus one of the central questions about the future of global capitalism is whether leading states, who make the rules, can come together in the WTO and other forums and agree on international capitalism with a human face – as they have done, after much political struggle, in their national political economies.[14] In other words, will economic globalization be accompanied by progressive social and political globalization?

In the national political economy, at least from the view of nationality and with class considerations aside, we are all "us." In the international political economy, there is an "in" group – us – and an "out" group – them. Nationalism being what it is, as long as the benefits flow to "us," as a political fact the moral imperative to show concern for "them" is reduced. The World Development Report, produced by the United Nations Development Program, regularly chronicles the large and growing gap between the wealthy global north and the impoverished global south. As one would expect in a situation of mostly unregulated international economics where a sense of global community is weak, the elites with property rights and capital prosper, and many of the have-nots live a life on the margins of human dignity. Dickens would not be surprised. Even as there was growing concern in some circles (but definitely not in others) about gross inequality within nations, there was not a comparable surge of interest in gross inequality between groups of nations – such as the global north and south, or more developed and less developed countries.

Against this background, one can easily find horror stories of unprincipled TNCs making handsome profits at the expense of clearly exploited employees and bystanders. Authors from Stephen Hymer to David

---

[14] See Rhoda Howard-Hassmann, *Can Globalization Promote Human Rights?* (University Park, PA: Penn State University Press, 2010). See also Jorge Heine and Ramesh Thakur, eds., *The Dark Side of Globalization* (Tokyo: United Nations University Press, 2011), for the same point in different terms. See further David Kinley, *Civilising Globalisation: Human Rights and the Global Economy* (Cambridge: Cambridge University Press, 2009), who argues for combining notions of social justice with pursuit of economic growth.

Korten have chronicled the record.[15] Relevant is the work of Sven Beckert, who shows conclusively that the cotton trade was made profitable first in the UK and then in the USA through ethnic cleansing, slavery, tenant farming as combined with racial discrimination, and other forms of exploitation on an international scale.[16] Economic globalization is partly the story of sweatshops, child labor, dangerous work, low pay, forced and slave labor, opposition to unions, and in extreme cases crimes against humanity and genocide. IBM and other outside companies were complicit in the German Holocaust.[17] As early as 1938, before Nazi Germany had invaded Poland and before Swiss leaders had reasonable concern about a Nazi invasion of Switzerland, some Swiss banks were stealing the property of Austrian Jews and turning it over to well-paying Germans.[18] More recently, Union Carbide has been less than exemplary in ensuring that those killed and hurt by the poisonous gas leak at its plant in Bhopal, India in 1984 have had their minimal rights to fair compensation respected.[19] The dark underside of globalized business is represented by trafficking in human beings, driven by the profit motive.[20]

Debora L. Spar of the Harvard Business School believes that the social record of TNCs engaged in the extraction of natural resources in foreign countries has been especially poor.[21] On the one hand, the TNC must have cozy relations with the (all-too-often reactionary or at least

---

[15] Stephen Hymer, "The Multinational Corporation and the Law of Uneven Development," in J. W. Bhagwati, ed., *Economics and World Order* (New York: Macmillan, 1971), 113–140; David Korten, *When Corporations Rule the World* (West Hartford: Kumarian Press, 1995). See also Richard J. Barnet and John Cavanagh, *Global Dreams: Imperial Corporations and the New World Order* (New York: Simon & Schuster, 1994).

[16] *Empire of Cotton: A Global History* (New York: Vintage, 2015), winner of the Bancroft Prize.

[17] See further Edwin Black, *IBM and the Holocaust: The Strategic Alliance Between Nazi Germany and America's Most Powerful Corporation* (New York: Random House, Crown, 2001). In general, however, on the role of business in the German Holocaust, see the scholarship of Peter Hayes, including a critical book review of Black's *IBM and the Holocaust*. A number of business deals between American corporations and German actors between 1933 and 1941 were negotiated by John Foster Dulles and the law firm for which he worked. Dulles of course later became Secretary of State in the Eisenhower Administration.

[18] William Glaberson, "For Betrayal by Swiss Bank and Nazis, $21 million," *New York Times*, April 14, 2005, www.nytimes.com/2005/04/14/nyregion/for-betrayal-by-swiss-bank-and-nazis-21-million.html?_r=0.

[19] Saritha Rai, "Bhopal Victims Not Fully Paid, Rights Group Says," *New York Times*, November 30, 2004, W3.

[20] See especially Siddharth Kara, *Sex Trafficking: Inside the Business of Modern Slavery* (New York: Columbia University Press, 2009).

[21] Debora L. Spar, "Multinationals and Human Rights: A Case of Strange Bedfellows," *Human Rights Interest Group Newsletter*, American Society of International Law, 8, 1 (Winter 1998), 13–16.

insensitive) government that controls access to the resource. The TNC and local government share an interest in a docile and compliant labor force. On the other hand, the TNC often shows little interest in other aspects of the local population. The resource is mostly sold abroad, with a certain amount of the profits going to the governmental elite. If that elite does not act progressively to reinvest the profit into infrastructures that improve the lot of the local population, such as education, health care, and ecological protection, the TNC has often seen little short-term economic interest in the situation. Profits are expatriated, and the condition of the local population is left to the tender mercies of the local government.

It is reasonably clear that Royal Dutch Shell in Nigeria cooperated closely with military governments and their security forces in suppressing local resistance to prevailing policies centering on extraction of oil in Ogoniland. Not only did Shell make it possible, at company expense, for the Abacha government to violently suppress those objecting to environmental degradation by Shell in Ogoniland. But also Shell refused to intercede with the government to object to the execution of Ken Saro-Wiwa, one of the most outspoken leaders of the Ogoni people in Nigeria. In reaction to considerable criticism, Shell took a number of steps to elevate the discourse about human rights as related to its business operations. But on balance the facts to date indicate that Shell has been less than fully socially responsible in its operations in Nigeria.[22]

The most fundamental *raison d'être* of the TNC is precisely economic self-interest, not to be a human rights actor. At least that has been the historical situation. "Investors and executives tended to see human rights as a matter for government officials and diplomats to implement, and resisted pressures to have their businesses used as tools for political reform . . . The globalization of the economy and the globalization of human rights concerns, both important phenomena in the second half of this century, developed separately from each other."[23]

Some TNCs went beyond cooperation with, and active support for, a reactionary elite. United Fruit in Guatemala (1954) and ITT in Chile (1973) actively cooperated with the US government in helping to overthrow politicians (Arbenz in Guatemala and Allende in Chile) who were

---

[22] For one overview out of a vast literature see Kenneth Omeje, *High Stakes and Stakeholders: Oil Conflict and Security in Nigeria* (Aldershot: Ashgate, 2006). See later in this chapter regarding the Kiobel case.

[23] Lance Compa and Tashia Hinchliffe-Darricarrere, "Enforcing International Rights through Corporate Codes of Conduct," *Columbia Journal of Transnational Law*, 33 (1995), 665.

champions especially of labor rights for their nationals.[24] Various TNCs, from United Fruit to Coca-Cola, actively opposed progressive governments and laws designed to advance labor rights and other human rights. There are powerful economic and political forces pushing corporations into exploitative and otherwise abusive policies. Economically there is the bottom line: companies must make a profit to stay in business. If the competition uses cheap labor, then it is difficult if not impossible for a company to use unionized, well-paid labor. The history of Levi Strauss demonstrates this clearly.[25] This San Francisco-based company, with a reputation for treating its labor force properly, has basically stopped manufacturing in the USA, and has felt compelled to outsource its production to foreign countries like China with poor human rights records, all because of pursuit of the bottom line. Within countries like the USA, when labor organized in northern cities like Detroit, management moved production to places like South Carolina and Alabama where labor was cheap and unions weak. The same process now characterizes business on a transnational or global scale. In this sense economic globalization does reflect a race to the bottom.[26]

Politically, when corporations deal with repressive governments and/or those known to violate international standards on human rights and humanitarian affairs, to get the business, companies tend to defer to governmental policies. This is true not just of IBM in Nazi Germany. The Caterpillar Company, when urged by certain human rights groups to not allow its bulldozers to be used by Israel in ways that violated international humanitarian law in the West Bank (collective punishments through destruction of houses alleged to be linked to "terrorists"), said it was a matter for the Israeli government.[27] Had Caterpillar withdrawn, it is likely that Israel would have continued the policy through a different company. When the USA prohibited its oil companies from doing business in Sudan, because of major human rights violations principally in the Darfur region, other oil companies took the business, especially those from China.

---

[24] On Arbenz and Guatemala, see especially Piero Gleijeses, *Shattered Hope: The Guatemalan Revolution and the United States 1944–1954* (Princeton: Princeton University Press, 1991). On Allende and Chile, see especially Richard Z. Israel, *Politics and Ideology in Allende's Chile* (Tempe: Arizona State University Press, 1989).

[25] See Karl Schoenberger, *Levi's Children: Coming to Terms with Human Rights in the Global Marketplace* (New York: Atlantic Monthly Press, 2000).

[26] See further Kimberly Ann Elliott and Richard B. Freeman, *Can Labor Standards Improve Under Globalization?* (Washington: Institute of International Economics, 2003).

[27] See Human Rights Watch, "Israel: Caterpillar Should Suspend Bulldozer Sales," www.hrw.org/news/2004/11/21/israel-caterpillar-should-suspend-bulldozer-sales.

The economic "laws" of competition, of supply and demand, tend to produce major human rights violations when markets are unregulated for social reasons.

One can find plenty of examples of "business as usual" and disregard for human rights. In the London area, human rights activists have noted the ease with which former foreign leaders can buy expensive property and live a life of luxury despite responsibility for past human rights violations and corruption abroad. Real estate agents and lawyers have not been inclined to ask questions about the sources of money involved or the conditions of past activity. At the time of writing, the British Parliament was considering a bill to at least delay if not restrict such rea-estate transactions in certain cases.[28]

A more positive view

At the same time that Professor Spar, as noted above, believes that extractive TNCs in particular have a poor social record, she observes that there are other types of TNCs: consumer products firms, manufacturing firms, service and information firms. Some of these, she argues, are engaged in business that is compatible with several human rights. She goes so far as to argue that TNCs sometimes export human rights values.[29] According to her research, some TNCs are interested in not just cheap labor but a good labor force that is highly educated and exists in the context of stable democracy. Thus Intel chose Costa Rica for one of its foreign plants. Firms intending to sell in foreign markets have an interest in a well-paid labor force with disposable income to buy their products.

Above all, Spar argues, all firms have an economic interest in avoiding negative publicity that might damage their sales. Thus TNCs do not want to face consumer boycotts and negative publicity because of the harsh, exploitative conditions in their foreign plants, or cooperation with pariah regimes. She cites a number of firms that have altered their policies, especially to establish codes of conduct for business practices

---

[28] Ben Judah, "London Rolls Out the Blood-Red Carpet for Kleptocrats," *New York Times*, December 29, 2016, www.nytimes.com/2016/12/29/opinion/london-rolls-out-the-blood-red-carpet-for-kleptocrats.html?emc=edit_tnt_20161229&nlid=40729248&tnte mail0=y.

[29] In addition to her views already noted, see her article "The Spotlight and the Bottom Line: How Multinationals Export Human Rights," *Foreign Affairs*, 77, 2 (March–April 1998), 7–12. See further Kenneth A. Rodman, "Think Globally, Punish Locally: Non-State Actors, Multinational Corporations, and Human Rights Sanctions," *Ethics & International Affairs*, 12 (1998), 19–42.

and to allow independent monitoring of labor conditions, in relation to widespread criticism: Starbucks Coffee, the Gap clothiers, Nike, Reebok, Toys R Us, Avon, etc. She notes that a number of firms pulled out of Myanmar, when a highly repressive military government was in control: Levi Strauss, Macy's, Liz Claiborne, Eddie Bauer, Heineken, etc. She cites as especially effective the international campaign against child labor in the making of soccer balls, which led major TNC sporting firms to certify that no child or slave labor was used in the making of the balls. After all, one might add, if it is common practice to certify that tuna are not caught with nets that endanger dolphins, why not certify that consumer products are not made with processes that violate human rights?

Moreover, beyond reacting to negative publicity that might hurt the firms' bottom line on their economic books, some observers note that TNCs export standard operating procedures that are sometimes an improvement over those previously existing in a developing country. TNC plants in the global south may provide infirmaries for health care, or improved safety conditions. TNCs, even while paying wages below standards in the global north, may pay wages in developing countries that permit growth, savings, and investment over time.

After all, the Asian Tigers such as Taiwan made remarkable economic progress from the mid-1950s to the mid-1990s on the basis of an economy open to TNCs. Countries like South Korea and Taiwan not only became more prosperous over time, with a skilled work force, but also became liberal and social democracies, at least relative to their past. Thus, it is argued, there is nothing inherent in the operations of TNCs that requires that they block beneficial change in host countries or that they oppose human rights standards. While they have certainly done so in the past on occasion, an emerging world of liberal market democracies, or even social democracies, would be perfectly compatible with a bottom line in the black for TNCs.

Also relevant is the fact that the major trading partners of the USA are other market democracies such as Canada and the states of the European Union. These states vigorously protect a wide range of human rights, including a right to health care and extensive unemployment and social security entitlements, while maintaining an economy that does very well over time. Clearly many states that recognize socioeconomic rights and manifest a relatively large social safety net score very well on indexes purporting to measure economic competitiveness. There is nothing inconsistent about being a competitive capitalist society and also providing for the socioeconomic needs of citizens and legal residents.

Some social science research finds a positive correlation between foreign economic penetration, or direct foreign investment, and the

Table 8.3 *Most competitive world economies 2010*

Singapore	1
Hong Kong	2
USA	3
Switzerland	4
Australia	5
Sweden	6
Canada	7
Taiwan	8
Norway	9
Malaysia	10
Luxemburg	11
Netherlands	12
Denmark	13
Austria	14
Qatar	15
Germany	16
Israel	17
China (mainland)	18
Finland	19
New Zealand	20
Ireland	21
United Kingdom	22
Korea	23
France	24
Belgium	25
Thailand	26
Japan	27
Chile	28
Czech Republic	29
Iceland	30
India	31
Poland	32
Kazakhstan	33
Estonia	34
Indonesia	35
Spain	36
Portugal	37
Brazil	38
Philippines	39
Italy	40
Peru	41
Hungary	42
Lithuania	43
South Africa	44
Colombia	45
Greece	46
Mexico	47

(cont.)

Table 8.3 (*cont.*)

Turkey	48
Slovak Republic	49
Jordan	50
Russia	51
Slovenia	52
Bulgaria	53
Romania	54
Argentina	55
Croatia	56
Ukraine	57
Venezuela	58

Source: www.imd.org/research/publications/wcy/upload/score board.pdf.
Note: The World Competitiveness Scoreboard presents the 2010 overall rankings for fifty-eight economies. The economies are ranked from the most to the least competitive.

respect for a wide range of human rights.[30] Another study has found similarly that the presence of TNCs and direct foreign investment is positively correlated with the practice of civil and political rights in developing countries. Those same civil and political rights were also positively correlated with higher GNP, US foreign assistance, and higher debt. Direct foreign investment was also positively correlated with the Physical Quality of Life Index, measuring longevity, nutrition, and education. Hence the author of this study concluded that in the modern world TNCs were engines of progressive development, associated with both improved civil-political and socioeconomic rights.[31] There are other optimistic accounts of the social and political workings of capitalism over time.[32] A 2009 study found that human rights clauses in trade agreements among governments had a positive effect on the practice of human rights, as these trade agreements set ground rules affecting corporate behavior.[33]

[30] David L. Richards, et al., "Money with a Mean Streak?: Foreign Economic Penetration and Government Respect for Human Rights in Developing Countries," *International Studies Quarterly*, 45, 2 (June 2001), 219–240.
[31] William H. Meyer, "Human Rights and Multi-National Corporations: Theory v. Quantitative Analysis," *Human Rights Quarterly*, 18, 2 (Spring 1996), 368–397; and his book making the same points, *Human Rights and International Political Economy in Third World Nations: Multinational Corporations, Foreign Aid, and Repression* (Westport: Praeger, 1998). There followed a debate about his methods and conclusions.
[32] Max Singer and Aaron Wildavsky, *The Real World Order: Zones of Peace, Zones of Turmoil*, rev. edn. (Chatham, NJ: Chatham House Publishers, 1996).
[33] Emilie Hafner-Burton, *Forced to Be Good: Why Trade Agreements Boost Human Rights* (Ithaca: Cornell University Press, 2009).

One does not need gross exploitation to make capitalism work, Marxist analysis notwithstanding. But one may need global social regulation to level the playing field, so that corporations are not tempted to move from rights-protective polities to oppressive ones.

A balance sheet

Two overviews of the effects of economic globalization on individuals and their human rights point in the same direction. Rhoda Howard-Hassmann concludes that global capitalism will be good for many individuals in the grand scheme of things over time, but that there will be the danger of many human rights abuses along the way.[34] The challenge is to leap over the human rights abuses that characterized the development of national capitalism in the industrialized West, so that the workings of global capitalism are more humane. Pietra Rivoli concludes likewise that capitalism works to the benefit of many, but that there are usually large numbers of individuals who are negatively affected either through exploitation or loss of jobs. She too sees an important role for public authorities in constructing a global capitalism with a more human face.[35]

It follows that if left unregulated, many TNCs will opt for short-term profits at the expense of human dignity for many persons affected directly and indirectly by their practices. It seems there must be countervailing power, either from public authorities, or from human rights organizations and movements, if TNC practices are to be made basically compatible with the International Bill of Rights (IBR). Given what I have noted before, namely that many elites are not enthusiastic about the IBR, effective human rights are usually wrestled from below in a tough struggle.[36] The clear experience of the global north is that unregulated capitalism is injurious to human dignity and social justice. Just as limitations on crude capitalism were achieved in western market democracies through tough struggle, sometimes bloody, so globalized economics is likely to be changed only in a similar process. Protests against the WTO in particular and economic globalization in general reflect this historical pattern. One salutary aspect of the rise of the "New Nationalism" circa

---

[34] "The Second Great Transformation: Human Rights Leapfrogging in the Era of Globalization," *Human Rights Quarterly*, 27, 1 (February 2005), 1–40. See also her book, *Can Globalization Promote Human Rights?*, on human rights and economic globalization.

[35] Pietra Rivoli, *The Travels of a T-Shirt in the Global Economy: An Economist Examines the Markets, Power, and Politics of World Trade* (New York: Wiley, 2005).

[36] See further, e.g., Rhoda Howard, *Human Rights in Commonwealth Africa* (Totowa, NJ: Rowman & Littlefield, 1986).

2016 was a willingness of nativist leaders on the political right wing to re-examine various international economic arrangements such as trade agreements that did not benefit broad sectors of society. Whether the critical rhetoric would be followed by beneficial policies is a question that will be answered by their actual policies over time. The central question is not just pursuit of economic growth per se, but what is the pattern of distribution of benefits. How is equity defined under capitalism, where some inequality is inherent?

Events in Indonesia during 1998 fit a larger pattern. The authoritarian Suharto government, with the support of many TNCs, clung to the *status quo* under the general banner of "Asian values" – meaning for present purposes that authoritarian Asian states had found a model of successful economics that did not require broad political participation, independent labor unions, and other manifestations of internationally recognized human rights. There was a pattern of impressive economic growth, but the continuation of much poverty – exactly as predicted by Novak and Lenkowsky.[37] But the "Asian flu" of economic recession caused a re-evaluation of "crony capitalism," led by students, labor groups, and others demanding more attention to human rights. Suharto stepped down, the succeeding government ceased to be a champion of "Asian values," and numerous changes occurred. Parts of the elite took reform measures, under popular pressures, which was precisely the pattern that had obtained in the West during earlier periods.

Relevant also was the history of Nike and Reebok in Asia. Both companies had sub-contracted the production of athletic shoes and soccer balls, *inter alia*, to firms that operated sweatshops, employed child labor, and otherwise violated internationally recognized labor rights. Negative publicity caused both companies to alter certain policies, and at one point Nike hired a prominent American public figure, Andrew Young, to examine some of its Asian operations. But a debate continued over whether the companies were engaged primarily in public relations and damage control, or in substantive change in keeping with human rights standards. (As noted in Chapter 3, certain labor rights such as freedom from slavery, freedom to bargain collectively, freedom of association, etc. are considered to be part of basic human rights.) The controversy was especially troubling to Reebok, which had pioneered certain policies related to human rights such as sponsoring rock concerts to benefit Amnesty International and making an annual human rights award. These two companies and others did participate in a program

---

[37] Cf. Novak and Lenkowsky, "Economic Growth."

designed to guarantee that child labor was not used in the manufacture of soccer balls carrying their brand name (small fingers had proved useful in sewing).[38] By 2005 Nike, under considerable pressure, had promised to disclose the location of all of its manufacturing, presumably to enhance transparency and convince consumers and others that it was not operating sweatshops.

Regulation for human rights?

Three points are noteworthy about TNCs and international regulation in the name of human rights:
(1) the weakness of current international law, especially as developed through the United Nations system, in regulating the social effects of international business;
(2) the growing importance of private activism, including law suits and consumer and other social movements, plus the communications media, in providing critiques of for-profit behavior; and
(3) the facilitative actions of some states, especially the USA during the Clinton Administration, but not Japan in general or the George W. Bush Administration, in trying to close the gap between much TNC practice and human rights standards.

Weakness of international law

As noted earlier in this chapter, international law has had little to say about the social effects of TNC action. International law is directed mostly to states. States are held responsible for human rights conditions within their jurisdiction. The basic rule of international law is that TNCs are not subjects of that law, but only objects through the intermediary role of the state where they are incorporated.[39] Thus, TNCs are not directly responsible to international law, and TNCs – outside the EU framework – have mostly escaped direct regulation under international law.

The example of the Convention on the Rights of All Migrant Workers and Members of their Families was instructive. Those bound by this multilateral treaty were states. The twenty-one ratifying states needed to bring the treaty into legal force was achieved in 2003. But no

---

[38] As with Shell in Nigeria, so with particularly Nike in Asia, there is a small library on the subject. See further, e.g., Philip Segal, "Nike Hones Its Image on Rights in Asia," *New York Times*, June 26, 1998, 1. In 1998 alone, the *New York Times* and other members of the global media carried numerous stories on this subject.

[39] See further the Barcelona Traction case, *International Court of Justice Reports*, 1970, 3.

industrialized country ratified, and it is these countries that serve as hosts to most migrant workers. It was the sending states that tended to ratify (e.g., Bosnia, Mexico, the Philippines, Uganda, etc.). So despite the treaty, most migrant workers and the companies that employed them remained outside the legal protections of the treaty, because the industrialized states refused to obligate themselves and then regulate their corporations under this part of international law.[40]

UN narrowly defined

During the 1970s when the United Nations was the scene of debates about a New International Economic Order (NIEO), there were demands from the global south, supported by the communist east, for a binding code of conduct on TNCs. Like the NIEO itself, this binding code for TNCs never came to fruition, due to blocking action by the capital exporting states whose primary concern was to protect the freedom of "their" corporations to make profits. (The OECD, made up of the westernized democracies, approved a non-binding code, but it has generated little influence.) A code of conduct for TNCs was negotiated in UNCTAD (UN Conference on Trade and Development) but never formally approved. A series of statements from UNCTAD, controlled by the developing countries, has been generally critical of the TNC record, but these statements were muted during the 1980s and thereafter. Attracting direct foreign investment via TNCs, not scaring it away, became the name of the game, especially after the demise of European communism.

For a time one could find a series of critical statements about TNCs from the former UN Human Rights Sub-Commission. A typical statement was issued by a Special Rapporteur in August 1998. El Hadji Guisse of Senegal called for criminal penalties in the national law of home states to regulate TNC actions that violated internationally recognized social and economic rights.[41] By 2003 the Sub-Commission, comprising independent experts rather than state representatives, had adopted a set of "Norms on the Responsibilities of Transnational Corporations and Other Business Enterprises with Regard to Human Rights."[42] Arguing that all corporations and business have an

---

[40] See Human Rights Watch, "Migrant Workers Need Protection," July 1, 2003, www.hrw.org/news/2003/06/30/migrant-workers-need-protection.
[41] Inter Press Service, "Human Rights: Holding Transnationals in Check," Global Policy Forum, www.igc.apc.org/globalpolicy/socecon/tncs/humrig.htm.
[42] UN Doc: E/CN.4/Sub.2/2003/12/Rev.2 (2003).

"obligation" (moral?, legal?) to protect the human rights recognized in national and international law, this UN document then goes on to elaborate such basic principles as equality and non-discrimination, personal security, labor rights, and so on.

In 2005, the UN Human Rights Commission, before it was sidelined in favor of the new UN Human Rights Council, itself appointed an individual to make a study of business and human rights. This move was opposed by the governments of Australia and the USA.

All of this effort directed to non-binding codes and further studies at the UN led into the creation of the Global Compact, an initiative of Secretary-General Kofi Annan to get TNCs to endorse a set of nine principles dealing mainly with human rights but also with ecological protection. The approach was traditional in the sense of asking business to police itself and accept certain standards of social responsibility. Whether all of this standard-setting and "social pressure light" would prove more effective than the various non-binding codes of conduct in the past remained to be seen.[43] It is possible that assertive pressure from civil society might cause corporations to take these UN norms at least somewhat seriously.[44] One study published in 2010 concluded that those TNCs that became parties to the UN Global Compact were more likely to adopt corporate statements on human rights and more likely to receive positive outside assessment of their human rights performance.[45] John Ruggie, who was the Secretary-General's representative on the subject, gave his views in a book published in 2013.[46] Traditional human rights advocacy groups continued to press for a stronger mechanism, whereas others thought there was still no political will among states for any instrument with legal teeth.

UN broadly defined

The International Labour Organization has not played a highly effective role in efforts after the Cold War to target abusive practices by TNCs. In part this was because national business associations made up one-third of

---

[43] See further Andreas Rasche and Georg Kell, eds., *The UN Global Compact: Achievements, Trends, and Challenges* (Cambridge: Cambridge University Press, 2010).

[44] See further Sean D. Murphy, "Taking Multinational Corporate Codes of Conduct to the Next Level," *Columbia Journal of Transnational Law Association*, 43 (2005), starting at 389.

[45] Patrick Bernhagen and Neil J. Mitchell, "The Private Provision of Public Goods: Corporate Commitments and the United Nations Global Compact," *International Studies Quarterly*, 54, 4 (December 2010), 1175–1187.

[46] John Ruggie, *Just Business: Multinational Corporations and Human Rights* (New York: Norton, 2013).

the membership of the ILO. Another reason was that some western states, chiefly the USA, did not favor channeling their major concerns through the ILO. During the Cold War the ILO had fallen out of favor with Washington due to various political battles. By the turn of the century the ILO had not recovered from these bruising struggles and had not proved to be a dynamic organization capable of achieving striking developments in defense of labor rights. The ILO had a role to play in long-term socialization. Its basic standards fed into other developments at the UN Human Rights Commission and the Global Compact. But its record of decisive, short-run improvements was not striking.

The ILO was old and distinguished, and it has long manifested a human rights program in relation to labor rights. As I noted in Chapter 3, since 1919 it had developed a series of reasonable – if sometimes vague – standards about international labor rights pertaining to a safe and healthy work environment, non-discrimination, fair wages, working hours, child labor, convict or forced labor, freedom of association, the right to organize, and the right to collective bargaining. But despite an elaborate system for reviewing and supervising its conventions, the ILO was unable to achieve very much "support in international practice – at least in the sense of universal compliance by multinational corporations with these standards."[47] The ILO Tripartite Declaration of Principles Concerning Multinational Enterprises and Social Policy (1977) also failed to affect the practice of many TNCs. In theory during the Cold War, labor rights should have been an area for cooperation between East and West, if not north and south. But the ILO was able to produce little progressive change during the Cold War,[48] as after. The abstract norms might remain valid. The principles underlying the basic conventions might have entered into customary law and become binding even on non-parties that were members of the ILO. The question was how to develop a political process that paid them some concrete attention.

A bright spot in the global picture after the Cold War was the growing attention to child labor.[49] The International Convention on the Rights of

[47] Diane F. Orentlicher and Timothy A. Gelatt, "Public Law, Private Actors: The Impact of Human Rights on Business Investors in China," *Northwestern Journal of International Law and Business*, 14 (1993), 116 and *passim*.

[48] Ernst A. Haas, *Human Rights and International Action* (Stanford: Stanford University Press, 1970).

[49] See Samantha Besson and Joanna Bourke-Martignoni, "Children's Convention (Convention on the Rights of the Child)," in David P. Forsythe, ed., *Encyclopedia of Human Rights* (New York: Oxford University Press, 2009), vol. I, 300–308. See further Burns H. Weston, ed., *Child Labor and Human Rights: Making Children Matter* (Boulder: Lynne Rienner, 2005).

the Child was almost universally accepted – only the USA and Somalia refused to ratify, the latter state often lacking effective government.[50] This law obligated states to protect child workers against forced and unsafe labor, *inter alia*.[51] UNICEF, the UN's premier agency dealing with children, was increasingly linking itself to this treaty and was seeing itself as much an actor for human rights as for relief and development. At a global conference in 1997 UNICEF expressed some optimism that the worst forms of exploitation of the 250 million working children could be successfully challenged, as had proved true with regard to much child labor in the garment industry.[52]

One needed to be careful, however, about a negative approach to the subject that insisted on a simple ban on child labor. This approach alone condemned children and their families to continued poverty and a denial of the recognized right to an adequate standard of living. What was required was a ban combined with positive developments. The source of child labor was underdevelopment. Small steps like providing the funds for better meals in schools could get children out of the fields and sweatshops. Overall development would have the same effect. Just removing children from the production of soccer balls in Pakistan did little but guarantee continued grinding poverty for them and their families, plus a boost for machine-made soccer balls in the sweatshops of China.[53]

Trade law

On the other side of the coin, embryonic trade law might not prove so supportive of growing attention to human rights. As noted earlier in this book, there was some fear that dispute panels under the new World Trade Organization would strike down national and sub-national legislation designed to curtail TNC activity in repressive states like Burma.

---

[50] Important circles in the USA championed parental and privacy rights and were skeptical of the intrusion of public authority into this domain, whether national or international. While some of the American opposition to this convention was irrational, it remained strong. Fears about the introduction of abortion rights or the undermining of parental authority in matters of religion might be misguided, but they were held intensely by some.

[51] Especially Article 32.

[52] UNICEF, "Conference Adopts Agenda against Child Labour," www.unicef.org/newsline/97pr53.htm.

[53] See further Mahmood Monshipoori, "Human Rights and Child Labor in South Asia," in David P. Forsythe and Patrice C. McMahon, eds., *Human Rights and Diversity: Area Studies Revisited* (Lincoln: University of Nebraska Press, 2003). See also a series of articles on this subject in the *New York Times* by Nicholas D. Kristof, as in "The Fuss over Child Labor Is Misguided," April 6, 2004.

Observers had been fearful that human rights legislation, such as from the state of Massachusetts, would be struck down in the WTO as an impermissible restraint on free trade. But the US Supreme Court made this particular point moot. Massachusetts had adopted a state law specifying that any company doing business in repressive Burma/Myanmar could not contract for services with Massachusetts. But the highest US court ruled unanimously that such internal state legislation was unconstitutional, as the US federal government had pre-empted legislation pertaining to Burma. Thus the Court held that Massachusetts was unconstitutionally interfering with the foreign policy power of the federal government.[54] (In the past, other internal legislation on human rights in foreign states, as in the Republic of South Africa under white minority rule, had been allowed, as the federal government had not tried to preempt internal state and local action.)

At the time of writing, efforts to interject stronger provisions into the WTO regarding human rights, and especially labor rights, had not been successful.[55] In 2014, the WTO struck down a US regulation requiring producers of meat to label the origin of their product. Intended as a matter of consumer protection, the regulation to divulge origin of the meat products was held to be a restraint on trade. Some critics feared that similar logic on behalf of free trade might be employed to strike down reasonable trade restrictions in the name of human rights.

The WTO continued to strongly endorse business prerogatives especially when buttressed by TRIPS – the agreement linked to the WTO protecting trade-related intellectual property rights. Among other issues, TRIPS protected the right of transnational drug companies under patent law to ensure the sale of their higher-priced drugs, and to block the sale of cheaper generic drugs that might impinge on those patents. But in places like sub-Saharan Africa, where HIV/AIDS was rampant, many human rights organizations pressured the drug companies to put people ahead of profits, to cooperate with the use of the cheaper generic drugs despite intellectual property rights. After much controversy the TNC pharmaceuticals did yield on a number of points, while making their own point that protection of patents was necessary to ensure some profitable return on

---

[54] For an analysis of *National Foreign Trade Council v. Crosby*, see Peter J. Spiro, "U.S. Supreme Court Knocks Down State Burma Law," *ASIL Insights*, American Society of International Law, June 2000, www.asil.org/insights/volume/5/issue/7/us-supreme-court-knocks-down-state-burma-law.

[55] See further Daniel B. Braaten, "World Trade Organization," in *Encyclopedia of Human Rights*, vol. V, 395–398; and Susan Ariel Aaronson and Jamie M. Zimmerman, *Trade Imbalance: The Struggle to Weigh Human Rights Concerns in Trade Policymaking* (New York: Cambridge University Press, 2007).

investments, it being those investments in costly research that led to new drugs. There were several barriers to an adequate response to the African HIV/AIDS pandemic, a situation that might repeat itself in parts of Asia as well. The arrangements for Africa showed both the clash of different human rights – to private property and to adequate health – as well as the prevalence of negotiated arrangements rather than general legal solutions.[56] The pharmaceuticals were concerned about damage to their brand names by a full and absolute insistence on their recognized property rights.

There is also regional trade law. In the North American Free Trade Agreement (NAFTA), unlike the WTO, there is a "side agreement" on labor rights (as well as on ecological protection). This reference to labor is relatively weak, at least in the view of Human Rights Watch and many other unions and human rights NGOs.[57] But one labor expert took a more positive view, arguing that NAFTA's labor provisions had legitimized the linkage between trade and human rights, while advancing a number of important principles as well as some regional cooperation on labor rights.[58] The same general situation characterizes the Central American Free Trade Agreement (CAFTA): there is some mention of labor rights, but the supervising and adjudicatory measures are weak. Given the influence of the Republican Party, the party of big business in US politics, it was difficult to get strong labor provisions in these regional arrangements in the Western Hemisphere. Even in the USA, a member of both CAFTA and NAFTA, and with its own federal and internal state legislation, there were significant labor abuses. In the state of Florida, for example, a number of agricultural workers existed in conditions of virtual forced labor and slavery, not to mention poor working conditions, lack of health care, and low wages.[59]

The only relatively strong protections for labor rights at the regional level are to be found in the European Union (EU).[60] Within the EU,

---

[56] For one view see Susan K. Sell and Aseem Prakash, "Using Ideas Strategically: The Contest Between Business and NGO Networks in Intellectual Property Rights," *International Studies Quarterly*, 48, 1 (March 2004), 143–175.

[57] Human Rights Watch, "Nafta Labor Accord Ineffective," April 16, 2001, www.hrw.org/English/docs/2001/04/16/global179.htm. See also the criticism in David Bacon, *The Children of NAFTA: Labor Wars on the US/Mexico Border* (Berkeley: University of California Press, 2004).

[58] Lance Compa, "A Glass Half Full: The NAFTA Labor Agreement and Cross-Border Labor Action," in George J. Andreopoulos, ed., *Concepts and Strategies in International Human Rights* (New York: Peter Lang, 2003).

[59] See further Human Rights Watch, "Human Rights of Florida's Farm Workers Are Under Serious Threat," March 2, 2005, www.hrw.org/english/docs/2005/03/02/usdom10284_txt.htm.

[60] See further Paul Craig and Grainne de Burca, *EU Law: Text Cases and Materials*, 3rd edn. (Oxford: Oxford University Presss, 2003), chs. 17 and 20.

treaty law and the case law of the European Court of Justice (ECJ) protect the free movement of workers within the EU without discrimination on grounds of nationality. ECJ cases also stipulate equal pay for men and women, and that such standards are directed not just to the goal of economic prosperity but to advancing the rights of individuals as part of the pursuit of social progress. Directives by the EU Council of Ministers endorse not only equal pay for equal work, but also equality in pension benefits and equal parental leave. Not just state members of the EU but corporations operating within the EU are obligated to follow these standards.

An ICC role?

The first prosecutor of the International Criminal Court suggested in several venues that he might be inclined to bring indictments against business leaders who are complicit in genocide, or crimes against humanity, or major war crimes.[61] There has been considerable discussion of the relevance of this possibility in situations like the Democratic Republic of the Congo. There, where public authority is weak and in some areas virtually non-existent, as in the Ituri district, a number of corporations are involved in extracting the abundant and valuable natural resources of the country – such as diamonds, gold, coltan (used in cell phones), and timber. The industries involved hire security firms to protect their operations, and allegedly these militia are some of the actors engaging in the atrocities often reported in various sources.[62] The long-running conflict in the DRC is the most disruptive and deadly in any country since World War II. The size and complexity of the problem makes it very difficult to find outside parties that want to seriously engage in order to manage the situation. There is little prospect of "humanitarian intervention" by states, and the IGOs controlled by states, like the UN or African Union, are only engaged in marginal ways. In this situation, where one finds "resource wars" and "blood diamonds," prosecution of corporate leaders under international criminal law might be one of the few promising avenues for doing something about systematic abuse, including murder, rape, persecution, and forced displacement.

Indictment of business leaders in the ICC, however, is not likely to encourage the USA to support or tolerate the Court, at least as long as the

---

[61] James Podgers, "Corporations in the Line of Fire," *ABA Journal*, January 2004, 13.
[62] See, e.g., Julia Graff, "Corporate War Criminals and the International Criminal Court: Blood and Profits in the Democratic Republic of Congo," *Human Rights Brief*, 11, 2 (Winter 2004), 23–26.

Republican Party, with its reluctance to link business and human rights, controls or substantially influences US foreign policy. On the other hand, some corporations are supportive of international action against those benefiting from these resource wars. The De Beers diamond company wants to shut off the flow of black market diamonds from places like Angola and Sierra Leone, in order to protect its market share. De Beers, with the support of Belgium, a traditional center for the diamond trade, would be only too happy to see the curtailment of black market diamonds.[63]

To date, none of the ICC investigations or cases has focused on corporations or corporate leaders, as previously discussed in Chapter 4. Increasingly, there were published reports critical of the first prosecutor of the ICC, Moreno-Ocampo, who had discussed the possibility of the ICC going after business leaders.[64]

Non-profit dynamism

Chapter 7 charted the growth of an international civic society in which various non-profit organizations and movements, including human rights groups, were increasingly active on public policy issues. This chapter follows up by showing that numerous organizations and movements have begun to focus on TNC practices in the light of human rights standards. One may use the broad phrase "social responsibility" in reference to TNCs, but human rights values are part of that concern (which also includes anti-bribery and anti-corruption measures, along with ecological matters).[65] As far back as 1972 the International Chamber of Commerce adopted a non-binding code of conduct for TNCs. Some business executives formed the Caux Round Table, which promotes TNC social responsibility, including "a commitment to human dignity, [and] political and economic freedoms."[66] Standard human rights organizations like Human Rights Watch and Amnesty International began to pay more attention to TNCs.[67] Groups that had long

---

[63] Alan Cowell, "De Beers Plans Guarantee: Diamonds Not from Rebels," *International Herald Tribune*, March 1, 2000, 15.

[64] See www.nytimes.com/2016/06/26/magazine/international-criminal-court-moreno-ocampo-the-prosecutor-and-the-president.html?_r=0.

[65] See further Lance A. Compa and Stephen F. Diamond, eds., *Human Rights, Labor Rights, and International Trade* (Philadelphia: University of Pennsylvania Press, 1996); John W. Houck and Oliver F. Williams, *Is the Good Corporation Dead?: Social Responsibility in a Global Economy* (Lanham: Rowman & Littlefield, 1996); and Lee Tavis, *Power and Responsibility* (Notre Dame: Notre Dame Press, 1997).

[66] See www.cauxroundtable.org/.

[67] On this point see especially the chapter by David P. Forsythe and Eric Heinze, "On the Margins of the Human Rights Discourse: Foreign Policy and International Welfare

tracked business practices in the interests of consumers, such as Ralph Nader's Global Trade Watch in Washington, began to focus more on human rights issues. Labor unions like the AFL-CIO were highly active on transnational labor issues. An important internet site was the Business and Human Rights Resource Center, created by AI and a number of other private groups, that provided broad monitoring of business and human rights issues (www.business-humanrights.org). There were other important websites run by NGOs as well, such as by Social Accountability International (www.sa-intl.org).

In some cases of private pressure there has been undeniable success. In response to a citizen boycott of its operations in south Florida over the treatment of immigrant workers picking tomatoes, Taco Bell agreed in 2005 to raise the wages of affected workers and imposed a tough code of conduct pertaining to its suppliers.[68] The "Sullivan Principles" at least directed attention to the effects of apartheid on working conditions in the Republic of South Africa under white minority rule, even if Reverend Sullivan of Philadelphia eventually concluded that his code – intended to affect investments – was inadequate for achieving major improvements in an integrated work force in South Africa during apartheid. The "McBride Principles" directed attention to sectarian discrimination in employment practices in Northern Ireland, as any number of investors in that British province tied their investments to these principles designed to reduce prejudice against Catholics or Protestants. As noted, other firms have been shamed into altering their policies in the light of human rights values. Starbucks Coffee opened its foreign operations to human rights monitors, Heineken withdrew from doing business in Burma, and Levi Strauss withdrew from manufacturing in China for a time.

In the fall of 1998, a group of companies in the apparel and footwear industries, including Liz Claiborne, Nike, Reebok, and others, agreed to open their overseas operations to independent human rights monitors under formal agreement. The "Apparel Industry Partnership" or "Fair Labor Association" provided for periodic inspection by the Lawyer's Committee for Human Rights, now renamed Human Rights First, based in New York, and other respected human rights NGOs under detailed provisions.[69] The deal was brokered by the Clinton Administration, which had worked for over two years to get such an agreement. While

---

Rights," in Howard-Hassmann and Welch, *Economic Rights in Canada and the United States*, 55–70. One has only to observe the websites or publication lists of these NGOs. See, e.g., www.hrw.org/about/initiatives/corp.html.

[68] Eric Schlosser, "A Side Order of Human Rights," *New York Times*, April 6, 2005, A29.

[69] For one summary, see www.fairlabor.org.

arrangements were criticized by various American labor groups, some American university students, and others as not going far enough, this development was hailed by its supporters as a major advance in providing specific attention to labor rights on a transnational basis.[70] About twenty major American universities with well-known sports programs and popular sports apparel, like Michigan, Notre Dame, and Nebraska, among others, joined this arrangement.[71]

When, for example, the University of Nebraska in 2005 concluded a new contract with Adidas for the provision of sports apparel, the contract contained a human rights clause that required the company and its sub-contractors to meet certain standards pertaining to freedom of association and collective bargaining, limitations on working hours, women's equality, prohibition of discrimination and harassment, etc. – a clause that would be independently supervised. The wording, however, did not address explicitly and specifically a fair or living wage.

Under the AIP/FLA, reports on companies are made public, allowing consumers to take whatever action they want on the basis of the reports. The reports focus on a workplace code, detailed in the agreement, and are based on a selected percentage of the companies' operating facilities. Analysis of wages is pegged to a US Department of Labor study regarding employee basic needs in the country at issue. There is also a procedure for filing complaints against the company. A "no sweat" label can be added to products made in compliance with this agreement.

Also in 1998, a number of companies including Toys R Us and Avon created the Council on Economic Priorities (CEP). This CEP deals with the usual labor rights in foreign subsidiaries or sub-contractors, but also with what constitutes a "living wage" in different countries. On this latter point, according to a specific formula, one calculates the cost of basic human need in caloric terms. This is done in a way that allows specific numbers to be provided country by country. The formula has been generally regarded as appropriate. But the CEP terms were sufficiently demanding for some business groups and commentators to endorse the AIP/FLA as indicated above, on the grounds that a specific "living wage" standard would curtail some foreign investment leading to loss of jobs in the global south.[72] After all, certain governments as in Malaysia have

---

[70] Steven Greenhouse, "Groups Reach Agreement for Curtailing Sweatshops," *New York Times*, November 5, 1998, A18.

[71] Steven Greenhouse, "17 Top Colleges Enter Alliance on Sweatshops," *New York Times*, March 16, 1999, A15.

[72] Aaron Bernstein, "Sweatshop Reform: How to Solve the Standoff," *Business Week*, May 3, 1999, 186–190.

been very explicit about low wages constituting one of their important comparative advantages in global markets.

Still other companies created the American Apparel Manufacturers Association. While this arrangement provided monitoring of labor rights, the standards were so low that it was generally discredited by most human rights groups, unions, attentive university students, and other observers outside the apparel industry.

Still further, some students and union leaders created the Worker Rights Consortium (WRC). This movement, excluding business leaders in the formulation of its plans, pushed for unannounced inspections of plants and factories as well as for a tough "living wage" for workers. Its approach was abrasive enough for Nike to break off arrangements with several major American universities, like Michigan, when they accepted WRC terms.[73] Later, however, Nike, while still not agreeing to WRC terms, did promise to open all of its foreign operations to public disclosure and did admit that a certain number of labor problems existed in its various facilities.[74]

A summary analysis of private action intended to make TNCs more sensitive to human rights standards is elusive. As noted already, Shell Oil was not forced out of Nigeria, nor into providing clearly different policies in Ogoniland where Shell operations had allegedly damaged the environment, nor into saving the life of Ken Saro-Wiwa and his Ogoni compatriots who had protested against Shell policies. At best Shell was forced into paying more attention to public relations and fending off calls for major boycotts and sanctions. Yet the story about Shell and Nigeria is not over, and it remains to be seen whether relations between this TNC and post-Abacha governments in Lagos remain the same as in the past. Private advocacy for better TNC policies may yet prove at least somewhat influential in this case. In Chapter 7 I noted the elusive nature of "success" for human rights groups and movements, as well as noting the importance of long-term, informal education in changing views over time.

Finally in this section I should note that some private actors have brought law suits in national courts against TNCs and their global operations. For example, in the USA, the Alien Tort Statute of 1789 allows civil suits against private parties where a violation of the law of nations is involved, regardless of the nationality of the parties.

---

[73] Mark Asher and Josh Barr, "Nike Pulls Funds from Campus Critics," *International Herald Tribune*, May 6–7, 2000, 9.
[74] Rukmini Callimachi, "Nike Reveals Overseas Factories," AP report, carried in *Lincoln Journal Star*, April 14, 2005, C1.

Most of the early case law under this statute concerned torture.[75] From 1980 and the final judgment in the Filartiga case, it was settled law that those victimized by pirates and torturers and other "enemies of mankind" who had been wronged in violation of international customary law could bring a civil suit for damages in US federal courts.[76] Thus the USA offered universal jurisdiction for civil torts in violation of the law of nations. Some human rights violations were included.

In the 1990s certain individuals as supported by human rights organizations and human rights lawyers began to go after TNCs for causing, or aiding and abetting states in, major human rights violations. Some early developments suggested progress was possible. Unocal Oil, based in California, was sued for engaging in – or allowing sub-contractors to engage in – forced labor and other human rights violations in its operations in Myanmar. The US district court in question, in a jurisdictional ruling of considerable importance, allowed the case to proceed. In the merits phase, however, the court held that plaintiffs had not proven legal culpability by Unocal. Despite this ruling, while the case was still under appeal, Unocal agreed to settle with the plaintiffs, thus giving the impression that civil litigation in US courts against TNCs for human rights violations might be effective in producing progressive settlements.[77]

However, while the US political branches had not reacted much to the Filartiga case and the use of US Federal courts to go after torturers in civil law cases, going after business corporations was another matter. The George W. Bush Administration tried to get US courts to narrow the scope of application of the Alien Tort Statute (ATS).[78] The Bush Administration, reflecting the pro-business and free-enterprise philosophy of the Republican Party, was not happy when businesses were made defendants in US courts regarding international human rights issues. And in March 2004, the US Supreme Court did try to narrow the application of the Alien Tort Statute.[79] In this important case, the Supreme Court held that

---

[75] Beth Stevens and Steven R. Ratner, *International Human Rights Litigation in US Courts* (Irvington-on-Hudson, NY: Transnational Publishers, 1996).

[76] Richard Alan White, *Breaking Silence: The Case that Changed the Face of Human Rights* (Washington: Georgetown University Press, 2004).

[77] For a good review of this general subject, see Beth Stephens, "Upsetting Checks and Balances," *Harvard Human Rights Journal*, 17 (Spring 2004), 169–205. See also her essay, "National Courts," in *Encyclopedia of Human Rights*, vol. IV, 41–49.

[78] See Daphne Eviatar, "A Big Win for Human Rights," *The Nation*, May 9, 2005, www.thenation.com/article/big-win-human-rights/. But see also Human Rights Watch, "US: Ashcroft Attacks Human Rights Law," May 15, 2003, www.hrw.org/press/2003/05/us051503.htm.

[79] For a readable analysis of the Alvarez-Machain case, see Warren Richey, "Ruling Makes It Harder for Foreigners to Sue in US Courts," *Christian Science Monitor*, June 30, 2004,

a Mexican doctor could not sue two American bounty hunters, who had been hired by the USA to capture and return him for trial, because the international law on arbitrary detention was not that clear and widely accepted and the detention not prolonged. Increasingly, different US Federal courts issued conflicting rulings about what violations of international law could and could not be litigated under the ATS. For example, in November 2004 a federal district court in New York threw out a suit against several major American corporations (e.g., General Electric, General Motors, etc.) for being complicit in the human rights violations in South Africa during the apartheid era.[80] If one looked at the history of US case law under ATS prior to the Kiobel case, plaintiffs were likely to lose when corporations were defendants and the Executive expressed interest in the case through a friend of the court brief.[81] The US Supreme Court had previously held that corporations were legal persons with a right of free speech, and that political donations were an expression of free speech that could not be regulated (Citizens United, 2009). In still another case, the US Supreme Court held that corporations were not legal persons in the sense of possessing a constitutionally protected right of privacy in the face of a request under the US Freedom of Information Act as related to a charge of violation of personal privacy (Federal Communications Commission v. AT&T, 2011). In still another case (Hobby Lobby), a presumed family business was seen as a legal person with rights of religious freedom, so that the large chain of stores did not have to cover women's reproductive health care in its insurance policies. So in the USA on the matter of rights and duties of US corporations where they were seen as legal persons, courts seemed to engage in judicial legislation without a great deal of consistency. On balance, courts seemed to favor corporate freedom from legal control in matters of violation of human rights abroad and political activity at home.

In 2013, the US Supreme Court finally disposed of the Kiobel case and in so doing severely restricted the impact of the preceding Filartiga case in so far as TNCs and human rights were concerned.[82] The Roberts court, consistently sympathetic to business interests, ruled in essence

---

as referenced in William J. Acheves, *The Anatomy of Torture: A Documentary History of Filartiga v. Pena-Irala* (Leiden and Boston: Nijhoff, 2007).

[80] For a readable analysis of the South African case, see Julia Preston, "Judge Dismisses Big Rights Suit on Apartheid," *New York Times*, November 30, 2004, A6.

[81] Jeffrey Davis, *Justice Across Borders: The Struggle for Human Rights in US Courts* (Cambridge: Cambridge University Press, 2008).

[82] The case is analyzed in many sources including in David P. Forsythe and Patrice C. McMahon, *American Exceptionalism Reconsidered: US Foreign Policy, Human Rights, and World Order* (New York and London: Routledge, 2016), ch. 5.

that US courts should be cautious in interfering in sensitive matters of international relations especially when the case in question did not "touch and concern" the USA in important ways. The Kiobel case involved Nigerian plaintiffs and Royal Dutch Shell, a British and Dutch company. The company was charged with a role in human rights violations in Nigeria. The Roberts court thus elevated technical matters about extra-territorial jurisdiction and concern for stable interstate relations over the role of various TNCs in aiding and abetting in gross violations of human rights. In effect, the court refuted the idea that abusive corporations were on a par with pirates as enemies of mankind.

The Kiobel judgment did not completely shut the door on use of the Alien Tort Statute in human rights matters. Enterprising human rights lawyers and organizations continued to look for cases that might fit with the Kiobel ruling. Yet once again the conservative Roberts court, supported by conservative business and political circles, had indicated a reluctance to use human rights law to restrict pursuit of profit on an international scale. Like Belgium regarding universal jurisdiction and criminal law (covered in Chapter 4), the USA no longer offered universal jurisdiction in civil cases without some link to the nation. It bears noting that it was the threat (promise?) of judicial action that caused Swiss banks to reach an out-of-court settlement about claims pertaining primarily to Jewish account-holders arising from the Holocaust era.[83] Likewise it was the prospect of similar judicial action that caused Volkswagen and other German corporations also to reach an out-of-court settlement that provided a fund to compensate slave laborers whose rights were violated in that same era.[84] The presence or absence of national legal proceedings on international human rights matters was an important subject.

Nation-state action

In the 1970s, as already noted, western or home state governments tried to fend off demands for new international law to regulate TNCs as part of the NIEO. By the 1990s this situation had partially changed, as a number of governments – including some that were pro-business and right-of-center – in westernized democracies advocated at least codes of conduct and other non-binding measures designed to advance social responsibility, including attention to human rights, in the activities of TNCs. The German government of Helmut Kohl underwrote the

---

[83] See Stuart E. Eizenstat, *Imperfect Justice: Looted Assets, Slave Labor, and the Unfinished Business of World War II* (New York: Public Affairs, 2003).
[84] "Volkswagen Joins Holocaust Fund," http://news.bbc.co.uk/2/hi/europe/279070.stm.

"Rugmark campaign," designed to ensure that Asian rugs were not made with child labor. The Chretian government in Canada also began to address the issue of child labor abroad. The Clinton Administration brokered the AIP/FLA arrangement discussed above, while trying to pressure Shell because of its policies in Nigeria. European governments, through the European Parliament, tried to embarrass British Petroleum over its policies in Colombia which allegedly led to the repression of labor rights through brutal actions by the army in constructing a BP pipeline. On the other hand I have noted the opposition of the George W. Bush Administration to linking TNCs to international human rights standards, an opposition which included voting against a measure which passed in the UN Human Rights Commission in the spring of 2005 calling for further attention to this subject. The Obama Administration did not emphasize the subject, being more "centrist" than the Bernie Sanders and Elizabeth Warren wing of the Democratic Party – the latter figures being critical of many corporate practices. The Trump Administration was pro-business, pro-growth, and not much interested in restricting TNCs in the name of human rights.

In general it can still be said that home state governments remain reluctant to firmly and effectively use public law to regulate TNCs in the name of international human rights. The real shift that is under way is for national governments, usually left of center, to prod "their" corporations to regulate themselves, under non-binding codes and now increasingly NGO monitoring. The sanction at work is that of negative publicity and consumer sanctions. This has proved somewhat effective for those companies that sell directly to individual consumers, as Heineken and Nike, *inter alia*, will attest.

A review of US foreign policy and TNC action for human rights, however, is an example that indicates more vague rhetoric than concrete examples of effective action – certainly beyond the AIP/FLA agreement.[85] The United States, especially under Republican administrations, is still wary of "statism" that would intrude deeply into the marketplace.

In 1996 the US Department of Commerce advanced a code called the Model Business Principles linked to universal human rights. The code referred to a safe and healthy workplace, fair employment practices, and free expression and opposition to political coercion in the workplace, along with environmental and anti-corruption concerns. But aside from the AIP/FLA agreement, it seems that nothing much has come about in the wake of this code. The Department of Commerce is normally

---

[85] See www.state.gov/p/io/humanrights/, especially para. 11 of the document.

pro-business, and was notably so in the Clinton Administration by comparison with the Labor Department under Robert Reich. As in most governments, there was tension between competing elements.

It is said that the State Department, the Office of the US Trade Representative, and other US bodies take up labor concerns in foreign countries. It is true that the Annual Country Human Rights Reports, compiled by the State Department's Bureau of Democracy, Human Rights, and Labor, consider labor issues. But it is well known that there has been a persistent gap between the recording of violations of internationally recognized human rights in these reports, which has been done fairly conscientiously since 1976, and any effective follow-up steps by the USA. Washington's trade statutes include language that allows trade to be made conditional on human rights behavior.[86] But as in EU relations with non-European trade partners, this conditionality is rarely if ever invoked in practice.

It is also true that US foreign policy officials make speeches on behalf of labor rights and corporate social responsibility, but concrete action by the USA in opposing certain TNC practices is not always easy to demonstrate. The United States has been more active, for a longer period of time, in opposing TNC bribery than in opposing child labor and other violations of labor rights.

It can be noted, however, that the USA joined a number of other actors like UNICEF in providing funds to allow underage children to return to school rather than work in Asian sweatshops. The Departments of Commerce and Labor do publish information on child labor abroad, and provide a list of codes of conduct and possible monitoring organizations for TNC use if they so choose. And the United States continues to support certain ILO programs, even if these have not always proved very effective.

Conclusions

Whereas not so long ago TNCs were urged not to get involved in the domestic affairs of host states, now there has been a considerable shift in expectations; TNCs are frequently urged by citizens and their governments to undertake a more active commitment to international human rights.[87] As a *New York Times* editorial noted: "A quarter-century ago,

---

[86] Compa and Hinchliffe-Darricarrere, "Enforcing International Rights," 667.
[87] The Dutch Sections of Amnesty International and Pax Christi International, *Multinational Enterprises and Human Rights* (n.p.: AI and PCI, n.d.), 22–23. See further Thomas Donaldson, "Moral Minimums for Multinationals," in Joel H.

business argued that protecting the environment was not their job. Few American companies would say so today. A similar change may be developing in corporate attitudes about human rights. Companies are increasingly recognizing that their actions can affect human rights, and that respecting rights can be in their business interest."[88]

Despite the fact that most public international law, and so far contemporary international criminal law, does not apply thus far to TNCs, there are ways to reorient private corporations to public standards of human rights. Non-binding codes of conduct, devoid of monitoring mechanisms, have proved uniformly weak in the 1970s and 1980s, whether originating from the International Chamber of Commerce, the OECD, the ILO, the US government, or in draft form from UNCTAD. But private codes, in the form of negotiated agreements, accompanied by independent monitoring and public reporting, hold some promise for changing corporate behavior. This is especially so when such agreements have the backing of governments which can be expected to assist in implementation. Recall that the AIP/FLA is underwritten by the US government, whose Department of Labor carries out studies, *inter alia*, to promote compliance. Recall that the Rugmark campaign was underwritten by the German government. Recall that the UN Global Compact can claim some modest successes.

It is in this a-legal gray area of public and private action that one is most likely to see progress in the near future in getting TNCs to pay more attention to human rights standards. The pressure will come mostly from the non-profit side, in the context of media exposure, with the threat of consumer or citizen action that endangers the corporation's profit margin. But socially responsible partners will exist within some corporations and governments. The process is likely to remain quasi-legal and extra-judicial, although national court cases making TNCs liable for civil penalties for human rights violations could be a factor of great significance. Most states, however, do not manifest their equivalent of the US Alien Tort Statute which opens up national courts to petitions about corporate violations of human rights globally. And even the USA has recently seen a reluctance of judges to hold corporations liable for complicity in human rights violations abroad.

Rosenthal, ed., *Ethics and International Affairs: A Reader*, 2nd edn. (Washington: Georgetown University Press, 1999), 455–480.

[88] Quoted in "Human Rights and Business: Profiting from Observing Human Rights," *Ethics in Economics*, 1998 (nos. 1 & 2), 2, 125 E. Broad St., Columbus, Ohio, www.businessethics.org.

Despite US judicial backsliding, globally speaking there is a new psychological environment in which TNCs are expected by many to engage in socially responsible policies. Many of these policies center on international standards of human rights. It was in this context that the JPMorgan Bank apologized for its role in supporting slavery in the past in the USA, and then set up a five-million-dollar program in Louisiana (where several of its acquired banks had operated) for African-American students to pursue higher education.[89]

Case study: Chinese oil companies and corporate social responsibility

There are three major Chinese oil companies that have become important international actors especially in African countries: China National Petroleum Corporation (CNPC), China Petroleum and Chemical Corporation (Sinopec), and China Offshore Oil Corporation (CNOOC).[90] They all profess commitment to the idea of corporate social responsibility (CSR), a composite non-binding or voluntary code of conduct consisting of segments on human rights, ecological protection, and good business practices including financial transparency. The central question here is the impact of CSR on these three Chinese oil firms and whether their relevant records are very different from those of western oil firms.

All three Chinese firms are members of the UN Global Compact and make voluntary public reports under this and other relevant international standards. They all profess allegiance to either the 1948 Universal Declaration of Human Rights or unspecified human rights values, to ecological protection, and to proper business practices. Information about these companies is available from the 2005–2006 era when the firms became important if relatively small players on the international oil scene.

In general the evidence shows that these Chinese oil companies seek the extraction of oil from countries such as Sudan, Nigeria, Equatorial Guinea, Angola, and elsewhere for international sale with the least degree of difficulty possible. They do not exist to advance democracy or promote human rights in any country, which of course one would not expect from firms based in authoritarian China. They do on occasion plow some of their profits back into the local communities through

---

[89] Associated Press, "JPMorgan: Banks Had Links to Slavery," *Lincoln Journal Star*, January 21, 2005, A9.
[90] Adapted from Scott Pegg, "Social Responsibility and Resource Extraction: Are Chinese Oil Companies Different?," *Resources Policy*, 37, 2 (2012), 160–167.

building schools or distributing water during the dry season. Their overall record on CSR is not significantly different from those of western-based oil companies over a longer time span.

To the extent that Nigeria, for example, has mismanaged its oil resources and in the process contributed to the violation of various human rights especially in the delta region of Ogoniland, the responsibility resides primarily with the Nigerian government as reinforced by western oil companies such as Royal Dutch Shell. The Chinese firms played no role. To the extent that oil resources in Angola prolonged the civil war there, feeding the conflict on both sides, the primary responsibility rested with the contesting factions as reinforced by the western oil companies that extracted the resources. The Chinese firms played no role, appearing on the scene after the conflict. To the extent that the Chinese firms moved into Sudan when western firms were compelled to withdraw because of human rights violations in Darfur, over time the record of China's oil firms has become more nuanced and is not radically different from the stated objectives of western governments.

It is true that the presence of these Chinese corporations gives contracting governments some leverage in bargaining with western entities as well as with the World Bank and IMF. But an African backlash against some early Chinese practices has caused the overall Chinese record especially in Africa to be similar to that of their western counterparts. Attacks on Chinese workers in Nigeria, much criticism of early Chinese policy in Sudan, and similar events have caused Chinese authorities to be more careful about local impact against the background of international scrutiny of international standards. For example, they changed course with regard to some dealings with the much-criticized Mugabe government in Zimbabwe.

One might keep in mind that, according to some analysts, the western-based oil firms do not have an outstanding record under CSR to begin with. So if we say that the Chinese oil firms have a record that is no worse, that is not holding those Chinese corporations to a very high standard. Nevertheless, the fear that the Chinese oil firms would greatly undermine democracy and human rights in Africa is, so far, much overstated. CSR is not a very powerful tool for promoting democracy and human rights to begin with; it cannot compel corporations interested in production and sales to become agents for progressive public policy. Primary responsibility for democracy and human rights in oil-producing states still rests with national governments. To the extent that an "oil curse" has led to negative human rights conditions in sub-Saharan Africa, one cannot look primarily to these Chinese firms.

Discussion questions

- Are transnational corporations too large and powerful for control by public authorities? To what extent are international authorities, compared with national authorities, important for the regulation of TNCs?
- What is the experience in OECD countries with regard to private, for-profit corporations and their impact on labor at home? Has the lesson of this experience been properly applied to international relations?
- Are human rights considerations, when applied to TNCs, actually a form of western imperialism in that the application of human rights standards to protect workers actually impedes economic growth and prosperity in the global south?
- If you are a stockholder in a TNC, do you really want "your" company to pay attention to human rights as labor rights if it reduces the return on your investment? What if you are both an owner and a consumer at the same time: does this change any important equation in your thinking? Why should we expect American and European owners or consumers to be concerned about Asian, African, or Latin American workers?
- Are companies like Nike and Reebok engaged in public relations maneuvers by joining a-legal codes of conduct like AIP/FLA, or do they show a real commitment to the human dignity of the workers in their Asian sub-contractors? Is there any real difference between Nike and Royal Dutch Shell when it comes to social issues in foreign countries?
- Can TNCs be effectively counterbalanced on sweatshop issues by a movement featuring primarily university students, unions, human rights groups, and the media? Is it necessary for governments to lend their support to such a movement? Can private a-legal codes of conduct be effective on TNC policies?
- Given that the ILO has been around since about 1920, why does so much action on labor rights take place outside the procedures of this organization? Can one make more progress on labor rights by circumventing international law and organization? Conversely, should we make TNCs directly accountable under international law, instead of indirectly accountable through nation-states? Is politics more important than law?
- Was the George W. Bush Administration correct in arguing that the Alien Tort Statute of 1789 was not intended to cover civil suits for violations of international human rights in the twenty-first century? Regardless of the original intent of those who drafted and passed that statute, was it proper policy for that administration to try to narrow the application of that law so as to exclude attempts to protect against corporate abuses?

SUGGESTIONS FOR FURTHER READING

Barnet, Richard J., and John Cavanagh, *Global Dreams: Imperial Corporations and the New World Order* (New York: Simon & Schuster, 1994). A hard look at TNCs and public policy from left of center.

Beckert, Sven, *Empire of Cotton: A Global History* (New York: Knopf, 2015). An outstanding study of the international economics of the cotton trade, showing the extent of human rights violations centrally involved through ethnic cleansing, slavery, and various forms of discrimination and persecution.

Compa, Lance A., and Stephen F. Diamond, eds., *Human Rights, Labor Rights, and International Trade* (Philadelphia: University of Pennsylvania Press, 1996). A good collection that provides a solid overview for its time.

Donaldson, Thomas, "Moral Minimums for Multinationals," in Joel H. Rosenthal, ed., *Ethics and International Affairs: A Reader*, 2nd edn. (Washington: Georgetown University Press, 1999), 455–480. A good, short treatment of ethical conduct in the world of TNCs.

Forsythe, David P., and Patrice C. McMahon, *American Exceptionalism Reconsidered: The United States, Human Rights, and World Order* (London and New York: Routledge, 2016). Chapter 5 presents a readable analysis of the Kiobel case in the US Supreme Court, in which the Roberts court greatly restricted the effort to use civil law in order to hold transnational corporations responsible for complicity in human rights violations abroad.

Frynas, Jedrzeg George, and Scott Pegg, eds., *Transnational Corporations and Human Rights* (London: Palgrave Macmillan, 2004). Useful short studies of private activism, codes of conduct, conflict situations, oil companies in Nigeria, mining in Papua New Guinea, the coffee industry, labor in South East Asia, community–corporate partnerships in Canada.

Gilpin, Robert, *The Political Economy of International Relations* (Princeton: Princeton University Press, 1987). A classic study. Chapter 6 deals with TNCs. Not much explicitly on human rights, but lots on TNC behavior in broad political perspective.

Haas, Ernst A., *Human Rights and International Action* (Stanford: Stanford University Press, 1970). Concludes that the ILO during the Cold War was not able to improve labor rights in the communist bloc.

Howard-Hassmann, Rhoda, "The Second Great Transformation: Leapfrogging in the Era of Globalization," *Human Rights Quarterly*, 27, 1 (February 2005), 1–40. A broad argument about the place of human rights in the transformation from national industrial capitalism to global technocratric capitalism.

Can Globalization Promote Human Rights? (University Park, PA: Penn State University Press, 2010). In this expansion of the 2005 article above, she discusses the interplay of political, social, and economic globalization. She holds that global capitalism can contribute to the protection of human rights if social and political developments keep pace with international economics.

Hymer, Stephen, "Multinational Corporations and the Law of Uneven Development," in J. W. Bhagwati, ed., *Economics and World Order* (New York: Macmillan, 1971), 113–140. A classic study of the evils TNCs can do.

Korten, David, *When Corporations Rule the World* (West Hartford: Kumarian Press, 1995). Another critical look, some would say hypercritical, at TNCs and the damage they can do.

Meyer, William H., *Human Rights and International Political Economy in Third World Nations: Multinational Corporations, Foreign Aid, and Repression* (Westport: Praeger, 1998). A quantitative study finding positive correlations, in general, between the presence of TNCs in the global south and lots of good things. The author's methodology has been questioned by other scholars.

Rasche, Andreas, and Georg Kell, eds., *The UN Global Compact: Achievements, Trends, and Challenges* (Cambridge: Cambridge University Press, 2010). Multiple authors provide an informed overview of the subject.

Rivoli, Pietra, *The Travels of a T-Shirt in the Global Economy: An Economist Examines the Markets, Power, and Politics of World Trade* (New York: Wiley, 2005). A broad and readable view of how global economics works, with attention to both benefits and problems – including why certain individuals will not benefit under free trade and the WTO.

Rodman, Kenneth A., "Think Globally, Punish Locally: Non-State Actors, Multinational Corporations, and Human Rights," *Ethics & International Affairs*, 12 (1998), 19–42. Notes the growing pressure on corporations to better respect labor rights, principally from human rights organizations and consumer movements.

Ruggie, John Gerard, *Just Business: Multinational Corporations and Human Rights* (New York: Norton, 2013). The UN Secretary-General's Special Representative for the global compact program reflects on corporations and social responsibility – the latter term encompassing human rights.

Schlesinger, Stephen C., and Stephen Kinzer, *Bitter Fruit: The Untold Story of the American Coup in Guatemala* (Garden City, NY: Doubleday, 1982). American corporations team with the US government to overthrow the Arbenz government in Guatemala, ushering in several decades of brutal repression.

Soros, George, "The Capitalist Threat," *Atlantic Monthly*, 279, 2 (February 1997). The successful Hungarian financier and philanthropist warns of the dangers of unregulated capitalism in Eastern Europe and the former Soviet Union. He sees pure *laissez-faire* economics as a threat to democracy.

Spar, Deborah, "The Spotlight and the Bottom Line: How Multinationals Export Human Rights," *Foreign Affairs*, 77, 2 (March–April 1998), 7–12. A short essay that is basically positive about the role of regulated or pressured corporations. The author notes that some corporations have a very poor record on human rights.

Vernon, Raymond, *Sovereignty at Bay: The Multinational Spread of US Enterprises* (New York: Basic Books, 1971). A classic study arguing that TNCs have not escaped control by the modern state.

9   The communications media and human
     rights: traditional and social domains

When it comes to the dissemination of news, traditionally one spoke of
hot and cool media. That referred to televised and print journalism.
In the past, such was the influence of the CBS evening news that
President Lyndon Johnson supposedly said that when anchor Walter
Cronkite became critical of US policies in Vietnam in 1968, he knew
he had lost the support of Middle America. In contemporary times one
has to also speak of social media in which every person might be considered a private journalist – choosing what to disseminate as newsworthy
"fact" and to whom. In 2016, various individuals in Aleppo used social
media to keep the world informed about conditions there in the midst of
the bloody Syrian war.[1] In 2009, various individuals in Iran kept the rest
of the world informed about the Green Revolution which sought more
democracy there, especially via Twitter, despite electronic jamming by
the regime.[2]

It was well known, witness the ample case law on the subject, that
traditional media activity involved a host of human rights questions
centered on freedom of belief and expression, and of privacy. The same
now is true for social media. Indeed, individual use of the internet has
expanded the list of thorny human rights questions not only for individuals, but also for those for-profit corporations like Facebook and Google
who saw themselves initially not as members of the media, but as technology or software companies. They are at least quasi-media actors,
however, because increasingly a high percentage of persons with internet

---

[1] See further the reporting by the Syrian Observatory of Human Rights, based in London.
     This was basically a one-man effort that was important enough to draw attention from the
     New York Times, www.nytimes.com/2013/04/10/world/middleeast/the-man-behind-the-
     casualty-figures-in-syria.html.
[2] Jared Keller, "Evaluating Iran's Twitter Revolution," *The Atlantic Magazine*,
     www.theatlantic.com/technology/archive/2010/06/evaluating-irans-twitter-revolution/
     58337/. It was reported that the Obama Administration asked Twitter on a certain day
     not to go offline for scheduled maintenance, such was the importance of that means of
     communication for keeping up with ongoing events.

access get their news, or fake news, from such electronic platforms – either singularly or in combination with television.[3] What circulates on Facebook, Google, and Twitter – and similar media actors – reaches billions of persons, which is precisely why these actors are at the center of discussion, debate, and legal and political action about their policies. What they allow to circulate or block is enormously important. Whether they cooperate with governmental spying programs is also hugely important.

It was obviously the case that traditional media could be important in drawing attention to human rights violations. This occurred as far back as the nineteenth century, when print journalism helped push Britain and other Western governments into interventions in response to Balkan atrocities during Ottoman rule.[4] Of these humanitarian interventions, the scholar Gary Bass has written, "The limits to the [British] expanding moral universe were the reach of the reporter and the run of the telegraph wire."[5] This occasional influence is now true also for social media and its ability to generate pressures on governments concerning situations in, say, the contemporary Middle East or Ukraine. Given this potential for traditional media to affect governmental policy, it was obviously the case that all governments sought to influence leading media outlets, at a minimum with a charm offensive or jawboning. US White House officials sometimes met with leading editors and asked them to withhold or delay some news story on the basis of national interest. Of course, some governments engaged in outright censorship and direct control of newspapers, radio, and television. Likewise, social media is now involved in a very tough struggle about independence and control, freedom and repression, as the same technology that might advance human rights can also be manipulated in ways that seriously violate human rights. In 2011, at the start of the Arab Spring in the Middle East, China cracked down on its dissidents and their use of the internet in East Asia lest the winds of revolution fan the flames of discontent there. The Arab Spring led to a Chinese Winter.[6]

---

[3] Pew Research Center, www.pewresearch.org/fact-tank/2016/11/21/tv-still-the-top-source-for-election-results-but-digital-platforms-rise/.
[4] Misha Glenny, *The Balkans: Nationalism, War, and the Great Powers 1804–2011* (New York: Penguin, 1999, 2012), 109–110 and passim.
[5] Gary Bass, *Freedom's Battle: The Origins of Humanitarian Intervention* (New York: Vintage, 2008), 38.
[6] James Fallows, "Arab Spring, Chinese Winter," *The Atlantic Magazine*, www.theatlantic.com/magazine/archive/2011/09/arab-spring-chinese-winter/308601/.

Norms and their fit with governmental policy

When it comes to the media and human rights, various norms could be cited, but two are central. In the Universal Declaration of Human Rights, Articles 18 and 19 read as follows:

(18) Everyone has the right to freedom of thought, conscience and religion; this right includes freedom to change his religion or belief, and freedom, either alone or in community with others and in public or private, to manifest his religion or belief in teaching, practice, worship and observance.

(19) Everyone has the right to freedom of opinion and expression; this right includes freedom to hold opinions without interference and to seek, receive and impart information and ideas through any media and regardless of frontiers.

These same norms were written into the International Covenant on Civil and Political Rights (ICCPR) which, as we have already noted, has been ratified by almost 170 states. In that treaty one finds a few additional words setting up a vague balance between these freedoms and other legitimate values. The ICCPR, Article 19 reads in part:

The exercise of the rights provided for in ... this article carries with it special duties and responsibilities. It may therefore be subject to certain restrictions, but these shall only be such as are provided by law and are necessary:

(a) For respect of the rights or reputations of others;
(b) For the protection of national security or of public order (ordre public), or of public health or morals.

The specifics of this are provided by national law and practice.

Some seventy years after the 1948 Universal Declaration, the private organization Freedom House based in New York provided one overview of the fate of these and related civil rights around the world.[7] If we look at its index on freedom of expression and belief for 2016 with its scale of zero (worst) to 20 (best), we find numerous countries scoring well, with ratings of 15 and 16. They are mostly in Europe and the Western Hemisphere, along with the Asian democracies, with a few from non-Western areas (e.g., Benin, Cap Verde, Cyprus, etc.). Scoring zero and hence the worst were Eritrea, North Korea, and Uzbekistan. Also scoring zero were certain territories such as Tibet as controlled by China. Scoring very low (zero to 5) were a large number of countries including,

---

[7] Readers can use the Freedom House website as a portal to the various indexes and commentary. There the organization explains its methodology and relationship among indexes. There are other relevant indexes by other organizations. The group Reporters Without Borders also presented a 2016 Press Freedom Index.

as examples, China, Cuba, Egypt, Ethiopia, Iran, Pakistan, Russia, Rwanda, Saudi Arabia, Vietnam, etc.

If we then look at the Freedom House index on press freedom for 2016, with zero as the best and 100 as the worst, we find as expected that most of the stable liberal democracies do well. Again, they are in Europe and the Americas, with some in East Asia (e.g., Japan and South Korea, Australia and New Zealand) and a smattering elsewhere (e.g., Malta, Micronesia, etc.). Scoring 80 and above, and thus poorly, were nineteen countries, including as examples: Bahrain, Belarus, Burundi, China, Cuba, Eritrea, Ethiopia, Iran, all the south Asian "Stans" such as Uzbekistan, Venezuela, Vietnam, Yemen, etc. Territories such as Crimea and also the West Bank and Gaza areas also scored poorly.

Finally, but importantly, if we look at the Freedom House index on Net Freedom for 2016, we find similar patterns regarding the internet for the fifty-six countries studied. Stable liberal democracies score well (0 is best), with a few surprises (e.g., Kenya, the Philippines, South Africa all scored in the 20s). Doing very well (under 20) were: Canada, Estonia, Iceland, and the USA. Many others score poorly (100 is worst) including those scoring over 75. Among these we find the usual suspects: China, Cuba, Ethiopia, Iran, Syria, and Uzbekistan.

Other information also makes the general point that much remains to be done to make UDHR, Articles 18 and 19 a reality in impacting behavior and public policy. According to the private group Committee to Protect Journalists, in 2016 a total of forty-eight journalists were killed, of whom twenty-six died in combat crossfires and eighteen were intentionally murdered. Others were said to have died on dangerous assignment.[8] Syria was said to be the country with the highest number of murders of journalists (five), followed by two each in Iraq, Somalia, India, and Mexico. The report gives information about whether the killings were by governmental or non-governmental agents. Some attacks were by narco-traffickers who obviously did not want attention to be drawn to their operations. By comparison, the organization Reporters Without Borders asserted that seventy-four journalists were killed in 2016, with a majority being intentionally targeted.[9] For a further comparison, one can consult the Index on Censorship.[10] Still further, the Organization of American States, through its Special Rapporteur on Freedom of Expression, also gave considerable attention to the problem

---

[8] See https://cpj.org/killed/2016/.   [9] See https://rsf.org/.
[10] See www.indexoncensorship.org/. See further Charlyne R. Berens, "Index on Censorship," in David P. Forsythe, ed., *The Encyclopedia of Human Rights* (New York: Oxford University Press, 2009), vol. 3, 1–4.

of attacks on journalists.[11] The Council of Europe mirrored this concern,[12] and at the time of writing it was undertaking a broad survey of leading problems for journalists.

To summarize the obvious, personal rights to freedom of opinion and expression are taken relatively seriously in certain countries, but not others. Those engaged in traditional and social media activities are sometimes protected, but in all too many cases repressed and even killed. In 2016, the UN Human Rights Council passed by consensus a resolution, proposed by mostly Western governments, endorsing again the norm of freedom of opinion and expression, including on the internet.[13] Joining in the consensus were several countries whose actual record on such matters was not good (e.g., Bangladesh, Burundi, China, Cuba, Ethiopia, Russia, Venezuela, Vietnam, etc.). State hypocrisy is a regular feature of international relations, often with unhappy consequences for those active on behalf of media freedom.

Traditional media

It is perfectly clear that newspapers and magazines along with television can have important effects on government and society. This is why it has often been said that the (traditional) media in reality constitutes a fourth branch of government along with the executive, legislature, and judiciary. And this importance is precisely why back in circa 1975 there was a grand debate at the UN about a New World Information and Communications Order (NWICO).[14]

Many developing and communist countries claimed to be interested in a responsible press that would be extensively regulated in the name of such values as fairness and balance. It was true, as a number of Western scholars pointed out, that much of the influential traditional media was based in the global northwest, focused primarily on events in that area, and contained various biases in its limited reporting on other parts of the

---

[11] Edison Lanza, "Annual Report: Freedom of Expression," OEA/Ser.L/V/II, Doc. 48/15, 31 December 2015, www.oas.org/en/iachr/expression/reports/annual.asp.

[12] Onur Andreotti, *Journalism at Risk: Threats, Challenges, and Perspectives* (Strasbourg: Council of Europe, 2015).

[13] See www.ohchr.org/EN/HRBodies/HRC/RegularSessions/Session32/Pages/ResDec Stat.aspx.

[14] In the USA, criticism of an unpopular traditional media in the 1940s led to the creation of the Hutchinson Commission, or Commission on Freedom of the Press. The central issues were similar to the UN debate some three decades later. One found a discussion of the social responsibility of the press to be fair and balanced and not destructive of important societal values. See Margaret A. Blanchard, "The Hutchins Commission, the Press and the Responsibility Concept," *Journalism Monographs* 49 (May 1977), 1–60.

world. This NWICO initiative emerged from a UNESCO that itself was viewed in some circles as autocratic and insensitive to various human rights issues at that time. The NWICO was fiercely resisted by most Western states and human rights organizations,[15] and the USA and Switzerland later withdrew from UNESCO for a time because of this issue, along with concern about treatment of Israel. With much discourse centering on debate about a responsible press versus a free press, the latter position carried the day. The supposed New World Information Order never came into being (with the related proposal for a New World Economic Order suffering the same fate). Still, it can be seen from the Freedom House indexes cited above that many governments, especially the more autocratic ones, remain opposed to a free press. It can be embarrassing, a challenge to elite power and perks. Both the USA and Russia prevented the media from photographing the return of the remains of soldiers killed in military actions abroad, lest the interventionist policy come under criticism.

This kind of potential impact is well demonstrated by a series of articles in 2007 by a team of *Washington Post* journalists headed by Dana Priest focusing on terrible conditions in the medical care of US military veterans.[16] The subject was on no one's radar screen up until that time. Congressional oversight was deficient. The military bureaucracy was uncaring. Other journalists had not discovered the subject. The President was unaware. After the stories, the head of the Veterans Agency was removed. Another was appointed. He too was removed after insufficient progress. Still another agency leader was installed. Funding was increased, as was monitoring of the situation. The problems were not immediately and fully rectified, but the subject was put on multiple official agendas and some progress was made. On the eve of taking office in late 2016, Donald Trump felt the need to address the subject some nine years after the first article appeared.

As for foreign policy, the media and the situation in Somalia in the early 1990s is often cited to similar effect. Widespread starvation in the context of lawlessness was reported by various media outlets. TV anchors "parachuted in" to report from the scene. To be sure many factors were in play. Various atrocities in the western Balkans centered on Bosnia competed with Somalia for coverage in the western press. The Cold War

---

[15] For a brief overview, see Roger Coate, "UNESCO," in David P. Forsythe, ed., *The Encyclopedia of Human Rights* (New York: Oxford University Press, 2009), vol. 5, 158–164.

[16] One can start with www.washingtonpost.com/wp-dyn/content/article/2007/02/17/AR2007021701172.html.

was over, and the 1992 presidential election was also over. The USA seemed to have a surplus of idle military power, and President George H. W. Bush was freed from domestic politics to think about his legacy. Some advising him were recommending action in Somalia, if only because it might take some of the pressure off getting further involved in the apparently more complicated Balkans. And so Bush the Elder authorized some 20,000 troops to provide security for a Red Cross feeding operation across Somalia. Here was another example of the apparent "CNN effect" in foreign policy. It was said that media coverage could force officials into new foreign policy directions, especially in responding to gross violations of human rights, similar to the British press and Balkan atrocities in the nineteenth century.[17]

Other cases, however, suggest otherwise. Where a government has firmly set views, extensive media reporting of this or that event may make no difference. In 1994, the genocide in Rwanda was well covered by Western media. Citizens could see graphic evidence of the atrocities on the nightly TV news, as well as in the print media. But the Bill Clinton Administration was determined not to get deeply involved after the US military deployment in Somalia had resulted in a debacle in 1993, with a number of American military personnel killed and wounded. Television recorded a dead American being dragged by a mob through the streets of Mogadishu. Public and congressional opinion became highly critical of the Clinton policy in Somalia. In the subsequent posture of non-intervention in Rwanda, the Clinton Administration was backed by key officials at UN headquarters who feared the end of UN-sponsored security deployments should such a mission to Rwanda end up like in Somalia.

The limits to any "CNN effect" were further confirmed by Syrian affairs from 2011 to about 2016. Again, the Western-based media daily covered the terrible death and destruction in that internationalized civil war. But the Obama Administration was determined not to get deeply involved in that complicated disaster after the long and inconclusive wars in Afghanistan (from 2001) and Iraq (from 2003). Obama authorized military strikes on the Islamic State Group in northern Syria and also Iraq. He put Special Forces on the ground to work especially with Iraqi security forces in contesting the Islamic State Group. But while pursuing an active diplomatic agenda on Syria, Obama firmly and consistently

---

[17] There was also "the Oprah Effect" which demonstrated again the impact of TV. The *Oprah Winfrey Show*, reaching over 40 million viewers, could certainly affect sales through her endorsement of commercial products. That being clear, various public figures appeared on her show to discuss this or that policy. Various studies followed on "the Oprah Effect" applied to the political domain.

rejected a major US military operation there, with or without a UN authorizing mandate. He did not contest major Russian involvement, which secured gains for the government of Bashar al-Assad. No amount of media coverage about Syria, and no amount of media commentary about Obama's alleged mistakes and weakness on that issue, changed his mind that Middle Eastern parties would have to sort out their problems themselves, and that the USA should "pivot to Asia" as much as possible.[18]

Given the different conclusions from different cases, scholars interested in the effect of the media on human rights undertook systematic studies trying to clarify when and under what conditions it might have important consequences for public policy. Clearly there were structural (meaning general and fundamental) pressures working against extensive coverage of human rights abroad. Much of the Western media was for-profit, dependent on subscriptions and, primarily, advertisements. This translated into a focus on financial viability, and hence often what was of interest near to home. This commercialization meant that coverage of atrocities in, say, Mali had limited sales appeal. The rise of news on social media (covered below) intensified the financial problems for traditional media. One could obtain a great deal of information via the internet without paying a subscription fee. Newspapers like the *Guardian* in the UK put out an online edition to compete, then asked readers for a voluntary contribution to finance it.

One also had to simplify for the typical main street audience. The complexities of the humanitarian disaster in South Sudan or Democratic Congo were not easy to cover with brevity. The twin factors of local interest and simplicity, plus the precarious financial bottom line, meant declining foreign coverage. Even non-profit media outlets such as the BBC and PBS needed to attract viewers and pay their bills, as well as avoid running afoul of governmental oversight.[19] Still, in general, it was known that the traditional media could help set the agenda for policy makers, generating pressures for action, as per the *Washington Post* and medical care for veterans.

An early careful study looked at foreign human rights coverage in several major Western media sources (*New York Times, Time Magazine, CBS Evening News*, and *The Times of London*) during 1978–1989.

---

[18] Likewise, media photos of Syria refugees fleeing toward Europe, including a widely circulated image of a dead child washed up on the shores of Turkey, did not alter the fact that many Europeans and their governments were firmly set against accepting more Syrian refugees. Shocking media images did not change set attitudes.
[19] PBS was sometimes accused by congressional Republicans of having a liberal bias.

The author found an emphasis on civil and political rights and rights of personal integrity, along with political participation. Few stories covered economic and social rights. The main regions covered toward the end of the Cold War were Eastern Europe and Latin America. A survey of congressional staffers revealed the view that media coverage of human rights issues was an important factor in perhaps 60 percent of the cases reviewed.[20]

A further study looked at Amnesty International advocacy and coverage of human rights violations by *Newsweek* and *The Economist* over about fifteen years. One conclusion was that this media tandem tended to highlight human rights violations in countries normally not well covered in the Western media. That is, the AI reports on lesser-known countries were picked up frequently by these two media actors, perhaps because *Newsweek* and *The Economist* were already covering major countries from other sources. This study did not ask whether the media reporting in question affected governmental policy.[21]

Another study found that media reports in *Newsweek* and the *New York Times* during 1976–2000 did have some significant effort on US sanctions policy toward certain countries for human rights violations, but this correlation was affected by other factors. Being an ally of the USA reduced the threat or imposition of economic sanctions by Washington, even if those violations were well covered in these two media sources.[22]

On this subject as on many others, the matter of cognitive dissonance might come into play. If the media reported something that either elites or various publics did not want to hear, there sometimes was a tendency to block out the media reports. It seemed clear that in early 2017 Donald Trump was inclined to build better relations with Putin's Russia. He therefore was initially reluctant to accept the judgment of US security agencies that Russian hackers had interfered with the 2016 presidential elections both to discredit the democratic process and help defeat Hilary Clinton. This same tendency to block out undesired facts (and often criticize the messenger) could be

[20] Jay S. Ovsiovitch, "News Coverage of Human Rights," *Political Research Quarterly*, 46, 3 (September 1993), 671–689. There did seem to be a more persistent bias in some Western media coverage of human rights violations in that a tendency to emphasize the Latin American region existed beyond the Cold War era. See Emile Hafner-Burton and James Ron, "The Latin Bias: Regions, the Anglo-American Media, and Human Rights," *International Studies Quarterly*, 57, 3 (September 2013), 474–491.

[21] Howard Ramos and James Ron, "Shaping the Northern Media's Human Rights Coverage, 1986–2000," *Journal of Peace Research*, 44, 4 (July 2007), 385–406.

[22] Dursun Peksen, Timothy M. Peterson, and A. Cooper Drury, "Media-driven Humanitarianism? News Media Coverage of Human Rights Abuses and the Use of Economic Sanctions," *International Studies Quarterly*, 58, 4 (December 2014), 855–866.

demonstrated on a broad scale.[23] For example, Republican supporters of President Trump were more likely to dismiss media reports about Russian interference in elections than Democratic critics.

While a wide range of scholars continued to seek a systematic understanding of the links among traditional media, coverage of human rights violations, and resulting public policies,[24] it remained obvious that threats to an independent media remained real and were sometimes fatal. The traditional media was often seen as a threat to ruling elites and/or their compatriots in the politicized public, whatever the media's real power to shape opinion and policy.

Two well-publicized cases highlight this latter point – the Danish cartoon controversy starting in 2005 and the *Charlie Hebdo* controversy centered on 2015. Angry Islamic militants attacked Western media actors apparently because of religious sensitivities. In some attacks there was eventual involvement by political actors such as the Islamic State Group, the Arab League, or the Organization for Islamic Cooperation, along with various governments. The latter sought to manipulate events for purposes of policy and power, whatever the purely religious factors.[25]

In 2005, the well-known Danish newspaper *Jylllands Posten* (*Jutland Post*) ran a serious of cartoons which were intended as a satirical commentary on the prevalence of Islamic terrorism. Among other cartoons, the Prophet Mohammed was pictured as a terrorist. A critical reaction by various Islamic circles in Denmark was later expanded to other parts of the world, particularly as the Danish government took the position that this media activity was to be defended as a normal part of a free and independent media. Danish courts eventually backed the government's position.

Particularly as taken up by various religious and political organizations, including the Arab League and the Organization of Islamic Cooperation, this controversy led to riots with fatalities in certain places like Pakistan, as well as broadly organized economic sanctions against Danish goods and services. Subsequently there were attempts at violent attacks on a range of Danish targets by Islamic militants, some of which were intercepted and some not. Several Danish embassies were damaged.

---

[23] Timothy Hilderbrandt, et al., "The Domestic Politics of Humanitarian Intervention: Public Opinion, Partisanship, and Ideology," *Foreign Policy Analysis*, 9, 1 (July 2013), 243–266.

[24] See further John C. Pollock, *Journalism and Human Rights* (New York and London: Routledge, 2015).

[25] In the various attacks, it was not always possible to say with certainty what organization might have been involved in planning them. But it was clear that certain organizations sought to manipulate reports of events after the fact.

Various Danish journalists were given police protection and some went into hiding. A considerable debate ensued not just about the proper limits of a free press, but about whether there should be a right for religions to be exempted from certain types of critical commentary. Should one be concerned about religious defamation?

Relatedly, the French satirical magazine *Charlie Hebdo*, which had re-published the Danish cartoons as well as running its own content critical of that part of Islam that was intolerant and militant, was firebombed in 2011 and then attacked by Islamic gunmen in 2015. The magazine manifested a clear history of being strongly secular and critical of various religions, including Catholicism and Judaism. It was critical of most established authority whether religious or secular. In the 2015 incident, the editor and eleven others were killed. There was other related violence. The French events rekindled the debate about a free press and religion. Particularly the *Charlie Hebdo* killings resulted in a strong defense of freedom of belief, opinion, speech, and press in the West. A follow-on and multilingual issue of *Charlie Hebdo* sold almost 8 million copies compared with a usual press run of about 60,000 copies in French. Like the Danish, the French government and courts strongly defended the rights of a free press even if persons might be offended. Short of libel, slander, and other intentional efforts to misrepresent and defame, Western governments defended a free press. So did a large number of human rights groups concerned about a free press such as PEN, International Federation of Journalists, and Article 19, not to mention Reporters Without Borders, Index on Censorship, and Committee to Protect Journalists – or Amnesty International and Human Rights Watch. Much of the Islamic world, however, which had never undergone their equivalent of the Protestant Reformation or Enlightenment, both centered on the individual and both wary of centralized authority, remained sensitive about any criticism of Islam and its main figure, the Prophet Mohammed. In places like Pakistan and Saudi Arabia, it was often supremely dangerous, aka fatal, to be perceived as blasphemous about Islam. In Indonesia, toward the close of 2016, when the mayor of Jakarta, an ethnic Chinese and a Christian, ran into political difficulties, he was charged with blasphemy against Islam.

Debates played out in the UN Human Rights Council and in various other places about rights to belief, expression, and communication on the one hand, and the wisdom of diplomatic and sensitive exercise of those rights on the other. One might have the legal right to use the word "nigger" or burn the national flag, but was it wise to do so? Likewise, one might have the legal right to harshly criticize or satirize this or that religion, to engage in what some termed the defamation of religion, but was it wise to do so? Did offensive wording or images advance worthwhile causes? Or was the right to be offensive, the right to be a prickly and provocative dissident, an important value? Was a sense of political correctness and diplomatic sensitivity overdone, or not?

Social media

Already existing controversies about traditional media and human rights have been greatly expanded by the rapid development of internet technology available to the attentive and mass publics. The emergence of social media, meaning for our purposes the use of the internet for communication of "newsworthy facts" by persons not representing the state or official media corporations, is of growing importance. Just who is a journalist these days? On the one hand, one sees the ability of citizens to communicate and organize about human rights. Social media played a significant role in the mass demonstrations that led to removing the strongman Hosni Mubarak from office in Egypt in 2011.[26] On the other hand, one also sees the ability of governmental elites to track the users of social media and block their efforts. We have already noted that China's party-state officials carefully monitor the internet and try to disrupt dissident social media users before they can mount any effective challenge.[27] In 2016, Apple developed new security software for its devices after discovering that some spyware, probably developed by an Israeli company, had been embedded by remote action in the iPhones of certain Arab political activists.[28] A myriad of other rights issues are now also debated. Certainly a major concern is the use of social media to spread hatred and organize violence, whether one speaks of the Islamic State Group or lone-wolf terrorists.

Without going into technical details, we can note that the internet and its worldwide web (www) were developed in the USA in the 1960s.[29] Its use exploded in the 1990s as regulated by several non-governmental expert bodies which try to maintain global digital interconnectivity without allowing control by any government, corporation, or interest group.

---

[26] Mahmood Monshipoori, ed., *Information Politics, Protests, and Human Rights in the Digital Age* (New York: Cambridge University Press, 2016).

[27] Fallows, "Arab Spring, Chinese Winter."

[28] Associated Press reports were picked up by various sources, including the *Chicago Tribune*, www.chicagotribune.com/bluesky/technology/ct-apple-iphone-security-spywa re-20160825-story.html.

[29] John Lannon, et al., "Internet," in David P. Forsythe, ed., *The Encyclopedia of Human Rights* (New York: Oxford University Press, 2009), vol. 3, 182–194. Crucial was Tim Berners-Lee and his discovery of the worldwide web and thus the ability to have interconnectivity via the internet.

Efforts to centralize internet governance, for example by putting control of specifications and access in the hands of a UN body, have been floated, but sunk so far. The US Constitution's First Amendment, providing broad scope for the legal right to free speech, has proven important since the USA is central to the internet's functioning, but is not controlling in other countries with different laws.

At the center of developments were not only the scientists who made the digital discoveries in the era 1960–1990. One also sees the importance of corporations like Microsoft and Apple, Facebook, Google, Twitter, and others, who developed the affordable technologies, platforms, and devices which "democratized" the internet, allowing typical citizens to use it. Facebook was reported to have about 1.8 billion monthly users. This evolution places these for-profit corporations at the center of debates affecting whether the internet will be used to advance human rights or undermine them.

Social scientists are in the early stages of trying to establish a systematic understanding of social media and politics, international politics included.[30] It is very clear that social media constitutes a new dimension of political activity – a playing field, as it were, where human rights are both defended and violated. It may also turn out to be the case that public authorities with media expertise can dominate citizens trying to use new media to limit and even change those authorities. But that is not yet certain.

A fundamental question is whether users of the internet have a right to privacy and anonymity, and a right to be forgotten. The US Constitution's Fourth Amendment does not mention, but implies, a right to privacy from unreasonable searches and seizures. Americans have a right to be secure in their person and effects. These basic concepts have led to numerous legal tangles, and much national case law has followed on that subject.[31] The matter is no less complicated internationally with regard to use of the internet. Each time a device is used to access the internet, that device's IP number (Internet Protocol) is recorded. But devices can be hacked and controlled by others, perhaps on the other side of the planet, or listed under a false name. Computer experts can try to obscure who is using the device to access the internet and where. Those operating under a different IP address can spread fake news, post revenge porn

---

[30] Leticia Bode, et al., "A New Space for Political Behavior: Political Social Networking and Its Democratic Consequences," *Journal of Computer-Mediated Communication*," 19, 3 (April 2014), 414–429.

[31] Jeffrey Rosen and Benjamin Wittes, *Constitution 3.0: Freedom and Technological Change* (Washington: Brookings, 2013).

(e.g., an embarrassing photo from a former relationship), or communicate to colleagues the plans for terrorism – among other nefarious
purposes.

But if true identities are required, unscrupulous authorities can use the
information to track dissidents, disrupt democracy movements, embarrass political opponents, and hamper human rights campaigns. It is
certainly of concern to those interested in human rights that China will
only allow companies like Facebook and Google to operate in China if
they agree to provide the technologies that allow Chinese authorities to
block certain websites and track virtually all users and their attempts at
internet access. China is clear about its desire for an Orwellian surveillance system utilizing the internet.[32] Hence China plans to extend its
"Great Firewall" in the elite's quest to ensure total stability and deference. The authorities even required Apple to remove the *New York Times*
app from its app store available in China. At the time of writing, Google,
Facebook, and others had not rejected outright this Faustian bargain,
since they want access to the huge Chinese digital market and conveni-
ently hope for a relaxation of Chinese restrictions over time.[33] In the
meantime, technologies developed in the democratic USA are being
used to suppress democracy and human rights efforts in places like
China.

But even in the world of Western-style democracies, there is the
Edward Snowden affair. As a contract employee of the USA, this former
employee of Dell computers and the CIA apparently downloaded possibly millions of documents from the National Security Agency (NSA)
and other security services in 2013. What he has released to selected
journalists thus far indicates a massive surveillance of the internet by the
USA and some of its closest allies, including Britain, Canada, Australia,
and New Zealand. Information was apparently collected on millions of
persons, with companies like Yahoo and Google perhaps being paid to
divulge certain data. Information was apparently collected in a broad
sweep, including of non-international telephone calls, far beyond the
subject matter of suspected terrorism or other legitimate national security
matters. For example, information was collected apparently on calls
within the USA by Verizon subscribers who had no apparent connection
to national security issues. Because of such revelations, some regard

---

[32] See www.cnbc.com/2016/11/07/china-approves-law-to-tighten-control-on-internet-use
.html.
[33] Kaveh Waddel, "Why Google Left China – and Why It's Heading Back," *The Atlantic
Magazine*, www.theatlantic.com/technology/archive/2016/01/why-google-quit-china-
and-why-its-heading-back/424482/.

Snowden as a defender of democracy and human rights. Snowden certainly believed that the US Executive was exceeding legal authorization granted by courts for spying programs such as PRISM – and then lying about it to Congress. But because Snowden also apparently disclosed sensitive information about US security plans and capabilities, even to the point of naming CIA operatives, others regard him as a malevolent traitor. Claiming that he could not get a fair hearing and trial in the USA, he fled first to Hong Kong and then to Russia, where he was granted temporary asylum. Public opinion polls indicate broad awareness of the Snowden affair, but opinion remains divided on whether he is to be cheered or jeered. There is discussion of whether he might be a spy for either China or Russia, given his interactions with authorities from those countries. Several studies indicate that in the wake of the Snowden disclosures a number of Americans have stopped using certain words in their electronic communications and have stopped visiting certain websites, in the belief that the USA continues to engage in unlawful search and "seizure" of personal information via the internet. Encryption has also increased. Hence it would appear that a number of citizens have reacted by taking steps to safeguard their electronic privacy, suspecting the US government – and others – of overreaching in internet matters. Also, in the wake of this prolonged incident, with stories continuing to trickle out, major media companies have had to deal more forthrightly with privacy concerns, lest they lose business because of the appearance of controversial cooperation with US authorities.[34]

It is also the case that companies like Facebook have been pressured into creating review boards to handle requests that certain content be removed from the internet. They already block material like child porn and discriminatory ads. Thus these companies have had to wrestle with what is fake news versus real news, what is revenge porn and what is free expression among consenting adults, what is incitement to violence and hate crimes, and other controversies. For years, Twitter has been wrestling with the problem of bullying, harassment, unwanted political pressures, and similar social attacks on individuals by individuals – with unknown involvement by governments.[35]

---

[34] For one overview, see Timothy H. Edgar, *Beyond Snowden: Privacy, Mass Surveillance, and the Struggle to Reform the NSA* (Washington: Brookings, 2017). For another, see the book authored by an involved journalist, Glen Greenwald, *No Place to Hide: Edward Snowden, the NSA, and the U.S. Surveillance State* (New York: Henry Holt/Metropolitan Books, 2014).

[35] Anna North, "Can Twitter Stop Harassment?" *New York Times*, December 3, 2014, http://op-talk.blogs.nytimes.com/2014/12/03/can-twitter-stop-harassment/?_r=0.

Within the EU, the Costeja case of 2014 established a right to be forgotten. A Spanish lawyer ran into financial difficulties, which like other official records in various countries was recorded on the internet. Eventually he got his financial affairs in better order and requested that records of his past financial difficulties be taken down, they being no longer relevant to any public purpose – in his view. The Spanish agency responsible for digital protection agreed with Mr Costeja. Google-Spain appealed to the EU Court of Justice, which affirmed the Spanish ruling. In the view of the court, material should be removed when the documents "appear to be inadequate, irrelevant or no longer relevant or excessive in the light of the time that had elapsed." But what if a convicted pedophile claimed to be reformed? What about a past terrorist conviction claimed to be mistaken? What about a past conviction for possessing or selling illegal drugs claimed to be no longer relevant and impeding employment? In a number of European states, as in Spain, there is a national digital board to review the decisions of Google and Facebook and other private media companies about what information should be removed. In the Costeja case, the material was removed from Google-Spain. But one could still find the information on Google-USA.

With regard to a right to privacy including a right to be forgotten, there is the related issue of not just passwords, but also encryption. One can put communication in code. But in the San Bernardino terrorism case of 2015, two apparently lone-wolf Islamic militants killed fourteen people and seriously injured twenty-two in California. After the terrorists were killed, authorities located one of their cell phones, but had trouble accessing information that might be on it. A debate ensued about whether the US authorities should compel Apple to provide assistance to the authorities, and/or whether Apple and similar companies should be required to provide a "backdoor" in their products – a point of access to "locked" information when national security, as affirmed by an independent court, so required. Apple, supported by various commentators, resisted any such outcome, arguing that such technology would open the door to broad spying and lack of privacy in many countries – with such backdoor technology also projected to lead to a drop in sales. It was reported that the terrorist's phone was eventually accessed with the help of an Israeli private security firm. The debate continued about the needs of public order and security versus the right to privacy in social media. On the market one could purchase various encryption programs, of use to law-abiding citizens who wanted to ensure their privacy. But that technology was also available to more devious persons.

In 2015, before the San Bernardino attack, the UN Special Rapporteur on Freedom of Opinion and Expression, who reports to the UN Human

Rights Council, issued a report strongly in favor of internet anonymity and encryption.[36] The companion UN Special Rapporteur on Right to Privacy had been of similar opinion.[37] Many advocates of a robust national security policy did not agree. And naturally enough, many autocratic governments were also opposed to a broad use of encryption, at least beyond their own security services.

There is also the matter of intentional fake news on the internet. In 2016, certain persons spread false information that Democratic presidential candidate Hillary Clinton was involved in a pedophile ring that was supposedly run out of a pizza restaurant in Washington. An individual crusader believed what he read on the internet without checking sources carefully. Heavily armed, he appeared at the restaurant but was detained and disarmed before he could do damage. Certain individuals, organizations, and no doubt governments are deeply invested in spreading false information – often in pursuit of political goals. In the fall of 2016, a widely circulated "news item" reported falsely that the Pope had endorsed Donald Trump. Private companies like Facebook have committed to fighting the problem, but policies are embryonic. Any number of media outlets now have an office for "fact-checking." The University of Pretoria in South Africa has set up an academic unit to do the same. But what is intentional fake news and what is simply an error in human and thus subjective reporting is not so easy to distinguish in a meaningful time frame. Many private citizens rush to spread information that fits with their beliefs; they do not always check on the reliability of the information they circulate. Results can damage reputations, the democratic process, and other important values.

Then there is the matter of hate speech and incitement to violence. The Islamic State Group recruits extensively on the internet, spreading hate for "Western crusaders." A video game developed and circulated in Australia showed an Aboriginal being beaten to death. The scenes were staged, but it appeared the creators might have intended to spread fear among local Aboriginals and their supporters. In the USA, hate speech was often said to be protected by the First Amendment, but incitement to violence was not so protected. There was a difference between hate speech and hate crimes. Distinguishing the one from the other, that is, passive hate speech from incitement to violence, was not always easy. Apple pulled the Australian violent video game about aboriginals from its

---

[36] A/71/373, 6 September 2016. This is the final report published by the UN General Assembly.

[37] A/HRC/31/64, 8 March 2016. This is the draft report as published by the UN Human Rights Council.

online app store. Once again we see media and technology companies in the front line of controversies about human rights and the internet, even before states and the courts they create take action.

Closely related is the matter of intentional discrimination and persecution. We referred earlier to Facebook and Twitter and attempts to control offensive use of the internet. Certain white supremacist or neo-nazi groups use the internet to circulate information about, for example, Jewish journalists and/or citizens who are known to be critical of, to take one example, Donald Trump. Personal contact information is provided online, after which the targeted individuals receive threatening messages. A collection of these ultra-conservative and racist groups, known loosely as the alt-right, concentrate on social media for their activities and have drawn the attention of various human rights groups, such as the Southern Poverty Law Center.[38]

To summarize, there clearly has been a digital revolution in much of the world. The internet has become significant for many business activities. One source suggested that by 2017 60 percent of all sales of consumer goods would be via the internet rather than in brick and mortar stores. The internet now also figures in many security policies. Cyber communication is now involved in the operation of many weapons systems and chains of command, and thereby opens up potential vulnerabilities in cyber war. Likewise, the internet has become significant for the future of many human rights – both as a threat to rights and as a means to implement them. This being so, a raft of non-governmental organizations has sprung up to fight for a free if properly regulated internet: the Global Network Initiative, Electronic Frontier Foundation, Global Internet Freedom Consortium, Global Network Initiative, Save the Internet/Free Press, etc. The human rights bureau in the US State Department (DRL, Bureau of Democracy, Rights, Labor) holds technology seminars for human rights NGOs and activists, trying to enable them to resist electronic manipulation by actors who are inimical to human rights.[39]

Probably all things ever invented have positive and negative characteristics or uses. The phone can be used to call for help in emergencies. It can also be used to coordinate a terrorist attack. Social media based on the internet present the same duality. Social media can aid in mobilizing for rights, or can be used to undermine and block rights.

---

[38] See www.splcenter.org/fighting-hate/extremist-files/ideology/alternative-right.
[39] See further Larry Diamond and Marc F. Plattner, eds., *Liberation Technology: Social Media and the Struggle for Democracy* (Baltimore: Johns Hopkins University Press, 2012).

Conclusion

In this day and age when talking about what personal rights are needed to ensure human dignity, or a life worth living, one has to address the role of the media – both traditional and social. A free traditional press, based on fundamental civil rights to free speech and communication, and exercising those rights, is essential to any rights-protective regime whether national or international. All governments including democratic ones spin, misrepresent, cover up, and lie. The Eisenhower Administration at first denied that Gary Powers in his U2 plane was spying on the Soviet Union when shot down and captured in 1960. President Kennedy's political team denied that he had Addison's disease. And these are just the milder examples of mendacious statements by democratic leaders. It is a free traditional media that is central to the search for truth in a free society – along with other actors such as institutions of higher education. The reason the Putin Administration in Russia gets away with so many blatant lies is that the traditional media there is not free – witness that country's ratings on Freedom House indexes and other relevant scales.

Social media based on the internet reinforces these conclusions. New digital developments have led to new debates about what personal rights should be internationally recognized: should a right to privacy include a right to anonymity and to be forgotten on the internet? What limitations on digital privacy should be recognized to protect national security and public order, to protect against libel and defamation, and to guarantee the integrity of voting and the democratic process? Perhaps the most important question is: how can the internet be utilized in mobilizing for the protection of human rights when numerous autocratic governments seek technology to block that very possibility – and when terrorists use technology to recruit, propagandize, organize, and kill?

To be sure, use of the internet to mobilize for rights does not ensure success. In Egypt, for example, social media helped produce the massive public demonstrations that drove Mubarak from power in 2011. But the demonstrators were badly organized for the subsequent elections won by the Muslim Brotherhood, and eventually the army installed al-Sisi as the new strongman. Events played out differently in neighboring Tunisia partly because the more a-political army did not impose the return of the old autocratic regime. In neither case did social media alone control the evolution of political developments.[40]

---

[40] See Monshipoori, *Information Politics*. Autocrats with modern technology can often control human rights campaigners despite their modern technology.

Nevertheless, a complicated reality persists. One needs rights to guarantee rights. One needs the rights to free speech, a free press, and a free internet in order to guarantee those and other internationally recognized human rights. There can be legitimate limitations on these rights crucial to a free media in order to protect order and to guard against abuses like child exploitation, human trafficking, or terrorism, *inter alia*. But limitations have to be limited. They should not undermine the essential personal freedoms at issue. How to get the fearful Chinese autocrats or the revolutionary Iranian autocrats, *inter alia*, to accept these values is a tough nut to crack.

Case study: Syrian refugees and the media

As mentioned in Chapter 3, by 2016, there were some 60 million persons in the world who were forced to leave their homes because of war, persecution, and other political causes. About 40 million of these were internally displaced (IDPs), and about 20 million were refugees. The latter had crossed an international frontier and had been unable to return in safety. Economic migrants are not included in these numbers.

As for the Syrian internationalized civil war during 2011–2016, out of a total national population of some 17 million, about 7 million became IDPs and another 5 million refugees. Hence over half of Syria's residents were uprooted because of the conflict. The focus here is on the refugees, but in some ways the IDPs were worse off, being still in a violent country and more difficult to reach by aid agencies or protective forces.

In general, the traditional Western-based media paid attention to Syrian refugees and covered the story regularly, especially as the numbers grew in 2015 and 2016.[41] It may have been rather late in giving prominence to the problem, but there was no lack of information in both hot and cool media. Several photos became iconic, such as that of Alan Kurdi, a 3-year-old Syrian boy washed up dead on the Turkish coast. While circulating widely, the photo did not alter various Western governmental policies which for the most part were already dealing with the refugee issue and which were under domestic pressures not to be generous regarding refugee admissions.

---

[41] This short case study is based primarily on: www.huffingtonpost.com/entry/refugee-crisis-media-coverage_us_5615952ce4b0cf9984d850ec; www.theguardian.com/media/greenslade/2015/dec/17/where-media-fails-on-the-reporting-of-migrants-and-refugees; www.usatoday.com/story/news/world/2016/01/26/migrants-smugglers-social-media-syria-turkey-greece-facebook/79347784/; www.reuters.com/article/us-refugees-media-idUSKBN0U129620151218; https://rctom.hbs.org/submission/digital-refugee-the-impact-of-technology-on-syrian-migrants-and-the-smugglers-who-profit/.

A number of studies have concluded that while the mainstream Western media covered the story, several biases or distortions were present. For one, the emphasis was on refugee affairs in Europe, to where many Syrian refugees hoped to move. There was some reason for this, as the numbers were sizable. There were about 520,000 refugee sea arrivals in Europe during 2015, and about 55 percent of these were from Syria. Yet the Western media did not often cover the story of how many other Syrian refugees fled to Lebanon and Jordan. In Lebanon, by 2016, every fourth person in the country was a refugee. Well-known media actors like *USA Today, New York Times, Washington Post*, PBS, etc. did run stories about Lebanon and refugees, but not frequently or with prominence. A regional bias was also found in African newspapers, which focused on the origins and routes for African refugees (and migrants) rather than European or US policies.

More prominent, according to several studies, was Western media emphasis on Western political statements opposing refugee admissions or denigrating refugees in general – whether by Donald Trump, or Victor Oban in Hungary, or elsewhere. Several studies concluded that it was these provocative or sensational aspects of the refugee story that were played up, rather than the personalized plight of the refugees themselves or their impact on neighboring countries like Jordan and Lebanon. The studies also found a relative lack of stories about how, in many refugee situations, their admission to a country had led to good things, such as a dynamic workforce or new start-up companies, etc.

Everyone agrees that social media was absolutely central to the Syrian refugee affair, whether as means of communicating "facts," or ability to organize, or capability to understand and react. The refugees, the refugee smugglers, and officials responsible for refugee policy – whether national or international – all relied on social media in essential ways. One study found that 86 percent of youth in a Jordanian refugee camp had a mobile device that connected to the internet.

Refugees, in order to flee, needed to know how to do it: what were the preferred routes (which changed frequently), where was the most reliable help, what were the costs, and what were the best destinations. For this, they relied heavily on social media. If their boat sank, the compass on a cell phone would tell them which way to swim – if they could swim.

The other side of the coin was that the underground or black-market smugglers who sought to make money from the refugee's plight also found social media to be central. They were only partially underground or in the shadows, because they created web pages on Facebook and elsewhere and became almost like traditional tourist agencies. They advertised family discounts, posted pictures of nice boats, listed peer reviews as if they had involved TripAdvisor, sometimes provided chat rooms and live blogs, listed fees for fake marriage licenses and passports. Of course, in general, they charged varying but high fees, often provided dangerous and overloaded boats, even sold fake life-vests that were not buoyant, and in general often exploited the refugees for monetary gain. In 2015, some 3,000 persons died crossing the Mediterranean and the straits from Turkey to Greece. Some of the smugglers were Syrian, often exploiting other Syrians. Perhaps 90 percent of Syrian refugees paid someone to help them move, with the black-market smuggling business making probably $3–6 billion by 2016. Facebook and others said they tried to remove the electronic advertising of smugglers as soon as possible. But the ads were often in languages that the monitors did not understand, and when one page was removed another sprang up to replace it somewhere else. There was also, of course, spread of information among friends, family, and acquaintances by "word of mouth" – partially communicated on the internet.

All of this being what it was, officials from governments and international organizations also utilized social media to plan and respond: who and where were the smugglers and how to arrest them; where were the refugees going and when; where were boats in distress and how many were on board or in the water or missing; what were the needs on arrival, how many, and where. Monitoring of social media and its use to respond to ever-changing refugee dimensions was crucial whether one speaks of Turkish, Greek, NGO, UN, or other officials. The UN refugee agency (UNHCR) in Greece and elsewhere provided not only tents and food, but also solar cell-phone charging stations so that refugees could stay in touch with relatives. In Jordanian refugee camps, the UNHCR used Twitter, *inter alia*, to communicate policies, rules, and regulations.

On this subject as on others in the modern world, both traditional and social media played a large role. Particularly social media could be used in positive ways – e.g., to help refugees find a safe route out of danger and locate the nearest UNHCR official. But it could also be used by refugee smugglers to deceive, endanger, and exploit. For refugee officials in national governments and international organizations, it was not possible to play a responsible role without monitoring and utilizing particularly social media.

Discussion questions

• Are Muslims right to be offended by cartoons and satire in Western media about Islam, in the same way that African-Americans are offended by use of the word "nigger" and blackface theatre, or the way Jews are offended by depictions of them as ugly and grasping? That is, regardless of legal rights in favor of free speech, is it wise to employ those rights in order to be offensive toward other groups? What are the proper lessons to be learned from the Danish cartoon controversy and the *Charlie Hebdo* affair?

• With regard to the internet, how can privacy, anonymity, and a right to be forgotten be combined with controls against harassment, discrimination, and threats to legitimate public order and security?

• Can traditional communications media like newspapers and television really aspire to objective news reporting on human rights, given that most of them are commercial and must sell a product and otherwise cater to the tastes of their consumers?

• In democratic countries, have Facebook, Twitter, Google, and similar corporations adequately protected human rights in their operations? To what extent should they cooperate with China and other autocratic counties which often violate many important human rights?

SUGGESTIONS FOR FURTHER READING

Diamond, Larry, and Marc F. Plattner, eds., *Liberation Technology: Social Media and the Struggle for Democracy* (Baltimore: Johns Hopkins University Press, 2012). Making a play on the phrase "liberation theology," two editors compile an excellent series of essays on social media and civil-political freedoms. The chapter by Daniel Calingaert is especially good.

Edgar, Timothy H., *Beyond Snowden: Privacy, Mass Surveillance, and the Struggle to Reform the NSA* (Washington: Brookings, 2017). Argues that the NSA in the USA is a threat to democracy, but that it can be adequately reformed if political will can be found for tough decisions. Thinks Snowden started a process for reform which Obama continued, but did not carry far enough. Thinks major threats to civil and political rights are both global and digital.

Fallows, James, "Arab Spring, Chinese Winter," *The Atlantic Magazine*, www.theatlantic.com/magazine/archive/2011/09/arab-spring-chinese-winter/308601/. A perceptive analysis showing how political protests in one part of the world, making use of social media, can affect politics in distant places.

Greenwald, Glen, *No Place to Hide: Edward Snowden, the NSA, and the U.S. Surveillance State* (New York: Henry Holt/Metropolitan Books, 2014). A journalist with the British newspaper the *Guardian*, who cooperated with Snowden in the release of stolen US classified documents based mostly on sweeping internet monitoring, gives his view of events and issues.

Monshipoori, Mahmood, ed., *Information Politics, Protests, and Human Rights in the Digital Age* (New York: Cambridge University Press, 2016). A good treatment of media and social protests, with much solid information, especially on the Middle East.

Pollock, John C., *Journalism and Human Rights* (New York and London: Routledge, 2015). Eight empirical studies reflecting a complex methods framework. Argues that traditional media can report stories that challenge elites, and thus that the media do not have to simply reflect existing power structures.

Rosen, Jeffrey, and Benjamin Wittes, *Constitution 3.0: Freedom and Technological Change* (Washington: Brookings, 2013). A very good analysis of the legal issues that have come to the fore with the intensified impact of social media.

Part III

Conclusion

Conclusion

10 The politics of liberalism in a realist world

This book has clearly shown the extent to which human rights has become a routine part of international relations. Michael Ignatieff has captured the trend succinctly but brilliantly: "We are scarcely aware of the extent to which our moral imagination has been transformed since 1945 by the growth of a language and practice of moral universalism, expressed above all in a shared human rights culture."[1] The language and practice of universal human rights, and of its first cousin, regional human rights, has been a redeeming feature of a very bloody and harsh twentieth century.

But the journalist David Rieff reminds us of a more skeptical interpretation of universal human rights. "The universalizing impulse is an old tradition in the West, and, for all the condemnations that it routinely incurs today, particularly in the universities, it has probably done at least as much good as harm. But universalism easily declines into sentimentalism, into a tortured but useless distance from the particulars of human affairs."[2] Or, to drive the same point home with a more concrete example, whereas virtually all states formally endorse the abstract principles of human rights in peace and war, "Combatants are as likely to know as much about the laws of war as they do about quantum mechanics."[3]

The international law of human rights is based on liberalism, but the practice of human rights all too often reflects a realist world. A classical example was provided by the situation in Syria from 2011: the Assad security forces and their allies killed and otherwise repressed those demanding more human rights and democracy; and various states such as Israel, Turkey, and the United States were reluctant to get deeply

---

[1] Michael Ignatieff, *The Warrior's Honor: Ethnic War and the Modern Conscience* (New York: Metropolitan, 1997), 8.
[2] David Rieff, "The Humanitarian Illusion," *New Republic*, March 16, 1998, 28.
[3] David Scheffer, "The Clear and Present Danger of War Crimes," Address, University of Oklahoma College of Law, February 24, 1998, unpublished.

involved, fearing a complicated quagmire. (In the midst of its bloody repression, Syria was at least blocked from sitting on the UN Human Rights Council.) State narrow interests rather than personal rights often prevail, interpersonal equality often gives way to disrespect for – if not hatred of – "others," violent conflict is persistent, and weak international institutions are easily demonstrated.[4]

It is a type of liberal progress in keeping with Ignatieff's view that we now recognize the enslavement and other exploitation of the persons in the Congo river basin between about 1460 and 1960 as a violation of their human rights.[5] It is a testament to the continuing explanatory power of David Rieff's realism that we note the lack of effective or decisive international response to the massacres and other gross violations of human rights in the Congo river basin after 1998, whether one speaks of Zaire or Democratic Republic of Congo. Approximately five million persons died from that conflict and its effects, and the rapes were perhaps too numerous to count precisely. (The DRC was the worst place in the world to be female, with on average over 1,000 raped *every day*.)[6] Yet the conflict continued at the time of writing, albeit on a lesser scale.

We recognize rights, but often we do not act to protect them. This provides one general answer to the frequently heard lament: "How could the rhetoric of human rights be so globally pervasive while the politics of human rights is so utterly weak?"[7]

Evidence suggests that the general and abstract idea of human rights still resonates well with publics, but whether governmental elites will follow that opinion is another question. In 2008, sixty years after the UN General Assembly adopted the Universal Declaration of Human Rights, a sample of 15,000 people in sixteen countries which reflected 59 percent of the world's population believed that there had been progress concerning sexism and racism. They believed that there was more equality in the world since 1948. Of this sample, 71 percent thought women had made progress in matters of equality. In fifteen of the sixteen countries large majorities indicated that governments should act to block

---

[4] To expand on notions of realism discussed in Chapter 1, see further among many sources Jack Donnelly, *Realism in International Relations* (Cambridge: Cambridge University Press, 2000). On the difference between human and national interests in international relations, see especially Robert C. Johansen, *The National Interest and the Human Interest: An Analysis of US Foreign Policy* (Princeton: Princeton University Press, 1980).

[5] Adam Hochschild, *King Leopold's Ghost: A Story of Greed, Terror, and Heroism in Colonial Africa* (Boston: Houghton Mifflin, 1998).

[6] See www.abc.net.au/pm/content/2011/s3215390.htm.

[7] Kenneth Cmiel, "The Recent History of Human Rights," *American Historical Review*, 109, 1 (February 2004), 118. For similar frustration, see also Emile M. Hafner-Burton, *Making Human Rights a Reality* (Princeton: Princeton University Press, 2013).

discrimination against ethnic and racial minorities. In the same year large majorities in twenty-one countries believed that governments were responsible for seeing that persons could achieve their basic needs in food, health care, and education. Even in the USA, which does not formally accept socioeconomic rights such as a human right to adequate health care, in 2008 even a small majority of John McCain supporters, not to mention an overwhelming majority of Barack Obama supporters, believed government should ensure adequate health care for all. In 2006 a poll of 27,000 people across twenty-five countries found 60 percent opposed to torture even if it were considered to protect innocent civilian lives from a terrorist attack. In the same year in the USA, a poll found that between 57 and 73 percent of those sampled were in favor of due process rights for terror suspects, ranging from freedom from threats of torture to rights of habeas corpus (right to challenge the reason for detention).[8] We should add, however, that public beliefs about torture being off-limits seemed to be in decline, with growing numbers in some places accepting the use of torture. See immediately below.

As for governmental policies, a careful study of the fate of thirteen human rights during 1981–2006, broken down into two segments, during and after the Cold War, mostly but not entirely focused on civil and political rights, found mixed results. This study attempted an objective measurement of the practice of rights, whatever publics might think. Most rights associated with democratic governance showed improvement. As for what the authors term physical integrity rights, freedom from arbitrary arrest and forced disappearance showed improvement. On the other hand, freedom from torture and extra-judicial killing did not. According to them, the decline in protection against torture started *before* 9/11 and the follow-on abusive counterterrorism policies. Women's political rights showed marked improvement; their economic and social rights did not.[9]

As already suggested, the fate of the values found in the Universal Declaration of Human Rights of 1948 is likely to mirror the fate of applying the principle of constitutional government as found in the

---

[8] See the data compiled and analyzed at worldpublicopinion.org run by the University of Maryland's Program on International Public Attitudes.

[9] David L. Cingranelli and David L. Richards, "The Cingranelli and Richards (CIRI) Human Rights Data Project," *Human Rights Quarterly*, 32, 2 (May, 2010), 401–424. Compare Todd Landman, *Protecting Human Rights: A Comparative Study* (Washington: Georgetown University Press, 2005). On women's rights see further International Center for Research on Women, "Recognizing Rights, Promoting Progress," 2010, www.icrw.org/publications/recognizing-rights-promoting-progress. This is a CEDAW impact report.

Magna Carta of 1215. There will be ups and downs, or successes and failures, dependent above all on the outcome of a very tough political struggle. Just as limited government under the rule of law has had its ups and downs in places like Turkey or Greece or Argentina or wherever, the same will be true for applied human rights. At the time of writing (winter 2016–2017), many internationally recognized human rights faced severe setbacks due to a variety of factors, but including prominently a resurgence of chauvinistic nationalism – make (White) America great again, make (Orthodox) Russia great again, make (Islamic) Turkey great again, make (Hindu) India great again, make (Han) China great again, etc.

To review

Given the ground covered in this work thus far, a brief review of main points is in order. Dichotomies and paradoxes characterize the turbulent international relations of the turn of the century in 2000, as noted in Chapter 1. International human rights are here to stay, but so is state sovereignty in some form. The latter notion is being transformed by the actions, *inter alia*, of intergovernmental and transnational nongovernmental organizations. But state consent still usually matters legally, and state policy and power still count for much in human affairs. One historian – tongue in cheek – quotes a British diplomat to the effect that we need an additional article in the UN Charter: "Nothing in the present Charter should be allowed to foster the illusion that [state] power is no longer of any consequence."[10] This remains relevant despite the rise of armed non-state actors and many non-state advocacy groups. Our moral imagination has been expanded by the language of universal rights, but we live in a world in which nationalism and the nation-state and national interests are frequently powerful barriers to effective action in the name of international human rights. Trade-offs and compromises between liberal and realist principles are legion, as human rights values are contextualized in a modified nation-state system of international relations.[11]

As covered in Chapter 2, the International Bill of Rights and supplemental standards give us the modern international law of global human rights. For all of its defects, noted in various critiques covered below, it is far more developed (meaning specified and structured) than some other parts of international law pertaining to such subject matter as ecology.

Like all law, the international law of human rights (including the law of armed conflict) is the result of a political process, frequently contentious.

[10] Geoffrey Best, Book Review, *Los Angeles Times*, August 16, 1998, 8.
[11] See further Rein Mullerson, *Human Rights Diplomacy* (London: Routledge, 1997).

Surely it comes as no surprise that transnational standards pertaining to the right to life or to the right of freedom of religion or to freedom from discrimination, *inter alia*, should prove controversial. The existence of international human rights law owes much to the western-style democracies – their liberal values and their hard power (the liberal values themselves can be a type of soft power). Still, internationally recognized human rights were also affected by the old communist coalition, and certainly by the newly independent states of the global south after about 1960. We should recall that the resurgence in attention to human rights in international relations circa 1970 was affected in part by the activism of certain Caribbean states.[12]

It cannot be stressed too much that whereas certainly the practice of politics on the basis of respect for the notion of human rights was extensively developed in certain western states, the idea of human rights is a defense against abuse of power everywhere.[13] Wherever the bicycle was invented, its utility is not limited to that historical and geographical situation. So it is also with the idea and practice of human rights.

The human dignity of especially those without great power and wealth normally benefits from the barriers to injurious acts of commission and omission provided by human rights standards. Intentional mass murder and neglectful mass misery are equal affronts to any conception of human dignity. Mass misery no less than mass murder can be changed by human endeavor, and is thus grist for the mill of human rights discourse. As often noted, there is no material or moral reason for world hunger, save for the way we choose to organize ourselves as inhabitants of the planet earth.[14]

We create territorial states whose governments are sometimes said to have responsibility only to their citizens; foster a type of nationalism that tends to restrict morality to within national borders; and internationally endorse a harsh form of *laissez-faire* economics despite its rejection on moral grounds at home. The idea of universal human rights seeks to change those mindsets. This will not occur easily, given the vested interests of the old order. There are always counter-narratives to arguments based on universal human rights: human rights are destabilizing in country X, human rights go against traditional values in country Y, human rights promote too much individualism and too little community

---

[12] Steven Jensen, *The Making of International Human Rights* (Cambridge: Cambridge University Press, 2016).

[13] See further Thomas M. Franck, "Is Personal Freedom a Western Value?," *American Journal of International Law*, 91, 4 (October 1997), 593–627.

[14] Thomas Pogge, *World Poverty and Human Rights: Cosmopolitan Responsibilities and Reforms* (Cambridge: Polity, 2002).

spirit in country Z, etc. Above all, serious attention to human rights restricts those in power.

Human dignity itself, and human rights as a means to that end, are contested constructs whose meaning must be established in a never-ceasing process of moral, political, and legal debate and review. Beyond mass murder and mass misery, the dividing line between fundamental personal rights held by all, and myriad optional legal rights properly varying by country, is a matter of considerable controversy.

In Chapter 3 we saw that the UN has moved beyond the setting of human rights standards toward the more demanding objective of systematic supervision of state behavior. This is a very broad and accelerating development, unfortunately partially undermined not only by a paucity of resources that states allow the overall UN human rights program, but also by the disjointed nature of the beast. The sum total of the diplomacy of shaming, or the politics of embarrassment, certainly has had an educative effect over time, even if the calculated violation continued in the short term. Moreover, the progress made immediately after the Cold War was under challenge by later developments featuring a resurgent traditional Russia and a more powerful autocratic China, not to mention a resurgence in illiberal Islam both governmental (e.g., Iran) and non-governmental (e.g., Al-Qaeda).

At least at first glance it was encouraging that the United Nations Security Council after the Cold War should pay so much attention to human rights issues in the guise of threats to international peace and security. The Council's deployment of field missions under the idea of second-generation or complex peacekeeping, mostly directed to producing a liberal democratic order out of failed states, showed a willingness to deal with many of the root causes of human rights violations – as long as the principal parties gave their consent to the UN presence. Such missions clearly were on the progressive side of history in places like El Salvador, Namibia, and Mozambique. The trend continued in places like Bosnia, Kosovo, East Timor, and Cambodia.

It was also noteworthy that the Council should authorize enforcement actions on behalf of democratic governance and other humane values in places such as Haiti, Somalia, and Libya, even if the job had to be contracted out to one or more member states, and even if the follow-up left something to be desired. Unfortunately the Council was heavily dependent on the one remaining superpower, the United States, to make its enforcement actions effective. The result was a very spotty record of UN accomplishments, especially where the USA saw few traditional national interests to sustain a complicated involvement. In the Kosovo crisis of 1999 the United States tried to enforce human rights protections via NATO, but without Security Council authorization and through a highly controversial military strategy.

On balance the UN was paying more attention to human rights, not less. It was being creative in the interpretation of Chapters VI and VII of the Charter, in calling emergency sessions of the Human Rights Council (as had the Commission), in expanding the authority of its monitoring mechanisms, in creating the office of the High Commissioner for Human Rights, in utilizing NGO information, and in other ways.

Some of this UN creativity had to do with the establishment of various *ad hoc* international or mixed criminal courts by the Security Council, as we saw in Chapter 4. The standing International Criminal Court, whose statute was overwhelmingly approved in 1998, and which began to function during 2002–2003, was loosely associated with the UN. This renewed foray into international criminal justice was a noteworthy development after a hiatus of some fifty years. It triggered a new round of debate about peace v. justice, and about what was central to peace as compared with a moral sideshow. Ignatieff is again brilliantly concise when he writes, "Justice in itself is not a problematic objective, but whether the attainment of [criminal] justice always contributes to reconciliation is anything but evident."[15] New efforts at international criminal justice also caused national policy makers to calculate carefully about how vigorously to go after those indicted for war crimes, crimes against humanity, and genocide, for fear of undermining larger objectives or incurring human costs difficult to justify according to traditional notions of national interest.

What started out in 1993 as partially as a public relations ploy, namely to create an *ad hoc* tribunal to appear to be doing something about human rights violations in Bosnia without major risk to outsiders, by 2016 had become an important global movement for international criminal justice formally accepted by more than 110 states. Such were the unexpected outcomes of a series of "accidental" or *ad hoc* decisions, as states muddled their way through complex calculations of media coverage, popular pressure, traditional national interests, and state power. Private armies might commit many of the violations of human rights, and private human rights groups might be players in the legislative process, but ultimately it was states that decided.

As should have been expected, a certain progress (six convictions in the ICC by early 2017) was followed by problems. Three African countries announced policies of withdrawal from the Court. The Court's

---

[15] Ignatieff, *The Warrior's Honor*, 170.

targeting of political leaders in Kenya reminded certain African leaders that their own policies might be subject to legal review for contributing to atrocities. More generally, these and other states were reminded that legal obligations to cooperate with the ICC might complicate diplomatic and trade arrangements. (China, like South Africa, hosted the indicted Sudanese leader al-Bashar rather than arresting him, as the Court had requested.) And so the struggle for an effective international criminal law continued.

Broad European support for the ICC was partly because, as we saw in Chapter 5, most European states had become accustomed to having supranational courts make judgments on human rights in both the Council of Europe and the European Union. French policy in particular had undergone a considerable change. Like the USA, France long considered its record on human rights beyond the need for the type of international review provided by individual petitions and a supranational regional court. But France – and Turkey – shifted over time, providing at least a glimmer of hope that eventually US nationalism might prove more accommodating to multilateral human rights developments.[16] This hope, to be sure, was at least temporarily derailed by the election of President Donald Trump in 2016 with his nativist policies of "America first."

Be that latter point as it may, European regional protections of civil and political rights remained relatively strong. The Council of Europe and the European Union proved that liberal principles of human rights could often be effectively combined with realist principles of the state system. Of course European developments transformed the regional state system in important ways, as states used their sovereignty to restrict their independence of policy making. Yet states continued to exist in meaningful ways, as did their views of their national interests. States such as Russia and Turkey remained difficult to regulate through regional human rights regimes. At the same time, an international view on protecting human rights also mattered in very important ways, mostly through the judgments of the supranational courts existing in Strasbourg (and Luxembourg for EU members). Once again, as usual, there was a bump in the road toward European protection of human rights, as the UK voted to leave the EU in 2016. In addition, there was an undercurrent of dissatisfaction with the Council of Europe with its human rights

---

[16] In *Of Paradise and Power: America and Europe in the New World Order* (New York: Vintage, 2003, 2004), Robert Kagan argues that European states are much more committed to international law and organization as essential public goods than is the USA.

treaty and powerful European Court of Human Rights. Especially in parts of England, there was a feeling of too much change that benefited foreign labor and refugees.

In less striking, more diplomatic (as compared with legal) ways the Organization for Security and Co-operation in Europe mattered regarding especially the diplomatic protection of national minorities. That NATO should be used to try to protect Albanian Kosovar rights in 1999 was indicative not only of the importance of regional organizations (NATO was a military alliance often considered a regional organization since it had non-military functions), but also of the importance of international action for human rights in Europe. It was not hyperbole to say that commitment to human rights was the central touchstone of being European.

Beyond Europe, the human rights agencies associated with the Organization of American States, especially the InterAmerican Commission on Human Rights, at least generated some impact sometimes on some issues. While the short-term view regarding African regional developments for human rights was even less encouraging, it was at least possible that the Banjul Charter and the African Commission on Human Rights were laying the foundations for long-term progress. After all, both the European Commission and Court had mostly undistinguished records during their first decade of operation, although both operated in an environment more conducive to real regional protection compared with Africa (and historically the Western Hemisphere). At least for Latin American states (but not so much the English-speaking states of the Western Hemisphere), there were more states (not less) accepting the jurisdiction of the InterAmerican Court of Human Rights, and that court was handing down more (not fewer) judgments.

Last but not least, NATO (or at least some of its member states) was an important actor in preventing governmental attacks on civilians in Kaddafi's Libya in 2011, even if the lack of proper follow-through still produced a humanitarian disaster of a different nature.

Permeating all these international developments on human rights was state foreign policy, as we saw in Chapter 6. It is states that take the most important decisions in most intergovernmental organizations, and it is states that are the primary targets of lobbying activities by traditional advocacy groups. It is states that decide on the legal rules for transnational corporations. State sovereignty is being transformed by transnational interests and movements, but states and their conceptions of sovereignty and sovereign foreign policy remain an important – indeed essential – aspect of world affairs at the turn of the century.

Contrary to some realist principles, rational states do not always adopt similar foreign policies despite their existing in anarchic international relations. Because of history, culture, ideology, and self-image, some states do strongly identify with international human rights – at least sometimes. They may take different slants and emphases when incorporating human rights into their foreign policies. But increasingly many states wish to stand for something besides independent existence and power. States certainly have not abandoned self-interest and pursuit of advantage, but more so than in the past they often seek to combine these traditional expediential concerns with concern for the human rights of others. The liberal framework of international relations, embedded in international law and organization, pushes them in that direction. Inconsistencies are legion, but some progress over time is demonstrable.

To be sure the result is usually inconsistent foreign policies that fall short of the goals demanded by the human rights advocacy groups. But in empirical and relative terms, there is now more attention to human rights in foreign policy than was the case in the League of Nations era. In a shrinking world, states that profess humane values at home find it difficult to completely ignore questions of human rights and dignity beyond their borders. Their self-image and political culture mandates that linkage. States that initially seek to bypass issues of individual human rights, like China and Iran, find themselves drawn into a process in which they at least endorse, perhaps in initially vague ways, human rights standards.

Traditional human rights advocacy groups have been active concerning both legislation and implementation of norms, as we traced in Chapter 7. Basing their actions mostly on accurate information, they have followed a self-defined moral imperative to try to "educate" public authorities into elevating their concerns for internationally recognized human rights. Frequently coalescing into movements or networks entailing diverse partners, they have engaged in soft lobbying (viz., lobbying that bypasses electoral and financial threat). Mostly relying on the politics of embarrassment or shaming, they have sought to use reason and publicity to bring about progressive change.

It has usually been difficult to factor out the general but singular influence of this or that human rights NGO, or even this or that movement. Nevertheless, given the flood of information they produce and the persistent dynamism the major groups such as Amnesty International or Human Rights Watch exhibit, it is difficult to believe that the same evolution concerning international human rights would have occurred over the past thirty years without their efforts. In some cases and situations NGO influence can indeed be documented. It is certainly true that the international system for provision of emergency relief in armed conflict and complex emergencies would not be the same without private groups such as the International Committee of the Red Cross. Likewise, there are numerous groups active for "development," or social and economic rights, like Oxfam, Save the Children, etc., and they often provide an important link between the donor agencies and the persons who presumably benefit from "development."

Increasingly it is necessary to look beyond not only states and their intergovernmental organizations, but also beyond the private groups active for human rights, relief, and development for an understanding of the fate of human rights in the modern world. We especially need to look at transnational corporations, as we did in Chapter 8. Given their enormous and growing power in international economics, and given the dynamics of capitalism, it is small wonder that their labor practices have come under closer scrutiny. It may be states that formally make and mostly enforce human rights norms. But it is private corporations, frequently acting under pressure from private groups and movements, that can have a great impact on the reality of human rights – especially in the workplace. Sometimes states are rather like mediators or facilitators, channeling concern from private advocacy groups and movements into arrangements that corporations come to accept.[17] Such was the case with the US government concerning labor standards in the apparel industry, and with the German government concerning child labor in the international rug industry.

One of the more interesting developments concerning international human rights at the close of the twentieth century was the linkage between student activism and labor standards at many universities in the global north. This merger resulted in growing pressure on particularly the apparel industry to end the use of not only child labor but sweatshops by their foreign sub-contractors. But progressive developments were not limited to that one industry, as corporations selling coffee and other products felt the need to protect their brand name and bottom line by opening their foreign facilities to international inspection under international labor standards. It was not so much muscular international law and established intergovernmental relations that brought about new developments. Rather it was a movement made up of consumer groups, unions, the communications media, student movements, churches, and traditional advocacy groups that brought about codes of conduct with

[17] See further B. Hocking, *Catalytic Diplomacy* (Leicester: Centre for Diplomatic Studies, 1996).

inspections and public reports.[18] Much has been written about the social media and grassroots networking that drove the Arab Spring of 2011 in places such as Tunisia and Egypt and the resulting demand for improved democracy and human rights.

Still, one should definitely not be Pollyannaish. Many of the corporations dealing in extraction of natural resources had compiled a record quite different from at least some TNCs in the American-based apparel industry. And many companies seemed more interested in public relations than in genuine commitment to either human rights or other means to human dignity. The corporate push to minimize expenses and maximize profits remained strong. The UN's Global Compact comprised a self-regulating regime that merited close study.

Toward the future

The future of international human rights is not easy to predict with any specificity. One might agree with the statement attributed to the Danish philosopher Kierkegaard: life is lived forward but understood backward. Or one might agree with a statement from Vaclav Havel, first President of the Czech Republic: "That life is unfathomable is part of its dramatic beauty and its charm."[19] Nevertheless, one point is clear about human rights in international relations. We will not lack for controversy.

Human rights has indeed been institutionalized in international relations, but that discourse will remain controversial. This is paradoxical but true. Debate is inherent in the concept of human rights. I do not refer now to the effort by philosophers to find an ultimate metaphysical source of, or justification for, the notion of human rights. Rather I refer to debates by policy makers and others interested in practical action in interpersonal relations. There is debate both by liberals of various sorts who believe in the positive contributions of human rights, and by non-liberals such as realists and Marxists.

---

[18] For example, the Presbyterian Church USA considered divesting from certain corporations providing military equipment to Israel, such was that church's concern about Israeli policies in the occupied territories. See Laurie Goodstein, "Threat to Divest is Church Tool in Israeli Fight," *New York Times*, August 6, 2005, A1.

[19] Vaclav Havel, *Summer Meditations* (New York: Vintage, 1993), 102. See further James F. Pontuso, "Vaclav Havel," in David P. Forsythe, ed., *Encyclopedia of Human Rights* (New York: Oxford University Press, 2009), vol. II, 361–364.

Controversies in liberalism

Enduring questions

Even for those who believe that international human rights constitute on balance a good thing, there are no clear and fixed, much less scientific, answers to a series of questions. What defines universal human dignity? What are the proper moral human rights that constitute the means to that dignity? Which are truly fundamental, and which are optional? Which are so fundamental as to be absolutely non-violable, even in war and other situations threatening national security or the life of the nation, and thus constituting part of *jus cogens* in international law (legal rules from which no conflicting rules or derogation is permitted)? What crimes are so heinous that the notion of universal jurisdiction attaches to them? When moral rights are translated into legal rights, and when there is conflict among legal rights, who resolves the conflicts, and on what principle? Which violations of internationally recognized human rights justify forceful intervention?

Traditional principles

If we focus on particular principles that are said to be human rights principles in contemporary international law, derived from liberalism, we still cannot avoid debate. Revisit, if you will, the principle discussed in Chapter 2 and codified in Article 1 of the two International Covenants in the International Bill of Rights: the collective right of the self-determination of peoples. How do we define a people with such a right – the Kosovars, the Quebecois, the Basques, the Ibos, the Kurds, the Slovaks, the Chechens, the Ossetians? Who is authorized to pronounce on such definitional issues? If we could define such a people, what form or forms can self-determination take? And why have states in contemporary international relations been unable to specify authoritative rules under this general principle that would prove relevant and helpful to conflicts over self-determination? Why is the evidence so overwhelming that most of these disputes are settled by politics, and frequently on the basis of superior coercive power, rather than on the basis of legal rules about collective rights?

Even if we take the widely shared principle of freedom from torture, we cannot avoid controversy. The classic counterexample involves the hypothetical prisoner who has knowledge of a "dirty bomb" that is about to explode. Is it moral to observe the no-torture principle if it results in death or serious injury and sickness to millions? As I noted especially in

Chapter 6, the USA from 2002 (with much support from allies) employed some coercive interrogation in its military detention centers, ran a secret detention system in which abusive interrogation was probably the norm (why else keep it secret?), and "rendered" persons to other states where mistreatment and even torture were widely regarded as prevalent. Was all of this truly necessary for US homeland security? Could the same information have been extracted by more humane methods? If one did obtain some "actionable intelligence," but in the process engaged in a widely known abusive process that produced even more "terrorists" because of their outrage, how should one evaluate the overall costs and benefits? How should one evaluate the experience of other countries that had employed mistreatment or torture, like France in the Algerian war, Britain in Northern Ireland, and Israel, say between 1967 and today? And why was it that almost 200 senior retired officers in the US military wrote President-Elect Trump advising him not to re-institute waterboarding, which they considered a form of torture?

Even if we take the widely shared principle about a right to religious freedom, we cannot escape controversy.[20] This is so even in countries that recognize the principle (and thus I exclude for the moment various controversies about Saudi Arabia and other states that reject the basic principle). What is a religion? The US government says that scientology is a religion, whereas the German government says it is a dangerous, perhaps neo-fascist cult. Do certain Native Americans in prison have a right to use marijuana as part of their claimed religious practices? Is religious belief a valid basis for refusal to serve in the military? Should religious freedom be elevated to those basic rights of the first order, as demanded at one point by the Republican-controlled Congress in the 1990s, and be made the object of special US concern? Or should religious freedom be considered one of many rights, and deserving of no automatic priority over other rights in state foreign policy? The latter was the position of the Clinton Administration, although as noted it did respond to congressional pressures by creating a special office in the State Department to deal with religious freedom.

Even if we note the central position in human rights discourse of the principle of non-discrimination, does the quest for personal equality extend to acceptance of sexual and gender diversity? The answer in much of the West tends toward the affirmative, as views have shifted over time.

---

[20] See further Kevin Boyle and Juliet Sheen, eds., *Freedom of Religion and Belief: A World Report* (London: Routledge, 1997).

But tolerance for gay and lesbian persons and acceptance of gay rights are markedly different in some other parts of the world.[21]

New claims

Certainly if we observe the demands for acknowledgment of a new, third generation of human rights in international relations, we cannot escape the reality of continuing controversy. Should the principle be recognized of a human right to a safe environment?[22] If so, would the enumeration of specific rules under this principle provide anything new, as compared with a repetition of already recognized civil rights about freedom of information, speech, association, and non-discrimination? On the other hand, is it not wise to draw further attention to ecological dangers by recasting norms as human rights norms, even at the price of some redundancy? Then again, given that many states of the global north already have extensive legal regulations to protect the environment, why is it necessary to apply the concept of human rights to environmental law?[23] Do we not have a proliferation of human rights claims already?[24] Do we not need a moratorium on new claims about human rights, perhaps until those rights already recognized can be better enforced?[25]

Process priorities

As should be clear by now, classical and pragmatic liberals do not always agree on how to direct attention to human rights, how much emphasis to give, and what priorities to establish when desired goals do not mesh

---

[21] See further Douglas Sanders, "Sexual and Gender Diversity," in *Encyclopedia of Human Rights*, vol. IV, 433–445.

[22] For starting points see Svitlana Kravchenko, "Environment," ibid., vol. II, 139–149; and Richard P. Hiskes, *The Human Rights to a Green Future: Environmental Rights and Intergenerational Justice* (Cambridge and New York: Cambridge University Press, 2008).

[23] See further W. Paul Gormley, *Human Rights and the Environment: The Need for International Co-operation* (Leiden: W. W. Sijthoff, 1976); and Human Rights Watch, *Defending the Earth: Abuses of Human Rights and the Environment* (New York: Human Rights Watch, 1992). See also Alan Boyle and Michael Anderson, eds., *Human Rights Approaches to Environmental Protection* (New York: Oxford University Press, 1996); Barbara Rose Johnston, ed., *Life and Death Matters: Human Rights and the Environment at the End of the Millennium* (Walnut Creek, CA: AltaMira Press, 1997).

[24] See further Carl Wellman, *The Proliferation of Rights: Moral Progress or Empty Rhetoric?* (Boulder: Westview, 1999).

[25] See Philip Alston, who opposes the development of most new categories of human rights when the older categories are not well enforced, in "Conjuring Up New Human Rights: A Proposal for Quality Control," *American Journal of International Law*, 78, 3 (July 1984), 607–621.

easily. The classical liberal places great faith in persistent emphasis on law, criminal justice, and other punishments for violation of the law. The pragmatic liberal argues for many avenues to the advancement of personal dignity and social justice, of which attention to legal rights, adjudication, and sanctions is only one. Classical liberals emphasize the hard law of adjudication. Pragmatic liberals aspire to that hard law on human rights but accept much soft law through diplomatic process – and even accept turning a blind eye to that law on occasion.

As a pragmatic liberal, I see no alternative to a case-by-case evaluation of when to stress human rights law and adjudication, hard law, that is, and when to opt for the priority of other liberal values through diplomacy. I believe, for example, that it was correct to pursue the Dayton accord in 1995 for increased peace in Bosnia, even if it meant at that time not indicting and arresting Slobodan Milosevic for his support for and encouragement of heinous acts. The persons of that area benefited from increased peace, decline of atrocities, and the attempt to establish liberal democracies in the region. I believe it was correct to go slow in the arrest of indicted persons in the Balkans, lest the United States and other western states incur casualties, as in Somalia in 1993, that would have undermined other needed international involvement, as in Rwanda in 1994.

I believe it was correct to emphasize truth commissions rather than criminal proceedings in places such as El Salvador and South Africa, despite the gross violations of human rights under military rule in San Salvador and under apartheid in Pretoria. Long-term national reconciliation and stable liberal democracy are better than before in those two countries, albeit with many remaining problems, whereas pursuit of criminal justice may have hardened animosities between the principal communities. On the other hand, I think it a good idea to try to hold Augusto Pinochet legally accountable for crimes against humanity, including torture and disappearances, when he ruled Chile. His extradition from Britain and prosecution in Spain, had that transpired, might have made other tyrants more cautious about violating human rights. At least the British legal judgment remains that he was liable to prosecution.

Given the Chinese elite's preoccupation with national stability, in the light of their turbulent national history and the closely watched disintegration of the Soviet Union during Gorbachev's political reforms, I believe it is correct to take a long-term, diplomatic approach to the matter of improvement of human rights in China. I believe we should use the international law of human rights as a guide for diplomacy and a goal for China's evolution. But in the absence of another massacre as in

Tiananmen Square in 1989, or some comparable gross violation of human rights, I believe that constructive engagement is the right general orientation.

None of these policy positions is offered as doctrinal truth. Many of them depend on the evolution of future events which are unknowable. All are offered as examples of policy choices that the typical pragmatic liberal might make, that are based on liberal commitment to the welfare of individuals over time regardless of nationality or gender or other distinguishing feature, and that sometimes avoid an emphasis on criminal justice and other forms of punishment in the immediate future.

The pragmatic liberal approach allows for a great deal of flexibility and guarantees a certain amount of inconsistency. The pragmatic liberal may support criminal justice for human rights violations in one situation, e.g., Spain regarding Chile (the Pinochet case), but not in another, e.g., Cambodia regarding the Khmer Rouge. The pragmatic liberal might well regard major sanctions as mostly inadvisable for Chinese violations of human rights, but find them useful in dealing with Iraq, or Afghanistan, or Burma, or Yugoslavia – or maybe not.

Characteristic of controversy about proper human rights policy was the western response to the Arab Spring of 2011 and the grassroots demand for human rights and genuine democracy across the region. There was military intervention in Libya and a *de facto* policy of regime change for Kaddafi, but a much weaker response in Syria that sought to regrettably leave the repressive Assad regime in charge for a time while hoping (improbably?) for moderation in the future. Was an uncertain future any more threatening in Syria than in Libya? And whose interests were threatened by the departure of Assad, such that protesting Syrians were left to pay the price for lack of regime change?

What we are certainly going to continue to see, even among liberals, is considerable debate about policy choice.

Feminist perspectives

Given that half of the planet's population is female, if we could continue to make major strides in better protecting women's rights, that would lead to a quantum leap in human rights protection overall.[26] And given

---

[26] On the progress that has been made since about 1970, in addition to Cingranelli and Richards, "The Cingranelli and Richards (CIRI) Human Rights Data Project," see Rhoda Howard-Hassmann, "Universal Women's Rights Since 1970: The Centrality of Autonomy and Agency," *Journal of Human Rights* 10, 2 (December 2011), 433–449. She notes the negotiation of CEDAW in 1981 (Convention on the Elimination of Discrimination against Women) and argues that three major issues were omitted:

the reality of "missing girls," namely that particularly in Asia there continues to be preference for male children, resulting in abortion of female fetuses and even infanticide of female babies, there is a pressing need to focus on women's rights. The great imbalance between males and females in the global population tells the distressing story, with perhaps 60–100 million "missing girls" overall.[27] Moreover we can note or already have noted various issues of women's rights requiring more attention: coercive sex trafficking (largely but not entirely pertaining to girls and women); rape as a political strategy (again largely but not entirely pertaining to girls and women); discrimination against women regarding compensation in the workplace; female cutting or genital mutilation; etc.[28]

Even the most radical feminists do not reject the international law of human rights, in the last analysis,[29] and thus I list feminist perspectives as part of liberalism despite great variety among feminist publicists. Much of the feminist critique of extant human rights actually turns out to be gendered liberalism or pragmatic liberalism.[30]

violence against women, abortion rights, and lesbian rights. See further Ann E. Towns, *Women and States: Norms and Hierarchies in International Society* (Cambridge: Cambridge University Press, 2010), who links the domestic status of women to foreign policy and global governance; and Niamh Reilly, *Women's Human Rights* (Cambridge: Polity, 2008), who links human rights to feminist perspectives. For a strong feminist approach to human rights, see Brooke Ackerly, *Universal Human Rights in a World of Differences* (Cambridge: Cambridge University Press, 2008).

[27] Compare Niall Ferguson, "Men Without Women: The Ominous Rise of Asia's Bachelor Generation," *Newsweek*, March 6, 2011, www.newsweek.com/2011/03/06/men-without-women.html; and Aarti Dhar, "'Missing Girls' Increasing in Asia: UNDP," *The Hindu*, March 9, 2010, www.thehindu.com/news/national/lsquoMissing-girls-increasing-in-East-Asia-UNDP/article16550176.ece.

[28] See Barbara Stark, "Women's Rights," in *Encyclopedia of Human Rights*, vol. V, 341–351. See further Howard B. Tolley, Jr., "Human Trafficking," ibid., vol. II, 494–502. See also Hope Lewis, "Female Genital Mutilation and Female Genital Cutting," ibid., vol. II, 200–213.

[29] Eva Brems, "Enemies or Allies?: Feminism and Cultural Relativism as Dissident Voices in the Human Rights Discourse," *Human Rights Quarterly*, 19, 1 (February 1997), 140–141.

[30] It can be noted in passing that one strand of feminism reflects a "post-modern" or "critical" or "essentialist" approach in that it argues that, unless one is female, one cannot understand female human dignity and the rights (and perhaps other institutions) needed to protect it. Male observers and scholars, as well as policy makers, are simply incapable of comprehending either the problem or its solution. I myself would not consider this approach part of the liberal tradition, for liberalism stresses a common rationality and scientific method available to all without regard to gender. See further Christine Sylvester, "The Contributions of Feminist Theory to International Relations," in Steve Smith, Ken Booth, and Marysia Zalewski, eds., *International Theory: Positivism and Beyond* (Cambridge: Cambridge University Press, 1996), 254–278.

The traditional feminist critique of human rights centers on the argument that those norms, being produced in a male-dominated legislative process, focus on the public rather than private domain.[31] The public arena is the man's world, while women have been confined to the home as sexual object, mother, unpaid domestic worker, etc. Thus it is said that international human rights fail to deal adequately with domestic abuse and oppression of women. International human rights have supposedly been gendered to the detriment of women, despite an active role for some women in the drafting of the Universal Declaration of Human Rights (as noted in Chapter 3).

One feminist critique attacks one half of the International Bill of Rights as it exists today, preferring to emphasize supposedly feminist values like caring and responsibility.[32] Here the argument is that a rights-based approach can only lead to negative rights of the civil and political variety. If one wishes to move beyond them to adequate food, clothing, shelter, and health care, one needs a feminist ethics of care that stresses not rights but the morality of attentiveness, trust, and respect.

Parts of international human rights law are being revised to respond to the first critique. International and more specifically comparative refugee law now stipulates that private abuse can constitute persecution and that women can constitute a social group subject to persecution. Thus a woman, crossing an international border to flee such behavior as female genital mutilation, or a well-founded fear of such behavior, particularly when the home government does not exercise proper protection, is to be provided asylum and is not to be returned to such a situation. Canada and the United States have led the way in reading this new interpretation into refugee law, acting under advisory guidelines established by the Office of the UN High Commissioner for Refugees.[33]

As for the second critique, it should be repeated that the discourse on human rights does not capture the totality of ethics pertaining to interpersonal relations. No doubt an ethics of care and responsibility has its place. Whether such an ethics in international relations is particularly feminine, and whether it can be specified and encouraged to better effect

---

[31] For a select bibliography on women's and human rights, see http://science.jrank.org/pages/9673/Women-s-Rights-BIBLIOGRAPHY.html.

[32] Fiona Robinson, "The Limits of a Rights-Based Approach to International Ethics," in Tony Evans, ed., *Human Rights Fifty Years On: A Reappraisal* (Manchester: Manchester University Press, 1998), 58–76.

[33] In general, see Stephen H. Legomsky, *Immigration and Refugee Law and Policy*, 2nd edn. (New York: Foundation Press, 1997). See also Connie M. Ericson, "In Re Kasinga: An Expansion of the Grounds for Asylum for Women," *Houston Journal of International Law*, 20, 3 (1998), 671–694.

than the human rights discourse, are interesting questions. It is by no means certain that a rights approach must be limited to negative rights, and cannot adequately lead to minimal floors for nutrition, clothing, shelter, and health care.[34]

The second feminist critique overlaps with parts of the pragmatic liberal argument in arguing the merits of at least supplementing legal rights with action not based on rights but still oriented to the welfare of individuals. Once again we find that much of the feminist critique of human rights reflects some form of liberalism, mostly gendered pragmatic liberalism. One needs the concept of human rights, if perhaps revised to take further account of special problems of dignity and justice that pertain to women, but one may also need to go beyond rights to extra-legal or a-legal programs that do not center on adjudication of rights.

Still, a reason for legal rights is the reliability and efficacy of thinking in terms of entitlements that public authority must respect. That is precisely why Henry Dunant and then the ICRC started with the notion of (Christian) charity toward those wounded in war, but quickly moved to trying to make medical assistance to the wounded a legal obligation in (secular) international law.

Controversies beyond liberalism

When considering the future of human rights, I have tried to indicate the tip of the iceberg of controversy even when one accepts the concept of human rights as a beneficial part of international relations. But there is controversy of a different order, based on a more profound critique of human rights as that notion has evolved in international relations. This second type of controversy, which takes different forms or schools of thought, is based on the shared view that individual human rights based on liberal philosophy is misguided as a means to human dignity. The dominant critique, at least for western liberals, has been by realists. But we should also note, at least in passing, the views of Marxists.[35]

---

[34] Paul Hunt, *Reclaiming Social Rights: International and Comparative Perspectives* (Aldershot: Dartmouth, 1996).

[35] It should be stressed that there are numerous approaches to understanding international relations and the place of human rights therein. A short introductory overview such as this one cannot be expected to be comprehensive. See further Scott Burchill and Andrew Linklater, eds., *Theories of International Relations* (New York: St. Martin's Press, 1996). As noted in Chapter 1, Michael Doyle has shown that one can gain many insights by concentrating on liberalism, realism, and Marxism/socialism. The present book follows that approach. Some authors stress not liberalism versus realism but liberalism versus communitarianism – the idea that the community, not the individual, is the proper

Realism

Realism in its various versions has historically captured some prevalent features of traditional international relations. Its strong point has been its emphasis on collective egoism, as numerous political leaders, claiming to speak for a nation, have indeed acted frequently on the basis of their view of narrow self-interest. It has also been accurate in emphasizing calculations of power and balance – or more precisely distribution – of power, however elusive the objective perception of power and its distribution might prove. Such calculations have indeed been a prevalent feature of international relations. In being state-centric, realism captures much of the real strength of nationalism and national identity.

The central weakness of realism has always been its inability to specify what comprises the objective national interest, and therefore its inability to say what is the rational pursuit of that interest based on power calculations. Realism assumes the permanence of a certain nineteenth-century view of international relations in which the dominant principles are state sovereignty understood to mean independence, non-intervention in the domestic affairs of states, and the inevitability of interstate power struggles culminating in war.

Most versions of realism discount the possibility that states would see their real security and other national interests advanced by *losing* considerable independence – e.g., by joining supranational organizations. Realism discounts the possibility of the rise of important transnational interests so that the distinction between domestic structure and issues and international relations loses much of its meaning. Realism discounts the possibility of a decline if not elimination of hegemonic global war among the great powers, and thus does not contemplate the irrationality of saving one's major preoccupations for a war that will not occur – perhaps at all and probably without great frequency.

Realism discounts the emergence of values such as real commitment to universal human rights and instead posits, in the face of considerable contradictory evidence, that states will always prefer separateness and independent policy making over advancement of human rights (or for that matter over quest for greater wealth through regulated trade or better environmental protection). Realists are prepared to look away when gross violations of human rights are committed inside states; morality and state obligation tend to stop at national frontiers – and

dominant concern. All liberal orders have to deal with individual rights and autonomy versus the rights and needs of the larger community. I have covered part of this controversy when discussing "Asian values."

anyway the game of correction is not worth the candle. To realists, international liberalism, and the international human rights to which it gives rise, is a utopian snare left over from the European enlightenment with its excessive belief in human rationality, common standards, and capacity for progress.

In situations *not* characterized by intense fear, suspicion, and the classic security dilemma, however, realism misses much of the real stuff of international politics. Where states and governments do not perceive threats to the life of the nation as they have known it, they behave in ways that realism cannot anticipate or explain. Realism is largely irrelevant to international integration in Europe through the Council of Europe and European Union. After all, French fears of German power led to integration between the two, not to French marshaling of separate military power. Realism has no explanation for NATO's unified commitment to a democratic Europe, and hence to its intervention in federal Yugoslavia to protect Kosovars, save for the argument that the entire policy of intervention was to demonstrate NATO's dominance (an argument much too simple). Realism cannot explain international human rights developments over the past fifty years, except to suggest that most of the states of the world have been either hypocritical or sentimental in approving human rights norms and creating extensive diplomatic machinery for their supervision. Realists like Kissinger were out of touch with important developments in international relations when he opposed the human rights and humanitarian aspects of the 1975 Helsinki Accord, and when he came to accept those principles only as a useful bargaining tool with, and weapon against, the European communists. Even then, he was more comfortable with traditional security matters as Metternich and other nineteenth-century diplomats would have understood them. His priority was stability among Great Powers, full stop.

In some types of international politics realists are relevant, but in other types they are anachronistic.[36] Realists well understand the prevalent negative correlation between war and protection of most human rights. Insecurity does indeed breed human rights violations. On the other hand, much of international relations cannot be properly understood by simple reference to "the prisoner's dilemma," in which fear of insecurity is the only attitude, explaining all policies. Some states will pursue human rights abroad only when such action can be made to fit with traditional national interests. But some states in some situations will

---

[36] See further Robert O. Keohane and Joseph H. Nye, *Power and Interdependence: World Politics in Transition* (Boston: Little, Brown, 1977). In their view, realism is not very relevant to that type of international relations called complex interdependence.

pursue human rights through international action even at the expense of certain traditional interests, such as independence in policy making, hence the Council of Europe and European Union. At least sometimes they will incur some costs for the rights of others, as NATO did over Kosovo and Libya, as the British did in Sierra Leone, etc. Realists do not understand that some states, like some natural persons, wish to stand for something besides independent power, obtained and used in other than a Machiavellian process.

Marxists

The Marxist and various neo-Marxist critiques of international human rights merit a separate book. But it is accurate to say here, albeit briefly, that classical Marxists consider individual legal rights a sham in the context of economic forces and structures that prevent the effective exercise of human rights. Legal human rights on paper are supposedly negated by exploitative capitalism that leads to the accumulation of profit rather than the betterment of human beings. When large parts of the world manifest persons earning less than one dollar per day, extensive human rights in legal form are meaningless. In this view international human rights have been used more since 1945 to legitimate international capitalism than to protect human beings from predatory capitalistic states which empower their corporations.[37] There is also the view, not based on strictly economic factors, arguing that the modern push for human rights, dominated as it has been by western states, is a new form of neo-colonialism.[38]

For a classical Marxist, "the contradictions that characterize human rights reflect the conflicts inherent in capitalist society, lead to pervasive violations of those rights, and make respect for them impossible, particularly in this era of global capitalism."[39] Thus, material conditions control, exercising rights depends on having wealth, corporate for-profit rights trump individual fundamental rights, and the Universal Declaration of Rights cannot be realized as long as international relations reflects global capitalism.

There is some overlap between Marxists and certain pragmatic liberals. Both would agree that the international financial institutions such

[37] See, e.g., Norman Lewis, "Human Rights, Law, and Democracy in an Unfree World," in Evans, ed., *Human Rights Fifty Years On*, 77–104.
[38] Makau Mutua, *Human Rights: A Political and Cultural Critique* (Philadelphia: University of Pennsylvania Press, 2002).
[39] Gary Teeple, *The Riddle of Human Rights* (Amherst, NY: Humanity Books, 2005). See also his "Karl Marx," in *Encyclopedia of Human Rights*, vol. III, 466–476.

as the World Bank and the International Monetary Fund need to consider further the human hardship caused by their structural adjustment programs. Both argue the futility of seeing and dealing with human rights apart from their socioeconomic context. Pragmatic liberals differ from Marxists in believing that regulated capitalism, and its primary global agent the transnational corporation, can be a force for progress and is not irredeemably exploitative. Pragmatic liberals also differ from Marxists in seeing in western history an effort to combine political freedom, economic freedom, and checks on gross abuses of human dignity, and not a record of unrelenting economic exploitation.

In summary of these two illiberal critiques, one can say that first of all realism has been the most important historically. Realism (meaning the varieties thereof) has been the dominant prism in the powerful western world for understanding international relations. Some realists have argued that national liberals, if rational, would not be liberal in anarchical international relations, or if they understood the evil "nature of man." Christian realists have argued, in effect, for realism with a human face (spiritually guided, of course) but this quest leads to a perpetually unsatisfying compromise between power and morality. Second, one can say that nowhere has the *practice* of Marxism led to an attractive model of human development entailing an acceptable degree of personal freedom.[40] Marxism, perhaps as one influence on democratic socialism, however, would seem to have continuing relevance by reminding us of the exploitative tendencies of unregulated capitalism, and of the weakness of legal rights when divorced from certain social and economic facts – e.g., minimal achievements in education and income.

In the final analysis even most of the critics of what I have termed classical political liberalism at the close of the twentieth century do not reject entirely the concept of universal human rights. They argue for its validity, but stress various cautions, reforms, and refinements. Even Kissinger and most other realists tolerate international human rights as a necessary if unwise addition to power calculations, although they do not give personal rights high priority and they are unwilling to greatly complicate traditional diplomacy with much attention to them.[41]

Francis Fukuyama, as discussed in Chapter 1, may yet be proved correct, however, in that no theory save some type of liberalism offers much prospect of a better world in the twenty-first century. The Arab

---

[40] See further Zbigniew Brzezinski, *The Grand Failure: The Birth and Death of Communism in the Twentieth Century* (New York: Scribner, 1989).

[41] In his book *Diplomacy* (New York: Simon & Schuster, 1994), Kissinger writes that pure realism is unsustainable at least in US foreign policy.

Spring of 2011 would seem to support his view that political liberalism based on human rights is the most appealing model for organizing national societies. A caution bears repeating. If Fukuyama is read to mean support for libertarianism and minimal governance, instability is the likely result. Libertarian liberalism wants to emphasize private property as a civil right, and to elevate it to a central and absolute position in its view of the good life. But the result of this view is Dickens' England, or the USA in the era of Henry Ford. There are definitely liberal interpretations that are injurious to human dignity, as recalled particularly in Chapter 8 where the misdeeds of certain private corporations were reviewed. It is no small task to combine property rights featuring "economic freedom" with other rights and freedoms so as to produce a widely shared view of social justice or human dignity.

The big picture

Are there important and enduring patterns and correlations on the subject of human rights in international relations? The answer is yes, with awareness of limitations and constant modification through new research.[42] If we focus on rights of personal integrity such as freedom from torture, forced disappearances, summary execution, and the like, we find that the protection of these rights is positively correlated with: democracy, economic development, peace, former status as British colony, and small population size. In other words, individuals are most at risk for torture and other violations of personal integrity in populous, authoritarian, poor states, facing international or internal armed conflict, and without the restraining traditions of British heritage.

If we inquire more carefully into why democracy seems to generally reduce violations of personal integrity, research by Bruce Bueno De Mesquita and others suggests that: full democracy through the form of multiparty competitive elections is necessary to get this effect; more limited forms of democracy short of multiparty elections do not produce the same effect; and the notion of real accountability to the electorate seems to be the key to the process.[43]

Such general trends are then crosscut by others. For example, economic development in Arab-Islamic states does not have a positive

---

[42] For an overview, see David P. Forsythe and Patrice C. McMahon, eds., *Human Rights and Diversity: Area Studies Revisited* (Lincoln: University of Nebraska Press, 2003), especially chs. 1 and 2, and the conclusion.

[43] Bruce Bueno De Mesquita, "Thinking Inside the Box: A Closer Look at Democracy and Human Rights," *International Studies Quarterly*, 49, 3 (September 2005), from 439.

correlation with protection of women's rights. Particular cultural factors intervene to block the normally beneficial impact of economic development.

Can we say for sure what produces democracy, with its civil and political rights? No, but there are some correlations between economic wealth and sustaining democracy. According to Adam Przeworski and Fernando Limongi, democracy does not last very long in the face of economic adversity.[44] During the Cold War more or less, a democratic polity with a per capita income of $1,500 lasted eight years or less; a per capita income up to $3,000 increased the longevity of a democratic state to an average of 18 years; above a per capita income of $6,000, democratic sustainability was largely assured. Against this background, it made complete sense that in 2004 citizens in relatively poor states like Russia or several states in the Western Hemisphere expressed considerable sympathy for a return to authoritarian government, given that existing democratic (or partially democratic) governments had compiled a poor record on increasing per capita income.[45] It merits reflection that very few states other than China have been able to achieve rapid and sustained economic growth without being at least a genuine electoral democracy.

One could group states in different ways, and inquire into correlations about different rights and types of rights, but it was clear that some insights into the fate of rights could be obtained through careful research.[46] One of the most persistent conclusions out of this type of research was that it was futile to focus on civil and political rights without regard to their socioeconomic and cultural context. From the time of Weimar Germany in the 1920s and 1930s to Afghanistan after the Taliban, holding elections would only mean so much over time. Without attention to economic development and equitable distribution of the fruits of that development, and without attention to cultural factors impeding equity if not equality, elections would not necessarily contribute to sustained human dignity.

One might recall at this point that the UN General Assembly has repeatedly endorsed the notion that civil, political, economic, social, and cultural rights are interdependent and equally important.

[44] Adam Przeworski and Fernando Limongi, "Modernization: Theories and Facts," *World Politics*, 49, 2 (January 1997), 155–183.
[45] Warren Hoge, "Latin Americans Are Nostalgic for Strongman Rule," *International Herald Tribune*, April 21, 2004.
[46] See Forsythe and McMahon, eds., *Human Rights and Diversity*, especially the chapter by David L. Richards. And recall his work with David Cingranelli, "The Cingranelli and Richards (CIRI) Human Rights Data Project," regarding the practice of rights during 1981–2006.

(At the same time, I noted that the same body had given priority to certain rights in the construction of international criminal courts and in endorsing the notion of R2P – namely preventing genocide, crimes against humanity, and major war crimes, and in the case of R2P ethnic cleansing.)

Balance sheet after seventy years

To end where we began: the future of human rights is not guaranteed, but rather depends on committed actors in a tough political struggle. Some champions of enlightenment values as centered on individual rights have been criticized for a naive optimism. They seem to assume that the justness of their cause is so evident that it is bound to triumph over time. But this kind of "Whig history," assuming a steady advance for moral progress through personal rights, is easily debunked. To repeat, those relying on the narrative of the 1948 Universal Declaration of Human Rights and its personal rights for all repeatedly encounter counter-narratives: that the West is decadent and its emphasis on individual rights misguided, leading to licentiousness; that the West uses (and has used) the language of universal rights as a political tool to undermine its adversaries and advance its imperial or hegemonic ambitions; that certain countries are too fragmented or uneducated for the successful practice of rights; that different cultures have alternative means for advancing human dignity, not centered on human rights, etc. To reduce to the absurd: it is fatuous to think that if Putin in Moscow or Xi in Beijing or al-Sisi in Cairo would only read carefully the Universal Declaration, all would be well in the world.

It is hard to think of an example of a major gain for fundamental personal rights that was not achieved through tough political struggle over time, with interim gains and losses along the way: reigning in the power of the monarchy in England or the power of a dictator in Tunisia; advancing civil rights for Blacks or voting rights for women in the USA; moving South Korea from military dictatorship to multi-party democracy; getting rid of apartheid in South Africa; reducing the frequency of personalized and militarized rule in South America; undermining the bogus claims to human liberation by a repressive European communism, etc. There were (and are) always defenders of an oppressive status quo. There were (and are) always those ready to elevate other concerns over individual human rights: quest for a perfect national security, need for economic growth, continuation of the ruling elite (the opposition always consisting of rascals and worse); fidelity to hierarchical religion and its sacred texts; glorification of the nation to such an extent that independent thought and dissent from current policy become treason.

Where then do we stand some seventy years after the UN General Assembly adopted the Universal Declaration on December 10, 1948? How far have we come in implementing what has been endorsed? Are the trends encouraging or disappointing?

As one might anticipate given the large number of rights found in treaties and major diplomatic agreements, the existence of over 190 states that are members of the UN, and the various cultures and levels of economic development of different nations and regions, the record is mixed. In general, there is now much more attention to human rights in international relations than was true of the League of Nations era. More specifically, one can start to identify major gains for, and major impediments to, internationally recognized human rights.[47]

Major progress

First one might cite the Renaissance of international criminal justice. As indicated in Chapter 4, after the Nuremberg and Tokyo Trials of the 1940s, international criminal justice went into eclipse as Great Power energies were channeled into the Cold War. But in 1993 with regard to the former Yugoslavia and then in 1994 with regard to Rwanda, a newly harmonious UN Security Council created ad hoc criminal courts. This was another Western-led development, and it was contingent on particular facts in particular times – mainly a desire in Washington and Paris to do something not too inconvenient about the human tragedies of the Balkan War of 1992–1995, and then a desire not to be obviously racist and manifestly double-dealing concerning Rwanda. But this is how change often occurs (probably almost always occurs) – by particular agents in particular contexts acting with mixed motives. It is then up to other actors to consolidate and possibly expand developments, as occurred with the creation of other criminal courts with limited jurisdiction, and then the emergence of the permanent International Criminal Court (ICC) by 1998–2000.

Certainly these criminal courts have not proven a panacea for all the defects of human dignity in places like Sierra Leone, Cambodia, East Timor, Lebanon, and elsewhere. This is certainly true of the ICC, with its slow, bumbling, and very limited record of convictions. And the more

---

[47] See further David P. Forsythe, "International Human Rights at 70: Has the Enlightenment Project Run Aground?," in Anthony Chase, ed., *Routledge Handbook on Human Rights in the Middle East and North Africa* (London and New York: Routledge, 2016), ch. 27.

active the ICC has become, the more particularly some African leaders have tended to see it as a threat to their freedom of policy making. This is not unexpected, given the unsavory nature of many policies by African leaders, as in Kenya. Governments often adopt human rights standards thinking they will be applied to others; then they dig in their metaphorical heels when the standards are applied to them. Nevertheless, a fair evaluation of the "justice cascade"[48] would indicate that the renewal of international criminal justice has taken any number of terrible leaders out of politics and into jail, as the story of Charles Taylor of Liberia would indicate. Indeed, from the Balkans to the Great Lakes region of Africa, prime ministers, mayors, war lords, militia leaders, and party activists have all felt the sharp edge of international criminal courts.

Relatedly there is the "Pinochet precedent" stemming from proceedings during 1998–2000. When UK courts ruled it was legal for the British government to extradite the Chilean former dictator to Spain to stand trial on charges of torture in Chile, that sent notice even to the powerful that national exercise of the principle of universal jurisdiction was in play in the game of international relations. Britain, a rule-of-law country, reaffirmed that under certain treaties, certain crimes like torture were so heinous that any state could try a defendant regardless of nationality or place of events, and that even claims to state sovereignty by high officials or former officials need yield to legal justice. The fact that the UK rewarded Pinochet for his past anti-communism by sending him home to Chile under the guise of "humanitarian" considerations of bad health did not change the potential sweep of the court's ruling.

Subsequently other officials and former officials from a variety of states carefully calculated where to travel, or when to cancel travel plans, for fear of being served with legal papers related to alleged atrocities. Who can be sure who is next, especially if from a small and weak government without powerful allies? One source found over 150 cases based on universal jurisdiction in recent years,[49] as exercised by nineteen countries.[50] Power still matters, and relatively weak states do not want to take on more powerful ones. Thus Belgium scaled back its universal jurisdiction law when the USA pressured it to do so. Still, there has been (incomplete) change in a positive direction.[51]

---

[48] Kathryn Sikkink, *The Justice Cascade* (New York: Norton, 2011).
[49] International Justice Resource Center, www.ijrcenter.org.
[50] For an overstatement about the impact of universal jurisdiction, see Philippe Sands, *Torture Team* (London: Palgrave-Macmillan, 2008).
[51] On double standards in the practice of international criminal justice, see David P. Forsythe, "The UN Security Council and Response to Atrocities," *Human Rights Quarterly*, 34, 3 (August 2012), 840–863. See also Klaus Bachmann and Aleksandar Fatic, *The UN International Criminal Courts* (London: Routledge, 2015).

A second overlapping area of progress concerns the attention now given to transitional justice. After the end of dictatorships, wars, and other situations involving gross violations of human rights and humanitarian law, there have been redoubled efforts, once again, to reinforce rights in order to prevent a recurrence of future wrongs. There is an effort at negative learning: how to transition to institutionalized human dignity, to avoid repeating the repressive and oppressive past. (Sometimes there is attention to gross violations of human rights and humanitarian law even while a situation is evolving, as per discussion of war crimes, crimes against humanity, and torture in the Syrian civil war. It is not always the case that all actors wait until the end of an era to address how to deter and rectify atrocious acts.)

Without spending much more time on criminal justice in this chapter, one can argue that in the aftermath of gross violations, *national* criminal justice is likely to be more about vindictive retribution than building future liberal and legitimate order. One has only to recall the spectacle of Shia Iraqis trying the Sunni Saddam Hussein, or some Polish democrats trying the former communist leader of martial law, Wojciech Jaruzelski, to appreciate the problems. Both judicial procedures constituted a circus – albeit a fatal one in Hussein's case. Then there was the debacle of one political faction in Bangladesh holding war crimes trials for a competing political faction, based on earlier behavior in the 1971 fighting that carved Bangladesh out of East Pakistan. So there is much to recommend international trials according to international standards. Unfortunately, as in Libya after 2010, headstrong local partisans often insist on running their own judicial show rather than involving the international community. The result in Libya was a failed effort to try some of those who had supported Kaddafi, resisting a role for the ICC, with the consequence that no trials occurred at all (at the time of writing) in that chaotic situation.

The larger point for present purposes is that there is now active discussion of a range of options concerning how best to institutionalize democratic and other rights after dictatorship and other rights violations. Almost always in the wake of fundamental change, whether pertaining to end of dictatorship, end of war, or end of instability, one moves to a debate about trials or reconciliation commissions or pardons (amnesties) or reparations or memorials. There is also an argument for doing nothing special in some situations, since after the Spanish Civil War and eventually the demise of autocrats like Franco and Salazar (in Portugal) one saw those Iberian countries successfully transition to stable liberal democracies without special look-back procedures (perhaps because of their integration into organizations like the EU, Council of Europe, and NATO).

There is now a vast literature exploring lessons learned from this menu of choice, with some finding a correlation between trials and stable liberal democracy, but others finding some linkage between trials and amnesties and liberal order. There is much discussion of how the South African Truth and Reconciliation Commission eased the way from white minority rule to multi-racial democracy circa 1994. There is also much discussion about how in some situations, advocates for the *ancien régime* are simply still too powerful for trials to occur, and so some actors, whether public or private (e.g., churches), seek an alternative reckoning. This occurred, for example, in Brazil (see the report, "Nunca Mais," compiled by the Catholic Church in Sao Paulo). Some scholars believe there is no science on the matter and that one needs to adopt policy choices on a case-by-case basis looking at the particular factors of each individual case.[52]

It is not irrelevant to note that Germany has faced up to its past with regard to the Nazis and the Holocaust, has to a considerable extent moved beyond those dark times, and emerged not only as a stable liberal democracy, but often a leader for human rights and humanitarian affairs. On the other hand, Japanese leaders continue to be ambivalent about taking clear and full responsibility for Japanese aggression and war crimes (including the practice of sexual slavery) in the 1930s and 1940s, with the result of facing continued friction with China, South Korea, and others. Turkey, for its part, continues to adamantly deny having conducted genocide against the Armenians circa 1915 and before, despite convincing evidence. Once again, the result has been continued controversy and friction rather than laying the matter to rest and moving on. And even in Spain, once thought to have successfully skipped over revisiting the atrocities of the Spanish Civil War and the Franco era, there emerged in recent years precisely argument, contention, and debate over that history. Efforts to avoid a historical reckoning in Spain have not in fact been fully successful.

In any event, it is now rare to find an end to repressive regimes or destructive wars without also finding a debate about how to ensure more personal rights in the future and avoid a return to repressive or destructive situations. Sri Lanka after the defeat of the Tamil Tigers is a clear example. This is progress, even if based on the negatives inherent in negative learning.

Another example of progress concerns R2P: the Responsibility to Protect. It had long been recognized that an absolute notion of state

---

[52] Martha Minow, *Between Vengeance and Forgiveness* (Boston: Beacon Press, 1998).

sovereignty was a recipe for internal atrocities. After all, for those concerned with how Hitler was treating German Jews and homosexuals and dissidents, international law provided no basis for action in that era. If a government was the supreme voice of a sovereign state, and if there was a prohibition on external interference into domestic affairs, efforts to stop domestic atrocities were legally blocked.

It was therefore important that the principle of R2P was unanimously adopted at a UN summit in 2005 and then was followed up by supportive action by others. Without doubt, the concept has gained acceptance over the years, despite the fact that the 2005 statement of principle consisted of two paragraphs in a long UN statement about all the good things that ought to occur in international relations. Once again, it was a matter of a particular proposal at a particular time that seemed of dubious importance, but was then pursued with considerable diligence by various actors.

As is reasonably well known by now, R2P implies that state sovereignty is not absolute, but rather depends on the sovereign state acting responsibly under international law. If a state is unwilling or unable to prevent genocide, crimes against humanity including ethnic cleansing, or major war crimes, outsiders have a duty to take corrective action in keeping with international law. This latter phrase was designed to counter a historical fact, namely that some powerful states intervened in the internal affairs of other states for self-interested and legally unjustifiable reasons – hence the misuse of the so-called humanitarian intervention doctrine. Putin's "humanitarian convoys" into eastern Ukraine in 2014 have kept alive the fear of the misuse of that doctrine.

Given this history and thus the taint on the humanitarian intervention doctrine, the authors of R2P went to great lengths to differentiate the new R2P concept, stressing the need for early and peaceful efforts to deal with situations that might turn into atrocities.[53] In this regard I would note an example of judicial R2P in the case of Kenya. Given past electoral violence, the ICC initiated an official inquiry into the role of certain Kenyan leaders in fomenting violence and displacement against political opponents. In fact, under the scrutiny of this ICC involvement in Kenyan affairs, the level of political persecution declined in subsequent elections. However, the targeted Kenyan leaders succeeded in stymying ICC judicial procedures by such measures as intimidating or paying off witnesses, while they mobilized regional support from certain other African leaders. So while the Kenyan electoral process was improved in relative terms at least for a time, the role of the ICC was

[53] Gareth Evans, *The Responsibility to Protect* (Washington: Brookings, 2008).

blocked by the self-serving and unprincipled maneuvers by the defendants and their supporters, as they trotted out the expected arguments about the ICC being part of renewed neo-colonialism (the ICC Prosecutor, however, was Gambian). Unfortunately, ethnic conflict seems on the rise once again in Kenya after the collapse of the ICC case.

Other examples are debated about the actual or potential activation of the principle of R2P concerning: (1) humanitarian relief after typhoon Nargis in 2008 in Myanmar (the junta seemed to be stalling in order to exclude outsiders, the French had warships off the coast, the junta allowed more international relief;) and (2) threats to civilians in Libya in 2011 (the Security Council authorized action for civilian protection, but not regime change). There is much to analyze about these and other cases of the actual or potential application of the principle, as in Democratic Congo, but space here does not allow it.

Suffice it to say for present purposes that the adoption of R2P, the practice of universal jurisdiction, and the workings of international criminal courts all made clear that in the world today, claims to absolute state sovereignty are not to be used to mask atrocious actions that violate international human rights and humanitarian law. State sovereignty properly conceived is relative, and its proper practice limited by, above all, avoiding atrocities as defined by international law.

It is of course true that diplomatic principles and international legal norms do not implement themselves. Some actors have to take the responsibility to see that the standards are upheld. The world being what it is and the UN Security Council being what it is, key states and especially the Permanent Five with the veto will almost always evaluate action with a view to their own self-interest. And so R2P was applied to Libya in 2011 but not Syria, despite the horrific internationalized internal armed conflict ongoing in the latter. For key Western states, Libya seemed "doable," whereas Syria seemed much more complicated. For Russia, Kaddafi was a pariah, whereas Assad comprised its only valuable ally in the Middle East. For China, most of its Arab oil suppliers wanted Kaddafi gone, whereas Assad had the backing of oil-rich Iran (and Hezbollah).

One could say in the last analysis that the adoption of R2P is an important and progressive step in making clear that state sovereignty is not a license to allow or commit atrocities against individuals. As usual, there will need to be continuing efforts to close the gap between lofty statements of principle and consistent and effective practice.

We should not forget regional human rights regimes, especially in Europe and also Latin America. We noted earlier that the one in Europe has been remarkable not only for the authority transferred to international institutions, but also for its general record of success until recent times. The one in the Western Hemisphere has been slowly gaining in scope as well as effectiveness, especially if one focuses on Central and South America and not the USA, Canada, and the English-speaking Caribbean.

The human rights institutions for Europe are exceedingly complex and no effort will be made here to review further the details of the Council of Europe, the European Union, and the Organization for Security and Cooperation in Europe (which deals with minority rights among other subjects, such as elections). All this was covered in Chapter 5. We saw that particularly the European Court of Human Rights is drowning in its caseload, demonstrating the point that if you give individuals the right to try to protect their rights, they will not be shy or passive about it. Private petitions are swamping the European Human Rights Court, with a sizable backlog of unfinished business.

We noted that in general states that have lost cases in these courts have implemented at least parts of the judgments. Thus as a general rule they have, for example, paid the ordered reparations to those wrongly treated, even if some states have not fully revised their legal code or legislative agenda to head off repeat violations. A major problem, but not the only one, for the European Court of Human Rights is Russia. Its membership in the Council of Europe leads to a large number of petitions against it, for Putin's Russia is increasingly autocratic and in violation of a large number of rights found in the European Convention on Human Rights and Fundamental Freedoms. After the Cold War it was said in some circles that it was politically impossible to keep Russia out of the Council of Europe, but it was legally impossible to manage Moscow once they were in. Other states subject to the European Court of Human Rights also present systematic problems because they are either illiberal democracies without full commitment to human rights,[54] or simply increasingly autocratic. Hungary and Turkey come to mind.

Nevertheless, for reasons well explained by Roger Kagan,[55] many European elites at least used to be aware of the dangers of unrestricted nationalism. Contemporary publics are a different matter. Traditional elites did not trust their nations not to fall back into policies of extremism and repression. Thus they were willing to delegate authority to international institutions in order to deter the return of those dangers. State historical rivalries, two disastrous world wars within twenty years, and the

---

[54] Fareed Zakaria, "The Rise of Illiberal Democracy," *Foreign Affairs*, 76, 6 (November–December 1997), 22–43.
[55] Robert Kagan, *Of Paradise and Power* (New York, Vintage, 2002).

record of European communism and fascism all contributed to the acceptance of muscular multilateralism with much attention to the protection of human rights. There are particular regional reasons why Europe manifested the best regional machinery for the protection of human rights, making possible, for example, regular supranational courts that are clearly premature on a global basis. (The ICC is a court of last resort and is not activated unless national procedures demonstrate the relevant state is "unwilling or unable" to do the right thing.)

More recent European public opinion, however, suggests that these historical lessons – painfully learned – have been forgotten or at least weakened in many countries. Those who voted for Britain to leave the EU, and who voted in various elections for nativist political parties, were clearly not thinking about the dangers of narrow nationalism. They were not only resentful of foreigners and their rights guaranteed by various international regimes, but also resentful of how the European Human Rights Court had mandated changes in national legal regimes.

The Inter-American human rights system, by comparison, does not have the impact of its European counterpart, but it is far superior to regional human rights developments in Africa or via the Arab League. Asia and its sub-regions show the least regional developments of all. The details were presented in Chapter 5.

We can summarily recall that the Inter-American system features an active Commission on Human Rights, while the supra-national Inter-American Court now has compulsory jurisdiction over about twenty states and is beginning to have an important impact on the public life of Central and South America. For example, the Court ruled in the Barrios Altos case that Peru under President Fujimori was responsible for death squads which had killed a number of citizens in 1991. The follow-on democratic Peruvian government paid reparations under that judgment and then used the case as part of its successful effort to have Fujimori extradited from Japan for a criminal trial. The principle was reaffirmed that even high state officials are not above the law.

There seems no consensus as to exactly why the English-speaking states of the Western Hemisphere have rejected the Inter-American Court of Human Rights. The US preference for unilateralism in these matters is clear, but the reasons for the Canadian record not as clear. Thus, unlike Europe, where all the major states are subject to binding rulings by the European Court of Human Rights, the Inter-American Court has made a growing impact on the region without the full support of the regional hegemon.

It is also not perfectly clear why about twenty states have bought into the supra-national IACHR. The lock-in theory, said to explain European developments, seems not to be applicable in the Western Hemisphere, as some important states accepted the Court's jurisdiction before their transition to full liberal democracy.[56] In any event, all the major Latin American states like Argentina, Brazil, Chile, and Mexico are parties to the Court. Thus we have another area that is Western by culture (most elites until recently have derived from Iberia in Europe) and which shows impressive human rights commitment – at least at the moment. At the time of writing, Brazil might be moving in a different direction with regard to regional human rights mechanisms.

Only Cuba and Venezuela lay outside the mainstream of liberal democracy in the region, although Honduras is borderline in that regard and certain other governments at times show tendencies toward a type of Huey Long authoritarian populism (not only in Venezuela, but also in Ecuador and Bolivia). There is much socio-economic inequality in the region which is a factor making for periodic protests and instability and the undermining of stable democracy based on a broad and effective welfare state (social democracy). As already noted, poverty does not correlate well with consolidated liberal democracy based on rights.[57] Nor does extreme inequality bode well for stable democracy, which is as true in places like the USA and India as in El Salvador.

Still, in relative terms, the Europeans and the Latinos of the Western Hemisphere manifest regional human rights developments far ahead of the rest of the world. There is some effective protection of rights through regional arrangements. Contemporary storm flags should not obscure what has been accomplished.

No doubt one could go on about positive human rights developments here and there. There is a rather long list of institutional and other advances in the UN system.[58] One could say that even the new UN Human Rights Council is slightly better than the old UN Human Rights Commission. The new Council now delegates, for example, a number of inquiries to panels of independent experts, which tends to reduce the politicization of reports at least at an early stage. (There is continuing controversy over the appointment of some of the experts, as some governments see them as biased from the start.) The Council now manifests the Universal Periodic Review, which subjects all member states to a debate on their human rights records, even if political alignment still

---

[56] Andrew Moravcsik, "The Origins of Human Rights Regimes: Democratic Delegation in Post-War Europe," *International Organization*, 54, 2 (Spring 2000), 217–252.

[57] Adam Prezworski, et al., *Democracy and Development* (Cambridge: Cambridge University Press, 2000).

[58] Andrew Gilmour, "The Future of Human Rights," *Ethics & International Affairs*, 28, 3 (Summer 2014), 239–250.

affects state commentary on their colleagues. If one excludes the question of Palestine, the Council's record is mixed – a blend of positive and negative developments.

Without continuing ad nauseam, it is safe to say that not all is gloom and doom since 1945 and that some real progress has been made not only normatively and institutionally, but also in the important matter of changing policies and practices for the betterment of individuals. But we need to be honest about the limitations, failures, and disappointments.

Structural barriers to progress

Professor Hafner-Burton is not altogether wrong when she writes that states endorse human rights commitments only to proceed to break those commitments when they prove inconvenient. David Rieff exaggerates only a little when he writes that all the human rights and humanitarian norms have not kept one jackboot off the neck of one victim. It is well known that there is a huge gap between the orgy of liberal rule-making in the world and the fate of those who lost the birth lottery and wound up in Afghanistan, Iraq, Syria, Somalia, South Sudan, Darfur, Congo, Myanmar, Central African Republic, northern Mali, northern Nigeria, etc., etc., etc. Have the norms helped Baha'i in Iran, women in Saudi Arabia, Muslims in northwest China, North Africans in France, Roma in Eastern Europe, African-Americans in Selma, Alabama or Ferguson, Missouri, etc., etc., etc.?

There are some persistent and fundamental barriers impeding the realization of human rights in policy and practice.

Illiberal nationalism

A first barrier to human rights progress is the continuation of the nation-state system and the continuing hold of narrow nationalism. All the inter-governmental organizations, from the UN to the WTO, have not so much replaced the nation-state system as they have just modified it. Particularly on security questions, it is up to states themselves to guarantee their continued existence. Poland has come and gone on various maps over time, and Ukraine (or parts thereof) may follow suit. The UN Security Council cannot be relied on to guarantee state security, much less to systematically stop atrocities because of: (1) the lack of independent hard power, all UN military power being tenuously borrowed from states; and (2) the veto by any of the P-5 (China, France, Russia, the UK, and the USA) which can block action in particular cases.

This being so, as Bernard Kouchner was bold enough to state, even democratic governments cannot do human rights consistently because they have to look out for their security and that of their allies.[59] The global security dilemma has not been solved, which means that governmental security concerns are the real trumps in foreign policy, often relegating human rights concerns to a secondary or tertiary ranking – if not to total oblivion. Hence when the USA was attacked by al-Qaeda on September 9, 2001, the George W. Bush Administration reacted with forced disappearances of terror suspects and their cruel and tortuous treatment. The British were not gentle in their treatment of prisoners in "The Troubles" in Northern Ireland. The Israelis have used physical and psychological pressures against Palestinian detainees (which is not to be confused with the Palestinian Authority's and Hamas's torture of Palestinians thought to be informers for Israel). To keep to this one genre of human rights violations, Rejali and others have made clear that even democracies torture in the name of national security – among other reasons.[60]

The security dilemma from the nation-state system (every state for itself) is compounded by various forms of national exceptionalism. Fueling the policies of the George W. Bush Administration was the belief that the USA was the engine for progress in the world, and that for al-Qaeda to attack New York and Washington was to engage in the worst form of uncivilized behavior which put the attackers beyond the pale of humane treatment. The British justified their colonial excesses as the price of bringing civilization to backward peoples (the White Man's burden), as did the French (their civilizing mission). Even a lying scoundrel like Vladimir Putin in Moscow sees himself as a moral force, resisting the decadent West and building a zone of progress in the Russian near-abroad which is blessed by the Russian Orthodox Church. This is not dissimilar from Pinochet's seeing himself as the savior of Christian civilization in Chile as he tortured and killed and stole children from suspected godless communists (or in some cases suppressed liberal Catholic priests). National leaders often have a romanticized and highly inflated view of themselves and their nation's place in the world. They, like the repressive Tzars of old, claim to be doing holy work. This often leads to human rights violations of the worst sort.[61]

---

[59] Bernard Kouchner, former French cabinet minister, quoted in the *New York Times*, December 11, 2008, p. A8.
[60] Darius Rejali, *Torture and Democracy* (Princeton: Princeton University Press, 2009).
[61] On how assumptions of cultural and racial superiority led to human rights violations in the Spanish Empire, see Helen M. Kinsella, *The Image before the Weapon* (Ithaca: Cornell University Press, 2011).

Even in less romanticized form, the nation-state system and narrow (parochial) nationalism leads to a brake on taking international human rights norms fully seriously. Most Western states resisted getting deeply involved in the Syrian quagmire from 2011 because it was Syrians and other Middle Easterners (e.g., from Hezbollah) getting killed and maimed, not Westerners. It was an obvious tragedy, but not a Western tragedy. Certainly in the USA, after long involvements in Afghanistan and Iraq, there was no groundswell of opinion in favor of costly involvement. It was only when radical Muslims operating from bases in Syria beheaded an American photojournalist in 2014 that the debate shifted, relatively speaking, in favor of more US involvement in the Syrian civil war. One shocking American death recorded on video could galvanize media coverage and policy debate in Washington, whereas many foreign deaths in Syria had not. (Other Americans were later killed.)

Because of the nation-state system and the pull of narrow or nativist nationalism, transnational morality and solidarity remain weak, while national morality and solidarity are often strong.[62] With an important exception noted below, it is only nationalism that allows most persons to pay taxes and put themselves in harm's way by serving in the military. In fact, given nations, nationalism, national identity, and national citizenship, some Western scholars view attachment to universal human rights without regard to nationality, race, religion, or other particular characteristics as utopian.[63]

Illiberal religion

Second on the list of persistent impediments to an effective human rights regime is misguided religious fervor which can overlap with chauvinistic nationalism as noted above, but which can also exist in the form of any holy war or extremist religious crusade. The Islamic State group (or ISIS, ISIL, or Daesh) is a good example of this phenomenon via initially an armed non-state actor, similar in some ways to the fractured al-Qaeda franchise system before it. Finding some Islamic religious figure to bless

---

[62] Thomas Pogge, *World Poverty and Human Rights* (Cambridge: Polity Press, 2008).
[63] Samuel Moyn, *The Last Utopia: Human Rights in History* (Cambridge, MA: Belknap for Harvard University Press, 2012). Some areas could benefit from *more* nationalism to forestall fragmentation and violent disputes as in former Yugoslavia circa 1990, Mali, Yemen, and Congo today, eastern, western, and southern Libya today and tomorrow, etc., etc., etc. The right kind of nationalism, a liberal nationalism, might be a relatively good thing as a blend of commitment to the national group while respecting international standards. See further Forsythe and McMahon, *Human Rights and Diversity*.

its cause, Islamic State killed and tortured with gusto, including presumably wrong-headed Muslims as well as non-believers, all the while claiming to be implementing the will of Allah. (Likewise, some Christians also adopt brutal actions as the Lord's will, and some Jews do the same because of being Yahweh's chosen people.) Islamic State proclaimed a transnational Caliphate in its zone of control, a multinational theocracy akin to some of the empires of the past in which transnational ambition was linked to religious inspiration (most of the Western empires, actually.) The Islamic Boko Haram based in Nigeria has also proclaimed a multinational Islamic Caliphate and has also used brutal tactics. The Republic of Iran also claims to be a theocracy implementing a Shia Islamic regime with regional ambitions.

These political-religious movements undertake total war of political action, limited only by the means at their disposal and the dangers of retaliation. They accept limits based on neither human rights nor humanitarian law. Much like the East and West during the Cold War, or various liberation movements fighting for de-colonization, they believe in a "higher morality" that transcends the secular limits of public law. Once the jihadists adopt a total-war approach, it is difficult for the other side to maintain limits. There is little limiting reciprocity in these mostly asymmetrical conflicts. Once the holy warriors attack civilians, aid workers, and hospitals, and out-group religious structures, and if they have some success, pressures build for opponents to also adopt any means, or at least questionable means, to stop the brutal jihadists. Religious total war tends to beget a more secular total war in return. (It was predictable that Islamic State would waterboard several American captives after the Bush Administration had waterboarded several Muslim captives after 9/11 – a kind of negative reciprocity. Some of those beheaded by ISIS wore orange prison attire, mimicking detainees at Guantanamo. George W. Bush claimed to be doing the Lord's work, as did al-Baghdadi, the shadowy leader of Islamic State.)

To be sure, there are secular factors mixed in with the religious ones. Osama bin-Laden was incensed that Saudi Arabia turned to the USA for protection against an expanding Saddam Hussein in Iraq, with Ridya spurning bin-Laden's offer of help. He was irritated by US support for Zionism and Israel, with terrible repercussions for many Palestinians (some of whom are in fact Christian). And so forth. But religious views, such as his concern about Western troops stationed in Islamic Saudi Arabia, and Israeli control of Jerusalem and its Islamic holy places, loomed large in his thinking. The same mix of factors, with religious views central, is no doubt true of al-Baghdadi. The brutal actions of the

Islamic State organization are repeatedly justified by reference to ancient Islamic texts.

Now some fighters for these jihadist groups are no doubt drawn to the cause because of their love of action and violence per se, not knowing what else to do with their unsatisfying lives. What the Western journalist Thomas Friedman has called the "stand around guys" can be mobilized into radical causes because of unemployment or other forms of social alienation. They are willing even to become suicide bombers. But the glue that holds these movements together is the view that "true" Islam has been attacked and exploited by the West and its allies. Because Mullah Omar or al-Baghdadi tells them that they represent the one true religion, then terror supposedly reflects the mind of a vengeful Allah.[64] Since one has religious Truth on his side, any brutality is justified and actually pleases God. The fact that other Islamic authorities, perhaps in Cairo, condemn their actions seems not to matter to them.

An age of terror, in contemporary times in the form of Muslim extremists, is not an age conducive to serious attention to human rights and humanitarian law. Insecure national governments tend to respond in kind – hence the linking of the first two negative factors.

Illiberal traditional practices

There is also the size of the problem to be overcome, since much of the world is characterized by traditional practices which are illiberal. Women are often seen as inherently unequal and second-class. There is female genital mutilation. The LGBT community is often attacked with no tolerance whatsoever for the different lifestyles that consenting adults may choose. Many political leaders succumb to the "Big Man" view of government, seeing autocratic rule as normal and in keeping with local history. One can recall the long (and disastrous) rule of Robert Mugabe in Zimbabwe. Such leaders have little commitment to the concept of government as existing to advance the rights and welfare of the people. In all too many places, from China to Congo, government is seen as an avenue to personal, family, and clan wealth. In a number of nations ruling elites believe only autocratic power can maintain stability and national cohesion. Whether in China or Egypt or elsewhere, authoritarian elites hold a dim view of democratic rights and show little interest in working for a gradual transition to a government by and for the people. In truth, given the way colonial powers drew national borders after 1919

---

[64] Mark Juergensmeyer, *Terror in the Mind of God* (Berkeley and Los Angeles: University of California Press, 2003).

(and again after 1945), that process did make national stability and cohesion a very complicated matter for many of the newer states. Iraq is a clear case in point.[65] In important places like China, past Western imperialism exploited weakness and opposed effective centralized government. Divide-and-rule was a Western approach often applied. This history taints and weakens today's human rights appeals coming from the West.

In sum, there are structural, meaning fundamental and contextual, problems to be overcome if the international law of human rights is to become broadly effective. The persistence of the national security dilemma and hence giving priority to national security issues, the deep roots of parochial and even chauvinistic nationalism, religious extremism, and many illiberal traditions especially in the non-Western world all present significant barriers to the practice of human rights (and humanitarian law).

The future

It took several hundred years for the state system of international relations to form (circa 1648 to 1975, the latter date being the end of the Portuguese Empire, or maybe we should use 1991 and the end of the Soviet Empire) with an absolute theory of state sovereignty at its core. I think it will take another very long time for the theory of human rights to result in the liberalized practices of that system.

Particularly once some nation-states have nuclear weapons, national power is not going to disappear. Moreover, the working of political psychology in much of the world means that national identity and national commitment are going to remain strong. This is especially so since states politicize education and teach a quasi-chauvinistic nationalism, as they gloss over national defects and inflate national accomplishments. At the time of writing, in almost every democratic state there were politically important factions that could be accurately termed nativist and anti-globalist.

The hope, therefore, is not for world government based on identity as world citizens. The hope, rather, is for a liberalized nationalism in which identification with nation is melded with a due appreciation of internationally recognized human rights and other international standards. In that regard I would say intuitively the glass is about 20 percent full. And if we are lucky, in the next century or so we might get it to 50 percent full.

---

[65] David Fromkin, *A Peace to End All Peace* (New York: Henry Holt, 2009).

The hope therefore is for a continuation of "determined incremental-ism."[66] The hope, in other words, is for a rooted cosmopolitanism based on a liberalized nationalism and liberalized realism.

Hopgood, in his important, readable, and often acerbic analysis of the fate of human rights, completely leaves out a crucial, maybe even decisive factor. This is the extent to which non-Western citizens of this or that nation buy into the human rights and humanitarian law paradigms – despite the latter's Western connections. There are, in fact, more than a few Syrians who have given their lives in the internationalized civil war there in order to carry out Henry Dunant's vision of neutral humanitarian assistance – forty-four from the Syrian Arab Red Crescent killed as of mid-2014. There are, in fact, more than a few Chinese who have been sent to prison, or even been killed, by their government, for demanding attention to human rights – who knows the exact number? Some of those tortured in Egypt, like Ahmed Seif, became human rights campaigners. There are non-Western states like South Korea and Indonesia that have evolved from autocratic repression to considerable attention to human rights without being occupied and controlled and reoriented by the USA or another Western power. In fact, public opinion polls show strong support for human rights across nations of different cultures. Other polls show strong public support for the principles undergirding the laws of war, such as restrictions on attacking hospitals, civilians, or captured combatants.

There are numerous non-Western human rights NGOs, like Muslim Women for Human Rights, who are seeking to transform their local political culture in a liberal direction. Frequently they cooperate with, and receive funding from, NGO partners based in the West. This can be a potent partnership over time.[67] So whereas it is often Amnesty International or Human Rights Watch that gets quoted in Western media, it is likely to be the numerous non-Western NGOs that make a difference especially in the non-Western world. For human rights to have local effect, some local person, persons, or groups need to adopt the international standards and push them in local politics.[68]

Two problems loom large in this process, namely: (1) Western and non-Western NGOs do not always have the same agendas and priorities,

---

[66] Philip Alston, "Against A World Court for Human Rights," *Ethics & International Affairs*, 28, 2 (Summer 2014), 212.

[67] Margaret Keck and Kathryn Sikkink, *Activists beyond Borders* (Ithaca: Cornell University Press, 1998); and Thomas Risse, Stephen C. Ropp, and Kathryn Sikkink, *The Persistent Power of Human Rights* (Cambridge: Cambridge University Press, 2013).

[68] Beth Simmons, *Mobilizing for Human Rights* (Cambridge: Cambridge University Press, 2009).

with locals often stressing poverty and its alleviation and those residing in New York and London pushing civil-political rights and criminal justice; and (2) illiberal elites are in a position to disrupt progress, as they have in China, Russia, and Egypt, inter alia, blocking outside funding for local human rights advocates and kicking expatriates out of the country.

At the risk of repetition, the key point is that human rights are not so much bestowed from heaven as they are wrestled into reality by a tough political struggle. Nelson Mandela showed this with regard to attaining a less racist South Africa. This process requires significant constituents to fight for rights in local politics by contesting military and other autocratic rule, fielding candidates via political parties, lobbying for welfare rights, pressing for a reduction in military spending to the benefit of health and education, pressing for an even-handed rule of law, etc., etc., etc. There is of course a role for outsiders to play in this process. But until locals press for rights in significant ways, those rights are unlikely to advance as policy and practice.

Unfortunately, examples like South Korea and Indonesia are counter-balanced by examples like Egypt. At the forefront of the Egyptian revolution of 2011 were secular liberals demanding the usual rights centered on civil and political freedoms, including especially media freedom, with much attention to gender equality. The movement for change was then captured by the well-organized and mostly illiberal Muslim Brotherhood, which was in favor of elections, but also opposed to much of the corpus of international human rights. And ultimately the secular and autocratic military launched a successful counter-revolution whose repression made the Muslim Brotherhood look positively liberal. The Obama Administration, which as in other cases lacked a strategy for dealing with affairs, eventually supported the counter-coup (without calling it that) and did not stand firm for democratic and progressive change. The Egyptian secular liberals were swept aside.

There is, of course, no guarantee of a teleological history in which human rights automatically advance. That should be clear when one recalls that Putin replaced Yeltsin, and al-Sisi controls Egypt. In Iraq, Prime Minister al-Maliki pursued a narrow, sectarian, and autocratic agenda, which alienated Iraqi Sunnis and Kurds. His record was so counter-productive to stability and progress that even his Iranian backers abandoned him in the face of Sunni extremist gains. Al-Maliki was no Mandela. More generally, brief moments of promise may be lost (repeatedly in Russian history) as progressives prove politically inept (El Baradei in Egypt in 2011?, Kerensky in Russia from the spring of 1917?). There are liberals in every country who support human rights, whether in Kenya or Myanmar. A crucial question is whether they can maneuver with adroitness in local politics, while maintaining support from international NGOs and helpful governments. There are usually liberal transnational advocacy networks in play, and the key question is their political influence vis-à-vis the ever-present illiberal factions.

Liberals usually have a good chance of advancing their values when an existing repressive regime has discredited itself through poor performance. That is, negative learning plays a large role in events. Mubarak fell in Egypt not so much because he was repressive, but because he was repressive and incompetent at providing jobs and a decent life for rank-and-file Egyptians. Much of the demand for increased freedoms in Egypt masked a deep demand for better economics. The same was true in Tunisia. The Argentine junta fell not simply because it was repressive, but because it was repressive and lost the Falklands/Malvinas war to Great Britain. (The other side of the coin is, if all democracies manifested the terrible finances of Argentina or Greece, the demand for civil-political rights would wither away and all would prefer the soft autocracy of Singapore.) There is a sense of legitimacy that comes from competence, and this can work against both autocrats and democrats (as social democrats in Weimar Germany came to learn all too well). Context matters, and awareness of the incompetence of autocrats is prime time to push human rights.

Finally, there is a certain serendipity in historical evolution that makes systematic analysis and prediction precarious. That the relatively liberal Yeltsin turned out to be an erratic drunk, and that the man selected as his successor, Putin, was a mendacious autocrat who prioritized reconstruction of a Soviet-like regime, was altogether unknown at key points. The Yeltsin people had little understanding of the man they elevated. Few predicted that a Burmese military man by the name of Thein Sein would turn out to be interested in major changes in a somewhat more liberal direction, as was true of Gorbachev (in limited ways) in the old Soviet Union. The advance of human rights protections is contingent on context and agency, with much uncertainty.

Discussion questions

• Do the past fifty years show that serious concern for personal rights can indeed improve the human condition in the state system of international relations?
• If one compares the Congo during King Leopold's time with the Democratic Congo (formerly Zaire) today, has anything changed about the human condition?

- When is it appropriate, if ever, to grant immunity for past violations of human rights, and otherwise to avoid legal proceedings about human rights violations, for the sake of improving the human condition?
- Are the demands for a third generation of human rights to peace, development, and a healthy environment well considered?
- Do internationally recognized human rights require radical change so as to properly protect women's dignity?
- Even after the political demise of European Marxism, are Marxists correct that capitalism and the transnational corporation are inherently exploitative of labor? What social values can markets advance (e.g., efficiency?), and what social values can they not advance (e.g., equity?)?
- Should one be optimistic or pessimistic about the future of human rights in international relations?

SUGGESTIONS FOR FURTHER READING

Alston, Philip, "Conjuring Up New Human Rights: A Proposal for Quality Control," *American Journal of International Law*, 78, 3 (July 1984), 607–621. A plea for a moratorium on endorsing more human rights until protection improves for those already recognized.

Brzezinski, Zbigniew, *The Grand Failure: The Birth and Death of Communism in the Twentieth Century* (New York: Scribner, 1989). An overview of what went wrong particularly with European communism, written in engaging style by the National Security Advisor to President Carter.

Cook, Rebecca J., ed., *Human Rights of Women: National and International Perspectives* (Philadelphia: University of Pennsylvania Press, 1994). A good and broad coverage of feminist perspectives on human rights.

Forsythe, David P., and Patrice C. McMahon, *American Exceptionalism Reconsidered: US Foreign Policy, Human Rights, and World Order* (New York and London: Routledge, 2016). Analyzes the difference between US talk about an exceptional commitment to human rights abroad, and the reality of unexceptional practice. Concludes by noting that a world order with China and Russia as hegemonic powers would be worse.

Franck, Thomas M., "Is Personal Freedom a Western Value?," *American Journal of International Law*, 91, 4 (October 1997), 593–627. Suggests that the West has no monopoly on the desire for personal freedom.

Gormley, W. Paul, *Human Rights and the Environment: The Need for International Co-operation* (Leiden: W. W. Sijthoff, 1976). An early study based on the premise that we need a third-generation human right to a healthy environment.

Grim, Brian J., and Roger Finke, *The Price of Freedom Denied: Religious Persecution and Conflict in the Twenty-First Century* (Cambridge: Cambridge University Press, 2010). A good study showing the extent of religious intolerance and its correlation with conflict. Shows how much illiberal religion is a problem in the modern world.

Hafner-Burton, Emilie M., *Making Human Rights a Reality* (Princeton: Princeton University Press, 2013). A hard look at actual human rights protection, stressing the hypocrisy of states. Recommends emphasizing those universal human rights that fit with Western foreign policy interests, since actual protection would result. This orientation, unfortunately, would increase those seeing action for international human rights as Western neo-colonialism.

Hiskes, Richard P., *The Human Right to a Green Future: Environmental Rights and Intergenerational Justice* (Cambridge and New York: Cambridge University Press, 2008). An argument for more attention to ecology based on the human rights of unborn generations.

Hochschild, Adam, *King Leopold's Ghost: A Story of Greed, Terror, and Heroism in Colonial Africa* (Boston: Houghton Mifflin, 1998). A gripping history of the lack of human rights in Central Africa when the Congo was the personal fiefdom of the King of Belgium.

Hocking, B., *Catalytic Diplomacy* (Leicester: Centre for Diplomatic Studies, 1996). Argues that in the modern world what governments frequently do is organize others for agreement and action, rather than establish a foreign policy completely independent from other actors.

Hopgood, Stephen, *The Endtimes of Human Rights* (Ithaca: Cornell University Press, 2013). A provocative polemic arguing that with the political decline of Western power, centralized attention to human rights through international law and organization will fade.

Ignatieff, Michael, *The Warrior's Honor: Ethnic War and the Modern Conscience* (New York: Metropolitan, 1997). A cosmopolitan and Renaissance man reflects on whether humane limits can be applied to ethnic war, arguing for the importance of traditional conceptions such as military honor.

Johansen, Robert C., *The National Interest and the Human Interest: An Analysis of US Foreign Policy* (Princeton: Princeton University Press, 1980). Shows clearly that if one starts with realist principles of state interest, one winds up with different policies than if one starts with liberal principles of human interest.

Kagan, Robert, *Of Paradise and Power: America and Europe in the New World Order* (New York: Vintage, 2004). Supposedly the Europeans are interested in human rights and international law and organization, while the USA is interested in the use of power to protect national security in a hostile world. Provides background to the question of whether the Europeans are now quite different.

Keohane, Robert O., and Joseph H. Nye, *Power and Interdependence: World Politics in Transition* (Boston: Little, Brown, 1977). A major study arguing that there are different types of international relations. Realism may be appropriate to some, liberalism or pragmatic liberalism to others. Argues that realism is less and less appropriate to contemporary international relations because of interdependence.

Pogge, Thomas, *World Poverty and Human Rights: Cosmopolitan Responsibilities and Reforms* (Cambridge: Polity, 2002). A leading philosopher reflects on, and provides data about, poverty, hunger, and human rights.

Sands, Phillippe, *East West Street: On the Origins of "Genocide" and "Crimes Against Humanity"* (New York: Knopf, 2016). Shows the interplay of context and agency, as Hersh Lauterpacht helped develop the concept of crimes against humanity, and Rafael Lemkin did the same regarding the idea of genocide.

Slaughter, Anne-Marie, *A New World Order* (Princeton: Princeton University Press, 2005). The former Dean of the Princeton Woodrow Wilson School and former State Department official in the Obama Administration argues that national authorities are cooperating with international courts in a way that is already producing considerable transnational protection of certain human rights.

Teeple, Gary, *The Riddle of Human Rights* (Amherst, NY: Humanity Books, 2005). A clearly argued Marxist analysis.

Towns, Anne E., *Women and States: Norms and Hierarchies in International Society* (Cambridge: Cambridge University Press, 2010). A transnational analysis linking the position of women inside states to various issues in foreign policy and international relations.

Index